INTERNATIONAL HANDBOOK OF INQUIRY AND LEARNING

International Handbook of Inquiry and Learning is an overview of scholarship related to learning through and engagement in inquiry. Education takes on complex dimensions when learners solve problems, draw conclusions, and create meaning not through memorization or recall but instead through active cognitive, affective, and experiential processes. Drawing from educational psychology and the learning sciences while encompassing key subdisciplines, this rigorous, globally attentive collection offers new insights into what makes learning through inquiry both possible in context and beneficial to outcomes. Supported by foundational theories, key definitions, and empirical evidence, the book's special focus on effective environments and motivational goals, equity and epistemic agency among learners, and support of teachers sets powerful, multifaceted new research directions in this rich area of study.

Ravit Golan Duncan is a Professor of Learning Sciences and Science Education with a joint appointment in the Graduate School of Education and the School of Environmental and Biological Sciences at Rutgers University, USA.

Clark A. Chinn is a Professor of Learning Sciences and Educational Psychology in the Graduate School of Education at Rutgers University, USA.

EDUCATIONAL PSYCHOLOGY HANDBOOK SERIES

Series Editor: Patricia A. Alexander

INTERNATIONAL HANDBOOK OF INQUIRY AND LEARNING
Edited by Ravit Golan Duncan and Clark A. Chinn

HANDBOOK OF EDUCATIONAL PSYCHOLOGY AND STUDENTS WITH SPECIAL NEEDS
Edited by Andrew J. Martin, Rayne A. Sperling, and Kristie J. Newton

HANDBOOK OF TEST DEVELOPMENT
Edited by Steven M. Downing and Thomas M. Haladyna

INTERNATIONAL HANDBOOK OF RESEARCH ON CONCEPTUAL CHANGE
Edited by Stella Vosniadou

HANDBOOK OF MOTIVATION AT SCHOOL
Edited by Kathryn Wentzel and Allan Wigfield

HANDBOOK OF MORAL AND CHARACTER EDUCATION
Edited by Larry P. Nucci and Darcia Narvaez

HANDBOOK OF SELF-REGULATION OF LEARNING AND PERFORMANCE
Edited by Barry J. Zimmerman and Dale H. Schunk

HANDBOOK OF RESEARCH ON LEARNING AND INSTRUCTION
Edited by Patricia A. Alexander and Richard E. Mayer

THE INTERNATIONAL GUIDE TO STUDENT ACHIEVEMENT
Edited by John Hattie and Eric M. Anderman

THE INTERNATIONAL HANDBOOK OF COLLABORATIVE LEARNING
Edited by Cindy E. Hmelo-Silver, Clark A. Chinn, Carol Chan, and Angela M. O'Donnell

INTERNATIONAL HANDBOOK OF INQUIRY AND LEARNING

Edited by
Ravit Golan Duncan and Clark A. Chinn

Routledge
Taylor & Francis Group
NEW YORK AND LONDON

First published 2021
by Routledge
605 Third Avenue, New York, NY 10158

and by Routledge
2 Park Square, Milton Park, Abingdon, Oxon, OX14 4RN

Routledge is an imprint of the Taylor & Francis Group, an informa business

Library of Congress Cataloging-in-Publication Data
Names: Chinn, Clark, editor. | Duncan, Ravit Golan, 1973– editor.
Title: International handbook of inquiry and learning / edited by Clark A. Chinn and Ravit Golan Duncan.
Description: New York, NY: Routledge, 2021. | Includes bibliographical references and index.
Identifiers: LCCN 2020054444 (print) | LCCN 2020054445 (ebook) | ISBN 9781138922594 (hardback) | ISBN 9781138922600 (paperback) | ISBN 9781315685779 (ebook)
Subjects: LCSH: Inquiry-based learning.
Classification: LCC LB1027.23 .I588 2021 (print) | LCC LB1027.23 (ebook) | DDC 371.39—dc23
LC record available at https://lccn.loc.gov/2020054444
LC ebook record available at https://lccn.loc.gov/2020054445

ISBN: 978-1-138-92259-4 (hbk)
ISBN: 978-1-138-92260-0 (pbk)
ISBN: 978-1-315-68577-9 (ebk)

Typeset in Bembo
by codeMantra

CONTENTS

CONTRIBUTOR BIOGRAPHIES

Jennifer D. Adams is a Tier 2 Canada Research Chair of Creativity and Science and Associate Professor at The University of Calgary where she holds a dual appointment in the Department of Chemistry and Werklund School of Education. Her research focuses on STEM learning and teaching and engagement in both formal and informal settings with an emphasis on integrating BIPOC peoples and perspectives. Her work emphasizes critical and sociocultural frameworks and participatory, qualitative, poststructural approaches. Her prior appointments include Brooklyn College and The Graduate Center, City University of New York, New York City Department of Education, and the American Museum of Natural History.

Na'ama Y. Av-Shalom is a PhD candidate at the Graduate School of Education at Rutgers University. Her research characterizes effective reasoning in students' written argumentation and classroom discourse. She is also examining teachers' implementations of model-based inquiry interventions to understand how teachers can best support students' reasoning. Collectively, the aim of her work is to establish an empirically grounded approach for evaluating dialogic instruction based on assessing students' epistemic performance and the ways in which instruction can promote epistemic growth.

Dan Battey is a Professor in the Graduate School of Education at Rutgers University. His work centers on engaging teachers in opportunities to learn within and from their practice in a way that sustains and generates change as well as challenges metanarratives that limit opportunities for African American and Latino students in mathematics. He is currently working on understanding mathematics education as a racialized space through researching relational interactions in classrooms.

Katerine Bielaczyc is the Director of the Hiatt Center for Urban Education and an Associate Professor at Clark University. Kate's scholarship involves collaborating with students, teachers, school districts, and community organizations to investigate new learning and teaching approaches, particularly the creation and impact of collectives such as learning communities and communities of researchers. As a design-researcher, she focuses on developing social and technological infrastructures to support participants in collective inquiry toward personal, pedagogical, and systemic transformation. Over the past 25 years, Kate has been part of an international research-practice network focused on knowledge building communities in K-12 and university settings.

Pia Bøgelund is an Associate Professor in the Department of Planning at Aalborg University. She holds a Master's degree and a PhD in Planning and is also trained as a coach and psychotherapist.

Her current fields of interest are the facilitation and retention of university students in a PBL context, group dynamics related to PBL projects, and supervision of international PhD students. She has published on student collaboration and skills development for supervisors. In her teaching, she works with the training and skills development of university staff in relation to PhD supervision, professional communication, and project planning.

Pablo Brocos is a young researcher in Science Education and currently employed as Assistant Professor at the Faculty of Education in the University of Santiago de Compostela, Spain. He is part of the research group RODA (Reasoning, Discourse and Argumentation), and his work deals with argumentation about socio-scientific issues, inquiry, sustainability, critical thinking, epistemic practices, and emotions in the classroom at different educational levels. His doctoral thesis addresses argumentation about sustainable and healthy dietary habits.

Clark A. Chinn is a Professor at the Graduate School of Education at Rutgers University. His research focuses on epistemic cognition, reasoning and argumentation, learning from multiple documents, conceptual change, and collaborative learning. His most recent work has focused on how to promote the goals of epistemic education—education that improves students' ways of knowing and thinking—with a particular focus on promoting better thinking in our so-called post-truth world. He has worked extensively on model-based inquiry in middle-school science classes—designing learning environments and investigating how these environments promote conceptual change and epistemic growth.

Ravit Golan Duncan is a Professor at the Graduate School of Education and the School of Environmental and Biological Science, Rutgers University. One of her research strands explores learning progressions in science education, in particular how instruction can support increasing sophistication in learning genetics from late elementary to high school. Her second research strand focuses on supporting epistemic growth through extensive engagement with shared epistemic norms and criteria that are used by students when constructing and evaluating epistemic products in the context of model-based inquiry learning environments.

Richard A. Duschl, Executive Director, Caruth Institute for Engineering Education and Texas Instruments; Distinguished Professor, Lyle School of Engineering, Southern Methodist University; Professor Emeritus, Penn State University. He has served as Editor, Science Education; President of US NARST (2009–2011); Director, Division for Research on Learning, NSF (2012–2015) and chaired the US National Research Council research synthesis report Taking Science to School: Learning and Teaching Science in Grades K-8. He received the JRST Award for best publication in 1989 and 2003. In 2014, he received the NARST Distinguished Career Research Award.

Drew Gitomer is the Rose and Nicholas DeMarzo Chair in Education at Rutgers Graduate School of Education. Gitomer's research has focused on the design and validation of assessments that support the improvement of instruction with particular focus on the assessment and evaluation of teaching. His research examines policy-related issues in teaching and teacher education and considers a range of measures and associated constructs of teaching quality, including observation, instructional artifacts, and assessments of teacher knowledge. Current work also is focused on research methods employed to study the use of research evidence in policy and practice.

Krista Glazewski, a former middle school science teacher, serves as Professor and Department Chair of Instructional Systems Technology at Indiana University exploring means of supporting teachers as they adopt new technological and curricular innovations. Her partnership work has spanned multiple regions in the U.S. to investigate how and under what conditions teachers might adopt and adapt new practices. She currently serves as Editor of the *Interdisciplinary Journal of Problem-Based Learning*, an open-access journal that publishes peer-reviewed articles of research, analysis, or promising practice related to all aspects of problem- or inquiry-based learning.

Kimberley Gomez, PhD, Professor of Education and Information Studies at UCLA, centers her research in the design and study of literate practices to enhance learning in STEM with an aim of informing theoretical and practical understandings. Her work focuses on helping urban, underserved youth experience more equitable opportunities to learn in secondary and postsecondary institutions. Her work is informed by participatory design, design-based research, and improvement science approaches. She designs and supports educational interventions and professional development opportunities working side-by-side with teachers, community partners, and other frontline practitioners. Gomez received the PhD in Educational Psychology from the University of Chicago.

Melissa Gresalfi is a Professor in Mathematics Education and the Learning Sciences, and Dean of the Martha Rivers Ingram Commons at Vanderbilt University. Her research considers how to design learning environments that support students' empowered engagement with mathematics. Her projects explore how tasks, social interactions, and norms and broader narratives support student learning and identity, with a current focus on textile craft, programming, and play. These projects share a commitment to understand how classroom structures and curricular designs create (or limit) opportunities for students to engage meaningfully with information.

Cindy E. Hmelo-Silver is the Barbara B. Jacobs Chair in Education and Technology, Professor of Learning Sciences, and Director of the Center for Research on Learning and Technology in the School of Education of Indiana University. Her research focuses on how people learn about complex phenomena and how technology can help support that learning. She studies problem-based learning, collaborative engagement, and computer-supported collaborative learning. Dr. Hmelo-Silver is an International Society for the Learning Sciences inaugural fellow as well as a fellow of the American Educational Research Association and International Society for Design and Development in Education.

Jette Egelund Holgaard is Associate Professor within the field of PBL, Sustainability, and Organizational Learning in the Department of Planning, Aalborg University; head of section at the Department of Planning. She has an MSc in Environmental Planning and a PhD in Environmental Communication from Aalborg University. Her primary research interests are PBL models and methodologies, with a specific focus on how PBL can frame and enhance engineering education for employability, sustainability, and a more contextual approach to engineering. She has published more than 140 articles in this research.

Ilana Horn is a Professor of Mathematics Education at Vanderbilt University, Nashville, TN. Her work lies at the intersection of several disciplines: mathematics education, the sociology of schooling, and learning sciences. She uses sociolinguistics and interpretive methods to examine secondary mathematics teachers' learning in the contexts of their workplace, yielding images of teachers' learning and practice that account for the institutional setting of schools and the pressures of policy. By understanding teachers' learning in the workplace, her research highlights ways to make teacher education and professional development usable and relevant to practicing educators.

Sanna Järvelä is a Professor in the field of Learning Sciences and Educational Technology and a head of the Learning and Educational Technology Research Unit (LET) in the Department of Educational Sciences, University of Oulu, Finland. Her main research interest deals with self-regulated learning and computer-supported collaborative learning. Järvelä and her research group are internationally recognized in theoretical and methodological advancement of social aspects of self-regulated learning (socially shared regulation in learning) and processes-oriented and multi-modal research methods.

Hanna Järvenoja is an Associate Professor (Tenure Track) at the University of Oulu, Learning and Educational Technology Research Unit (LET) and an adjunct professor in the University of Turku, Finland. Järvenoja's research interest is in the field of self-regulated learning, particularly motivation and emotion in individual and social levels. She is also interested in how to utilize technology for supporting collaborative groups in their regulation processes.

Marilar Jiménez-Aleixandre is Ad Honorem Professor of Science Education at the University of Santiago de Compostela, Spain. Her research focuses on students' engagement in argumentation and epistemic practices, through classroom studies and longitudinal designs. Her recent work explores the use of evidence by kindergarteners and the interface between critical thinking and argumentation on socioscientific issues. Outside science education, Marilar is an award-winning author of poetry, fiction, and children's fiction, and she has been recently elected for the Royal Galician Academy (RAG).

Yael Kali is a professor of technology-enhanced learning at the Technologies in Education Graduate Program, Faculty of Education, University of Haifa, and the director of the Learning In a NetworKed Society (LINKS) Israeli Center of Research Excellence (I-CORE), and the Taking Citizen Science to School (TCSS) research center. Using design-based research (DBR) and design-based implementation research (DBIR), Kali explores technology-enhanced learning and teaching at various contexts and age levels, from junior high school to higher education. Since 2012 Kali has been serving as an associate editor for the journal *Instructional Science*.

Anette Kolmos is Professor of Engineering Education and PBL; Director for the UNESCO Category 2 Centre: Aalborg Centre for Problem-Based Learning in Engineering Science and Sustainability, Aalborg University, Denmark. She has been Guest Professor at the KTH Royal Institute of Technology; President of SEFI 2009–2011 (European Society for Engineering Education); and Founding Chair of the SEFI-working group on Engineering Education Research. She was awarded the IFEES Global Award for Excellence in Engineering Education, 2013. Dr. Kolmos has around 300 publications on management of change and problem- and project-based learning (PBL) in engineering education.

Carol D. Lee is Professor Emeritus—Learning Sciences Program, School of Education and Social Policy—at Northwestern University. She is President-Elect of the National Academy of Education, member of the American Academy of Arts and Sciences, member of the Reading Hall of Fame, and former President of the American Educational Research Association. Her research focuses on cultural supports for literacy learning and pedagogical supports for holistic development during adolescent literacy learning, with special attention to reading across the disciplines. She formally taught high school, primary school, and community college.

Nicole Mancevice is an Assistant Professor-in-Residence in Education at the University of California, Los Angeles. Her research focuses on disciplinary literacy, curriculum design, and teachers' professional learning. She is committed to building collaborative research partnerships with educators to both support local goals and generate knowledge about teaching and learning. Her projects draw on design-based research, collaborative or participatory design, and action research approaches. In a recent project, she partnered with teachers to co-design and study instructional routines for teaching elementary school students how to read and evaluate historical texts.

As a postdoctoral Educational Research Scientist **Claudia Mazziotti** develops, evaluates, and implements 21st-century learning approaches. These learning approaches include adaptive educational technologies, collaborative learning elements, and opportunities for students to productively fail. In her new role as researcher in the Clearing House Unterricht she supports evidence-based teaching by qualifying teachers and teacher educators in dealing with evidence in their professional practice.

Susan McCullough is a Distinguished Lecturer and Program Director for Art Education at Queens College. She worked in museum education for over 20 years at various art museums, including the Brooklyn Museum, the Museum of Modern Art (MoMA), and the Whitney Museum of American Art. Her research interests include gender and education, art and museum education, and the development of teacher professional identity. Her book, *Latina Students' Experiences in Public Schools: Educational Equity and Gender*, was published by Routledge in 2020.

Emily Wolf McMichael is a former K-12 educator with an MEd in English Education as well as an MEd in Counseling Psychology. She has worked as a researcher on projects that examine race and student-teacher relationships in K-12 English classrooms as well as the COURAGE project in undergraduate mathematics.

Barbara Means examines the effectiveness of innovative education approaches supported by digital technology, including evaluating the implementation and impacts of adaptive learning software. She is also studying the long-term effects that attending an inclusive STEM-focused high school has for students from underrepresented minorities. A fellow of the American Educational Research Association, Dr. Means has served on many study committees of the National Academies of Science, Engineering, and Medicine. She has advised the U.S. Department of Education on national education technology plans and authored or edited more than a half-dozen books.

Hanni Muukkonen is a Professor in Educational Psychology at the Faculty of Education, University of Oulu, Finland. Her research areas include collaborative learning, knowledge creation, technology in education, and methodological development. Her current research focuses on higher education collaborative inquiry, particularly pedagogical designs fostering knowledge creation and the development of capabilities to solve complex challenges in interdisciplinary collaboration. In learning analytics, she presently studies supporting and monitoring fluent academic paths and student engagement, design of tools and visualizations, and the questions of user needs and ethical practices

Bill Penuel is a Professor of Learning Sciences and Human Development at the University of Colorado Boulder. He designs and studies curriculum materials, assessments, and professional learning experiences for teachers in science. He works in partnership with school districts and state departments of education, and the research he conducts is in support of educational equity in three dimensions: (1) equitable implementation of new science standards; (2) creating inclusive classroom cultures that attend to students' affective experiences and where all students have authority for constructing knowledge together; and (3) connecting teaching to the interests, experiences, and identities of learners.

Ashley Potvin is research faculty in the Renée Crown Wellness Institute at the University of Colorado Boulder. Her work focuses on employing design-based implementation research and co-design to collaborate with practitioners in ways that value their expertise and experiences and support their professional growth. Her research interests/areas include educator wellness and agency, teacher-student relationships, and caring and inclusive classrooms and schools.

Chris Quintana is an Associate Professor in the School of Education, University of Michigan, where he applies his background in learning sciences, human-computer interaction, and computer science to explore how different technologies and media can support learning. Much of his work has focused on software-based scaffolding, including the development of scaffolded software tools and frameworks, and learner-centered design processes. His recent work is exploring how emerging technologies, from wearable and mobile computers, to virtual and augmented reality, can be used for learning environments that incorporate inquiry practices.

Maya Resnick is a PhD student at the Hebrew University of Jerusalem and is the research coordinator and a researcher in The Research Center for Teachers' Learning and Development. Her studies focus on teacher knowledge and thinking, primarily in the context of teaching higher-order thinking, and the ways in which teachers and teacher candidates engage with their students' thinking. Her PhD dissertation strives to promote the understanding of how teachers notice, analyze, and address their students' thinking.

Alina Reznitskaya is a Professor at the Department of Educational Foundations at Montclair State University. Her research interests include investigating the role social interaction plays in the development of argument literacy, designing measures of argumentation, and examining professional development efforts. In one of her recent projects, she designed and validated an observational rating scale to assess the quality of teacher facilitation and student argumentation during group discussions of texts. In another project, she worked collaboratively with elementary school teachers to develop and test curriculum materials and activities that support teacher learning of argumentation and facilitation.

Jeremy Roschelle applies learning science theories and methods to understand how, when, and why technology can enable improved teaching and learning. He is nationally and internationally recognized for research in computer-supported collaborative learning; learning with connected, mobile devices; and technology in mathematics learning. He has conducted rigorous efficacy research on personalized, adaptive learning, on online homework tools, and on dynamic visualizations for mathematics learning. Roschelle has a long-standing role as Associate Editor for the *Journal of the Learning Sciences* and leads a large community of National Science Foundation-funded projects in the area of cyberlearning.

Asmalina Saleh is a Research Scientist at the Center for Research in Learning and Teaching in Indiana University. Her work focuses on the intersection of learning theories, design, and research methodologies in computer-supported collaborative learning (CSCL) environments, ranging from 2D to mixed-reality environments. This work is instantiated in three ways: leveraging 1) theories of play and problem-based learning to design and implement computer-supported and intelligent game-based learning environments for teaching and learning, 2) scaffolding frameworks to shape the design and analysis of collaborative inquiry play, and 3) learning analytics to explore ways to document and understand collaborative learning processes.

Gerhard Stoel is a Postdoctoral Researcher and teacher educator of learning and instruction in history education at University of Amsterdam. His research focuses on educational design, teacher professionalization, self-regulated learning, causal historical reasoning, and the role of epistemological beliefs in history. He is currently involved in several professional development programs that aim at developing teachers' explicit knowledge of domain-specific (historical or social-scientific) reasoning and support them in designing learning environments that foster this reasoning with students.

Armend Tahirsylaj, PhD, is an Associate Professor of Education at Department of Teacher Education, Norwegian University of Science and Technology (NTNU), Norway. His research encompasses curriculum theory, Continental/Nordic Europe Didaktik, Bildung, education policy, teacher education, international large-scale assessments, and international comparative education. His latest research examines the spread of competence-based curriculum models internationally and related implications for curriculum policymaking and implementation within national contexts. In addition, his work has examined teacher education programs and their outcomes, as well as trends in teacher monitoring methods across curriculum and didaktik traditions in the Western hemisphere.

Carla van Boxtel is Professor of History Education at the Research Institute of Child Development and Education and the Amsterdam School of Historical Studies of the University of Amsterdam. Her research focuses on the learning and teaching of history, particularly historical thinking and reasoning. Her research fields include components and resources of historical reasoning (e.g. historical contextualization, causal historical reasoning, the critical examination of historical sources and epistemological beliefs) and pedagogic approaches to improve historical reasoning.

Michiel Voet is a Postdoctoral Researcher at Ghent University's Department of Educational Studies. His main research interest lies with inquiry-based learning in history education. In his research, he has investigated topics such as cognitive processes involved in inquiries, student motivation, teachers' instructional decision-making, and the impact of teacher training.

Ian Wilkinson is Professor in the Department of Teaching and Learning at The Ohio State University and Honorary Professor in the School of Curriculum and Pedagogy at the University of Auckland, Aotearoa/New Zealand. His research focuses on school and classroom contexts for literacy learning and the cognitive consequences for students with particular interests in classroom discussion, dialogue, and argumentation. Most recently, he has conducted research on the impact of classroom talk on students' reading comprehension and argument literacy and the implications for professional development of teachers.

Anat Zohar holds the Besen Family Chair at the Seymour Fox School of Education, the Hebrew University of Jerusalem, and is the director of the Research Center for Teachers' Learning and Development. Her main interests are the development of students' higher-order thinking (including argumentation and inquiry learning) and metacognition, teachers' knowledge, and the challenges involved in scaling up instructional innovations. Between 2006 and 2009, she was Director of Pedagogical Affairs in the Israeli MOE, leading a national pedagogical reform aimed at teaching higher-order thinking. She recently chaired the committee "Adapting Curricula and Study Materials for the 21st Century."

1

INQUIRY AND LEARNING

Clark A. Chinn and Ravit Golan Duncan

This volume—*The International Handbook of Learning and Inquiry*—provides an overview of scholarship related to learning through inquiry. The chapters focus broadly on how to promote learning through engaging learners in inquiry. Collectively they discuss what it means to engage in inquiry, what learners gain through engaging in inquiry, how to structure inquiry environments to promote greater learning as well as equity in learning, and how to support teachers and other educators (including designers of learning environments) as they engage students in learning through inquiry. The handbook is intended to be a resource both for scholars new to the field and for scholars who specialize in issues related to inquiry and learning. While summarizing and reviewing existing scholarship, the chapters also advance new ways of thinking about effective inquiry environments that foster student learning.

In this introductory chapter, we will begin with a discussion of several foundational issues related to inquiry. These include defining inquiry and learning through inquiry, identifying the goals of inquiry-based learning environments, and issues of domain and topic specificity. Then we turn to an overview of the chapters in the handbook.

Foundational Issues

What Is Inquiry?

What does it mean to engage in inquiry as a means of learning in and out of schools? We asked authors of each chapter to explain what they mean by inquiry but did not charge them with adopting a particular definition. The resulting variation reflects the variety that exists in the field. Nonetheless, we think that their approaches to understanding what inquiry is overlap substantively, along the lines of our analysis below.

What, then, is inquiry? In common terms, we could say that inquiry occurs when people "find things out." In turn, finding things out is a complex notion with at least six components. First, finding things out means that one is in fact gaining new ideas or new knowledge. There is no inquiry when one already knows the answer to a question. For instance, if a person can answer a question by recalling an answer that is already stored in memory, nothing new has been learned—nothing new has been found out. Many laboratory exercises in science classes fall into this category: The teacher explicitly teaches a scientific principle to the students, and the students carry out a laboratory experiment as an illustration of this principle. There is no inquiry in such activities, as students already know what the experiment is to show.

Second, finding things out means that one is not simply told an answer; the inquirers must engage in active work to think through and work conclusions out. When a teacher poses a question and then tells the answer, there is no inquiry for the students, because the students have engaged in no effort to figure out the answer. If a teacher develops a rich set of mathematical materials from which students could potentially engage in finding out new mathematical principles, but then the teacher does all the work of inquiry, modeling each thinking process for the students, then the students have not engaged in any inquiry. If the teacher already knew the principles in advance, the teacher has not engaged in inquiry, either, but has only pretended to do so. Thus, inquiry needs to involve active work to think through and work out some conclusions anew.

Third, finding things out involves the use of some sort of evidence to reach some kind of conclusion. In this analysis, we construe *evidence* very broadly, in the broad philosophical sense of including all the considerations that are used to support or refute a claim (Kelly, 2014). Thus, evidence can be empirical evidence, testimony from an expert or a friend, prior memories and experiences, and so on. Conclusions similarly refer to a broad range of epistemic products developed on the basis of this evidence, from simple propositions to historical narratives to scientific models. In science, evidence may include empirical studies, results of simulations, and established principles of other theories; the conclusions can be laws, models, explanations, theories, and so on. In mathematics, the evidence may include basic axioms or givens in a problem, and the conclusion could be the final proved claim (in a proof). In literary inquiry, the evidence may be the corpus of texts under consideration, and the conclusions may be claims about the characters, about the work of fiction, about a genre of writing, and so on. Finding things out means using a set of considerations (the evidence) to reason through to a conclusion.

Fourth, finding things out requires that inquirers have epistemic agency. Epistemic agency means that inquirers have the authority to express their own ideas, share these ideas with the communities engaged in inquiry, advance their own proposed ways of knowing about the matters at hand, and to reach their own conclusions. All the inquirers in a community are "allowed to propose and shape the community's knowledge production and practices" (Stroupe, Caballero, & White, 2018, p. 1180). Learning activities can masquerade as inquiry when they provide the resources that could be used for inquiry, but teachers end up doing all the intellectual work (Miller, Manz, Russ, Stroupe, & Berland, 2018). For instance, imagine a history unit intended to engage students in reaching historical conclusions using multiple documentary sources. If the teacher walks the students through each document, steering them to the teacher's (or the curriculum's) predetermined conclusion about each document and how they should be interpreted, there is no real inquiry going on, because the students have little or no epistemic agency to propose their own interpretations, suggest ways of approaching the thinking about the documents, or reach their own conclusions. In a similar way, there is little epistemic agency in a cookbook lab in which every step is clearly spelled out in the instructions, and the questions asked point strongly to the normative conclusions.

Fifth, finding things out entails that there is some degree of complexity in the reasoning involved. Finding things out involves enough reasoning so as not to be trivial. There is no hard-and-fast boundary as to what should be regarded as simple inferences that do not rise to the level of inquiry. But we can classify some instances as clearly on one side of the line or the other. Showing students a graph indicating an increase in immigration over time and then asking students how immigration changes over time do not rise to the level of inquiry. The inference is too simple. Inquiry generally involves considering, evaluating, and weighing multiple pieces of information (often from different information sources) as students attempt to reach conclusions from the complex of information. An inquiry task might give students a set of a dozen written and/or video documents providing conflicting information about the economic effects of immigration and then ask students to determine the relationship between immigration and economic conditions. This is a complex task that involves complex forms of analysis, evaluation, interpretation, and integration of information across multiple sources of information as well as the use of prior knowledge.

Finally, full-fledged inquiry requires engagement within communities. In any real inquiry, the ideas developed by an individual or a team must be subjected to the appraisal of others in their community (Longino, 2002). Finding things out requires that the community of knowers validate the new ideas developed by any individuals or groups within the community. A single individual or group that propounds a new idea has merely proposed an idea for consideration. To say that something has been found out requires further that the community has evaluated the claim and endorses it (Chinn, Buckland, & Samarapungavan, 2011; Code, 1991). In addition, the community is the home of the practices that guide the inquiry. The principles of reasoning themselves need to be endorsed by the community, and thus the community establishes norms and practices that are accepted as legitimate, reasonable ways of knowing. Thus, inquiry in learning environments needs to involve communities of students working socially to establish through their collective epistemic agency both the conclusions that they accept and the reasoning practices that are used to reach the conclusions.

The chapters in this handbook discuss a variety of learning environments that engage students in inquiry. All of them generally engage students in activities that, in varying degrees, meet the above six characteristics of inquiry, in terms of *finding things out*. Collectively, they scrutinize the conditions under which engaging students in inquiry can foster learning.

Goals of Inquiry-Based Learning

The goals of inquiry-based learning vary but generally encompass some combination of motivational and learning goals. Motivational goals include increasing students' engagement, enhancing interest in topics and subjects, promoting intrinsic caring about learning, and advancing goals for learning rather than just getting good grades or other such ends. Learning tasks can be made as consequential as possible, which means that tasks engage students in matters that they care about (e.g., analyzing and proposing solutions to various social injustices in one's community); in this way, students will perceive the direct relevance of what they are learning to addressing problems that matter to them.

Other goals involve gaining knowledge, understanding, and skills. A distinction discussed by Andriessen (2006) with respect to argumentation pertains more generally to learning through inquiry. Andriessen (2006) distinguished between arguing to learn and learning to argue. Arguing to learn means that students engage in argumentation to learn about the content of a topic; for instance, students engaged in argumentation about how to address poverty are learning about the topic of poverty and how policies might affect poverty levels. Learning to argue means that students engage in argumentation to learn how to argue more effectively. With this goal, the primary intent is not for students to learn about poverty but instead to learn about how to argue more effectively—by using evidence, counterarguments, rebuttals, and so on. Of course, argumentation-based learning may focus on one goal or the other or focus on both goals simultaneously.

The analogous distinction can be made for inquiry learning more generally. One goal of inquiry-based learning could be that students learn more about the content (we could call this "inquiring to learn"); a second goal is that students learn how to engage in inquiry ("learning to inquire"). Many contemporary curriculum standards envision that both goals can be achieved simultaneously (e.g., NGSS Lead States, 2013). Many chapters in this handbook describe learning environments that seek to foster both. For example, the environment that we ourselves have developed for science learning aims for students to learn science content about topics such as genetics while also learning to engage in inquiry with models (Duncan et al., this volume).

Inquiring to learn. When inquiring to learn is the focus, the specific goals of the learning environment will vary widely—from learning models of photosynthesis to understanding historical events. In schools, the content learning goals will usually be determined by curriculum standards, although many scholars also advocate affording students more autonomy to choose topics that are consequential to them (Hall & Jurow, 2015). Content goals may involve topic-specific concepts and principles as well as more generalizable concepts and principles. In science, an example of the former is the concepts and principles of evolution; an example at a more general level is the concepts and principles that govern complex systems, which are applicable to many topics in science. In history, an example at the topic level is learning about the Industrial Revolution; a more general topic would be learning about historical causation more generally (Van Boxtel et al., this volume).

Learning to inquire. Learning to inquire involves learning a range of reasoning practices to construct and critique conclusions (Ford, 2008). Two distinct subgoals of learning to inquire can be broadly distinguished. The first is that students learn some of the disciplinary practices of a field. For example, through engaging in inquiry, history students can experience and learn some of the practices that historians use to develop their historical narratives; in the same way, science students can experience and learn some of the practices that scientists use to generate scientific knowledge and consensus. This approach treats learners themselves as young or budding scientists, historians, mathematicians, and so on. In an analysis of science education, Feinstein and Waddington (2020) refer to this approach as an internalist approach—students are learning to be scientists as if they are internal to science, as scientists are. We extend this notion more broadly to all disciplines.

The second subgoal is learning to inquire not as a specialist in an area but as a layperson. In science education, Feinstein and Waddington (2020) refer to this as a contextual approach to science—students are learning not to be scientists but to be "competent outsiders" (Feinstein, 2011) who are external to science but nonetheless can interact with scientists and scientific information in ways that enable them to address issues of importance to them in personal and social contexts relevant to them. The same contextual approach can be applied to any field.

In reality, working as a scientist, as a historian, or as any other expert requires vast content knowledge and methodological knowledge of the domain. For instance, research on climate change involves in-depth knowledge of detailed models of climate change, sophisticated and technical methods of analysis, and so on (Chinn & Duncan, 2018). Laypeople cannot be expected to engage in such original inquiry themselves, nor do they have the domain knowledge to evaluate original research (Chinn & Duncan, 2018; Duncan, Chinn, & Barzilai, 2018). Instead, students should learn to engage in the forms of inquiry that they themselves will use as a lay adult (Duncan et al., 2018). In other words, educators should enable people to be competent outsiders in science (Feinstein, 2011) and in other fields—that is, people who are not specialists but can reason about information to address issues that they encounter in their lives, from decisions about personal and family health to reasoning about economic policies. This can involve learning to evaluate whether those who promulgate information are sufficiently expert, what counts as expertise on a topic, whether experts have reached consensus, and so on.

One value of learning about how disciplinary experts engage in inquiry is that it can give students a deeper sense of how these experts work and why (and when) their conclusions are worthy of trust (Chinn & Duncan, 2018; Duncan et al., 2018). For example, as students learn that the social processes of science can produce scientific knowledge but only through ongoing struggles to resolve the many challenges that arise in the search for truth (Duschl, 2020), they can better appreciate how science unfolds as it addresses new problems such as the COVID-19 pandemic.

Most chapters in the handbook discuss empirical evidence that pertains to one or both of these goals. Especially common in the chapters is evidence that supports the development of internalist and contextual goals for learning to inquire. Promoting greater competence in inquiry is a main goal of many approaches to inquiry-based education. Many chapters also document the value of inquiry-based learning for student motivation and engagement. Other chapters highlight that inquiry-based learning can also promote content goals.

The Goals of Learning to Inquire: The Apt-AIR Framework

The goals of learning to inquire can be described in terms of the Apt-AIR analysis of the ends of epistemic education developed by Barzilai and Chinn (2018) (see also Chinn, Barzilai, & Duncan, 2020a, 2020b). This analysis specifies the goals of epistemic education—that is, education directed at improving epistemic thinking (reasoning, engaging in inquiry, etc.). Building on the epistemology of Sosa (2015), the Apt-AIR framework posits that the objective of epistemic education is to promote *apt epistemic performance*. This means the successful achievement of valued epistemic aims (e.g., developing a good understanding of how inequities arise in society) through epistemic competence (e.g., developing this understanding through the use of effective strategies for evaluating evidence and expert claims about these issues).

One part of the Apt-AIR framework is the categorization of the component of epistemic thinking into three components: epistemic Aims and value, epistemic Ideals, and Reliable epistemic processes. (a) In inquiry, epistemic aims are the goals one sets for finding things out. Epistemic aims can include knowledge, explanations, models, understanding, and so on. Inquirers may value particular epistemic aims, such as explaining why cancer occurs, due to their value in achieving other goals or for their intrinsic interest. (b) Epistemic ideals refer to the standards or criteria used to evaluate whether epistemic aims have been achieved. For example, scientific explanations can be evaluated according to the epistemic ideals of fit with evidence, fit with other established theories, scope of evidence covered, and so on (Kuhn, 1977). (c) Reliable epistemic processes are the procedures, strategies, methods, and forms of collective interaction that have a good likelihood of achieving epistemic aims successfully. For example, scientific methods such as systematic experimentation and careful statistical analyses, as well as collaborative interactive patterns such as ongoing peer critique of work, are reliable epistemic processes for producing new scientific knowledge.

The Apt-AIR framework further posits that apt epistemic performance involves five aspects of competent engagement with epistemic aims, ideals, and reliable processes (Barzilai & Chinn, 2018):

1. In apt-epistemic performance, people *engage cognitively* with appropriate epistemic aims, ideals, and reliable processes to achieve valued epistemic aims. For instance, citizens who want to know why economic inequality is increasing and what policies could ameliorate it could seek to achieve these aims by setting ideals of ensuring that conclusions accord with sociological and economic evidence, as well as the consensus of experts where such consensus exists. And they could use reliable processes such as seeking out multiple sources of information, favoring the most trustworthy sources, and integrating information from such sources.
2. Epistemic aims, ideals, and reliable processes should be used *adaptively* for successful performance across diverse situations. This can involve selecting appropriately among different aims, ideals, and processes for use in different situations, or adjusting them in some way to fit a new situation. On topics where people have sufficient expertise, they may apply processes to evaluate evidence themselves; on topics where they lack the expertise to evaluate evidence themselves, they can instead focus on identifying the views of relevant experts, including whether there is expert consensus (Chinn et al., 2020b).
3. People have *epistemic metacognitive understanding* of valuable aims, ideals, and reliable processes, why they are valuable or reliable, and the conditions on their usefulness; they also engage in *epistemic metacognitive regulation* of their epistemic performance, such as appropriately evaluating whether ideals have been properly met (for a discussion of epistemic metacognitive

knowledge and skills, see Barzilai & Zohar, 2014). For instance, a person inquiring into causes and remedies of economic inequality would understand why fit with evidence is a better ideal than fit with prior beliefs (e.g., because prior beliefs are frequently incorrect but hard to dislodge due to motivated reasoning) and why seeking out multiple sources of information is more effective than just seeking out information from one source (e.g., because psychological research shows that considering alternative explanations tends to combat motivated reasoning and is a more reliable means to gain knowledge). They use this understanding to plan their inquiry, to regulate their activities, and to monitor and evaluate their progress.

4 People *care about* valuable epistemic aims and ideals and about using reliable epistemic processes; they are thus motivated to engage with them, and they further *enjoy* doing so. They form motivational-affective dispositions to achieve valuable epistemic aims. For instance, even though sorting through conflicting information on economic inequality is effortful, people whose epistemic performance is apt will care enough about gaining knowledge that meets valued ideals that they will engage in the needed processes and to engage with others in sometimes-tense discussions of how to move forward. And they will even enjoy the experience of identifying and trying to resolve conflicts.

5 Finally, in apt epistemic performance, people participate in epistemic performance together with others. That is, in apt epistemic performance involving inquiry, people are able to achieve their epistemic aims in concert with others, working together as communities of inquirers as they apply shared ideals and reliable social processes of developing knowledge. Citizens in a community seeking to understand economic inequality might come together to study the problem, agree on shared ideals such as fit with empirical evidence, and together brainstorm, argue about, and develop solutions to help remediate the problem.

The Apt-AIR framework can thus be used to identify the specific aims, ideals, and reliable processes to be set as the goals of education for particular topics (see Barzilai & Chinn, 2018). As we discuss in the next section, apt epistemic performance can differ from discipline to discipline, and even topic to topic. Thus, comprehensive efforts to develop effective inquiry learning environments will likely need to develop analyses of apt epistemic performance for many different inquiry problems and topics.

Domain Specificity or Generality of Inquiry

The AIR components of the Apt-AIR model can be used to compare the reasoning practices in different disciplines. Chinn and Sandoval (2018) used this approach to contrast the practices of scientists and historians through the lens of the AIR model of epistemic cognition. This analysis illustrates the substantive differences in inquiry practices across different disciplines or fields within disciplines.

Aims, ideals, and reliable processes in science and history. In their analysis of the practices of scientists versus historians, Chinn and Sandoval (2018) identified significant differences in the aims, ideals, and processes used in these two disciplines.

Both groups pursue a wide variety of aims. Central aims of science are to develop models and general explanations (Giere, 1988). Although some historians have also aspired to general explanations, many other historians deny this as a proper aim of history (Tucker, 2011), and historians do not aim to create models (Tucker, 2011). In contrast, some historians (but not scientists) aim to construct narratives with elements such as plots, characters, settings, and literary devices (Green & Troup, 1999). Scientists also seek to establish laws and estimate parameters (e.g., the gravitational constant)—aims not found in history. Conversely, historical aims such as establishing document authenticity and understanding the perspective of historical actors are not pursued by most scientists. On the basis of this analysis, we conclude that the aims of science and history are clearly different.

Epistemic ideals also vary substantively across science and history. Although both may profess to use fit with evidence, scientists and historians employ different conceptions of the meaning of evidence. Evidence in science typically involves empirical studies with patterns of analyzed data; evidence in history comes from documentary and other testimonies. Moreover, many other espoused ideals are different across the two fields. Scientists often hold up simplicity and elegance of explanation as an ideal (Kuhn, 1977), whereas historians instead hold the ideal of complexity and richness of description and narrative (Tucker, 2011). For scientists, theories, models, and explanations—when possible—should meet the ideal of making successful predictions; such an ideal is not part of the ideals of history, as historians do not expect their historical narratives to have direct predictive value. Ideals for good evidence in science may include conclusiveness (ruling out confounds for findings) and valid statistical inference. In contrast, ideals for good evidence in history may include contextualization within its local and historical setting (Wineburg, 2001) as well as trustworthiness of primary source documents (Goldman et al., 2016).

Finally, reliable processes for achieving epistemic aims vary across science and history. Central to the repertoire of processes regarded as reliable in science are experimentation, live observations of behaviors and activities (e.g., observations of chimpanzees in the wild), careful measurement (e.g., careful measurement of the weight and temperature of reactants in an experiment in chemistry), and synthetic analytic methods such as meta-analysis. Historians typically engage in none of these processes. Instead, they may deploy processes such as assuming the perspective of historical actors using empathy (Breisach, 2007) and thinking through and elaborating counterfactual scenarios to support claims (Wainryb, Shaw, Laupa, & Smith, 2001).

This analysis demonstrates that there can be significant differences in the aims, ideals, and reliable processes in different disciplines of inquiry. But differences can also occur within a single discipline. Within science, the field of paleontology uses historical methods of observation and analysis (Cleland, 2002). In contrast, tightly controlled experimentation is prevalent in fields such as microbiology, whereas more complex and less carefully controlled field studies are more common in ecology. In some fields, formal and informal replication is common (Greene et al., 2021); in others, the empirical studies are so expensive that they cannot be rerun (see Latour & Woolgar, 1986). Simulations provide significant sources of evidence in some fields; in others, they play no role at all (Lenhard, 2019).

Even when an ideal or process shares the same label across fields, the meaning may be quite different. Ecologists, particle physicists, and historians may all agree that "fit with evidence" is an important ideal, yet the nature of evidence across these three fields is dramatically different, and the means of determining fit with evidence is similarly different. In some scientific and social scientific fields, meta-analyses might be used to determine fit with evidence, but coherence of narratives with documentary evidence would be more appropriate in history. Similarly, although experimentation is common to many science and social science fields, the specifics of experimentation vary greatly. Threats to validity that are problematic in education (e.g., participants finding out about which condition they are in and adjusting their behavior accordingly) play no role in experiments in microbiology. Furthermore, knowing what needs to be controlled in research on different topics requires extensive knowledge of the causal factors that are operative within that field. Thus, even though certain aims, ideals, and processes may share some features across domains, they may differ in other, important respects.

Mid-level of generality. Given the challenges of differences in apt inquiry practices across topics, we believe that two consequences follow. First is that it is important that students learn about the deep entanglement of inquiry with domain knowledge (Duncan et al., 2018; Leung,

2020); awareness of these entanglements can enable students to appreciate the difficulty of evaluating evidence oneself when one lacks the domain knowledge (Chinn et al., 2020b). Second, instruction might most productively focus on aims, ideals, and processes that have a mid-level (or intermediate-level) generality, together with an emphasis that these need to be adapted across different disciplines, fields, and topics. Aims, ideals, and processes with a *mid-level of generality* are those that span many, but not all, domains. Students can learn what is common to these across fields and what differs. For example, students could learn about features of experimentation that are widely shared across fields (e.g., random assignment, the justifications for drawing causal conclusions from experiments) while also learning about some of the critical differences (e.g., particular challenges for implementing random assignment in educational research that do not exist in microbiology). Similarly, students could learn about the challenges that are presented by valid and reliable measurement across fields. They could come to appreciate that the particular challenges and remedies differ across fields (e.g., the challenges of measuring population size of animals based on samples differ qualitatively from the challenges of measuring human racial attitudes), as well as that measurement is seldom straightforward. This is a mid-level understanding of measurement that can be generative in understanding inquiry across a variety of fields. As one additional example, learning to evaluate source expertise and bias is a mid-level process that can benefit students across many domains, although the specifics of evaluating online sources for bias differ from the specifics of evaluating historical documents for bias (Wineburg & McGrew, 2019).

Inquiry-Based Learning versus Direct Instruction

In education, there has been an ongoing debate about the efficacy of inquiry-based learning versus direct instruction. Kirschner, Sweller, and Clark (2006) argued that constructivist approaches to education—including inquiry-based learning—are inferior to direct instruction methods in promoting learning. Their arguments were grounded in the limitations of working memory: Working memory is limited, and constructivist methods place too much of a burden on working memory for learning to occur. Hmelo-Silver, Duncan, and Chinn (2007) presented a detailed rebuttal of this conclusion Hmelo-Silver et al., (2007) agreed that working memory constraints are an important consideration in designing learning environments; constructivist learning environments in fact take this into account by providing various kinds of scaffolding that ease the working memory burden.

In addition, although Kirschner et al. (2006) provided extensive, persuasive evidence for working memory constraints, their review provided scant evidence that these working memory constraints render constructivist approaches ineffective. That is, they presented little direct evidence that scaffolded constructivist approaches were either ineffective or less effective than direct instruction approaches. Furthermore, the review omitted consideration of extensive research that supported the use of constructivist methods over alternatives, including direct instruction, such as the research on problem-based learning (Hmelo-Silver et al., 2007). Problem-based learning can be viewed as a type of inquiry learning that engages students in using various sources of information to solve problems. In contrast to the claims of Kirschner et al. (2006), who dismissed scaffolded forms of constructivist instruction as ineffective, Mayer (2004) presented cogent evidence that guided discovery methods (which are typical of inquiry-based learning) are superior to pure discovery methods of learning and also to direct instruction methods.

Subsequent research supports these positive conclusions about the efficacy of inquiry-based learning. In a more recent meta-analysis of problem-based learning in Dutch medical schools, Schmidt, Van Der Molen, Te Windel, and Wijnen (2009) reported that problem-based learning (in comparison to more traditional modes of instruction based largely on direct instruction) improved medical knowledge by small amounts and improved medical skills by larger amounts.

Chinn, Duncan, Dianovsky, and Rinehart (2013) reviewed additional evidence in science education that supported the efficacy of inquiry-based approaches to science education. Kapur (2016) also reviewed evidence that learning through inquiry or problem-solving is effective in promoting learning.

Kapur (2016) synthesized evidence on the effects of engaging students in exploratory problem-solving (or inquiry) prior to receiving normative explanations. He concluded that such problem-solving is highly effective when students engage in effortful work to solve a problem (even though they typically do not succeed) and then receive an explanation. He has termed this form of learning *productive failure*, because students initially fail to solve the problem but are subsequently better able to learn from explanations provided to them. Students' struggles to solve the problem appear to cue them to important features of the problem that better prepare them to grasp an explanation when they receive it. Thus, direct instruction is less effective than instruction that engages students in efforts to make discoveries. Kapur (2016) argued further that direct instruction promotes short-term learning but not long-term retention or transfer to new problems. Summarizing evidence that indicates that direct instruction "does not fare well over the longer term" (p. 295), Kapur (2016) argued that direct instruction might be regarded as promoting unproductive success—that is, it promotes short-term learning gains but not longer-term or transferrable gains in learning.

Recent analyses by Chinn et al. (2020a, 2020b) cast further doubt on the potential of direct instruction to prepare students to engage in inquiry in the real world. They analyzed reasoning in the contemporary "post-truth" world, which is rife with conflicting claims in proliferating digital media outlets. They proposed that instruction that is effective in preparing students to engage with the complex, emotion- and identity-laden messages in digital media requires engaging them with tasks that expose them more consistently to the messy complexity of this world. Students need to be engaged in tasks that tempt them to reason poorly, so that they can learn to cope with these situations. This can be done only by engaging students in such reasoning tasks, not by telling them how to do it.

Furthermore, Chinn et al. (2020a, 2020b) and Barzilai and Chinn (2020) argued that people frequently are committed to alternative ways of knowing that differ from what they are formally taught in school. Chinn et al. (2020a) showed that people who oppose vaccinations have often adopted ways of knowing (aims, ideals, and processes) that differ from those of scientists. For example, while scientists view systematic data collected by scientists as the most reliable forms of knowing, many who oppose vaccination believe that scientists who test vaccinations are deeply biased by financial interests and thus use unreliable processes. They may also view direct, personal experiences as more reliable than scientific studies. Leung (2020) presented data indicating that some undergraduates may resist the idea that peer review renders scientific findings trustworthy; rather, some view peer review as a highly subjective process in which reviewers endorse only those old ideas that conform to their preexisting beliefs. In such contexts, simply telling these students how to know through direct instruction is insufficient; they are committed to alternative ways of knowing. A student whose family and community are committed to the view that mainstream media are unreliable sources of news will not be persuaded by instruction that simply tells them that sources like the *New York Times* are trustworthy. They may "play along" within school in order to get good grades, but such instruction is unlikely to change their minds. Instead, to engage students in seriously considering alternative ways of knowing, students need to engage in inquiry about ways of knowing. They need to be given the epistemic agency to consider and weigh, and potentially be persuaded by, arguments for different ways of knowing (Miller et al., 2018).

Finally, it is worth noting that, in practice, inquiry environments often meld together many different forms of instruction within an overall inquiry framework. For instance, in our own inquiry learning environments, the overall inquiry tasks engage students in developing and choosing among alternative models using evidence. But a unit may include elements of direct instruction as embedded sub-components (e.g., explaining components of good arguments to help students strengthen the argumentative essays they write as one of their inquiry products; directly explaining key terms after they have developed the concepts themselves). Students may also engage in practice in some lessons (e.g., solving Mendelian inheritance problems as part of a unit once they have constructed a model of Mendelian inheritance). Thus, inquiry environments are often eclectic in the choices of particular instructional tactics within an overall inquiry task.

Overall, then, empirical research supports the conclusion that inquiry-based forms of learning can be highly effective. Pure discovery methods, however, are generally ineffective. Effective methods must be properly scaffolded. Further, inquiry environments may also include elements of direct instruction to explain particular points to students that they can use in inquiry. Many of the chapters in this volume focus on the variety of ways in which inquiry-based learning can be productively scaffolded to support learning.

Inquiry learning and equity. An increasingly central issue in the design of inquiry learning environments is how to engage students in inquiry learning in ways that are equitable for all students, including students from minoritized and marginalized communities and groups. A number of chapters throughout this handbook address how to design effective instruction that promotes equitable treatment of students and equity in learning outcomes. Central to these efforts is according epistemic agency and authority to students from diverse backgrounds to advance their own ideas and perspectives (Bang & Medin, 2010; Bang, Warren, Rosebery, & Medin, 2013; Stroupe, 2014). Positioning students as strong epistemic contributors to the inquiry is also vital. Choosing problems that address issues of concern to students is another approach for deepening the engagement of all students (e.g., Rubel, Hall-Wieckert, & Lim, 2017; Tan, Calabrese Barton, & Benavides, 2019).

Organization of the Handbook

Given this backdrop of analysis of what inquiry-oriented learning involves, we turn now to a brief overview of *The Handbook of Inquiry and Learning*. The chapters are authored by leading scholars working on inquiry and learning across the globe. The chapters thus include attention to inquiry and learning from a variety of perspectives—from different countries, from different disciplines that engage students in inquiry, and from different lenses on inquiry (e.g., focus on equity issues, focus on assessment).

The handbook is divided into three sections, which we summarize below.

The design of learning environments. The first section addresses the design of inquiry learning environments. This section leads off with a chapter by Richard A. Duschl and Armend Tahirsylaj (Chapter 2), who discuss major curricular trends that have shaped educators' conceptions of how to design learning environments; they point to major shifts in thinking that have influenced conceptions of learning through inquiry. The remaining chapters in this section discuss critical dimensions of how to design learning environments that engage students in inquiry. Yael Kali (Chapter 3) presents an overview of basic theoretical perspectives on inquiry learning, and how these connect to three frameworks for designing learning environments, including designs for inquiry as knowledge integration, designs for inquiry as a community endeavor, and designs for inquiry in the networked society. Kimberley Gomez and Nicole Mancevice (Chapter 4) discuss how to establish and run design teams leveraging a participatory approach—with a focus on activities including developing project vision and goals, understanding context for design, establishing roles and expectations, and fostering participation. The chapter by William R. Penuel and Ashley Seidel Potvin (Chapter 5) discusses design from the perspective of design-based implementation research, which focuses on creating ongoing, sustainable innovations in partnership with stakeholders; their analysis points to the need for extensive collaborative work with the stakeholders who will be involved with implementation. Extensive interactions with those who will implement the designs are also a focus of the chapter by Jeremy Roschelle, Claudia Mazziotti, and Barbara Means (Chapter 6), who discuss the critical issue of how to scale up the design of inquiry environments. They discuss why scaling up inquiry learning environments is hard and suggest effective strategies for successful scale-up. One element of design that is critical to efforts to implement and scale up inquiry learning environments is effective professional development for teachers who will be implementing these environments; in Chapter 7, Anat Zohar and Maya S. Resnick discuss how to design professional development successfully. They review central pedagogical features of PD programs that can promote successful implementation. In Chapter 8, the final chapter in this section, Drew H. Gitomer lays out a framework for thinking about how to assess inquiry learning; grounding his analysis in evidence-centered design of assessment, he reviews and evaluates a comprehensive array of approaches that have been used to date.

Components of Inquiry Environments. The second section of the handbook analyzes core components of effective inquiry environments. Each chapter spotlights one of these components and its role in supporting learning and engagement in inquiry environments. Chapter 9, the first chapter in this section, by Sanna Järvelä, Hanna Järvenoja, and Hanni Muukkonen, addresses the role of motivation in inquiry environments and how inquiry environments can be designed to foster motivation. They focus particularly on how to support motivation in the social contexts that are featured in inquiry learning environments. As we discussed earlier, guidance is needed to effectively support learning in inquiry learning environments. Chris Quintana (Chapter 10) provides an overview of critical issues in how to successfully scaffold inquiry in these environments. Quintana reviews the core features of scaffolding and how our conceptions of scaffolding have changed over time, providing examples of various forms and functions of scaffolding in action. Dan Battey and Emily Wolf McMichael (Chapter 11) turn to the role of teachers in leading and orchestrating equitable learning environments; they focus on how teachers' moves can support equitable learning for children from diverse backgrounds in inquiry environments, or how teachers can conversely exacerbate problems of inequity. The next two chapters both address argumentation as a critical discourse of inquiry (because argumentation is, by definition, a discourse involving the giving of reasons and evidence to support claims). Alina Reznitskaya and Ian A. G. Wilkinson (Chapter 12) take the perspective of argumentation as a form of dialogic discourse that embodies principles of sociocultural learning theories; they discuss the critical role of dialogic discourse in mediating learning in inquiry environments and the need for research that investigates these sociocultural processes in greater detail. María Pilar Jiménez-Aleixandre and Pablo Brocos (Chapter 13) discuss argumentation using the lens of the AIR model discussed earlier; they examine critical epistemic goals, ideals, and reliable processes for engaging in argumentation within various instructional contexts. Argumentation is part of the social, discursive dimension of inquiry environments. The final two chapters in this section extend the analysis of social aspects of inquiry to other dimensions beyond argumentation. Asmalina Saleh, Cindy Hmelo-Silver, and Krista D. Glazweski (Chapter 14) examine the collaborative interactions that support successful inquiry learning; they discuss how to scaffold productive collaborative inquiry, as well as technological tools that can provide the needed support. Katerine Bielaczyc (Chapter 15) takes a higher-level view of inquiry at the social level; she explicates four design considerations that focus on the community level of inquiry (e.g., cultivating a social identity of a collective enterprise; framing social interactions using multiplayer epistemic games).

Inquiry and Learning across Different Disciplines and Contexts. The third and final section of the handbook examines inquiry and learning across different disciplines and contexts. Carol D. Lee (Chapter 16) explicates the engagement of students in inquiry with literature. She explains what inquiry in literature means, shows what it looks like, and examines how to promote learning through inquiry effectively and equitably. Carla van Boxtel, Michiel Voet, and Gerhard Stoel (Chapter 17) focus on inquiry and learning in history. They examine both how to promote student learning and how to support teachers' professional development in the context of history education. Ilana Seidel Horn and Melissa Gresalfi (Chapter 18) address how the design of inquiry environment can broaden participation in inquiry in mathematics classes; they examine four key leverage points (including teachers' knowledge, classroom norms and practices) for improving classrooms as interactive systems engaged in inquiry. Ravit Golan Duncan, Na'ama Y. Av-Shalom, and Clark A. Chinn (Chapter 19) examine inquiry learning in science, with a focus on model-based inquiry. They discuss a wide range of issues needed to design effective inquiry environments in science, with a particular focus on how to enable science learners to become competent outsiders. Anette Kolmos, Pia Bøgelund, and Jette Egelund Holgaard (Chapter 20) present a comprehensive overview of inquiry in engineering education. They contrast views of inquiry in engineering education and science education, as well as different, related approaches within engineering education including inquiry-based learning, design-based learning, and problem-based learning. Finally, turning to learning environments out of school, Jennifer D. Adams and Susan McCullough discuss inquiry and learning in informal settings. They discuss the opportunities that informal learning environments (in science and art) provide for both student and teacher inquiry in terms of knowledge construction and the pedagogies to support it.

Summary. Collectively, the chapters in this handbook provide a comprehensive picture of how to design and develop inquiry learning environments across a variety of disciplines and settings. They identify critical components of learning environments that support learning, and they document the effects of inquiry-based learning environments. They also provide guidance on how to plan and design effective learning environments that engage students in inquiry. We hope that the handbook will help inspire new rounds of research and innovation that will further advance the field's ability to leverage inquiry to promote students' learning and motivation.

References

Andriessen, J. (2006). Arguing to learn. In R. K. Sawyer (Ed.), *The Cambridge handbook of the learning sciences* (pp. 443–459). Cambridge: Cambridge University Press.

Bang, M., & Medin, D. (2010). Cultural processes in science education: Supporting the navigation of multiple epistemologies. *Science Education, 94*(6), 1008–1026. https://doi.org/10.1002/sce.20392

Bang, M., Warren, B., Rosebery, A. S., & Medin, D. (2013). Desettling expectations in science education. *Human Development, 55*(5–6), 302–318. https://doi.org/10.1159/000345322

Barzilai, S., & Zohar, A. (2014). Reconsidering personal epistemology as metacognition: A multifaceted approach to the analysis of epistemic thinking. *Educational Psychologist, 49*(1), 13–35. https://doi.org/10.1080/00461520.2013.863265

Barzilai, S., & Chinn, C. A. (2018). On the goals of epistemic education: Promoting apt epistemic performance. *Journal of the Learning Sciences, 27*, 353–389.

Barzilai, S., & Chinn, C. A. (2020). A review of educational responses to the "post-truth" condition: Four lenses on "post-truth" problems. *Educational Psychologist, 55*, 107–119. https://doi.org/10.1080/00461520.2020.1786388

Breisach, E. (2007). *Historiography: Ancient, medieval, & modern* (3rd ed.). Chicago, IL: University of Chicago Press.

Chinn, C. A., Barzilai, S., & Duncan, R. G. (2020a). Disagreeing about how to know: The instructional value of explorations into knowing. *Educational Psychologist, 55*(3), 167–180. https://doi.org/10.1080/00461520.2020.1786387

Chinn, C. A., Barzilai, S., & Duncan, R. G. (2020b). Education for a "post-truth" world: New directions for research and practice. *Educational Researcher, 50*(1), 51–60. https://doi.org/10.3102/0013189x20940683

Chinn, C. A., Buckland, L. A., & Samarapungavan, A. (2011). Expanding the dimensions of epistemic cognition: Arguments from philosophy and psychology. *Educational Psychologist, 46*, 141–167. https://doi.org/10.1080/00461520.2011.587722

Chinn, C. A., & Duncan, R. G. (2018). What is the value of general knowledge of scientific reasoning? In F. Fischer, C. A. Chinn, K. Engelmann, & J. Osborne (Eds.), *Scientific reasoning and argumentation: The roles of domain-specific and domain-general knowledge* (pp. 77–101). New York: Routledge.
Chinn, C. A., Duncan, R. G., Dianovsky, M., & Rinehart, R. (2013). Promoting conceptual change through inquiry. In S. Vosniadou (Ed.), *International handbook of conceptual change* (2nd ed., pp. 539–559). New York: Taylor & Francis.
Chinn, C. A., & Sandoval, W. A. (2018). Epistemic cognition and epistemic development. In F. Fischer, C. Hmelo-Silver, S. Goldman, & P. Reimann (Eds.), *International handbook of the learning sciences* (pp. 24–33). New York: Routledge.
Cleland, C. E. (2002). Methodological and epistemic differences between historical science and experimental science. *Philosophy of Science, 69*, 474–496.
Code, L. (1991). *What can she know? Feminist theory and the construction of knowledge*. Ithaca, NY: Cornell University Press.
Duncan, R. G., Chinn, C. A., & Barzilai, S. (2018). Grasp of evidence: Problematizing and expanding the next generation science standards' conceptualization of evidence. *Journal of Research in Science Teaching, 55*(7), 907–937. https://doi.org/10.1002/tea.21468
Duschl, R. A. (2020). Practical reasoning and decision making in science: Struggles for truth. *Educational Psychologist, 55*(3), 187–192. https://doi.org/10.1080/00461520.2020.1784735
Feinstein, N. (2011). Salvaging science literacy. *Science Education, 95*(1), 168–185. https://doi.org/10.1002/sce.20414
Feinstein, N. W., & Waddington, D. I. (2020). Individual truth judgments or purposeful, collective sensemaking? Rethinking science education's response to the post-truth era. *Educational Psychologist, 55*(3), 155–166. https://doi.org/10.1080/00461520.2020.1780130
Ford, M. (2008). "Grasp of practice" as a reasoning resource for inquiry and nature of science understanding. *Science & Education, 17*, 147–177.
Giere, R. N. (1988). *Explaining science: A cognitive approach*. Chicago, IL: University of Chicago Press.
Goldman, S. R., Britt, M. A., Brown, W., Cribb, G., George, M., Greenleaf, C., ... Project READI. (2016). Disciplinary literacies and learning to read for understanding: A conceptual framework for disciplinary literacy. *Educational Psychologist, 51*, 219–246.
Green, A., & Troup, K. (Eds.). (1999). *The houses of history: A critical reading in twentieth century history and theory*. New York: New York University Press.
Greene, J. A., Chinn, C. A., & Deekins, V. M. (2021). Experts' reasoning about the replication crisis: Apt epistemic performance and actor-oriented transfer. *Journal of the Learning Sciences*. Advance online publication.
Hall, R., & Jurow, A. S. (2015). Changing concepts in activity: Descriptive and design studies of consequential learning in conceptual practices. *Educational Psychologist, 50*(3), 173–189. https://doi.org/10.1080/00461520.2015.1075403
Hmelo-Silver, C. E., Duncan, R. G., & Chinn, C. A. (2007). Scaffolding and achievement in problem-based and inquiry learning: A response to Kirschner, Sweller, and Clark (2006). *Educational Psychologist, 42*, 99–107.
Kapur, M. (2016). Examining productive failure, productive success, unproductive failure, and unproductive success in learning. *Educational Psychologist, 51*, 289–299.
Kelly, T. (2014). Evidence. Retrieved from https://plato.stanford.edu/entries/evidence/
Kirschner, P. A., Sweller, J., & Clark, R. E. (2006). Why minimal guidance during instruction does not work: An analysis of the failure of constructivist, discovery, problem-based, experiential, and inquiry-based teaching. *Educational Psychologist, 41*, 75–86.
Kuhn, T. S. (1977). *The essential tension: Selected studies in scientific tradition and change*. Chicago, IL: University of Chicago Press.
Latour, B., & Woolgar, S. (1986). *Laboratory life: The construction of scientific facts*. Princeton, NJ: Princeton University Press.
Lenhard, J. (2019). *Calculated surprises: A philosophy of computer simulation*. Oxford: Oxford University Press.
Leung, J. S. C. (2020). Students' adherences to epistemic understanding in evaluating scientific claims. *Science Education, 104*(2), 164–192. https://doi.org/10.1002/sce.21563
Longino, H. E. (2002). *The fate of knowledge*. Princeton, NJ: Princeton University Press.
Mayer, R. E. (2004). Should there be a three-strikes rule against pure discovery learning? The case for guided methods of instruction. *American Psychologist, 59*, 14–19.
Miller, E., Manz, E., Russ, R., Stroupe, D., & Berland, L. (2018). Addressing the epistemic elephant in the room: Epistemic agency and the next generation science standards. *Journal of Research in Science Teaching, 55*(7), 1053–1075. https://doi.org/10.1002/tea.21459

NGSS Lead States. (2013). *Next generation science standards: For states, by states.* Washington, DC: National Academies Press.

Rubel, L., Hall-Wieckert, M., & Lim, V. (2017). Making space for place: Mapping tools and practices to teach for spatial justice. *Journal of the Learning Sciences*, *26*(4), 643–687. https://doi.org/10.1080/10508406.2017.1336440

Schmidt, H. G., Van Der Molen, H. T., Te Winkel, W. W. R., & Wijnen, W. H. F. W. (2009). Constructivist, problem-based learning does work: A meta-analysis of curricular comparisons involving a single medical school. *Educational Psychologist*, *44*, 227–249.

Sosa, E. (2015). *Judgment and agency.* Oxford: Oxford University Press.

Stroupe, D. (2014). Examining classroom science practice communities: How teachers and students negotiate epistemic agency and learn science-as-practice. *Science Education*, *98*, 487–516. https://doi.org/10.1002/sce.21112

Stroupe, D., Caballero, M. D., & White, P. (2018). Fostering students' epistemic agency through the co-configuration of moth research. *Science Education*, *102*(6), 1176–1200. https://doi.org/10.1002/sce.21469

Tan, E., Calabrese Barton, A., & Benavides, A. (2019). Engineering for sustainable communities: Epistemic tools in support of equitable and consequential middle school engineering. *Science Education*, *103*(4), 1011–1046. https://doi.org/10.1002/sce.21515

Tucker, A. (Ed.). (2011). *A companion to the philosophy of history and historiography.* Malden, MA: Wiley-Blackwell.

Wainryb, C., Shaw, L. A., Laupa, M., & Smith, K. R. (2001). Children's adolescents', and young adults' thinking about different types of disagreements. *Developmental Psychology*, *37*, 373–386.

Wineburg, S. (2001). *Historical thinking and other unnatural acts: Charting the future of teaching the past.* Philadelphia, PA: Temple University Press.

Wineburg, S., & McGrew, S. (2019). Lateral reading and the nature of expertise: Reading less and learning more when evaluating digital information. *Teachers College Record*, *121*, 1–40.

SECTION 1

The Design of Inquiry Learning Environments

2

EVOLVING CONCEPTIONS OF EDUCATIONAL RESEARCH AND INQUIRY

Richard A. Duschl and Armend Tahirsylaj

Introduction

Looking across the 20th century, the guiding conceptions for educational research and inquiry—from problem selection to choice of methods and theories—have varied widely and progressed differentially. Educational practices and policy over the past 100 years reveal a narrative of oscillating changes and developments (Lagemann, 2000; Rudolph, 2019). The recurring introduction of new theories, tools, and technologies has shaped, and will continue to shape, how we conceptualize teaching, learning, and the design of learning environments. Across the decades, researchers and policymakers have taken various stances (e.g., epistemological, ontological, historical, pedagogical, psychological, sociological, cultural, and economical) to inform and represent how knowledge is established, refined, transmitted, and changed.

In very broad brushstrokes, 20th-century developments in education inquiry can be summarized along a continuum where inquiry has been conceived as an experiment-driven enterprise, a theory-driven enterprise, and a model-driven enterprise. Such stances have influenced the dynamics of educational inquiry and research. In turn, these deliberations and debates have affected what is considered to be, at any point in time, the knowledge that is most worth knowing. We live in a rapidly changing world, and we are learning how to learn as well as learning how to learn about learning. This chapter will trace some of these developments in educational research and inquiry, with a focus on how these developments have influenced curricula design and research on learning.

Looking back, there was one highly influential decade that wrought dynamic changes in educational inquiry. The 1950s were a pivotal turning point, a disruptive decade, when significant changes occurred to psychological, philosophical, and pedagogical frameworks—three core domains that inform education theory and practice. For psychology, the emergence through the 1950s to 1970s of cognitive and constructivist learning theories challenged the tenets of behavioral learning theory (National Research Council [NRC], 1999). In philosophy, the adoption of historical and cognitive frameworks for depicting the growth of scientific knowledge challenged logical positivistic images with respect to how building and refining scientific theories, models, and explanations occurs (Kuhn, 1970; Giere, 1988). The major 1950s pedagogical shift regarding curriculum and instruction was adopting disciplinary-based "enquiry into enquiry" stances for education (Schwab, 1962; Duschl, 1988, 1990; Connelly, 2013; Rudolph, 2019). Collectively, these changes summarily influenced and ignited considerations regarding the central roles that epistemic and scientific practices (e.g., systems thinking, digital literacies, modeling, argumentation, computational thinking) play in learning in the sciences, mathematics, and humanities.

The first section of the chapter begins with an overview of the major mid-century shifts to educational inquiry more generally. The second section delves into curriculum theory and learning theory debates and examines two major, and very different, models for teaching and learning—constructivism and Bildung-centered Didaktik.[1] We then examine reforms in science and mathematics education and in literacy traditions. The final section examines the emergence of the learning sciences in education, which is then followed by the chapter summary.

Paradigmatic Shifts in Educational Inquiry

There were several key catalysts spurring rapid changes in educational inquiry and curriculum following WWII. One catalyst in the 1950s was the reaction to the launching of the USSR satellite Sputnik. Another was the post-WWII reconstruction of Europe and the Cold War. Other influences were the explosion in population and the introduction of new technologies. Within one decade, 1955–1965, hundreds of millions of dollars were invested in the development of school curriculum and facilities, employing a top-down process from high schools first, followed by middle and elementary grades. Once the curricula were established, National Science Foundation (NSF) funding in the US and Nuffield funding in the UK was then directed to establish teacher education programs with broad goals toward enhancing and promoting the next-generation workforces (Duschl, 1990; DeBoer, 1991; Rudolph, 2002; Black & Atkin, 2003). More recent reforms in Europe include Spain's national educational reforms in the 1970s, following the removal of the Franco regime and the establishment of the Autonoma Universities network, and Germany's education recalibration following the PISA Shock (Tahirsylaj, Niebert, & Duschl, 2015).

Curriculum and instruction reforms beginning in the 1950s were taking place concurrently with the deliberations to shift from modernism to postmodernism frameworks (Doll, 1993). Curriculum study during the interwar years began to pursue human developmental perspectives over determinism in education and to examine the dynamics between curriculum and instruction (Lagemann, 2000). In the 1950s, philosophers and psychologists began to question and alter many of the foundational guiding conceptions and tenets about the growth of scientific knowledge and theories for learning (Hanson, 1958; Kuhn, 1970; Chomsky, 1986). Sociological perspectives, particularly in European nations (e.g., Vygotsky, Piaget, Bernstein, Habermas, Foucault, among others), were also shaping educational theory and practice principally within the didaktik traditions (Tahirsylaj, 2019). The point is that during the post-WWII decades (1950–1970), when psychological and educational researchers and disciplinary experts (e.g., scientists, mathematicians, historians) were revamping education theory and education systems (Bruner, 1960), there were concurrent major revisions among historians and philosophers of science and cognitive psychologists pertaining to the core ideas about the nature of scientific inquiry and about the nature of learning, respectively.

In psychology, associative and behavioral learning theory tenets came under attack in the 1950s and 1960s. Psychological skepticism toward educational research began to wane, but skepticism regarding the value of basic research to inform educational practice and decision-making persisted up to the 1970s (Getzel, 1978). Robert Glaser (1978) wrote:

> We are at a kind of juncture (between the) extrapolation of behavioristic animal learning lab studies, concepts and techniques to practical human affairs. At the same time, cognitive theories of human performance, influenced by a concern for realistic complex human endeavors, have stimulated the present major theoretical orientation in psychology.
>
> *(p. 257)*

By the 1990s, cognitive, information-processing, and sociocultural tenets of learning theory were firmly in place (Greeno, Collins, & Resnick, 1997; NRC, 2001). Furthermore, the cognitive, social, and cultural dynamics of learning were held to be mutually supportive of one another and intertwined such that "you cannot strip learning of its content, nor study it in a 'neutral' context. It is always situated, always related to some ongoing enterprise" (Bruner, 2004, p. 20). These trends will be elaborated on further later in this chapter.

Perspectives on the Foundations of Education

Knowledge growth and reasoning in the disciplines are grounded philosophically, psychologically, and socially (Giere, 1988; Knorr-Cetina, 1999; Longino, 2002). When considered together in application to conducting scientific inquiries, these disciplinary frameworks shape investigative practices in research settings (Pickering, 1995) and learning settings (Lehrer & Schauble, 2004; NRC, 2008). What counts as appropriate and rational knowledge seeking and building practices has been debated. Many scholars of science drew a distinction between "contexts of discovery" (i.e., where, when, and how new models, explanations, and theories emerge) and "contexts of justification" (i.e., how new models, explanations, and theories are rationalized and verified). In response to debates regarding the validity and reliability of scientific theories and laws, coupled with the emergence of history of science as scholarly field which showed that the practices of scientists did not fit with earlier assumptions, new images of scientific inquiry emerged in the philosophy and history of science. Contemporary philosophical, anthropological, and sociological accounts of the growth of knowledge (Longino, 1990; Knorr-Cetina, 1999) adopted naturalistic approaches to explain the emergence of new conceptual (what we know), methodological (how we know), and epistemological (why we believe) criteria or standards for understanding and explaining the growth of scientific knowledge and the mechanisms of scientific reasoning. In the Preface to *The Cognitive Basis of Science*, Carruthers, Stich, and Siegal (2002) state:

> It became important, then, to see science, too, as a natural phenomenon, somehow recruiting a variety of natural processes and mechanisms—both cognitive and social—to achieve its results. Philosophers of science began to look, not just to history, but also to cognitive psychology in their search for an understanding of scientific activity.
>
> *(p. 4)*

The prevailing view up to the 1970s to account for and justify the rationality of scientific knowledge was to examine how the practices of science fell into either the context of discovery (e.g., how were questions and problems identified) or the context of justification (e.g., how was empirical evidence obtained and used to test hypotheses). A movement called *naturalized philosophy of science* focused careful attention on how scientists actually worked to create knowledge. The ideas that emerged were a recognition that the bulk of knowledge-building or epistemic activities involved attending to anomalies and incorporating new evidence, as well as refining theories, models, and mechanisms (Kuhn, 1970; Suppe, 1977). That is, scientific practice involves ongoing modifications that facilitate improvement and refinement of theories, models, mechanisms, and/or explanations. The prevalent and persistent epistemic game came to be seen as the refinement and restructuring of knowledge systems to enhance explanatory coherence (Longino, 2002; Zammito, 2004; NRC, 2007; Thagard, 2007; Duschl & Grandy, 2008).

This body of scholarship also showed that the values, beliefs, methods, and guiding conceptions or theoretical frameworks (e.g., Cell Theory, Plate Tectonic Theory, Periodic Law, Newton's Laws) adopted by researchers were paramount. Schwab's conceptualization of inquiry (Schwab, 1962) was based on such commitments to guiding conceptions. These served as frameworks that influenced the problem choice, the questions asked, the measurements taken, the data analysis and interpretations, and the findings and outcomes. These "steps" constituted the "Pattern of Enquiry" framework (Finegold, Clipsham, & Wahlstrom, 1977) developed as an instructional tool for reading original science research in high school and college science programs. Schwab's recognition of the role of guiding conceptions strongly influenced the 1960s and 1970s adoption of inquiry approaches in science education curriculum (Rudolph, 2002; Connelly, 2013).

As such, shifts in researchers' guiding conceptions serve as signals to frame the history of 20th-century educational inquiry in terms of the philosophical, psychological, and pedagogical frameworks used by researchers. Surveying the adopted and debated guiding conception frameworks that embrace different, shifting, and sometimes competing, philosophical, psychological, and pedagogical conceptions and commitment reveals a series of scholarly debates that capture, in part, the salient developments of 20th-century educational research and inquiry. To that we now turn, beginning with reforms in science education and then turning to other areas.

Science Education Reforms

Among pedagogues, traditional curriculum development and teaching practices in the 1950s were under review in both science and mathematics. Reformers favored approaches that were grounded more in inquiry and discovery and that were historically grounded (Easley, 1959; DeMott, 1962; Schwab & Brandwein, 1962; Phillips, 2014). Since the first NSF-funded era of science education reform, begun in the 1950s and extending through the 1960s into the 1970s, there have been numerous revisions and changes in science educators' thinking about the nature of knowledge, the nature of learning, and the nature of teaching. The slow progression of changes during the second half of the 20th century reflects the challenging modifications to basic and applied research on learning, reasoning, communicating, and teaching imparted to educational theory, policy, and practice. Building out from the dynamic changes of the 1950s in the fields of psychology, epistemology, pedagogy, and in the emergent STEM disciplines themselves, educational researchers, developmental psychologists, and curriculum developers redesigned the landscapes of both formal and informal education.

The curriculum reforms in the 1950s and 1960s funded by NSF in the US and Nuffield in the UK were guided by groups of scientists working with science and mathematics educators in different disciplinary domains (Rudolph, 2002; Black & Atkin, 2003). Connelly (2013) captures the spirit of the shift in curriculum design:

> One of the main educational critiques leading to these reforms … was that educators controlled the curriculum of the 1950s, offering "soft" progressive education ideas on student interest and learning.
>
> *(p. 624)*

Connelly goes on to describe the tug-of-war that ensued between the "subject-centered curriculum" developed by disciplinary specialists (e.g., scientists, historians, mathematicians) and the "student-centered life-adjustment curriculum" developed by curriculum designers adopting more learner/child-centered cognitive and sociocultural teaching and learning frameworks.

> [T]here was a shift in educational reform workers from educationists to researchers in disciplines. The school reforms … were driven by academic professional associations in mathematics, biology, physics, chemistry and history. So, … *educational reform in the middle of the last century focused explicitly on recognizable curriculum matters.* It did so by marginalizing curriculum scholars in favor of disciplinary scholars.
>
> *(Connelly, 2013, p. 624. Emphasis in original)*

Examining teaching of the scientific method, Rudolph (2019) reveals how political, economic, pedagogical, psychological, philosophical, and technological forces all influenced education to swing back and forth during the 20th century between teaching knowledge (e.g., what we know), and teaching scientific methods, processes, and practices (e.g., how and why we know).

Joseph Schwab was influential in establishing a push to undo the subject-matter-coverage orientation of school science. Schwab's contributions to educational reform were motivated in part by his commitment to place philosophical over psychological tenets. In "On the corruption of education by psychology" (Schwab, 1958), he did so by advocating for a shift away from behavioral psychological tenets to philosophical tenets about scientific inquiry. He argued that science education should be designed so that learning is an "enquiry into enquiry" and not a rhetoric of conclusions, e.g., teaching only what we know (Schwab, 1962). As introduced above, his study of scientists reveal a "Pattern of Enquiry" that went well beyond a stepwise scientific method for testing hypotheses. A biologist himself, Schwab was appointed the first director of the NSF-funded BSCS (Biological Sciences Curriculum Study), center for the reform of high school biology. But his seminal contributions to teaching science as enquiry (Schwab, 1962) and reframing the language of curriculum (Schwab, 1969) were influenced by the significant changes in how science itself was being enacted but not yet reflected in educational models. His position recognized that there was a "transformation from a literal-minded empiricism to a complex in which conceptual invention plays a vast role, determining the facts we seek and conditioning the meaning we confer upon them" (Schwab, 1960, pp. 176–177). Thus, the guiding conceptions adopted by researchers, scientists, historians, or anyone engaged in inquiry, shaped choices, decisions, and, ultimately, reasoning.

Mathematics Education Reforms

Concurrent with the revisionary curriculum activities taking place in the US science classrooms, mathematicians also set out to reform math education. Over the preceding 60 years, a revolution in mathematics had occurred making obsolete the math being taught in secondary schools. Areas of mathematics that were emerging in post-World War II technologies and industrial practices included computers, programming, telecommunications, data analysis, probability, and statistics. Two reform episodes, the first in the 1950s and the second in the 1960s, sought to introduce a new math movement in the secondary grades that targeted these emerging new topics (DeMott, 1962; Phillips, 2014; Kilpatrick, 2015). The new math sought to introduce new topics into the secondary school curriculum, including symbolic logic, Boolean algebra, set theory, groups and fields, probability, and statistics. The argument was that the acquisition of mathematical ideas would be best approached by developing students' instincts for abstraction.

In the 1950s, two programs for revising the mathematics curriculum were formed. One was the School Mathematics Study Group (SMSG) formed in 1958 and directed by E. G. Beagle, first at Yale University and then later at Stanford University, that sought to design, develop, and try out a new secondary-level curriculum in mathematics. The other, involving The Carnegie Corporation and the University of Illinois and begun in 1952, was the Curriculum Study in Mathematics. They produced several texts "emphasizing ... the structure of mathematics and the 'discovery theory' of learning; these texts had been tested in several states before the SMSG project was undertaken" (DeMott, 1962, p. 300).

By the 1960s, conferences were being held to discuss which stream of mathematics to include in the new curriculum. Kilpatrick (2017) reports that at the 1966 New Orleans meeting university mathematicians, high school mathematics teachers, and mathematicians from industry gathered and produced three recommendations for secondary (grades 7–12) mathematics curriculum:

1 Frequent consideration of mathematical models of significant and interesting problem situations;
2 An introduction to those mathematical concepts that are important for general citizenship;
3 In addition to traditional topics, some consideration for probability, logic, computing and flowcharts, and the concept of function (pp. 168–169).

The subsequent curriculum materials represent the first time that mathematical modeling was introduced to the US math textbooks. Following tryouts of the new curriculum materials, a major obstacle that emerged was the intent to teach the same math curriculum to all secondary-grade students. Designing one curriculum suitable for all levels of mathematical abilities proved to be an impossible task, according to Kilpatrick (2017). Preparing teachers to handle the new content and arranging for pupils to take the appropriate course each year turned out to be too challenging. Furthermore, the US secondary teachers were not familiar with the applications of new mathematics—e.g., mathematical modeling, computer mathematics, probability, and statistics. An additional obstacle for the new math curricula was the elimination of funding for curriculum development in the 1970s by the NSF based on political arguments that the NSF was promoting national curriculum and usurping State's rights for local control of schools and schooling (Crane, 1976; Duschl, 1985, 1990).

Between 1960 and 1990, mathematical modeling and applications were gradually recognized by mathematics education researchers. The *Common Core State Standards in Mathematics* listed, for example, "model with mathematics" as one of eight standard's practices. A comprehensive analysis of the political history of the 1960s new math movement can be found in Phillips (2014).

Teaching for Understanding

By the 1990s the US began to engage in K-12 standards-based reforms in the sciences, mathematics, and English language arts (ELA). This work included the *Common Core State Standards Initiative* as well as the *National Science Education Standards* (NRC, 1996) and *AAAS Benchmarks* (1993) in the sciences. Similar reform efforts were also taking place in the UK (Millar & Osborne, 1998) and European Union (European Commission, 2007; Rocard et al., 2007; Osborne & Dillon, 2008).

Accompanying these developments was the emergence of a pedagogical perspective labeled "Teaching for Understanding" (Romberg, Carpenter, & Demock, 2005). The shift was away from the mechanistic rote learning views of the 19th century toward newer views that promoted examining the dynamics and abstractions of the new technological world. Akin to the arguments made in the 1950s by the School Mathematics Study Group to emphasize the language of sets, functions, programing, probability, and statistics, scholars who emphasized teaching and learning for understanding also adopted perspectives that treated mathematics and science as languages and literacies. It wasn't enough just to know the language resources of concepts, procedures, and design features in math and science. Equally important was to learn how to deploy them; e.g., to know how to model, to problem solve, to develop explanations, to acquire evidence, to argue, to reason (Gravemeijer, 1994).

According to Romberg et al. (2005), the features of mathematical and scientific literacy included domain-based knowledge (i.e., a recognition that there are discipline-specific routines and practices with respect to measuring, modeling, representing), learning corridors (i.e., a recognition that past experiences and prior knowledge influence and guide learning), and science and mathematical practices (i.e., a recognition that a set of representational, reasoning, modeling, and computational practices are fundamental for engaging in mathematical and scientific inquiries). These approaches taken up by the US reforms drew heavily on European didactical perspectives and phenomenology:

> Students are, as Freudenthal (1983) noted, "entitled to recapitulate in a fashion the learning processes of mankind" (p. ix) and the activities that they engage in can more effectively arise from reality itself, which is not a fixed datum, but expands continuously in individual and collective learning process (Freudenthal, 1987, p. 280)."
>
> *(Romberg et al., 2005, p. 10)*

Chief among Freudenthal's "learning processes of mankind" are two information technologies identified by historians—literacy and numeracy. Hobart (2018) posits that these two literacies were influential in the emergence of mathematical abstractions and modern science—a kind of learning corridor. The first information age was literacy and the development of the Greek alphabet and phonetic letter symbols that enabled encoding of information. By the Renaissance new information technology that rivaled and challenged the alphabetic literacy was developing as modern relational numeracy:

- Numerals gave rise to new counting systems and place value.
- Symbolic representation of zero lead to seeing numbers as relations and not just collections of things.
- Musical notations brought about first representations and measurements of time units.
- The emergence of linear perspectives in the visual arts developed ideas in geometry such as perspective grids, spatial proportions, and one-to-one mappings between object and representations.
- The joining of motion and time into mathematical formula; Galileo's incline plane experiments that generated the law of freefall.

The *Teaching for Understanding* agenda rested on teaching the language of mathematics and sciences and as such naturally drew on the practices of science and of mathematics to engage learners in literacy and relational numeracy. From the focus on language, researchers began to carefully examine classroom discourses and the dynamics of representation, critique, and communication practices:

- *Models and Modeling*: Process, representations, and inscriptions, and using explanatory and representational models in classrooms (Lehrer & Schauble, 2003, 2006) and
- *Argumentation*: Study of discourse in the classroom, articulation of ideas verbally, with writing, or with pictures, diagrams, models, and flowcharts to support conjectures (Forman, 2001; Engle & Conant, 2002; Ford & Forman, 2006).
- *Teaching and Design Experiments*: Carefully constructed pedagogical sequences to better illuminate students' reasoning and learning and inform instructional strategies, pathways, and learning trajectories (Cobb, Confrey, diSessa, Lehrer, & Schauble, 2003).

Pedagogical Debates in Curriculum and Learning Theory

The previous section examined broad paradigmatic shifts in the visions of the goals for education, especially science and mathematics education. This section examines parallel changes in curriculum and learning theory. We discuss several historical debates and changes and note some landmark works that illustrate key changes underway.

In a critical review of curriculum theory, William Doll (1993) examined the limitations of "scientific" and "technical rationality" (Schön, 1983) and the transitions during the 20th-century from Modern to Post-Modern perspectives. Doll conjectured that "a new sense of educational order will emerge, as well as new relations between teachers and students, culminating in a new concept of curriculum" (p. 3). According to Doll, the linear and sequential will give way to "a more complex, pluralistic, unpredictable system or network ... a transformative network" (p. 3). We view the transformative network as the blending of conceptual, epistemic, and social knowledge-building dynamics located in the learning sciences-guided designs of curriculum and pedagogical enactments (Duschl, 2008). A more recent depiction of the role of transformative network is through the lens of assessment frameworks. Penuel and Shepard (2016a, 2016b) reviewed four formative assessments frameworks that best support feedback and guidance on learning and reasoning. They assert that situating learning in domain-specific assessment frameworks such as culturally relevant "sociocultural" place-based contexts (e.g., impacts on communities and groups) and/or relevant "sociocognitive" problem-based contexts (e.g., impacts on environmental, nutritional, or ecological systems or services) is more effective than "data dashboard driven" and "Strategy-focused" domain-general assessment frameworks.

A confrontation between "knowing" and "doing" guiding conceptions is one that has persisted within curriculum theory throughout the 20th century and continues to prevail today. In the opening decades of the 20th century, three new curriculum ideologies emerged within curriculum theory and development in the US, namely, social efficiency, learner-centered, and social reconstruction, to compete against the traditional ideology of scholar academic that relied on mastery of academic knowledge (Schiro, 2013). Among the four ideologies, we see the clash of visions for personal growth between development of the technical skills, i.e. technical skills needed to complete an existing job in the labor market, and the transformative enactments, i.e. betterment of individuals and society beyond the status quo, respectively, in the framings of Thorndike's Administrative Progressive Education versus Dewey's Pedagogical Progressive Education (Connelly & Xu, 2008). Thorndike-influenced "Administrative progressives had most impact on curriculum structure and practice" while Dewey-influenced "pedagogical progressives had most impact on curriculum rhetoric" (Connelly & Xu, 2008, pp. 523–524). The development of technical skills relied on the curriculum ideology of social efficiency, which promoted development of specific skill sets that learners would need to perform as adult members of the society (Kliebard, 2004). Thorndike's introduction of educational or "intelligence" measurement from psychology to education gave rise to social efficiency as a social ideal and educational doctrine (Kliebard, 2004; Tahirsylaj, 2017). The transformative enactment of personal growth relied on learner-centered and social reconstruction curriculum ideologies that promoted more holistic education of the individual student as well as aiming for resolving broader societal issues through education (Schiro, 2013). Dewey's ideas on Pedagogical Progressive Education contributed to development of learner-centered and social reconstruction curriculum ideologies. The Pedagogical Progressive Education has had the most impact on curriculum rhetoric, and the Administrative Progressive Education has had the most impact on curriculum structure and practice. This scenario is often referred to as a battle between Dewey and Thorndike where Thorndike won and Dewey lost (Lagemann, 1989; Labaree, 2005; Connelly & Xu, 2008; Tahirsylaj, 2019).

In the second half of the 20th century, research on learning began moving away from a strict focus on general psychological principles of learning to a more diverse focus on the psychological, social, and cultural factors that influence the development of learning. New images of educational inquiry coupled with new images of learning have led to heterogenetic foundations of education. Is learning influenced by the epistemological framework of the discipline? Or is it shaped by the sociological contexts of the investigative communities? Is it cognitive mechanisms that govern thinking and reasoning? Or is it the cultural contexts that shape what it is that is important to know and to do? Such epistemic, social, cognitive, and cultural perspectives have spawned a wide array of frameworks and debates for how to conceptualize learning and teaching. As an example, in the US, an influential study that resulted from the new thinking in educational inquiry in the second half of the 20th century was *The Equality of Educational Opportunity*—often referred to as *Coleman Report* (Coleman et al., 1966)—which concluded that out-of-school factors, such as socioeconomic status of the students' families, had stronger effects on students' learning than school factors. The *Coleman Report* initiated hundreds of other studies examining how school inputs (e.g., teacher qualification, school resources) generate any given school outputs (e.g., test scores). Two influential outcomes were the economics-based human capital theory developed by Nobel Prize winners Theodore Schultz and Gary Becker, and the sociology-based social reproduction theory by French sociologist Pierre Bourdieu. Studies of educational opportunity sought to examine public and private investments in education and the role of education in fostering a nation's economic growth (Murnane & Willett, 2011).

Within pedagogical work, the influence of new emerging guiding conceptions for teaching and learning created a period of ongoing tensions between the alternative perspectives. In 1986, White and Tisher (1986) edited the *Handbook of Teacher Education Research*, which had as its principal focus the conceptual change in learning environments and the then-competing perspectives between two education research programs: (a) Piagetian domain-general stages view of cognitive development with an emphasis on the distinctions between concrete-abstract stages of reasoning, and (b) the information-processing/metacognitive view of cognitive development with an emphasis on prior knowledge, information processing, and short-term/long-term memory.

In the *Handbook of Research on Science Teaching and Learning* (Gabel, 1994), sponsored by the US National Science Teaching Association (NSTA), we see further developments of how competing guiding conceptions for learning influenced research. Chapter summaries on cognition and learning were parceled out into two sections, one on Learning and the other on Problem-Solving. Like *The Handbook of Teacher Education Research*, the topics and paradigms within the chapters demonstrate the progress and the tensions operating between stage development and information-processing views in research on science learning. For example, one chapter on learning examined and used Piaget's process of equilibration to examine knowledge acquisition and to consider neurological mechanisms involved in learning and knowing. The focus was strongly on the domain-general logical-mathematical reasoning constructs that guide deduction, induction, inference, and analogy. In contrast, a second chapter on learning examined the research on alternative conceptions in science with a strong focus on domain-specific characteristics of emergent knowledge claims. Here the review of research was grounded in Ausubel's (1963) meaningful learning theory and focused on the methodological practices for conducting research on children's images of science. These tensions have continued to some extent through to the present day.

The chapters on problem-solving, however, take up domain-specific research summaries in six contexts: elementary school, middle school, Earth science, genetics, chemistry, and physics. Here we begin to see a decisive turn in educational inquiry, particularly in the Stewart and Hafner's (1994) genetics chapter, toward domain-specific research in science education. The trend toward domain-specific research in science education is further evidenced in the *International Handbook of Science Education* (Fraser & Tobin, 1998) section on Learning. The lead chapter by Duit and Treagust "Learning in Science—From Behaviourism Towards Social Constructivism and Beyond" provides a concise overview of 20th-century developments on views of learning in education. The remaining seven chapters take up the role of language in science, cultural aspects, models and modeling, teaching that attends to students' informal conceptions, young children's inquiry reasoning, theories of knowledge acquisition, and students' epistemologies.

As stated above, the closing decades of the 20th century were a period of adopting and debating guiding conceptual frameworks for teaching and learning. Viewed through the lens of science education, different, shifting, and sometimes competing, philosophical, psychological, social, and pedagogical conceptions and commitment spawned a series of scholarly debates that capture, in part, the salient developments of 20th-century educational research and inquiry.

The focus on designing knowledge-building learning environments has brought about some consilience regarding design principles and what constitutes best practices. There is the aforementioned recognition by Penuel and Shepard that domain-specific formative assessment approaches that are guided by sociocognitive and sociocultural framings enhance the quality of feedback. Then there's the consensus recognition of the importance of discourse practices that promote epistemic cognition and reasoning from/with evidence (Lemke, 1990; Engle & Conant, 2002; Sandoval, 2003). Another point of convergence is that of conceiving classrooms as places where students' learning occurs individually and collaboratively within groups creating a "communities of practice" (Brown, 1997) in the classroom learning environment. These more dynamic and complex perspectives of classrooms influenced the considerations for how lesson plans and curriculum designs were viewed. The emergent thinking was that both students and teachers needed guidance about learning. Thus, the advancement of "educative curriculum materials" was put forth as a strategy to support both teachers' and students' learning (Davis & Krajick, 2005; Davis, Palincsar, Smith, Arian, & Kademian, 2017).

However, there remain among educational scholars many unresolved debates and stances regarding competing commitments to guiding conceptions and theoretical frameworks applied to establishing teaching and learning goals and for designing curriculum and assessment materials. In addition to the evolution of competing perspectives mentioned above, a specific current case in point is the review of learning frameworks by Sandoval, Greene, and Bråten (2016) that examines the psychological and educational research that frames epistemic cognition. What they found is there exist "various fault lines that currently prevent coherent synthesis of theoretical models and empirical findings" (p. 457). The fault lines they report are due to the salient differences among researchers regarding guiding conceptions, e.g. the adoption of competing frameworks regarding individuals' cognitive development and the deployment of radically different research methods for measuring reasoning and knowing. Their warning is that such fault lines will compromise the aggregation of results, the attainment of coherent models and thus interfere with theory building in the learning sciences. Once again, guiding conceptions are at the core of conducting inquiries (Schwab, 1960; Finegold et al., 1977) in that they influence and determine the problems selected or questions asked, the measures/observations taken and patterns recognized or missed, the evidence selected or dismissed, and the development and refinement of models/explanations.

In the following subsections, we shine a spotlight on three particular issues and trends that are interwoven to the broad historical trajectory that we have discussed. These are the debates on constructivism, Bildung-centered didaktik, and the emergence of the learning sciences.

Constructivism

One ongoing pedagogical debate that merits additional discussion is the debate centering around constructivism (Doll, 1993). The continued clash and questioning of modernist perspectives and postmodernist conceptions is vividly displayed in *Constructivism: Success or Failure?* (Tobias & Duffy, 2009). On one side of the debate are theorists and researchers who claim that our models of cognitive architecture support the need to retrieve knowledge efficiently and to develop usable knowledge through a directive and guided approach to science instruction. The thesis is that cognitive architecture and working memory theory dictate that instruction should be direct and explicit (Kirschner, Sweller, & Clark, 2006; Sweller, Kirschner, & Clark, 2007). In contrast, the other side of the debate focuses on the need for authenticity of learning contexts. That is, the need to situate the development of relevant knowledge and skills within social and collaborative context that parallel the contexts within which that knowledge (e.g., scientific, historical, mathematical, linguistic) is developed, used, and modified (Hmelo-Silver, Duncan, & Chinn, 2007; Kuhn, 2007; Schmidt, Loyens, van Gog, & Paas, 2007). The focus of the latter approach, which is not strictly postmodern, is to engage learners in activities that will encourage the construction of knowledge within authentic settings, e.g. knowledge-building learning environments, and the development of learning progressions which are coherent sequences of instruction.

The conceptualization of knowledge-building learning environments for young children and the considerations for developmental pathways and coherent sequences for learning that promote and sustain "deep learning" have done much to advance the field's thinking about learning goals. Learning progressions help align systems between curriculum, instruction, and assessment that strive to elevate students' understandings and reasoning from simpler to integrated levels. In the Learning Progressions' chapter of *Taking Science to School* (NRC, 2007), learning progressions are defined as research-based pathways of how students build knowledge and expertise within and across a disciplinary domain over a broad span of grade levels. In such knowledge-building and refining learning environments, the development of practices and expertise span the spectrum of conceptual, epistemic, and social learning goals (Duschl, 2008). We now recognize, for example, the importance of adopting learning proficiency goals to serve as guiding conceptions for instructional, curricular, and assessment models. These include goals for science education such as generating and evaluating scientific evidence and explanations and goals for mathematics education such as adaptive reasoning (capacity for logical thought, reflections, explanation, and interpretation) (NRC, 2001, 2007).

Bildung-Centered Didaktik

In continental Europe, from the 20th century to the present day, educational thinking and school practice have been dominated by different didaktik models as specific ways to achieve school knowledge transformation, with German "Bildung-centered didaktik" being the most dominant (Hopmann, 2007). The modern and postmodern didaktiks build upon a long tradition of educational thinking, starting from Aristotle's definitions of three forms of knowledge, including *episteme* (academic knowledge contained in intellectual disciplines), *techne* (related to crafts and skills), and *phronesis* (pertaining to practical wisdom in specific practical and complex situations) (Deng & Luke, 2008; Tahirsylaj & Wahlström, 2019). *Bildung* is a Germanic concept without a direct translation into English but is often described in terms of being educated and cultivated through education originating from the German enlightenment era (Hopmann, 2007). Bildung is an encompassing and evolving concept that describes education both as a process (through teaching and learning) and an outcome (being educated) that constantly needs updating to match the ever-changing societal goals and aspirations. For example, a key tenet of Bildung in the 21st century is being prepared to live in a world of plurality and difference (Biesta, 2002). Bildung entails all three forms of knowledge as defined by Aristotle and expands further toward subjectivity and who we are as individuals in the world.

> The concept of Bildung brings together the aspirations of all those who acknowledge—or hope—that education is more than the simple acquisition of knowledge and skills, that it is more than simply getting things "right," but that it also has to do with nurturing the human person, that it has to do with individuality, subjectivity, in short, with "becoming and being somebody."
>
> *(Biesta, 2002, p. 343)*

Within German Bildung-centered didaktik, Wolfgang Klafki's critical constructive didaktik has had the most influence on teaching and learning practices, with the focus on an operationalization of Bildung into three core elements: self-determination, co-determination, and solidarity (Klafki, 1998). In the didaktik perspective, "The purpose of teaching and schooling is [...] the use of knowledge as a transformative tool of unfolding the learner's individuality and sociability, in short: the Bildung of the learners by teaching" (Hopmann, 2007, p. 115). At the institutional level, didaktik is divided into general didaktik (Allgemeine Didaktik) and subject matter didaktik (Fachdidaktik), where the first centers around broader issues of teaching and learning, while the second deals with analysis, organization, and preparation of subjects of teaching (Künzli, 1998).

Related to the rise of didaktik among continental Europe nations, a dialogue between British and continental Europe scholars has focused on why education developed *as an academic discipline* on its own in continental Europe, whereas education arose *as an interdisciplinary field* relying on theoretical input from other "fundamental" disciplines (e.g., philosophy, history, psychology, and sociology) in English-speaking countries (Simon, 1981; Alexander, 2004; Biesta, 2011). The primary rationale for the distinctive development of education in English-speaking countries rests on the claim that educational theory does not generate a unique form of understanding about education beyond what is generated by "fundamental disciplines" (Hirst, 1966; Biesta, 2011).

Unlike the US institutions of higher education, science professors of didaktiks typically reside in academic disciplinary departments. In addition, traditional approaches to didaktik (Lijnse, 1995) frequently forgo psychological tenets of learning in favor of disciplinary epistemological and philosophical structures that initiate and offer learners a framework for formative development or Bildung. In science education, this didaktik transition was shaped by the research on conceptual change (Treagust & Duit, 2008), on discourse practices (Mortimer & Scott, 2003; NRC, 2008), and on domain-specific subject matter learning (Hamilton & Duschl, 2017). Under these approaches, the disciplinary content decided internally and developed by scientists and science educators takes primacy over externally developed learning outcomes by social scientists often defined and measured through psychological modeling. Consider the example of the Model of Educational Reconstruction (MER) research program (Duit, Gropengießer, & Kattman, 2005). The MER coordinates three domains of research: (1) investigations into students' perspectives, (2) clarification and analysis of subject matter content, and (3) design of learning environments. Derived from the German Didaktik tradition and culture of pedagogy, the MER offers a well-conceived framework for educational research as well as a context for conducting theoretical, basic, and applied research.

Emergence of Learning Sciences

As discussed above, post-WWII there were major changes to research frameworks and paradigms in the domains of psychology, social psychology, cultural psychology, and educational psychology. Many of these changes to psychological frameworks, coupled with concomitant complementary changes with philosophical and sociological frameworks, contributed to the emergence of the learning sciences as a guiding conceptual framing for education. In her comprehensive historical review of research in education, Lagemann (2000) discussed the transition from behaviorism to cognitive sciences, which preceded the emergence of learning sciences, and asserted it began in earnest at two US centers for cognitive study. These centers formed "stimulating work on all aspects of mental activities—memory, perception, grammar, artificial intelligence, sentence parsing, acoustics, learning, and much more" (Lagemann, 2000, p. 217). One was the Harvard University Center for Cognitive Sciences under the direction of George A. Miller and Jerome Bruner; the other was a collaboration in Pittsburgh between the Learning Research and Development Center at the University of Pittsburgh and Carnegie Mellon University, which involved Robert Glaser, Lauren Resnick, Allan Newell, and Herbert Simon.

In addition to the emergence of cognitive science, the adoption of sociocultural or situative perspectives help to reveal how the nature of social interactions and agency influence learning and, thus, the design of learning environments. From this guiding conception perspective, learning involves the adoption of sociocultural practices, including the situated epistemic practices within particular academic domains. Students of science, for example, not only learn the content of science; they also develop an "intellective identity"(Greeno, 2002) as scientists by becoming acculturated, akin to Bildung, to the tools, practices, and discourse of the sciences (Bazerman, 1988; Rogoff, 1990; Lave & Wenger, 1991; Roseberry, Warren, & Contant, 1992). The sociocultural and situative perspectives grew out of the influential ideas and research of Vygotsky (1978) and were further developed in the 1980s (Wertsch, 1985; Lave, 1988). See Jerome Bruner's *The Culture of Education (*1996) for a comprehensive reporting of the emergence of cultural psychology in education. The stance taken within sociocultural perspectives is that learning as well as developing reasoning and knowledge-building practices are situated in epistemic contexts and social interactions and, as such, cannot be nurtured solely by cognitive orientations.

In 1978 the National Academy of Education published an edited volume of case studies that looked back to examine the impact research had on education policy and practice (Suppes, 1978). The transitional decades of interest for the case studies were the 1960s and 1970s. Getzel's (1978) case study commented that skepticism about the value of basic research informing educational practice and decision-making held strong up into the 1970s. The case study by Robert Glaser (1978) posits:

> We are at a kind of juncture (between the) extrapolation of behavioristic animal learning lab studies, concepts and techniques to practical human affairs. At the same time, cognitive theories of human performance, influenced by a concern for realistic complex human endeavors, have stimulated the present major theoretical orientation in psychology.
>
> *(p. 257)*

By the 1970s, cognitive and sociocultural tenets of learning theory were firmly in place (Greeno, Pearson, & Schonfeld, 1997; NRC, 2001). Furthermore, the cognitive, social, and cultural dynamics of learning were held to be mutually supportive of one another and intertwined such that "you cannot strip learning of its content, nor study it in a 'neutral' context. It is always situated, always related to some ongoing enterprise" (Bruner, 2004, p. 20).

The National Research Council synthesis research reports—*How People Learn* (NRC, 1999) and *Knowing What Students Know* (NRC, 2001—which examined the disciplinary domains of history, science, and mathematics education, provide rich examples regarding the 20th-century transitions through Associative, Behavioral, Cognitive, and Sociocultural-Situative Perspectives. One major development that is reported in the two NRC reports is the central role building and reasoning with models has on learning. Research on learning, with an eye toward informing educational processes from a domain-general prospective, posited that we must attend to the development of four types of knowledge: declarative "what we know" knowledge, procedural "how we know" knowledge, systemic "why we know" knowledge, and strategic "thinking about thinking" knowledge. The stance taken in these two synthesis research reviews is that the adoption of new research-based models of learning can better facilitate the mediation of learning by teachers and peers, too. One example of this is Ann Brown's "community of practice" depiction of classrooms.

Robert Glaser (1991, 1992, 1997) provides an overview of how findings from cognitive and social psychology research can be used to inform educational practices. He developed and outlined components of a coherent learning theory that inform instruction, curriculum, and assessment designs. The seven research findings Glaser identified to guide the structure and design of learning environments were:

1. **Structured Knowledge**—Instruction should develop conceptual structures to support inference and reasoning.
2. **Prior Knowledge**—Learner intuition is a source of cognitive ability that supports and promotes new learning.
3. **Metacognition**—Reflecting on learning, meaning making, and reasoning strategies provide learners a sense of agency.
4. **Procedural Knowledge in Meaningful Contexts**—Learning information should be connected with its use.
5. **Social participation and cognition**—Social display of cognitive competence via group dialog helps individuals acquire knowledge and skill.
6. **Holistic Situation for Learning**—Competence is best developed through cognitive apprenticeship within larger task contexts.
7. **Make Thinking Overt**—Design situations in which the thinking of the learner is made apparent and overt to the teacher and to students.

The learning sciences emerged from this pioneering research in the cognitive sciences and the socio-cultural research revealing that children's thinking is fundamentally different from that of adults. Expert/novice studies revealed how the characteristics of expertise (e.g., employing heuristics and representations) impacts reasoning, thinking, and problem-solving. Such insights led to establishing one guiding tenet of the learning sciences; "students learn deeper knowledge when they engage in activities that are similar to the everyday activities of professionals who work in a discipline" (Sawyer, 2006, p. 4). Subsequent research on informal out-of-school learning further revealed the importance of participation structures and the development of practices in culturally valued activities (Cole, 1996). Focusing on sociocultural dynamics such as scaffolding, apprenticeship, legitimate peripheral participation, and guided participation, informal learning researchers provided both broader units of analysis and signaled the importance of understanding how learning occurs in social groups, families, and communities (Bransford et al., 2006).

Yet another learning sciences development was the study of knowledge-building workers (e.g., scientists, engineers, mathematicians, historians, writers, medical doctors). Cognitive, historical, sociological, and anthropological studies of knowledge workers demonstrated the central role of social practices in reasoning, critiquing, and communicating. With respect to the scientific disciplines and other epistemic cultures, cognitive models of science (c.f., Goldman, 1986; Giere, 1988; Thagard, 1992; Kitcher, 1993) coupled with sociocultural models of science (c.f., Kuhn, 1970; Longino, 1990, 2002; Knorr-Cetina, 1999) demonstrated the critical roles models, mechanisms, and peers have in the advancement and refinement of scientific knowledge and the methods regarding the growth of scientific knowledge. The epistemic game is the refinement of knowledge systems to enhance explanatory coherence (NRC, 2007; Thagard, 2007; Duschl & Grandy, 2008).

In an extended review of Glasers' framework, Gitomer and Duschl (2007) assert that adding in the epistemic perspective helps inform the design of formative assessments by situating the cognitive and sociocultural approaches into specific activities and contexts that involve the growth of knowledge practices. Their position is that there are two general elements to the epistemic perspective—one disciplinary, the other methodological. Knowledge-building traditions across the natural and social science disciplines, while sharing many common features, are actually quite distinct when the tools, technologies, and theories each deploys are considered. Such distinctions naturally shape the adopted inquiry methods. The second methodological element of the epistemic perspective includes the shared practices of modeling, measuring, and explaining that frame investigations and inquiries.

Summary

The changes that began in the 1950s ignited the notion that education needed to be more than learning about what we know—mere mastery learning. Newer images of learning focus on how ideas and concepts build together in contexts that involve using knowledge or doing. That is, by taking science and engineering as participatory practices, history as posing fair depictions of events, or mathematics as "productive dispositions" we can inquire about how we come to know the natural world and how we select and use evidence to explain why we believe a scientific, mathematical, or historical explanation in the face of alternative competing ideas. The storyline of 20th-century educational models of inquiry is one that involves philosophy, psychology, and pedagogy. The pedagogical and psychological trends and shifts in guiding conceptions outlined above have been decidedly toward engaging students in using knowledge and in discipline-based epistemic and scientific practices (Duschl & Jimenez-Aleixandre, 2012). This amounts to a rediscovery of Dewey's progressive education of doing. The new emerging models have led researchers and educators to advance positions that learning ought to be coordinated and coherently sequenced over time. The emergent pedagogical perspectives include conceptual trajectories (Driver, Leach, Scott, & Wood-Robinson, 1994), developmental corridors (Brown, 1997), historical problem-solving (Wineburg, 1991), learning trajectories (Simon, 1995), and learning progressions (NRC, 2005, 2007).

From the 1950s to 1990s, developments taking place in the learning sciences and science studies—history, philosophy, sociology, anthropologies, and economics of science—have ignited efforts to understand how we have learned how to learn about nature. But this scientific interrogation of nature has also shaped our understandings of how to learn about learning itself and the design of learning environments as well. John Rudolph's *How We Teach Science: What's Changed and Why It Matters* (2019) scrutinizes the various and sundry 20th-century efforts, policies, and products that constitute the emergence of science education through the lens of teaching the scientific method. Rudolph has presented much more than a descriptive narrative of events, institutions, and people involved in science education. Rudolph has crafted an engaging tapestry of how political, economic, pedagogical, psychological, philosophical, and technological forces have all influenced and been influenced by matters of science causing the focus of science education to swing back and forth between teaching knowledge and teaching practices.

Internationally, the proliferation of large-scale assessments such as Trends in Mathematics and Science Study (TIMSS) since 1960s and Programme for International Student Assessment (PISA) since 2000 have brought the battle between knowing and doing to an international stage. The TIMSS focused on "knowing," testing knowledge of the disciplines of mathematics and sciences, whereas the PISA focused on "doing," testing students in mathematics, science, and reading focused on the application of knowledge. The era of measuring "the other," i.e. other countries and education systems, has been accelerated by the agenda that a quality education gives countries a competitive edge in the global economy. International assessments and comparative education have often been conducted in relation to other countries. This makes it possible to compare countries and education systems internationally. Over time, the focus on international comparisons with other nations has shifted from "knowing the other" in the 1880s, to "understanding the other" in the 1920s, to "constructing the other" in the 1960s, to "measuring the other" in recent decades (Nóvoa & Yariv-Mashal, 2003, p. 424).

The pathways of inquiry over the last few centuries has been dynamic. From the Renaissance forward, there has been a persistent evolution of technologies for acquiring information, for both literacy (e.g., printing press, alphabetic systems, libraries) and numeracy (e.g., arithmetic, music, geometry, and astronomy) (Hobart, 2018). The evolution of technologies continues to provide humanity with newer abstract means for processing and storing information. New tools, technologies, and theories have shaped pathways first in physics and chemistry for the early paradigmatic sciences; in population biology through Darwinian Evolution, the Great Synthesis and on to molecular biology and medical sciences; in quantum mechanics; in material, communication, and information sciences; in geosciences and Earth systems sciences; in the social sciences; and in neurosciences and brain sciences, among others. The historical development of information technologies, initially literacy and then numeracy via relational mathematics (Hobart, 2018), has segued to computational reasoning and data analytics. Indeed, the dynamics of inquiry in the 20th century is revealed and explained through the lenses of competing and shifting guiding conceptual frameworks.

In *The Structure of Scientific Revolutions*, Thomas Kuhn postulated that one characteristic episode of scientific revolutions is a period when competing ideas and guiding conceptions begin to proliferate and abound. During this period, new paradigmatic shifts are being contemplated to explain and account for new evidence and evidentiary anomalies. Kuhn refers to this dynamic as moving into "crisis," where competing theories and models vie to explain both the established knowledge claims while also reconciling the growing number of anomalies—unexplained yet undismissable events and findings—generated by older or alternative paradigms. If the past century of developments in educational inquiry is viewed as typically characteristic, with the continued and increasingly more rapid development of new regimes of tools, technologies, and theories (e.g., data analytical, AI, and learning engineering models), then the next century may well be more of the same contemplations for the design of learning environments as ever-newer guiding conceptions emerge. Educators are learning how to learn about learning.

Over the 20th century, education proved to be a contested field, viewed cyclically either as a source of evil or a panacea, or both, for understanding or solving larger social issues. Educational inquiry practices and methods in the 21st century will inevitably follow similar cyclic trajectories as in the past century, primarily due to the ever-growing uncertainties of life in the interconnected and globalized world. The worldwide disruption caused by Covid-19 disease at the beginning of 2020 is an example and a stark warning of what the future might hold. If social distancing becomes the norm rather than a one-time experience, how will it affect education delivery, and by extension educational inquiry, in the times ahead? While the future is hard to predict, we can safely speculate that information and communication technologies (ICTs) will gain a more prominent role both in education delivery and educational inquiry. As a result, the recent emergence of learning engineering and learning analytics will play a key role on the design of learning environments and associated research infrastructure.

Irrespective of challenges in worldwide public health, humanity is moving toward the fourth industrial revolution or the Age of Innovation (Tahirsylaj, Matson, & Gashi, 2019). As Klaus Schwab (2017) notes, while the three previous revolutions liberated humankind from animal power, brought mass production, and introduced digital capabilities to billions of people, respectively, the fourth industrial revolution is creating dramatic shifts on how people live and work. These shifts will have strong implications to learning and educational inquiry. The Organisation for Economic Co-operation and Development (OECD) is leading the efforts internationally to design forward-looking curriculum, instruction, and assessment policies that take into consideration the challenges faced by societies presently. The OECD 2030 Learning Framework paves the way for an ambitious education agenda for individual countries around the world, as the OECD attempts to address two far-reaching questions for the state of education worldwide:

(1) What knowledge, skills, attitudes, and values will today's students need to thrive and shape their world? and (2) How can instructional systems develop these knowledge, skills, attitudes, and values effectively? (OECD, 2018, p. 2). The OECD rationale for reconsidering the future of education is driven by the need for new solutions to ongoing or emerging environmental, economic, and social challenges.[7] If the 20th century taught us anything, it was this: Crises represent critical moments in time when attention turns to education as a solution, and ongoing robust educational inquiry that is based on diverse epistemological frameworks and modes of inquiry will better prepare societies to face upcoming challenges and to find solutions for ill-defined or yet-unknown problems.

How do we respond? Handling anomalies that arise from new insights and the adoption of new tools and technologies are at the heart of engaging in inquiry. Building, polishing, and refining our questions, theories, and models is the name of the game. Consider our 150 years of developing the theory of evolution and our understandings of the brain and mind; first at the macro organismic level, next at the cellular genetic level, and now at the molecular level. What are the salient features of the modifications and anomalies in educational inquiry during periods of crisis? Is there consensus agreement on goals, as advocated in improvement science approaches? Ought there be agreement about evidence or do heterogeneities prevail? Or, are we bound to be forever embroiled and steeped in incommensurability battles? What are the methods, procedures, and pathways to achieve systemic and individualistic goals to bring educational inquiry out of crisis and continue on evolutionary and revolutionary pathways? What more do we need to know, to do, and to adapt to?

Notes

1 The chapter uses the original German term *didaktik* throughout as already established in the literature (Westbury, Hopmann, & Riquarts, 2000; Tahirsylaj, 2019; Werler & Tahirsylaj, 2020) and to avoid the use of the English term *didactics*, which is often ascribed negative connotations such as lecture-based teaching (Kansanen, 1995). *Bildung* is also used in the original German because of a lacking established translation into English; however, some approximate meanings include "self-cultivation," "self-formation," and "self-development."

2 See Duschl, Jorde, McLoughlin, and Osborne (in press) for a discussion of recent policy reports on science and STEM education.

References

Alexander, R. (2004). Still no pedagogy? Principle, pragmatism and compliance in primary education. *Cambridge Journal of Education, 34*(1), 7–33. https://doi.org/10.1080/0305764042000183106

American Association for the Advancement of Science (AAAS). (1993). *Benchmarks for scientific literacy.* Oxford: Oxford University Press.

Ausubel, D. (1963). *The psychology of meaningful verbal learning.* New York: Grune & Stratton.

Bazerman, C. (1988). *Shaping written knowledge: The genre and activity of the experimental article in science.* Madison: University of Wisconsin Press.

Biesta, G. (2002). Bildung and modernity: The future of Bildung in a world of difference. *Studies in Philosophy and Education, 21*(4–5), 343–351. https://doi.org/10.1023/A:1019874106870

Biesta, G. (2011). Disciplines and theory in the academic study of education: A comparative analysis of the Anglo-American and continental construction of the field. *Pedagogy, Culture & Society, 19*(2), 175–192. https://doi.org/10.1080/14681366.2011.582255

Black, P., & Atkin, J. M. (2003). *Inside science education reform: A history of curricular and policy change.* New York: Teachers College Press.

Bransford, J., Barron, B., Pea, R., Meltzoff, A., Kuhl, P., Bell, P., Stevens, R., Schwartz, D., Vye, N., Reeves, B., Roschelle, J., & Sabelli, N. (2006). Foundations and opportunities for an interdisciplinary science of learning. In K. Sawyer (Ed.), *The Cambridge handbook of the learning sciences* (pp. 19–34). Cambridge: Cambridge University Press. https://doi.org/10.1017/CBO9780511816833.003

Brown, A. (1997). Transforming schools into communities of thinking and learning about serious matters. *American Psychologist, 52*(4), 399–413. https://doi.org/10.1037/0003-066X.52.4.399

Bruner, J. (1960). *The process of education*. Cambridge, MA: Harvard University Press.

Bruner, J. (1996). *The culture of education*. Cambridge, MA: Harvard University Press.

Bruner, J. (2004). The psychology of learning: A short history. *Daedalus*, Winter, 13–20. https://doi.org/10.1162/001152604772746657

Carruthers, P., Stich, S., & Siegal, M. (Eds.). (2002). *The cognitive basis of science*. Cambridge: Cambridge University Press. https://doi.org/10.1017/CBO9780511613517

Chomsky, N. (1986). *Knowledge of language, Its nature, origin and use*. West Port, CT: Praeger.

Cobb, P., Confrey, J., diSessa, A., Lehrer, R., & Schauble, L. (2003). Design experiments in educational research. *Educational Researcher, 32*(1), 9–13. https://doi.org/10.3102/0013189X032001009

Cole, M. (1996). *Cultural psychology: A once and future discipline*. Cambridge, MA: Belknap Press.

Coleman, J. S., Campbell, E. Q., Hobson, C. J., McPartland, J., Mood, A. M., Weinfeld, F. D., & York, R. L. (1966). *Equality of educational opportunity*. Washington, DC: U. S. Government Printing Office.

Connelly, F. M. (2013). Joseph Schwab, curriculum, curriculum studies and educational reform. *Journal of Curriculum Studies, 45*(5), 622–639. https://doi.org/10.1080/00220272.2013.798838

Connelly, M. F., & Xu, S. (2008). The landscape of curriculum and instruction: Diversity and continuity. In F. M. Connelly, M. F. He, & J. Phillion (Eds.), *The Sage handbook of curriculum and instruction* (pp. 514–533). Sage. https://doi.org/10.4135/9781412976572.n26

Crane, L. T. (1976). *The National Science Foundation and precollege science education: 1950–1975*. Washington, DC: U. S. Government Printing Office.

Davis, E. A., & Krajcik, J. (2005). Designing educative curriculum materials to promote teacher learning. *Educational Researcher, 34*(3), 3–14. https://doi.org/10.3102/0013189X034003003

Davis, E. A., Palincsar, A. S., Smith, P. S. Arias, A., & Kademian, S. M. (2017). Educative curriculum materials: Uptake, impact, and implications for research and design. *Educational Researcher, 46*(6), 293–404. https://doi.org/10.3102/0013189X17727502

DeBoer, G. (1991). *A history of ideas in science education: Implications for practice*. New York: Teachers College Press.

DeMott, B. (1962). An unprofessional eye: The math wars. *American Scholar, 31*(2), 296–310.

Deng, Z., & Luke, A. (2008). Subject matter: Defining and theorizing school subjects. In F. Michael Connelly, M. Fang He, & J. Phillion (Eds.), *The sage handbook of curriculum and instruction* (pp. 66–87). Sage. https://doi.org/10.4135/9781412976572.n4

Doll, W. J. (1993). *A post-modern perspective on curriculum*. New York: Teachers College Press.

Driver, R., Leach, J., Scott, P., & Wood-Robinson, C. (1994). Young people's understanding of science concepts: Implications of cross-age studies for curriculum planning. *Studies in Science Education, 24*, 75–100. https://doi.org/10.1080/03057269408560040

Duit, R., Gropengieβer, H., & Kattman, U. (2005). Towards science education research that is relevant for improving practice: The model of educational reconstruction. In H. Fisher (Ed.), *Developing standards in research on science education: The ESERA Summer School 2004*. Oxfordshire: Taylor & Francis.

Duschl, R. (1985). Science education and philosophy of science: Twenty-five years of mutually exclusive development. *School Science and Mathematics, 85*(7), 541–555. https://doi.org/10.1111/j.1949-8594.1985.tb09662.x

Duschl, R. (1988). Abandoning the scientistic legacy of science education. *Science Education, 72*(1), 51–62. https://doi.org/10.1002/sce.3730720105

Duschl, R. (1990). *Restructuring science education: The role of theories and their importance*. New York: Teachers College Press.

Duschl, R. (2008). Science education in 3 part harmony: Balancing conceptual, epistemic and social learning goals. *Review of Research in Education, 32*, 268–291. https://doi.org/10.3102/0091732X07309371

Duschl, R., & Grandy, R. (2008). Reconsidering the character and role of inquiry in school science: Framing the debates. In R. Duschl & R. Grandy (Eds.), *Teaching scientific inquiry: Recommendations for research and implementation*. Rotterdam: Sense Publishers. https://doi.org/10.1163/9789460911453

Duschl, R., & Jimenez-Aleixandre, M. P. (2012). Epistemic foundations of conceptual change. In S. Carver & J. Shrager (Eds.), *The journey from child to scientist: Integrating cognitive development and the education sciences* (pp. 245–262). Washington, DC: American Psychological Association. https://doi.org/10.1037/13617-012

Duschl, R., Jorde, D., McLoughlin, & Osborne, J. (in press). Policy and pedagogy: International reform and design challenges for science and science education, In O. Levrini, G. Tasquier, T. Amin, L. Branchetti, & M. Levin (Eds.), *ESERA 2019 book of selected papers*. Berlin: Springer.

Easley, J. (1959). The physical science study committee and educational theory. *Harvard Educational Review, 29*(1), 4–11. https://doi.org/10.2307/3204594

Engle, R., & Conant, F. (2002). Guiding principles for fostering productive disciplinary engagement: Explaining an emergent argument in a community of learner's classroom. *Cognition and Instruction, 20*, 399–483. https://doi.org/10.1207/S1532690XCI2004_1

European Commission. (2007). *Science education now: A renewed pedagogy for the future of Europe: Report of the high-level group on science education*. EC Directorate-General for Research: Retrieved from http://ec.europa.eu/research/science-society/document_library/pdf_06/report-rocard-on-science-education_en.pdf

Finegold, M., Clipsham, J., & Wahlstrom, M. W. (1977). *Scientific enquiry and the teaching of science: Pattern of enquiry project*. Toronto: OISE Press.

Ford, M. J., & Forman, E. A. (2006). Redefining disciplinary learning in classroom contexts. *Review of Research in Education, 30*, 1–32. https://doi.org/10.3102/0091732X030001001

Forman, E. (2001). *Classroom discourse project*. Madison: National Center for Improving Student Learning and Achievement in Mathematics and Science, Wisconsin Center for Educational Research.

Fraser, B., & Tobin, K. (Eds.). (1998). *International handbook of research in science education*. Kluwer. https://doi.org/10.1007/978-94-011-4940-2

Freudenthal, H. (1983). *Didactical phenomenology of mathematical structures*. Dordrecht: Reidel.

Freudenthal, H. (1987). Mathematics starting and staying in reality. In I. Wirszup & R. Street (Eds.), *Proceedings of the USCMP conference on mathematics education on development in school mathematics education around the world* (pp. 279–295). Reston, VA: National Council of Teachers of Mathematics.

Gabel, D. L. (Ed.). (1994). *Handbook of research on science teaching and learning*. New York: Macmillan.

Getzel, J.W. (1978). Paradigm and practice: On the impact of basic research in education. In P. Suppes (Ed.), *Impact of research on education: Some case studies* (pp. 477–521). Washington, DC: National Academy of Education.

Giere, R. (1988). *Explaining science: A cognitive approach*. Chicago, IL: University of Chicago Press. https://doi.org/10.7208/chicago/9780226292038.001.0001

Gitomer, D., & Duschl, R. (2007). Establishing multi-level coherence in assessment. In P. Moss (Ed.), *Evidence and decision making, NSSE 2007 yearbook*, (Vol. 106, Issue 1, pp. 288–320). https://doi.org/10.1111/j.1744-7984.2007.00106.x

Glaser, R. (1978). The contributions of B.F. Skinner to education and some counter interfluences. In P. Suppes (Ed.), *Impact of research on education: Some case studies* (pp. 199–260). Washington, DC: National Academy of Education.

Glaser, R. (1991). The maturing of the relationship between the science of learning and cognition and educational practice. *Learning and Instruction, 1*(2), 129–144. https://doi.org/10.1016/0959-4752(91)90023-2

Glaser, R. (1992). Expert knowledge and processes of thinking. In D. F. Halpern (Ed.), *Enhancing thinking skills in the sciences and mathematics* (pp. 63–75). Mahwah, NJ: Lawrence Erlbaum Associates.

Glaser, R. (1997). Assessment and education: Access and achievement. *CSE Technical Report 435*. National Center for Research on Evaluation, Standards, and Student Testing (CRESST).

Goldman, A. (1986). *Epistemology and cognition*. Cambridge, MA: Harvard University Press.

Gravemeijer, K. P. E. (1994). *Developing realistic mathematics instruction*. Utrecht: Freudenthal Institute.

Greeno, J., Collins, A., & Resnick, L. (1996). Cognition and learning. In D. C. Berliner and R. C. Calfee (Eds.), *Handbook of educational psychology* (pp. 15–46). New York: Macmillan.

Greeno, J. G. (2002). *Students with competence, authority, and accountability: Affording intellective identities in classrooms*. New York: College Board.

Greeno, J. G., Pearson, P. D., & Schoenfeld, A. H. (1997). Implications for the National Assessment of Educational Progress of research on learning and cognition. In *Assessment in transition: Monitoring the nation's educational progress: Background studies* (pp. 152–215). Stanford, CA: National Academy of Education.

Hamilton, R., & Duschl, R. (2017). Learning, science. In R. Mayer & P. Alexander (Eds.), *Handbook of research on learning and instruction*. 2nd ed. London: Routledge. https://doi.org/10.4324/9781315736419

Hanson, N. R. (1958). *Patterns of discovery: An inquiry into the conceptual foundations of science*. Cambridge: Cambridge University Press.

Hirst, P. H. (1966). Educational theory. In J. W. Tibble (Ed.), *The study of education* (pp. 29–58). London: Routledge and Kegan Paul.

Hmelo-Silver, C., Duncan, R., & Chinn, C. (2007). Scaffolding and achievement in problem-based and inquiry learning: A response to Kirschner, Sweller, and Clark (2006). *Educational Psychologist, 42*(2), 99–107. https://doi.org/10.1080/00461520701263368

Hobart, M. E. (2018). *The great rift: Literacy, numeracy and the religion-science divide*. Cambridge, MA: Harvard University Press. https://doi.org/10.4159/9780674985186

Hopmann, S. (2007). Restrained teaching: The common core of Didaktik. *European Educational Research Journal, 6*(2), 109–124. https://doi.org/10.2304/eerj.2007.6.2.109

Kansanen, P. (1995). The Deutsche Didaktik. *Journal of Curriculum Studies, 27*(4), 347–352. https://doi.org/10.1080/0022027950270401

Kilpatrick, J. (2015). Curriculum and the cold war: A closer look at the "new math" movement of the 1960s. *Science, 327*(6220), 380. https://doi.org/10.1126/science.aaa1471

Kilpatrick, J. (2017). Changing direction: The "Second Round" of the school mathematics study group. In K. Bjarnadottir, F. Furinghetti, M. Menghini, J. Prytz, & G. Schubring (Eds.), "Dig where you stand" 4, Proceedings of the Fourth International Conference on the History of Mathematics Education (pp. 167–174). Edizioni Nuova Cultura.

Kirschner, P., Sweller, J., & Clark, R. (2006). Why minimal guidance during instruction does not work: An analysis of the failure of constructivist, discovery, problem-based, experiential and inquiry-based teaching. *Educational Psychologist, 41*, 75–86. https://doi.org/10.1207/s15326985ep4102_1

Kitcher, P. (1993). *The advancement of science: Science without legend, objectivity without illusions.* Oxford: Oxford University Press.

Klafki, W. (1998). Characteristics of critical-constructive Didaktik. In B. Gundem & S. Hopmann (Eds.), *Didaktik and/or curriculum* (pp. 29–46). New York: Peter Lang.

Kliebard, H. M. (2004). *The struggle for the American curriculum, 1893–1958.* London: Routledge. https://doi.org/10.4324/9780203339985

Knorr-Cetina, K. (1999). *Epistemic cultures: How science makes knowledge.* Cambridge, MA: Harvard University Press.

Kuhn, D. (2007). Is direct instruction an answer to the right question? *Educational Psychologist, 42*(2), 109–113. https://doi.org/10.1080/00461520701263376

Kuhn, T. (1970). *The structure of scientific revolutions*, 2nd ed. Chicago, IL: The University of Chicago Press. Originally published 1962.

Künzli, R. (1998). The common frame and places of Didaktik. In B. Gundem & S. Hopmann (Eds.), *Didaktik and/or curriculum* (pp. 29–46). New York: Peter Lang.

Labaree, D. F. (2005). Progressivism, schools and schools of education: An American romance. *Paedagogica historica, 41*(1–2), 275–288. https://doi.org/10.1080/0030923042000335583

Lagemann, E. C. (1989). The plural worlds of educational research. *History of Education Quarterly, 29*(2), 185–214. https://doi.org/10.2307/368309

Lagemann, E. C. (2000). *An elusive science: The troubling history of education research.* Chicago, IL: The University of Chicago Press.

Lave, J. (1988). *Cognition in practice: Mind, mathematics and culture in everyday life.* Cambridge: Cambridge University Press. https://doi.org/10.1017/CBO9780511609268

Lave, J., & Wenger, E. (1991). *Situated learning: Legitimate peripheral participation.* Cambridge: Cambridge University Press. https://doi.org/10.1017/CBO9780511815355

Lehrer, R., & Schauble, L. (2003). Origins and evolution of model-based reasoning in mathematics and science, In R. Lesh (Ed.), *Models and modeling in mathematics teaching learning a problem solving* (pp. 59–70). Mahwah, NJ: Erlbaum Associates Publishers.

Lehrer, R., & Schauble, L. (2004). Modeling natural variation through distribution. *American Educational Research Journal, 41*(3), 635–679. https://doi.org/10.3102/00028312041003635

Lehrer, R., & Schauble, L. (2006). Cultivating model-based reasoning in science education. In K. Sawyer (Ed.), *The Cambridge handbook of the learning sciences* (pp. 371–388). Cambridge: Cambridge University Press. https://doi.org/10.1017/CBO9780511816833.023

Lemke, J. (1990). *Talking science: Language, learning, and values.* Norwood, NJ: Ablex.

Lijnse, P. (1995). "Developmental Research" as a way to an empirically based "Didactical Structure" of science. *Science Education, 79*, 189–199. https://doi.org/10.1002/sce.3730790205

Longino, H. (1990). *Science as social knowledge.* Princeton, NJ: Princeton University Press. https://doi.org/10.1515/9780691209753

Longino, H. (2002). *The fate of knowledge.* Princeton, NJ: Princeton University Press. https://doi.org/10.1515/9780691187013

Millar, R., & Osborne, J. F. (Eds.). (1998). *Beyond 2000: Science education for the future.* London: Nuffield Foundation.

Mortimer, E. F., & Scott, P. (Eds.). (2003). *Meaning making in secondary science classroom.* London: Open University Press.

Murnane, R. J., & Willett, J. B. (2011). *Methods matter: Improving causal inference in educational and social science research.* Oxford: Oxford University Press.

National Research Council. (1996) *National science education standards*. Washington, DC: National Academy Press.

National Research Council. (1999). *How people learn*. In J. Bransford, A. Brown, & R. Cocking (Eds.). Washington, DC: Center for Education, Division of Behavioral and Social Sciences. The National Academy Press.

National Research Council. (2001). *Knowing what students know: The science and design of educational assessment*. In J. Pellegrino, N. Chudowsky, & R. Glaser (Eds.). Washington, DC: Center for Education, Division of Behavioral and Social Sciences. The National Academy Press.

National Research Council. (2005). *Adding it all up: Helping children learn mathematics*. In J. Kilpatrick, J. Swafford, & B. Findell (Eds.). Washington, DC: Center for Education, Division of Behavioral and Social Sciences. The National Academy Press.

National Research Council. (2007). *Taking science to school: Learning and teaching science kindergarten to eight grade*. In R. A. Duschl, H. A. Schweingruber, & A. W. Shouse (Eds.). Washington, DC: Center for Education, Division of Behavioral and Social Sciences. The National Academy Press.

National Research Council. (2008). *Ready, set, science!:Putting research to work in K-8 science classrooms*. In S. Michaels, A. W. Shouse & H. A. Schweingruber (Eds.). Washington, DC: The National Academy Press.

Nóvoa, A., & Yariv-Mashal, T. (2003). Comparative research in education: A mode of governance or a historical journey? *Comparative Education*, *39*(4), 423–438. https://doi.org/10.1080/0305006032000162002

Organisation for Economic Co-operation and Development. (2018). *The future of education and skills: Education 2030*. http://www.oecd.org/education/2030/E2030%20Position%20Paper%20(05.04.2018).pdf

Osborne, J., & Dillon, J. (2008). *Science education in Europe: Critical reflections*. London: The Nuffield Foundation.

Penuel, W. R., & Shepard, L. A. (2016a). Sociocognitive and sociocultural models of assessment. In A. Rupp & J. P. Leighton (Eds.), *Cognitive models of assessment* (pp. 146–173). Hoboken, NJ: Wiley. https://doi.org/10.1002/9781118956588.ch7

Penuel, W. R., & Shepard, L. A. (2016b). Teaching and assessment. In D. Gitomer & C. Bell (Eds.), *Handbook of research on teaching* (pp. 787–851). Washington, DC: AERA. https://doi.org/10.3102/978-0-935302-48-6_12

Phillips, C. J. (2014). *The new math: A political history*. Chicago, IL: University of Chicago Press. https://doi.org/10.7208/chicago/9780226185019.001.0001

Pickering, A. (1995). *The mangle of practice: Time, agency and science*. Chicago, IL: University of Chicago Press. https://doi.org/10.7208/chicago/9780226668253.001.0001

Rocard, M. et al. (2007). *Science education now – A renewed pedagogy for the future of Europe*. Luxembourg: Office for Official Publications of the European Communities.

Rogoff, B. (1990). *Apprenticeship in thinking: Cognitive development in a social context*. Oxford: Oxford University Press.

Romberg, T. A., Carpenter, T. P., & Demock, F. (Eds.). (2005). *Understanding mathematics and science matters*. Mahwah, NJ: Lawrence Erlbaum Associates, Publishers. https://doi.org/10.4324/9781410612618

Roseberry, A., Warren, B., & Contant, F. (1992). Appropriating scientific discourse: Findings from language minority classrooms. *The Journal of the Learning Sciences*, *2*, 61–94. https://doi.org/10.1207/s15327809jls0201_2

Rudolph, J. (2002). *Scientists in the classroom: The cold war reconstruction of American science education*. Palgrave Macmillian. https://doi.org/10.1057/9780230107366

Rudolph, J. (2019). *How we teach science: What's changed and why it matters*. Cambridge, MA: Harvard University Press. https://doi.org/10.4159/9780674240377

Sandoval, W. A. (2003). Conceptual and epistemic aspects of students' scientific explanations. *The Journal of the Learning Sciences*, *12*(1), 5–51. https://doi.org/10.1207/S15327809JLS1201_2

Sandoval, W. A., Greene, J. T., & Bråten, I. (2016). Understanding and promoting thinking about knowledge: Origins, issues, and future directions of research on epistemic cognition. *Review of Research in Education*, *40*, 457–496. https://doi.org/10.3102/0091732X16669319

Sawyer, R. K. (Ed.). (2006). *The Cambridge handbook of the learning sciences*. Cambridge: Cambridge University Press. https://doi.org/10.1017/CBO9780511816833

Schiro, M. S. (2013). *Curriculum theory: Conflicting visions and enduring concerns*, 2nd ed. Los Angeles: Sage.

Schmidt, H. G., Loyens, S. M. M., van Gog, T., & Paas, F. (2007). Problem-based learning is compatible with human cognitive architecture: Commentary on Kirschner, Sweller, and Clark (2006). *Educational Psychologist*, *42*(2), 91–97. https://doi.org/10.1080/00461520701263350

Schön, D. (1983). *The reflective practitioner: How professionals think in action*. New York: Basic Books.

Schwab, J. (1958). On the corruption of education by psychology. *The School Review, 66*(2), 169–184. https://doi.org/10.1086/442438

Schwab, J. (1960). Inquiry, the science teacher, and the educator. *The School Review, 68*(2), 176–195. https://doi.org/10.1086/442536

Schwab, J. (1962). The teaching of science as inquiry. In J. Schwab & P. Brandwein (Eds.), *The teaching of science* (pp. 1–101). Cambridge, MA: Harvard University Press

Schwab, J. (1969). The practical: A language for curriculum. *School Review*, 78, 1–23. https://doi.org/10.1086/442881

Schwab, J., & Brandwein, P. (1962). *The teaching of science*. Cambridge, MA: Harvard University Press.

Schwab, K. (2017). *The fourth industrial revolution*. New York: Crown Business.

Simon, B. (1981). Why no pedagogy in England? In B. Simon & W. Taylor (Eds.), *Education in the eighties: The central issues*. London: Batsford.

Simon, M. (1995). Reconstructing mathematics pedagogy from a constructivist perspective. *Journal for Research in Mathematics Education, 26*, 114–145. https://doi.org/10.5951/jresematheduc.26.2.0114

Stewart, J., & Hafner, R. (1994). Research on problem solving: Genetics. In D. Gabel (Ed.), *Handbook of research on science teaching and learning* (pp. 284–300). New York: Macmillan.

Suppe, F. (Ed.). (1977). *The structure of scientific theories*. Champaign: University of Illinois Press.

Suppes, P. (1978). Impact of research on education: Some case studies. Washington, DC: National Academy of Education.

Sweller, J., Kirschner, P., & Clark, R. (2007). Why minimally guided teaching techniques do not work: A reply to commentaries. *Educational Psychologist, 42*(2), 115–121. https://doi.org/10.1080/00461520701263426

Tahirsylaj, A. (2017). Curriculum field in the making: Influences that led to social efficiency as dominant curriculum ideology in progressive era in the U.S. *European Journal of Curriculum Studies, 4*(1), 618–628.

Tahirsylaj, A. (2019). Revisiting 'curriculum crisis' dialogue: In search of an antidote. *Nordic Journal of Studies in Education Policy, 5*(3), 180–190. https://doi.org/10.1080/20020317.2019.1664217

Tahirsylaj, A., Matson, J., & Gashi, L. (2019). Educating minds for the age of innovation. *International Journal of Innovation, Creativity and Change, 5*(1), 15–32.

Tahirsylaj, A., Niebert, K., & Duschl, R. (2015). Curriculum and didaktik in 21st century: Still divergent or converging? *European Journal of Curriculum Studies, 2*(2), 262–281.

Tahirsylaj, A., & Wahlström, N. (2019). Role of transnational and national education policies in realisation of critical thinking: The cases of Sweden and Kosovo. *The Curriculum Journal, 30*(4), 484–503. https://doi.org/10.1080/09585176.2019.1615523

Thagard, P. (1992). *Conceptual revolutions*. Princeton, NJ: Princeton University Press. https://doi.org/10.1515/9780691186672

Thagard, P. (2007). Coherence, truth, and the development of scientific knowledge. *Philosophy of Science, 74*(1), 28–47. https://doi.org/10.1086/520941

Tobias, S., & Duffy, T. (Eds.). (2009). *Constructivist instruction: Success or failure?* London: Routledge. https://doi.org/10.4324/9780203878842

Treagust, D. F., & Duit, R. (2008). Conceptual change: A discussion of theoretical, methodological and practical challenges for science education. *Cultural Studies in Science Education, 3*, 297–328. https://doi.org/10.1007/s11422-008-9090-4

Vygotsky, L. S. (1978). *Mind in society*. Cambridge, MA: Harvard University Press.

Werler, T. C., & Tahirsylaj, A. (2020). Differences in teacher education programmes and their outcomes across *Didaktik* and curriculum traditions. *European Journal of Teacher Education*. https://doi.org/10.1080/02619768.2020.1827388

Wertsch, J. (Ed.) (1985). *Culture, communication and cognition: Vygotskian perspectives*. Cambridge: Cambridge University Press.

Westbury, I., Hopmann, S., & Riquarts, K. (Eds.). (2000). *Teaching as a reflective practice: The German Didaktik tradition*. Mahwah, NJ: Lawrence Erlbaum Associates.

White, R., & Tisher, R. (1986). Research on natural sciences. In M. Wittrock (Ed.), *Handbook of research on teaching* (3rd ed., pp. 874–905). New York: Macmillan.

Wineburg, S. S. (1991). Historical problem solving: A study of cognitive processes used in the evaluation of documentary and pictorial evidence. *Journal of Educational Psychology, 83*, 73–87. https://doi.org/10.1037/0022-0663.83.1.73

Zammito, J. H. (2004). *A nice derangement of epistemes: Post-positivism in the study of science from Quine to Latour*. Chicago, IL: University of Chicago Press.

3

GUIDING FRAMEWORKS FOR THE DESIGN OF INQUIRY LEARNING ENVIRONMENTS

Yael Kali

Introduction: The "What & Why" versus the "How" in Designing Inquiry Learning Environments

In their seminal book, *The Design Way*, Nelson and Stolterman (2012) maintain that design is a tradition of human inquiry and action. As such, they juxtapose design to science, art, and humanities. Research, they claim, is an inherent part of any design process, mirroring a similar reversed assertion that design is an inherent part of scientific inquiry. In the past two decades, the integration of both traditions, design and research in education, has been developed into a methodological approach. The design-based research (DBR) approach is conducted as theory-driven and iterative cycles of design, implementation in real-world contexts, analysis, and revision of the design, with a goal of advancing both theory and practice (Barab & Squire, 2004; Design-Based Research Collective, 2003; Kali & Hoadley, in press; McKenney & Reeves, 2018). This iterative and integrated approach, which has gradually become an accepted genre of research in education and the learning sciences has fostered the development of numerous learning environments (oftentimes technology-enhanced). Inquiry learning has been the focus of many of these studies, advancing our current understanding of what the learning process entails and how it can be supported.

Various frameworks have been developed in an attempt to synthesize the knowledge that is gradually accumulating regarding how people learn in such designed inquiry learning environments and encapsulate this knowledge as pragmatic guidelines for design. Such frameworks seek to consolidate lessons learned that cut across disciplinary domains and educational contexts regarding *what* characterizes productive designs and *why* they are productive (informing design products) as well as *how* to go about designing such environments (informing design processes). Guidelines informing design products seek to abstract generalized constructs of learning environments that have been shown to productively support inquiry for the purpose of advancing learning theory. Whereas guidelines informing design processes explore effective mechanisms to design and develop such environments. These two types of guidelines, or frameworks, typically originated from research fields, which, in spite of many overlaps, were conducted by research communities that up to two decades ago had only little interaction but have become less isolated in recent years. Specifically, frameworks that guide design products typically stem from research in the learning sciences, while frameworks that guide design processes stem from the field of instructional design (Carr-Chellman & Hoadley, 2004; McKenney & Kali, 2017). Accordingly, the former aim at delineating generalized design heuristics, principles, and patterns, which have been shown to promote pedagogical goals and can help further advance learning theory, while the latter aim at developing productive design mechanisms and methodologies to do so. Despite the growing cross-fertilization between these lines of research, they have still remained relatively separate.

An example set of guidelines informing the design of technology-enhanced learning environments (design products) is Bielaczyc's social infrastructure framework (2006), which was developed to assist learning scientists in making fine-grained decisions to design and explore learning in social contexts. Bielaczyc delineates four critical socially driven design elements: "(a) cultural beliefs of the people who are to use the designed product, (b) their practices in engaging in both online and offline activities, (c) the socio-techno-spatial relations (d) their interaction with the 'outside world'" (p. 301). For each dimension, she describes design considerations and example questions that need to be answered to design a socially sensitive design product. For instance, in the cultural beliefs dimension, one design consideration is "how a student's social identity is understood" (p. 314). A question that can guide this consideration: "How are students meant to view each other—as learning resources, as team members, as competitors?" (p. 314).

Guidelines informing design processes usually follow an iterative staged sequence including the core elements of analyzing, designing, developing, implementing, and evaluating (ADDIE; Gustafson and Branch, 1981). The way each stage is executed is further informed by other forms of design knowledge. For example, the work of Hoadley and Cox (2009) emphasizes design values and roles (e.g., the notion that we should examine our designs from different perspectives, such as that of the user, the implementer, and the critic), which commonly shape the overall design process.

As one manifestation of the growing cross-fertilization between the fields of learning sciences and instructional design (Carr-Chellman & Hoadley, 2004; McKenney & Kali, 2017), learning scientists have begun exploring and developing guidelines to inform design processes with an emphasis on the role of teachers-as-designers (Goodyear, 2015; Kali, McKenney, & Sagy, 2015; Laurillard, 2012), research-practice partnerships (Coburn & Penuel, 2016; Kali, Eylon, McKenney, & Kidron, 2018), and design-based implementation research (Fishman, Penuel, Allen, Haugan-Cheng, & Sabelli, 2013; Penuel, Fishman, Haugan-Cheng, & Sabelli, 2011). Since later chapters (see Chapters 7–10, this volume) include discussions of these topics, the current chapter focuses on the type of frameworks that characterize productive design products that emerge from and guide DBR studies and that have advanced our understanding of inquiry learning. The chapter concludes with describing a future trajectory, with promising seeds in the present, highlighting the value of integrating guidelines for design products and processes.

The sections following this introduction describe three groups of guidelines for designing learning environments that support: (a) inquiry as knowledge integration, (b) inquiry as a community endeavor, and (c) inquiry in the context of the 21st century's networked society. As illustrated in Table 3.1, despite many commonalities, each group of guidelines represents a unique

Table 3.1 Theoretical perspectives, unit of analysis, and disciplinary perspectives represented in the three groups of design guidelines in this chapter

	Designs for inquiry as knowledge integration	*Designs for inquiry as a community endeavor*	*Designs for inquiry in the networked society*
Theoretical perspective on inquiry learning	Socio-constructivist	Sociocultural	Cyberlearning
Unit of analysis	Learning of individuals or dyads	Learning of the whole class	Learning that transcends the classroom
Disciplinary perspectives	Typically, physical, life, and earth sciences		Physical, life, earth, social, and humanistic

theoretical perspective on inquiry learning (socio-constructivist, sociocultural, and cyberlearning, respectively). They also represent expanding units of analysis. The first group of guidelines focuses on the learning of individuals or dyads, with an emphasis on supporting knowledge integration. The second group of guidelines emphasizes the learning of the whole class as a community endeavor. The third group attends to learning that transcends the classroom, where larger communities and geographical settings are involved. The disciplinary perspectives taken by the developers of each group of guidelines also differ, with a focus on physical, life, and earth sciences in the first and second groups, and a wider disciplinary range including also social sciences and the humanities in the third. Consequently, each group of guidelines emphasizes different values that are likely to affect the designed learning environments. Despite these differences, it is important to note that the sets of design guidelines described in this chapter can certainly complement each other to inform the design of learning environments that seek to integrate the perspectives each of them offers.

Designs for Inquiry as Knowledge Integration

The knowledge integration framework's theoretical foundation lies within constructivist and socio-constructivist conceptions of learning and specifically highlights the importance of helping learners make connections among ideas (Roseman, Linn, & Kopal, 2008). It builds on Bruner's (1960, 1995) argument that knowledge of the relationships among ideas and of the fundamental principles that connect these ideas enables learners to integrate new ideas into what they already know. As Bruner puts it, "the only possible way in which individual knowledge can keep proportional pace with the surge of available knowledge is through a grasp of the relatedness of knowledge" (1995, p. 333). The empirical foundation of the knowledge integration framework stems from three decades of DBR studies capitalizing on the *Web-based Inquiry Science Environment* (WISE) (Slotta & Linn, 2009). The WISE infrastructure enabled close examination of ideas that students bring to science classes, illustrating the multiple, conflicting, and often confusing ideas about scientific phenomena, as well as exploration and testing of technology-enhanced knowledge integration supports designed to assist students in developing coherent understanding of science (Kali, Linn, & Roseman, 2008; Linn & Eylon, 1996; Linn & Hsi, 2000). Syntheses efforts have carefully examined design considerations, and their embodiment within dozens of WISE units has led to the identification of *design principles* (Linn, Bell, & Davis, 2004) and *design patterns* (Linn & Eylon, 2006) that have been productive in supporting students' inquiry learning (Linn & Eylon, 2011). The following sections provide a brief overview of the design principles and design patterns approaches for synthesizing design knowledge and illustrate how they complement each other.

Design Principles for Knowledge Integration

The design principles approach uses design principles as an organizational unit for synthesizing design knowledge (for more on the notion of design knowledge, see Hoadley & Cox, 2009; Merrill, 2002; Quintana et al., 2004). Bell, Hoadley, and Linn (2004) describe design principles as follows:

> an intermediate step between scientific findings, which must be generalized and replicable, and local experiences or examples that come up in practice. Because of the need to interpret design principles, they are not as readily falsifiable as scientific laws. The principles are generated inductively from prior examples of success and are subject to refinement over time as others try to adapt them to their own experiences.
>
> *(Bell et al., 2004, 83)*

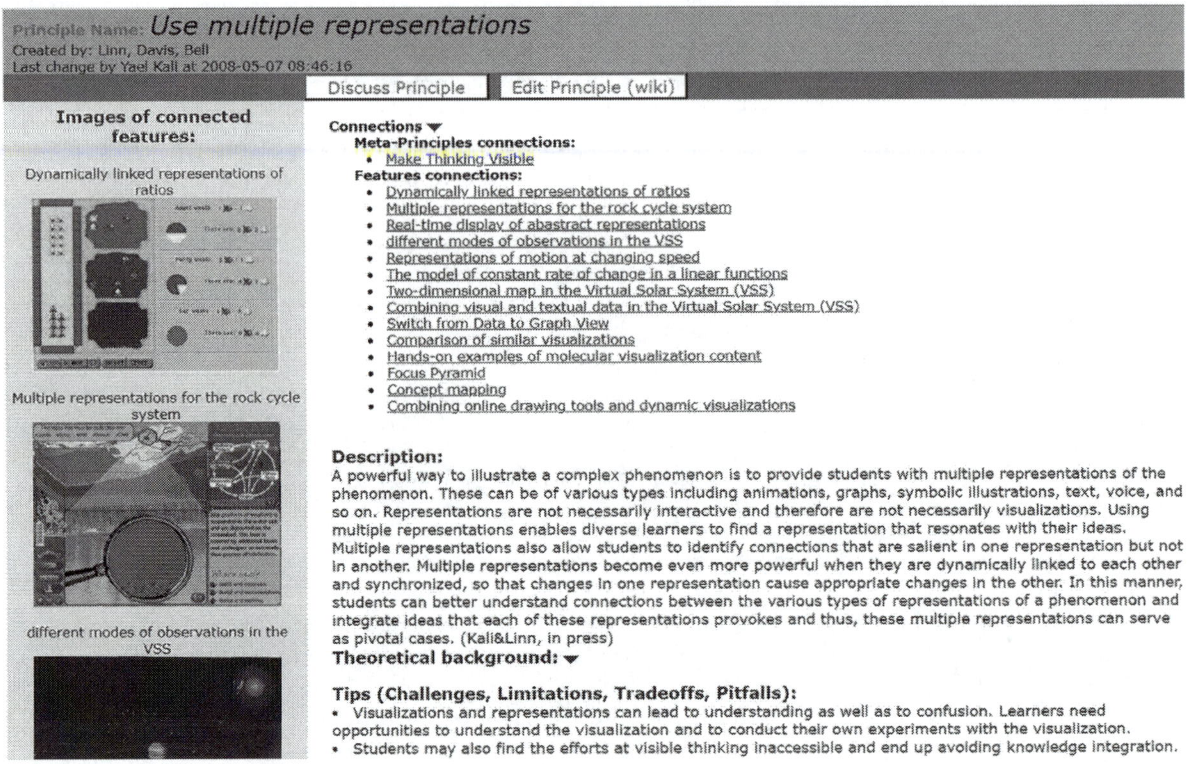

Figure 3.1 Example of a design principle from the Design Principles Database

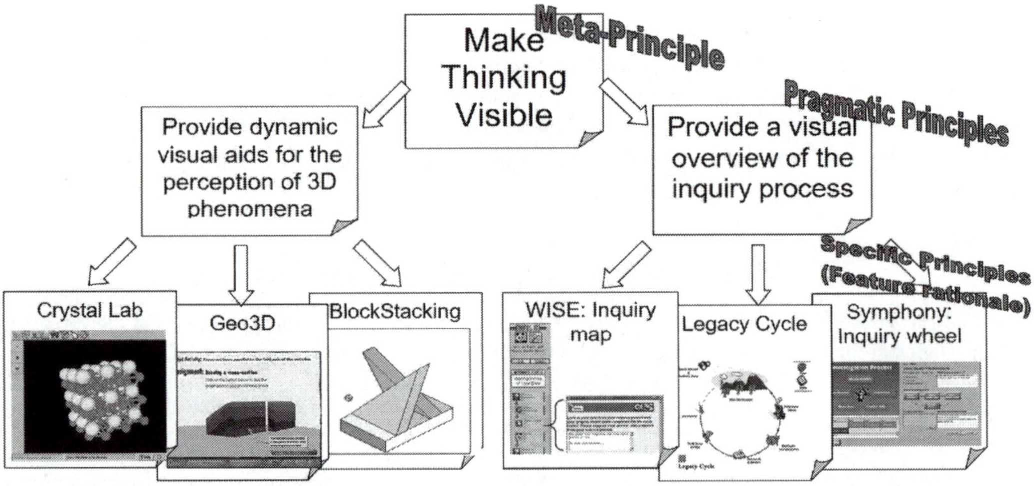

Figure 3.2 Schematic representation of the three levels of design principles in the Design Principles Database with examples from various DBR studies on inquiry learning at the specific level (http://www.edu-design-principles.org/)

Based on this approach, the *Design Principles Database* (Kali, 2006, 2008; Kali & Linn, 2008) was developed. Between 2003 and 2008, it served as a digital platform and public infrastructure to support researchers from a broad spectrum of DBR projects to share their design knowledge on inquiry learning and design. Participants contributed insights from their studies in various ways, such as: (a) linking existing principles with example features in their own learning environments; (b) suggesting new or refining existing design principles; (c) adding tips in the form of limitations, tradeoffs, and pitfalls for designing according to a principle (Figure 3.1). These insights served the community to further advance design knowledge via additional DBR studies. In this manner, the *Design Principles Database* served as a collaborative knowledge-building tool as well as a mechanism to support DBR on inquiry learning (Kali, 2006, 2008).

Having originated from design principles that were abstracted based on DBR studies in WISE, knowledge integration principles of inquiry learning served as a backbone within the Design Principles Database. It comprised three levels of design principles (meta, pragmatic, and specific), to which design knowledge regarding inquiry learning and design was advanced (Figure 3.2).

Design Patterns for Knowledge Integration

Design patterns is a different approach that is complementary to the design principles approach. It has been adopted by educational researchers and learning scientists (e.g., Goodyear & Retalis, 2010) to guide the design of learning environments. The notion of design patterns has been adapted in education from its origins in fields such as architecture (Alexander, Ishikawa, & Silverstein, 1977) and computer science (Gamma, Helm, Johnson, & Vlissides, 1995). For instance, Linn and Eylon (2006) defined design patterns for knowledge integration as "tested sequences of learning activities, such as discussing, modeling, or reading that take advantage of the variety of student ideas and promote integrated understanding" (p. 513). These sequences involved four basic processes (eliciting student ideas, adding new, pivotal ideas, developing criteria for distinguishing among ideas, and sorting out ideas), which play out in ten design patterns that have been shown to promote knowledge integration.

One of the patterns described by Linn and Eylon (2006) is predict, observe, and explain. This involves introducing a demonstration of a scientific phenomenon, eliciting predictions, running the demonstrations, and encouraging students to reconcile contradictions. This pattern has a long history of employment in many science-related learning environments and especially in those involving modeling tools (e.g., Gobert & Pallant, 2004; Krajcik, Blumenfeld, Marx, & Soloway, 1994). It has been shown to productively assist students in expressing and then re-examining their alternative ideas using evidence. To illustrate the employment of this pattern, as well as to illuminate how design principles and design patterns complement each other, Kali and Linn (2010) analyzed a curricular unit in thermodynamics (Sampson & Clark, 2008), using these two lenses. The juxtaposition of the two lenses highlights the different ways in which each of the approaches guides design of knowledge integration activities (Figure 3.3).

Designs for Inquiry as a Community Endeavor

One of the most compelling notions that has advanced our current understanding of inquiry learning has been consideration of the social and cultural contexts in which inquiry takes place, whether in formal or informal settings. Building on theoretical foundations developed in the 1990s on communities of practice and situated learning (Brown, Collins, & Duguid, 1989; Lave, 1991; Lave & Wenger, 1991), an influential body of scholarship began to develop, examining how

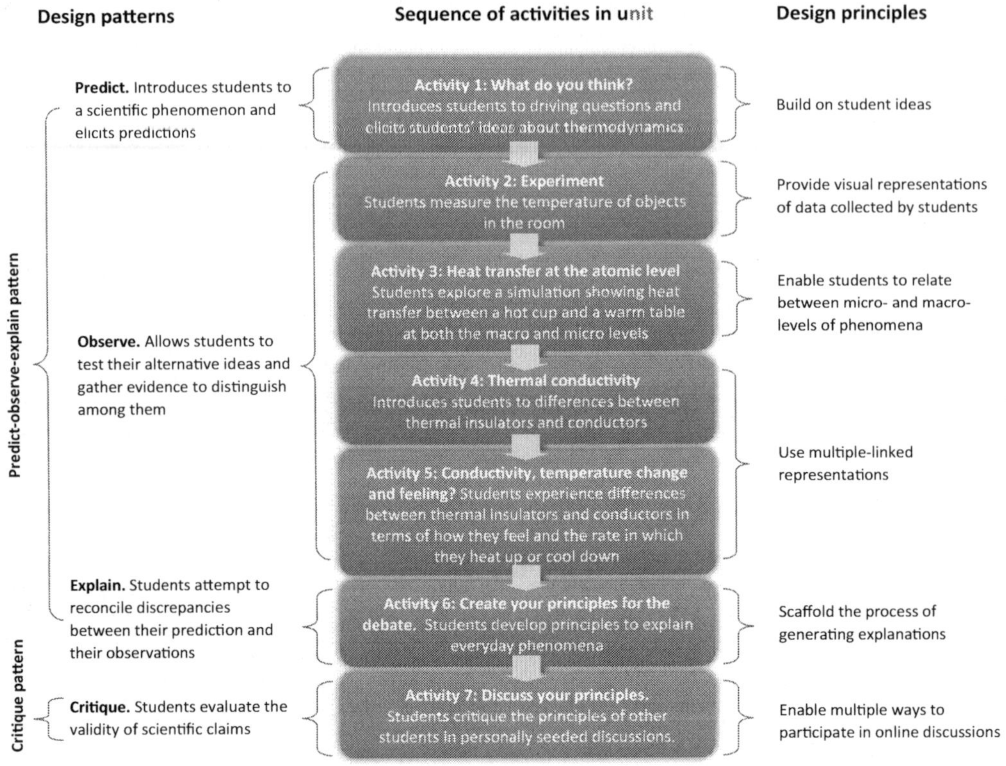

Figure 3.3 Sequence of activities in the thermodynamics curriculum unit described in terms of design patterns (left) and design principles (right) (adapted from Kali and Linn, 2008)

practices of inquiry learning found "in the wild" can play out in classrooms, and what are the consequences of implementing the idea of "learning communities" on students' inquiry learning. Two outstanding examples that have propelled the field's conceptualization of this approach are: *knowledge-building communities* (Scardamalia & Bereiter, 1991, 1994), and *Fostering Communities of Learners* (Brown, 1992; Brown & Campione, 1994). For a detailed comparison between these models, see Scardamalia and Berieter (2007). Despite some differences, there are also many commonalities between them, which have advanced the field's understanding of school-based inquiry as a community endeavor. Slotta and Najafi (2010) describe the commonalities as follows:

> Broadly cast, this approach involves giving students a much higher level of agency and responsibility for developing their own questions, exchanging and critiquing ideas with peers, and even evaluating their own progress. Teachers become members of the classroom knowledge community, and participate as knowledgeable mentors. The students in a knowledge community typically create a knowledge base of commonly held resources that are negotiated and continuously revised through their activities conducted in the classroom, at home, or on the playground. Often, this knowledge is situated in a technology-mediated environment that scaffolds students as they add new ideas to the knowledge base, revise materials, or synthesize the contents into new organizations, designs, or arguments.
>
> *(Slotta & Najafi, 2010, p. 190)*

Since the development of the knowledge-building communities and the fostering communities of learners models, the notion of learning communities has intrigued numerous researchers, and its theorization has continually evolved. Two cornerstone efforts in synthesizing this work have been Bielaczyc and Collins' seminal article "Learning Communities in Classrooms: A Reconceptualization of Educational Practice" (1999), and, almost 20 years later—Hod, Bielaczyc, and Ben-Zvi's introduction to the special issue they edited on learning communities in *Instructional Science*—"Revisiting Learning Communities: Innovations in Theory and Practice" (2018).

In the earlier synthesis, Bialaczyc and Collins identified four main characteristics of learning communities based on their analysis of three instructional models (including the two described above) as:

> (1) diversity of expertise among its members, who are valued for their contributions and given support to develop, (2) a shared objective of continually advancing the collective knowledge and skills, (3) an emphasis on learning how to learn, and (4) mechanisms for sharing what is learned.
>
> *(p. 269)*

In the recent synthesis, however, Hod, Bielaczyc, and Ben-Zvi (2018) analyze a much wider range of contexts, focusing on papers included in the special issue that highlighted studies on learning communities in elementary science classes (Fong & Slotta, 2018; Tao & Zhang, 2018), graduate classes on education, and even a high-school marching band (Ma & Hall, 2018). Although Hod et al.'s analysis shows that the four attributes characterizing learning communities were maintained throughout the years, their broader perspective on the field's history and practice enabled important new insights regarding cross-cutting issues and directions that learning communities research was beginning to take. One issue, specifically relevant to this chapter, is the tremendous challenge in implementing the learning communities approach in classrooms, which often requires a teacher to "radically revise his or her classroom methods ... to embrace the required epistemological commitments" (Slotta & Najafi, 2010, p. 194).

Alongside theoretical insights, and specifically to address implementation challenges, the learning communities approach has spurred the development of various frameworks that have guided the design and implementation of this ambitious approach to inquiry learning in classrooms. The following sections describe two such frameworks. The first set of guidelines developed throughout, what Bereiter (2006) calls, one of the "longest running design experiments in education" (p. 18)—the aforementioned knowledge-building communities endeavor (Scardamalia, 2002; Zhang, Hong, Scardamalia, Teo, & Morley, 2011). The second represents a model and instructional design framework developed more recently from this endeavor, in an attempt to bridge its underlying principles with those of the fostering communities of learners approach described above (Brown, 1997; Brown & Campione, 1994), namely—the knowledge community and inquiry model (Fong & Slotta, 2018; Lui & Slotta, 2014; Slotta, 2019; Tissenbaum & Slotta, 2019). Both design frameworks suggest means to address the challenge of implementing learning communities in classrooms, though in quite different ways.

Knowledge-Building Design Principles

The guiding framework for knowledge building (Figure 3.4) encompasses 12 principles that Scardamalia (2002) has synthesized following more than a decade of research on transformative discourse (Scardamalia & Bereiter, 1987), intentional learning (Scardamalia & Bereiter, 1991), and creative expertise (Bereiter & Scardamalia, 1993). Rather than aiming to guide researchers and

1. *Real Ideas and Authentic Problems.* Students identify problems that arise from their efforts to understand the world and pursue sustained creative work surrounding them.
2. *Improvable Ideas.* Ideas are treated as improvable rather than simply accepted or rejected; students work continuously to improve the explanatory power, coherence, and utility of ideas.
3. *Epistemic Agency.* Students set goals, assess their work, engage in long-range planning, monitor idea coherence, use contrasting ideas to spark and sustain knowledge advancement, and engage in high-level knowledge work normally left to the teacher.
4. *Collective Responsibility for Community Knowledge.* All participants are legitimate contributors to community goals and take high-level responsibility for advancing the community's knowledge, not just for their individual learning.
5. *Democratizing Knowledge.* All participants are empowered as legitimate contributors to the shared goals; all take pride in knowledge advances of the community. Diversity and divisional differences are viewed as strengths rather than as leading to separation along knowledge have/have-not lines.
6. *Idea Diversity.* Knowledge advancement depends on the diversity of ideas, just as the success of an ecosystem depends on biodiversity. To understand an idea is to understand the ideas that surround it, including those that stand in contrast to it.
7. *Knowledge Building Discourse.* Students engage in discursive practices that not only share but transform and advance knowledge, with problems progressively identified and addressed and new conceptualizations built.
8. *Rise Above.* Students work with diverse ideas in complex problem spaces; they transcend trivialities and oversimplifications and work toward more inclusive principles and higher level formulations of problems.
9. *Constructive Use of authoritative Sources.* Participants access and critically evaluate authoritative sources and other information. They use these sources to support and refine their ideas, not just to find "the answer."
10. *Pervasive Knowledge Building.* Knowledge Building is not confined to particular occasions or subjects but pervades mental life—in and out of school and across contexts.
11. *Symmetric Knowledge Advance.* Expertise is distributed within and between communities and team members, with knowledge exchange and co-construction reflecting the understanding that "to give knowledge is to get knowledge."
12. *Embedded and Transformative Assessment.* Assessment is integral to Knowledge Building and helps to advance knowledge through identifying advances, problems, and gaps as work proceeds.

Figure 3.4 The 12 principle of knowledge-building communities (adapted from Scardamalia & Bereiter, 2002)

designers in developing learning activities, as the design principles approach described above do (Bell, Hoadley, & Linn, 2004; Kali, 2006, 2008; Kali & Linn, 2008, 2010), these 12 principles are intended for teachers and students, guiding their functioning as a learning community. In other words, this approach "defines core values and principles, leaving to teachers the challenge of engaging in reflective interpretation, using discretionary judgment, and making adaptive classroom decisions to accommodate their different contexts and possibilities" (Zhang et al., 2011 p. 263). To support teachers and students, a technology-enhanced learning environment—*Knowledge Forum*—has been designed, which embeds these principles as designed features. For example, to promote "idea diversity" (principle 6 in Figure 3.4), *Knowledge Forum* supports include notes that students and teachers can write and connect: "linking and rise-above facilities bring different combinations of ideas together in different notes and views; semantic analysis and visualizations convey the diversity and connectedness of ideas" (p. 268).

The capacity of the knowledge-building approach to promote students' learning as well as teachers' design practices has been examined in numerous research studies. An especially comprehensive study was conducted by Zhang et al. (2011) involving analysis of 39 knowledge-building initiatives, each focused on a different curriculum theme and facilitated by different teachers over a period of eight years. Students' discourse in *Knowledge Forum* indicated that across projects they were engaged in work of growing scope and depth, taking collective responsibility for knowledge advances, conceptual content of growing scope and depth, and collective responsibility for knowledge advancement. At the same time, the knowledge-building principles supported teachers' pedagogical thinking, decision-making, experimentation, and reflection on practice.

Knowledge Community and Inquiry Design Principles

As described above, the knowledge, community, and inquiry model (Fong & Slotta, 2018; Lui & Slotta, 2014; Slotta, 2019; Tissenbaum & Slotta, 2019) was developed in an attempt to bridge the approaches of knowledge-building communities and fostering communities of learners. As such, it adopted some of the core values of knowledge building, such as enabling students to collectively build their knowledge, giving voice and shared authority to students, distributing expertise, and encouraging cognitive responsibility. But it also acknowledges an important value from the fostering communities of learners approach, that is, the commitment to targeted predefined learning goals, which is a departure from the knowledge-building communities approach. In fostering communities of learners, a curricular domain is divided into subtopics, with groups of students assigned to each subtopic. First, they explore the domain using designated resources, and then, they share their expertise with the other groups in class. This is conducted by each group's co-designing of "textbooks" that other groups use for their learning of these subtopics. "Overall, the collaborative activity in fostering communities of learners might be characterized as 'learning in order to teach' and in knowledge building as 'working to advance the state of knowledge in the community'" (Scardamalia & Bereiter, 2007, p. 201).

The uniqueness of the knowledge, community, and inquiry approach is that this combination of values is embedded within smart classroom infrastructures that "scaffold students and teachers in new forms of collaboration and inquiry, including a substantive role for large projected displays and small touch surfaces, as well as a dependency on students' physical location within the room" (Tissenbaum & Slotta, 2019, p. 423). Figure 3.5 delineates the design principles that guide Knowledge Community and Inquiry environments.

Findings from studies on knowledge, community, and inquiry to date (Slotta, 2019) include evidence that this approach can promote students' co-regulation in collaborative inquiry as well as their productive co-construction of knowledge. For instance, co-regulation scaffolds in a global climate change unit designed in the knowledge, community, and inquiry approach encouraged tenth-grade students to support each other's co-construction of a classroom knowledge base. This was evident by the notes that students left to each other within the unit's web platform. Some of

1. Students work collectively as a learning community to produce a knowledge base that is indexed to learning goals and pedagogical variables.
2. The knowledge base is accessible for editing and improvement by all members, and serves as a primary resource for ongoing inquiry.
3. Collaborative inquiry activities are designed that ensure the coverage of targeted science learning goals, including assessable outcomes.
4. The teacher plays a critical role defined within the inquiry script, but also a general orchestration role, scaffolded by the technology environment.

Figure 3.5 Design principles guiding knowledge community and inquiry learning environments (adapted from Fong & Slotta, 2018) these notes specifically encouraged less active members to participate and guided their participation to balance factual information already contributed to the knowledge base with explanatory elaborations. This resulted not only in deepening the knowledge base but also in a more equitable co-construction process (Slotta et al., 2019). Findings also illuminate the critical role that teachers play in orchestrating student activity within knowledge, community, and inquiry learning environments. For instance, an emergent *reflect-refocus-release* pattern was revealed in teachers' support, where "the *reflective* community discussions culminated in teacher-issued instructions or guidance to *refocus* the learning community's subsequent inquiry tasks or goals, just prior to their *release* into autonomous inquiry pursuits" (Fong & Slotta, 2018, p. 551). The refocusing instructions typically synthesized or responded to ideas that emerged in the discussion. In this way, teachers' orchestration was crucial in supporting students' collective knowledge-building processes regarding the "big ideas" embedded within the curricular unit.

Designs for Inquiry in a Networked Society

Many aspects of human learning have not changed much throughout history; however, the settings in which learning occurs nowadays are quite different from those of even a decade ago. Having access to unprecedented amounts of the human knowledge and cultural heritage at the tip of the finger, up-to-the-moment information concerning almost every aspect of our lives, endless channels for communicating and co-creating of ideas and artifacts with others in the multiple networks we are part of—put together, all these create a very different context (whether viewed as utopic or dystopic, or anywhere in between) for today's being and learning. Tabak, Ben-Zvi, and Kali (2019) describe learning in today's networked society as a process of shared meaning-making in which people co-create knowledge in technology-enhanced learning environments and communities. They claim that within this realm, many incidental opportunities for learning occur—for instance, when youths develop shared insights concerning techniques to determine top-achieving players in a massively multiplayer online roleplaying game. The networked society is not merely a new context for learning; rather, it has been conceptualized as a distinct characteristic of today's learning, named cyberlearning (Roschelle, Martin, Ahn, & Schank, 2017). In contrast, as Tabak et al. (2019) claim, "in-school learning interactions are … technologically impoverished … as a result, students mostly view schools and schooling as irrelevant to their current and future lives, remaining largely unreceptive to the curriculum" (p. 26). This phenomenon has been referred to as a school-society digital disconnect (Selwyn, 2006, 2014).

In recent years, several pedagogical approaches have been developed that seek to adopt promising trajectories of spontaneous learning within the networked society and bring them to school, without "schoolifying" them—that is, without trivializing them to align with standardized academic requirements (for the notion of schoolification see Blikstein, 2013 or Ring & O'Sullivan, 2018). Two such approaches, which are specifically relevant for inquiry learning, build on the trajectories of (a) mobile learning and (b) citizen science. The next sections provide a brief overview of each of these trajectories and then highlight guiding frameworks for designing environments that can support inquiry learning within the networked society, spanning contents related to natural sciences (e.g., biology), social sciences (e.g., history), and humanities (e.g., art).

Mobile Learning to Support Out-of-School Inquiry

The use of mobile devices for educational purposes has been growing rapidly in the past decade (Metz, 2014). In this context, the notion of mobile learning, defined as "the processes of coming to know through conversations across multiple contexts amongst people and personal interactive technologies" (Sharples, Taylor, & Vavoula, 2007, p. 225), has gained much interest among education researchers. One of the reasons for this interest is that mobile technologies have the potential to address a most challenging aspect of inquiry learning—connecting between various contexts of learning, including the connection between school and the outdoor environment, or other informal learning settings such as museums.

Research shows that when properly designed, out-of-school inquiry can enhance meaningful learning in various aspects and domains, from fostering students' self-confidence, to their development of deep knowledge (Bamberger & Tal, 2008; NRC, 2009). Being properly designed means that the inquiry addresses unique features of the local environment, makes connections to students' life experiences, enables choice, encourages social interaction, and is well-mediated (Dillon et al., 2006; Orion, 1993; Tal, 2016). Despite its benefits, when it comes to implementation, teachers struggle to support students to actively engage in exploration and meaning-making outside the safe environment of the classroom, where they are required to deal with issues such as safety, and students' attention in environments that are full with stimulations, especially in the realm of large classes, and limited support (Dillon et al., 2006).

The affordances of mobile technologies to connect in-classroom inquiry learning with out-of-classroom settings have been studied in various contexts and domains such STEM (Kali, Levy, Levin-Peled, & Tal, 2018; Maldonado & Pea 2010; Seow, Zhang, Chen, Looi, & Tan, 2009), geography (Medzini, Meishar-Tal, & Sneh, 2015), history (Sun et al., 2008), language learning, (Ogata et al., 2008), and art (Kali, Sagy, Kuflik, Mogilevsky, & Maayan-Fanar, 2014). In the latter study, for example, a technology-enhanced learning environment was designed to support students in developing artwork analysis skills as part of an undergraduate-level introductory course in art history. The course intertwined learning using a cognitive apprenticeship approach (Collins, 2006) within three settings: (a) in-class instruction, where theoretical foundations were introduced and discussed (focused on the instructor's modeling); (b) several visits to an on-campus archeological museum, where students conducted small-group collaborative inquiry of ancient artwork (focused on students' active inquiry with coaching of the instructor); and (c) off-campus work (labeled "home"), where students continued their collaborative inquiry online with feedback from the instructor (focused on greater independence of students' inquiry work, while fading the instructor's coaching role).

To support a seamless flow of learning activities between these settings, the learning environment provided full connectivity between: (a) the course website with a responsive design to enable both desktop and mobile use, which included resources prepared by the instructor (annotated artwork studied as part of theoretical foundations, scaffolds for the inquiry work, etc.); (b) two mobile apps: a location-aware visitor's guide to the museum providing information on exhibits, and an app enabling students to record insights during the inquiry work (photos with text, audio, or video annotations, which were automatically transferred to the teams' private collaborative space within the course website); and (c) collaborative documents within designated spaces for each group to document the inquiry work. Findings from two enactments of the course, each with about 50 students, indicated that the design of the learning environment enabled the instructor to provide students with much more opportunities to actively engage in art inquiry than in her previous teaching of the course, even though they originally included visits to the museum. The seamless flow of learning activities across the three settings enabled students to gradually develop competence in analyzing artwork and gradually become more confident and independent in doing so (Kali et al., 2015).

Learning across settings and contexts has been shown to be a prominent characteristic of learning in the networked society, known as mobile seamless learning. Chan et al. (2006) described mobile seamless learning situations as those in which students can "...learn whenever they are curious in a variety of scenarios and that they can switch from one scenario to another easily and quickly using the personal device as a mediator" (p. 6). The "seamlessness" within such learning, as identified in Wong and Looi's (2011) thorough review of the literature, encompasses ten dimensions across which mobile technologies can support learning (Right column in Table 3.2). Wong and Looi do not view the mobile seamless learning (MSL) dimensions as a design framework, but rather as a type of meta-design framework. As such, the MSL dimensions are not aimed at delineating generalized design heuristics for designing activities that promote certain pedagogical goals. Rather, the MSL framework aims at assisting designers of mobile seamless learning environments:

> to situate the dimensional space where the constraints or parameters of his or her design problem lie, and look at relevant design and research-based evidence of other related MSL systems to refine her own design.
>
> *(p. 1504)*

An example of how this meta-design framework can guide more specific design considerations for particular contexts is described in the development process of the Supporting Outdoor Inquiry Learning (SOIL) framework (Kali, Levy, et al., 2018). The SOIL framework stemmed from a design-based research study with two iterations, which explored a teacher professional development model for supporting teachers in designing technology-enhanced learning environments for their students' outdoor inquiry. The first iteration of the study revealed four dimensions by which teachers' designs were lacking in terms of supporting seamless outdoor inquiry learning (left column in Table 3.2). These dimensions encompass supports for assisting students to connect between: (a) various type of scientific practices such as asking questions, designing investigation, data analysis and interpretation, communicating knowledge (SOIL-1); (b) in-class preparation work, the fieldwork itself, and in-class follow-up activities (SOIL-2); (c) learning that occurs at home (e.g., via homework), within class, and in the outdoor environment (SOIL-3); and (d) learning as individuals, within groups, and as a whole class (SOIL-4).

Challenges to support seamless learning across scientific practices (SOIL-1), for instance, were evident in teachers' designs, which required students to carry out various scientific processes as part of an outdoor inquiry sequence of activities. In most teams in the first iteration of the study, coherence and seamlessness between these activities were lacking. One team, for example, designed a learning environment with good explanations for using sticky-traps to estimate the number of insects, but supports were missing to assist students decide where to place these traps in relation to a water source. Another team developed well-designed supports for students to collect data on plankton in the field but provided no instructions or supports for their interpretation in class. Guided by the scientific practices dimension (SOIL-1), teachers who participated in the second iteration of the study were more aware of using the (mobile and non-mobile) technology to incorporate supports that will assist students to see the connections between the scientific practices they engaged with at different parts of the activity sequence.

Although the guidance in this example was directed specifically to support seamless learning across the various scientific practices (SOIL-1), it aligns with three more general dimensions of seamless learning that Wong and Looi (2011) suggest to support using mobile technology. The first is seamless switching between multiple types of learning tasks (MSL8 in the right column of Table 3.2); the second is synthesizing knowledge across such tasks, especially when they require different levels of thinking (MSL9); and the third is seamless learning across time (MSL3). The alignment between all SOIL dimensions and the MSL framework dimensions, although rough, and sometimes overlapping, illustrates how the SOIL framework constitutes a particular instantiation of the MSL meta-design framework.

Citizen Science and Supporting Mutualistic Ecologies of Learning and Inquiry

Connectivity is one of the key characteristics of the networked society. People who might otherwise have little interaction with each other can become part of technology-enhanced communities

Table 3.2 Alignment between guidelines for supporting outdoor inquiry learning (SOIL) and for supporting mobile seamless learning

Dimensions across which supporting seamlessness is suggested in the Supporting Outdoor Inquiry Learning (SOIL) in Kali et al. (2018)		*Dimensions of seamlessness identified in Wong and Looi's review of mobile learning, which mobile technologies can support (2011)*	
SOIL-1	**Seamless learning across scientific practices** Because outdoor inquiry activity sequences may span considerable time (see SOIL 2), it is crucial to design supports to foster students' awareness of connections between activities along the sequence where they engage in asking questions, designing investigation, analyzing and interpreting data, and communicating their ideas	MSL8	**Seamless learning across tasks** For example, making connections between data collection, analysis, and communication.
		MSL9	**Seamless learning across levels of thinking skills** For example, synthesizing ideas across activities
		MSL3	**Seamless learning across time** For example, connecting between learning at school (morning) and after-school (afternoon)
SOIL-2	**Seamless learning across preparation, fieldwork, and follow-up activities** In planning valuable outdoor inquiry, it is important that good preparation for fieldwork as well as follow-up activities are planned and executed in order to promote seamless learning across contexts and active learning in various scientific practices	MSL1	**Seamless learning across formal and informal settings** For example, schools and museums
		MSL5	**Seamless learning through various techniques to access information** For example, ubiquitous Internet access, augmented reality, context-aware technology
SOIL-3	**Seamless learning across physical settings** Mobile technologies enable seamless flow of learning across the outdoor, home, and classroom settings. When designing outdoor inquiry learning environments, incorporation of mobile technologies is crucial to support the seamlessness between these physical settings	MSL4	**Seamless learning across locations** For example, school, the natural environment, home, and museums
		MSL6	**Seamless learning across physical and digital worlds** For example, fieldtrips and the World Wide Web
		MSL7	**Seamless learning across multiple types of devices** For example, "stable" technologies such as desktop computers, and mobile devices
SOIL-4	**Seamless learning across social activity structures** Designing activity sequences that support a seamless flow of learning between individual, group, and whole-class learning can be beneficial in various learning environments, especially when students reuse each other's knowledge artifacts. In outdoor inquiry learning this is specifically important due to the variety of learning contexts involved, each with its unique challenges and affordances	MSL2	**Seamless learning across social forms of learning** For example, personalized and social learning
		MSL10	**Seamless learning across pedagogical approaches** For example, various combinations of sequencing between exploration, guided inquiry, and creating artifacts.

in which a variety of stakeholders meet to promote a common goal and co-create knowledge. Citizen science (including community-driven science) is a genre of research in which such a meeting point brings together participants from the general public and scientists around projects involving various fields of science (Hecker et al., 2018; National Academies of Sciences, Engineering and Medicine, 2018; Sagy et al., 2019). This genre has become much more prominent in the past decade, as mobile technologies have become commonplace and enable volunteers around the world to actively participate in different aspects of scientific research. The "science" in citizen science encompasses a vast array of disciplinary areas including various research projects initiated by the public, communities, or scientists. This richness is expressed, for instance, in the Zooniverse website (2019), the world's largest citizen science web-portal, accommodating more than 100 citizen science projects in areas categorized into arts, biology, climate, history, language, literature, medicine, nature, physics, social science, and space. Zooniverse projects have already yielded dozens of scientific publications.

Some citizen science projects have been specifically designed for participation by school students. For example, "Community Drive" (Magnussen, Hamann, & Stensgaard, 2019) engaged middle-school students in redesigning their under-resourced neighborhood by generating solutions to problems they explored in their local area. These solutions were co-designed by the students with Copenhagen City Council urban planners. Findings from this project with two seventh-grade classes indicated that students became aware of the value of their own knowledge about their urban area as they realized connections with professional principles of urban planning during the project.

Due to the proliferation of citizen science projects in the past decade and the growing awareness of their potential for democratization of science as well as learning (Hecker et al., 2018), several frameworks have been developed to classify citizen science projects and abstract design guidelines for citizen science endeavors. Two seminal efforts have recently been accomplished in parallel, one based in Europe and the other in the United States, to coalesce such frameworks. The European effort, led by a working group within the European Citizen Science Association (ECSA), resulted in the Ten Principles of Citizen Science framework (Figure 3.6), which has been

1. *Citizen science projects actively involve citizens in scientific endeavor that generates new knowledge or understanding.* Citizens may act as contributors, collaborators or as project leaders and have a meaningful role in the project.
2. *Citizen science projects have a genuine science outcome.* For example, answering a research question or informing conservation action, management decisions or environmental policy.
3. *Both the professional scientists and the citizen scientists benefit from taking part.* Benefits may include the publication of research outputs, learning opportunities, personal enjoyment, social benefits, satisfaction through contributing to scientific evidence, for example, to address local, national and international issues, and through that, the potential to influence policy.
4. *Citizen scientists may, if they wish, participate in multiple stages of the scientific process.* This may include developing the research question, designing the method, gathering and analyzing data, and communicating the results.
5. *Citizen scientists receive feedback from the project.* For example, how their data are being used and what the research, policy or societal outcomes are.
6. *Citizen science is considered a research approach like any other, with limitations and biases that should be considered and controlled for.* However unlike traditional research approaches, citizen science provides opportunity for greater public engagement and democratization of science.
7. *Citizen science project data and metadata are made publicly available and where possible, results are published in an open-access format.* Data sharing may occur during or after the project, unless there are security or privacy concerns that prevent this.
8. *Citizen scientists are acknowledged in project results and publications.*
9. *Citizen science programs are evaluated for their scientific output, data quality, participant experience and wider societal or policy impact.*
10. *The leaders of citizen science projects take into consideration legal and ethical issues surrounding copyright, intellectual property, data-sharing agreements, confidentiality, attribution and the environmental impact of any activities.*

Figure 3.6 The 10 principles of citizen science (adapted from ECSA website, 2020) disseminated internationally in 26 languages (European Citizen Science Association, 2020; Robinson, Cawthray, West, Bonn, & Ansine, 2018). In formulating the principles, the group viewed their mission as follows:

> supporting those new to citizen science to deliver high-quality projects and providing a benchmark against which to examine existing citizen science programs ... to be applicable across a broad spectrum of citizen science activities.
>
> *(Robinson et al., 2018, p. 28)*

As illustrated by the Ten Principles—citizen science holds much potential to promote various types of values, one of which is inquiry learning among participants. However, many of the principles are not related to the depth of learning among participants, and inquiry learning is certainly not a requirement for well-designed citizen science projects. Therefore, when seeking to adopt citizen science into schools with the intention of promoting meaningful inquiry learning in any disciplinary topic (e.g., science, history, art, geography), additional guidelines are needed. One of the greatest challenges is to avoid the pitfall described above as "schoolification," which can occur when employing pedagogical approaches that do not align with, and may even suppress, the innovative spirit that citizen science affords. To avoid this detrimental route, and to develop the foundation for leveraging citizen science in bridging various school-society disconnects, the *Taking Citizen Science to School* (TCSS) center developed the notion of a school-based Mutualistic Ecology of Citizen Science (MECS) (Atias et al., 2017; Hod, Sagy, Kali, & TCSS, 2018; Sagy et al., 2019). The notion of MECS highlights values that guide the incorporation of citizen science into school education with three main design principles (Figure 3.7).

The growing awareness about the notion of school participation in citizen science has resulted in promising findings in recent years with regard to three main dimensions: (a) student learning, with a focus on enhanced epistemic thinking of science (Atias et al., 2020; Ballard, Dixon, & Harris, 2017; Golumbic, Fishbain, & Baram-Tsabari, 2019; Harris, Dixon, Bird, & Ballard, 2019); (b) teachers' professional growth, with a focus on enhanced inquiry teaching skills within citizen science contexts (Kali, Sagy, Benichou, Atias, & Levin-Peled, 2019); and (c) participation of schools in leading educational change (Hod, Sagy, et al., 2018) with a focus on practitioner teams' involvement in decision-making processes regarding the design of inquiry learning environments within such contexts. These findings emphasize the important role that inquiry learning and teaching play within the school participation in citizen science movement and provide a unique lens for studying inquiry learning.

1. Connect between the learning of students, school practitioners and scientists in a mutualistic manner (e.g., by making visible and committing to address the various parties' goals)
2. Support students' enculturation of norms and practices characteristic of citizen science (e.g., building on diverse expertise, advancing knowledge collectively, contributing to and using shared databases)
3. Adopt a societal situated approach (e.g., situate problems of inquiry in real, important, and even controversial issues that gain the public's interest).

Figure 3.7 MECS design principles

Future Trajectory: Integrating Guidelines for Design Products and Processes

The distinction between the "what" & "why" and the "how" type of guidelines for designing productive inquiry learning environments introduced at the beginning of this chapter represents a chasm that will require further investigation and bridging efforts. Despite the growing cross-fertilization between research trajectories for guiding design products and design processes (Carr-Chellman & Hoadley, 2004; McKenney & Kali, 2017), research projects tend to favor one or the other. Although we have focused on principles for design products in this chapter, we would like to close by emphasizing that the integration of the two research trajectories holds great potential. Such integration can produce the type of knowledge on inquiry learning that Bereiter (2014) framed as "principled practical knowledge," that could "provide a ladder leading to sometimes radical design improvement" (p. 4). Exciting insights are emerging from research studies that have begun to develop such integration. For example, in their Multilevel Learning for Scaling Up Systemic ICT-Enabled Learning Innovations, Law and her colleagues (Law, Kapylis, & Punie, 2015; Law, Yuen, & Lee, 2015) explain how scaling innovation can be guided by "architectures for learning" that include:

> (1) organizational structures (designed or pre-existing, which could be formal, or informal but stable), and (2) interaction mechanisms for interaction and participation, as well as (3) reification artifacts that communicate ideas and consolidate consensus and alignment.
>
> *(Law, Yuen et al., 2015, p. 3)*

The first two components of this architecture—organizational structures and interaction mechanism—represent the type of guidelines for informing design processes, because they are methods for designing learning environments and, thus, address the "how" question. The third component—reification artifacts—represents the type of guidelines for informing design products, because they provide characterization of such products and, thus, address the "what" & "why" questions. As Law and her colleagues (Law, Yuen, et al. 2015) argue, sustained scalability can be obtained only by integrating all three components of learning architectures.

If the issue of scaling educational innovation that involves design for inquiry learning is to be taken seriously, the field will need to advance such efforts of integrating guidelines for design products and design processes. The following chapters, focusing on guiding design processes, such as establishing and running design teams (Chapter 4, this volume), developing designs through design-based research and design-based implementation research (Chapter 5, this volume), and scaling up design of inquiry environments (Chapter 6, this volume), provide insights into how such an ambitious goal can be achieved.

References

Alexander, C., Ishikawa, S., & Silverstein, M. (1977). *A pattern language: Towns, buildings, and construction.* New York: Oxford University Press.

Atias, O., Benichou, M., Sagy, O., Ben-David, A., Kali, Y., & Baram-Tsabari, A. (2020). "Sometimes you're not wrong, you're just not right": Advancing students' epistemic thinking about science through in-school citizen science programs. *Proceedings of the 12th Chais Conference for the Study of Innovation and Learning Technologies: Learning in the Technological Era*, Ra'anana: The Open University of Israel.

Atias, O., Sagy, O., Kali, Y., Angel, D., & Edelist, D. (2017). Jellyfish and people—A citizen-science collaboration with mutual benefits to citizens and scientists. Poster presented at the *American Educational Research Association Conference*, San Antonio, Texas, April.

Ballard, H. L., Dixon, C. G., & Harris, E. M. (2017). Youth-focused citizen science: Examining the role of environmental science learning and agency for conservation. *Biological Conservation, 208*, 65–75. https://doi.org/10.1016/j.biocon.2016.05.024

Bamberger, Y., & Tal, T. (2008). Multiple outcomes of class visits to natural history museums: The students' view. *Journal of Science Education and Technology, 17*(3), 274–284.

Barab, S. A., & Squire, K. D. (2004). Design-based research: Putting our stake in the ground. *Journal of the Learning Sciences, 13*(1), 1–14. https://doi.org/10.1207/s15327809jls1301_1

Bell, P., Hoadley, C. M., and Linn, M. C. (2004). Design-based research in education. In M. C. Linn, E. A. Davis, & P. Bell (Eds.), *Internet environments for science education* (pp. 73–85). Mahwah, NJ: Lawrence Erlbaum Associates. https://doi.org/10.4324/9781410610393

Bereiter, C. (2006). Design research: The way forward. *Education Canada, 46*(1), 16–19. ISSN-0013-1253

Bereiter, C. (2014). Principled practical knowledge: Not a bridge but a ladder. *Journal of the Learning Sciences, 23*(1), 4–17. https://doi.org/10.1080/10508406.2013.812533

Bereiter, C., & Scardamalia, M. (1993). Surpassing ourselves. *An inquiry into the nature and implications of expertise.* Chicago, IL: Open Court.

Bielaczyc, K. (2006). Designing social infrastructure: The challenge of building computer-supported learning communities. *Journal of the Learning Sciences, 15*(3), 301–329. https://doi.org/10.1207/s15327809jls1503_1

Bielaczyc, K., & Collins, A. (1999). Learning communities in classrooms: Advancing knowledge for a lifetime. In C. M. Reigeluth (Ed.), *Instructional design theories and models design theories and models A new paradigm of instructional theory* (Vol. II, pp. 269–292). Mahwah, NJ: Lawrence Erlbaum Associates.

Blikstein, P. (2013). Digital fabrication and "making" in education: The democratization of invention. *FabLabs: Of Machines, Makers and Inventors, 4*, 1–21. https://doi.org/10.14361/transcript.9783839423820.203

Brown, A. L. (1992). Design experiments: Theoretical and methodological challenges in creating complex interventions in classroom settings. *Journal of the Learning Sciences, 2*(2), 141–178.

Brown, A. L. (1997). Transforming schools into communities of thinking and learning about serious matters. *American psychologist, 52*(4), 399.

Brown, A. L., & Campione, J. C. (1994). Guided discovery in a community of learners. In K. McGilly (Ed.), *Classroom lessons: Integrating cognitive theory and classroom practice* (pp. 229–270). Cambridge, MA: MIT Press/Bradford Books.

Brown, J. S., Collins, A., & Duguid, P. (1989). Situated cognition and the culture of learning. *Educational Researcher, 18*(1), 32–42.

Bruner, J. S. (1960). *The process of education.* Cambridge, MA: Harvard University Press.

Bruner, J. S. (1995). Seventy-fifith anniversary retropective: On learning mathematics. *Mathmatics Teacher, 8*(4), 330–335. (Reprinted from *Mathematics Teacher,* 53, 610–619, December, 1960).

Carr-Chellman, A. A., & Hoadley, C. (2004). Learning sciences and instructional systems: Beginning the dialogue [Special issue]. *Educational Technology, 44*(3).

Chan, T. W., Roschelle, J., Hsi, S., Kinshuk, Sharples, M., Brown, T., ... & Soloway, E. (2006). One-to-one technology-enhanced learning: An opportunity for global research collaboration. *Research and Practice in Technology Enhanced Learning, 1*(01), 3–29. https://doi.org/10.1142/s1793206806000032

Coburn, C. E., & Penuel, W. R. (2016). Research-practice partnerships in education: Outcomes, dynamics, and open questions. *Educational Researcher, 45*(1). https://doi.org/10.3102/0013189x16631750

Collins, A. (2006). Cognitive apprenticeship. In R. K. Sawyer (Ed), *The Cambridge handbook of the learning sciences* (pp. 205–221). New York: Cambridge University Press. https://doi.org/10.1017/cbo9780511816833.005

Design-Based Research Collective. (2003). Design-based research: An emerging paradigm for educational inquiry. *Educational Researcher, 32*(1), 5–8. https://doi.org/10.3102/0013189x032001005

Dillon, J., Rickinson, M., Teamey, K., Morris, M., Choi, M.-Y., Sanders, D., & Benefield, P. (2006). The value of outdoor learning: Evidence from research in the UK and elsewhere. *School Science Review, 87*, 107–111.

European Citizen Science Association (2020, September, 03). Retreived from https://ecsa.citizen-science.net

Fishman, B. J., Penuel, W. R., Allen, A.-R., Haugan Cheng, B., & Sabelli, N. (2013). Design-based implementation research: An emerging model for transforming the relationship of research and practice. *National Society for the Study of Education, 112*(2), 136–156.

Fong, C., & Slotta, J. D. (2018). Supporting communities of learners in the elementary classroom: The common knowledge learning environment. *Instructional Science, 46*(4), 533–561. https://doi.org/10.1007/s11251-018-9463-3

Gamma, E., Helm, R., Johnson, R., & Vlissides, J. (1995). *Design patterns: Elements of reusable object-oriented software.* Reading, MA: Addison-Wesley.

Gobert, J. D., & Pallant, A. (2004). Fostering students' epistemologies of models via authentic model-based tasks. *Journal of Science Education and Technology, 13*(1), 7–22. https://doi.org/10.1023/b:jost.0000019635.70068.6f

Golumbic,Y. N., Fishbain, B., & Baram-Tsabari, A. (2019). User centered design of a citizen science air-quality monitoring project. *International Journal of Science Education*, Part B, 1–19. https://doi.org/10.1080/21548455.2019.1597314

Goodyear, P. (2015). Teaching as design. *HERDSA Review of Higher Education Volume 2, 2*, 27–50.

Goodyear, P., & Retalis, S. (2010). *Technology-enhanced learning: Design patterns and pattern languages*. Education for primary care: An official publication of the Association of Course Organisers, National Association of GP Tutors, World Organisation of Family Doctors (Vol. 23). Rotterdam: Sense Publishers. https://doi.org/10.1163/9789460910623

Gustafson, K., & Branch, R. (1981). *Survey of instructional development models*. Syracuse: ERIC Clearinghouse on Information & Technology.

Harris, E. M., Dixon, C. G., Bird, E. B., & Ballard, H. L. (2019). For science and self: Youth interactions with data in community and citizen science. *Journal of the Learning Sciences, 29*(2), 224–263. https://doi.org/10.1080/10508406.2019.1693379

Hecker, S., Haklay, M., Bowser, A., Makuch, Z., Vogel, J., & Bonn, A. (2018). *Citizen science: Innovation in open science, society and policy*. London: UCL Press. https://doi.org/10.2307/j.ctv550cf2

Hoadley, C. M., & Cox, C. (2009). What is design knowledge and how do we teach it? In C. DiGiano, S. Goldman, & M. Chorost (Eds.), *Educating learning technology designers: Guiding and inspiring creators of innovative educational tools* (pp. 19–35). London: Routledge. https://doi.org/10.4324/9780203357217

Hod, Y., Bielaczyc, K., & Ben-Zvi, D. (2018). Revisiting learning communities: Innovations in theory and practice. *Instructional Science, 46*(4), 489–506. https://doi.org/10.1007/s11251-018-9467-z

Hod, Y., Sagy, O., Kali, Y., & TCSS. (2018). The opportunities of networks of research-practice partnerships and why CSCL should not give up on large-scale educational change. *International Journal of Computer-Supported Collaborative Learning, 13*(4), 457–466. https://doi.org/10.1007/s11412-018-9287-9

Kali, Y. (2006). Collaborative knowledge building using the design principles database. *International Journal of Computer Support for Collaborative Learning, 1*(2), 187–201. https://doi.org/10.1007/s11412-006-8993-x

Kali, Y. (2008). The design principles database as means for promoting design-based research. In A. E. Kelly, R. A. Lesh, & J. Y. Baek (Eds.), *Handbook of design research methods in education: Innovations in science, technology, engineering, and mathematics learning and teaching* (pp. 423–438). Mahwah, NJ: Lawrence Erlbaum Associates. https://doi.org/10.4324/9781315759593

Kali, Y., Eylon, B.-S., Mckenney, S., & Kidron, A. (2018). Design-centric research-practice partnerships: Three key lenses for building productive bridges between theory and practice. In J. M. Spector, B. Lockee, & M. Childress (Eds.), *Learning, design, and technology* (pp. 1–30). Cham: Springer. https://doi.org/10.1007/978-3-319-17727-4_122-1.

Kali, Y., & Hoadley, C. (in press). Design-based research methods in CSCL: Calibrating our epistemologies and ontologies. In U. Cress, C. Rosé, A. Wise, and J. Oshima (Eds.), *International handbook of computer-supported collaborative learning*. Springer. https://doi.org/10.13140/RG.2.2.31503.20642

Kali, Y., Levy, K. S., Levin-Peled, R., & Tal, T. (2018). Supporting outdoor inquiry learning (SOIL): Teachers as designers of mobile-assisted seamless learning. *British Journal of Educational Technology, 49(*6), 1145–1161. https://doi.org/10.1111/bjet.12698

Kali, Y., & Linn, M. C. (2008). Technology-enhanced support strategies for inquiry learning. In J. M. Spector, M. D. Merrill, J. J. G. V. Merriënboer, & M. P. Driscoll (Eds.), *Handbook of research on educational communications and technology* (3rd ed., pp. 445–461). Mahwah, NJ: Erlbaum.

Kali, Y., & Linn, M. C. (2010). Curriculum design—as subject matter: Science. In B. McGraw, E. Baker & P. Peterson (Eds.), *International Encyclopedia of Education* (3rd ed., pp. 468–474). Philadelphia, PA: Elsevier. https://doi.org/10.1016/b978-0-08-044894-7.00081-6

Kali, Y., Linn, M. C., & Roseman, J. E. (2008). *Designing coherent science education: Implications for curriculum, instruction, and policy*. Technology, Education – Connections (Vol. 37). New York: Teachers College Press.

Kali, Y., McKenney, S., & Sagy, O. (Eds.). (2015). Teachers as designers of technology-enhanced learning [Special issue]. *Instructional Science, 43*(2). https://doi.org/10.1007/s11251-014-9343-4

Kali, Y., Sagy, O., Benichou, M., Atias, A., & Levin-Peled, R. (2019). Teaching expertise reconsidered: The Technology, Pedagogy, Content, and Space (TPeCS) knowledge framework. *British Journal of Educational Technology, 50*(5), 2162–2177. https://doi.org/10.1111/bjet.12847

Kali, Y., Sagy, O., Kuflik, T., Mogilevsky, O., & Maayan-Fanar, E. (2014). Harnessing technology for promoting undergraduate art education: A novel model that streamlines learning between classroom, museum, and home. *IEEE Transactions on Learning Technologies, 8*(1), 5–17. https://doi.org/10.1109/TLT.2014.2365810

Krajcik, J. S., Blumenfeld, P. C., Marx, R. W., & Soloway, E. (1994). A collaborative model for helping middle grade science teachers learn project-based instruction. *The Elementary School Journal, 94*(5), 483–497.

Laurillard, D. (2012). *Teaching as a design science: Building pedagogical patterns for learning and technology*. London: Routledge. https://doi.org/10.1080/00071005.2012.742279

Lave, J. (1991). Situating learning in communities of practice. *Perspectives on Socially Shared Cognition, 2*, 63–82.

Lave, J. J., & Wenger, E. (1991). Situated learning: Legitimate peripheral participation. In R. Pea & J. S. Brown (Eds.), *Learning in doing: Social, cognitive, and computational perspectives*. Cambridge: Cambridge University Press.

Law, N., Kampylis, P., & Punie, Y. (2015). Pathways to enhance multilevel learning for scaling up systemic ICT-enabled learning innovations: Lessons from 7 European and Asian cases. In C-K. Looi & L-W. Teh (Eds.), *Scaling educational innovations* (pp. 197–223). Singapore: Springer. https://doi.org/10.1007/978-981-287-537-2_10

Law, N. W. Y., Yuen, J. K. L., & Lee, Y. (2015). Precarious school level scalability amid network level resilience: Insights from a multilevel multiscale model of scalability. In *Annual Meeting of the American Educational Research Association*, AERA 2015. Chicago, IL. Retreived from http://hub.hku.hk/bitstream/10722/219242/1/Content.pdf

Linn, M. C., Bell, P., & Davis, E. A. (2004). Specific design principles: Elaborating the scaffolded knowledge integration framework. In M. C. Linn, E. A. Davis, & P. Bell (Eds.), *Internet environments for science education* (pp. 315–340). Mahwah, NJ: Lawrence Erlbaum. https://doi.org/10.4324/9781410610393

Linn, M. C., & Eylon, B.-S. (1996). Lifelong science learning: A longitudinal case study. In Garrison, W. Cottrell (Ed.), *Proceedings of cognitive science society, 1996* (pp. 597–602). Mahwah, NJ: Lawrence Erlbaum Associates.

Linn, M. C., & Eylon, B.-S. (2006). *Science education: Integrating views of learning and instruction. Handbook of educational psychology* (2nd ed.). Mahwah, NJ: Lawrence Erlbaum Associates. https://doi.org/10.4324/9780203874790.ch22

Linn, M. C., & Eylon, B.-S. (2011). *Science learning and instruction: Taking advantage of technology to promote knowledge integration*. New York: Taylor & Francis. https://doi.org/10.4324/9780203806524

Linn, M. C., & Hsi, S. (2000). *Computers, teachers, peers: Science learning partners*. Mahwah, NJ: Lawrence Erlbaum Associates. https://doi.org/10.4324/9781410605917

Lui, M., & Slotta, J. D. (2014). Immersive simulations for smart classrooms: Exploring evolutionary concepts in secondary science. *Technology, Pedagogy and Education, 23*(1), 57–80. https://doi.org/10.1080/1475939x.2013.838452

Ma, J. Y., & Hall, R. (2018). Learning a part together: Ensemble learning and infrastructure in a competitive high school marching band. *Instructional Science, 46*(4), 507–532. https://doi.org/10.1007/s11251-018-9455-3

Magnussen, R., Hamann, V. D., & Stensgaard, A. G. (2019). Educating for co-production of community-driven knowledge. *Electronic Journal of E-learning, 17*(3), 222–233. https://doi.org/10.34190/jel.17.3.005

Maldonado, H., & Pea, R. D. (2010). LET's GO! to the creek: Co-design of water quality inquiry using mobile science collaboratories. *The 6th IEEE International Conference on Wireless, Mobile, and Ubiquitous Technologies in Education*, 81–87. https://doi.org/10.1109/wmute.2010.50

Metz, S. (2014). Science teaching and learning in the 21st century. *The Science Teacher,* 81(6), 6. http://dx.doi.org/10.2505/4/tst14_081_06_6

McKenney, S., & Kali, Y. (2017). Design methods for TEL. In E. Duval, M. Sharples, & R. Sutherland (Eds.), *Technology enhanced learning: Research themes* (pp. 37–46). Springer. https://doi.org/10.1007/978-3-319-02600-8_4

McKenney, S., & Reeves, T. C. (2018). *Conducting educational design research*. New York: Routledge. https://doi.org/10.4324/9781315105642

Medzini, A., Meishar-Tal, H., & Sneh, Y. (2015). Use of mobile technologies as support tools for geography field trips. *International Research in Geographical and Environmental Education, 24(*1), 13–23. https://doi.org/10.1080/10382046.2014.967514

Merrill, M. D. (2002). First principles of instruction. *Educational Technology Research and Development, 50*(3), 43–59. https://doi.org/10.1007/bf02505024

National Academies of Sciences, Engineering, and Medicine. (2018). *Learning through citizen science: Enhancing opportunities by design*. National Academies Press. DOI: 10.17226/25183

Nelson, H. G., & Stolterman, E. (2012). *The design way: Intentional change in an unpredictable world* (2nd ed.). Cambridge, MA: MIT Press. https://doi.org/10.7551/mitpress/9188.001.0001

NRC. (2009). *Learning science in informal environments*. Washington, DC: National Research Council.

Ogata, H., Hui, G. L., Yin, C., Ueda, T., Oishi, Y., & Yano, Y. (2008). LOCH: Supporting mobile language learning outside classrooms. *Mobile Learning and Organisation, 2*(3), 271–282. https://doi.org/10.1504/ijmlo.2008.020319

Orion, N. (1993). A model for the development and implementation of field trips as an integral part of the science curriculum. *School Science and Mathematics*, *93*(6), 325–331.

Penuel, W. R., Fishman, B. J., Haugan-Cheng, B., & Sabelli, N. (2011). Organizing research and development at the intersection of learning, implementation, and design. *Educational Researcher*, *40*(7), 331–337. https://doi.org/10.3102/0013189x11421826

Quintana, C., Reiser, B. J., Davis, E. A., Krajcik, J., Fretz, E., Duncan, R. G., & Soloway, E. (2004). A scaffolding design framework for software to support science inquiry. *The Journal of the Learning Sciences*, *13*(3), 337–386. https://doi.org/10.1207/s15327809jls1303_4

Ring, E., & O'Sullivan, L. (2018). Dewey: A panacea for the "schoolification" epidemic. *Education*, *46*(4) , 3–13, 402–410. https://doi.org/10.1080/03004279.2018.1445474

Robinson, L. D., Cawthray, J. L., West, S. E., Bonn, A., & Ansine, J. (2018). Ten principles of citizen science. In S. Hecker, M. Halay, A. Bowser, Z. Makuch, J. Voger, & A. Bonn (Eds.), *Citizen science: Innovation in open science, society and policy* (p. 582). London: UCL Press. https://doi.org/10.2307/j.ctv550cf2.9

Roschelle, J., Martin, W., Ahn, J., & Schank, P. (Eds.). (2017). *Cyberlearning community report: The state of cyberlearning and the future of learning with technology*. Menlo Park, CA: SRI International. https://doi.org/10.1007/978-3-319-66610-5_69

Roseman, J. E., Linn, M. C., & Koppal, M. (2008). Characterizing curriculum coherence. In Y. Kali, M. C. Linn, J. E., Roseman (Eds.), *Designing coherent science education: Implications for curriculum, instruction, and policy*. New York: Teachers College Press.

Sagy, O., Golumbic, Y., Abramsky, H., Benichou, M., Atias, O., Manor, H., Baram-Tsabari, A., Kali, Y., Ben-Zvi, D., Hod, Y., Angel, D., (2019). Citizen science: An opportunity for learning in a networked society. In Y. Kali, A. Baram-Tsabary, & A. Schejter (Eds.), *Learning in a networked society: Spontaneous and designed technology enhanced learning communities* (pp. 97–115). Cham: Springer. https://doi.org/10.1007/978-3-030-14610-8_6

Sampson, V., & Clark, D. B. (2008). Assessment of the ways students generate arguments in science education: Current perspectives and recommendations for future directions. *Science Education*, *92*(3), 447–472. https://doi.org/10.1002/sce.20276

Scardamalia, M. (2002). Collective cognitive responsibility for the advancement of knowledge. In B. Smith (Ed.), *Liberal education in a knowledge society* (pp. 67–98). Chicago, IL: Open Court.

Scardamalia, M. and Bereiter, C. (1987). Knowledge telling and knowledge transforming in written composition. In S. Rosenberg (Ed.), *Advances in Applied Psycholinguistics, Vol. 2: Reading, Writing and Language Learning* (pp. 142 175). Cambridge: Cambridge University Press.

Scardamalia, M., & Bereiter, C. (1991). Higher levels of agency for children in knowledge building: A challenge for the design of new knowledge media. *Journal of the Learning Sciences*, *1*(1), 37–68.

Scardamalia, M., & Bereiter, C. (1994). Computer support for knowledge-building communities. *Journal of the Learning Sciences*, *3*(3), 265–283.

Scardamalia, M., & Bereiter, C. (2007). Fostering communities of learners and knowledge building: An interrupted dialogue. In J. Campione & K. Metz (Eds.), *Children's learning in the laboratory and in the classroom: Essays in honor of Ann Brown* (pp. 197–212). London: Routledge.

Selwyn, N. (2006). Exploring the "digital disconnect" between net-savvy students and their schools. *Learning, Media and Technology*, *31*(1), 5–17. https://doi.org/10.1080/17439880500515416

Selwyn, N. (2014). *Distrusting educational technology: Critical questions for changing times*. New York: Routledge. https://doi.org/10.4324/9781315886350

Seow, P., Zhang, B., Chen, W., Looi, C.-K., & Tan, N. (2009). Designing a seamless learning environment to learn reduce, reuse and recycle in environmental education. *International Journal of Mobile Learning and Organisation*, *3*(1), 60–83. https://doi.org/10.1504/ijmlo.2009.023053

Sharples, M., Taylor, J., & Vavoula, G. (2007). A theory of learning for the mobile age. In R. Andrews & C. Haythornthwaite (Eds.), *The Sage handbook of Elearning research* (pp. 221–247). London: Sage. https://doi.org/10.4135/9781848607859.n10

Slotta, J. D., Kali, Y., Najafi, H., Lui, M., Tissenbaum, M., Acosta, A., Zhao, N., Quintana, R. M., Ehrlick, S. P., Schwartz, N., Cavalho, R., Fong, C., Servetas, M. (2019). *The knowledge community and inquiry model: Synthesizing a decade's research for a widening audience*. Session Presented at the Annual Meeting of the American Educational Research Association. April 5–9. Toronto.

Slotta, J. D., & Linn, M. C. (2009). *WISE Science: Web-based inquiry in the classroom*. New York: Teachers College Press. ISBN-0-8077-4950-8

Slotta, J. D., & Najafi, H. (2010). Knowledge communities in the classroom. In P. L. Peterson, E. Baker, & B. McGaw (Eds.), *International ecyclopedia of education* (Vol. 8, pp. 189–196). Elsevier. https://doi.org/10.1016/b978-0-08-044894-7.00742-9

Sun, Q., Ardito, C., Buono, P., Costabile, M. F., Lanzilotti, R., Pederson, T., & Piccinno, A. (2008). Experiencing the past through the senses: An m-learning game at archaeological parks. *IEEE MultiMedia, 15*(4), 76–81. https://doi.org/0.1109/mmul.2008.87

Tabak, I., Ben-Zvi, D., & Kali, Y. (2019). Technology-enhanced learning communities on a continuum between spontaneous and designed. In Y. Kali, A. Baram-Tsabary, A., Schejter (Eds.), *Learning in a networked society: Spontaneous and designed technology enhanced learning communities* (pp. 25–37). Cham: Springer. https://doi.org/10.1007/978-3-030-14610-8_2

Tal, T. (2016). From schools to nature: Bridging learning environments in Israel. In M.-H. Chiu (Ed.), *Science education research and practices in Asia: Challenges and opportunities* (pp. 539–552). Singapore: Springer. https://doi.org/10.1007/978-981-10-0847-4_29

Tao, D., & Zhang, J. (2018). Forming shared inquiry structures to support knowledge building in a grade 5 community. *Instructional Science, 46*(4), 563–592. https://doi.org/10.1007/S11251-018-9462-4

Tissenbaum, M., & Slotta, J. D. (2019). Developing a smart classroom infrastructure to support real-time student collaboration and inquiry: A 4-year design study. *Instructional Science, 47*(4), 423–462. https://doi.org/10.1007/s11251-019-09486-1

Wong, L.-H., & Looi, C.-K. (2011). What seams do we remove in mobile assisted seamless learning? A critical review of the literature. *Computers & Education, 57*(4), 2364–2381. https://doi.org/10.1016/j.compedu.2011.06.007

Zhang, J., Hong, H. Y., Scardamalia, M., Teo, C. L., & Morley, E. A. (2011). Sustaining knowledge building as a principle-based innovation at an elementary school. *The Journal of the Learning Sciences, 20*(2), 262–307. https://doi.org/10.1080/10508406.2011.528317

Zooniverse. (2019, September 28). Retrevied from https://www.zooniverse.org.

4
ESTABLISHING AND RUNNING DESIGN TEAMS

Kimberley Gomez and Nicole Mancevice

Introduction

Learning scientists have a rich history of designing curricular and instructional resources to support inquiry learning in classrooms and out-of-school settings. To design these curricular and instructional resources, interdisciplinary teams of university researchers have typically collaborated to develop resources and pilot them in classrooms with the aim of studying student learning (Fishman & Davis, 2006). Early design research (e.g., Brown, The Learning through Collaborative Visualization [CoVis] Project, Blumenthal, Palincsar) reflected this emphasis in collaboration and a focus on studying student learning. Although teachers may have been involved in piloting and sharing feedback on the resources (e.g., usability, student interest) in the early years of design research, they were not likely to be privy to design decisions and were not encouraged to engage in much adaptation; fidelity to the innovation was much preferred (Snyder, et al., 1992). In fact, reports from that period suggest that researchers were concerned with potential variation, particularly in how teachers might enact the instruction (Brown & Campione, 1996). While such efforts to rein in "undesirable" variation resulted in high-quality resources, they were not necessarily well-aligned with teachers' professional needs or the mutually adaptive (Berman & McLaughlin, 1975) needs of the local classroom contexts in which they taught.

Researchers have increasingly recognized the importance of including teachers in the design of curricular and instructional resources (see Gomez et al., 2018, for a recent discussion of collaborative design with teachers), which has involved discussing design rationale and limitations. By designing *with*, not for, teachers, researchers are able to develop resources that will be more usable in classrooms. As researchers have expanded their focus to include inquiry learning in school and out-of-school settings, stakeholders involved in designing resources for these diverse settings have also expanded. This shift has benefits for the design and use of curricular and instructional resources. Not only are the resources more usable, research suggests that the stakeholders involved have more ownership over the final product (Gomez et al., 2015; Penuel et al., 2007). Studies have reported additional benefits for participants, such as professional development and learning (Bang et al., 2010; Kyza & Nicolaidou, 2017).

As design-based research continues to establish a foothold within designer-stakeholder efforts, the literature describing these efforts spans many contexts, including classroom inquiry activities (Ching et al., 2015), inquiry efforts with school practitioners (Coburn & Penuel, 2016), and community organizations (Gutiérrez & Jurow, 2016). These research and design activities have examined the curricular and instructional resources that support inquiry, as well as the design processes that led to their development. Studies have reported stakeholders' involvement in the design processes and the ways that organizational roles and constraints impact the process and outcomes (Severance et al., 2016). Moving beyond the what, i.e., design outcomes, the literature has also highlighted stakeholders' perceptions of benefits and challenges (D'Amico, 2010; Penuel et al., 2007). While these reports serve an important purpose to guide and inform future scholarship, specific details about how to launch a design team and how to support and maintain such a team remain relatively absent. As designers in the health disciplines recently noted, "the *process* of co-creation is as important as any particular products or services generated" (Greenhalgh et al., 2016, p. 406). Far too often, many researchers have had to figure out how to facilitate the process of design while doing design work (Stieff & Ryan, 2016).

This chapter responds to a need for a detailed discussion of how to establish, facilitate, and sustain design teams with stakeholders. We write from the perspective of researchers who are convening and facilitating design teams. The role of researcher as facilitator is consistent with the literature (Penuel et al., 2007). Our stance is that designing curriculum, tools, or instruction without input from teachers, students, community youth, and the organizations that serve them, is not far afield from the cognitive laboratory design and testing approach from which much of the field of learning sciences originated (Brown, 1992) and from which it has determinedly moved beyond, philosophically and practically. Designing for, rather than designing with, stakeholders is likely to yield a less-than-satisfactory outcome in classroom implementation and is less likely to lead to sustained use in classroom implementation (Shrader et al., 2001). Ideally at every stage, and with respect to the various components of design (aim, activities, materials, technology, and assessment), practitioners and other stakeholders work alongside researchers to provide ideas and feedback and to share and build their collective expertise. This stance drives the guidance offered in this chapter.

To situate recommendations on how to establish and run design teams, we begin with a brief background on the rationale for a participatory approach to designing curriculum, tools, and instruction to support inquiry learning. We offer examples of the design teams' constitution and the work of design teams. We then present recommendations based on our own experiences as well as from the work of researchers in the United States and Europe. We have organized these recommendations in four categories: developing project vision and goals, understanding context for design, establishing roles and expectations, and fostering participation. To elaborate on these recommendations, we present examples from design studies that developed and studied curriculum, tools, and instruction. We highlight issues specific to designing inquiry-based teaching and learning throughout our discussion of the recommendations. Although we center this discussion primarily on the design of inquiry learning environments in K-12 classrooms, we also acknowledge important design work done in community and out-of-school settings. We conclude with some thoughts about what design teams can learn from the process of design and implications for future research on collaborative design processes.

Design Teams and the Role of Participatory Approaches

The central focus of this chapter is starting and sustaining design teams to develop or refine curriculum, tools, and instruction in education. We highlight design approaches that are participatory in nature. The studies we cite involve stakeholders (e.g., teachers, students, community members, software designers) with the expertise and knowledge to develop materials that will be usable in specific contexts. While relatively new to education, participatory approaches to design, however, have been used extensively outside the field. Arising in the 1970s in Scandinavia, a central aim of participatory design was to prepare non-management employees to understand tools and systems (Nygaard & Bergo, 1973). By engaging in design, employees developed conceptual knowledge and language related to technology, and they worked with management to shape the production and use of technology (Nygaard & Bergo, 1973).

In education, the primary aim of participatory design approaches is to develop an educational product (e.g., a curriculum) that is usable and useful to educators and learners. The curricular and instructional resources should be locally usable because the educators and learners, or the "end users" of the resources, contributed to their development and refinement. The participatory process intentionally leverages distributed intelligence (Pea, 1993) among the stakeholders on the team. For example, Gomez et al. (2006) described a project to incorporate literacy supports in an existing science inquiry curricular unit. The university researchers brought knowledge of curriculum development, literacy instruction, and the role of literacy skills in science inquiry. Teachers brought extensive experience in working with the student population at the school as well as pedagogical knowledge. One of the teachers, in particular, in the co-design group, "sought to provide challenging texts for students to read" (Gomez et al., 2006, p. 34). Similarly, when designing for out-of-school settings, team members might bring knowledge of the community, user design activities, and specific technology integrative expertise. Design teams should involve stakeholders with the necessary expertise to develop usable educational products; the design process needs to draw on stakeholders' respective expertise.

Participatory design approaches anticipate what happens, "in real life" in the field, when everyday users take the artifact in hand. Variation happens. "Systemic disparities are proof that the services we have created selectively fail for some people" (Gomez et al., 2020, p. 196). To that end, participatory design approaches guide us to avoid a practice of walling off our theoretical underpinnings. What does it look like when theoretical underpinnings are kept separate from the participatory design practices? When we create our designs "in-house" without participant collaboration, and then share them for a review with practitioners, or simply find sites for trying out the designed tools and materials, we lose the opportunity to share our knowledge, beliefs, and experience about how the theory informs practice with our design partners. Keeping the design in-house also reduces the adaptability of the design and the likelihood that the design will meet the needs of the variety of learning contexts and learners who may encounter it. Furthermore, with respect to researcher and designer learning, we limit what we might learn when we fail to engage the expertise of practitioners. It then becomes all the more difficult to glean practitioners' and stakeholders' experiences relative to the theoretical framing that we believe guides the design. In an essay examining equity and variation in the improvement of science reform designs, Gomez et al. (2020) remind that there is almost, if not, always, variability in use and outcome. They argue that "designers of educational innovations must bear in mind—which seems obvious—that interventions seldom meet with complete success or failure" (Gomez et al., 2020, p. 197). Variability naturally occurs as users try to understand how to adopt and when, where, and why to adapt designs to fit their understandings of local needs. As such, we suggest that designers strive to explicitly build theoretical linkages around the relationships between tools and expected outcomes and identify the variability that may be necessary, for example, to support accessibility and inclusion. Lacking a theoretical bridge, natural in-the-field adaptations whether large (substantial changes) or minor (in keeping with the intended design) in form, use, or content may instead be viewed as "lethal mutations" (Brown & Campione, 1996, p. 291) that subvert the theoretical underpinnings of the designed artifact. To this latter point, Trigg and Clement (2000) urged us to be willing to see our theories in design as inseparable from practice. It is in practice that our theories come alive and are made manifest as designed materials and tools. Participatory design research, they argued, is committed to improving both (Trigg & Clement, 2000).

Often, teachers use curricular materials, and related tools, "implicitly based on experiences and past practices, but not based on intentionally articulated and theoretically grounded principles" (Garcia et al., 2014, p. 494). In addition to more usable curricular and instructional resources, practitioners who participate in design develop ownership of the resources and knowledge of curriculum design (Gomez et al., 2018). They are aware of the theory underlying the resources, and they can use that knowledge to productively adapt the resources in the future. Both in school and out-of-school settings, stakeholders and researchers learn by participating in design processes (Bang et al., 2010; Kyza & Nicolaidou, 2017). Participatory design also requires researchers to negotiate issues of values, power, and authority in design (Bang et al., 2016; Carroll & Rosson, 2007; Kyza & Nicolaidou, 2017). As Carroll and Rosson (2007) point out, there is a "moral proposition" (p. 243) inherent in participatory design: The people who will be affected by a design have a right to contribute to its creation. To this end, learning scientists have taken up issues of power and equity in learning and design by involving community members in design (Bang et al., 2016; Penuel, 2017).

In the examples of projects that follow, researchers used a variety of ways to identify and describe a particular design approach: community-based design research (Bang et al., 2010, 2013, 2016), critical design ethnography (Barab et al., 2004, 2007), design experimentation (Herrenkohl et al., 2010), co-design (Kyza & Nicolaidou, 2017; Penuel et al., 2007; Severance et al., 2016), participatory design (Cober et al., 2015; Kyza & Georgiou, 2014), and research-practice partnerships (Penuel, 2017). While it is beyond the scope of this chapter to define and characterize the similarities and differences between these respective approaches, central to each is that they involved researchers working in partnership with stakeholders to design a curriculum or technology that is locally useful. In this chapter, we focus on what we can learn from the ways these different projects involved stakeholders and the process of facilitating design.

Impetus for the Design Effort

Researchers launch design teams in response to myriad aims and local needs. A researcher's grant funding is often the impetus for forming a team. The researcher's reported aims are often to develop, adapt, or study inquiry curricula aligned with particular instructional reforms or learning standards (Kyza & Nicolaidou, 2017; Severance et al., 2016). In one multi-year research and design effort, researchers from the University of Michigan School of Education developed a partnership with the Detroit Public Schools District (Marx et al., 2004). The researchers formed design teams with teacher and administrative partners to create science inquiry curricular materials that were grounded in big driving questions that allowed students to engage with and learn both content and inquiry practices. In other cases, teams form because of a local policy requirement or administrator request. For example, Gomez et al. (2019) began working with a school after the school's faculty became concerned about the number of students who did not pass an introductory biology course. The principal asked the researchers to work collaboratively with science teachers to help students recover their biology credits and helped to form the design team.

Researchers typically form design teams as a way to involve the population who will use the final products or at the behest of the community of users. Researchers may bring the research concern as well as research expertise "to the table," or they may jointly develop the research and design agenda with the practitioners (Penuel et al., 2011). There are a number of such examples in the field of science education. In one example, Gomez et al. (2006) explained that researchers formed a design team with high school science teachers in response to the presumptive literacies (Williams & Gomez, 2002) present in the types of public reports and other trade materials frequently included in inquiry science curricular units. These units included public reports and trade materials as a way to provide more authentic connections to science learning. However, the reports and trade materials included text structures and vocabulary that made them difficult to read, especially for English language learners. The design team worked to identify and refine the text structures and vocabulary to support teaching and learning.

Recommendations for Establishing and Running Design Teams

Expertise in Membership

Design teams need stakeholders with the necessary expertise to develop usable educational products. By involving diverse stakeholders, design teams leverage distributed intelligence (Pea, 1993). When designing for school settings, researchers often involve teachers as team members (Kyza & Nicolaidou, 2017; Penuel et al., 2007; Stieff & Ryan, 2016). Teachers can contribute a variety of valuable expertise, such as knowledge of pedagogy, curriculum, learning standards, and students, to the design of curricula and tools. For example, Kyza and Nicolaidou (2017) described a research project that aimed to create an online inquiry learning environment. The researchers worked with science teachers to design a biotechnology and genetic engineering online inquiry for students in 11th grade. Design teams might also include students, disciplinary experts, software developers, and other technology experts. In the Kyza and Nicolaidou (2017) example, the researchers involved a biotechnology scientist and other experts at different stages in the process. Researchers select team members based on the expertise and knowledge needed to accomplish the project goal.

Design teams work to develop and study inquiry learning in out-of-school settings too (Bang et al., 2010, 2013, 2016; Barab et al., 2007). When designing for out-of-school settings, researchers have partnered with a wide variety of community members. Bang et al. (2013) described a community-based design research effort with an after-school science program for Indigenous youth in Chicago. As a community-based design effort, the researchers believed it was important for the Indigenous community to be included in design decisions related to education for Indigenous youth. Bang et al. (2013) explained that design team members included Indigenous community elders, parents, teachers, community content experts, other experts, interested adults, and youth.

To identify and select team members, researchers have reported different strategies. Some projects involved screening potential participants to determine if they had the interest and expertise to participate (Stieff & Ryan, 2016). Stieff and Ryan (2016) explained that researchers in the Connected Chemistry project interviewed teachers to select participants who wanted to be involved and were interested in working collaboratively. Kyza and Nicolaidou (2017) described a co-design project in which they reviewed teacher applications to select participants based on their knowledge of science and technology, as well as their teaching experience and interest in participating in co-design. Being a member of a design team typically involves an extended time commitment (Penuel et al., 2007). It is an additional work responsibility for participants. By inviting participants who have the expertise and vested interest in the work, projects are more likely to sustain involvement over time.

Developing a Project Vision and Goals

Before design teams can begin the iterative work of developing, enacting, and refining an instructional tool or curricular innovation, participants need time to develop a shared vision for the work. Researchers often facilitate conversations for participants to learn about the experiences, expertise, and interests of all team members (Cober et al., 2015; D'Amico, 2010). Writing about community-based design research, for example, Bang et al. (2010) described meeting monthly or bimonthly with a team of community stakeholders to establish a shared vision and goals for a science curriculum in an out-of-school setting. The team focused on understanding science issues in relation to participants' histories and experiences during the first year of the collaboration.

Researchers have a purpose in mind when forming a team. This purpose might originate with the researcher, a funding institution, or local stakeholders. If the project is grant-funded, then there is likely a proposed project outcome. A characteristic of designing with stakeholders, however, is that the process might unfold in unexpected directions (D'Amico, 2010; Penuel et al., 2007). For example, practitioner stakeholders, given their knowledge of the context, may have particular concerns for the design direction. The LeTUS project is an example of the way a project focus can shift based on participants' interests, needs, and expertise (D'Amico, 2010). The LeTUS project involved partnerships between universities and school districts in Chicago and Detroit to develop curriculum and teacher professional development (D'Amico, 2010). As with other projects cited here, researchers began early meetings with a focus on understanding the stakeholders' points of reference, expertise, interests, and needs (D'Amico, 2010). Researchers had to be open to shifting the project focus, within the parameters of the grant funding, based on these conversations with educators. In retrospective interviews about the project, the researchers reflected that curriculum became a greater focus than they had originally anticipated (D'Amico, 2010).

Design is time-intensive work. Taking the time to develop shared vision and goals for the project is a critical first step to build trust among participants and manage inequities in power and privilege. Researchers might also consider holding meetings in district and school offices (D'Amico, 2010), spending extended amounts of time in a setting (Barab et al., 2007), and providing volunteer services to the community (Bang et al., 2013). These activities can help to build and foster trust and level the playing field somewhat in terms of power and privilege.

When working with practitioners, researchers and designers should also recognize their unique privilege as university or institutional professionals. Researchers and designers often study others, but they are rarely the subject of inquiry themselves. In describing a collaborative relationship with a K-12 teacher, Moje (2000) noted her embodied power as she traversed the school and university communities at will. While teachers worked daily within the bounds of a school day, Moje (2000) was free to come and to leave. She reminded researchers that our discursive practices may also reflect our power, and she urged researchers to talk openly with practitioners about our epistemological, philosophical, and other differences (Moje, 2000). Lee et al. (under review) extended these ideas to highlight the ways that such differences may also influence research-practice partnerships when seemingly agreed-upon and shared values, like equity, are not openly examined for subtle and not-so-subtle differences in meaning.

Understanding Context for Design

Taking the time to learn more about a design context is important to the design process. Researchers need to learn about the context in which people will enact the curricula or use the tools. Regardless of the model or approach, there appears to be consensus that learning about context is an important aspect of a design process (Barab et al., 2007; Penuel et al., 2007). What is often less explicit in the literature are descriptions and characterizations of the current practices, educational initiatives, resources, norms, and routines of the settings in which a curriculum or tool will be used (Penuel et al., 2007). This knowledge is important for designing inquiry learning opportunities as well as for creating opportunities for all team members to engage in the process (Penuel et al., 2007).

In reflecting on challenges to enacting inquiry-based learning, Edelson et al. (1999) emphasized the importance of understanding resources and scheduling in the instructional context. It might matter whether students have access to computers in the classroom and whether those computers have reliable connection to the Internet (Edelson et al., 1999). Similarly, it might matter whether instructional periods are 40 minutes or 180 minutes (Edelson et al., 1999). One way for teams to develop this understanding of the instructional setting is to hold meetings in the classrooms and other spaces where teachers, students, and other community members will enact curricula and tools (Cober et al., 2015). It might be productive to spend time in these spaces;

however, Penuel et al. (2007) recommended that co-design take place outside of participants' work contexts so they are not distracted by their daily professional duties. Regardless of the location of team meetings, participants need to attend to the local context in addition to the proposed learning goals when designing curricula and technology (Edelson et al., 1999). Design teams will be more likely to create a curriculum or tool that can be used in current contexts if they attend to the constraints and needs of teachers, students, and community members (Edelson et al., 1999; O'Neill, 2016).

Researchers need to understand schools, museums, and community organizations as contexts for learning; they also need to consider the ways these contexts can impact team members' participation in the design process (Severance et al., 2016). District and school calendars will affect when teachers can participate in the process and the pacing of design cycles (Penuel et al., 2007; Stieff & Ryan, 2016). Researchers will also want to consider how they enlist the support of administrators (Stieff & Ryan, 2016) and facilitate opportunities for participants to work together (Severance et al., 2016). The literature on design teams highlights visible and invisible professional hierarchies that may affect how team members interact (Severance et al., 2016; Stein & Coburn, 2010). In teams with teachers and students, for example, students might look to teachers as having the authority to respond (Stieff & Ryan, 2016). Teachers might look to researchers as experts (Stieff & Ryan, 2016). Community members might be skeptical of researchers' stated intent to work collaboratively (Druin, 2002). Collaborative work requires researchers to rethink their relationship with practitioners and other stakeholders (Stein & Coburn, 2010). By attending to social and physical contexts in these ways, researchers can ensure that all team members can participate and contribute their expertise to the design process.

Establishing Roles and Expectations

Although team members might be initially skeptical about their role on the design team (Druin, 2002), each participant has unique and valuable expertise to contribute to the process. Participants likely bring different workplace experiences and norms to the project (Penuel et al., 2007). To ensure that all participants can fully participate, it is important to explicitly engage in conversations about roles, expectations for the design process, and the day-to-day work of team members (Druin, 2002; Penuel et al., 2007), while acknowledging the individual demands participants face in their lives. Researchers often take on the task of facilitating these conversations among participants (Penuel et al., 2007; Stieff & Ryan, 2016). They may use a variety of protocols (Stieff & Ryan, 2016) and design practices (Bang et al., 2016) to guide the discussion and encourage participation.

When researchers initiate a design project with practitioners or other stakeholders, how the design project is introduced can set the stage for how team members contribute and interact. For example, practitioners and stakeholders, involved in design with researchers, often have histories of being "the researched," the "informants," or the end users. They might expect, therefore, that the design project will follow a similar approach. We have found that it is not enough to plainly describe an aspiration for a distributed context of expertise and participation. Instead, inscribing such commitments in both words and actions matters for the design team's experience. Researchers can collaborate with stakeholders on the research agenda, in identifying common misconceptions, and establishing values and an agreed-upon meaning of terms. In describing a co-design project to develop a technological tool, Penuel et al. (2007) explained that researchers wanted to include teachers as co-designers but were aware that teachers had felt excluded from past efforts to integrate technology in classrooms. Therefore, to be clear about their intentions, the researchers shared their core commitments and research questions with the teachers. The researchers' core commitments included that they would attend to the community members' concerns and learn from the co-design process. Researchers also made it clear to the design group that they did not have the answers to the research questions; they would answer the questions alongside the teachers and other team members. By having these conversations about the research questions and core commitments, Penuel et al. (2007) asserted that the researchers presented themselves as fellow learners. Grossman et al. (2001) addressed how there may be the appearance of a community in professional learning community groups without substantial examination of intellectual and epistemological beliefs. Similarly, we suggest that researchers must be willing to shed the expectation of researching others, embrace the notion of engaging in mutual learning, and explicitly communicate what they hope to learn. Researchers will need to continue to attend to how all participants are involved in the design work and assigned tasks throughout the process (Stieff & Ryan, 2016).

Depending on the model or approach to design, there will be differences in the work expectations and design-making process. Some models or approaches involve distributing different responsibilities in the design process. As part of the Connected Chemistry Project, for example, Stieff and Ryan (2016) wrote that there were three subgroups within their "work circle" configuration: development, evaluations, and teacher implementers. Researchers, teachers, students, and software designers were part of these subgroups, and each subgroup had different responsibilities at different stages of the design process. Other models or approaches involve participants in all aspects of the project. As part of a community-based design research project, Bang et al. (2010) described how the project involved community members throughout the design and research process. Community members helped to identify and define problems and how to address those problems. They were central to enacting the design as well as collecting and analyzing data. Bang et al. (2010) characterized this level of community involvement as a basic principle for community-based design.

In school settings, students are another important, but frequently overlooked, stakeholder group. Druin (2002) described four possible roles for students to play in designing technology: user, tester, informant, and design partner. These roles can be described along a continuum regarding the degree to which students are involved in the design process. In the user role, children use the technology and adults study how they use it. In a modified user role, children use the technology and provide adults with feedback about the affordances of the tools (e.g., Gomez & Lee, 2017; Richards & Gomez, 2010). In the design partner role, children are full participants and stakeholders in the design process. Druin (2002) explained that researchers may select different roles for children based on their goals, resources, and timelines. Georgiou and Kyza (2014) reported on an effort to include students in the design process related to the PROFILES Cyprus professional development program. They posited that students should be part of the design of science instruction to ensure it addresses their needs and interests. Working with teachers to co-design an inquiry learning environment, Georgiou and Kyza (2014) reported that some of the teachers asked for their students' perspectives on the characteristics of the ideal learning environment for chemistry. Barton and Tan (2009) reported that they included students in a design process to increase students' engagement in middle-school science. They worked with students and teachers to adapt lessons to incorporate a set of pedagogical strategies for connecting home and school. They asked the students to share their experiences related to a particular unit; they also asked students to share what they thought their peers needed to know on the topic. After each lesson, students participated in a focus group interview to offer their feedback on the lesson. Similarly, recent work by Pinkard et al. (2017) also involved youth as designers of narrative stories that served to launch the creative designs of digital artifacts in the Digital Youth Divas out-of-school program. Pinkard et al. (2017) demonstrated that "narrative artifacts provided … [students] with a shared resource that energized conversation and relationship development" (p. 507). In addition, the co-designed tools served to strengthen students' relationships with STEM, as they "wrote themselves" (Pinkard et al., 2017, p. 506) into the narratives, and with co-design partner-mentors (Pinkard et al., 2017).

Grant and budget responsibilities are another important factor related to the project structure and decision-making. Shrader et al. (2001) described the challenges inherent in collaboratively designing curricular materials when funding constrains content and form. Similarly, in describing the co-design project, Severance et al. (2016) explained that the design process was not fully democratic because the researchers were accountable to a funding agency for project outcomes. In contrast, Bang et al. (2010) described a community-based design research project that was funded by a grant with three budgets. The researchers did not control all of the budget responsibilities. This structural decision was an intentional effort to address power and equity in institutional relationships (Bang et al., 2010).

Fostering Participation

Throughout the design process, researchers need to attend to ways to support participation of all team members—but not simply participation. It is important to create opportunities for people to work together, especially because participants do not likely work together in their day-to-day professional lives. Researchers can create these opportunities by articulating a design process and allowing that process to take the project in unexpected directions (Cober et al., 2015). It is especially important for participants to see that their ideas are valued (Cober et al., 2015). One exciting approach to explicitly building opportunities for ideas to be recognized as valuable is idea elaboration. In Druin's (2002) work with children as design partners in the University of Maryland's Human-Computer Interaction Lab, an important part of the design process involved a steady development of an initial seed idea. When either a child or adult shared an idea with the team, the other participants would then build on that idea. Writing about the Connected Chemistry Project, Stieff and Ryan (2016) explained that they also worked hard to show teachers and students how their recommendations contributed to the designs. Researchers also made sure to acknowledge all participants on print materials.

Enactment seems to be an especially valuable component of the design process (Cober et al., 2015; Kyza & Nicolaidou, 2017). Kyza and Nicolaidou (2017) described a co-design process that involved multiple stages: initial design, first enactment, redesign, and second enactment. They highlighted a design principle that the co-design process should include both design and enactment phases. These cycles of planning, enactment, and refinement can allow teams to become clearer in their theories for how a tool or curricular resources will lead to the intended outcomes (Ko et al., 2016). Teachers are better able to inform the redesign if they have participated in the design and enactment phases. Penuel et al. (2007) suggested that opportunities to test designs through enactment allow team members to take ownership of the designed artifact. It can also be motivating for participants to work together with a shared interest on improving learning environments for students (Cober et al., 2015; Herrenkohl et al., 2010).

Diversity and Inclusion as a Social Good

In his acceptance speech, after receiving the 2007 Nobel Peace Prize, Vice President Al Gore quoted an African proverb, "If you want to go quickly, go alone. If you want to go far, go together." Here we are reminded of the power in moving outside of individual strengths and, instead, leveraging the power and the presence of other perspectives. In design, leveraging the power of the few or many, through consciously attending to diversity and inclusion in selecting design team composition, offers the possibility of creating a designed context that represents part of a social good. In Ancient Greece, philosophers characterized a social good as something that offers a significant and positive benefit to many people, the aim of which is also present in individual people (Kraut, 2002). Why does diversity matter for design teams? We draw from a

2017 Interaction Design and Children Conference workshop on Equity and Inclusivity (Sobel et al., 2017) that noted "[t]hese issues—equity and inclusivity—complement each other as we can use equitable practices and approaches to promote inclusion in our designs and methods" (p. 762). Boivin et al. (2014) suggested diverse partnerships require consideration of credibility of each voice, legitimacy of knowledge each person brings and contributes, and paying attention to power. We suggest that inclusion benefits team members as well as the designed product through the representation of diverse experiences and perspectives.

Over the past decade, researchers aiming to build and support design teams have been reflecting on personal, professional, and community concerns about the limitations of design efforts that lack representation from multiple stakeholders and the limitations of designed products that fail to reflect representation from multiple perspectives and experiences (Bang & Vossoughi, 2016). Our design community is also recognizing our responsibility in actively making space for diverse representation—social, economic, ethnic, religious, linguistic, community, and related considerations—in design team membership (Penuel, 2017). Diversity in representation on design teams can be deliberately sought and strategically leveraged. Characterizing their pioneering work with Quest Atlantis, Barab et al. (2004) described the effort as critical design ethnography grounded in an inquiry approach to instruction. They suggested that it is helpful to address/reflect on the social implications/agenda of design. To understand the contexts for which they hoped to contribute design, the researchers spent an extended period of time in the Boys and Girls Club and schools to learn about the spaces (2004). They considered the club and school staff, students, and parents their co-designers, and they developed an agenda with these practitioners and youth. Because they spent an extended amount of time at the site, which was not their initial plan, they developed an understanding of what participants/collaborators wanted the outcomes to be. This critical approach to design led to the development of social commitments and critical commitments that were then build into the design. These commitments informed the collaborative design process with teachers and children as they collectively sought to understand what children would find interesting and what features would make the program usable for teachers.

Conclusion and Future Directions for Research

We began this chapter with a set of claims about the benefits of leveraging a participatory approach to designing curriculum, tools, and instruction that support inquiry learning. We described considerations for design team composition and work. We offered four categories of recommendations for organizing and facilitating design teams: developing project vision and goals, understanding context for design, establishing roles and expectations, and fostering participation. We provided examples based on our own experiences, as well as from the work of researchers in the United States and Europe, designing and studying curriculum, tools, and instruction in a variety of learning contexts. To close this chapter, we offer reflections about what design teams can learn from the process of design. We also suggest some paths for future research on collaborative design processes.

The practice of design aims to create knowledge and support knowledge use. In our view, the best examples of design team efforts keep relationships (Pressman et al., 2017) in the first position, and these efforts keep context (Barab & Squire, 2004) and usability (Dede, 2005) at the center of the work. When creating design teams, researchers need to consider who they are inviting to participate, their rationale for including these participants, and how the participants' experiences and training will likely shape the direction of the designed effort (Bang et al., 2013; Kyza & Nicolaidou, 2017; Stieff & Ryan, 2016). Researchers also need to plan for ways to acknowledge participants' contributions so they feel valued in the effort (e.g., being able to see evidence of their expertise in the design process or in the designed product as it evolves; Cober et al., 2015; Druin, 2002; Penuel et al., 2007; Stieff & Ryan, 2016). With an aim to create a colleagueship among team members, researchers need to devote time and effort to tease out the differences in how participants understand "commonly understood" pedagogical, epistemological, and social-emotional concepts (D'Amico, 2010; Grossman et al., 2001; Moje, 2000). A lack of shared language, awareness of differences, and efforts to build shared understanding can fracture the design effort. Last, in facilitating and maintaining effective design team processes, researchers need to attend to how all team members are contributing to an understanding of how features of the learning context relate to successful implementation of the design (D'Amico, 2010; Penuel et al., 2007). Working successfully as a design team, as in most relationships, requires attention to shared values, shared vision, and regular communication.

Future research into starting and facilitating design teams would benefit from attention to understanding how the elements described above create strong and effective design team relationships and usable products that participants can successfully implement in the learning contexts. While we recognize the importance of the designed curricular or instructional resource, we encourage research that attends to what different stakeholders on the design team are learning and how their experiences become evident in the process and designed product. For example, what do researchers learn about the instructional context that would not have been knowable without the design team members? What differences are evident between participants who seem to share similar backgrounds—how might the intersectionality of race, gender, social class, community, and other elements that constitute humanity (Crenshaw, 1989) be a factor in design team effectiveness? In what ways do researchers iteratively learn from attention to these issues as they create, facilitate, and participate in design teams from one project to the next? These aspects of the experience of facilitating and participating in design teams have been sorely neglected in the literature. Given the increased interest in collaborations between researchers and local stakeholders, we urge researchers to attend to these issues of researcher learning, design team membership, and fostering working relationships among team members in future scholarship.

References

Bang, M., Faber, L., Gurneau, J., Marin, A., & Soto, C. (2016). Community-based design research: Learning across generations and strategic transformations of institutional relations toward axiological innovations. *Mind, Culture, and Activity, 23*(1), 28–41. https://doi.org/10.1080/10749039.2015.1087572

Bang, M., Marin, A., Faber, L., & Suzukovich, E. S., III. (2013). Repatriating indigenous technologies in an urban Indian community. *Urban Education, 48*(5), 705–733. https://doi.org/10.1177/0042085913490555

Bang, M., Medin, D., Washinawatok, K., & Chapman, S. (2010). Innovations in culturally based science education through partnerships and community. In M. S. Khine & I. M. Saleh (Eds.), *New science of learning* (pp. 569–592). New York: Springer.

Bang, M., & Vossoughi, S. (2016). Participatory design research and educational justice: Studying learning and relations within social change making. *Cognition and Instruction, 34*(3), 173–193. http://dx.doi.org/10.1080/07370008.2016.1181879

Barab, S., Dodge, T., Thomas, M. K., Jackson, C., & Tuzun, H. (2007). Our designs and the social agendas they carry. *The Journal of the Learning Sciences, 16*(2), 263–305. https://doi.org/10.1080/10508400701193713

Barab, S., & Squire, K. (2004). Design-based research: Putting a stake in the ground. *The Journal of the Learning Sciences, 13*(1), 1–14. https://doi.org/10.1207/s15327809jls1301_1

Barab, S. A., Thomas, M. K., Dodge, T., Squire, K., & Newell, M. (2004). Critical design ethnography: Designing for change. *Anthropology and Education Quarterly, 35*(2), 254–268. https://doi.org/10.1525/aeq.2004.35.2.254

Barton, A. C., & Tan, E. (2009). Funds of knowledge and discourses and hybrid space. *Journal of Research in Science Teaching, 46*(1), 50–73. https://doi.org/10.1002/tea.20269

Berman, P., & McLaughlin, M. W. (April, 1975). Federal programs supporting educational change. Vol. IV, Findings in Review. Santa Monica, CA: Rand Corporation. R-1589/4-HEW.

Boivin, A., Lehoux, P., Lacombe, R., Burgers, J., & Grol, R. (2014). Involving patients in setting priorities for healthcare improvement: A cluster randomized trial. *Implementation Science, 9*, 1–10. https://doi.org/10.1186/1748-5908-9-24

Brown, A. L. (1992). Design experiments: Theoretical and methodological challenges in creating complex interventions in classroom settings. *The Journal of the Learning Sciences*, *2*(2), 141–178. https://doi.org/10.1207/s15327809jls0202_2

Brown, A. L., & Campione, J. C. (1996). Psychological theory and the design of innovative learning environments: On procedures, principles, and systems. In L. Schauble & R. Glaser (Eds.), *Innovations in learning: New environments for education* (pp. 289–325). Mahwah, NJ: Erlbaum.

Carroll, J. M., & Rosson M. B. (2007). Participatory design in community informatics. *Design Studies*, *28*(3), 243–261. https://doi.org/10.1016/j.destud.2007.02.007

Ching, D., Santo, R., Hoadley, C., & Peppler, K. (2015). *On-ramps, lane changes, detours and destinations: Building connected learning pathways in Hive NYC through brokering future learning opportunities* [White paper]. Hive Research Lab. https://hiveresearchlab.files.wordpress.com/2015/05/hive-research-lab-2015-community-white-paper-brokering-future-learning-opportunities2.pdf

Cober, R., Tan, E., Slotta, J., So, H., & Könings, K. D. (2015). Teachers as participatory designers: Two case studies with technology-enhanced learning environments. *Instructional Science*, *43*, 203–228. https://doi.org/10.1007/s11251-014-9339-0

Coburn, C. E., & Penuel, W. R. (2016). Research–practice partnerships in education: Outcomes, dynamics, and open questions. *Educational Researcher*, *45*(1), 48–54. https://doi.org/10.3102/0013189X16631750

Cornfield, J., & Tukey, J. W. (1956). Average values of mean squares in factorials. *Annals of Mathematical Statistics*, *27*(4), 907–949.

Crenshaw, K. (1989). Demarginalizing the intersection of race and sex: A Black feminist critique of antidiscrimination doctrine, feminist theory and antiracist politics. *University of Chicago Legal Forum*, *1989*, 139–167.

D'Amico, L. (2010). The Center for Learning Technologies in Urban Schools: Evolving relationships in design-based research. In C. E. Coburn & M. K. Stein (Eds.), *Research and practice in education: Building alliances, bridging the divide* (pp. 37–53). Lanham, MD: Rowman & Littlefield.

Dede, C. (2005). Why design-based research is both important and difficult. *Educational Technology*, *45*(1), 5–8. https://www.jstor.org/stable/i40186159

Druin, A. (2002). The role of children in the design of new technology. *Behaviour and Information Technology*, *21*(1), 1–25. https://doi.org/10.1080/01449290110108659

Edelson, D. C., Gordin, D. N., & Pea, R. D. (1999). Addressing the challenges of inquiry-based learning through technology and curriculum design. *The Journal of the Learning Sciences*, *8*(3–4), 391–450. https://doi.org/10.1080/10508406.1999.9672075

Fishman, B. J., & Davis, E. A. (2006). Teachers learning research and the learning sciences. In R. K. Sawyer (Ed.), *The Cambridge handbook of the learning sciences* (pp. 535–559). Cambridge: Cambridge University Press.

Garcia, I., Barberà, E., Gros, B., Escofet, A., Fuertas, M., Noguera, I., López, M., Cortada, M., & Marimón, M. (2014). Analysing and supporting the process of co-designing inquiry-based and technology-enhanced learning scenarios in higher education. In S. Bayne, C. Jones, M. de Laat, T. Ryberg, & C. Sinclair (Eds.), *Proceedings of the 9th international conference on networked learning* (pp. 493–501). Edinburgh: University of Edinburgh.

Georgiou, Y., & Kyza, E. A. (2014). "Can you listen to my voice?" Including a student voice in the design of a chemistry module aiming to increase students' learning and motivation. In C. Bolte, J. Holbrook, R. Mamlok-Naaman, & F. Rauch (Eds.), *Science teachers' continuous professional development in Europe: Case studies from the PROFILES Project* (pp. 94–102). Freie Universität Berlin; Alpen-Adria-Universität Klagenfurt.

Gomez, K., Gomez, L. M., Cooper, B., Lozano, M., & Mancevice, N. (2019). Redressing science learning through supporting language: The biology credit recovery course. *Urban Education*. https://doi.org/10.1177/0042085916677345

Gomez, K., Gomez, L. M., Rodela, K. C., Horton, E. S., Cunningham, J., & Ambrocio, R. (2015). Embedding language support in developmental mathematics lessons: Exploring the value of design as professional development for community college mathematics instructors. *Journal of Teacher Education*, *66*(5) 450–465. https://doi.org/10.1177/0022487115602127

Gomez, K., Kyza, E. A., & Mancevice, N. (2018). Participatory design and the learning sciences. In F. Fischer, C. E. Hmelo-Silver, S. R. Goldman, & P. Reimann (Eds.), *International handbook of the learning sciences* (pp. 401–409). London: Routledge.

Gomez, K. & Lee, U.-L. (2015). Situated cognition and learning environments: Implications for teachers on- and offline in the new digital media age. *Interactive Learning Environments*, *23*(5), 634–652. https://doi.org/10.1080/10494820.2015.1064447

Gomez, K., Sherrer, J., Borg, T., Dowling, J., & Evans, D. (2006). Literacy infusion in a high school environmental science curriculum. *Spectrum*, *31*(3), 31–38.

Gomez, L., Bryk, A., & Bohannon, A. (April, 2020). Reliability: A path to fairness? Revue de international d'education de Sèvres. https://journals.openedition.org/ries/9447#tocfrom2n2

Gore, A. (2007). *Nobel lecture*. Nobel Media AB 2020. https://www.nobelprize.org/prizes/peace/2007/gore/26118-al-gore-nobel-lecture-2007/

Greenhalgh, T., Jackson, C., Shaw, S., & Janamian, T. (2016). Achieving research impact through co-creation in community-based health services: Literature review and case study. *The Milbank Quarterly*, *94*(2), 392–429. https://doi.org/10.1111/1468-0009.12197

Grossman, P., Wineburg, S., & Woolworth, S. (2001). Toward a theory of teacher community. *Teachers College Record*, *103*(6), 942–1012.

Gutiérrez, K. D., & Jurow, A. S. (2016). Social design experiments: Toward equity by design. *The Journal of the Learning Sciences*, *25*(4), 565–598. https://doi.org/10.1080/10508406.2016.1204548

Herrenkohl, L. R., Kawasaki, K., & Dewater, L. S. (2010). Inside and outside: Teacher- researcher collaboration. *The New Educator*, *6*(1), 74–92. https://doi.org/10.1080/1547688X.2010.10399589

Ko, M., Goldman, S. R., Radinsky, J., James, K., Hall, A., Popp, J., Bolz, J., & George, M. (2016). Looking under the hood: Productive messiness in design for argumentation in science, literature, and history. In V. Svihla & R. Reeve (Eds.), *Design as scholarship: Case studies in the learning sciences* (pp. 71–85). London: Routledge.

Kraut, R. (2002). *Aristotle: Political philosophy*. Oxford: Oxford University Press.

Kyza, E. A., & Georgiou, Y. (2014). Developing in-service science teachers' ownership of the PROFILES pedagogical framework through a technology-supported participatory design approach to professional development. *Science Education International*, *25*(2), 55–77.

Kyza, E. A., & Nicolaidou, I. (2017). Co-designing reform-based online inquiry learning environments as a situated approach to teachers' professional development. *CoDesign*, *13*(4), 261–286. https://doi.org/10.1080/15710882.2016.1209528

Langley, J., Wolstenholme, D., & Cooke, J. (2018). 'Collective making' as knowledge mobilisation: The contribution of participatory design in the co-creation of knowledge in healthcare. *BMC Health Services Research*, *18*, 1–10. https://doi.org/10.1186/s12913-018-3397-y

Lee, U.-L., DeLiema, D., & Gomez K. (under review). Equity conjectures: A methodological tool for centering social change in learning and design.

Marx, R. W., Blumenfeld, P. C., Krajcik, J. S., Fishman, B., Soloway, E., Geier, R., & Tal, R. T. (2004). Inquiry-based science in the middle grades: Assessment of learning in urban systemic reform. *Journal of Research in Science Teaching*, *41*(10), 1063–1080. https://doi.org/10.1002/tea.20039

Moje, E. B. (2000). Changing our minds, changing our bodies: Power as embodied in research relations. *International Journal of Qualitative Studies in Education*, *13*(1), 25–42. https://doi.org/10.1080/095183900235717

Nygaard, K., & Bergo, O. T. (1973). Planlegging, styring og databehandling. *Grunnbok for fagbevegelsen ("Planning, management and data processing. Basic reader for trade unions"). Volume I.* Tiden Norsk Forlag.

O'Neill, D. K. (2016). Designing the collaboratory notebook: "Building the future, the night before it's due." In V. Svihla & R. Reeve (Eds.), *Design as scholarship: Case studies in the learning sciences* (pp. 11–25). London: Routledge.

Pea, R. D. (1993). Practices of distributed intelligence and designs for education. In G. Salomon (Ed.), *Distributed cognitions: Psychological and educational considerations* (pp. 47–87). Cambridge: Cambridge University Press.

Penuel, W. R. (2017). Research–practice partnerships as a strategy for promoting equitable science teaching and learning through leveraging everyday science. *Science Education*, *101*(4), 520–525. https://doi.org/10.1002/sce.21285

Penuel, W. R., Fishman, B. J., Cheng, H., & Sabelli, N. (2011). Organizing research and development at the intersection of learning, implementation, and design. *Educational Researcher*, *40*(7), 331–337. https://doi.org/10.3102/0013189X11421826

Penuel, W. R., Roschelle, J., & Shechtman, N. (2007). Designing formative assessment software with teachers: An analysis of the co-design process. *Research and Practice in Technology Enhanced Learning*, *2*(1), 51–74. https://doi.org/10.1142/S1793206807000300

Pinkard, N., Erete, S., Martin, C. K., & McKinney de Royston, M. (2017). Digital youth divas: Exploring narrative-driven curriculum to spark middle school girls' interest in computational activities. *The Journal of the Learning Sciences*, *26*(3), 477–516. https://doi.org/10.1080/10508406.2017.1307199

Pressman, E., Gomez, L. M., Gomez, K., & Rodela, K. (2017). *Pedagogical design capacity and improving developmental mathematics teaching* [Paper]. Annual Meeting of the American Educational Research Association, San Antonio, TX.

Richards, K. A., & Gomez, K. (2011). Participant understandings of the affordances of Remix World. *International Journal of Learning and Media, 2*(2–3), 101–121.

Severance, S., Penuel, W. R., Sumner, T., & Leary, H. (2016). Organizing for teacher agency in curricular co-design. *The Journal of the Learning Sciences, 25*(4), 531–564. https://doi.org/10.1080/10508406.2016.1207541

Shrader, G., Williams, K., Lachance-Whitcomb, J., Finn, L.-E., & Gomez, L. (2001). *Participatory design of science curricula: The case for research for practice* [Paper]. Annual Meeting of the American Educational Research Association, Seattle, WA.

Snyder, J., Bolin, F., & Zumwalt, K. (1992). Curriculum implementation. In P. W. Jackson (Ed.), *Handbook of research on curriculum: A project of the American Educational Research Association* (pp. 402–435). New York: Macmillan.

Sobel, K., Kientz, J. A., Clegg, T. L., Gonzalez, C., & Yip, J. C. (2017). Equity and inclusivity at IDC. *Proceedings of the 2017 Conference on Interaction Design and Children*, 761–767. http://dx.doi.org/10.1145/3078072.3081313

Stein, M. K., & Coburn, C. E. (2010). Reframing the problem of research and practice. In C. E. Coburn & M. K. Stein (Eds.), *Research and practice in education: Building alliances, bridging the divide* (pp. 1–13). Lanham, MD: Rowman & Littlefield.

Stieff, M., & Ryan, S. (2016). Designing the connected chemistry curriculum. In V. Svihla & R. Reeve (Eds.), *Design as scholarship: Case studies in the learning sciences* (pp. 100–114). London: Routledge.

Trigg, R., & Clement, A. (2000). *Participatory design.* Computer Professionals for Social Responsibility. http://cpsr.org/prevsite/program/workplace/PD.html/

Williams, K., & Gomez, L. (2002). Presumptive literacies in technology-integrated science curriculum. In G. Stahl (Ed.), *Computer support for collaborative learning: Foundations for a CSCL community* (pp. 599–600). Mahwah, NJ: Lawrence Erlbaum.

5

DESIGN-BASED IMPLEMENTATION RESEARCH TO SUPPORT INQUIRY LEARNING

William R. Penuel and Ashley Seidel Potvin

Design-based implementation research (DBIR) is a collaborative approach to research and development anchored in problems of practice. Researchers and practitioners work together to design and test innovations, with the goals of building knowledge, theory, and innovations to bring about and sustain equitable change in educational systems (Penuel, Fishman, Cheng, & Sabelli, 2011). It integrates the wisdom of practice into innovations and studies implementation in a way that informs ongoing design. DBIR is not a method but rather an approach that employs multiple research methods, depending upon a study's aims. DBIR is especially suitable for the study of inquiry learning environments for both students and teachers, when the goal is to understand the conditions needed to support equitable implementation in such environments.

DBIR is not a new approach to research and development, but a synthetic approach that draws from multiple traditions. Primary antecedents of DBIR are the two traditions of education research from which the approach takes its name: design-based research and implementation research. Like design research, DBIR develops and tests innovations through an iterative process involving both design and research. In addition to innovations, the products of design research include new theories of learning, new learning goals and theories of how to support them, as well as theories of design (Cobb, Confrey, DiSessa, Lehrer, & Schauble, 2003; Edelson, 2002). A distinctive focus of DBIR is a focus on implementation, a topic that is part of a different tradition of education research—implementation research. Implementation research seeks to develop explanatory accounts of how, when, why, and for whom policies and programs can be implemented effectively (McLaughlin, 2006). Equity is a central concern of DBIR, through the promotion of participation of stakeholders in design and in its attention to variation in implementation and outcomes.

This chapter presents the core principles of DBIR and examples that embody those principles, along with guidance for planning a DBIR study and descriptions of dilemmas that can arise within DBIR studies.

An Example of DBIR

We begin with an example of a larger-scale DBIR project called the "Scaled Impact" project, an initiative of the Inquiry Hub research-practice partnership. This research-practice partnership seeks to support the design and implementation of curriculum materials in mathematics and science that align to the Common Core State Standards in Mathematics and the Next Generation Science Standards (NGSS; NGSS Lead States, 2013). District leaders from Denver Public Schools and researchers from the University of Colorado, who make up the core of this partnership, share a commitment to building and supporting inquiry-based learning environments, that is, environments that engage students directly with disciplinary uncertainties and practices, using authentic tools of the discipline to do so (Chinn & Malhotra, 2002; Engle, 2012; Stein & Kaufman, 2010).

A key focus of activity between 2014 and 2018 for the partnership was on developing new curriculum materials that were aligned to the NGSS. Although Colorado had not yet adopted the standards, Denver Public Schools was committed to preparing for adoption, and leaders wanted all students to have access to free, high-quality curriculum materials. Over the course of four years, teachers in the district and researchers co-designed these inquiry-based materials, producing a year-long high school curriculum that has been recognized for its quality by Achieve, Inc., an independent organization that has supported implementation of the NGSS nationwide.

While developing the curriculum, the team undertook a number of research studies that focused on the design process, effects on students, and the development of supports for implementation. One study documented how the co-design process evolved and supported teacher agency (Severance, Penuel, Sumner, & Leary, 2016). Another focused on the assessments developed to evaluate the curriculum and presented evidence that students could learn from the materials (Penuel, Turner, Jacobs, Van Horne, & Sumner, 2019). A third study focused on efforts to integrate those assessments into the district's own educational infrastructure (Penuel, 2019a).

It was a fourth study, coupled informal observations of district leaders, that led to a shift in focus for the partnership. Our research documented wide variability in the student experience of inquiry learning in their classrooms, as evident in differences across classrooms in the perceived relevance of lessons to students of different races, genders, and home languages (Penuel, Van Horne, Severance, Quigley, & Sumner, 2016). In some classrooms, teachers were able to foster a sense that the curriculum was relevant to their interests and concerns of communities and put students in the driver's seat of their own learning. But in others, few students saw the curriculum as relevant to their lives, and students had little sense of how lessons were helping them build toward an understanding of the phenomena that anchored the units.

The partnership sought and won funding for a grant from the William and Flora Hewlett Foundation, to support teachers in developing inclusive, inquiry-focused culture of learning in their classrooms across all high schools in Denver. What was co-designed in this project were professional development supports for teachers, an infrastructure for gathering and using data on student experience in the classroom, and a set of culminating design challenges that can be used as assessments of student learning. In the project, two cohorts of teachers each have experienced collaboratively designed workshops focused on building inclusive classroom culture, phenomenon-based teaching, and curriculum materials anchored in phenomena.

For the co-design effort, Denver Public Schools and the University of Colorado Boulder broadened the membership to include partners with relevant expertise needed for the effort. Already on the team were leaders with expertise in science education, curriculum, professional development, and assessment design and validation. But the partnership needed assistance in providing professional development at scale, and so a new partner, Tidemark Institute, was brought in to assist. In addition, the partnership added a youth organization, Project VOYCE, whose members are helping with developing engineering design challenges that connect with community concerns of youth.

The research has continued to examine implementation variation across classrooms, using a revised version of the measure of student experience that was used to identify the focal problem for the project. The measure of student experience is an example of a *practical measure*, designed to be administered quickly, frequently, and easily so that it can be embedded into school practice (Yeager, Bryk, Muhich, Hausman, & Morales, 2013). The practical measure used in the Scaled Impact project is a brief, nine-item survey that students complete online in three to five minutes at the end of a lesson. The survey asks questions about the perceived coherence of the day's lesson from the students' point of view, the perceived relevance of the lesson to self and community, and perceived contributions of individuals to the class discussion. Importantly, students provide background information on race and gender, so that responses can be aggregated across classrooms and measured over time to gauge progress toward the partnership's overall mission. In accordance with principles for the design of practical measures, the research team has developed evidence that the measure can be used frequently in practice and that responses to items predict subsequent learning outcomes (Penuel, Van Horne, Jacobs, & Turner, 2018). A small design study is investigating how best to support teachers in making use of the data from student experience to adjust their strategies for creating inclusive classroom cultures.

Principles of DBIR

In this section, we describe the four principles that characterize DBIR studies and how the Scaled Impact project and other DBIR projects embody them. There are four principles that characterize DBIR studies:

1. A focus on persistent problems of practice to address concrete goals for improvement from multiple stakeholders' perspectives;
2. A commitment to building and testing innovations through iterative, collaborative design;
3. A concern with developing theory and knowledge related to both classroom learning and implementation through systemic inquiry; and
4. A concern with developing capacity for sustaining change in systems.

Identifying Goals and a Shared Problem of Practice

In contrast to many forms of research, the focus of joint work reflects the goals and concerns of both research and practice partners. In the Inquiry Hub, the initial focus on developing new materials was agreed upon by partners, and the partnership's shift to focus on teaching was too. Importantly, both evidence from research studies and education leaders' own observations informed the shift, illustrating how different forms of implementation evidence can inform an evolution in focus from one project to the next, as partnerships address problems that arise during implementation.

Identifying a shared problem of practice requires ongoing negotiation, as well as some common values across partners (Penuel & Gallagher, 2017). Without common values, it may be too difficult to come to agreement on key components of learning environments to promote (e.g., the value of inquiry or giving students a say in the direction of investigations). Therefore, a number of researchers who employ DBIR seek out partners who they know share their values and ideas about teaching and learning. The MIST Project, for example, sought out partners that shared a commitment to promoting ambitious mathematics instruction in mainstream classrooms for all students (Cobb, Jackson, Smith, Sorum, & Henrick, 2013). This enabled them to maintain a partnership even in the face of significant turnover and reorganization in some partner districts (Davidson & Penuel, 2019).

The problem of practice is frequently revisited and may be revised as the team engages in ongoing study of the problem. In addition, the design and testing of solutions to problems create new problems that must be addressed. Particularly when implementation of inquiry learning environments demands significant changes to practice, new policies and capacities of adults in systems may need to be developed (Blumenfeld, Fishman, Krajcik, Marx, & Soloway, 2000). In order to negotiate a problem of practice, teams often engage in facilitated and structured activities meant to surface diverse perspectives across and within groups (e.g., Dolle, Gomez, Russell, & Bryk, 2013).

Negotiating the focal problem and goals for joint work demands attention to power, the distribution of resources, and history. Teams need to take time to explore different ways to build equitable relationships in the face of power differences and mistrust arising from historical and continuing marginalization of communities (Vakil, de Royston, Nasir, & Kirshner, 2016). Such teams might also be observed sharing leadership in design and explicitly negotiating sharing of resources to support this process (Bang, Medin, Washinawatok, & Chapman, 2010).

An example comes from a DBIR project that linked researchers from a science museum with several after-school programs focused on creating inquiry environments using making and tinkering activities, the California Tinkering Afterschool Network. That team was particularly focused on creating more equitable opportunities for children in programs to engage in making activities, but they quickly realized they did not have a shared definition of equity. They engaged together in a "value mapping" exercise to clarify definitions of equity (Ryoo, Choi, & McLeod, 2015). This activity led to identification of common commitments and opened the door for the team to begin to identify and study facilitation strategies for promoting equity.

Collaborative Design and Testing of Solutions

The process of co-design begins with the formation of a design team. The teams that form are often both cross-sector and cross-disciplinary. In the Scaled Impact project, researchers from multiple organizations, district leaders, veteran teachers involved in the design, and representatives from a youth organization and professional development provider all attended project meetings. Each brought a different and important perspective to the table. Teachers and district leaders brought ideas about how best to articulate standards and teacher evaluation systems at the system and school level. Researchers from the professional development organization brought the theoretical lens of epistemic justice (Fricker, 2009) to help sharpen the partnership's goals for equity to focus on supporting contributions of students from nondominant groups to knowledge building in the classroom.

Once teams have formed around a problem of practice and have explored potential causes of the problem, teams engage in collaborative and iterative design to improve teaching and learning practice at scale. To engage in collaborative work, teams make a number of important decisions, including determining the composition of the design team, processes for iteration, and what evidence and rationales will form the basis for making changes to designs (Fishman, Penuel, Allen, Cheng, & Sabelli, 2013). In DBIR the objects of design are not limited to classrooms but also include system-level improvements and interventions that cross settings (Fishman et al., 2013). The objects of design, for instance, may include not only curriculum materials and professional development supports needed to implement an innovation but also involve redesign of system supports and tools for monitoring instructional quality in a district. In the Scaled Impact project, for example, the team engaged not only in design of materials but also district unit assessments and guidance for teacher evaluators that were core parts of the partner district's educational infrastructure (Penuel, 2019b).

As in other forms of design-based research, teams in DBIR engage in iterative cycles of design and study to refine innovations, build knowledge, and elaborate theories (Gravemeijer & Cobb, 2013). In contrast to some examples of design research, however, the design process is *always* participatory, involving representatives from multiple stakeholder groups throughout the research and development process. In addition, a key source of evidence to inform iterations is variation in implementation across multiple classrooms, as illustrated by the Scaled Impact project described above. In smaller-scale DBR studies involving only one or two classrooms, such variation is less likely to be observable.

Building Knowledge and Theory

In the Scaled Impact project, a key goal of the research is to develop the field's understanding of how to support inquiry learning at the scale of a district. The project draws on a range of theoretical perspectives to inform its work, from research on how students learn to engage meaningfully in science practices (e.g., Schwarz, Passmore, & Reiser, 2017) to theories focused on how to redesign educational infrastructures to support ambitious, equitable changes to instruction (e.g., Hopkins & Woulfin, 2015).

DBIR has helped develop knowledge and theory in a number of domains. For example, DBIR studies have examined the consequences of different forms of organizing collaborative design (Potvin, Kaplan, Boardman, & Polman, 2018; Severance et al., 2016). Studies have also contributed knowledge and theory related to the implementation of ambitious instructional practices at the scale of a district (e.g., Cobb, Jackson, Henrick, & Smith, 2018). And studies have used randomized controlled trials to study the impacts of curricular activity systems that educators and researchers have refined after many cycles of iterative design (e.g., Harris et al., 2015).

In DBIR, theories-in-development in projects typically have the character of bricolage, that is, a mashup of different prototype theories borrowed from past projects and the literature (Gravemeijer, Rainero, & Vonk, 1994). The bricolage is often made up of multiple kinds of theories—ones that apply to supporting young people's learning in particular settings, to supporting learning of educators and caregivers charged with supporting learning in those settings, and to creating organizational conditions for equitable implementation (Russell, Jackson, Krumm, & Frank, 2013). Because of the character of educational research as a field—which promotes the development of scholars who specialize in learning research or policy and organizational studies, but not both—these theories often employ different concepts, methods, and language for describing similar phenomena. It can therefore take time to develop a common language across theories (Lehrer & Schauble, 2015) and a sense of when theories need to be refined to account for phenomena in novel contexts.

As an example, a recent DBIR study focused on supporting implementation of the Common Core State Standards in Mathematics brought together theory related to inquiry mathematics instruction and theory related to design. In the study, teachers, district leaders, and researchers were engaged in identifying rich mathematical tasks that aligned with the standards. For tasks that were identified, teachers developed analyses of tasks and supports for implementing them in linguistically diverse classrooms on a digital platform to be shared with other teachers in the district (Leary et al., 2016). The focus on tasks was informed by a body of empirical research that indicates task analysis is a powerful vehicle for teacher learning in mathematics (Boston, 2013; Boston & Smith, 2015). The theory underlying a focus on task analysis is that it helps teachers to notice key features of tasks that promote student engagement in disciplinary practices and to implement them with integrity (Boston, 2013). The team brought a different theory to analyze what happens when task-focused professional development takes place collaboratively, as opposed to in the context of a workshop led by an expert facilitator. The design tensions framework (Tatar, 2007) drew attention to how balancing goals of promoting teacher learning, teacher agency, and implementation led to compromises and a recognition that past professional development research had offered too little guidance to designers about how to integrate teacher learning supports into complex educational systems.

Developing Capacity

DBIR teams work toward developing capacity for sustaining change in systems. DBIR moves beyond a focus of developing the capacity of individuals, to focus on sustaining change in systems. Sustaining change in systems involves building human, social, and/or material capital necessary to persist in implementation. Developing capacity for sustaining change requires that teams plan ahead for such efforts to determine how the innovation will scale across the system (Weinbaum & Supovitz, 2010). Some DBIR teams have successfully built capacity for sustaining change by creating robust "curricular activity systems" and processes for supporting ongoing learning in networks or partnerships (e.g., Anderson et al., 2018). In the Inquiry Hub partnership, for example, researchers have done so by creating digital infrastructures and routines to support peer sharing and learning (e.g., Leary et al., 2016) and by creating assessments and guidance for teacher evaluators that align with curricular goals as noted above (Penuel, 2019b).

A good example of a robust curricular activity system was developed by the SunBay partnership, a partnership focused on bringing inquiry-oriented mathematics to scale in an urban school district in Florida. The center of the system was a replacement unit that had been tested elsewhere and found to be effective for a wide range of students (Roschelle et al., 2018). The partnership created a set of assessments and professional development supports that were adapted for the new Florida context and, as part of the curricular activity system, established a process for preparing local teachers to become leaders in the professional development process (Vanover, Roy, Unal, Fueyo, & Vahey, 2012). As part of the research, the team studied the effects on students and demonstrated that they could replicate the earlier experimental findings using a partnership approach (Vahey, Roy, & Fueyo, 2013). This approach differs from a typical approach taken by researchers seeking to replicate findings from an innovation, in that there was explicit attention to building local capacity to adapt and sustain the innovation.

Planning and Implementing DBIR Study: An Example

Planning for and implementing a DBIR study is more complex than planning for a small researcher-led design study or for an observational implementation study. First, in order to be problem-centered, prior to design, there must be some negotiation of what problems are to be solved and what goals are to be met by engaging in joint work. In a research-practice partnership, moreover, the study's relationship to the overall goals of the partnership must be articulated. Second, because DBIR involves the partners actively in shaping the innovation design and what aspects of it will be tested in learning environments, the project requires planning for how to structure the co-design process. Finally, researchers must decide how implementation evidence from a range of classrooms will not only be developed but also used to inform improvements to designs after testing.

Below, we describe the planning and implementation process developed by Ashley Potvin, the second author of this chapter, of a small-scale DBIR study with teachers to illustrate how these decisions can be made in ways that adhere to the core principles of DBIR. Small efforts like this may involve a design team of no more than three or four people. In this case, what makes it a DBIR effort is the purpose (attention to equitable implementation across settings) and the focus of design (at least two levels of settings are brought into coordination). In addition, it was part of a larger research-practice partnership that is focused on promoting inquiry learning environments in high school English language arts classrooms.

Deciding on a Focus for Joint Work

This particular study was situated within a larger DBIR study, Compose Our World, that aimed at co-designing ninth-grade language arts curriculum with teachers (Boardman, Garcia, Dalton, & Polman, 2021). Potvin brought a particular interest in the importance of teachers building productive relationships with students to this work, and she sought teachers who were part of the larger project to engage in joint inquiry about how they could improve the quality of relationships they had with students. She composed a design team of three volunteers from among a group of teachers she had been observing regularly as part of the larger project's research activities.

At an initial meeting with the group of teachers, Potvin facilitated an activity to help them identify a concrete challenge to tackle. In the activity, teachers developed personas that described specific students in their classrooms who they were struggling to engage in some way. Often used in design, personas are concrete representations of people that are being "designed for." Designers and product developers use personas to "help keep the assumptions [about the target audience] and decision-making criteria explicit" (Grudin & Pruitt, 2002, p. 149). In this case, Potvin hoped the teachers could use these personas to not only identify specific challenges in engaging students but also in designing strategies for reaching those students. The activity was successful, in that it led to defining the challenge as helping build relationships with students whom teachers felt they did not know well. In addition, teachers referred back to their personas during parts of the design process and considered ways to revise the design based on their interactions with their persona students.

Structuring a Design Process

Every DBIR project needs a process for designing, testing, and iterating upon an innovation. Potvin chose to organize her process around a set of Plan-Do-Study-Act cycles, a method that she adapted from improvement scientists in education (Bryk, Gomez, Grunow, & LeMahieu, 2015). In each design cycle, teachers reviewed either research on building productive relationships with students or data from their students to set a concrete, measurable aim for improving their instruction and to make a plan to introduce a new teaching routine into their classes (Plan). They tried the routine in their classrooms and collected data from students on their perceptions of the routine (Do). Then, they met as a design team to review their data (Study) and refined the routine for use in another cycle (Act).

Potvin chose this approach because it was well-suited for what in improvement science is called a "small test of change." Her plan was to engage teachers in making a focused addition to their practice, rather than a wholesale change to it. The change, moreover, needed to be practical to implement within the curriculum the larger project was testing and to support that curriculum's goals. She needed teachers to be able to support data collection directly and to generate data quickly that could inform iterations to the designed routines.

In the initial Plan phase of the cycle, the team designed a routine to develop relationships with students as a change strategy and, in doing so, worked toward creating caring classrooms. The team called the routine Dig Deep. Teachers had a number of goals for Dig Deep, including to provide an opportunity for students to share about themselves, including their culture, interests, background, home, and family, and to expand upon the kinds of things considered acceptable to share in the classroom. In this routine, teachers, and in some cases students, posed prompts to the class designed to be playful and exploratory, inviting students to share about their lives. Students shared in small groups, and teachers sat intentionally with students who they did not yet know well, including their persona students. Teachers also shared their responses to prompts. Artifacts created to support the implementation of the routine included a teacher guide, a list of ideas for prompts, and a template for students to generate their own prompts.

Potvin and her team drew on multiple theories to create these routines. The team drew on research from user-centered design that used cultural probes to engage participants in a responsive way and to encourage play and inspirational responses (Gaver, Dunne, & Pacenti, 1999). Literature on teacher-student relationships (e.g., Cooper & Miness, 2014; Moje, 1996; Reddy, Rhodes, & Mulhall, 2003) and creating caring classrooms (e.g., Gay, 2000; Noddings, 1998, 2013) also informed the research efforts.

Creating a Measure to Inform Iteration: A Student Survey

In addition to the routine, the team also designed as part of the Plan phase a student survey to collect data on students' experiences. This was a key source of evidence related to implementation for the study that informed iterative design. In the Study phase, the team analyzed survey data in meetings to guide revisions to the routine and to the survey items, as well as to understand students' feelings and experiences in teachers' classrooms. Students' responses also helped the team refine its working theory of change and encouraged teachers to reflect on their relationships with students. Through iterating on the design, implementing the design, and studying the progress of the innovation, the team began to broaden the scope of the goal to also include students developing caring relationships with one another.

The student survey allowed the team to understand students' experiences in teachers' classrooms. By the end of the project, the student survey included 13 survey items, 10 of which asked students to *agree* or *disagree* with statements (e.g., "Today the opening routine made me feel like I matter in this classroom"). Three questions required an open-ended response from students. The team wrote the items to ask students specifically about their experiences with the opening routine designed. Students completed the surveys at the end of the class period, about the opening routine in that day's class.

The data collected from the practical measure differed from traditional forms of data collected to monitor and improve classroom practice, in that the data focused on students' experiences rather than on academic outcomes. The practical measure was "practical" in two senses: (1) It was designed to gather information about student experiences that might be altered through changes in teacher practice, and (2) it was designed to be feasible to implement in the context of teaching. Analyzing the data together provided opportunities for teachers to discuss their teaching practice and problem-solve together as they worked on shared goals of creating caring classrooms (see Potvin, 2020).

The overall findings were that the routines did help teachers build better relationships with their students (Potvin, 2018), though they did not continue to use them once the research had ended. The routines, however, were incorporated into the larger curriculum project and continue to inform that team's efforts to promote social and emotional learning goals in the context of literacy instruction. One teacher continued to use the student surveys as a way to gather student perceptions on their experiences in the classroom and to make adjustments to her teaching based upon trends she noticed in her data. In addition, for teachers who participated in the project, there was evidence of a shift toward viewing students from a strengths-based perspective.

Dilemmas in DBIR

For teams engaged in DBIR studies, there are some dilemmas that can be anticipated related to its core principles, specifically those related to how the enactment of the core principles requires departures from typical, researcher-defined and researcher-led studies. Below, we describe these dilemmas and how they can manifest within projects.

Negotiating a Shared Focus for Joint Work

In deciding on a focus for joint work, differences in priorities and values can arise that seem too wide to bridge. For researchers committed to inquiry learning, partners who prioritize memorization of facts, engaging in designs for innovations that prepare students to do well on tests that focus on low-level knowledge and skills, would be an example of a "bridge too far." Under such circumstances, it may be necessary to explore if there are any areas of overlapping commitments using a values-mapping exercise such as the one described above or if the project's partners do not share enough of a common vision for teaching and learning to find a project to undertake together.

Ideally, DBIR studies are undertaken by partners who have developed close working relationships with one another. Research-practice partnerships are long-term collaborations that aim to promote educational improvement or transformation through the production and use of findings, tools, and ideas from research (Farrell, Penuel, Daniel, Steup, & Coburn, 2020). Such partnerships are intentionally organized to engage diverse forms of expertise and to ensure that all partners have a say in the joint work. Partnerships facilitate the ambitious work of most DBIR projects, and the trust that can develop within partnership enables teams to confront challenges and failures that inevitably arise in equity-focused change efforts (Penuel & Gallagher, 2017).

Many researchers worry about spending time building such partnerships. They are concerned that school systems are too chaotic and that their designs and research plans are likely to be at risk when districts change their priorities or a key member of the team leaves or changes jobs. In fact, to survive, any team engaged in innovation must adapt to the continuously changing environments surrounding educational systems (Peurach & Glazer, 2012), and churn is a reality of many educational systems (Daly, Finnigan, & Liou, 2016). Key to survival in such cases is developing multiple relationships with partners in education systems, including some who can serve in boundary-spanning roles (Davidson & Penuel, 2019).

Eliciting and Making Use of Diverse Forms of Expertise

Effective partnerships depend on valuing different forms of expertise partners bring. This includes but goes beyond the expertise that researchers may bring to the project, such as a deep knowledge of inquiry learning and methods for evaluating the effectiveness of innovations. It requires the elicitation of teacher and education leader experience and perspectives, as well as those of youth, parents, and communities, depending on the focus of the effort (Bang & Vossoughi, 2016; Zuiker, Piepgrass, & Evans, 2017). For researchers accustomed to being experts or in settings where research evidence is valued above all other forms of evidence, DBIR can be difficult.

Teams can employ specific strategies to ensure that all forms of expertise are valued and used to help design and iterate upon solutions to pressing educational problems. One strategy is to organize a meeting at the conclusion of a testing cycle for an innovation where different stakeholder groups first get to present their perspectives on implementation. During the meeting, researchers might present research evidence, teachers might report on their experiences of enacting the innovation with students, and a school leader might share observations from classroom visits. Once all stakeholder groups have had a chance to present, all groups together make sense of the different forms of evidence presented to inform decision making about how to improve the innovation. To be sure, while such a process can provide opportunities for each group to have a voice, team members must still attend to ways that power and authority dynamics between researchers and practitioners can undermine efforts to promote an equal partnership (Denner, Bean, Campe, Martinez, & Torres, 2019).

Negotiating Participant Roles

For many participants, roles in DBIR are unfamiliar. As a result, participants may initially be confused about the roles they are expected to play. Teachers may be unfamiliar with being asked to co-design materials that will be used by other teachers, and researchers may be unfamiliar with giving participants in research a say in the focus of that research (Penuel, Roschelle, & Shechtman,

2007). Clarifying roles not only of individuals but also of organizations often takes time, in part because turnover is common in systems and also because as the work evolves, roles often need to change as well (Farrell, Harrison, Coburn, 2019).

Matching the Scope of Work with Team Capacity

DBIR studies are in many respects ambitious, not just because of the range of expertise that is needed but also because of the scale of projects. As illustrated above, there are ways to engage in DBIR on a small scale, within a larger project. But teams can also easily get in over their heads if they begin a partnership with an exceptionally large study rather than starting small (Penuel & Gallagher, 2017). Efforts to promote equitable implementation can and do fall short, disappointing the partners. But such failures can and should become a locus for further investigation and theory refinement (Penuel, 2019b). Indeed, herein lies the driving force behind DBIR as an approach: the continuous pursuit of educational equity and justice in complex educational systems.

The Future of DBIR

A key task ahead is for the field to establish shared norms and practices related to theory development within DBIR, or what Kelly (2004) has described as an *argumentative grammar* of a subfield. That is, needed are norms for what counts as evidence for claims that an innovation works under certain conditions or for certain groups of students. Needed are not only agreements about when measures of conditions and contexts that shape implementation are appropriate but also when to use particular methods, such as ethnography or an efficacy study. Developing such norms is a challenge in the absence of specific methods (DBIR borrows methods from other fields) or publication venues. Many accounts of DBIR projects can only be fully rendered through multiple articles. In addition, because the audiences for DBIR studies include school and district leaders interested in understanding how to sustain an innovation in varied contexts across the system, the degree to which arguments are compelling to these audiences is an important consideration. Promising approaches to evaluating the value to practitioners are now beginning to be developed (see Cobb et al., 2018).

DBIR is one among many emerging forms of research that seek closer relationships among research, policy, and practice. In its focus on the iterative design and testing of innovations for schools, DBIR shares with many "family resemblances" (Wittgenstein, 1953) with such models as the Strategic Education Research Partnership (Donovan, Wigdor, & Snow, 2003) and Improvement Science (Bryk et al., 2015), for example. In its commitment to equity, it is similar to Community-Based Design Research (Bang, Faber, Gurneau, Marin, & Soto, 2016), in which co-design takes place in teams that often include youth and their families as well as representatives from organizations in the community. For DBIR to develop, it will be critical to articulate ways that these different models relate to, and can build on, one another.

The future of DBIR also depends on preparing scholars to engage in this kind of work. A multiday workshop is offered regularly in Boulder, Colorado that focuses on partnership development, negotiating the focus of joint work, co-design, and the development and use of implementation evidence. These skillsets are all important to develop, and a workshop alone is insufficient to prepare researchers to engage in the work. Needed in graduate study are opportunities for developing scholars to apprentice to partnership work in ways that provide them with opportunities to take on different roles in partnerships and observe first-hand how partners come to agree on goals and activities. Coursework that prepares students with the theories and methods appropriate to designing for different levels of a system and different settings is needed as well.

As DBIR grows, the focus of work is likely to remain at the level of systems but expand in new directions to meet the equity challenges of education. This includes an expansion of theory relevant to informing design to consider, for example, politics and race more explicitly (Khalil & Kier, 2017; Politics of Learning Writing Collective, 2017; Vakil et al., 2016). It also likely includes the development of novel approaches to co-design that more fully include parents and community members in design (e.g., Ishimaru & Takahashi, 2017). Finally, in addition to school districts as systems, DBIR will need to expand to consider state systems and community-wide learning ecosystems.

References

Anderson, C. W., de Los Santos, E. X., Bodbyl, S., Covitt, B. A., Edwards, K., Hancock, B., ... & Welch, M. (2018). Designing educational systems to support enactment of the Next Generation Science Standards. *Journal of Research in Science Teaching, 55*(7), 1026–1052. https://doi.org/10.1002/tea.21484

Bang, M., Faber, L., Gurneau, J., Marin, A., & Soto, C. (2016). Community-Based design research: Learning across generations and strategic transformations of institutional relations toward axiological innovations. *Mind, Culture, and Activity, 23*(6), 28–41. https://doi.org/10.1080/10749039.2015.1087572

Bang, M., Medin, D., Washinawatok, K., & Chapman, S. (2010). Innovations in culturally based science education through partnerships and community. In M. S. Khine & M. I. Saleh (Eds.), *New science of learning: Cognition, computers, and collaboration in education* (pp. 569–592). New York: Springer. https://doi.org/10.1007/978-1-4419-5716-0_28

Bang, M., & Vossoughi, S. (2016). Participatory design research and educational justice: Studying learning and relations within social change making. *Cognition and Instruction, 34*(3), 173–193. https://doi.org/10.1080/07370008.2016.1181879

Blumenfeld, P., Fishman, B. J., Krajcik, J., Marx, R. W., & Soloway, E. (2000). Creating usable innovations in systemic reform: Scaling up technology-embedded project-based science in urban schools. *Educational Psychologist, 35*(3), 149–164. https://doi.org/10.1207/S15326985EP3503_2

Boardman, A. G., Garcia, A., Dalton, B., & Polman, J. (2021). Compose Our World: Project-based learning in secondary English language arts. Teachers College Press.

Borko, H., Carlson, J., Mangram, C., Anderson, R., Fong, A., Million, S., Mozenter, S., & Villa, A. M. (2017). The role of video-based discussion in model for preparing professional development leaders. *International Journal of STEM Education, 4*, 1–15. https://doi.org/10.1186/s40594-017-0090-3

Boston, M. D., & Smith, M. S. (2009). Transforming secondary mathematics teaching: Increasing the cognitive demands of instructional tasks used in teachers' classrooms. *Journal for Research in Mathematics Education*, 119–156. http://www.jstor.org/stable/40539329

Bryk, A. S., Gomez, L. M., Grunow, A., & LeMahieu, P. G. (2015). *Learning to improve: How America's schools can get better at getting better.* Cambridge, MA: Harvard University Press.

Chinn, C. A., & Malhotra, B. A. (2002). Epistemologically authentic inquiry in schools: A theoretical framework for evaluating inquiry tasks. *Science Education, 86*(2), 175–218. https://doi.org/10.1002/sce.10001

Cobb, P., Confrey, J., DiSessa, A., Lehrer, R., & Schauble, L. (2003). Design experiments in educational research. *Educational Researcher, 32*(1), 9–13. http://www.jstor.org/stable/3699928

Cobb, P., Jackson, K., Henrick, E., & Smith, T. M. (2018). Investigating and supporting instructional improvement. In P. Cobb, K. Jackson, E. Henrick, T. M. Smith, & t. M. Team (Eds.), *Systems for instructional improvement: Creating coherence from the classroom to the district office* (pp. 1–14). Cambridge, MA: Harvard Education Press.

Cobb, P. A., Jackson, K., Smith, T., Sorum, M., & Henrick, E. C. (2013). Design research with educational systems: Investigating and supporting improvements in the quality of mathematics teaching at scale. In B. J. Fishman, W. R. Penuel, A.-R. Allen, & B. H. Cheng (Eds.), *Design-based implementation research: Theories, methods, and exemplars. National Society for the Study of Education Yearbook* (pp. 320–349). New York: Teachers College Record.

Cohen, D. K. (2011). *Teaching and its predicaments.* Cambridge, MA: Harvard University Press. https://doi.org/10.4159/harvard.9780674062788

Cooper, K. S., & Miness, A. (2014). The co-creation of caring student-teacher relationships: Does teacher understanding matter? *The High School Journal, 97*(4), 264–290. https://doi.org/10.1353/hsj.2014.0005

Daly, A. J., Finnigan, K. S., & Liou, Y.-H. (2016). How leadership churn undermines learning and improvement in low-performing school districts. In A. J. Daly & K. S. Finnigan (Eds.), *Thinking systemically: Improving districts under pressure* (pp. 183–208). Washington, DC: AERA. https://doi.org/10.3102/978-0-935302-46-2_7

Davidson, K. L., & Penuel, W. R. (2019). How brokers negotiate joint work at the boundaries. In J. Malin & C. Brown (Eds.), *The role of knowledge brokers in education: Connecting the dots between research and practice* (pp. 154–167). New York: Routledge. https://doi.org/10.4324/9780429462436-11

Denner, J., Bean, S., Campe, S., Martinez, J., & Torres, D. (2019). Negotiating trust, power, and culture in a research–practice partnership. *AERA Open*, *5*(2), 1–11. https://doi.org/10.1177/2332858419858635

Dolle, J., Gomez, Russell, & Bryk, A. S. (2013). More than a network: Building professional communities for educational Improvement. *National Society for the Study of Education*, *112*(2), 443–463.

Donovan, M. S., Wigdor, A. K., & Snow, C. E. (2003). *Strategic education research partnership*. Washington, DC: National Research Council.

Edelson, D. C. (2002). Design research: What we learn when we engage in design. *The Journal of the Learning Sciences*, *11*(1), p. 105-121. https://doi.org/ 10.1207/S15327809JLS1101_4

Engle, R. A. (2012). The productive disciplinary engagement framework: Origins, key concepts, and developments. In Y. Dai (Ed.), *Design research on learning and thinking in educational settings: Enhancing intellectual growth and functioning* (pp. 161–200). New York: Routledge.

Farrell, C. C., Harrison, C., & Coburn, C. E. (2019). "What the hell is this, who the hell are you?" Role and identity negotiation in research-practice partnerships. *AERA Open*, *5*(2), 1–13. https://doi.org/10.1177/2332858419849595

Farrell, C. C., Penuel, W. R., Daniel, J., Steup, L., & Coburn, C. E. (2020). *Taking stock of today's research-practice partnerships: Current practices and future possibilities*. Boulder: National Center for Research in Policy and Practice, University of Colorado Boulder.

Fishman, B. J., Penuel, W. R., Allen, A.-R., Cheng, B. H., & Sabelli, N. (2013). Design-based implementation research: An emerging model for transforming the relationship of research and practice. *National Society for the Study of Education*, *112*(2), 136–156.

Fricker, M. (2009). *Epistemic injustice: Power and the ethics of knowing*. New York: Oxford University Press.

Gaver, W. W., Dunne, T., & Pacenti, E. (1999). Cultural probes. *Interactions, January + February*, pp. 21–29.

Gay, G. (2000). *Culturally responsive teaching: Theory, practice and research*. New York: Teachers College Press.

Gravemeijer, K., & Cobb, P. (2013). Design research from a learning design perspective. In J. van den Akker, K. Gravemeijer, S. E. McKenney, & N. Nieveen (Eds.), *Educational design research* (pp. 73–112). New York: Routledge.

Gravemeijer, K., Rainero, R., & Vonk, H. (1994). *Developing realistic mathematics education*. Utrecht: Freudenthal Institute.

Grudin, J. & Pruitt, J. (2002). Personas, participatory design and product development: An infrastructure for engagement. In T. Binder, J. Gregory, & I. Wagner (Eds.), *Proceedings of the Participatory Design Conference* (pp. 144–152). Malmo, Sweden.

Gutiérrez, K. D., & Vossoughi, S. (2010). Lifting off the ground to return anew: Mediated praxis, transformative learning, and social design experiments. *Journal of Teacher Education*, *61*(1–2), 100–117. https://doi.org/10.1177/0022487109347877

Harris, C. J., Penuel, W. R., D'Angelo, C., DeBarger, A. H., Gallagher, L. P., Kennedy, C. A., & Cheng, B. H. (2015). Impact of project-based curriculum materials on student learning in science: Results of a randomized controlled trial. *Journal of Research in Science Teaching*, *52*(10), 1362–1385. https://doi.org/10.1002/tea.21263

Henrick, E. C., Muñoz, M. A., & Cobb, P. (2016). A better research-practice partnership. *Phi Delta Kappan*, *98*(3), 23–27. https://doi.org/10.1177/0031721716677258

Hopkins, M., & Woulfin, S. L. (2015). School system (re)design: Developing educational infrastructures to support school leadership and teaching practice. *Journal of Educational Change*, *16*(4), 371–377. https://doi.org/10.1007/s10833-015-9260-6

Ishimaru, A. M., & Takahashi, S. (2017). Disrupting racialized institutional scripts: Toward parent-teacher transformative agency for educational justice. *Peabody Journal of Education*, *92*(3), 343–362. https://doi.org/10.1080/0161956X.2017.1324660

Johnson, R., Severance, S., Penuel, W. R., & Leary, H. A. (2016). Teachers, tasks, and tensions: Lessons from a research-practice partnership. *Journal of Mathematics Teacher Education*, *19*(2), 169–185. https://doi.org/10.1007/s10857-015-9338-3

Kelly, A. E. (2004). Design research in education: Yes, but is it methodological? *The Journal of the Learning Sciences*, *13*(1), 115–128. https://doi.org/10.1207/s15327809jls1301_6

Khalil, D., & Kier, M. (2017). Critical race design: An emerging methodological approach to anti-racist design and implementation research. *International Journal of Adult Vocational Education*, *8*(2), 54–71. https://doi.org/10.4018/IJAVET.2017040105

Leary, H., Severance, S., Penuel, W. R., Quigley, D., Sumner, T., & Devaul, H. (2016). Designing a deeply digital science curriculum: Supporting teacher learning and implementation with organizing technologies. *Journal of Science Teacher Education*, *27*(1), 61–77. https://doi.org/10.1007/s10972-016-9452-9

Lehrer, R., & Schauble, L. (2015). Learning progressions: The whole world is NOT a stage. *Science Education*, *99*(3), 432–437. https://doi.org/10.1002/sce.21168

McLaughlin, M. W. (2006). Implementation research in education: Lessons learned, lingering questions and new opportunities. In M. Honig (Ed.), *New directions in education policy implementation: Confronting complexity* (pp. 209–228). Albany, NY: SUNY Press.

Moje, E. B. (1996). "I teach students, not subjects": Teacher-student relationships as contexts. *Reading Research Quarterly*, *31*(2), 172–195. https://doi.org/10.1598/RRQ.31.2.4

NGSS Lead States. (2013). *Next Generation Science Standards: For states, by states*. Washington, DC: National Academies Press.

Noddings, N. (1988). An ethic of caring and its implications for instructional arrangements. *American Journal of Education*, *96*(2), 215–230. https://doi.org/10.1086/443894

Noddings, N. (2013). *Caring: A relational approach to ethics and moral education*. Berkeley: University of California Press. https://doi.org/10.1525/9780520957343

Penuel, W. R. (2019a). Co-Design as infrastructuring with attention to power: Building collective capacity for equitable teaching and learning through Design-Based Implementation Research. In J. M. Pieters, J. M. Voogt, & N. N. P. Roblin (Eds.), *Collaborative curriculum design for sustainable innovation and teacher learning* (pp. 387–401). Dordrecht: Springer.

Penuel, W. R. (2019b). Infrastructuring as a practice of design-based research for supporting and studying equitable implementation and sustainability of innovations. *Journal of the Learning Sciences*, *28*(4–5), 659–677. https://doi.org/10.1080/10508406.2018.1552151

Penuel, W. R., Fishman, B. J., Cheng, B.H., & Sabelli, N. (2011). Organizing research and development at the intersection of learning, implementation, and design. *Educational Researcher*, *40*(7), 331–337. https://doi.org/10.3102/0013189X11421826

Penuel, W. R., & Gallagher, D. (2017). *Creating research-practice partnerships in education*. Cambridge, MA: Harvard Education Press.

Penuel, W. R., Roschelle, J., & Shechtman, N. (2007). Designing formative assessment software with teachers: An analysis of the co-design process. *Research and Practice in Technology Enhanced Learning*, *2*(1), 51–74. https://doi.org/10.1142/S1793206807000300

Penuel, W. R., Tatar, D., & Roschelle, J. (2004). The role of research on contexts of teaching practice in informing the design of handheld learning technologies. *Journal of Educational Computing Research*, *30*(4), 331–348. https://doi.org/10.2190/FJ51-5W3V-GGMC-4A92

Penuel, W. R., Van Horne, K., Jacobs, J., & Turner, M. (2018). *Developing a validity argument for practical measures of student experience in project-based science classrooms*. Paper presented at the Annual Meeting of the American Educational Research Association, New York.

Penuel, W. R., Van Horne, K., Severance, S., Quigley, D., & Sumner, T. (2016). Students' responses to curricular activities as indicator of coherence in project-based science. In C.-K. Looi, J. L. Polman, U. Cress, & P. Reimann (Eds.), *Proceedings of the 12th International Conference of the Learning Sciences* (Vol. 2, pp. 855–858). Singapore: International Society of the Learning Sciences.

Peurach, D. J., & Glazer, J. L. (2012). Reconsidering replication: New perspectives on large-scale school improvement. *Journal of Educational Change*, *13*(2), 155–190. https://doi.org/10.1007/s10833-011-9177-7

Politics of Learning Writing Collective. (2017). The learning sciences in a new era of U.S. nationalism. *Cognition and Instruction*, *35*(2), 91–102. https://doi.org/10.1080/07370008.2017.1282486

Potvin, A. S. (2018). *Designing for teacher-student relationships: An investigation into the emotional and relational dimensions of co-design*. (PhD), University of Colorado.

Potvin, A. S. (2020). "Students speaking to you": Teachers listen to student surveys to improve classroom environment. *Learning Environments Research*. https://doi.org/10.1007/s10984-020-09330-1

Potvin, A. S., Kaplan, R. G., Boardman, A., & Polman, J. L. (2018). Configurations in codesign: Participant structures in partnership work. In B. Bevan & W. R. Penuel (Eds.), *Connecting research and practice for educational improvement: Ethical and equitable approaches* (pp. 135–149). New York: Routledge. https://doi.org/10.4324/9781315268309-9

Reddy, R., Rhodes, J. E., & Mulhall, P. (2003). The influence of teacher support on student adjustment in the middle school years: A latent growth curve study. *Development and Psychopathology*, *15*, 119–138. https://doi.org/10.1017.S0954579403000075

Roschelle, J., Shechtman, N., Tatar, D., Hegedus, S., Hopkins, B., Empson, S., Knudsen, J., & Gallagher, L. P. (2010). Integration of technology, curriculum, and professional development for advancing middle school mathematics: Three large-scale studies. *American Educational Research Journal, 47*(4), 833–878. https://doi.org/10.3102/0002831210367426

Russell, J. L., Jackson, K., Krumm, A. E., & Frank, K. A. (2013). Theories and research methodologies for design based implementation research: Examples from four cases. *National Society for the Study of Education Yearbook, 112*(2), 157–191.

Ryoo, J., Choi, M., & McLeod, E. (2015). *Building equity in research-practice partnerships.* San Francisco, CA: Research+Practice Collaboratory.

Severance, S., Penuel, W. R., Sumner, T., & Leary, H. (2016). Organizing for teacher agency in curriculum design. *Journal of the Learning Sciences, 25*(4), 531–564. https://doi.org/10.1080/10508406.2016.1207541

Stein, M. K., & Kaufman, J. H. (2010). Selecting and supporting the use of mathematics curricula at scale. *American Educational Research Journal, 47*(3), 663–693. https://doi.org/10.3102/0002831209361210

Schwarz, C. V., Passmore, C., & Reiser, B.J. (Eds.) (2017). *Helping students make sense of the world using next generation science and engineering practices.* NTA Press.

Tatar, D. (2007). The design tensions framework. *Human-Computer Interaction, 22*(4), 413–451. https://doi.org/10.1080/07370020701638814

Vahey, P., Roy, G. J., & Fueyo, V. (2013). Sustainable use of dynamic representational environments: Toward a district-wide adoption of SimCalc-based materials. In S. Hegedus & J. Roschelle (Eds.), *Democratizing access to important mathematics through dynamic representations: Contributions and visions from the SimCalc research program* (pp. 183–202). New York: Springer. https://doi.org/10.1007/978-94-007-5696-0_11

Vakil, S., de Royston, M. M., Nasir, N. S., & Kirshner, B. (2016). Rethinking race and power in design-based research: Reflections from the field. *Cognition and Instruction, 34*(3), 194–209. https://doi.org/10.1080/07370008.2016.1169817

Vanover, C., Roy, G. J., Unal, Z., Fueyo, V., & Vahey, P. (2012). The SunBay digital mathematics project: An infrastructural and capacity-based approach to improving mathematics teaching and learning at scale. In J. van Aalst, K. Thompson, M. J. Jacobson, & P. Reimann (Eds.), *The future of learning: Proceedings of the 10th international conference of the learning sciences (ICLS 2012) – Volume 1, short papers, symposia, and abstracts* (pp. 192–197). Sydney: ISLS.

Weinbaum, E., & Supovitz, J. A. (2010). Planning ahead: Make program implementation more predictable. *Phi Delta Kappan, 91*(7), 68–71. https://doi.org/10.1177/003172171009100714

Wittgenstein, L. (1953). *Philosophical investigations.* London: Blackwell Publishing.

Yeager, D., Bryk, A., Muhich, J., Hausman, H., & Morales, L. (2013). *Practical measurement.* Retrieved from https://labs.la.utexas.edu/adrg/files/2013/12/Practical-Measurement.pdf

Zuiker, S. J., Piepgrass, N., & Evans, M. D. (2017). Expanding design research: From researcher ego-systems to stakeholder ecosystems. In M. J. Spector, B. B. Lockee, & M. D. Childress (Eds.), *Learning, design, and technology: An international compendium of theory, research, practice, and policy* (pp. 1–28). Basel: Springer International Publishing. https://doi.org/10.1007/978-3-319-17727-4_74-1

6
SCALING UP DESIGN OF INQUIRY ENVIRONMENTS

Jeremy Roschelle, Claudia Mazziotti, and Barbara Means

Introduction

Researchers, developers, and educators often describe their motivation for designing inquiry learning environments as a response to societal challenges. In today's global economy, many routine tasks may be performed by machines, and people may be called upon to address complex problems requiring innovative, insightful solutions. All students need to be able to think critically and solve problems given the accelerating economic, technical, political, and cultural changes. Thus, we need inquiry learning opportunities that will make an impact at scale and thereby broaden participation in inquiry-related learning and careers. How should developers, researchers, innovators, and educators who are advancing inquiry think about scale?

The literature on scaling up educational innovations has intensified over the past two decades, spurred by funding both for bringing innovations to scale and for studying the scaling process itself. For example, in the United States, the Interagency Educational Research Initiative (IERI, n.d.) was launched in 1999 and led to over 70 research projects and over 100 publications documenting the scaling process across projects. Two edited volumes provide an overview (Schneider & McDonald, 2007a, 2007b). This program was followed in the United States by an Investing in Innovation Fund and later by the Education Innovation Research program, cumulatively investing hundreds of millions of dollars in scaling up promising educational programs. Similarly, Singapore invested in scaling up inquiry-based technologies (e.g., Looi & Woon Teh, 2015), and the United Kingdom created the Educational Endowment Fund (https://educationendowmentfoundation.org.uk/). Many other countries undertook similar efforts to scale up promising education programs and approaches. But perhaps even more consequential than this surge in funding for scaling up was the increased availability of the Internet and inexpensive, powerful computing devices. Greater availability of devices and connectivity have enabled technology-based products to reach large numbers of people with unprecedented speed and sometimes at no cost (e.g., open educational resources) or low cost. Another stream of contributions to the intensification of work on scaling up was the engagement of multidisciplinary scholars, moving beyond traditional educational evaluators to also include computer scientists, domain experts, statisticians, sociologists, educational data mining experts, and other social scientists. Additional forms of expertise become necessary when the problem shifts from defining an innovative support for inquiry to understanding how and why use of that inquiry support spreads or fails to spread (Roschelle, Tatar, & Kaput, 2008). For example, sociologists can shed light on the role that context plays in the implementation of a new educational approach (McDonald et al., 2006). Furthermore, as focus shifts to school district uptake and improvement, data mining, learning analytic, and improvement science can become valuable for monitoring and adjusting improvement (Krumm, Means, & Bienkowski, 2018).

In this chapter, we review definitions of scaling up, causes of failure, strategies linked to success, and remaining challenges with a focus on inquiry learning environments

Definitions and Key Aspects of Scaling Up

Building on McDonald et al. (2006), we define scaling up as "achieving greater reach with predictable, measurable impact." In contrast to McDonald et al. (2006), we do not assume that scaling up occurs after something is first "proven," because as we discuss later, there are multiple pathways to scale and some begin before an innovation is proven.

"Greater reach" captures the essence of "scaling up" as "expanding" without being prescriptive about how a particular initiative defines growth. As we will discuss, there can be good reasons to conceptualize growth as something more nuanced than counting the number of users. "Predictable, measurable impact" indicates that the purpose of scaling up is to improve learning for a large population of students, and we need to measure learning to know whether it has improved. Furthermore, we add the word "predictable" because understanding variability is important. Variability is intrinsic to scaling up because of the many local factors in education that vary from place to place; the important thing is to be able to make sense of and predict the variability that will occur when an approach is scaled and to identify strategies for adapting to or otherwise addressing this variability. Greater reach and predictable, measurable impact should be complementary objectives for scaling efforts, but we recognize that progress in these dimensions does not always occur at the same time. Now we proceed to discuss some key additional aspects of scaling up.

In education, scale often takes a long time and may be achieved in different ways. Research on scaling educational innovation goes back to the mid-20th century. Mort (1953, as reported in Dearing et al., 2015) observed that educational change often takes 25 years or more. Subsequent studies of how research-based innovations move into practice have articulated two contrasting perspectives (Dearing et al., 2015): (1) a linear knowledge transfer model in which researchers create and test the innovations and then pass them on to others for dissemination to those who will implement them and (2) a nonlinear, participant-centered model in which educational stakeholders play a decisive role in the design, refinement, and spread of an innovation. The linear view has been embodied in the structure of many funding programs, which progress from exploratory studies to development of innovations with efficacy and effectiveness testing and finally to scale (see, for example, the "common guidelines" issued by the Institute of Education Sciences and the National Science Foundation, 2013). A seminal reference for the contrasting, participant-centered view of scaling is provided by Rogers' (1962) description of "Diffusion of Innovation" and usefully elaborated in von Hippel's (2005) discussion of democratizing innovation. In the nonlinear model, researchers and developers may collaborate with practitioners throughout the project, for example, to respond to a newly identified problem of practice, help define generalizable components of the innovation, and to study emerging impacts or challenges. The border between research and practice may seem more fluid in the case of nonlinear scaling but is still important to identify, investigate, and consolidate an emerging innovation.

Scale as an Experiment with a Large Sample and Sound Measurement

In its most conventional form, research on scale can be operationalized as an experimental comparison that demonstrates a statistically significant effect on an appropriate outcome in a suitably large sample population and across settings. The nature of the outcome and its measurement need to be carefully defined. For example, whereas research intended to generate scientific knowledge might choose a measure for its bearing on a particular scientific theory, scale-up research usually focuses on measures that are relevant to educational policy. A challenge for research on scaling up inquiry environments is that policy-relevant measures (such as an end-of-year assessment mandated by a state) may not capture the outcomes of inquiry learning well; yet an expectation for scale-up research is often that it will focus on policy-relevant measures. Hence, scale-up research may challenge the existing assessment regime. An example is research on the nature of science learning that informed the Next Generation Science Standards in the United States with the standards then exerting pressure for new kinds of assessments capturing the "three-dimensional learning" embodied in the standards (e.g., DeBarger et al., 2016).

Scale-up research is sometimes differentiated from effectiveness and efficacy research (Flay et al., 2005). Efficacy research must be rigorous and sound in experimental design and statistical analysis but can be conducted with "best case" levels of support to practitioners. Effectiveness research aims to evaluate the approach in realistic (not "best case") conditions (and with realistic variation across settings) and thus to better establish the practical significance of the approach. Scale-up research may add information about program costs and tools to monitor and improve the quality of implementation. Summarizing with regard to inquiry environments, scale-up research in education should examine a novel approach "under circumstances that would typically prevail in the target context" (IES & NSF, 2013, p. 9) without substantial developer involvement in implementation or evaluation and should include practical information about program costs and how practitioners can monitor and improve implementations.

The stipulation of typical circumstances is important because if one scales only to those participants who are most willing, or have the most support, the program may scale to "early adopters" but never "cross the chasm" to broader populations (e.g., Moore, 2014). If the sample does not reflect the variation in contexts and capacities in the eventual target population, using statistics to support the generalization of inferences based on the sample to the target population is not possible (Tipton, 2014). Cartwright (2012, 2013) adds concerns for the degree to which an experimental trial is sufficient to answer practical questions about whether and how an inquiry approach will scale. For example, there are differences between finding that an approach works in an initial collection of settings, that it works in a wide variety of settings, and that it is likely to "work here" (in a practitioner's particular setting). At the heart of Cartwright's argument, external validity of research requires attention to both capacities of an approach (e.g., how a particular inquiry approach drives learning) and the capacities of settings (e.g., the people, policies, and practices in schools); the subtle interrelations between the two is often not captured in reporting on randomized controlled trials. Furthermore, measuring outcomes for inquiry environments is challenging. Measured impact is almost always stronger with proximal measures that are closely aligned to the new learning environment than to more distal outcomes such as end-of-year mandated tests (Ruiz-Primo, et al., 2002). For example, in the study of scaling up the SimCalc learning environment (Roschelle, Shechtman, et al., 2010), researchers found significant positive impacts for assessment items related to the conceptual skills emphasized in the SimCalc mathematical inquiry environment but no significant difference in students' performance on items chosen from the relevant state test.

Researchers can also conceptualize scaling research as applying the method of meta-analysis to many related studies. When many studies have been conducted on an approach, each in different settings, a meta-analysis can combine the findings through statistical methods, resulting both in a more precise estimate of the impact of the approach and also in identification of variables that moderate or mediate the effect. For example, Furtak et al. (2012) identified 37 studies of inquiry-based instruction and found an overall positive effect. In addition, they were able to identify some key variables that mediate the size of the effect, such as the degree of focus on epistemic activities and whether instruction was led by a teacher. The availability of many studies conducted by different teams in different locations is prima facie evidence that an approach is scaling up. Furthermore, by pooling data from unrelated experiments, researchers can increase their confidence in their estimation of the average size of the effect and ascertain the degree to which it is dependent on factors unique to one setting or one implementation. The combination of prima facie evidence of use in many different settings along with evidence of consistent effects across settings can be used to argue that the approach effectively scales up and can also address the issue of replicability (e.g., Makel, Plucker, & Hegarty, 2012).

Scale Is Not Just a Bigger "n"

When we think about scale, it is important to consider not only the number of participants but also the qualitative nature of their participation, which can include changes in depth, sustainability, ownership, and the evolution of an approach.

Coburn (2003) describes how two innovations may reach a similar number of participants but still vary in what she describes as the *depth* of scaling. For example, an inquiry approach may be superficially employed by asking students to conduct a fixed lab experiment that is related to instruction or more deeply employed by having students design their own investigation of a driving question. Likewise, two approaches may each reach 200 teachers but vary in the density of penetration. One approach may penetrate a school district thoroughly, reaching every science teacher in the district. Another may choose friendly teachers in 200 different school districts, which has less depth from a district's perspective. Another depth factor may be the degree to which the outcome measure aligns to a deep conception of inquiry; a performance task or scenario-based task is generally regarded as a deeper assessment of inquiry than a set of multiple-choice items (Scalise & Gifford, 2006). Likewise, an innovation that is used for a very short amount of curricular time would be considered to have less depth than an inquiry approach used for an entire block of instruction or school year.

Another measure of scaling depth is *sustainability:* how easy or difficult it is to keep the approach going after an initial usage in a new setting or after research-based support is withdrawn. A related indicator of scaling depth is *shift in ownership*, with educators coming to view the innovation as "their" approach rather than something coming from an external entity. For scaling to occur, educators must come to feel ownership of the innovation.

To Coburn's list of characteristics, Clarke and Dede (2009) added *evolution*, by which they mean the degree to which the adopters, in collaboration with the developers of the approach, are learning and revising as scale occurs and improving the fitness of the approach for further scaling. Realistically, few things scale without adaptation to local settings, and an evolution dimension of scaling can reflect a process of making an approach adaptable without sacrificing its integrity.

For Whom and under What Conditions?

Building on the brief discussion of moderator variables above, a further important set of considerations regarding scale has to do with *for whom and under what conditions* an innovative approach delivers improvements. Typical moderator variables can include the age of the students, their gender, ethnicity, or language-learner status, socioeconomic status, and prior achievement scores. Thus, it is important to find out whether an inquiry learning environment is scaling only to boys or only to students for whom English is their first language. Furthermore, researchers are often concerned with the "Matthew Effect" (Kerckhoff & Glennie, 1999), whereby students who already have an advantage benefit more from a novel learning approach relative to students who have less incoming advantage. When the Matthew Effect is present, an innovative approach may increase achievement gaps between advantaged and less advantaged students, which is not desirable. Furthermore, higher-income settings may have more capacity to sustain novel learning approaches. If the approach is more effective and is better sustained in high-income settings, then scaling the approach could increase achievement gaps. The level of school capacity is one example of a "condition" that might moderate the effectiveness of an approach; other typical influential conditions include alignment to standards and accountability, degree of support from administrative leadership, the degree and nature of support for teacher learning, alignment to other materials in use with the same students, and availability and quality of necessary technology or other infrastructure.

One powerful way to conceptualize research on "for whom and under what conditions" an innovation is effective is in terms of the generalizability or external validity of a program of research (Hedges, 2018; Tipton, 2014). Generalizability is also sometimes called "external validity." Analyzing generalizability in a research study requires two things. First, the study must capture a set of variables that describe the study participants ("for whom") and contexts ("what conditions") and that could plausibly moderate the effectiveness or impact of the inquiry learning approach. Second, one needs a data set that describes the prevalence and distribution of those variables in the broader population beyond the study. If these conditions are met, then one can estimate the range of situations to which the approach's measured impact may be reasonably expected to generalize. Imagine that a study finds inquiry learning is working well for both low- and high-SES students but that the study's sample did not include many students who are English Language Learners (ELL). Furthermore, imagine that the study's sample found the approach was more effective in districts that use performance tasks as a district-wide assessment of science learning. If a database with these variables is available for all the schools in a state or country, one could color a map green (the results are likely to generalize), yellow (the results may generalize, but effects may be weaker), or gray (no match between the place and places in the existing data and thus not enough information) to show the approach's demonstrated potential for scalability (see Roschelle et al., 2018, for an example of such maps). Cartwright (2012, 2013) further argues that determining which variables are relevant requires a lot of specific knowledge about how new approaches and existing conditions/practices may or may not fit together. We should not be content to analyze generalizability merely in terms of well-known policy variables, such as ELL status, reduced price and free lunch status, or student race, ethnicity, and gender.

Alternative Research Designs

As mentioned above, the conventional scaling method has been to stage experiments with larger and larger groups of participants, while also measuring impact by contrasting outcomes of a treatment to an untreated condition. For example, the U.S. Institute of Education Sciences has programs that provide funding for larger-scale and rigorously controlled research on implementations of a program. Budgets increase as an investigator goes from exploratory studies to development projects then efficacy projects and finally scaling projects, a progression that also involves increasing the number of students and classrooms experiencing the intervention. Furthermore, the standards of evidence strengthen from correlational and quasi-experimental methods to randomized controlled trials. In some cases, there is also attention to cost-effectiveness, which involves both measuring program costs (which in the case of inquiry-based learning might include instructional materials, experimental apparatus, teacher professional development, and other costs) and program impacts (Levin & Belfield, 2015).

A set of complementary methods focus on the design dimension of scaling up. These methods recognize that scale involves not only testing something with more people but also designing it to be more adaptable and robust in varied implementation environments. Researcher-Practitioner Partnerships (e.g., Coburn & Penuel, 2016; Coburn, Penuel, & Geil, 2013) emphasize the importance of identifying authentic problems of practice and having researchers and educators work together to address them. Design-based Implementation Research (e.g., Penuel et al., 2011) emphasizes the layers of design needed to support uptake and high-quality implementation of an approach at scale. Networked Improvement Communities in education (see LeMahieu et al., 2017) combine improvement science approaches and a focus on measuring variability and finding ways to retain program integrity and impacts while allowing for adaptations (e.g., Lewis, 2015). Improvement science is one of many continuous improvement approaches (with roots going back to Total Quality Management, e.g., Sallis, 2002) that involve a series of successive advances on a defined metric and thus emphasize iterating toward the future state rather than a single definitive experiment to estimate the impact of an intervention. Like scaling up research, improvement science has an interest in examining local conditions and in analyzing changes caused by an intervention on many different levels (rather than just on student learning outcome measures). In a Networked Improvement Community, multiple entities in the network are employing improvement science practices in designing, implementing, and refining approaches to address a common aim. Variation in the conditions in which the different entities operate becomes a source of information about what's necessary and sufficient for the approach to work. The six core principles for running Networked Improvement Communities involve focusing on a problem of practice, attuning to variation, taking a systems perspective, using measurement to drive improvement, anchoring specific improvements in collaborative investigations, and accelerating overall improvement by sharing in networked communities (LeMahieu et al., 2017).

When Does Scaling up Happen?

Finally, we observe that the phrase "scaling up," like the linear knowledge transfer model, misleadingly implies a discrete phase that happens some time later, after initial research and development is complete. Yet in reality the path to scale is rarely linear or stage-like (Prewitt, Schwandt, & Straf, 2012). Some educational programs with inquiry potential, such as the Scratch computing environment (https://scratch.mit.edu/) and the FIRST Lego League robotics competition (https://www.first-lego-league.org/en/general/what-is-fll.html) have scaled very rapidly, often before early stage R&D focusing on efficacy was available or published. As initial versions of these environments scaled, the researchers and developers working on them continued to define and develop multiple components—technological, human, and organizational—to maximize the learning value of students' engagement (e.g., Melchior et al., 2016). Thus, it is possible for either scaling or program refinement to happen first, and these processes can also occur simultaneously.

A disadvantage of the traditional stepwise approach to getting education innovations to scale is that years of R&D may be devoted to developing and refining an approach, only to find later that it doesn't scale well. This realization can make it worthwhile to seek alternatives to the traditional strategy of first getting an inquiry learning environment working in one or two classrooms, then expanding to 6–10 classrooms, then 100 classrooms and so on—the conventional, "step-by-step" scaling up process. For example, one can scale a digital infrastructure for inquiry learning first and gather data from it to drive improvement research. For example, the Scratch programming environment scaled quickly; this allowed researchers to later look for programming constructs which students are learning or not learning to use (e.g., Aivaloglou & Hermans, 2016). The technology sector often espouses this approach—releasing a "minimum viable product" intended to attract large numbers of users and then leveraging user feedback and data to inform cycles of product refinement (e.g., Münch et al., 2013); increasingly, technology and publishing companies also care about conducting high-quality research (Newman, Jaciw, & Lazarev, 2018).

By making scale an intentional focus early in an R&D program, teams may become aware of pitfalls and address these earlier. Nonetheless, in the field of education as in medicine, a first principle should be "do no harm." If the inquiry learning system will supplant a significant part of existing instruction in areas for which there are serious stakes for students and teachers, launching an ineffective product at scale may be unacceptably risky. Regardless of the path chosen by a particular inquiry environment team, the lessons about scaling up in this chapter should be considered early in the process, as scaling any ambitious learning activity system (and all inquiry learning environments) is sure to require the disciplined effort of a dedicated team over a long period of time.

Summary

Scaling up is a complex process involving not only reaching more participants but also strengthening measurement and prediction of impacts in varied environments. As one scales, there are changes both to design and in the types of research. Within the notion of "reach," it is important to consider metrics other than the number of participants served and the estimated treatment effect. Additional metrics include shift of ownership, sustainability, and evolution. Furthermore, it is highly important to better understand for whom and under what conditions an approach to inquiry-based learning works. Experimental methods are valuable, as they enable measuring impacts under variable conditions, and much can be learned by doing them. However, complementary design and improvement methods are also valuable and important. Starting small and gradually increasing reach is not necessarily the only or best scaling plan. Especially when technology or favorable policies are available and risks to participants are low, it may make sense to begin implementation at scale. In any event, scaling should be a design consideration early in any significant program of education research and development.

Why Is Scaling Hard?

Scaling inquiry learning environments would seem to be obviously desirable, because opportunities to learn through inquiry respond to pressing needs to educate future citizens for the realities of the future society, culture, and workforce. And yet it is hard to scale inquiry learning environments. Why?

We conjecture that inquiry environments are challenging to scale because they are "Ambitious Learning Activity Systems" (building on the phrase in Roschelle, Knudsen, & Hegedus, 2010). They are "ambitious" because introducing inquiry is typically a big change from existing educational practice (Anderson & Helms, 2001; Roehrig & Luft, 2004). They involve new roles and responsibilities for both teachers and students (van der Valk & de Jong, 2009). Teachers may also be reluctant to implement inquiry-based learning systems because they emphasize depth rather than breadth of content, whereas testing regimes often stress the latter (Penuel et al., 2009). With regard to "learning," because inquiry environments stress the active, mindful engagement of the learner, they cannot be scaled simply by distributing new teaching resources. Teachers often find that they have not experienced inquiry learning themselves, and they cannot be assumed to have the content background and instructional strategies needed to produce supports for this kind of learning successfully (Donelly, Linn, & Ludvigsen, 2014). With regard to "activity," inquiry learning requires changing how students and teachers interact with each other and with resources. Thus, what is to be scaled is not just a new or better piece of content but rather a different form of participation in cognitive and social interactions with resources, peers, and teachers. And finally, conceptualizing a "system" is necessary, because changing learning at scale requires changing many factors at once in a coherent way. A systems perspective can organize the different inputs (like curriculum materials, technologies, teacher professional development) and processes (like new uses of classroom discussions, small-group work, and assessments) into a well-organized and coherent approach to change. Consequently, this chapter focuses on what can be learned from efforts to scale ambitious learning activity systems, with an eye to applying those lessons to inquiry environments.

A good place to contextualize our intuitions about the difficulty of scaling ambitious learning activity systems is a recent broad historical review of efforts to change education by Cohen and Mehta (2017). Their review focuses on adoption of education "reforms" in general rather than inquiry learning environments per se, but the lessons they draw are highly relevant to instructional reforms such as inquiry-based learning. They examine reasons why reform is not easy, particularly in countries like the United States, Canada, Germany, and India, with decentralized control of education.

A first challenge is ***local adoption***. In the United States, for example, education is primarily a function of the states and local education agencies (e.g., school districts). The U.S. Department of Education does not have the authority to impose a curriculum or a teaching approach on the nation's schools. As a consequence, any effort to introduce an educational innovation cannot succeed by winning over a single centralized, national education authority. Instead, reformers must win over each of the 50 states and often tens of thousands of school districts one by one. Furthermore, when adoption is local, one must convince not only educational professionals but also parents and school board officials, and thus a corollary to local adoption is the wide span of stakeholders who must be engaged and convinced. Different communities may have different sensibilities with regard to inquiry; people with different political, religious, or cultural perspectives may want to emphasize (or de-emphasize) different aspects of inquiry in their local schools.

A second challenge for educational innovations is their requirement for extensive ***professional learning*** on the part of teachers, school leaders, and district administrators. Many innovators have failed to consider the amount of learning time and support educators will need if they are to implement new ways of doing things successfully (Cobb et al., 2013). Not only does a reform effort need to design and offer the tools and professional learning experiences needed to implement the reform well, it also needs to solve the problem of finding times when that learning can take place. Time for teacher learning, for example, is very limited in the United States (Darling-Hammond et al., 2017). For working in inquiry learning environments, professional learning is very important, because teachers need to learn not just how to use a specific inquiry tool but also how to change their role in the classroom from that of authority to that of facilitator. This change in roles can be ambiguous in practice (Russ & Berland, 2019).

Finally, at every level of the education system (federal, state, local), there is what Cohen and Mehta characterize as "***remarkable vulnerability to public opinion and political pressure***" (p. 5). Plans in the 1980s to encourage more consistency in what is taught at each grade level in the United States by developing and administering a national test were quickly scuttled in the face of deep-seated political opposition. Similarly, activities encouraging adoption of the Common Core State Standards during the Obama Administration were perceived by many as overstepping the appropriate federal role in K-12 education, and citizens in many states rejected the new standards out of hand. More generally, public dissatisfaction with the functioning of their local school district has resulted in an average tenure for the superintendent in large U.S. school districts of fewer than three years. Elected school boards may not resonate with reform goals or approaches and can fire leaders who introduce them. Battles in the specification of approaches to teaching reading or mathematics (Nicholson & Tunmer, 2010; Schoenfeld & Pearson, 2012) may be instructive to proponents of inquiry learning; one dimension of recurrent policy tension in reading and mathematics is between (a) direct, prescriptive and (b) meaning-making approaches; inquiry learning environments may incur similar debates.

Despite these challenges, some educational changes have scaled successfully (examples follow). Cohen and Medha (2017) report that education reforms that have scaled successfully provided a solution to something that was a problem in the minds of educators or addressed a broader issue perceived by the general public or government (e.g., the need to provide a safe and supportive environment in which five-year-olds could acquire the social and behavioral competencies needed to benefit from academic instruction in first grade). Successful reforms offered the guidance, tools, and resources educators would need to implement them, and they were consistent with the values of most educators, parents, and students (Cohen & Mehta, 2017).

Going beyond Cohen and Mehta's historical review, researchers and innovators have identified specific factors that can make instructional innovations, such as inquiry learning environments, hard to scale (see Cohen, Raudenbush, & Ball, 2003 for an overview). First, there are three qualities that affect adoption and implementation:

- **Degree of ambition**. The bigger the change from standard instruction and the more it requires revamping the basic organization of education, the more challenges an innovation will encounter, including resistance from those who have a vested interest in the current system or who are simply risk-averse. Thus, an inquiry learning environment that is used as a supplemental or enrichment activity for a topic that is broadly taught is easier to scale than one that would require an entirely new approach to mathematics learning with most of the instruction conducted online. Inquiry environments are often quite ambitious.
- **Complexity**. Complexity often goes hand-in-hand with ambition but is conceptually distinct from it. The more complex the target educational practice, the harder it is likely to be for educators to learn how to do it, and the more pieces of the reform will need to be developed and aligned so that educators can achieve the desired practice. Inquiry environments are often complex, with long-term, multistage activities that a teacher must orchestrate smoothly.
- **Resource-intensiveness**. The more resources an innovation requires, the fewer classrooms, schools, and systems will be willing and able to assemble them in order to implement the innovation. If teachers require 40 hours of training and additional coaching to learn to implement an inquiry learning environment as intended, many decision-makers will judge the intervention as too costly. In addition, inquiry environments sometimes require unusual and specific technology.

Accompanying these three adoption and implementation dimensions, there are two additional factors that influence the likelihood that an effective intervention will retain its efficacy when implemented on a broader scale:

- **Degree of specification**. The clearer and more detailed the description of a desired new practice, the better educators and education systems know what they're aiming for and the easier it is to measure the presence or absence of the target practice. If educators do not have a clear understanding of what constitutes inquiry or of the practices teachers need to implement, their chances of really implementing the innovation are small. When specification is weak, "lethal mutations" can emerge (Brown & Campione, 1996), where the adaption no longer honors the original vision.
- **Adaptability to fit local capacity, conditions, and practices**. At the same time, as an innovation is tried in more contexts, unforeseen difficulties and tensions with some portions of the ambitious learning activity system are likely to arise. If implementers do not adapt to fit their circumstances, the "replica trap" (Dede, 2005) can occur, because identical materials and teacher moves may be understood and perceived quite differently in different contexts and settings. Most importantly, a clear goal of inquiry learning is for students to experience ownership of an authentic driving question; doing so often involves developing culturally relevant pedagogies (Ladson-Billings, 1995) and this is not always conceptualized as part of the inquiry environment.

There are tensions among these principles that can only be addressed while considering the specifics of a particular inquiry learning approach. One tension is between ambition and complexity.

Inquiry learning is ambitious and yet designers may need to reduce ambition in order not to become overly complex for educators to adopt. Likewise, there is a tension between adaptability and specification. One way it can be partially resolved is for the design team to become more specific about what is adaptable in their approach and what should be changed only with great caution. This is hard to do a priori, and thus design teams typically capture information about variability and then respond. In one example, a research team found some teachers adapted to the pace of a mathematics curriculum by skipping part of every lesson so they could initiate the next lesson on the prescribed pace (Dunn, 2009. This was maladaptive and led to guidance to skip some optional lessons entirely rather than skipping parts of the most important lessons. Another step is often to be clear with those who will make adaptations about what principles are to be honored. In another example from the SimCalc research, when some teachers did not have access to a computer lab on the right day, they were able to keep the student-centered intention of a curriculum by having students plan investigations as a class, and then have one student perform the investigation on a projected computer. This honored the student-centered intent. Another adaptation, where the teacher demonstrated on the computer instead of allowing students to drive the work, did not honor the intent.

Finally, many scaling efforts, such as the Building Blocks (Sarama & Clements, 2013, discussed in more detail below), are framed in terms of equity challenges. Inquiry learning opportunities need to become more common overall, and it is especially important that they become as common in the classrooms of underserved students as they are in classrooms serving predominantly white and higher-income students. Indeed, investigators have found that inquiry activities can be especially beneficial for students in low-income schools (Ben-David & Zohar, 2009). Yet some inquiry learning environments require resources that are less available in schools that serve low-income students. Some of them require teachers with knowledge and skills that are in short supply in the teacher labor force (e.g., computer science skills for computational thinking initiatives) and are inequitably allocated across schools. Or they may call on skills that take extended practice for teachers to acquire, and higher rates of teacher mobility in low-income areas may impede progress. Thus, the issue of **equity and access** adds another layer to the challenge of scaling up an inquiry environment.

Strategies for Scaling Inquiry Environments

In this section, we focus on successful examples of scaling inquiry for approaches that are implemented in schools. We selected six well-known inquiry environments for which there is published evidence with regards to efficacy as well as scholarly reflections on the scaling up process. Our intention in choosing these cases was to illustrate the variety of inquiry environments that have scaled up as well as common issues that were addressed within the scaling efforts. In the scope of this chapter, we did not have space for a comprehensive review of every case.

In each of these cases, the R&D team reflected on its scaling process after they had made significant progress and overcome some major obstacles. Each team explicitly took on the challenge of scaling up themselves, rather than expecting it to happen spontaneously or planning to hand off the scaling process to someone else (e.g., a publisher). The project teams put in "multiple coordinated efforts" to not only "let it happen" but to actually "make it happen" (Sarama & Clements, 2013, p. 176). Each team made scaling up their inquiry learning environment a programmatic feature of their work and organized their leadership to manage this aspect of the work. Each team found the process challenging and sought to learn from their initial experiences and make improvements to improve their ability to scale further.

For each of the six cases, Table 6.1 provides a brief description of the inquiry learning environment as well as evidence for its efficacy and scale.

Table 6.1 Six examples for scaled and efficient inquiry learning environments entailing common inquiry learning features

Project	*Inquiry learning features*	*Content and target group*	*Example efficacy studies*	*Scale metrics*
GLOBE	1 exploration and 3 collaboration	Environmental science (e.g., atmospheric science) Grades K-12	Quasi-experiment (*N* = 123): EG GLOBE (*n* = 60 students) vs. CG Non-GLOBE (*n* = 63 students) EG outperformed CG on hydrology assessment scores with an effect size of 0.10 (Penuel et al., 2005)	In 2020, the project scaled to approximately 37,000 schools, 40,000 teachers, 7000 teacher trainees, and 809,000 students worldwide (see GLOBE Homepage, 2020)
Building Blocks/ TRIAD	1 exploration and 2 visualization	Mathematics Pre K to grade 2	Experiment (*N* = 25 classrooms, 209 students): EG Building Blocks (*N* = 13 classrooms) vs. CG Non-Building Block (*N* = 12 classrooms) EG outperformed CG on Research-based Early Mathematics Assessment scores with an effect size of 0.62 Follow-up experiment with 42 schools, 106 classrooms, and 1375 preschoolers replicated the beneficial effect (g = 0.72) of learning with Building Blocks (Sarama, Clements, Starkey, Klein, & Wakeley, 2008; Clements et al., 2011)	In 2018, the project scaled to approximately 180 Pre-K teachers, 2160 children from MA, Buffalo, NY and Nashville, TN often coming from HeadStart and low-resources schools (see TRIAD Homepage)
LASER	1 exploration and 3 collaboration	STEM disciplines Mainly grades 1–5 but also grades 6–8 and kindergarten	Matched-paired RCT (*N* = 2601 students): EG LASER (*n* = 1429 students) vs. CG Non-LASER (1172 students) EG outperformed CG on Partnership for the Assessment of Standards-Based Science performance assessment scores (Smithsonian Science Education Center, 2015)	In 2015, the project scaled to 60,000 students mainly from different U.S. school districts but is also used in other countries such as Mexico, Sweden, and Chile (Smithsonian Science Education Center, 2015; Devés & Lopez, 2007)

SimCalc	1 exploration and 2 visualization	Mathematics (rate and proportionality) Grades 7–8 (originally)	RCT (N = 1621 students): EG SimCalc (n = 796 students) vs. CG Non-SimCalc (n = 825 students) EG outperformed CG rate and proportionality understanding scores with an effect size of 0.63 Follow-up experiments with another 1048 seventh graders and 825 eighth graders replicated the beneficial effect of learning with SimCalc with effect sizes of 0.50 and 0.56 (Roschelle, Shechtman et al., 2010)	The SimCalc approach scaled to 4 regions of Texas, 95 teachers (in 7th grade) and 56 teachers (in 8th grade) and thousands of students with diverse backgrounds (SES levels, ethnicity, region) Later, the SunBay environment scaled to over 25 000 students per year in Florida. The Cornerstone work in the United Kingdom scaled to over 100 schools and 203 teachers (Roschelle, Shechtman et al., 2010; Vahey et al., 2013; Clark-Wilson et al., 2015)
River City	1 exploration and 4 metacognitive learning	Science (infectious disease) K-12	Quasi-experiment (N = 1000 students; 11 teachers): EGs with 2 variants of River City vs. Non-River City CG Both EGs outperformed CG on biology posttest (Clarke et al., 2006)	In 2009, the project scaled to 250 teachers, 15,000 students from the United States and Canada (Clarke & Dede, 2009)
WISE	1 exploration, 2 visualization, 3 collaboration, and 4 metacognitive learning	Science (physics, chemistry, life science, earth science) K-12	Two-time delayed experimental groups (N = 4328 students; 26 teachers) EG WISE vs. CG Non-WISE EG outperformed CG on explanation-based knowledge integration scores with an effect size of 0.32 (Linn et al., 2006)	In 2018, 73 different WISE-projects were listed in the project library; 5 projects are in Dutch and 4 projects are in Spanish (WISE Homepage, 2020)

* in Table 6.1 with examples for successful scale-up projects
Note: EG = experimental group; CG = control group; RCT = randomized controlled trial. When available, sample sizes and effect sizes were reported. References listed in Table 6.1 are marked with a star in the reference list. Inquiry learning features are adopted from Donelly, D. F., Linn, M. C., & Ludvigsen, S. (2014). Impacts and Characteristics of Computer-Based Science Inquiry Learning Environments for Precollege Students, *Review of Educational Research*, *84*(4), 572–608.

To illustrate how these environments support inquiry learning, we draw on the four inquiry learning features identified in a review of inquiry learning environments (Donelly et al., 2014). These features are elements that allow students to (1) explore meaningful and authentic scientific contexts, (2) use powerful visualizations, (3) collaborate with others, and (4) develop autonomous, metacognitive learning practices (Donnelly et al., 2014, p. 4). Like most inquiry learning environments, all of the examples in Table 6.1 engage students in exploration and investigation. LASER and GLOBE, in particular, are noteworthy for involving students in working with scientists in authentic scientific investigations. Second, many inquiry environments support students in visualizing concepts or empirical evidence. SimCalc and Building Blocks, our two mathematics examples, introduce technology-supported visualizations. Third, some inquiry environments focus on student collaboration and argumentation; WISE is our example that best illustrates this characteristic. Finally, River City and WISE are examples of inquiry learning environments that emphasize metacognitive learning as well as learning in the field of study.

In all six cases, R&D teams were concerned with establishing efficacy, that is, providing evidence for a causal argument that implementing their approach would improve student learning outcomes. For two of the cases (Building Blocks and SimCalc), researchers conducted randomized controlled trials to establish efficacy. In other cases, an efficacy case was built through a series of design studies, case studies, and quasi-experimental evaluations. See Table 6.1 for more details.

In terms of scale, each of our example cases sought to test inquiry learning across diverse settings beyond the setting in which the approach was first designed (most often, inquiry learning environments are tested in a single context or several similar contexts). Each reached thousands of students. GLOBE and LASER in particular had ambitious scaling goals right from the beginning, even as they were still under development. Both of these inquiry learning environments met their objective of scaling internationally and involved hundreds of thousands of students.

Through our review of each team's reflections on these cases, we identified five useful scaling strategies. We see these as complementary strategies, not alternatives.

Strategy 1: Understand the Context. Teams that succeed in scaling up inquiry environments invest considerable energy in understanding and defining the niche in which they can scale and the needs of the educators who will adopt their approach. Although they may have ambitions for universal adoption, realistically they focus on niches where growth is possible. They define stakeholders in their approach and seek to learn more about what those stakeholders care about, what obstacles they face, and what supports they need. For example, the SimCalc team started with a vision of "simulations for calculus learning" (hence "SimCalc") but later focused on student learning of ratio and proportion in their scaling activities because these topics were a bigger problem for schools than precalculus was. The GLOBE program initially emphasized its data collection protocols and the accuracy of the data students submitted on their local study site. Over time, however, the GLOBE leaders realized that winning time for their environmental inquiry program within the regular school schedule required mapping the curriculum onto the standards for which teachers and schools are held accountable. The program even developed GLOBE books for early readers that teachers in the early elementary grades could use to teach literacy and environmental inquiry concepts at the same time.

Strategy 2: Engage a Breadth of Expertise. Teams that succeed in scaling their innovations incorporate multiple types of talent within their teams specifically to help with problems of scale. This means going beyond the small group that developed the initial design concept. For example, the LASER team included experts in curriculum, assessment, professional development, administrative and community support, and materials delivery. The Building Blocks team (see Sarama et al., 2008) focused on developing strong relationships with stakeholders in their implementation sites and invited input and feedback from stakeholders. The SimCalc program incrementally added experts with additional expertise as the range of concerns to be addressed expanded (Roschelle et al., 2008). In general, a design-based implementation research approach—which emphasizes inclusion of practitioners in decision-making and focuses specifically on the layers of additional design needed to support implementation—becomes highly relevant in scaling up inquiry approaches (Penuel et al., 2011).

Strategy 3: Develop a Coherent Learning Activity System. Teams that succeed in bringing inquiry learning innovations to scale integrate the many different elements needed to support the desired change in teaching and learning into an ambitious learning activity system (defined above). For example, they take care to pull together and align the curriculum, technology, professional development, and assessment components of their approach. In the Scaling Up SimCalc project (Roschelle et al., 2010), this entailed writing replacement curriculum units that were specific about how and when dynamic representations on a computer were to be used, and interconnecting the technology activities with non-technology activities. Furthermore, teacher professional development was very tightly synchronized to what teachers would need to know to use the curriculum workbooks and technology together. More broadly, we noted that successful scale-up designs carefully consider what educators need at different stages of experience with the innovation—for example, to make the decision to adopt the approach, to learn how to initially use it, to become expert in their use of the approach, and eventually to sustain it on their own and help others learn to use it. Overall, teams that succeed at scaling view their work as building systems for teaching and learning, not just disseminating an isolated tool or material, and they focus on a clear image of the teaching and learning activity that every aspect of the system will work to support (Clements et al., 2011; Sarama et al., 2008).

Strategy 4: Work with Practitioners to Improve Implementation. Teams that scale their innovations successfully use design methods that invite participation of practitioners early on and throughout the design and scaling process. These methods include co-design, design-based implementation research, and researcher-practitioner partnerships. One especially important focus for co-design is on the teacher professional development that will be needed to support scaling up an inquiry learning environment. A recent meta-analysis (Lynch et al., 2019) is a good starting point for considering the nature of effective teacher professional development for scaling STEM inquiry approaches. Reviews and syntheses of best practices in STEM teacher professional development for inquiry also offer guidance (i.e., Capps, Crawford, & Constas, 2012; Gerard et al., 2011; Lederman & Lederman, 2012; Wilson, 2013). All projects acknowledge that designing an inquiry environment for scale requires allowing for its adaptation to fit different contexts and its expandability to additional content and needs (Clark & Dede, 2009). For example, to promote depth of scaling, the River City team "employs design-based research methods in order to understand what conditions are more flexible and adaptable to meet needs of students and teachers in various conditions" (Clark & Dede, 2009, p. 358).

Strategy 5: Measure and Iterate. To meet the scaling criterion of "predictable, measurable impact at scale," teams develop measures they can use to monitor their progress. This often includes designing student learning measures that fit the intention of their inquiry environment, as most large-scale assessments fail to measure what students learn from inquiry environments. Effort is often made to show the relationships between the newly designed measures and aspects of curricular standards or frameworks that are important. In some cases, studies seek to measure both more aligned and accountability-oriented measures. For example, the Scaling Up SimCalc program (Roschelle, Shechtman et al., 2010) included two subscales, one of which was better aligned to the curriculum's inquiry goals and the other which used relevant items from the state accountability assessment. Teams also develop indicators of the ease of use of their materials, ways of monitoring how frequently and in what ways their various tools are used, and likelihood of continued usage. Although most developers of inquiry learning environments have leaned toward the idea of adaptation of their system to local conditions as opposed to strict "fidelity of implementation" (e.g., Dede, 2005), successful scaling efforts nonetheless develop ways to detect inappropriate or weak uses of their system and to help implementers improve. All the projects in Table 6.1 describe the scaling up process as highly iterative, with many cycles covering a wide range of issues that arise during implementations. The teams built systems and practices to collect examples of implementation issues that they used to plan future versions of their learning environments.

Partnerships for Sustaining Inquiry Environments

The six cases in Table 6.1 were selected in part because both evidence of impact and scholarly reflections on the scaling process were available. Application of these criteria ruled out many successful cases of scaling involving partnerships where the scaling work was performed by a company. A reason to also focus attention on partnerships is their relationship to sustainability.

Scale and sustainability are interrelated, but they are not the same. Scale is spreading a practice; sustainability is keeping it in use for a longer period of time. There are economic dimensions of both scale and sustainability. Programs that are very expensive can have a hard time attracting initial adoptions. Economics comes into play with sustainability because it involves recurrent costs as well as initial costs. For an innovation to be sustained, a mechanism for covering recurring costs must be identified. These costs may be easily measured direct costs (such as annual licensing fees) or may be more subtle and even nonmonetary in nature—such as the costs of maintaining a pool of talented teachers who can enact the innovation or the need to refresh and refine the innovation on a regular basis in response to changing circumstances or even just the cost of keeping the focus on continuing to implement the innovation in the face of other shiny, new objects promoted by others.

One way to address sustainability is through partnerships with business. Businesses are structured to sustain their offerings in a market. We offer some examples, but then turn to other means of sustainability. Read180 is one well-known example where the scale and sustainability of an ambitious learning activity system was led by a company. Read180 is a reading program by the company HMH which configures the classroom as a series of stations in which different modes of reading activity occur. Research conducted by Ted Hasselbring and Laura Goin (e.g., Hasselbring & Goin, 1988) at Vanderbilt University provided the underpinnings for the initial design of Read180. Another example of scale and sustainability is Carnegie Learning, a company that scaled up intelligent tutoring technologies developed in partnership with researchers at Carnegie Mellon University (Ritter et al., 2007).

Two additional examples that have achieved remarkable scale and sustainability highlight the parallel and coordinated contributions from researchers and companies. The prominence of graphing calculators arose from separate but related efforts of Texas Instruments (a company) and university professors. Ohio State professors Frank Demana and Bert Waits were integral to the drive for calculator adoption and use in mathematics classroom (e.g., Waits & Demana, 1998). Furthermore, Demana and Waits developed a large teacher professional development network that was independent of, yet closely affiliated with, Texas Instruments. Texas Instruments often shaped their product development roadmap in response to suggestions from this network. Subsequently, independent researchers analyzed the impact of graphing calculator use; for example, a meta-analysis by Ellington (2003) found graphing calculators were effective for developing conceptual understanding (this is likely because teachers use calculators to free students from doing tedious calculations and thus can focus more on concepts). Graphing calculators were first developed in the 1990s and remain prominent in mathematics and science classrooms 20 years later.

In a closely related example, probes and sensors were developed through separate but interrelated efforts of researchers and several small companies. Probes and sensors are used to foster hands-on inquiry instruction (Soloway et al., 1999). Early research on microcomputer-based labs (e.g., Mokros & Tinker, 1987) and subsequent research to further develop probes and sensors were closely related to long-standing efforts at many companies to develop commercially viable probes and sensors, resulting in wide availability of low-cost technologies. The Concord Consortium nurtured a symbiotic connection between researchers and industry to continue advancing the scalable technologies along with related science inquiry research.

We would also caution that such success stories involve partnerships and collaboration that span decades of back-and-forth dialogue on an educational problem and approach. Despite the involvement of a commercial entity, they are not well described by terms such as "transferring" or "commercializing" a research-based discovery or invention. Furthermore, a partnership like this is not necessarily the only route available to innovators who would like to scale an inquiry learning environment. In some cases, a university-affiliated group itself becomes the long-term engine scaling an innovation, though usually outside the tenure track demands of a university department. Such is the case with FOSS (Powell & Wells, 2002), a hands-on inquiry activity system that has been sustained by the Lawrence Hall of Science, which is affiliated with the University of California, Berkeley. It is also possible that the thrust of an inquiry-based approach may be sustained as a school of thought and thus by a person, team, or institution providing intellectual thought leadership. For example, the Exploratorium, an informal science institution in San Francisco, could be said to have had this effect with its "to do and notice" approach to engaging wonder and investigation through physical activities (Oppenheimer & Cole, 1974). Likewise, sustainability may be created institutionally, such as when inquiry-based learning environments or approaches become the basis of policies that are adopted by school systems. In such cases, the exact tool or environment may not be sustained, but the core features of the inquiry approach may be. One might see the growing adoption of maker spaces by schools in this light; they create a dedicated school space where inquiry practices might be sustained.

With regard to sustainability, there are also limitations to what can be learned from studying existing cases. Leaders who develop inquiry learning environments may find the niche for inquiry learning within schools may be too small, the possible adopters too hard to reach, or the available financing too little. Faced with these challenges, the team may simply move on to a new research topic. We have noted that public-private partnerships can sometimes overcome these barriers, but few scholarly reflections on the nature of educational public-private partnerships are available. The other key feature we identified in this context was the shift of ownership, where institutions different from those who developed an inquiry learning innovation take on the life of an innovation. The thought-leadership approach requires new owners who take on and sustain the thoughts. The institutional space approach requires new owners who independently figure out how to cover the initial and recurrent costs of the new space. As ownership shifts either to partnerships or to new institutions come to the fore, issues of maintaining the quality of the innovation continually come to the fore—the innovation may become less ambitious, mutate fatally to become something different, or become less identifiable or prominent. Sustainability of ambitious learning activity systems remains a "wicked problem," not a well-mapped challenge.

Discussion: The State of the Art and Remaining Challenges

Bringing inquiry learning environments to scale is an important issue for society, especially given the needs for stronger inquiry skills among future citizens, employees, and leaders. Scaling up is a complex challenge for any educational innovation, and we have argued particularly so for ambitious inquiry learning innovations that may not find a good fit with prevailing priorities in many of today's classrooms and communities. Nonetheless, it can be done: We have described six examples of inquiry learning environments that achieved considerable scale and four additional long-term partnerships. To tackle the challenges of scaling, the example projects planned for scaling from the earliest stages of their work. They invested in scaling up for a long period of time, and their approach evolved to incorporate insights gained through their experience in the field. They also reflected on which principles helped them reach scale on many different dimensions.

The principles presented above are interwoven, and implementing them is labor-intensive. Overcoming the many obstacles to realizing a vision is a long-term commitment best undertaken with a highly dedicated team. Although there is still much to be learned about how to work effectively on scaling up an inquiry learning environment, due to an expansion of research on scaling education innovations in the past two decades, there are now proof points that it is possible and there is much less mystery about how to do it.

There are also limitations to what can be learned from studying existing cases. Sustainability after R&D funding is exhausted and in the face of changing education priorities and staffing remains a major challenge. Inquiry projects can achieve scale, and yet the learning environment may not continue to spread or keep going after the funding ends. The niche for inquiry learning within schools may be too small, the available financing too little, or the team may simply move on to a new research topic. We have noted that public-private partnerships can sometimes overcome these barriers, but few scholarly reflections on the nature of educational public-private partnerships are available. Other models are available as well, as noted above, but the paths to sustainability can appear to be idiosyncratic to the personalities of the individuals involved. Further insights on how inquiry teams could achieve sustainability are very much needed.

A second enduring challenge is addressing equity. We found that few scale-up examples were as specific as we would like about the degree to which they overcame the pervasive equity issues. Absent intentional strategies to counteract preconceptions about who can and should engage in inquiry learning, inquiry learning environments may scale primarily to classrooms that are already doing student-centered instruction. For the most part, scale has been achieved by what Cohen and Mehta characterize as "niche reforms." This type of reform fits a place within the educational system but does not challenge the system as a whole. For those aspiring to make inquiry learning the centerpiece of systemic reform—to design entire school systems for the purpose of fostering inquiry among all students (see, for example, Collins, 2017)—more research is needed.

A third challenge regards incentivizing researchers to focus on scaling. Given how slow and hard scaling work is, working on this issue may detract from building the kind of publication track record prized by universities. Scaling work tends to force one to become a generalist, because of the range of problems one encounters—and this too runs counter to academic career rewards for specialization. Scaling efforts may not fit the mission of a department, lab, or institution. And scaling requires patience, because the costs and problems arrive early, and the benefits and successes materialize more slowly.

Future research and funding initiatives related to scaling inquiry learning environments should pay attention to the limitations noted above to what has been achieved thus far. The field has much to learn about how to achieve sustainability, equity, and aligned incentive systems for the implementation of inquiry learning systems at scale.

Acknowledgments

This material is based upon work supported by the National Science Foundation under grants 2021159 (CIRCLS) and 1837463 (CIRCL). Any opinions, findings, and conclusions or recommendations expressed in this material are those of the author(s) and do not necessarily reflect the views of the National Science Foundation.

References

Aivaloglou, E., & Hermans, F. (2016). How kids code and how we know: An exploratory study on the Scratch repository. In *ICER '16 Proceedings of the 2016 ACM Conference on International Computing Education Research* (pp. 53–61). New York: ACM. http://doi.org/10.1145/2960310.2960325

Anderson, R., & Helms, J. (2001). The ideal of standards and the reality of schools: Needed research. *Journal of Research in Science Teaching*, 38, 3–16. http://doi.org/10.1002/1098-2736(200101)38:1<3::AID-TEA2>3.0.CO;2-V

Ben-David. A., & Zohar, A. (2009). Contribution of meta-strategic knowledge to scientific inquiry learning. *International Journal of Science Education*, *31*(12), 1657–1682. http://doi.org/10.1080/09500690802162762

Brown, A. L., & Campione, J. C. (1996). Psychological theory and the design of innovative learning environments: On procedures, principles, and systems. In L. Schauble & R. Glaser (Eds.), *Innovations in learning: New environments for education* (pp. 289–325). Mahwah, NJ: Erlbaum.

Capps, D. K., Crawford, B. A., & Constas, M. A. (2012). A review of empirical literature on inquiry professional development: Alignment with best practices and a critique of the findings. *Journal of Science Teacher Education*, *23*(3), 291–318. https://doi.org/10.1007/s10972-012-9275-2

Cartwright, N. (2012). Presidential address: Will this policy work for you? Predicting effectiveness better: How philosophy helps. *Philosophy of Science*, *79*(5), 973–989. https://doi.org/10.1086/668041

Cartwright, N. (2013). Knowing what we are talking about: Why evidence doesn't always travel. *Evidence & Policy: A Journal of Research, Debate and Practice*, *9*(1), 97–112. https://doi.org/10.1332/174426413X662581

*Clarke, J., & Dede, C. (2009). Design for scalability: A case study of the River City curriculum. *Journal of Science Education and Technology*, *18*, 353–365. https://doi.org/10.1007/s10956-009-9156-4

*Clarke, J., Dede, C., Ketelhut, D. J., Nelson, B., & Bowman, C. (2006). A design-based research strategy to promote scalability for educational innovations. *Educational Technology*, *46*(3), 27–36. [Faculty Publication]

*Clark-Wilson, A., Hoyles, C., Noss, R., Vahey, P., & Roschelle, J. (2015). Scaling a technology-based innovation: Windows on the evolution of mathematics teachers' practice. *ZDM Mathematics Education*, *47*, 79–92. https://doi.org/10.1007/s11858-014-0635-6

*Clements, D. H., Sarama, J., Spitler, M. E., Lange, A. A., & Wolfe, C. B. (2011). Mathematics learned by young children in an intervention based on learning trajectories: A large scale cluster randomized trial. *Journal of Research in Mathematics Education*, *2*, 127–166. https://doi.org/10.5951/jresematheduc.42.2.0127

Cobb, P., Jackson, K., Smith, T., Sorum, M., & Henrick, E. (2013). Design research with educational systems: Investigating and supporting improvements in the quality of mathematics teaching and learning at scale. In B. J. Fishman, W. R. Penuel, A.-R. Allen & B. Haugan Cheng (Eds.), *Design-based implementation research: Theories, methods and exemplars, Yearbook of the National Society for the Study of Education*, *112*(2), 320–349. New York: Teachers College, Columbia University.

Coburn, C. E. (2003). Rethinking scale: Moving beyond numbers to deep and lasting change. *Educational Researcher*, *32*(6), 3–12. https://doi.org/10.3102/0013189X032006003

Coburn, C. E., & Penuel, W. R. (2016). Research-practice partnerships in education: Outcomes, dynamics, and open questions. *Educational Researcher*, *45*(1), 48–54. https://doi.org/10.3102/0013189X16631750

Coburn, C. E., Penuel, W. R., & Geil, K. (2013). *Research-practice partnerships at the district level: A new strategy for leveraging research for educational improvement*. New York: Wiilliam T. Grant Foundation.

Cohen, D. K., & Mehta, J. D. (2017). Why Reform Sometimes Succeeds: Understanding the Conditions That Produce Reforms That Last, *American Educational Research Journal*, *54*(4), 644–690, https://doi.org/10.3102/0002831217700078

Cohen, D. K., Raudenbush, S. W., & Ball, D. L. (2003). Resources, instruction, and research. *Educational Evaluation and Policy Analysis*, *25*(2), 119–142. https://doi.org/10.3102/01623737025002119

Collins, A. (2017). *What's worth teaching? Rethinking curriculum in the age of technology*. New York: Teachers College Press.

Darling-Hammond, L., Hyler, M. E., Gardner, M., & Espinoza, D. (2017). *Effective teacher professional development*. Palo Alto, CA: Learning Policy Institute.

Dearing, J. W., Dede, C., Boisvert, D., Carrese, J., Clement, L., Craft, E. et al. (2015). How educational innovators apply diffusion and scale-up concepts. In C. K. Looi & L. W. Teh (Eds.), *Scaling educational innovations* (pp. 81–104). Singapore: Springer. https://doi.org/10.1007/978-981-287-537-2_5

DeBarger, A. H., Penuel, W. R., Harris, C. J., & Kennedy, C. A. (2016). Building an assessment argument to design and use next generation science assessments in efficacy studies of curriculum interventions. *American Journal of Evaluation*, *37*(2), 174–192. https://doi.org/10.1177/1098214015581707

Dede, C. (2005). Scaling up: Evolving innovations beyond ideal settings to challenging contexts of practice. In R. K. Sawyer (Ed.), *Cambridge handbook of the learning sciences*. Cambridge: Cambridge University Press. https://doi.org/10.1017/CBO9780511816833.034

*Devés, R., & López, P. (2007). Inquiry-based science education and its impact on school improvement: The ECBI program in Chile. In T. Townsend (Ed.), *International handbook of school effectiveness and improvement*. Springer International Handbooks of Education (vol. 17). Dordrecht: Springer. https://doi.org/10.1007/978-1-4020-5747-2_48

Donelly, D. F., Linn, M. C., & Ludvigsen, S. (2014). Impacts and characteristics of computer-based science inquiry learning environments for precollege students. *Review of Educational Research, 84*(4), 572–608. https://doi.org/10.3102/0034654314546954

Dunn, M. B. (2009). *Investigating variation in teaching with technology-rich interventions: What matters in training and teaching at scale?* Unpublished doctoral dissertation, Rutgers University, New Brunswick, NJ.

Educational Endowment Foundation. (n.d.). Retrieved from https://educationendowmentfoundation.org.uk/

Ellington, A. (2003). A meta-analysis of the effects of calculators on students' achievement and attitude levels in precollege mathematics classes. *Journal for Research in Mathematics Education, 34*(5), 433–463. https://doi.org/10.2307/30034795

First Lego League. (n.d.). Retrieved from https://www.first-lego-league.org/en/general/what-is-fll.html

Flay, B. R., Biglan, A., Boruch, R. F., Castro, F. G., Gottfredson, D., Kellam, S., ..., & Ji, P. (2005). Standards of evidence: Criteria for efficacy, effectiveness and dissemination. *Prevention science, 6(3),* 151–175. https://doi.org/10.1007/s11121-005-5553-y

Furtak, E. M., Seidel, T., Iverson, H., & Briggs, D. C. (2012). Experimental and quasi-experimental studies of inquiry-based science teaching: A meta-analysis. *Review of Educational Research, 82*(3), 300–329. https://doi.org/10.3102/0034654312457206

Gerard, L. F., Varma, K., Corliss, S. B., & Linn, M. C. (2011). Professional development for technology-enhanced inquiry science. *Review of Educational Research, 81*(3), 408–448. https://doi.org/10.3102/0034654311415121

*Globe Home Page. (2020, October 13). Retrieved from https://www.globe.gov/de/about/impact-and-metrics

Hasselbring, T. S., & Goin, L. I. (1988). Microcomputer applications to instruction. In E. A. Polloway, J. S. Payne, J. R. Patton, & R. A. Payne (Eds.), *Strategies for teaching retarded students* (4th ed.). Columbus, OH: Charles E. Merrill Publishing Company.

Hedges, L. V. (2018). Challenges in building usable knowledge in education. *Journal of Research on Educational Effectiveness, 11*(1), 1–21. https://doi.org/10.1080/19345747.2017.1375583

Institute for Educational Sciences and National Science Foundation. (2013). *Common guidelines for educational research and development*. Washington, DC: US Department of Education and National Science Foundation. Retrieved January 30, 2019 from https://ies.ed.gov/pdf/CommonGuidelines.pdf

Interagency Educational Research Initiative (IERI). (n.d.). Retrieved from https://drdc.uchicago.edu/community/main.php

Kerckhoff, A. C., & Glennie, E. (1999). The Matthew effect in American education. *Research in Sociology of Education and Socialization, 12*(1), 35–66.

Krumm, A., Means, B., & Bienkowski, M. (2018). *Learning analytics goes to school*. New York: Routledge. https://doi.org/10.4324/9781315650722

Ladson-Billings, G. (1995). Toward a theory of culturally relevant pedagogy. *American Educational Research Journal, 32*(3), 465–491. https://doi.org/10.3102/00028312032003465

Lederman, N. G., & Lederman, J. S. (2012). Nature of scientific knowledge and scientific inquiry: Building instructional capacity through professional development. In *Second international handbook of science education* (pp. 335–359). Dordrecht: Springer. https://doi.org/10.1007/978-1-4020-9041-7_24

LeMahieu, P., Grunow, A., Baker, L., Nordstrum, L., & Gomez, L. (2017). Networked improvement communities. *Quality Assurance in Education, 25*(1), 5–25. https://doi.org/10.1108/QAE-12-2016-0084

Levin, H. M., & Belfield, C. (2015). Guiding the development and use of cost-effectiveness analysis in education. *Journal of Research on Educational Effectiveness, 8*(3), 400–418. https://doi.org/10.1080/19345747.2014.915604

Lewis, S. (2015). Qualitative inquiry and research design: Choosing among five approaches. *Health Promotion Practice, 16*(4), 473–475. https://doi.org/10.1177/1524839915580941

*Linn, M. C., Lee, H.-S., Tinker, R., Husic, F., & Chiu, J. L. (2006). Teaching and assessing knowledge integration in science. *Science, 313*(5790), 1049–1050.

Looi, C.-K., & Woon, T. L. (2015). *Scaling educational innovations*. Singapore: Heidelberg.

Lynch, K., Hill, H., Gonzalez, K., & Pollard, C. (2019). Strengthening the research base that informs STEM instructional improvement efforts: A meta-analysis. *Educational Evaluation and Policy Analysis*. https://doi.org/10.3102/0162373719849044

Makel, M. C., Plucker, J. A., & Hegarty, B. (2012). Replications in psychology research: How often do they really occur? *Perspectives on Psychological Science*, *7*(6), 537–542. https://doi.org/10.1177/1745691612460688

McDonald, S.-K., Keesler, V. A., Kauffman, N. J., & Schneider, B. (2006). Scaling-up exemplary interventions. *Educational Researcher*, *35*(3), 15–24. https://doi.org/10.3102/0013189X035003015

Melchior, A. L., Burack, C., Hoover, M., & Marcus, J. (2016). *FIRST longitudinal study: Participant characteristics, program experience, and impacts at follow-up (year 3 report)*. Waltham, MA: Center for Youth and Communities, Heller School, Brandeis University. Prepared for US FIRST.

Mokros, J. R., & Tinker, R. F. (1987). The impact of microcomputer-based labs on children's ability to interpret graphs. *Journal of Research in Science Teaching*, *24*(4), 369–383. https://doi.org/10.1002/tea.3660240408

Moore, G. (2014). *Crossing the Chasm. Marketing and selling disruptive products to mainstream customers* (3rd ed.). New York: Harper Collins Business.

Mort, P. R. (1953). Educational adaptability. *The School Executive*, *71*, 1–23. https://doi.org/10.1111/j.2044-8279.1953.tb02842.x

Münch, J., Fagerholm, F., Johnson, P., Pirttilahti, J., Torkkel, J., & Järvinen, J. (2013). Creating minimum viable products in industry-academia collaborations. In B. Fitzgerald, K. Conboy, K. Power, R. Valerdi, L. Morgan, & K. J. Stol (Eds.), *Lean enterprise software and systems. LESS 2013. Lecture Notes in Business Information Processing* (vol. 167). Heidelberg: Springer. https://doi.org/10.1007/978-3-642-44930-7_9

Newman, D., Jaciw, A. P., & Lazarev, V. (2018). *Guidelines for conducting and reporting edtech impact research in U.S. K-12 schools*. Washington, DC: Educational Technology Network of Software and Information Industry Association. Retrieved from https://www.empiricaleducation.com/pdfs/guidelines.pdf (Accessed November 7, 2019).

Nicholson, T. W., & Tunmer, W. E. (2010). Reading: The great debate. In C. M. Rubie-Davies (Ed.), *Educational psychology: Concepts, research and challenges* (pp. 50–64). London: Routledge.

Oppenheimer, F. J., & Cole, K. C. (1974). The Exploratorium: A participatory museum. *Prospects*, *4*(1), 21–34. https://doi.org/10.1007/BF02206525

*Penuel, W. R., Bienkowski, M., Korbak, C., Molina, A., Russo, D., Shear, L., Toyama, Y., & Yarnall, L. (2005). Globe year 9 evaluation: Implementation supports and student outcomes. SRI International. https://www.globe.gov/documents/10157/6afb66ed-24de-4d2e-800f-ba26abf7028c

Penuel, W. R., Fishman, B. J., Cheng, B., & Sabelli, N. (2011). Organizing research and development at the intersection of learning, implementation and design. *Educational Researcher*, *40*(7), 331–337. https://doi.org/10.3102/0013189X11421826.

Penuel, W. R., McWilliams, H., McAuliffe, C., Benbow, A., Mably, C., & Hayden, M. (2009). Teaching for understanding in Earth science: Comparing impacts on planning and instruction in three professional development designs for middle school science. *Journal of Science Teacher Education*, *20*(5), 415–436. https://doi.org/10.1007/s10972-008-9120-9

Powell, K., & Wells, M. (2002). The effectiveness of three experiential teaching approaches on student science learning in fifth-grade public school classrooms. *The Journal of Environmental Education*, *33*(2), 33–38. https://doi.org/10.3102/0013189X11421826

Prewitt, K., Schwandt, T. A., & Straf, M. L. (Hrsg.). (2012). *Using science as evidence in public policy*. Washington, DC: National Academies Press.

Ritter, S., Anderson, J. R., Koedinger, K. R., & Corbett, A. (2007). Cognitive tutor: Applied research in mathematics education. *Psychonomic Bulletin & Review*, *14*(2), 249–255. https://doi.org/10.3758/BF03194060

Roehrig, G. H., & Luft, J. A. (2004). Constraints experienced by beginning secondary science teachers in implementing scientific inquiry lessons. *International Journal of Science Education*, *26*(1), 3–24. https://doi.org/10.1080/0950069022000070261

Rogers, E. M. (1962). *Diffusion of innovations* (3rd ed.). New York: A Division of Macmillan Publishing.

Roschelle, J., Knudsen, J., & Hegedus, S. (2010). From new technological infrastructures to curricular activity systems: Advanced designs for teaching and learning. In M. J. Jacobson & P. Reimann (Eds.), *Designs for learning environments of the future: International perspectives from the learning sciences* (pp. 233–262). New York: Springer. https://doi.org/10.1007/978-0-387-88279-6_9

*Roschelle, J., Shechtman, N., Tatar, D., Hegedus, S., Hopkins, B., Empson, S., Knudsen, J., & Gallagher, L. P. (2010). Integration of technology, curriculum, and professional development for advancing middle school mathematics: Three large-scale studies. *American Educational Research Journal*, *47*(4), 833–878. https://doi.org/10.3102/0002831210367426

Roschelle, J., Tatar, D., & Kaput, J. (2008). Getting to scale with innovations that deeply restructure how students come to know mathematics. In A. E. Kelly, R. Lesh & J. Y. Baek (Eds.), *Handbook of design research methods in education* (pp. 369–395). New York: Routledge.

Roschelle, J., Tipton, E., Shechtman, N., & Vahey, P. (2018). *Generalizability of a technology-based intervention to enhance conceptual understanding in mathematics* (SimCalc Technical Report 10). Menlo Park, CA: SRI International. https://doi.org/10.13140/RG.2.2.31260.13442

Ruiz-Primo, M. A., Shavelson, R. J., Hamilton, L., & Klein, S. (2002). On the evaluation of systemic science education reform: Searching for instructional sensitivity. *Journal of Research in Science Teaching, 39*(5), 369–393. https://doi.org/10.1002/tea.10027

Russ, R. S., & Berland, L. K. (2019) Invented science: A framework for discussing a persistent problem of practice. *Journal of the Learning Sciences, 28*(3), 279–301. https://doi.org/10.1080/10508406.2018.1517354

Sallis, E. (2002). *Total quality management in education* (3rd ed.). London: Taylor & Francis.

Sarama, J., & Clements, D. H. (2013). Lessons learned in the implementation of the TRIAD scale-up model. Teaching early mathematics with trajectories and technologies. In T. G. Halle, A. J. Metz & I. Martinez Beck (Eds.), *Applying implementation science in early childhood programs and systems* (pp. 173–191). Baltimore, MD: Brookes.

*Sarama, J., Clements, D. H., Starkey, P., Klein, A., & Wakeley, A. (2008). Scaling up the implementation of a pre-kindergarten mathematics curriculum: Teaching for understanding with trajectories and technologies. *Journal of Research on Educational Effectiveness, 1*, 89–119. https://doi.org/10.1080/19345740801941332

Scalise, K., & Gifford, B. (2006). Computer-based assessment in E-learning: A framework for constructing "Intermediate Constraint" questions and tasks for technology platforms. *The Journal of Technology, Learning and Assessment, 4*(6). Retrieved from https://ejournals.bc.edu/index.php/jtla/article/view/1653 (Accessed May 15, 2019).

Schneider, B., & McDonald, S. K. (Eds.). (2007a). *Scale-up in education: Vol. 1: Ideas in principle.* Lanham, MD: Rowman & Littlefield.

Schneider, B., & McDonald, S. K. (Eds.). (2007b). *Scale-up in education: Vol. 2: Issues in practice.* Lanham, MD: Rowman & Littlefield.

Schoenfeld, A. H., & Pearson, P. D. (2012). The reading and math wars. In G. Sykes, B. Schneider & D. N. Plank (Eds.), *Handbook of education policy research* (pp. 576–596). London: Routledge.

Scratch Computing Environment. (n.d.). Retrieved from https://scratch.mit.edu/

*Smithsonian Science Education Center. (2015). *The LASER model: A systemic and sustainable approach for achieving high standards in science education. Executive summary.* Washington, DC: Smithsonian Institution. Retrieved from https://ssec.si.edu/laser-i3

Soloway, E., Grant, W., Tinker, R., Roschelle, J., Mills, M., Resnick, M., Berg, R., & Eisenberg, M. (1999). Science in the palm of their hands. *Communications of the ACM, 42*(8), 21–26. https://doi.org/10.1145/310930.310953

Tipton, E. (2014). How generalizable is your experiment? An index for comparing experimental samples and populations. *Journal of Educational and Behavioral Statistics, 39*(6), 478–501. https://doi.org/10.3102/1076998614558486

*Vahey, P., Knudsen, J., Rafanan, K., & Lara-Meloy, T. (2013). Curricular activity systems supporting the use of dynamic representations to foster students' deep understanding of mathematics. In *Emerging technologies for the classroom* (pp. 15–30). New York: Springer. https://doi.org/10.1007/978-1-4614-4696-5_2

Van der Valk, T., & de Jong, O. (2009). Scaffolding science teacher in open-inquiry teaching. *International Journal of Science Education, 31*(6), 829–850. https://doi.org/10.1080/09500690802287155

Von Hippel, E. (2005). *Democratizing innovation.* Cambridge, MA: MIT Press. https://doi.org/10.7551/mitpress/2333.001.0001

Waits, F., & Demana, B. K. (1998). The role of graphing calculators in mathematics reform. Retrieved from https://files.eric.ed.gov/fulltext/ED458108.pdf (Accessed January 31, 2019).

Wilson, S. M. (2013). Professional development for science teachers. *Science, 340*(6130), 310–313. https://doi.org/10.1126/science.1230725

*WISE Homepage. (2020, October, 13). Retrieved from https://wise.berkeley.edu/features

7

PROFESSIONAL DEVELOPMENT FOR THE SUPPORT OF TEACHING THROUGH INQUIRY

Anat Zohar and Maya S. Resnick[1]

The implementation of quality inquiry learning (IL) in classrooms requires broad and intricate actions, some of which focus on teachers' professional development (PD). In this chapter we (a) describe what we mean by thoughtful inquiry; (b) present the essential knowledge base teachers need for teaching authentic and thought-provoking inquiry; (c) examine the characteristics of PD programs aimed at developing teaching through inquiry; and (d) discuss and critique these findings.

Inquiry Learning (IL)

Inquiry learning was introduced into the field of education by John Dewey, who believed that the child is an active learner who learns best by doing. Dewey viewed inquiry as a process in which the undefined and unkown is turned gradually and intentionally into a clear entity. According to Dewey, IL has four distinct stages: sensing a problem, defining the problem, searching for a solution, and finding the solution (Dewey, 1902, 1938). There are numerous more recent definitions that refer to inquiry in school as instructional methods that, instead of providing students with the question and the answer, encourage teachers to create more room for students to formulate and explore their answers to the posed questions (Loyens & Rikers, 2011). One example definition of IL would be that of Linn, Davis, and Bell (2004), who define IL in the discipline of science education as "Engaging students in the intentional process of diagnosing problems, critiquing experiments, distinguishing alternatives, planning investigations, researching conjectures, searching for information from experts, and forming coherent arguments" (p. xvi). In science and social studies, IL usually consists of empirical studies that may be qualitative, quantitative, or mixed. In the humanities, IL is usually conducted around texts, with students engaging in analysis, interpretation, comparison, and integration of written resources. IL may take the form of either a whole inquiry process that may be summarized in a written paper, or a smaller, shorter inquiry task (Ministry of Education, 2015). Researchers argue that IL comprises a broad range of student-centered approaches to learning such as IL itself (also termed inquiry-based learning), problem-based learning, or project-based learning (for more details, see Loyens & Rikers, 2011).

Currently, IL is highly regarded as a valuable form of learning and as a desired form of instruction (Calder, 2015; Crawford, 2016; Justice, Rice, Roy, Hudspith, & Jenkins, 2009; Salovaara, 2005; Wells et al., 2015). It is recognized by scholars and policymakers as an important component of a critical education (Crawford, 2016; Turnip, Wahyuni, & Tanjung, 2016; Wells et al., 2015) and valued both as a tool for achieving conceptual learning and as an educational objective for developing higher-order thinking and skills (Anderson, 2002; Lotter, Harwood, & Bonner, 2007). Policy papers in numerous countries advocate the implementation of inquiry in K-12 classrooms (e.g., Australian Curriculum Assessment and Reporting Authority [ACARA], 2012; Israeli Ministry of Education, 2012; NRC, 2012; NGSS, 2013). Accordingly, IL can be found in many different disciplines—sciences (Crawford, 2007; Sadeh & Zion, 2009), mathematics (Calder, 2015; Makar & Fielding-Wells, 2018), agriculture (Wells et al., 2015), history (Callahan, Saye, & Brush, 2016; Reisman, 2012), civics (LeCompte & Blevins, 2015; Setiani & MacKinnon, 2015), and arts (Danker, 2015; Heid, Estabrook, & Nostrant, 2009) (yet as we will see further along in this chapter, the natural sciences seem at present to be the most prominent in terms of implementation of IL in schools and of research on that implementation).

Quality of Inquiry Conducted in Classrooms: Thoughtful versus Technical Inquiry

Although students in many classrooms may be engaged in conducting scientific experiments, going through primary historical sources, or constructing graphs based on neighborhood surveys, one can see they are not necessarily engaged in *learning through inquiry* (Crawford & Capps, 2018; Seraphin et al., 2012). Many such activities practiced by students are critiqued for being technical and lacking the central objectives of inquiry, as expressed by Chinn and Malhotra (2002): "many scientific inquiry tasks given to students in schools do not reflect the core attributes of authentic scientific reasoning" (p. 175). Too often inquiry activities focus on the mechanical aspects of conducting an experiment, running through prescribed processes, or conducting "confirmatory lab experiments," while overlooking the use of logic, reasoning, and higher-level critical thinking (Capps & Crawford, 2013; Crawford, 2016; Zohar & Dori, 2003). Although IL has numerous facets and challenges, we wrote this chapter with a focus on the challenges involved in enacting **thoughtful** IL.

In order to explain this idea, we need to go a bit deeper over what is higher-order thinking (abbreviated HOT). Although it is difficult to precisely define HOT, Resnick (Resnick & SNRC,1987) provided a useful list addressing some of its key features that can help us recognize it when it occurs. These key features include the following: HOT is non-algorithmic, it tends to be complex, it often yields multiple criteria and solutions, and it often involves uncertainty. In general terms, HOT refers to cognitive activities that are beyond the stage of recall and comprehension/understanding, according to Bloom's (1956) taxonomy and according to more recent revised models (Krathwohl, 2002). Applying, analyzing, evaluating, and creating are key elements at the HOT level. HOT cognitive activities also include constructing and evaluating arguments, asking research questions, dealing with controversies, making comparisons, designing, controlling variables, drawing conclusions, corroborating information sources, and establishing causal relationships (Zohar, 2004). As a concept, HOT is relatively recent; however, it overlaps to a large extent with the more classic, longstanding concept of critical thinking. This can be seen for example by the following definition of critical thinking which includes many of the elements that are also considered part of HOT: "Critical thinking is the intellectually disciplined process of actively and skilfully conceptualizing, applying, analysing, synthesizing, and/or evaluating information gathered from, or generated by, observation, experience, reflection, reasoning, or communication, as a guide to belief and action" (The Foundation for Critical Thinking, retrieved June 2019).

Examining how researchers refer to the concepts of inquiry, HOT, and critical thinking shows that HOT and critical thinking share many features with IL. Indeed, over the years, prominent educational researchers have defined critical thinking and scientific reasoning as the core objectives of IL. More than a century ago, Dewey advocated for an emphasis on teaching how to *think* about the way science works (1910). Researchers today, such as Crawford (2000, 2014, 2016), Anderson (2002), Zohar and Dori (2003), and Zohar and Barzilai (2015), continue to argue that higher-order thinking is an important focus of IL. Current educational policies also declare support for the notion that HOT is an important focus of IL and set goals of using logical thinking (NRC, 1996), developing critical-thinking skills (NRC, 2000), modeling scientific thinking (AAAS, 1990), and increasing the level and use of thinking skills (NGSS, 2013).

In order to better understand the integral and critical role of HOT in IL, let us look at an example that demonstrates the necessity of various thinking strategies in an inquiry process. *The example that we will use throughout the chapter is of students who conduct IL in civics education, about the working conditions of teenagers (Zohar & Cohen, 2016). The background to this topic is that employers too often take advantage of teenager employees, overlooking pertinent occupational laws. Students investigating this problem may ask research questions about laws and regulations, about their enforcement, about youngsters' actual experiences, about what would be an ideal situation, and about comparative issues between adults and teens. They may base their inquiry on various written information sources, and/or on data collection conducted through surveys, questionnaires, interviews, etc. Students' investigations would call for the use of multiple higher-order thinking skills such as formulating research questions and hypotheses, planning, integrating/synthesizing data from various sources, and analyzing data. Finally, students would need to draw conclusions and discuss them. The conclusions section is tightly related to the HOT strategy of argumentation; students would need to formulate statements (i.e., the conclusions) and support them with the evidence they had collected from the previous parts of their investigation, while explaining how the evidence supports the statements and discussing counterevidence, possible counterarguments, and their refutations. Students whose argumentative skills are not well developed will be unable to write well-supported conclusions in their final research paper and to discuss them in a profound way, nor will they be able to discuss and criticize inquiry processes conducted by others. Importantly, teachers who do not have a clear notion of what high-quality argumentation looks like will be unable to support their students in developing this strategy and may, for instance, be ineffective in providing students with useful feedback that could guide them toward drawing more coherent conclusions.*

The example of the civics IL demonstrates the central role of HOT in conducting meaningful IL. This notion is also explicitly supported by both policy documents and scholars. One must therefore consider what can explain the gap between the *view of inquiry* as an enactment of thinking and the common *practice of inquiry* as conducting "cookbook experiments" and "hands- on rather than minds-on" learning.

Teacher Knowledge

While many different factors play a role in explaining this gap, studies in recent years identify limited teacher knowledge regarding various aspects of inquiry as a decisive factor (Crawford, 2016). Inquiry-based teaching is a complex and sophisticated way of teaching, requiring complex and sophisticated teacher knowledge (Capps, Crawford, & Constas, 2012). The lack of such complex knowledge can be a major inhibitor of "authentic" thinking-rich inquiry. Unfortunately, a review of teachers' intuitive knowledge of teaching through inquiry shows that teachers often hold insufficient knowledge and detrimental beliefs (through no fault of their own) (e.g., Crawford, 2014; Duncan, Pilitsis, & Piegaro, 2010; Roth, McGinn, & Bowen, 1998; Zohar, 2007).

More specifically, studies show deficits regarding teachers' knowledge about IL (Anderson, 2002; Crawford, 2007), beliefs regarding the nature of science (Anderson, 2002; Duncan et al., 2010), epistemic beliefs (Maor & Taylor, 1995), pedagogical knowledge regarding inquiry instruction (Anderson, 2002; Duncan et al., 2010), and knowledge of thinking related to inquiry processes (Crawford, 2014; Roth et al., 1998; Zohar, 2007). For example, teachers' knowledge of the scientific process is frequently lacking (Kazempour & Amirshokoohi, 2013; Miranda &

Damico, 2015), with teachers often perceiving scientific inquiry as a linear and one-lane process (Crawford, 2016; Gyllenpalm, Wickman, & Holmgren, 2010; Seraphin et al., 2012). This often coincides with limited perceptions of the nature of science (NOS) and epistemic beliefs regarding the way scientific knowledge is constructed and evaluated. Various studies point to the fact that teachers often hold personal epistemologies which are detrimental to the implementation of authentic classroom inquiry, perceiving knowledge as absolute, certain, and generated by external sources (absolutist) rather than as tentative and constructed by experimentation (evaluative) (Duncan et al., 2010; Pilitsis & Duncan, 2012; Roth & Lucas, 1997; Seraphin et al., 2012). In addition, teachers frequently appear to lack the pertinent pedagogical knowledge necessary for teaching inquiry. For example, studies document deficiencies in teachers' knowledge regarding assessment and monitoring of inquiry processes (Schmidt & Fulton, 2016; Van Der Valk & De Jong, 2009), in their ability to address students' prior knowledge (Peters-Burton, Merz, Ramirez, & Saroughi, 2015), and in their ability to scaffold the learning process (Furtado, 2010; Gutierez, 2015). Lastly, teachers' grasp of metacognitive knowledge and skills seems also to be lacking. Studies relating to teachers' metacognition regarding IL are rare, but those that do refer to it portray a picture of limited metacognitive knowledge and skills, especially on an explicit level (Seraphin et al., 2012; Zohar, 2006).

Teaching through inquiry is a new form of instruction for most teachers. Many teachers have never themselves experienced conducting authentic inquiry (Kazempour & Amirshokoohi, 2013; Pilitsis & Duncan, 2012; Seraphin et al., 2012), especially elementary school teachers (Kazempour & Amirshokoohi, 2013). More so, many teachers have rarely experienced IL throughout their own education (preschool through to higher education) (Crawford, 2007; Duncan et al., 2010). This unfortunate state of affairs is succinctly demonstrated in the following citation:

> Carrie openly admitted she had limited knowledge of teaching science as inquiry and of the nature of scientific inquiry. She stated, "the problem is the science education department tells you inquiry is a great approach to take, but nobody ever teaches you inquiry. I have never experienced inquiry per se. Yeah, but if you were to say to me, think back on your experiences in the lab, would you consider them inquiry based? I would say, no."
>
> *(Crawford, 2007, p. 631)*

Needless to say, this is in no way an accusation of the teachers. On the contrary, as all professionals, teachers should be supported in learning the skills and knowledge necessary for the kinds of sophisticated teaching practices needed for doing their job, in this case, inquiry teaching (Crawford, 2016; Zohar, 2020). Teachers' PD programs therefore have a critical role in supporting teachers' knowledge, beliefs, and pedagogical skills related to teaching inquiry.

Teacher Professional Development (PD)

Teacher PD (for both pre- and in-service teachers) is considered a central tool for the promotion of teacher knowledge and skills (Timperley, Wilson, Barrar, & Fung, 2008; Yoon, Duncan, Lee, Scarloss, & Shapley, 2007) and of students' learning outcomes (Ingvarson, Meiers, & Beavis, 2005). Teachers' capacity building through PD programs is considered essential for implementing pedagocial changes such as IL (Darling-Hammond & McLaughlin, 2011; Dede, 2006; Penuel, Fishman, Yamaguchi, & Gallagher, 2007). Teacher PD has also been recognized specifically as supporting teachers in conducting inquiry-based instruction in science classrooms (Loucks-Horsley, Love, Stiles, Mundry, & Hewson, 2009).

However, before discussing professional learning programs aimed at teaching inquiry, let us take a step back to examine what should be the goals of such programs.

A Theoretical Model of the Knowledge Teachers Need for Teaching Thoughtful Inquiry

An old and widely accepted proposition asserts that "one cannot teach what one does not know." Consequently, it is obvious that teachers need at least some level of familiarity with IL in order to teach it. This however is a simplistic and general assertion. This section elaborates this assertion by discussing a theoretical model with five categories for the knowledge teachers need in order to teach inquiry (see Figure 7.1). It should be noted that when talking about teacher knowledge we're not referring only to theoretical knowledge but also to knowledge in action (Schön, 2005) that is included in PCK. This includes, for example, knowledge of how to implement different aspects of inquiry in the classroom, how to design relevant materials, and how to adjust curriculum to diverse students. The following sections explain each of the categories.

a **Teachers' beliefs about inquiry learning**: Studies have found a variety of teacher beliefs that influence the implementation of IL in the classroom. For example, teachers' views of assessment and their feeling of the need to "teach students for the test" as well as their commitment to "coverage" interfere with devoting the time that is necessary for IL (Anderson, 2002); beliefs regarding teachers' self-efficacy have an effect on the frequency of teachers' IL instruction (Furtado, 2010; Miranda & Damico, 2015); and beliefs concerning students' ability to benefit from IL play a central role in the quantity and depth in which teachers engage in IL with their students (Gutierez, 2015; Arce, Bodner, & Hutchinson, 2014). For example, teachers' belief that only high-achieving students benefit from IL results in a reduced amount and depth of IL lessons when teaching low-achieving students (Zohar, A., Degani, A., & Vaaknin, E.., 2001).

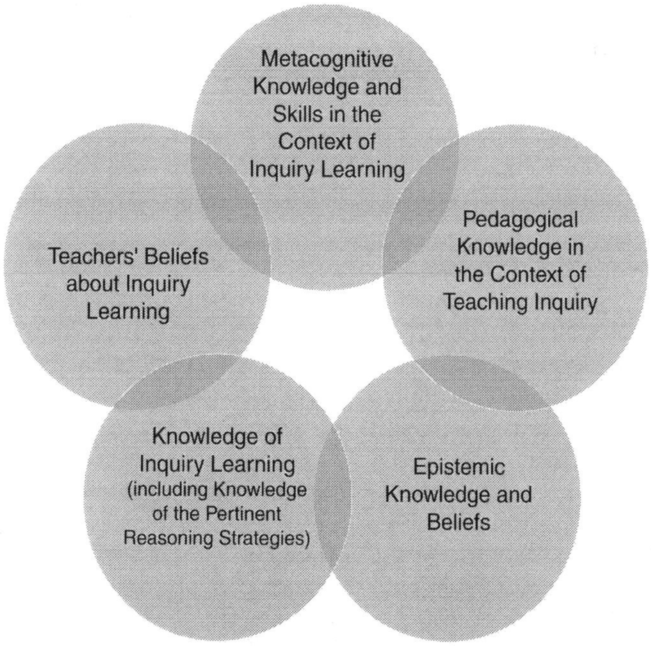

Figure 7.1 Knowledge and beliefs required of teachers in order to teach inquiry

b **Knowledge of inquiry learning (including knowledge of the pertinent thinking strategies)**: One meaning of teachers' knowledge of IL is their own ability to conduct IL. Clearly, teachers have to experience IL first-hand as learners before they can reliably lead students in their investigations (and, as we have noted, teachers rarely experienced IL as learners themselves). A second meaning is teachers' knowledge *about* IL: What are the goals of IL? What constitutes IL and what types of IL exist (i.e., IL, project-based learning or problem-based learning)? This also includes the effectiveness of IL in general and for various age groups and students' ability levels in particular; the connections between IL and subject matter knowledge; and the connections between IL and thinking strategies (i.e., HOT).

The latter component requires further elaboration. Interestingly, the literature about inquiry teaching does not often lean on the vast literature about teaching critical thinking or HOT strategies or skills. Yet, as noted earlier, an examination of more than a hundred years of educational scholarly work about IL shows clearly that even though the terminology used has been constantly changing, cognitive activities that are in fact HOT strategies/skills (according to more recent terminologies) have a central role in many discussions of IL. Without delving into the complexity of the numerous definitions of the concepts involved, it seems intuitive that in all cases, IL consists of a central question that leads to investigation and exploration (e.g., Abd-El-Khalick et al., 2004; Ader, 2013; Tamir & Lunetta, 1978; Schwab, 1962; Germann, Haskins, & Auls, 1996; PRIMAS, 2011). For example, in a recent paper Crawford (2014) offered the following definition of scientific IL:

> Teaching science as inquiry involves engaging students in using critical thinking skills, which includes asking questions, designing and carrying out investigations, interpreting data as evidence, creating arguments, building models, and communicating findings, in the pursuit of deepening their understanding by using logic and evidence about the natural world.
>
> *(Crawford, 2014, p. 515)*

Additional thinking strategies that are often used during IL consist of evaluating the quality and relevance of information sources, integrating information from multiple sources, making comparisons, drawing conclusions, making decisions, and more. In fact, thinking strategies are the building blocks of any sound inquiry process. Consequently, teachers need sound knowledge of the pertinent thinking strategies in order to both conduct investigations and to teach them. As we shall argue in what follows, teachers' insufficient knowledge of the pertinent thinking strategies is one of the main reasons that often makes IL shallow and "mechanical."

What makes the required reasoning even more demanding is that thinking strategies have not only general but also subject-specific characteristics (Fischer, Chinn, Engelmann, & Osborne, 2018). For instance, in order to ask a good inquiry question, teachers (like any other thinker) not only need to know what is a good question in general; they must also understand what type of questions can be asked in particular subjects, because, for example, questions arising while examining historical sources are different from questions asked while conducting scientific investigations. Consequently, the knowledge of how exactly such questions need to be formulated, and what are the criteria for their quality, differs across disciplines. Likewise, in order to formulate high-quality conclusions while carrying out investigations, teachers need to know how to write a good argument, including familiarity with the function of justifications, counterarguments, and refutations. Yet, the nature of justifications, or what counts as evidence in history or in science varies. Teachers' knowledge of inquiry therefore needs to be comprehensive, complex, and, for the most part, subject-specific.

c **Metacognitive knowledge and skills in the context of inquiry learning**: A third component of relevant teachers' knowledge pertains to metacognition. Many studies show that using metacognition in the classroom may improve learning in general (see Veenman, 2011, for review) and learning of higher-order thinking in particular (see Zohar & Barzilai, 2015, for review). Both metacognitive skills—such as planning, monitoring, and evaluating one's thinking—and metacognitive knowledge (Veenman, 2015) are important for this purpose. One of the components of metacognitive knowledge that is particularly significant here is meta-strategic knowledge (MSK). MSK consists of general knowledge about thinking strategies, i.e., *what* is the strategy and *when, why*, and *how* it should be used.

> Going back to the example of students' inquiry about working conditions for teenagers, MSK concerning the conclusions and discussion component of the pertinent inquiry process consists of the following components: (a) knowledge that drawing conclusions calls for argumentation because in order to be valid the statements that comprise the conclusions of an inquiry process must be supported by evidence (i.e., the task characteristics or **when** and **why** to use a thinking strategy); (b) knowledge of what constitutes argumentation and of the "language of thinking" that is associated with it (for example, statement, justification, evidence, explanation, counter argument, refutation, etc., that is **what** is the thinking strategy); (c) knowledge of how to formulate statements (i.e., **how** to use a thinking strategy) and to support them with evidence that come from the empirical data and other information sources students had collected in the preceding parts of their inquiry. At a more advanced stage, students would also need to know how to construct more complex argumentative processes (such as develop counter arguments and refute them, evaluate arguments according to criteria of reliability, truthfulness, clarity and the quality of the relationship between a statement and its supporting evidence). In actually carrying out these thinking processes, students would need to apply their MSK, which is general knowledge about the thinking strategy of argumentation, to their specific investigation, in this case—teens working conditions.

In order to develop such complex knowledge on the part of the students, teachers must first master this knowledge themselves. Teachers need metacognitive skills to actively plan, monitor, evaluate, and regulate their own inquiry processes as well as those of their students and to be able to apply that knowledge to concrete teaching practices. Since inquiry processes are complex and often quite long, learning how to reflect upon them and self-regulate one's progress throughout the various phases of the inquiry cycle is particularly significant (White & Frederiksen, 1998). Teachers, just like other thinkers, also need metacognitive knowledge and, particularly MSK, regarding the particular thinking strategies that they and their students apply during their inquiry processes. It should be noted, however, that metacognitive knowledge and skills are interrelated. For example, one cannot evaluate (i.e., carry out a metacognitive skill) the ways they had used a particular thinking strategy during inquiry if they do not have the general meta-level knowledge of just what that thinking strategy entails and of when and how that thinking strategy should be used. For example, the general meta-level knowledge about argumentation described earlier can help a student in evaluating a conclusion he or she had written in his or her inquiry paper by asking himself or herself questions such as: *does the evidence I obtained from interviewing 20 teenagers support the conclusion I wrote? And does my explanation of how the evidence support the conclusion make sense and is it expressed clearly?* In the absence of the relevant MSK, efforts to evaluate the quality of one's conclusions cannot be fruitful.

d **Teachers' epistemic cognition**: Epistemic cognition is an umbrella term for epistemic beliefs, epistemic development, and personal epistemology. It is defined by many as individuals' knowledge about the nature of knowledge and how one comes to know (Bondy et al., 2007; Hofer, 2001; Hofer & Pintrich, 1997; Pintrich, 2002; Schommer, 1990). It is a wide and complex construct that refers to knowledge about what knowledge is; about the way it is constructed; how it is processed, stored, and evaluated; how simple or complex it is; and how certain it is, as well as beliefs about the way people achieve a state of knowing (Bondy et al., 2007). Research has shown relationships between epistemic cognition and cognitive processes of thinking and reasoning and of metacognitive processes (Barzilai & Zohar, 2014; Hofer, 2001; Hofer & Pintrich, 1997; Kuhn, 1990, 1999; Schommer, 1990). More specifically, IL clearly requires a sophisticated epistemic view of knowledge that is tentative, actively constructed, and based on evidence rather than a simplistic view of knowledge as fixed and based on authority. Inquiry environments that include argumentation activities involve more attention to epistemic-sophisticated thinking, because they require learners to explicitly address competing explanations and claims (Tabak & Weinstock, 2011).

Practicing teachers' epistemic cognition has been shown to influence their teaching approach, the strategies they employ in the classroom, and their expectations for students (Brownlee, Ferguson, & Ryan, 2017). There is strong evidence that teachers' epistemic knowledge has an impact on their instructional decisions and classroom interactions (Brickhouse, 1990; Hashweh, 1996; Hofer & Pintrich, 1997; King & Kitchener, 2004). Among other things, teachers' epistemic knowledge has been shown to affect their use of teaching strategies (Hashweh, 1996) and their students' use of higher-level thinking skills and of IL (Maor & Taylor, 1995; Bondy et al., 2007). Teachers with more sophisticated epistemic knowledge were found to be more democratic, empathetic, innovative, able to use more effective teaching strategies, and more able to conceive of teaching as facilitating rather than transmitting knowledge (for example, use many open-ended activities; encourage students to think and to solve problems). Teachers who hold less sophisticated epistemic knowledge were more likely to hold perceptions of teaching as a simple act of transmitting knowledge (Brownlee & Berthelson, 2006; Richardson, 2003) and lack the understanding of the nature of knowledge or the ways of reasoning that would enable them to make evidence-based, defensible judgments. Feucht (2011) also showed specific links between teachers' epistemic cognition and practice. It was found that teachers' holding absolutist views of knowledge as true and stable resulted in "step-by-step recipe" instruction and asking questions to determine "correct understanding."

e **Pedagogical knowledge in the context of teaching inquiry**: The knowledge components described in the previous sections are necessary rather than sufficient for active classroom instruction. What is missing is pedagogical knowledge that enables teachers to actively lead inquiry-related activities in the classroom. In the areas of teaching HOT and metacognition one of us had suggested in previous studies to use the term "pedagogical knowledge in the context of teaching HOT and/or metacognition" rather than the term pedagogical content knowledge (PCK) (Zohar & Barzilai, 2015). This term delineates the distinctive nature of teachers' knowledge in this area that has unique characteristics and is neither general nor content-specific pedagogical knowledge. Our analysis indicates that a similar term—"pedagogical knowledge in the context of teaching inquiry"—is appropriate for the present discussion.

Because IL is a form of constructivist learning, many principles of instruction aimed at fostering constructivist learning are relevant for teaching inquiry. One prominent principle is a radical change in teachers' role from transmitting information to leading students' active knowledge construction. As IL in classrooms often takes the form of students' collaborative work, knowledge of how to lead fruitful students' collaboration is essential. More specifically, teachers need to know how to lead students through the various stages of the inquiry cycle; how to tailor the degree of openness of an inquiry task to students' needs, age, and ability; how to support students in using the thinking strategies they need to apply; how to design relevant investigations; how to connect deep subject matter knowledge to students' investigations, how to assess IL, and how to make IL accessible to all learners. Another (related) principle of instruction that teachers must master for fruitful IL is scaffolding. Extensive scaffolding reduces the considerable cognitive load characterizing IL and allows students to learn in complex domains (Hmelo-Silver, Duncan, & Chin, 2007). Scaffolding is also significant for adjusting IL to students of diverse cultural backgrounds and levels of academic achievements.

Finally, because (as explained earlier) reasoning and metacognition have such an important role in meaningful IL, pedagogical knowledge in the context of teaching HOT and metacognition is essential for planning, teaching, and assessing IL (Zohar, 2007; Zohar & Barzilai, 2015). One principle of such pedagogical knowledge pertains to deliberate attention to general thinking structures and skills. As they engage with a variety of inquiry teaching situations that are often "messy" in terms of their rich contents and inquiry-related activities, teachers need to be able to clearly maintain in their minds the relevant general thinking strategies. Such awareness contributes to teachers' ability to treat thinking strategies and metacognition in the classroom in an intentional and planned way, rather than intuitively. A second principle is knowledge of how to foster students' explicit awareness of the type of cognitive and metacognitive procedures being used. The explicitness helps make learners' thinking visible and an object for reflection, discussion, and evaluation. In terms of teaching practices, the construction of thinking strategies and of metacognitive knowledge and skills can be mediated by: (a) explicit discussions of the generalizations and rules that are relevant to a thinking strategy, (b) naming the thinking strategies and engaging students with additional aspects of the "language of thinking," and (c) discussing explanations as to when, why, and how the thinking strategy should be used. In addition, teachers need to know how to apply metacognitive prompts and reflective writing. Explicitness is also regarded in the literature as an important instructional approach for remedying limitations in learners' personal epistemology. Researchers suggest that in order to overcome such limitations teachers should encourage reflection and debate on epistemic practices (e.g., Brownlee, Ferguson, & Ryan, 2017; Chinn & Buckland, 2012; Khishfe & Abd-El-Khalick, 2002).

Our model shows the width and depth of the knowledge teachers need for quality teaching of IL. Theoretically, PD programs need to target all aspects of this knowledge in order to prepare teachers for IL in an effective way. In order to find out whether and in what ways PD programs indeed address the various components of the model, we reviewed a number of recent studies. The following section presents this review.

Examination of Professional Development (PD) Programs

Many existing PD programs attempt to offer teachers support in introducing IL to the classroom or in refining existing inquiry instruction. Moreover, a great amount of resources (both time and money) has been spent on such programs, and yet studies systematically assessing their effectiveness are still scarce (Capps et al., 2012).

For the purpose of this review, we evaluated empirical studies pertaining to PD interventions designed to support teachers in the instruction of IL. We searched for peer-reviewed studies from the last decade (2008–2017) relevant to IL instruction in schools. This search located 25 relevant articles. The analysis was based on features of effective inquiry PD (see Table 7.1) provided by previous studies (Darling-Hammond & McLaughlin, 1995; Garet, Porter, Desimone, Birman, & Yoon, 2001; Loucks-Horsley et al., 1999; Penuel et al., 2007), alongside themes which arose from close reading of the articles. The first round of analyses revealed very little explicit attention to teacher thinking, and the significance of that preliminary finding led us to conduct a deeper examination of this issue. An additional reading of all papers was therefore conducted focusing on detecting and analyzing references to teacher thinking.

Review of the Programs

Program Characteristics

An examination of the 25 studies indicated that they were overall well aligned with the features of PD that are highly recommended by the collective research in this area (see Capps et al., 2012 for review). Frequent features included classroom implementation (23/25), teachers' active participation in inquiry (22/25), reflection (19/25), developing lesson plans (18/25), and extended contact and support (11/21).[2]

It was also evident that the majority of PDs were aimed at practicing teachers rather than preservice teachers and that all PD programs were conducted within a specific discipline. The length of the PD programs varied greatly from five lessons in a preservice course to three years of participation in an ongoing PD program.

Table 7.1 provides an overview of several central pedagogical characteristics and whether and how frequently they were manifested in the 25 reviewed PDs. Table 7.2 provides a list of the articles used in the IL PD review (see p. 122).

Beliefs and Knowledge in the PDs

An overview of the goals and questions of the studies we reviewed reveals that the most prevalent research goal addressed teacher beliefs (20/25). A large emphasis was put on the significance of teachers' beliefs in affecting their learning in the PDs and in shaping their classroom actions. Most frequently, studies examined teachers' beliefs regarding NOS (n = 11), which often went hand in hand with epistemic beliefs (n = 8), self-efficacy beliefs regarding teachers' ability to teach through inquiry (n = 10), and beliefs concerning their students' ability to learn through inquiry (n = 8). In addition, programs addressed, and studies examined, teacher beliefs and conceptions regarding the effectivity of IL (n = 5), teachers' beliefs regarding what inquiry teaching is (n = 4), and more general beliefs regarding the nature of learning and teaching (n = 4).

Obstacles for Implementation

The studies identified numerous factors perceived as inhibiting the implementation of IL. Some were external factors such as time limitations in the classroom due to curriculum pressures, state standards and high-stakes testing (n = 10), lack of time for planning (n = 4), and lack of cooperation or support from superiors, including lack of funding and resources (n = 5). Students' motivation and abilities as perceived by the teachers were also stated as challenges for implementing inquiry in the classroom (n = 6). In terms of teachers' beliefs, self-efficacy (e.g., fear of conducing inquiry in contents that teachers are not knowledgeable about) (n = 10) and epistemic beliefs (n = 4) were most significant.

Yet shortcomings in teachers' knowledge appeared to be the most central obstacle, with teachers and researchers identifying deficiencies in a number of elements: content knowledge (n = 5), knowledge regarding the process of scientific inquiry (n = 6), and pedagogical knowledge in the context of teaching inquiry (n = 15). The pedagogical knowledge addressed by the studies consisted of the following issues: development of learning units, guidance through open or semi-structured inquiry, assessing and monitoring of students' progress and learning outcomes,

Table 7.1 The manifestation of central pedagogical characteristics in the 25 reviewed PDs

Pedagogical characteristic	*Number of PD programs in which the characteristic/feature was or was not manifested*		*Notes*
	Manifested	*Was not manifested*	
Active participation in inquiry	22	3	Significant variance in the type of inquiry in which teachers participated (ranging from conducting the inquiry expected of their students[a] to conducting teachers' own research alongside scientists).
Taught within specific disciplinary content	25	0	The promotion of inquiry in a specific discipline indicates an understanding that instruction of innovative pedagogies and of skills needs to be combined with the conceptual parts of the curriculum. All but one of the PDs were in the sciences, an issue which requires further examining.
Long-term contact and support	11/21	10/21	Teachers' main claim was that the follow-ups assisted in supporting the practice of inquiry in their classrooms by helping to counterbalance the challenges teachers face in teaching IL.
Lesson plan development	18	7	Was regarded as essential so that the teachers would be able to take what they had learnt "in theory" and make it happen in their own classrooms.
Application of the acquired knowledge in a classroom setting	23	2	Application served multiple goals, such as practicing new strategies, tackling obstacles with expert guidance, and increasing self-efficacy.
Reflection	17	8	Reflection (either collaborative or individual) was used to connect teachers' theory and practice, evaluate their teaching or students' learning, and infrequently to reflect metacognitively on chosen inquiry strategies.
Stage	21 In-service	4 Preservice	Suggests a perception that a teacher must have significant previous knowledge in order to teach inquiry or to be able to benefit from an inquiry learning PD and could perhaps imply that teacher education programs do not trust that their preservice teachers hold sufficient knowledge.

a Crawford and Capps (2012) consider this type of teacher inquiry as participation in modeling of IL and not as participation in "authentic inquiry."

incorporating students' prior knowledge, distinguishing between teachers' and students' roles in science-based inquiry classes, scaffolding the lesson so that all students can feel involved, and guiding students to see the importance and benefits of scientific inquiry. Deficiencies in teacher knowledge were overall the most frequently considered obstacle in the implementation of authentic classroom inquiry; more than all external factors combined and more than teachers' beliefs.

Table 7.2 Articles used in the IL PD review

#	*Article reference*
1	Eckhoff, A. (2017). Partners in inquiry: A collaborative life science investigation with preservice teachers and kindergarten students. *Early Childhood Education Journal, 45*(2), 219–227. https://doi.org/10.1007/s10643-015-0769-3
2	Schmidt, M., & Fulton, L. (2016). Transforming a traditional inquiry-based science unit into a STEM unit for elementary pre-service teachers: A view from the trenches. *Journal of Science Education and Technology, 25*(2), 302–315. https://doi.org/10.1007/s10956-015-9594-0
3	McKeown, T. R., Abrams, L. M., Slattum, P. W., & Kirk, S. V. (2016). Enhancing teacher beliefs through an inquiry-based professional development program. *Journal of Education in Science, Environment and Health (JESEH), 2*(1), 85–97. https://doi.org/10.21891/jeseh.30143
4	Kazempour, M., & Amirshokoohi, A. (2013). Exploring elementary pre-service teachers' experiences and learning outcomes in a revised inquiry-based science lesson: An action research. *Journal of Education and Learning, 2*(2), 144. https://doi.org/10.5539/jel.v2n2p144
5	Hollingsworth, H. L., & Vandermaas-Peeler, M. (2017). "Almost everything we do includes inquiry": Fostering inquiry-based teaching and learning with preschool teachers. *Early Child Development and Care, 187*(1), 152–167. https://doi.org/10.1080/03004430.2016.1154049
6	Peters-Burton, E. E., Merz, S. A., Ramirez, E. M., & Saroughi, M. (2015). The effect of cognitive apprenticeship-based professional development on teacher self-efficacy of science teaching, motivation, knowledge calibration, and perceptions of inquiry-based teaching. *Journal of Science Teacher Education, 26*(6), 525–548. https://doi.org/10.1007/s10972-015-9436-1
7	Blanchard, M. R., Southerland, S. A., & Granger, E. M. (2009). No silver bullet for inquiry: Making sense of teacher change following an inquiry-based research experience for teachers. *Science Education, 93*(2), 322–360. https://doi.org/10.1002/sce.20298
8	Gutierez, S. B. (2015). Collaborative professional learning through lesson study: Identifying the challenges of inquiry-based teaching. *Issues in Educational Research, 25*(2), 118–134.
9	Brand, B. R., & Moore, S. J. (2011). Enhancing teachers' application of inquiry-based strategies using a constructivist sociocultural professional development model. *International Journal of Science Education, 33*(7), 889–913. https://doi.org/10.1080/09500691003739374
10	Nichols, K., Burgh, G., & Kennedy, C. (2017). Comparing two inquiry professional development interventions in science on primary students' questioning and other inquiry behaviours. *Research in Science Education, 47*(1), 1–24. https://doi.org/10.1007/s11165-015-9487-5
11	Preston, L., Harvie, K., & Wallace, H. (2015). Inquiry-based learning in teacher education: A primary humanities example. *Australian Journal of Teacher Education, 40*(12), 6. https://doi.org/10.14221/ajte.2015v40n12.6
12	Ødegaard, M., Haug, B., Mork, S. M., & Sørvik, G. O. (2014). Challenges and support when teaching science through an integrated inquiry and literacy approach. *International Journal of Science Education, 36*(18), 2997–3020. https://doi.org/10.1080/09500693.2014.942719
13	Wuttiprom, S., Wuttisela, K., Phonchaiya, S., Athiwaspong, W., Chitaree, R., & Sharma, M. D. (2016). Preliminary results of professional development program for school science research. *Universal Journal of Educational Research, 4*(4), 842–848. https://doi.org/10.13189/ujer.2016.040421
14	Clayton, C. D., Kilbane, J., & McCarthy, M. R. (2017). Growing into inquiry: Stories of secondary school teachers using inquiry for themselves and their students. *Journal of Inquiry and Action in Education, 8*(2), 1.
15	Almuntasheri, S., Gillies, R. M., & Wright, T. (2016). The effectiveness of a guided inquiry-based, teachers' professional development programme on Saudi students' understanding of density. *Science Education International, 27*(1), 16–39.
16	Yezierski, E. J., & Herrington, D. G. (2011). Improving practice with target inquiry: High school chemistry teacher professional development that works. *Chemistry Education Research and Practice, 12*(3), 344–354. https://doi.org/10.1039/C1RP90041B

#	*Article reference*
17	Arce, J., Bodner, G. M., & Hutchinson, K. (2014). A study of the impact of inquiry-based professional development experiences on the beliefs of intermediate science teachers about "Best Practices" for classroom teaching. *International Journal of Education in Mathematics, Science and Technology, 2*(2).
18	Kazempour, M. (2009). Impact of inquiry-based professional development on core conceptions and teaching practices: A case study. *Science Educator, 18*(2), 56.
19	Capitelli, S., Hooper, P., Rankin, L., Austin, M., & Caven, G. (2016). Understanding the development of a hybrid practice of inquiry-based science instruction and language development: A case study of one teacher's journey through reflections on classroom practice. *Journal of Science Teacher Education, 27*(3), 283–302. https://doi.org/10.1007/s10972-016-9460-9
20	Van Der Valk, T., & De Jong, O. (2009). Scaffolding science teachers in open-inquiry teaching. *International Journal of Science Education, 31*(6), 829–850. https://doi.org/10.1080/09500690802287155
21	Pérez, M. d. Carmen B., & Furman, M. (2016). What is a scientific experiment? the impact of a professional development course on teachers' ability to design an inquiry-based science curriculum. *International Journal of Environmental and Science Education, 11*(6), 1387–1401. https://doi.org/10.12973/ijese.2016.353a
22	Lotter, C. R., & Miller, C. (2017). Improving inquiry teaching through reflection on practice. *Research in Science Education, 47*(4), 913–942. https://doi.org/10.1007/s11165-016-9533-y
23	Furtado, L. (2010). Kindergarten teachers' perceptions of an inquiry-based science teaching and learning professional development intervention. *New Horizons in Education, 58*(2), 104–120.
24	Seraphin, K. D., Philippoff, J., Kaupp, L., & Vallin, L. M. (2012). Metacognition as means to increase the effectiveness of inquiry-based science education. *Science Education International, 23*(4), 366–382.
25	Miranda, R. J., & Damico, J. B. (2015). Changes in teachers' beliefs and classroom practices concerning inquiry-based instruction following a year-long RET-PLC program. *Science Educator, 24*(1), 23.

Teachers' Thinking

In their literature reviews, all papers but one addressed the reasoning processes required of students when conducting inquiry. They frequently listed a variety of skills/procedures students need to carry out, such as identifying and asking questions, designing and conducting investigations, choosing appropriate tools, learning to develop logical conclusions, and communicating understandings to peers. Most papers ($n = 19$) also used terms related to higher-order thinking, reasoning, or critical thinking, though fewer were explicit in characterizing the relations between HOT and IL and in defining inquiry as consisting of higher-order thinking strategies. Yet, despite prevalent acknowledgment of the theoretical central role of reasoning in thoughtful inquiry, elaborations on the means by which teachers might achieve this goal were significantly less frequent.

Considering the central role these papers attributed to goals involving students' thinking, one would have expected to see how these goals are expressed de facto in the PD programs by devoting ample efforts to develop teachers' ability to foster students' thinking. However, in comparison to the frequency of addressing students' thinking in the theoretical part of the studies, the frequency of addressing teacher thinking during the PD was substantially lower. Less than half of the papers recognized the importance of addressing teachers' thinking and/or provided evidence that the PD programs promoted teacher engagement with higher-order thinking in a practical way. Of the 12 papers that did address teachers' thinking, five engaged predominantly with teachers' pedagogical thinking, attempting to understand or affect teachers' pedagogical reasoning and decision-making. An emphasis on teacher reflection in a manner that puts teachers' own thinking at the forefront was described in two papers, both focusing on reflection as a tool for pedagogical development. Two papers very explicitly recognized the importance of teachers' engagement in thinking about the inquiry process but did not follow through by addressing the knowledge teachers need to support such practices in the classroom. Two other papers addressed teachers' thinking about the inquiry process but included no evidence of in-depth engagement with the thinking strategies required for each step.

Finally, only three of the 25 papers included reference of activities that engaged teachers with the thinking strategies comprising the inquiry process—for example, "using techniques to gather, analyse, and interpret data, developing descriptions, explanations, predictions, and models grounded on evidence, thinking critically and logically to make relations between evidence and explanations, recognizing and analysing alternative explanations and predictions" (Wuttiprom et al., 2016, p. 842). In these papers, we detected active use of thinking strategies on the cognitive, procedural level by way of examples of the questions used during the PDs (e.g., "How do you explain the flotation of the popped popcorn? What evidence supports your explanation?" "How could the mass and volume of the popped and un-popped popcorn be compared?" "If the masses of both were almost the same, what do you think was the cause of the flotation of the popped corn?" (Almuntasheri, Gillies, & Wright, 2016, p. 24).

One IL PD program (Seraphin et al., 2012) stood out with its engagement with teachers' metacognition. In this PD program, teachers were taught to "help students evaluate and decide which inquiry techniques to use during their investigations." Yet teachers' meta-level knowledge about thinking skills (MSK) was not highlighted by any of the papers, neither explicitly nor implicitly. For example, the MSK regarding argumentation discussed earlier was not the goal of any of the papers, nor was the MSK regarding any other thinking skill.

Considering the central role of reasoning we found in the theoretical sections of the papers we reviewed, as well as the findings from previous studies documenting ample challenges in teachers' knowledge of thinking strategies and in their pedagogical knowledge in the context of teaching HOT and metacognition, this finding is alarming.

Summary, Discussion, and Implications

Teachers' knowledge base for teaching was rarely addressed: It was encouraging to see that the PD programs we reviewed aligned with many of the features of effective PDs. It was also reassuring that the programs had embraced the understanding that it is essential to acknowledge teachers' beliefs and to address them in a substantial way. However, in contrast to the wide recognition of the significance of teachers' beliefs, teachers' knowledge base for teaching was only rarely addressed. In the studies we reviewed, deficiencies in teacher knowledge were overall the most frequently considered obstacle in the implementation of authentic classroom inquiry and, still, teacher knowledge was a central variable of examination in only ten of the 25 studies. These finding together are of great importance.

Insufficient explicit engagement with higher-order thinking: Genuine, thinking-rich inquiry relies on various thinking strategies. In order to lead thoughtful IL, teachers need sufficient explicit knowledge and deep understanding of complex strategies (as demonstrated by the example of argumentation provided earlier). Such knowledge cannot be achieved by providing teachers with specialized materials and reconstructed curriculum units alone (Zech, Gause-Vega, Bray, Secules, & Goldman, 2000). If our goal is to develop teachers who will be able to support genuine, thinking-rich inquiry rather than merely playing the role of "inquiry-technicians," sufficient PD must be provided. Yet the PD programs we reviewed facilitated only limited explicit engagement with teachers' higher-order thinking. Of the papers that addressed teachers' thinking, most addressed pedagogical thinking or reflective thinking or merely stated the importance of addressing teachers' reasoning but de facto did not act upon that statement. The programs in which teachers did engage with inquiry-related reasoning were few, and even in those programs explicit engagement with MSK was insufficient.

Promoting IL that can support genuine thinking requires deep involvement with the thinking strategies which make up the inquiry process. When teachers do not engage with this knowledge in an explicit way, the chances of student engagement are meager. As we stated earlier, teachers need sound knowledge of the pertinent thinking strategies in order to conduct their own sound inquiry and in order to teach it. Meta-strategic knowledge is essential for teachers so that they can plan and regulate their own inquiry processes and that of their students and for making effective decisions regarding the choice and use of appropriate thinking strategies. Teachers' practice and modeling of inquiry-related thinking strategies in the classroom, and the direct and explicit reference to such strategies, has a beneficial effect on the development of students' higher-order thinking as well as on their NOS and epistemic beliefs (Baumfield, 2015; Crawford, 2016; Zohar & Barzilai, 2015).

To achieve a slightly more concrete understanding of what fostering such knowledge in the setting of a PD might look like, we provide a short description of a relevant PD. *In recent years, we have experimented with various PD programs that foster the pertinent knowledge for both pre- and in-service teachers. Our experiences point to several components that seem to be useful. According to the time allocated, these programs consist of the following components: (a): Teachers (working in small groups) engage in ample opportunities of experiencing metacognitive thinking "as learners." In these experiences, teachers engage in short IL activities requiring the activation of various HOT skills on both the cognitive and the metacognitive levels. (b) Teachers study some theoretical concepts and ideas related to IL, HOT, and metacognition. (c) Teachers study about various ways to promote students' HOT and metacognition. The latter two components employ both "top-down" deductive instruction and inductive instruction in which teachers discuss their own learning experiences and construct from them explicit principles of thinking and of instruction. For example, teachers may receive data regarding the exploitation of teenagers' labor rights in a certain town, and they discuss the data and draw conclusions. Then, through guided activities, teachers will assess their work, leading to a conceptualizing of the MSK regarding argumentation and the criteria of a good argument. Similarly, working on a different concrete topic such as a contaminated water source, they may experience activities aimed at additional thinking skills (such as asking research questions or making comparisons). Then, through reflections and discussions, teachers (led by the workshop's leader) construct the pedagogical knowledge used in the learning activities they had participated in. (d) "Creative workshops" in which small groups of teachers apply the knowledge constructed in stages a to c to design new learning activities in additional concrete topics. (e) Throughout the programs teachers try out some of the learning activities in their classrooms and then discuss these lessons and reflect on them.*

Going back to Figure 7.1, we can see that these PD programs target at least three of the knowledge components presented in the theoretical model of the knowledge teachers need for teaching thoughtful inquiry: knowledge of IL (including knowledge of the pertinent reasoning thinking strategies), metacognitive knowledge and skills in the context of IL, and pedagogical knowledge in the context of teaching inquiry.

In conclusion, we found that PD programs rarely address the knowledge teachers need to support thoughtful inquiry. It is important to clarify that there is no claim that these programs are necessarily shallow or technical and do not require teachers to think. Rather we claim that there is a lack of explicit and systematic engagement with pertinent higher-order thinking and metacognition and with developing teachers' pedagogical knowledge in these contexts. We also note that time in PD programs is often a significant constraint, and, therefore, goals should be adjusted in a thoughtful manner so that they may be dealt with in profound and significant ways and not become technical. Yet the scarcity of addressing the crucial components we discussed can be explained by a lack of acknowledgment of the significance of the relevant teachers' knowledge for sound inquiry teaching and/or by a lack of know-how to foster that knowledge in PDs. We argue that in either case our findings highlight the need for change. If teachers are to facilitate and support students' reasoning, more time and attention in PD programs must be paid to supporting the development of teachers' own strategic and metacognitive thinking and to their pedagogical knowledge in these contexts. These issues must therefore become prevalent and explicit goals in future PDs in the area of IL.

Notes

1 This chapter was written with the support of the Besen Family endowment for Integrated Studies in Education and the Reaserch Center on Teachers' Learning and Development, the Seymour Fox School of Education, Hebrew University of Jerusalem.

2 Ten of 21 PDs for in-service teachers.

References

Abd-El-Khalick, F., Boujaoude, S., Duschl, R., Lederman, N. G., Mamlok-Naaman, R., Hofstein, A., ... & Tuan, H. L. (2004). Inquiry in science education: International perspectives. *Science Education, 88*(3), 397–419. https://doi.org/10.1002/sce.10118

Ader. E. (2013). A framework for understanding teachers' promotion of students' metacognition. *International Journal for Mathematics Teaching and Learning.* http://www.cimt.org.uk/journal/ader.pdf (ERIC)

Adey, P., & Shayer, M. (2006). *Really raising standards: Cognitive intervention and academic achievement.* London: Routledge. https://doi.org/10.4324/9780203137284

Almuntasheri, S., Gillies, R. M., & Wright, T. (2016). The effectiveness of a guided inquiry-based, teachers' professional development programme on Saudi students' understanding of density. *Science Education International, 27*(1), 16–39.

American Association for the Advancement of Science (AAAS). (1990). *Science for all Americans.* New York: Oxford University Press.

Anderson, R. D. (2002). Reforming science teaching: What research says about inquiry. *Journal of Science Teacher Education, 13*(1), 1–12. https://doi.org/10.1023/ A:1015171124982

Arce, J., Bodner, G. M., & Hutchinson, K. (2014). A Study of the Impact of Inquiry-Based Professional Development Experiences on the Beliefs of Intermediate Science Teachers about' Best Practices' for Classroom Teaching. *International Journal of Education in Mathematics, Science and Technology, 2*(2).

Australian Curriculum, Assessment and Reporting Authority (ACARA). (2012). National report on schooling in Australia 2012.

Banilower, E. R., Heck, D. J., & Weiss, I. R. (2007). Can professional development make the vision of the standards a reality? The impact of the national science foundation's local systemic change through teacher enhancement initiative. *Journal of Research in Science Teaching: The Official Journal of the National Association for Research in Science Teaching, 44*(3), 375–395. https://doi.org/10.1002/tea.20145

Barzilai, S., & Zohar, A. (2014). Reconsidering personal epistemology as metacognition: A multifaceted approach to the analysis of epistemic thinking. *Educational Psychologist, 49*(1), 13–35. https://doi.org/10.1080/00461520.2013.863265

Baumfield, V. (2015). Tools for inquiry: The role of thinking skills approaches in developing pedagogy as theory. In Rupert Wegerif Li Li and James C. Kaufman (Eds.) *The Routledge international handbook of research on teaching thinking* (pp. 95–103). London: Routledge.

Bloom, B. S. (1956). *Taxonomy of educational objectives. Vol. 1: Cognitive domain.* New York: McKay, 20–24.

Bondy, E., Ross, D., Adams, A., Nowak, R., Brownell, M., Hoppey, D., Kuhel, K., McCallum, C., & Stafford, L. (2007). Personal epistemologies and learning to teach. *Teacher Education and Special Education, 30*(2), 67–82. https://doi.org/10.1177/088840640703000202

Brickhouse, N. W. (1990). Teachers' beliefs about the nature of science and their relationship to classroom practice. *Journal of Teacher Education, 41*(3), 53–62. https://doi.org/10.1177/002248719004100307

Brownlee, J., & Berthelsen, D. (2006). Personal epistemology and relational pedagogy in early childhood teacher education programs. *Early Years, 26*(1), 17–29. https://doi.org/10.1080/09575140500507785

Brownlee, L. J., Ferguson, L. E., & Ryan, M. (2017). Changing teachers' epistemic cognition: A new conceptual framework for epistemic reflexivity. *Educational Psychologist, 52*(4), 242–252.

Calder, N. (2015). Student wonderings: Scaffolding student understanding within student-centred inquiry learning. *ZDM, 47*(7), 1121–1131. https://doi.org/10.1080/00461520.2017.1333430

Callahan, C., Saye, J., & Brush, T. (2016). Interactive and collaborative professional development for in-service history teachers. *The Social Studies, 107*(6), 227–243. https://doi.org/10.1080/00377996.2016.1214905

Capps, D. K., Crawford, B. A., & Constas, M. A. (2012). A review of empirical literature on inquiry professional development: Alignment with best practices and a critique of the findings. *Journal of Science Teacher Education, 23*(3), 291–318. https://doi.org/10.1007/s10972-012-9275-2

Capps, D. K., & Crawford, B. A. (2013). Inquiry-based instruction and teaching about nature of science: Are they happening? *Journal of Science Teacher Education, 24*(3), 497–526. https://doi.org/10.1007/s10972-012-9314-z

Chinn, C. A., & Buckland, L. A. (2012). Model-based instruction: Fostering change in evolutionary conceptions and in epistemic practices. In Rosengren, K. S., Brem, S. K., Evans, E. M., & Sinatra, G. M. (Eds.) *Evolution Challenges: Integrating Research and Practice in Teaching and Learning about Evolution* (pp. 211–232). Oxford University Press.

Chinn, C. A., & Malhotra, B. A. (2002). Epistemologically authentic inquiry in schools: A theoretical framework for evaluating inquiry tasks. *Science Education, 86*(2), 175–218. https://doi.org/10.1002/sce.10001

Crawford, B., & Capps, D. (2018). Teacher cognition of engaging children in scientific practices. In Dori, J., Mevarech, Z., & Baker D. (Eds.) *Cognition, metacognition, and culture in STEM education* (pp. 9–32). New York: Springer.

Crawford, B. A. (2000). Embracing the essence of inquiry: New roles for science teachers. *Journal of Research in Science Teaching: The Official Journal of the National Association for Research in Science Teaching, 37*(9), 916–937. https://doi.org/10.1002/1098-2736(200011)37:9<916::aid-tea4>3.0.co;2-2

Crawford, B. A. (2007). Learning to teach science as inquiry in the rough and tumble of practice. *Journal of Research in Science Teaching, 44*(4), 613–642. https://doi.org/10.1002/tea.20157

Crawford, B. A. (2014). Invited chapter. From inquiry to scientific practices in the science classroom. In N. Lederman & S. Abell (Eds.), *Handbook of research on science education.* Vol. II. New York: Routledge. https://doi.org/10.4324/9780203097267.ch26

Crawford, B. A. (2016, January). Supporting teachers in inquiry/science practices, modeling, and complex reasoning in science classrooms. South Africa, Pretoria: Paper Presented at the Southern Africa Association of Maths, Science, and Technology Education Annual Conference.

Danker, B. (2015). Using flipped classroom approach to explore deep learning in large classrooms. *IAFOR Journal of Education, 3*(1), 171–186. https://doi.org/10.22492/ije.3.1.10

Darling-Hammond, L., & McLaughlin, M. W. (1995). Policies that support professional development in an era of reform. *Phi delta kappan, 76*(8), 597–604. https://doi.org/10.1177/003172171109200622

Darling-Hammond, L., & McLaughlin, M. W. (2011). Policies that support professional development in an era of reform. *Phi delta kappan, 92*(6), 81–92. https://doi.org/10.1177/003172171109200622

Dede, C. (2006). *Online professional development for teachers: Emerging models and methods.* Cambridge, MA: Harvard Education Press. https://doi.org/10.5860/choice.44-3983

Desimone, L. M. (2009). Improving impact studies of teachers' professional development: Toward better conceptualizations and measures. *Educational Researcher, 38*(3), 181–199. https://doi.org/10.3102/0013189X08331140

Dewey, J. (1902). *The child and the curriculum (No. 5).* Chicago, IL: University of Chicago Press.

Dewey, J. (1910). Science as subject-matter and as method. *Science, 31*(787), 121–127.

Dewey, J. (1938). *Logic, the theory of inquiry.* New York: H. Holt and Company, 9, 104–105.

Duncan, R. G., Pilitsis, V., & Piegaro, M. (2010). Development of preservice teachers' ability to critique and adapt inquiry-based instructional materials. *Journal of Science Teacher Education, 21*(1), 81–102. https://doi.org/10.1007/s10972-009-9153-8

Feucht, F. C. (2011). The epistemic underpinnings of Mrs. M's reading lesson. on drawing conclusions: A classroom-based research study. In J. Lunn Brownlee, G. Schraw, & D. Berthelsen (Eds.), *Personal epistemology and teacher education* (pp. 3–21). New York: Routledge.

Fischer, F., Chinn, C. A., Engelmann, K., & Osborne, J. (Eds.). (2018). *Scientific reasoning and argumentation: The roles of domain-specific and domain-general knowledge.* London: Routledge.

Furtado, L. (2010). Kindergarten teachers' perceptions of an inquiry-based science teaching and learning professional development intervention. *New Horizons in Education, 58*(2), 104–120.

Garet, M. S., Porter, A. C., Desimone, L., Birman, B. F., & Yoon, K. S. (2001). What makes professional development effective? Results from a national sample of teachers. *American Educational Research Journal, 38*(4), 915–945. https://doi.org/10.3102/00028312038004915

Germann, P. J., Haskins, S., & Auls, S. (1996). Analysis of nine high school biology laboratory manuals: Promoting scientific inquiry. *Journal of Research in Science Teaching: The Official Journal of the National Association for Research in Science Teaching, 33*(5), 475–499. https://doi.org/10.1002/(SICI)1098-2736(199605)33:5<475::AID-TEA2>3.0.CO;2-O

Gutierez, S. B. (2015). Collaborative professional learning through lesson study: Identifying the challenges of inquiry-based teaching. *Issues in Educational Research, 25*(2), 118–134.

Gyllenpalm, J., Wickman, P. O., & Holmgren, S. O. (2010). Teachers' language on scientific inquiry: Methods of teaching or methods of inquiry? *International Journal of Science Education, 32*(9), 1151–1172. https://doi.org/10.1080/09500690902977457

Hashweh, M. Z. (1996). Effects of science teachers' epistemological beliefs in teaching. *Journal of Research in Science Teaching: The Official Journal of the National Association for Research in Science Teaching, 33*(1), 47–63. https://doi.org/10.1002/(sici)1098-2736(199601)33:1<47::aid-tea3>3.0.co;2-p

Heid, K., Estabrook, M., & Nostrant, C. (2009). Dancing with line: Inquiry, democracy, and aesthetic development as an approach to art education. *International Journal of Education & the Arts, 10* (Portrayal 3). Retrieved [28.2.2021] from http://www.ijea.org/v10p3/.

Hofer, B. K. (2001). Personal epistemology research: Implications for learning and teaching. *Educational Psychology Review, 13*(4), 353–383. https://doi.org/10.1023/A:1011965830686

Hofer, B. K., & Pintrich, P. R. (1997). The development of epistemological theories: Beliefs about knowledge and knowing and their relation to learning. *Review of Educational Research, 67*(1), 88–140. https://doi.org/10.3102/00346543067001088

Hmelo-Silver, C. E., Duncan, R. G., & Chinn, C. A. (2007). Scaffolding and achievement in problem-based and inquiry learning: A response to Kirschner, Sweller, and Clark (2006). *Educational Psychologist, 42*(2), 99–107. https://doi.org/10.1080/00461520701263368

Ingvarson, L., Meiers, M., & Beavis, A. (2005). Factors affecting the impact of professional development programs on teachers' knowledge, practice, student outcomes & efficacy. *Education Policy Analysis Archives/Archivos Analíticos de Políticas Educativas, 13.* https://doi.org/10.14507/epaa.v13n10.2005

Israel Ministry of Education. (2015). Pathways to meaningful learning. http://meyda.education.gov.il/files/MinhalPedagogy/netivim.pdf (Retrieved September, 2017). (In Hebrew).

Israeli Ministry of Education. (2012). Learning through inquiry: Explicit teaching of scientific inquiry skills- Measurement, observation and experimentation. https://cms.education.gov.il/NR/rdonlyres/375D7610-BB39-4A99-8035-8C8489EAD794/163682/4doc1.doc (Retrieved September, 2017). (In Hebrew).

Justice, C., Rice, J., Roy, D., Hudspith, B., & Jenkins, H. (2009). Inquiry-based learning in higher education: Administrators' perspectives on integrating inquiry pedagogy into the curriculum. *Higher Education, 58*(6), 841. https://doi.org/10.1007/s10734-009-9228-7

Kazempour, M., & Amirshokoohi, A. (2013). Exploring elementary pre-service teachers' experiences and learning outcomes in a revised inquiry-based science lesson: An action research. *Journal of Education and Learning, 2*(2), 144. https://doi.org/10.5539/jel.v2n2p144

Khishfe, R., & Abd-El-Khalick, F. (2002). Influence of explicit and reflective versus implicit inquiry-oriented instruction on sixth graders' views of nature of science. *Journal of Research in Science Teaching, 39*(7), 551–578. https://doi.org/10.1002/tea.10036

King, P. M., & Kitchener, K. S. (2004). Reflective judgment: Theory and research on the development of epistemic assumptions through adulthood. *Educational Psychologist, 39*(1), 5–18. https://doi.org/10.1207/s15326985ep3901_2

Krathwohl, D. R. (2002). A revision of Bloom's taxonomy: An overview. *Theory into Practice, 41*(4), 212–218. https://doi.org/10.1207/s15430421tip4104_2

Kuhn, D. (1999). A developmental model of critical thinking. *Educational Researcher, 28*(2), 16–46. https://doi.org/10.3102/0013189X028002016

Kuhn, D. E. (1990). *Developmental perspectives on teaching and learning thinking skills.* Basel: Karger.

LeCompte, K., & Blevins, B. (2015). Building civic bridges: Community-centered action civics. *The Social Studies, 106*(5), 209–217. https://doi.org/10.1080/00377996.2015.1059792

Linn, M. C., Bell, P., & Davis, E. A. (2004). Specific design principles: Elaborating the scaffolded knowledge integration framework. In Linn, M.C., Davis, E.A., & Bell, P. (Eds.) *Internet Environments for Science Education* (pp. 315–340).

Lotter, C., Harwood, W. S., & Bonner, J. J. (2007). The influence of core teaching conceptions on teachers' use of inquiry teaching practices. *Journal of Research in Science Teaching, 44*(9), 1318–1347. https://doi.org/10.1002/tea.20191

Loucks-Horsley, S., Love, N., Stiles, K. E., Mundry, S., & Hewson, P. W. (2009). *Designing professional development for teachers of science and mathematics* (2nd ed.). Thousand Oaks, CA: Corwin Press. https://doi.org/10.4135/9781452219103

Loucks-Horsley, S., & Matsumoto, C. (1999). Research on professional development for teachers of mathematics and science: The state of the scene. *School Science and Mathematics, 99*(5), 258–271. https://doi.org/10.1111/j.1949-8594.1999.tb17484.x

Loyens, S. M., & Rikers, R. M. J. P. (2011). Instruction based on inquiry. In *Handbook of research on learning and instruction* (pp. 361–381). New York: Routledge. https://doi.org/10.4324/9780203839089-27

Luft, J. A. (2001). Changing inquiry practices and beliefs: The impact of an inquiry-based professional development programme on beginning and experienced secondary science teachers. *International Journal of Science Education, 23*(5), 517–534. https://doi.org/10.1080/09500690121307

Luft, J. A., & Hewson, P. W. (2014). Research on teacher professional development programs in science. *Handbook of Research on Science Education, 2*, 889–909. https://doi.org/10.4324/9780203097267.ch44

Makar, K., & Fielding-Wells, J. (2018). Shifting more than the goal posts: Developing classroom norms of inquiry-based learning in mathematics. *Mathematics Education Research Journal, 30*(1), 53–63. https://doi.org/10.1007/s13394-017-0215-5

Maor, D., & Taylor, P. C. (1995). Teacher epistemology and scientific inquiry in computerized classroom environments. *Journal of Research in Science Teaching, 32*(8), 839–854. https://doi.org/10.1002/tea.3660320807

Miranda, R. J., & Damico, J. B. (2015). Changes in teachers' beliefs and classroom practices concerning inquiry-based instruction following a year-long RET-PLC program. *Science Educator, 24*(1), 23.

National Research Council. (1996). *National science education standards*. Washington, DC: National Academies Press.

National Research Council. (2000). *Inquiry and the national science education standards: A guide for teaching and learning*. Washington, DC: National Academies Press.

National Research Council. (2012). *A framework for K-12 science education: Practices, crosscutting concepts, and core ideas*. Washington, DC: National Academy Press.

Next Generation Science Standards. (2013). *Benchmarked standards for K-12 science education*. Retrieved from http://www.nextgenscience.org/

Pajares, M. F. (1992). Teachers' beliefs and educational research: Cleaning up a messy construct. *Review of Educational Research, 62*(3), 307–332. https://doi.org/10.3102/00346543062003307

Penuel, W. R., Fishman, B. J., Yamaguchi, R., & Gallagher, L. P. (2007). What makes professional development effective? Strategies that foster curriculum implementation. *American Educational Research Journal, 44*(4), 921–958. https://doi.org/10.3102/0002831207308221

Peters-Burton, E. E., Merz, S. A., Ramirez, E. M., & Saroughi, M. (2015). The effect of cognitive apprenticeship-based professional development on teacher self-efficacy of science teaching, motivation, knowledge calibration, and perceptions of inquiry-based teaching. *Journal of Science Teacher Education, 26*(6), 525–548. https://doi.org/10.1007/s10972-015-9436-1

Pilitsis, V., & Duncan, R. G. (2012). Changes in belief orientations of preservice teachers and their relation to inquiry activities. *Journal of Science Teacher Education, 23*(8), 909–936. https://doi.org/10.1007/s10972-012-9303-2

Pintrich, P. R. (2002). The role of metacognitive knowledge in learning, teaching, and assessing. *Theory into Practice, 41*(4), 219–225. https://doi.org/10.1207/s15430421tip4104_3

PRIMAS. (2011). The PRIMAS project: Promoting inquiry based learning (IBL) in mathematics and science education across Europe: PRIMAS guide for professional development providers. www.primas-project.eu. Downloaded June 2012.

Reisman, A. (2012). The "Document-Based Lesson": Bringing disciplinary inquiry into high school history classrooms with adolescent struggling readers. *Journal of Curriculum Studies, 44*(2), 233–264. https://doi.org/10.1080/00220272.2011.591436

Resnick, L. B. (1987). *Education and learning to think*. Washington, DC: National Academies. https://doi.org/10.17226/1032

Resnick, L. B., & Science National Research Council (US). Committee on Research in Mathematics. (1987). Education and learning to think.

Richardson, V. (2003). Preservice teachers' beliefs. *Teacher Beliefs and Classroom Performance: The Impact of Teacher Education, 6*, 1–22.

Roth, W. M., McGinn, M. K., & Bowen, G. M. (1998). How prepared are preservice teachers to teach scientific inquiry? Levels of performance in scientific representation practices. *Journal of Science Teacher Education, 9*(1), 25–48. https://doi.org/10.1023/ A:1009465505918

Roth, W. M., & Lucas, K. B. (1997). From "truth" to "invented reality": A discourse analysis of high school physics students' talk about scientific knowledge. *Journal of Research in Science Teaching: The Official Journal of the National Association for Research in Science Teaching, 34*(2), 145–179. https://doi.org/10.1002/(sici)1098-2736(199702)34:2<145::aid-tea4>3.0.co;2-t

Sadeh, I., & Zion, M. (2009). The development of dynamic inquiry performances within an open inquiry setting: A comparison to guided inquiry setting. *Journal of Research in Science Teaching, 46*(10), 1137–1160. https://doi.org/10.1002/tea.20310

Salovaara, H. (2005). An exploration of students' strategy use in inquiry-based computer-supported collaborative learning. *Journal of Computer Assisted Learning, 21*(1), 39–52. https://doi.org/10.1111/j.1365-2729.2005.00112.x

Schmidt, M., & Fulton, L. (2016). Transforming a traditional inquiry-based science unit into a STEM unit for elementary pre-service teachers: A view from the trenches. *Journal of Science Education and Technology, 25*(2), 302–315. https://doi.org/10.1007/s10956-015-9594-0

Schommer, M. (1990). Effects of beliefs about the nature of knowledge on comprehension. *Journal of Educational Psychology, 82*(3), 498. https://doi.org/10.2307/747695

Schön, D. A. (2005). *The reflective practitioner: How professionals think in action*, 2nd ed. Aldershot: Ashgate Publishing. https://doi.org/10.1016/b978-0-7506-6465-3.50019-3

Schraw, G., McCrudden, M. T., Lehman, S. and Hoffman, B. (2011). An overview of thinking skills. In G. Schraw, & D. R. Robinson (Eds.), *Assessment of higher order thinking skills* (pp. 1–18). Charlotte, NC: Information Age Publisher.

Schwab, J. J. (1962). The teaching of science as enquiry. In J. J. Schwab & P. F. Brandein (Eds.), *The teaching of science*. Cambridge, MA: Harvard University Press.

Seraphin, K. D., Philippoff, J., Kaupp, L., & Vallin, L. M. (2012). Metacognition as means to increase the effectiveness of inquiry-based science education. *Science Education International, 23*(4), 366–382.

Setiani, M. Y., & MacKinnon, A. M. (2015). A community of inquiry-based framework for civic education at Universitas Terbuka, Indonesia. *Distance Education, 36*(3), 351–363. https://doi.org/10.1080/01587919.2015.1081740

Supovitz, J. A., & Turner, H. M. (2000). The effects of professional development on science teaching practices and classroom culture. *Journal of Research in Science Teaching: The Official Journal of the National Association for Research in Science Teaching, 37*(9), 963–980. https://doi.org/10.1002/1098-2736(200011)37:9<963::aid-tea6>3.0.co;2-0

Tabak, I., & Weinstock, M. (2011). If there is no one right answer? The epistemological implications of classroom interactions. In Brownlee, J., Schraw, G., & Berthelsn, D. (Eds.) *Personal epistemology and teacher education* (pp. 180–194). Routledge, New York.

Tamir, P., & Lunetta, V. N. (1978). An analysis of laboratory inquiries in the BSCS yellow version. *American Biology Teacher, 40*(6), 353–357. https://doi.org/10.2307/4446267

The Foundation for Critical Thinking, retrieved June 2019, http://www.criticalthinking.org/pages/critical-thinking-where-to-begin/796, retrieved June 2019.).

Timperley, H., Wilson, A., Barrar, H., & Fung, I. (2008). Teacher professional learning and development. Educational Practices Series, volume 18. International Bureau of Education.

Turnip, B., Wahyuni, I., & Tanjung, Y. I. (2016). The effect of inquiry training learning model based on just in time teaching for problem solving skill. *Journal of Education and Practice*, 7(15), 177–181.

Van Der Valk, T., & De Jong, O. (2009). Scaffolding science teachers in open-inquiry teaching. *International Journal of Science Education, 31*(6), 829–850. https://doi.org/10.1080/09500690802287155

Veenman, M. V. (2011). Alternative assessment of strategy use with self-report instruments: A discussion. *Metacognition and Learning, 6*(2), 205–211. https://doi.org/10.1007/s11409-011-9080-x

Veenman, M. V. (2015). Thinking about metacognition improves thinking. In Rupert Wegerif Li Li and James C. Kaufman (Eds.) *The Routledge international handbook of research on teaching thinking*, 280–288. London: Routledge.

Wells, T., Matthews, J., Caudle, L., Lunceford, C., Clement, B., & Anderson, R. (2015). The infusion of inquiry-based learning into school-based agricultural education: A review of literature. *Journal of Agricultural Education, 56*(4), 169–181. https://doi.org/10.5032/jae.2015.04170

White, B. Y., & Frederiksen, J. R. (1998). Inquiry, modeling, and metacognition: Making science accessible to all students. *Cognition and Instruction, 16*(1), 3–118. https://doi.org/10.1207/s1532690xci1601_2

Wuttiprom, S., Wuttisela, K., Phonchaiya, S., Athiwaspong, W., Chitaree, R., & Sharma, M. D. (2016). Preliminary results of professional development program for school science research. *Universal Journal of Educational Research, 4*(4), 842–848.

Yoon, K. S., Duncan, T., Lee, S. W. Y., Scarloss, B., & Shapley, K. L. (2007). Reviewing the evidence on how teacher professional development affects student achievement. Issues & Answers. REL 2007-No. 033. *Regional Educational Laboratory Southwest (NJ1).*

Zech, L. K., Gause-Vega, C. L., Bray, M. H., Secules, T., & Goldman, S. R. (2000). Content-based collaborative inquiry: A professional development model for sustaining educational reform. *Educational Psychologist, 35*(3), 207–217. https://doi.org/10.1207/ S15326985EP3503_6

Zohar, A. (2004). *Higher order thinking in science classrooms: Students' learning and teachers' professional development* (Vol. 22). Dorchester: Springer Science & Business Media.

Zohar, A. (2006). The nature and development of teachers' metastrategic knowledge in the context of teaching higher order thinking. *The Journal of the Learning Sciences, 15*(3), 331–377. https://doi.org/10.1207/s15327809jls1503_2

Zohar, A. (2007). Science teacher education and professional development in argumentation. In *Argumentation in science education* (pp. 245–268). Dordrecht: Springer. https://doi.org/10.1007/978-1-4020-6670-2_12

Zohar, A. (2020). *Connecting the islands to form a continent: Improving education by deep learning across the school system.* Jerusalem: Magnes. (In Hebrew).

Zohar, A., & Barzilai, S. (2015). Metacognition and teaching higher order thinking (HOT) in science education: Students' thinking, teachers' knowledge, and instructional practices. In R. Wegerif, L. Li & J. Kaufman (Eds.), Routledge international handbook of research on teaching thinking (pp. 229–242). Oxon, UK: Routledge. Zohar, A., & Cohen, A. (2016). Large scale implementation of higher order thinking (HOT) in civic education: The interplay of policy, politics, pedagogical leadership and detailed pedagogical planning. *Thinking Skills and Creativity, 21*, 85–96. https://doi.org/10.1016/j.tsc.2016.05.003

Zohar, A., Degani, A., & Vaaknin, E. (2001). Teachers' beliefs about low-achieving students and higher order thinking. *Teaching and Teacher Education, 17*(4), 469–485.

Zohar, A., & Dori, Y. J. (2003). Higher order thinking skills and low-achieving students: Are they mutually exclusive? *The Journal of the Learning Sciences, 12*(2), 145–181. https://doi.org/10.1207/S15327809JLS1202_1

8
ASSESSING INQUIRY

Drew H. Gitomer

What does it mean to assess inquiry? How have educators, researchers, assessment specialists, and policymakers all engaged with this challenge—one that has been intertwined with the full range of reform efforts that have centered the teaching and learning of inquiry skills, understandings, and practices as core to education? This chapter attempts to provide a lens for examining a broad range of research on and development of tools and strategies for assessing inquiry.

The chapter draws primarily from the field of science education for two related reasons. First, in many domains such as mathematics and English language arts, inquiry is most often considered as a pedagogical strategy to interrogate the domain (see Battey & McMichael, 2021, this volume; Lee, 2021, this volume). Inquiry is not treated as a core disciplinary target in these domains as evidenced by the term *inquiry's* minimal or absent treatment in disciplinary standards documents (National Governors Association Center for Best Practices & Council of Chief State School Officers, 2010a, 2010b). Consequently, there has not been significant research and development on the explicit assessment of inquiry understanding or skills. Even assessment of inquiry processes (e.g., argumentation in mathematics) is very limited.

One exception to this relative inattention to inquiry is in the domain of history. The assessment of inquiry in history education is overviewed briefly throughout the chapter. Ultimately, though, the most substantial research and development work on inquiry and assessment has been in science education.

Concepts are drawn from Mislevy's evidence-centered design (ECD; Mislevy, 2011; Mislevy & Haertel, 2006) to organize the chapter and highlight the core issues that are germane to characterizing assessments of science inquiry. In his writing on ECD, which is widely accepted as best practice in test development, Mislevy emphasizes the importance of building an evidentiary argument to support the development and interpretation of an assessment. This requires developing "an argument from what we observe students say, do, or make in a few particular circumstances, to inferences about what they know, can do, or have accomplished more generally" (Mislevy & Haertel, 2006, p. 7). The ECD process involves multiple steps, starting with modeling the relevant knowledge, skills, and abilities that characterize the domain, then developing tasks that elicit responses that provide evidence of those skills, and finally building assessments that map to the domain to allow for drawing reliable and valid inferences from test scores. Although each issue is treated somewhat separately for clarity of presentation, there are substantial interdependencies that constrain and support particular features of inquiry assessment and are organized in the chapter as follows:

1 *Conceptions of Inquiry.* All assessments begin with a set of beliefs and understandings of what is important for students to know and/or be able to do. Certainly, state, national, and international standards drive the design of large-scale assessments (e.g., National Research Council [NRC], 2001), but this would also be true of classroom assessments: What is it that teachers believe is important for their students to know? Conceptions of inquiry are quite variable and have certainly evolved over time. These various conceptions have profound implications for what and how assessment of inquiry has been conducted.

2 *The Purpose of Assessing Inquiry.* As Messick (1989) argued, the validity of any assessment must be considered in terms of its intended purpose(s). Assessments of inquiry have been used as accountability measures in, for example, state assessments. They have also been used in national and international surveys such as the National Assessment of Educational Progress (NAEP; U. S. Department of Education, 2003) and the Trends in International Mathematics and Science Study (TIMSS; Gonzales et al., 2008), respectively. In history, the most prolific use of inquiry assessments has been the document-based questions (DBQs) in the U.S. History Advanced Placement® (AP®) Exams (College Board). For these *summative* purposes, the primary goal is to draw inferences about what a student, or group of students, knows with respect to inquiry. Inquiry assessment tools and strategies have also been developed for more *formative* purposes. Here, the goal is to gather and evaluate information that can be acted upon during the course of some instructional experience.

3 *The Tasks Used to Assess Inquiry.* Assessment tasks are used to capture evidence about what a student knows and can do with respect to inquiry. Tasks vary both in the aspects of inquiry they probe and in terms of how students engage with and provide responses. These tasks can range from traditional selected-response (e.g., multiple-choice) items on tests, to more open-ended constructed-response items, to performance tasks. Tasks can be stand-alone questions embedded within more complex problems or integrated within simulated environments that make use of modern technologies. Assessment tasks can also include classroom activities and questions posed to elicit student understanding. Current conceptions of inquiry also call for assessment tasks that reflect the social dimensions of inquiry in which one is not just displaying understanding but engaging in processes like argumentation and explanation in which one is participating in a discourse with others in the discipline to both build on and confront different perspectives (see Duncan et al., 2021, this volume).

4 *Evaluating Evidence of Inquiry.* Responses to assessment tasks provide the basis for evidence about what students know and are able to do. Student responses provide data that only become evidence, however, when some interpretations are made about the data (e.g., correct responses, actions taken in a simulation) to support inferences about student understanding (Mislevy, 1994). Assessments also require the aggregation of smaller pieces of evidence into broader claims about students. These aggregations can be represented in the form of assessment scores or in more qualitative interpretations.

The chapter is organized along these four issues. In each section, relevant theory and assessment examples are drawn upon. The chapter is not intended to be an exhaustive literature review, however. The focus is on K-12 education, so studies of higher education are not included.

Conceptions of Inquiry for Education

Science education has grappled with the nature of science inquiry for a very long time, certainly predating the various standards reform efforts that have been put forth beginning almost 30 years ago (Project 2061; American Association for the Advancement of Science [AAAS], 1993). Joseph

Schwab made an argument in the 1950s that the teaching of science needed to move to one in which students actually engaged in the practice of inquiry (Schwab, 1958). This represented a substantial contrast with models of science education in which students were presented with what Duschl (1990, 2008) referred to as *final form* science. In this view, the science enterprise involved the study of a "permanent, inflexible, and given world" that had the sole purpose of "seeking and finding unalterable truths" (Schwab, 1958, p. 375). He pointed to three properties of science that were, and still are, true for much of science education, providing students with idealized, and incorrect, views of science.

The first concern Schwab (1958) raised is that students were presented information about science that was abstracted from any context in which the originating science inquiries took place, thereby making conclusions provided to students as "unintelligible or misleading unless they are known in the context of inquiry which structured and bounded the matters to which they refer" (p. 375). The second issue Schwab raised involved the tentative or revisionary nature of scientific theories (Kuhn, 1996; Suppe, 1977). Schwab's final concern about final form science is what he called *plurality*—the idea that any particular inquiry will lead only to a partial and often ambiguous scientific understanding of a phenomenon. In school, however, students were presented with a view of science in which particular experiences were designed to yield complete and certain truths.

Despite inquiry being accepted as a goal for science education, its implications have certainly been, and continue to be, a subject of much discussion. In 1993, Project 2061 (AAAS, 1993) presented a set of benchmarks for scientific literacy. This document largely defined inquiry as scientific literacy. This approach does not prioritize the doing of inquiry (*inquiry as means*) but rather understanding about inquiry (*inquiry as ends*) (see Abd-El-Khalick et al., 2004). The valuing of scientific literacy as the goal of science education was prominently argued for by Lederman et al. (1998) and embodied in Project 2061 benchmarks that were very much focused on declarative knowledge about reasoning (see Figure 8.1).

A view of inquiry has clear implications for its assessment. For example, Lederman et al. (2014) developed the *Views about Scientific Inquiry* (VASI) questionnaire to explore what students know

By the end of the 8th grade, students should know that

- Scientists differ greatly in what phenomena they study and how they go about their work. Although there is no fixed set of steps that all scientists follow, scientific investigations usually involve the collection of relevant evidence, the use of logical reasoning, and the application of imagination in devising hypotheses and explanations to make sense of the collected evidence. 1B/M1
- If more than one variable changes at the same time in an experiment, the outcome of the experiment may not be clearly attributable to any one of the variables. It may not always be possible to prevent outside variables from influencing the outcome of an investigation (or even to identify all of the variables), but collaboration among investigators can often lead to research designs that are able to deal with such situations. 1B/M2
- What people expect to observe often affects what they actually do observe. Strong beliefs about what should happen in particular circumstances can prevent them from detecting other results. Scientists know about this danger to objectivity and take steps to try and avoid it when designing investigations and examining data. One safeguard is to have different investigators conduct independent studies of the same questions. 1B/M3

Figure 8.1 Example benchmarks from Project 2061 (American Association for the Advancement of Science, 1993) about inquiry and the nature of science. Instead of focusing on the doing of science, the VASI focused on how students understand critical features of inquiry including that:

1 scientific investigations all begin with a question and do not necessarily test a hypothesis;
2 there is no single set of steps followed in all investigations (i.e., there is no single scientific method);
3 inquiry procedures are guided by the question asked;
4 all scientists performing the same procedures may not get the same results;
5 inquiry procedures can influence results;
6 research conclusions must be consistent with the data collected;
7 scientific data are not the same as scientific evidence; and
8 explanations are developed from a combination of collected data and what is already known.

Subsequently, the National Science Education Standards (NSES; NRC, 1996) moved from literacy to a greater commitment to engaging with inquiry skills. The NSES claimed that students need to develop three types of skills and understandings including: the principles and concepts of science, the reasoning and procedural skills of scientists, and the nature of science as a particular form of human endeavor (see NRC, 2000, p. xiii). The standards tried to accommodate a range of practices, from learning specific inquiry skills to engaging in broad investigations of substantial time duration. The underlying view of inquiry was that discrete skills and understandings accrete over time into more integrated and complex inquiry activities. The focus was largely on conducting experimentation, though the NSES also committed to students being able to produce and consider evidence through the use of explanation, justification, and communication (NRC, 2000). Inquiry was defined as having five essential features:

- Learners are engaged by scientifically oriented questions.
- Learners give priority to evidence, which allows them to develop and evaluate explanations that address scientifically oriented questions.
- Learners formulate explanations from evidence to address scientifically oriented questions.
- Learners evaluate their explanations in light of alternative explanations, particularly those reflecting scientific understanding.
- Learners communicate and justify their proposed explanations. (NRC, 2000, p. 25)

Importantly, the inquiry standards were treated separately from any considerations of science content or context. While examples of using inquiry were certainly grounded in content and context, there were no standards that addressed the specifics of what kinds of science content were to be the targets of inquiry.

This componential view of inquiry, together with avoiding considerations of content, supported particular ways of assessing inquiry. First, the standards embraced and suggested multiple formats and procedures to assess student inquiry (see Figure 8.2). Second, the standards led to assessment designs that were used widely and that tended to focus on items, either selected-response (first column of Figure 8.2) or constructed-response items, that were designed to assess specific inquiry skills independent of content. These kinds of items were most prominently featured in the NAEP (National Assessment Governing Board, 2010).

A very different representation of the nature of inquiry in science education was provided by the Next Generation Science Standards (NGSS; NRC, 2013), which built on a consensus framework for K-12 science education (NRC, 2012). The NGSS work represents a fundamental shift from the NSES in conceptualizing inquiry at the heart of the standards in which three

Illustrative Item

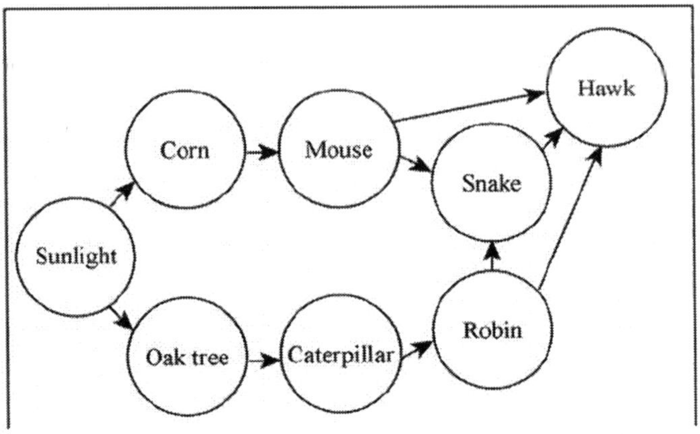

Look at the food web above. If the corn crop failed one year, what would most likely happen to the robin population? Explain your answer.

(See appendix C for item scoring guides.)

L8.6, Using Science Principles
Source: TIMSS 1999, Grade 8.

Figure 8.2 Constructed response: Verbal task example

dimensions intersect: *Science and Engineering Practices*, *Crosscutting Concepts*, and *Disciplinary Core Ideas* (see Appendix).

Central to inquiry in NGSS are the science and engineering practices of:

- asking questions (for science) and defining problems (for engineering);
- developing and using models;
- planning and carrying out investigations;
- analyzing and interpreting data;
- using mathematics and computational thinking;
- constructing explanations (for science) and designing solutions (for engineering);
- engaging in argument from evidence; and
- obtaining, evaluating, and communicating information.

Whereas NSES focused primarily on skills involved in conducting and interpreting experiments, NGSS placed a much greater emphasis on scientific reasoning, including question-asking, problem definition, data interpretation, argumentation, modeling, explaining, and communicating.

NRC (2014) considered the core aspects of NGSS that would ultimately affect the design and implementation of assessments:

1 a focus on developing students' understanding of a limited set of core ideas in the disciplines and a set of crosscutting concepts that connect them;
2 an emphasis on how these core ideas develop over time as students progress through the K-12 system and how students make connections among ideas from different disciplines;

3 a definition of learning as engagement in the science and engineering practices to develop, investigate, and use scientific knowledge; and

4 an assertion that science and engineering learning for all students will entail providing the requisite resources and more inclusive and motivating approaches to instruction and assessment, with specific attention to the needs of disadvantaged students. (pp. 25–26)

The implications for assessment under NGSS are profound. First, NGSS defines a limited set of core ideas as the object of inquiry. Second, in an attempt to create coherence across the K-12 curriculum, the concept of learning progressions is central (see Duschl et al., 2011; Jin et al., 2019). NGSS stresses the importance of recognizing the course of student development while also raising the concern that inquiry in science education classrooms is not necessarily faithful to science practice (Chinn & Malhotra, 2002; Duncan et al., 2021, this volume). Together, this led to performance objective descriptions that integrate across the three dimensions and also across grades K-12. Third, students need to be engaged in the socially situated science and engineering practices that define inquiry. Finally, there is an inextricable link between classroom instruction and assessment practice.

These changes led to recommendations for what NGSS assessments should look like (National Academies of Sciences, Engineering, and Medicine, 2017). Assessments would be required to:

- examine how students use science and engineering practices in the context of crosscutting concepts and disciplinary core ideas;
- use a variety of tasks and challenges to give students multiple opportunities and ways to demonstrate what they have learned;
- provide diverse and specific information that shows teachers where students are struggling in their learning and helps them decide on next steps; it also helps students understand the progress they have made and where they need to go next; and
- focus on students' progress along a learning pathway rather than what is correct or incorrect at a particular time. (pp. 18–19)

In history education, the push for inquiry has been relatively absent and critiqued by Bain and Mirel (2006), Reisman and Fogo (2016), and Wineburg (2001), among others. These researchers have noted that the dominant focus on learning about history has negated engagement in the practices of historical inquiry, which include the search for and evaluation of evidence that underlies the final form narratives to which they are typically exposed. While there are calls for the use of primary documents in structuring historical arguments, inquiry is largely treated as a means to learn about history rather than as a fundamental goal of history education articulated by the National Council for History Education (2020).

Independent of discipline, views of inquiry have explicit implications for assessment that have permeated education over the past few decades. For the purposes of this chapter, some of the diversity of ideas are glossed over in order to focus on the larger trends that have shaped initiatives in assessing inquiry learning. In the next sections, connections are drawn between conceptions of the nature of inquiry and its assessment.

Purposes for Assessing Inquiry

Assessment of inquiry has been used for a variety of purposes. This section describes three dominant purposes and their implications for how assessments have been designed and enacted. A first purpose has been to make summative claims about what students know about inquiry. Such assessments have been developed not only for annual student testing but also for national and international surveys that examine science understanding within and across groups of students. A second purpose has been to assess inquiry as a means to evaluate the impact of instructional or other interventions. The third purpose has been to use assessment of inquiry as a formative tool in order to support instructional decisions made primarily by teachers. Purposes of inquiry can, and have been, generally guided by different conceptions of inquiry. However, the focus on formative purposes of inquiry has been more recent and has coincided with the emergence of conceptions of inquiry embodied in the NGSS (see NRC, 2014) as well as the work of independent research groups.

The Summative Use of Inquiry Assessment

Summative uses of inquiry assessment have been used within state testing accountability systems and Advanced Placement tests, as well as part of national and international surveys that are designed to provide pictures of academic performance within groups of students along with comparisons among different groups.

There have been long-standing criticisms that traditional state accountability systems have been sorely lacking in terms of assessing performance and reasoning skills that are embodied in science inquiry (e.g., Clarke-Midura & Dede, 2010; NRC, 2001). These critiques have focused both on the underlying conceptual models of student understanding and on the limited repertoire of assessment tasks that have been used. Traditional selected-response, paper-and-pencil test items are ill-suited to assess much of what is important to gauging what a student understands and can do with respect to science inquiry.

Although there have been some recent efforts (e.g., Quellmalz et al., 2013) to enhance the assessment of inquiry in the context of accountability assessments, there is not a strong research literature that has studied these assessments. Large numbers of sample items are not available, nor is there much clarity about the extent to which the actual test content maps onto the conceptual frameworks of, say, the NGSS. Independent analyses of what is measured in state accountability assessments will be important gauges of the extent to which practices are changing with respect to modern conceptions of science inquiry.

In history education, the most prominent summative inquiry assessment has been the DBQ section of the College Board's Advanced Placement assessment of U.S. History. Items in this section ask students to engage with multiple primary documents to structure and support an argument.

Assessment of inquiry has been much more prevalent in national and international surveys of academic performance. Rakow et al. (1984) described the science assessment of the NAEP given in 1981–1982, which was based on frameworks that included inquiry (Education Commission of the States & National Assessment of Educational Progress, 1979). Items classified as inquiry made up almost half of the test questions for 9-year-olds and almost 1/3 of items for 13- and 17-year-olds. However, all items were selected-response, paper and pencil items. One of the core purposes of NAEP is to compare performance over time. Rakow et al. (1984) reported small declines in performance on inquiry items, for example, over the years 1969–1970 to 1981–1982.

Later NAEP frameworks and corresponding assessments adopted a more robust conception of inquiry consistent with the NSES (National Assessment Governing Board, 2008, 2010) by focusing on the following key inquiry practices: designing or critiquing aspects of scientific investigations, conducting scientific investigations using appropriate tools and techniques, identifying patterns in data and/or relating patterns in data to theoretical models, and using empirical evidence to validate or criticize conclusions about explanations and predictions (National Assessment Governing Board, 2010, p. 69). Performance assessments had a significant role in assessing these practices.

The more recent NAEP framework (National Assessment Governing Board, 2014) represented a synthesis of emerging national and international frameworks and created a two-dimensional framework that crossed science content (physical science, life science, earth and space sciences) with science practices (identifying science principles, using science principles, using scientific inquiry, using technological design). The basic division of inquiry into specific practices remained consistent with prior frameworks. However, the assessments included not only performance tasks but also tasks that leveraged advances in computer technology and simulated problem environments.

There is also a long history of international assessments of science literacy that have included inquiry. Broadly used as a way of comparing performance across countries, these assessments' conceptual and implementation development have paralleled developments in NAEP. Perhaps the most visible of these assessments has been the TIMSS. The most recent framework includes two domains: content (life, physical, and earth science) and cognitive (knowing, applying, and reasoning). Inquiry practices explicitly featured in the framework include: asking questions based on observations, generating evidence, working with data, answering the research question, and making an argument from evidence (Mullis & Martin, 2017, p. 55). The newest TIMSS assessment will be administered completely online and will make significant use of simulation tasks.

The Evaluative Use of Science Inquiry Assessment

Given the centrality of inquiry throughout the last several decades of educational reform, inquiry assessments have also been used to evaluate the impact of interventions designed to improve students' scientific literacy, particularly with respect to inquiry skills.

One common approach in these types of evaluations is to, first, determine changes or differences in qualities of teaching in terms of their alignment with models of inquiry teaching and, second, evaluate the relationship between the quality of practice and assessment outcomes that are presumed to be related to inquiry understanding. Unforunately, in many of these studies, the assessment outcome measures themselves are not described in much detail.

Examples include Sawada et al. (2002), who developed a classroom observation protocol, *The Reformed Teaching Observation Protocol* (RTOP), to capture the extent to which science education reforms were being enacted. Observers used RTOP to make judgments about qualities of classrooms that were grounded in existing science standards (e.g., NRC, 2000) and made judgments on indicators of inquiry such as whether student ideas were acknowledged and respected or whether students engaged in exploratory activities, made predictions and/or estimations, or generated hypotheses and ways of testing them. While RTOP has been used in many evaluation studies that attempt to establish relationships between practice and student learning (Furtak et al., 2012), the learning measures in this and other studies are often given very brief attention.

A second approach has focused on how student assessments can provide insight into the effectiveness of science educational reforms. Ruiz-Primo et al. (2002) developed a "multilevel-multifaceted" approach to evaluate educational reform efforts. They considered a range of assessments in terms of how closely linked they were to classroom instruction, identifying five levels of achievement indicators associated with the assessments:

- Remote: Standardized National Science Achievement Tests;
- Distal: Large-scale Assessment from State/National Curriculum Framework;
- Proximal: Same Concept/Principle—New Assessment;
- Close: Embedded Assessments—Assessments from Slightly More Advanced Activities in the Units; and
- Immediate: Science Journals/Notebooks and Classroom Tests.

Several examples highlight these distinctions. Schneider et al. (2002) evaluated an initiative in Project-based Science (PBS; Marx et al., 1994, 1997), a pedagogical approach focused on developing inquiry skills characterized by: asking a driving question, investigations and artifacts, and collaboration and technological tools. The study used items from the 1996 NAEP science exam and compared performance of students who were in a high school PBS program with the national sample and also examined performance across items. The largest differences, in favor of the PBS students, were for items focused on scientific investigation and extended constructed response, leading the authors to conclude that PBS was successful in developing general inquiry skills. Geier et al. (2008) studied the effects of a highly related intervention and found that students who participated in the inquiry curriculum outperformed student peers on a state standardized science assessment.

DeBarger et al. (2016) proposed an evaluative framework that could potentially be used to address the NGSS. They used the evidence-centered design perspective of Mislevy and Haertel (2006) to clarify both the range of measures that address what students need to know about inquiry and the extent to which the programs provide students opportunities to develop these inquiry skills. They developed tasks to assess students' ability to develop and use models using design patterns (Mislevy & Haertel, 2006) that provide a generalized conceptual structure for the creation of tasks. In order to assess modeling, for example, tasks would include features that examine students' ability to construct and use models to explain or make predictions, evaluate the quality of models for explaining a phenomenon, and/or use a given model to make predictions about a phenomenon (DeBarger et al., 2016, p. 9).

The Formative Use of Science Inquiry Assessment

Over the past several decades, there has been an increasing focus on using assessment as a means for contributing to improved instruction in classrooms (e.g., NRC, 2001, 2003). The call for such approaches has included several core features. First, there should be coherence among what is assessed at different levels of the educational system (Bennett & Gitomer, 2009; Gitomer & Duschl, 2007; NRC, 2003). Second, the focus is on how assessment can support informed instructional decisions. Third, assessment is positioned as a critical component of the instructional process. Fourth, students act as assessors of their own learning, in contrast to summative approaches in which the student role is only as the object of assessment (see Black & Wiliam, 1998; Heritage, 2010; NRC, 2000). Formative assessments have been used to support inquiry learning in several ways.

Duschl and Gitomer (1997) proposed the idea of an *assessment conversation* as part of curricular reform in middle-school science classrooms in which students participate in an instructional dialog that embeds assessment into the activity structure of classrooms. Using shared and recognized criteria for the production of scientific ideas and evaluation in the context of evidence and argumentation, students learned to apply these criteria to publicly evaluate their ideas and those of other students in the classroom as they proceeded through relatively expansive curricular units. Teachers would use such information to make instructional decisions to support student understanding of the core concepts critical to the curricular unit.

Cowie and Bell (1999) distinguished two kinds of formative assessment that could be used in science classrooms. The first, *planned formative assessment*, involves designed instructional activities in which teachers establish an instructional purpose, elicit student thinking, interpret that thinking, and then act on the thinking as part of instructional decision-making. The second, unplanned kind of formative assessment was called *interactive formative assessment*. Such unplanned assessments arise during the course of conducting a learning activity. The process of classroom noticing cues gives insight into student understanding about the concepts or skills they are exploring.

Carrying out formative assessment of inquiry presents significant conceptual and logistical challenges for teachers (see Duschl & Gitomer, 1997; Grob et al., 2017). Ruiz-Primo and Furtak (2006) studied three teachers' formative assessment practices using an analytic framework that considered how teachers elicited questions, how students responded, how teachers recognized the information contained in the students' responses, and how teachers used such information to influence instruction.

Formative assessment approaches to inquiry have also been embedded within computer simulations designed to support inquiry assessment (e.g., Gobert et al., 2013; Zapata-Rivera et al., 2016). In these approaches, a student works within a problem-based environment, and, based on actions taken by the student, assessments of student understanding are made, which then influence actions taken by the instructional system.

Tasks Used to Assess Inquiry

Given the broad range of conceptions of inquiry and the purposes for assessing inquiry, a vast array of approaches have been developed to assess student skills and understanding of inquiry. Twenty years ago, the NRC (2000) report on inquiry and the NSES provided a taxonomy of assessment contexts, formats, and procedures (see Table 8.1) and the timeframes within which they unfold. On-demand assessments such as standardized achievement tests are associated with short-answer, multiple-choice assessments, while project and portfolio assessments occur over a substantially longer period of time.

While this taxonomy remains relevant, three additional considerations would be added today. First, a taxonomy would include classroom assessment centered around forms of discourse such as argumentation. Second, the taxonomy would address the use of computer technology. Third, there exist on-demand assessments, largely technology-based, that include richer assessment tasks than simple forced-choice items.

Table 8.1 Assessment formats and procedures

	On demand	⟶		*Over time*
Formats	*Multiple choice, true/false, matching*	*Constructed response, essays*	*Investigations, research reports, projects*	*Portfolios, journals, lab notebooks*
Amount of time	Typically ~1 min 2–3 min with justifications	1–2 min short answers 5–15 min open-ended responses	Days, weeks, or months	Months or even years
Whose questions? (audience for the answer)	Anonymous or the teacher's	Anonymous or the teacher's	The teacher's or the student's	The teacher's or the student's
What kind of questions?	Posed narrowly	Posed narrowly	Posed more openly	Varies
Source of answer	Anonymous or the teacher's	The student's	The student's	The student's
What kind of answers?	Right/wrong	Extent of correctness	Standards or criteria for quality	Standards or criteria for quality
Resources available during assessment	Usually none	None or some equipment	Equipment, references	Equipment, references
Opportunity for feedback, revision	None	Usually none	Usually some from teachers and peers	Usually some from teachers and peers

This section samples a broad array of assessment formats and tasks to illustrate the various ways that inquiry has been assessed. For each format, common contexts of use and assessment of inquiry purpose are highlighted.

Selected-Response Format

Multiple-choice and other selected-response items are very commonly used in large-scale assessments as well as in various kinds of surveys. Such tasks have typically not been used to measure inquiry skills because of their inherent limitation to elicit direct evidence about student reasoning and social dimensions of disciplinary practices.

However, several researchers have attempted to develop selected-response items that can be used to assess inquiry skills. Nowak et al. (2013) developed a multiple-choice assessment based on a two-dimensional framework designed to assess inquiry in biology. Item stems contained descriptions of a biological context and then asked students to choose the best option on questions addressing aspects of inquiry such as hypothesis generation, experimental design, model interpretation, and data analysis. Liu et al. (2010) developed *explanation multiple-choice* items, which began with a multiple-choice item (e.g., predict a particular outcome) and then asked students to explain their choice using constructed-response formats. While such efforts are attempts to provide evidence of inquiry within the constraints of particular testing programs, there is little evidence that scientific inquiry can be well measured by selected-response items alone.

Constructed Response: Verbal Tasks

There have been many attempts to assess inquiry through the presentation of problems that ask students to demonstrate their understanding by providing a written response. This type of item has been widely used in national and international science assessments and has included tasks that ask students to interpret data, make predictions. explain observations, and evaluate explanations and/or models (e.g., National Assessment Governing Board, 2008), often in response to graphical models or data tables. Such items have been used in the TIMSS assessments (Mullis & Martin, 2017), an example of which is presented in Figure 8.2.

Lederman et al. (2014) probed student understanding of the nature of science through responses to statements such as (1) *Inquiry procedures are guided by the question asked* or (2) *Research conclusions must be consistent with the data collected.* Still other examples have inquiry prompts within comprehensive curricular units designed to support inquiry of important scientific concepts and principles (e.g., Gotwals & Songer, 2009; Liu et al., 2011). These problems ask students to complete tasks such as making predictions, interpreting data, and providing explanations as they reason around rich science content.

In history, the Advanced Placement DBQ exam asks students to consider 10–12 documents and develop a written argument within one hour. Young and Leinhardt (1998) observed that such time constraints limited students' ability to engage in the kind of in-depth historical analysis that might be possible using primary documents. Breakstone et al. (2013) have developed Historical Assessments of Thinking (HATs; Stanford History Education Group, 2020), which ask students to briefly respond to primary documents from the Library of Congress. HATs can be embedded within teachers' curricular units to probe specific historical issues raised by the particular document(s).

Constructed-response items are almost always scored using rubrics that each contain multiple-ordered score points. Each score point is described by one or more critical features of a student's response. Almost always, human judges, including classroom teachers, interpret the student response with respect to the rubric to assign a score.

Constructed Response: Hands-on Performance Tasks

Hands-on performance tasks were first used in the 1996 NAEP assessments (O'Sullivan et al., 1997). Consistent with views of inquiry focused on developing investigative skills, these tasks involved students working with physical materials to make observations, perform investigations, evaluate experimental results, and apply problem-solving skills (p. 2) but were disconnected from substantive consideration of science content or any substantial scientific reasoning. Thus, tasks might ask students to use materials to take measurements (e.g., using rulers, scales, graduated cylinders), graph data, or physically separate materials (e.g., with magnets) and to explain their rationale behind carrying out these processes.

As views of inquiry became more comprehensive, tasks considered issues of content such that the goal of hands-on tasks was to probe students' abilities to combine their science knowledge with the investigative skills that reflect the nature of science and inquiry. The goal was to move beyond the "recipe" types of exercises that characterized prior hands-on assessments (National Assessment Governing Board, 2008, p. 106). The 2009 NAEP framework highlighted an earlier task developed by Shavelson et al. (1992) (see Figure 8.3) to illustrate how hands-on tasks could be used to explore inquiry reasoning to investigate science principles (e.g., electrical circuits). For these hands-on tasks, assessment of students' performance remained based on the written work that students produced.

A more ambitious effort was undertaken by Emden and Sumfleth (2016), who created a set of more ambitious hands-on group tasks that were administered as part of multi-lesson curricular units. Students were video-recorded as they engaged in the inquiry (as was the intermediate work that they did), and all of this was used as evidence to be considered as group performances were scored. Individuals also produced written responses to some aspects of the task, and these were also scored. Thus, scores were produced for both the inquiry process and the inquiry outcomes, permitting interrogations of how inquiry processes were related to student learning.

Constructed Response: Technology Simulations

For large-scale assessments like NAEP and TIMSS, computer technologies began to replace hands-on tasks. One of the obvious motivations for this was that coordinating hands-on tasks with the requisite materials was a substantial logistical undertaking (National Assessment Governing Board, 2008). The move to technology simulations made performance assessment more tenable

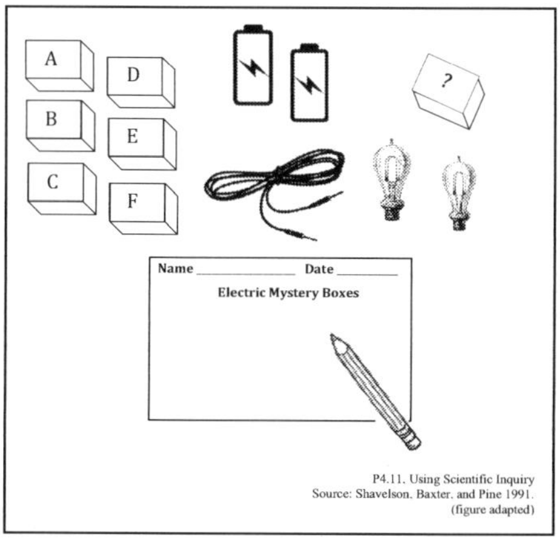

Figure 8.3 Constructed response: Hands-on performance task example

as scoring transitioned from human judgments to automated scoring. The increasing power of computational environments coincided with broadened conceptions of inquiry and inquiry assessment in science education, resulting in far more ambitious assessments of inquiry (see Means & Haertel, 2002).

Early technology-based assessments tended to mirror hands-on tasks in asking students to take measurements, make predictions, observe patterns in data, and manipulate variables in order to understand relationships among those variables, all within a simulated task environment. For example, Bennett et al. (2003) reviewed items used in NAEP Technology-Rich Environment (TRE) modules (see Figure 8.4). Students are presented with a problem: *How do different payload masses affect the altitude of a helium balloon?* Students can manipulate a set of variables (e.g., altitude, balloon volume, payload mass), make predictions, "run" experiments, display data, and evaluate and interpret experimental results as they develop their responses.

In such tasks, far more evidence than the final response is collected. The computer collects and analyzes the logic of testing (e.g., the choice of variable values) and how students' interpretations align with the simulated experimental results. As these tasks were developed from models that conceptualized inquiry as a set of skills, there was substantial focus on logical reasoning but relatively little focus on the underlying scientific principles and concepts associated with the phenomena being simulated.

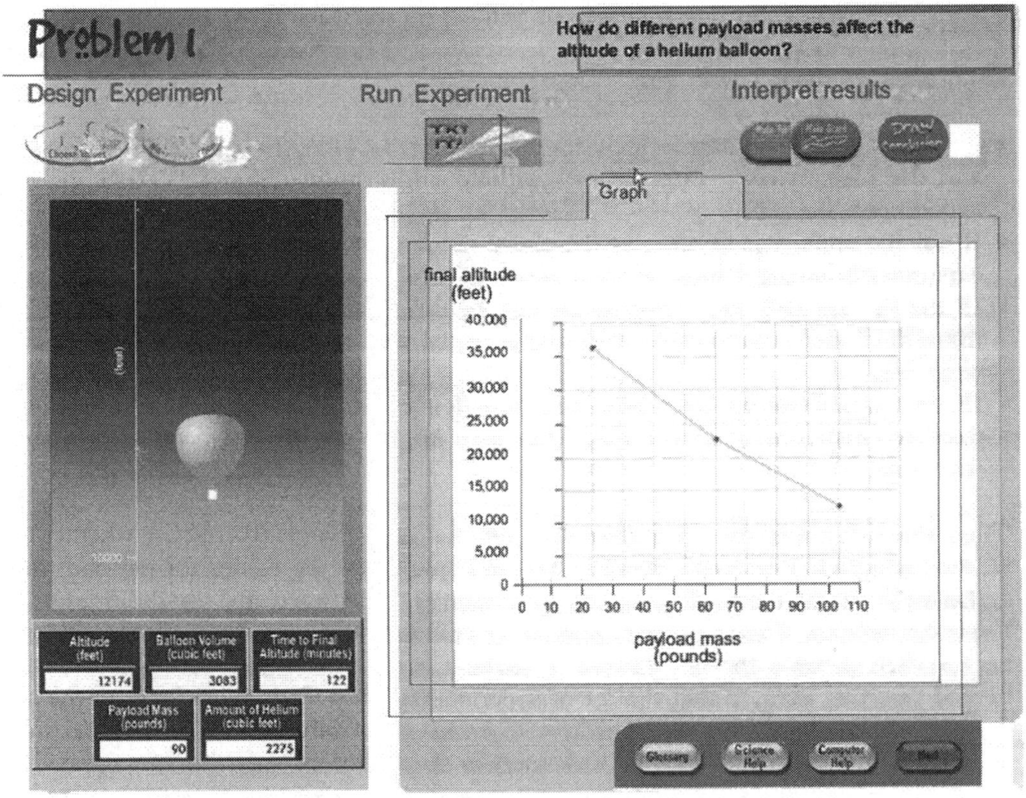

A set of data points qualifying for the highest 'Ran Best Experiments' score category.

Figure 8.4 Computer-based inquiry reasoning task (Bennett et al., 2003)

Assessment environments have become increasingly complex and robust and have become what is known as *immersive environments*—simulation contexts in which students can engage with a rich problem context and deeper content along with a much broader set of actions available to them. Some of these systems allow for multiple users. In addition, these environments often have feedback systems that can provide hints and redirection to students.

Building such assessments requires detailed underlying models—models of target skills, knowledge, and abilities (the domain model) and models of how actions taken by the student provide evidence of what the student understands with respect to the domain model (the student model). Insight about these models, as well as how tasks elicit such evidence (the task model), particularly in the context of science inquiry assessment, have been specified in an approach to assessment design called evidence-centered design (Mislevy et al., 2017).

Davenport and Quellmalz (2017) distinguished differences in technology-based formats as *static*, *active*, and *interactive*. Static formats use graphical representations, but what is presented is not changed through actions of the student and, thus, are not conducive to eliciting evidence of inquiry. Active formats include representations that are dynamic but that are not changed by the actions of the student and also do not lend themselves readily to assessing inquiry. For example, students might "run" a simulation that describes the relationship of two variables over time. Only in interactive simulations can students manipulate parameters in the simulation that change the behavior of the simulation. With such simulations, information about how students design an experiment, select appropriate tools, and carry out procedures correctly can be elicited (DeBoer et al., 2014). Davenport and Quellmalz (2017) developed interactive assessments that made extensive use of dynamic visualizations—systems in which phenomena were presented with visual fidelity and in which the behavior within the simulation was dynamic and reponsive to user actions. These assessments were also followed by off-line written reflections that provided opportunities for scientific discourse, argumentation, and presentations (Quellmalz et al., 2013).

Other examples of assessing inquiry in such interactive and immersive environments include Gobert et al. (2013), who developed a system to support and assess students' ability to design controlled experiments. Ketelhut et al. (2010) developed a multiuser virtual environment in which students engaged in scientific inquiry within a gaming environment to research the issue of how water systems might be affecting disease within a city. The system tracked and assessed behaviors such as gathering data, making observations, posing questions, planning investigations, and using different sources of evidence. Skill in argumentation was assessed by having students write letters to the "mayor" of the city.

Zapata-Rivera et al. (2016) used natural language processing technologies to support inquiry dialogs between students and intelligent agents. Given a particular problem, students could ask questions, make predictions, and collect and analyze data in rich problem contexts (e.g., the probability of a volcano erupting). One of two intelligent actors then reacted to each student action/statement. In these kinds of immersive environments, there are no linear paths toward solution. Students have the option to enter into and pursue the problem, and every action taken by students results in some change in the status of the simulation and can include feedback about their actions. Nevertheless, the systems do constrain actions and responses in order to provide sufficient control to support the embedded algorithmic scoring approaches.

Assessment Strategies for Promoting Inquiry in Classrooms

Assessments of inquiry have been used not only to provide insight about students but also as tools to promote inquiry. For example, Duschl and Gitomer (1997) developed the pedagogical strategy of the *assessment conversation* in which teachers would elicit student understanding of science concepts and then use that understanding as the instructional basis for achieving conceptual and reasoning goals in the classroom. Teachers worked with students to develop assessment criteria by which they could learn to judge and communicate the quality of explanations, models, and experimentation produced by themselves and/or student peers. The elicitation of student understanding often happened by asking students to complete classroom tasks that required them to do things such as develop a model or write an explanation. Other approaches to formative assessment have been developed by Davies et al. (2012), Dori and Herscovitz (1999), and Grob et al. (2017). In all of these efforts, student thinking is captured through either public discourse or classroom artifacts, and some determination of student understanding is made and acted upon, often by the students themselves. Assessment does not produce scores or reports but provides a set of tools that support students' development of inquiry processes (e.g., evaluating evidence, arguments, and models produced by the students themselves). Indeed, the line between assessment and instruction is deliberately blurred as interrogating student understanding moves instruction forward and functions as a core aspect of the instructional curriculum.

Coherence of Assessment Systems

The broad range of inquiry tasks and assessment contexts described in this section is designed to satisfy particular goals within different sets of constraints. For many years, educators and policymakers have been concerned that desired objectives of educational reform can be subverted when the assessments used in classrooms and in large-scale assessments, and those used formatively and summatively, are not coherent (e.g., NRC, 2001).

Coherence does not mean that assessments of inquiry at different levels of the system need to be isomorphic. Rather, the essential learning goals that are valued in the classroom need to be valued in high-stakes standardized assessments and vice versa (Gitomer & Duschl, 2007). In order to address issues of coherence, Ruiz-Primo et al. (2002) proposed a multilevel-multifaceted approach that embraced a common learning framework but recognized that assessments would vary in terms of how tied they were to a particular curriculum. The more standardized assessments are, the less likely they are to be connected to any particular curriculum.

Harlen (2013) and NRC (2014) expanded the idea of coherent assessment systems. NRC argued for three dimensions of a coherent assessment system. *Horizontal* coherence refers to the idea that curriculum, instruction, and assessment should all be aligned and target the same goals for learning. *Vertical* coherence implies that all levels of the educational system use assessments that share the same goals for learning. Finally, *developmental* coherence suggests a system of assessments that takes into account how students develop with respect to these common goals for student learning.

Evaluating Evidence of Inquiry

Assessment requires processes in which the evidence from student responses is interpreted in order to draw inferences and make some claims about the student (see Kane, 1990; Messick, 1989; Mislevy, 1994). Evidence can be drawn from all of the various task structures discussed to this point. This section overviews a highly varied set of methods that has been used to interpret and evaluate assessment evidence.

Applying Traditional Psychometric Analysis

Common assessment formats, particularly selected-response items, are often analyzed using customary psychometric tools such as classical test theory or item-response theory. In these models, the fundamental data consist of whether or not a student responds correctly to a prompt. Results from these analyses are then placed on some type of scale that can rank-order responses. This results in scores that enable global interpretations of groups of students (e.g., how well students are doing with respect to the measured construct) as well as comparisons among students and groups of students. However, in and of itself, typical approaches are atheoretical and do not necessarily provide insight into the nature of the construct.

More theoretically developed approaches to item and assessment development have also been used, which then permits more interpretable results about student inquiry development. Wilson (2009) used Rasch modeling to analyze assessments and evaluate theoretical models of student development based on learning progressions—descriptions of how students learn and progress though domains of understanding while attending to dimensions of content and inquiry reasoning, for example, understanding and reasoning about particular science content (e.g., skills in measurement and data handling and conceptual knowledge relevant to molecular theory). In Wilson's BEAR Assessment System (BAS), the first step is to develop a construct map from which item design proceeds. The construct map for a learning progression requires a theoretical model that has a developmental orientation. For example, understanding Earth and the solar system may progress from a second grader's understanding that the Sun appears to move across the sky every day and that the moon changes shape over a month to a fifth grader's understanding of the day/night cycle, the phases of the moon, and the seasons. Responses to assessment prompts are assigned to ordered levels based on the extent to which the response, as defined by how the student understands what is measured, is best described by a particular level.

These item scores are then modeled using the Linacre and Wright (2002) partial-credit Rasch modeling approach, an approach that Liu et al. (2008) also used to evaluate performance on a theory-based curricular assessment consisting of multiple-choice and constructed-response items. The advantage of these Rasch model approaches is that the difficulty of a particular assessment or task and the level of skill of the student can all be characterized along the same measurement scales.

Kind (2013) crafted an assessment instrument that included selected-response inquiry assessment tasks that were deliberately chosen from a variety of research studies and focused on one of three inquiry constructs: hypothesizing, experimenting, and evaluating evidence. Kind (2013) combined evidence-centered design and learning progression approaches, respectively, (Mislevy et al., 2003) to map particular assessment tasks to evidence about the target constructs and then used traditional Rasch analysis (Linacre & Wright, 2002) and factor analysis to develop separate scales for each of the constructs.

Rubric-Based Evaluation

Constructed-response tasks and hands-on performance tasks are most often scored using rubrics and human raters. Assigned scores vary for multiple reasons. First, students bring different levels of understanding to tasks, which should result in differing scores. Second, scores can also vary because different raters assign discrepant scores to the same performance. However, research on tasks of the type described in the previous section suggests that score variation across raters is not particularly problematic (Shavelson et al., 1992; Stecher et al., 2000).

If one is trying to make claims about a student's general inquiry ability across different problem contexts, then it is important that there be some degree of consistency in performance across problems as well as across testing occasions. However, studies have found substantial, yet unexplained, variation across problem contexts (Shavelson et al., 1992; Stecher et al., 2000) and occasions (Ruiz-Primo et al., 1993). For example, Stecher et al. (2000) were not able to find any systematic relationship of content, inquiry demands, or task structure that could explain the observed variation in performance across tasks.

Simulation-Based Evaluation

As computer simulation technologies allow students to engage in more ambitious and less structured inquiry tasks, there is a commensurate need to interpret student responses in order to make appropriate inferences about the student actions. Such interpretations might be used to make summative judgments of student performance as well as to make more formative judgments that enable feedback to the student.

Earlier, more structured simulations constrained student responses to a limited set of options. Evaluation of those responses relied on rule-based systems that connected specific actions or sets of actions to particular inferences. A set of rules for the task represented in Figure 8.4 specified the following guidelines for judging the quality of a student's understanding of experimentation by considering the tests that were run by the student during the simulation:

- IF the list of payload masses includes the low extreme (10), the middle value (50), and the high extreme (90) with or without additional values, THEN the *best* experiments were run.
- IF the list omits one or more of the above required values but includes at least three experiments having a range of 50 or more, THEN *very good* experiments were run.
- IF the list has only two experiments but the range is at least 50 OR the list has more than two experiments with a range equal to 40, THEN *good* experiments were run.
- IF the list has two or fewer experiments with a range less than 50 OR has more than two experiments with a range less than 40, THEN *insufficient* experiments were run. (Bennett et al., 2003, p. 353)

More immersive environments permit students to engage without many restrictions on the ordering or structuring of actions. Assessment tools must be able to make sense of such varied and somewhat idiosyncratic sets of responses. One very promising approach involves the use of data mining (see Slater et al., 2017) of student log files.

As students move through a problem space each action they take is logged and stored in a log file. Using a range of methods that include natural language processing, statistical modeling, and rule-based approaches, series of actions in the log file are inferred to represent evidence of some knowledge or skill understanding. Given the very large number of potential patterns of actions that could be observed, it is impossible to prespecify all possible outcomes as is done in rule-based systems.

In order for a system to be sufficiently robust to make inferences about all potential patterns of actions, researchers have incorporated machine learning into their assessment systems (e.g., Gobert et al., 2013; Sao Pedro et al., 2014). Key steps in this process involve, first, human experts making judgments about segments in log files. Given that a student made moves *a*, *b*, and *c*, for example, an expert might say that this is evidence that the student knows about control variables. After a large number of these judgments are made, machine learning methods are applied to extract key features of each of the human-scored patterns that lead to detectors or models that are characterized by these features. When a novel set of actions are produced by a new student in the simulation, the assessment system probabilistically selects the detector that best matches the student responses. Gobert et al. (2013) built such a system and then conducted validation studies of the quality of inferences made about students' inquiry skills within experimentation simulations.

Other research teams have employed different approaches to interpret actions within immersive systems. Clarke-Midura and Dede (2010) and Ketelhut et al. (2010) used Bayesian inference statistical methods to classify sets of actions. Gerard et al. (2016) used natural language processing methods to characterize student verbal responses in order to tailor feedback to students. All of these methods offer the potential to make sense of student responses using probabilistic methods within relatively open inquiry environments.

Summary

The assessment of inquiry has undergone profound shifts during the last half-century and arguably represents as exciting and dramatic a transformation as has occurred in any educational discipline. Such development has only been possible because of significant and interdependent advances with respect to the four core issues introduced at the outset of this chapter.

First, there has been a fundamental shift in what is the appropriate focus of inquiry in K-12 classrooms. Early foci on knowing about inquiry evolved into having students engage in learning specific skills of inquiry. We then witnessed a deeper focus on the cognitive and sociocognitive aspects of inquiry as argumentation, explanation, and models became prominent. Within the umbrella of NGSS, we now see an integrated three-dimensional framework that clarifies the interrelationships among content, core concepts, and science practices.

Second, the purposes of assessment have been broadened. For one, the focus on inquiry, particularly in science education, has become more central. There has also been a broad focus on formative assessment across education writ large. With respect to science inquiry, formative approaches to assessment have been the subject of a great deal of attention. This has included embedding assessments within curricular units as well as substantially focusing on the dynamics and pedagogy of formative assessment with very specific emphasis on inquiry skills such as argumentation and models. Across several iterations of science education reform, there has been substantial attention to building coherent systems in which assessments at state and national levels support the work of classroom teachers in developing inquiry skills and understanding.

Third, there has been a dramatic evolution in the nature of assessment tasks used to capture evidence of inquiry thinking and skill. This has included movement from paper-and-pencil instruments, including selected- and constructed-response items, to hands-on tasks that ask students to engage in skills of inquiry. There are robust curricula that probe student understanding and ask them to engage in reasoning at the heart of inquiry through creative inquiry problems. Finally, the emergence and continued development of computer-based environments is providing ways of assessing inquiry.

Fourth, new approaches to evaluating evidence elicited by these different kinds of assessment tasks have been introduced. To the extent that these tools are robust, students will have the opportunity to engage in learning and inquiry activities that are not artificially constrained by technology or assessment requirements. These tools have the promise of developing assessments that operate completely in the background of rich simulation environments that are designed to have fidelity with legitimate inquiry engagement.

The future will, no doubt, be one in which the sophistication of simulation and evaluative tools continues to develop. In doing so, there will be increasing ability for assessments to automatically make sense of and make inferences about a broader range of inquiry responses in a broader range of modes. Whether it is through classroom discourse, student writing, or actions around physical models or simulations, there no doubt will be increasingly robust inquiry learning environments supported by ambitious assessment methods and strategies.

Appendix

Three Dimensions of the Next Generation Science Standards (NGSS) Framework

(National Research Council [NRC], 2013)

Scientific and Engineering Practices

1 Asking questions (for science) and defining problems (for engineering)
2 Developing and using models
3 Planning and carrying out investigations
4 Analyzing and interpreting data
5 Using mathematics and computational thinking
6 Constructing explanations (for science) and designing solutions (for engineering)
7 Engaging in argument from evidence
8 Obtaining, evaluating, and communicating information

Crosscutting Concepts

1 *Patterns.* Observed patterns of forms and events guide organization and classification, and they prompt questions about relationships and the factors that influence them.
2 *Cause and effect.* Mechanism and explanation. Events have causes, sometimes simple, sometimes multifaceted. A major activity of science is investigating and explaining causal relationships and the mechanisms by which they are mediated. Such mechanisms can then be tested across given contexts and used to predict and explain events in new contexts.
3 *Scale, proportion, and quantity.* In considering phenomena, it is critical to recognize what is relevant at different measures of size, time, and energy and to recognize how changes in scale, proportion, or quantity affect a system's structure or performance.
4 *Systems and system models.* Defining the system under study—specifying its boundaries and making explicit a model of that system—provides tools for understanding and testing ideas that are applicable throughout science and engineering.
5 *Energy and matter.* Flows, cycles, and conservation. Tracking fluxes of energy and matter into, out of, and within systems helps one understand the systems' possibilities and limitations.
6 *Structure and function.* The way in which an object or living thing is shaped and its substructure determine many of its properties and functions.
7 *Stability and change.* For natural and built systems alike, conditions of stability and determinants of rates of change or evolution of a system are critical elements of study.

Disciplinary Core Ideas

Physical Sciences

PS1: Matter and its interactions
PS2: Motion and stability: Forces and interactions

PS3: Energy
PS4: Waves and their applications in technologies for information transfer

Life Sciences

LS1: From molecules to organisms: Structures and processes
LS2: Ecosystems: Interactions, energy, and dynamics
LS3: Heredity: Inheritance and variation of traits
LS4: Biological evolution: Unity and diversity

Earth and Space Sciences

ESS1: Earth's place in the universe
ESS2: Earth's systems
ESS3: Earth and human activity

Engineering, Technology, and Applications of Science

ETS1: Engineering design
ETS2: Links among engineering, technology, science, and society

References

Abd-El-Khalick, F., BouJaoude, S., Duschl, R., Lederman, N. G., Mamlok-Naaman, R., Hofstein, A., Niaz, M., Treagust, D., & Tuan, H. (2004). Inquiry in science education: International perspectives. *Science Education, 88*(3), 397–419. https://doi.org/10.1002/sce.10118

American Association for the Advancement of Science. (1993). *Benchmarks for science literacy: Project 2061*. New York: Oxford University Press.

Bain, R., & Mirel, J. (2006). Setting up camp at the great instructional divide: Educating beginning history teachers. *Journal of Teacher Education, 57*(3), 212–219. https://doi.org/10.1177/0022487105285892

Battey, D., & McMichael, E. W. (2021). Inquiry-based practices: Opening possibilities for (in)equitable interactions in classrooms. In R. G. Duncan & C. A. Chinn (Eds.), *International handbook of inquiry and learning* (pp. 189–203). New York: Routledge.

Bennett, R. E., & Gitomer, D. H. (2009). Transforming K–12 assessment: Integrating accountability testing, formative assessment and professional support. In C. Wyatt-Smith & J. Cumming (Eds.), *Educational assessment in the 21st century* (pp. 43–61). Dordrecht: Springer.

Bennett, R. E., Jenkins, F., Persky, H., & Weiss, A. (2003). Assessing complex problem solving performances. *Assessment in Education: Principles, Policy & Practice, 10*(3), 347–359. https://doi.org/10.1080/0969594032000148181

Black, P., & Wiliam, D. (1998). Assessment and classroom learning. *Assessment in Education: Principles, Policy & Practice, 5*(1), 7–74. https://doi.org/10.1080/0969595980050102

Breakstone, J., Smith, M., & Wineburg, S. (2013). Beyond the bubble in history/social studies assessments. *Phi Delta Kappan, 94*(5), 53–57. https://doi.org/10.1177/003172171309400512

Chinn, C. A., & Malhotra, B. A. (2002). Epistemologically authentic inquiry in schools: A theoretical framework for evaluating inquiry tasks. *Science Education, 86*(2), 175–218. https://doi.org/10.1002/sce.10001

Clarke-Midura, J., & Dede, C. (2010). Assessment, technology, and change. *Journal of Research on Technology in Education, 42*(3), 309–328. https://doi.org/10.1080/15391523.2010.10782553

Cowie, B., & Bell, B. (1999). A model of formative assessment in science education. *Assessment in Education: Principles, Policy & Practice, 6*(1), 101–116. https://doi.org/10.1080/09695949993026

Davenport, J. L., & Quellmalz, E. S. (2017). Assessing science inquiry and reasoning using dynamic visualizations and interactive simulations. In R. Lowe & R. Ploetzner (Eds.), *Learning from dynamic visualization:*

Innovations in research and application (pp. 203–232). Cham: Springer International Publishing. https://doi.org/10.1007/978-3-319-56204-9_9

Davies, D., Collier, C., & Howe, A. (2012). Assessing scientific and technological enquiry skills at age 11 using the e-scape system. *International Journal of Technology and Design Education, 22*(2), 247–263. https://doi.org/10.1007/s10798-011-9191-3

DeBarger, A. H., Penuel, W. R., Harris, C. J., & Kennedy, C. A. (2016). Building an assessment argument to design and use Next Generation science assessments in efficacy studies of curriculum interventions. *American Journal of Evaluation, 37*(2), 174–192. https://doi.org/10.1177/1098214015581707

DeBoer, G. E., Herrmann-Abell, C. F., Quellmalz, E. S., Davenport, J. L., Buckley, B. C., Jordan, K. A., Huang, C.-W., Timms, M. J., & Flanagan, J. C. (2014). Comparing three online testing modalities: Using static, active, and interactive online testing modalities to assess middle school students' understanding of fundamental ideas and use of inquiry skills related to ecosystems. *Journal of Research in Science Teaching, 51*(4), 523–554. https://doi.org/10.1002/tea.21145

Dori, Y. J., & Herscovitz, O. (1999). Question-posing capability as an alternative evaluation method: Analysis of an environmental case study. *Journal of Research in Science Teaching, 36*(4), 411–430. https://doi.org/10.1002/(SICI)1098-2736(199904)36:4<411::AID-TEA2>3.0.CO;2-E

Duncan, R. G., Av-Shalom, N. Y., & Chinn, C. A. (2021). Inquiry and learning in science. In R. G. Duncan & C. A. Chinn (Eds.), *International handbook of inquiry and learning* (pp. 325–344). New York: Routledge.

Duschl, R. (1990). *Restructuring science education: The importance of theories and their development.* New York: Teachers College Press.

Duschl, R. (2008). Science education in three-part harmony: Balancing conceptual, epistemic, and social learning goals. *Review of Research in Education, 32*(1), 268–291. https://doi.org/10.3102/0091732X07309371

Duschl, R. A., & Gitomer, D. H. (1997). Strategies and challenges to changing the focus of assessment and instruction in science classrooms. *Educational Assessment, 4*(1), 37–73. https://doi.org/10.1207/s15326977ea0401_2

Duschl, R., Maeng, S., & Sezen, A. (2011). Learning progressions and teaching sequences: A review and analysis. *Studies in Science Education, 47*(2), 123–182. https://doi.org/10.1080/03057267.2011.604476

Education Commission of the States, & National Assessment of Educational Progress. (1979). *Science objectives for the third assessment.* Washington, DC: Department of Health, Education, and Welfare, Education Division, National Institute of Education,

Emden, M., & Sumfleth, E. (2016). Assessing students' experimentation processes in guided inquiry. *International Journal of Science and Mathematics Education, 14*(1), 29–54. https://doi.org/10.1007/s10763-014-9564-7

Furtak, E. M., Seidel, T., Iverson, H., & Briggs, D. C. (2012). Experimental and quasi-experimental studies of inquiry-based science teaching: A meta-analysis. *Review of Educational Research, 82*(3), 300–329. https://doi.org/10.3102/0034654312457206

Geier, R., Blumenfeld, P. C., Marx, R. W., Krajcik, J. S., Fishman, B., Soloway, E., & Clay-Chambers, J. (2008). Standardized test outcomes for students engaged in inquiry-based science curricula in the context of urban reform. *Journal of Research in Science Teaching, 45*(8), 922–939. https://doi.org/10.1002/tea.20248

Gerard, L. F., Ryoo, K., McElhaney, K. W., Liu, O. L., Rafferty, A. N., & Linn, M. C. (2016). Automated guidance for student inquiry. *Journal of Educational Psychology, 108*(1), 60–81. https://doi.org/10.1037/edu0000052

Gitomer, D. H., & Duschl, R. A. (2007). Establishing multilevel coherence in assessment. *Yearbook of the National Society for the Study of Education, 106*(1), 288–320. https://doi.org/10.1111/j.1744-7984.2007.00106.x

Gobert, J. D., Sao Pedro, M., Raziuddin, J., & Baker, R. S. (2013). From log files to assessment metrics: Measuring students' science inquiry skills using educational data mining. *Journal of the Learning Sciences, 22*(4), 521–563. https://doi.org/10.1080/10508406.2013.837391

Gonzales, P., Williams, T., Jocelyn, L., Roey, S., Kastberg, D., & Brenwald, S. (2008). *Highlights from TIMSS 2007: Mathematics and science achievement of U.S. fourth- and eighth-grade students in an international context* [NCES 2009–001 Revised]. Washington, DC: National Center for Education Statistics, Institute of Education Sciences, U.S. Department of Education. Retrieved from http://nces.ed.gov/pubs2009/2009001.pdf

Gotwals, A. W., & Songer, N. B. (2009). Reasoning up and down a food chain: Using an assessment framework to investigate students' middle knowledge. *Science Education, 94*(2), 259–281. https://doi.org/10.1002/sce.20368

Grob, R., Holmeier, M., & Labudde, P. (2017). Formative assessment to support students' competences in inquiry-based science education. *Interdisciplinary Journal of Problem-Based Learning, 11*(2). https://doi.org/10.7771/1541-5015.1673

Harlen, W. (2013). Inquiry-based learning in science and mathematics. *Review of Science, Mathematics and ICT Education,* 7(2), 9–33. https://doi.org/10.26220/rev.2042

Heritage, M. (2010). *Formative assessment: Making it happen in the classroom*. Thousand Oaks, CA: Corwin. https://doi.org/10.4135/9781452219493

Jin, H., Mikeska, J. N., Hokayem, H., & Mavronikolas, E. (2019). Toward coherence in curriculum, instruction, and assessment: A review of learning progression literature. *Science Education*, *103*(5), 1206–1234. https://doi.org/10.1002/sce.21525

Kane, M. T. (1990). *An argument-based approach to validation* (ACT-RR-90-13). Iowa City, IA: American College Testing (ACT) Program. Retrieved from files.eric.ed.gov/fulltext/ED336428.pdf

Ketelhut, D. J., Nelson, B. C., Clarke, J., & Dede, C. (2010). A multi-user virtual environment for building and assessing higher order inquiry skills in science. *British Journal of Educational Technology*, *41*(1), 56–68. https://doi.org/10.1111/j.1467-8535.2009.01036.x

Kind, P. M. (2013). Establishing assessment scales using a novel disciplinary rationale for scientific reasoning. *Journal of Research in Science Teaching*, *50*(5), 530–560. https://doi.org/10.1002/tea.21086

Kuhn, T. S. (1996). *The structure of scientific revolutions* (3rd ed.). Chicago, IL: University of Chicago Press.

Lederman, J. S., Lederman, N. G., Bartels, S. L., Bartos, S. A., Meyer, A. A., & Schwartz, R. S. (2014). Meaningful assessment of learners' understandings about scientific inquiry—The Views About Scientific Inquiry (VASI) questionnaire. *Journal of Research in Science Teaching*, *51*(1), 65–83. https://doi.org/10.1002/tea.21125

Lederman, N. G., Wade, P. D., & Bell, R. L. (1998). Assessing the nature of science: What is the nature of our assessments? *Science & Education*, 7(6), 595–615. https://doi.org/10.1023/A:1008601707321

Lee, C. D. (2021). Inquiry and learning in literature. In R. G. Duncan & C. A. Chinn (Eds.), *International handbook of inquiry and learning* (pp. 277–295). New York: Routledge.

Linacre, J. M., & Wright, B. D. (2002). Construction of measures from many-facet data. *Journal of Applied Measurement, 3*(4), 486–512.

Liu, O. L., Lee, H.-S., Hofstetter, C., & Linn, M. C. (2008). Assessing knowledge integration in science: Construct, measures, and evidence. *Educational Assessment*, *13*(1), 33–55. https://doi.org/10.1080/10627190801968224

Liu, O. L., Lee, H.-S., & Linn, M. C. (2010). Multifaceted assessment of inquiry-based science learning. *Educational Assessment*, *15*(2), 69–86. https://doi.org/10.1080/10627197.2010.491067

Liu, O. L., Lee, H.-S., & Linn, M. C. (2011). An investigation of explanation multiple-choice items in science assessment. *Educational Assessment*, *16*(3), 164–184. https://doi.org/10.1080/10627197.2011.611702

Marx, R. W., Blumenfeld, P. C., Krajcik, J. S., Blunk, M., Crawford, B., Kelly, B., & Meyer, K. M. (1994). Enacting project-based science: Experiences of four middle grade teachers. *The Elementary School Journal*, *94*(5), 517–538. https://doi.org/10.1086/461781

Marx, R. W., Blumenfeld, P. C., Krajcik, J. S., & Soloway, E. (1997). Enacting project-based science. *The Elementary School Journal*, *97*(4), 341–358. Retrieved from https://www.jstor.org/stable/1002351

Means, B., & Haertel, G. (2002). Technology supports for assessing science inquiry. In National Research Council, *Technology and assessment: Thinking ahead—Proceedings from a workshop* (pp. 12–25). Washington, DC: The National Academies Press. https://doi.org/10.17226/10297

Messick, S. (1989). Validity. In R. Linn (Ed.), *Educational measurement* (3rd ed., pp. 13–103). New York: Macmillan and American Council on Education.

Mislevy, R. J. (1994). Evidence and inference in educational assessment. *Psychometrika*, *59*(4), 439–483. https://doi.org/10.1007/BF02294388

Mislevy, R. J. (2011). *Evidence-centered design for simulation-based assessment* (CRESST Report 800). Los Angeles: University of California, Los Angeles, National Center for Research on Evaluation, Standards, and Student Testing (CRESST). Retrieved from http://cresst.org/publications/cresst-publication-3170/

Mislevy, R. J., & Haertel, G. D. (2006). Implications of evidence-centered design for educational testing. *Educational Measurement: Issues and Practice*, *25*(4), 6–20. https://doi.org/10.1111/j.1745-3992.2006.00075.x

Mislevy, R. J., Haertel, G. D., Riconscente, M., Rutstein, D. W., & Ziker, C. (2017). *Assessing model-based reasoning using evidence-centered design: A suite of research-based design patterns*. Cham: Springer International Publishing.

Mislevy, R. J.,Wilson, M. R., Ercikan, K., & Chudowsky, N. (2003). Psychometric principles in student assessment. In T. T. Kellaghan & D. Stufflebeam (Eds.), *International handbook of educational evaluation* (pp. 489–531). Dordrecht: Kluwer Academic Press.

Mullis, I. V. S., & Martin, M. O. (Eds.). (2017). *TIMSS 2019 assessment frameworks*. Chestnut Hill, MA: TIMSS & PIRLS International Study Center, Lynch School of Education, Boston College, and International Association for the Evaluation of Educational Achievement (IEA). Retrieved from Boston College, TIMSS & PIRLS International Study Center website: http://timssandpirls.bc.edu/timss2019/frameworks/

National Academies of Sciences, Engineering, and Medicine. (2017). *Seeing students learn science: Integrating assessment and instruction in the classroom*. Washington, DC: The National Academies Press. https://doi.org/10.17226/23548

National Assessment Governing Board. (2008). *Science framework for the 2009 National Assessment of Educational Progress*. Washington, DC: Author. Retrieved from https://www.nagb.gov/naep-frameworks/science/2009-science-framework.html

National Assessment Governing Board. (2010). *Science framework for the 2011 National Assessment of Educational Progress*. Washington, DC: Author. Retrieved from https://www.nagb.gov/naep-frameworks/science/2011-science-framework.html

National Assessment Governing Board. (2014). *Science framework for the 2015 National Assessment of Educational Progress*. Washington, DC: Author. Retrieved from https://www.nagb.gov/naep-frameworks/science/2015-science-framework.html

National Council for History Education. (2020, June 26). *Blueprint for student learning*. University Heights, OH: National Council for History Education. https://ncheteach.org/Blueprint-for-Student-Learning

National Governors Association Center for Best Practices, & Council of Chief State School Officers. (2010a). *Common Core State Standards for English language arts & literacy in history/social studies, science, and technical subjects*. Washington, DC: Author. Retrieved from http://www.corestandards.org/ELA-Literacy/

National Governors Association Center for Best Practices, & Council of Chief State School Officers. (2010b). *Common Core State Standards for mathematics*. Washington, DC: Author. Retrieved from http://www.corestandards.org/Math/

National Research Council. (1996). *National science education standards*. Washington, DC: The National Academies Press. https://doi.org/10.17226/4962

National Research Council. (2000). *Inquiry and the National Science Education Standards: A guide for teaching and learning*. Washington, DC: The National Academies Press. https://doi.org/10.17226/9596

National Research Council. (2001). *Knowing what students know: The science and design of educational assessment*. Washington, DC: The National Academies Press. https://doi.org/10.17226/10019

National Research Council. (2003). *Assessment in support of instruction and learning: Bridging the gap between large-scale and classroom assessment: Workshop report*. Washington, DC: The National Academies Press. https://doi.org/10.17226/10802

National Research Council. (2012). *A framework for K-12 science education: Practices, crosscutting concepts, and core ideas*. Washington, DC: The National Academies Press. https://doi.org/10.17226/13165

National Research Council. (2013). *Next Generation Science Standards: For states, by states*. Washington, DC: The National Academies Press. https://doi.org/10.17226/18290

National Research Council. (2014). *Developing assessments for the Next Generation Science Standards*. Washington, DC: The National Academies Press. https://doi.org/10.17226/18409

Nowak, K. H., Nehring, A., Tiemann, R., & Upmeier Zu Belzen, A. (2013). Assessing students' abilities in processes of scientific inquiry in biology using a paper-and-pencil test. *Journal of Biological Education, 47*(3), 182–188. https://doi.org/10.1080/00219266.2013.822747

O'Sullivan, C. Y., Reese, C. M., & Mazzeo, J. (1997). *NAEP 1996 science report card for the nation and the states: Findings from the National Assessment of Educational Progress*. Washington, DC: National Center for Education Statistics. Retrieved from https://nces.ed.gov/nationsreportcard/pubs/main1996/97497.aspx

Quellmalz, E. S., Davenport, J. L., Timms, M. J., DeBoer, G. E., Jordan, K. A., Huang, C.-W., & Buckley, B. C. (2013). Next-generation environments for assessing and promoting complex science learning. *Journal of Educational Psychology, 105*(4), 1100–1114. https://doi.org/10.1037/a0032220

Rakow, S. J., Welch, W. W., & Hueftle. S. J. (1984). Student achievement in science: A comparison of national assessment results. *Science Education, 68*(5), 571–578. https://doi.org/10.1002/sce.3730680507

Reisman, A., & Fogo, B. (2016). Contributions of educative document-based curricular materials to quality of historical instruction. *Teaching and Teacher Education, 59*, 191–202. https://doi.org/10.1016/j.tate.2016.05.018

Ruiz-Primo, M. A., Baxter, G. P., & Shavelson, R. J. (1993). On the stability of performance assessments. *Journal of Educational Measurement, 30*(1), 41–53. https://doi.org/10.1111/j.1745-3984.1993.tb00421.x

Ruiz-Primo, M. A., & Furtak, E. M. (2006). Informal formative assessment and scientific inquiry: Exploring teachers' practices and student learning. *Educational Assessment, 11*(3–4), 237–263. https://doi.org/10.1080/10627197.2006.9652991

Ruiz-Primo, M. A., Li, M., Tsai, S.-P., & Schneider, J. (2010). Testing one premise of scientific inquiry in science classrooms: Examining students' scientific explanations and student learning. *Journal of Research in Science Teaching, 47*(5), 583–608. https://doi.org/10.1002/tea.20356

Ruiz-Primo, M. A., Shavelson, R. J., Hamilton, L., & Klein, S. (2002). On the evaluation of systemic science education reform: Searching for instructional sensitivity. *Journal of Research in Science Teaching, 39*(5), 369–393. https://doi.org/10.1002/tea.10027

Sao Pedro, M. A., Gobert, J. D., & Betts, C. G. (2014). Towards scalable assessment of performance-based skills: Generalizing a detector of systematic science inquiry to a simulation with a complex structure. In S. Trausan-Matu, K. E. Boyer, M. Crosby, & K. Panourgia (Eds.), *Intelligent tutoring systems: 12th international conference, ITS 2014, proceedings* (LNCS 8474, pp. 591–600). Cham: Springer International Publishing. https://doi.org/10.1007/978-3-319-07221-0_75

Sawada, D., Piburn, M. D., Judson, E., Turley, J., Falconer, K., Benford, R., & Bloom, I. (2002). Measuring reform practices in science and mathematics classrooms: The Reformed Teaching Observation Protocol. *School Science and Mathematics*, *102*(6), 245–253. https://doi.org/10.1111/j.1949-8594.2002.tb17883.x

Schneider, R. M., Krajcik, J., Marx, R. W., & Soloway, E. (2002). Performance of students in project-based science classrooms on a national measure of science achievement. *Journal of Research in Science Teaching*, *39*(5), 410–422. https://doi.org/10.1002/tea.10029

Schwab, J. J. (1958). The teaching of science as inquiry. *Bulletin of the Atomic Scientists*, *14*(9), 374–379. https://doi.org/10.1080/00963402.1958.11453895

Shavelson, R. J., Baxter, G. P., & Pine, J. (1992). Performance assessments: Political rhetoric and measurement reality. *Educational Researcher*, *21*(4), 22–27. https://doi.org/10.2307/1177207

Slater, S., Joksimović, S., Kovanovic, V., Baker, R. S., & Gasevic, D. (2017). Tools for educational data mining: A review. *Journal of Educational and Behavioral Statistics*, *42*(1), 85–106. https://doi.org/10.3102/1076998616666808

Stanford History Education Group. (2020, June 26). *History assessments*. Stanford, CA: Stanford History Education Group. https://sheg.stanford.edu/history-assessments

Stecher, B. M., Klein, S. P., Solano-Flores, G., McCaffrey, D., Robyn, A., Shavelson, R. J., & Haertel, E. (2000). The effects of content, format, and inquiry level on science performance assessment scores. *Applied Measurement in Education*, *13*(2), 139–160. https://doi.org/10.1207/S15324818AME1302_2

Suppe, F. (Ed.). (1977). *The structure of scientific theories* (2nd ed.). Champaign: University of Illinois Press.

U.S. Department of Education. (2003). *The nation's report card: Science 2000* (NCES 2003–453). Washington, DC: Author. Retrieved from https://nces.ed.gov/nationsreportcard/pdf/main2000/2003453.pdf

Wilson, M. (2009). Measuring progressions: Assessment structures underlying a learning progression. *Journal of Research in Science Teaching*, *46*(6), 716–730. https://doi.org/10.1002/tea.20318

Wineburg, S. S. (2001). *Historical thinking and other unnatural acts: Charting the future of teaching the past*. Philadelphia, PA: Temple University Press.

Young, K. M., & Leinhardt, G. (1998). Writing from primary documents: A way of knowing in history. *Written Communication*, *15*(1), 25–68. https://doi.org/10.1177/0741088398015001002

Zapata-Rivera, D., Liu, L., Chen, L., Hao, J., & von Davier, A. A. (2016). Assessing science inquiry skills in an immersive, conversation-based scenario. In B. K. Daniel (Ed.), *Big data and learning analytics in higher education* (pp. 237–252). Cham: Springer International Publishing. https://doi.org/10.1007/978-3-319-06520-5_14

SECTION 2

Components of Inquiry Environments

9
MOTIVATION IN COLLABORATIVE INQUIRY ENVIRONMENTS

Sanna Järvelä, Hanna Järvenoja, and Hanni Muukkonen

Introduction

Inquiry learning at school has been a success. Inquiry activities provide a valuable context for learners to learn how to reason and to learn concepts in different domains. The results indicate that inquiry learning tasks and environments also foster productive task-related interaction and enhance student motivation in general (Blumenfeld et al., 1991; Rogat, Linnenbrink-Garcia, & DiDonato, 2013). This chapter will focus on motivational effects on inquiry learning and their contribution to the learning outcomes.

Inquiry-based instructional approaches propose techniques for active learning pedagogy that requires learners to observe, generate questions, discover gaps in their knowledge base, and study resources in order to overcome these gaps (O'Donnell & Hmelo-Silver, 2013). Learners are given meaningful tasks, such as problems or cases presented in a realistic context. Such instruction demands that the students take responsibility for their learning processes (Mäkitalo-Siegl & Fischer, 2013). Students need to plan learning activities and monitor and evaluate their progress regularly, and these activities are closely related to strategic learning skills (Hadwin, Oshige, Gress, & Winne, 2010; Järvelä et al., 2014). In sum, inquiry learning creates an optimal context for learners' task engagement, but motivational involvement is also a prerequisite, as individuals' motivational characteristics, such as interest, influence forethought and goal setting (Zimmerman, 1989).

Researchers have extensively investigated implementations of inquiry learning in diverse contexts and have documented its cognitive and strategic consequences. In this chapter, we complement these discussions of cognitive aspects of inquiry learning by focusing on the motivational prerequisites and consequences of inquiry learning. We consider inquiry learning not only as a method for disciplinary learning but also as a potential and timely context for training 21st-century learning skills, such as collaborative problem-solving (Griffin, McGaw, & Care, 2012). Challenging learning tasks and situations are opportunities for students to train their motivation (e.g., interest) and regulation of learning during engagement in collaborative inquiries. Accordingly, in this chapter, we will discuss two main themes: (a) *How does inquiry learning challenge or support students' motivation to learn?* and (b) *If both pathways, challenging and supporting, occur, what settings and supports create a learning environment for motivating inquiries?* We build our understanding not based specifically on any "traditional theoretical paradigm" but instead on a perspective of motivation as a social phenomenon (Järvelä, Volet, & Järvenoja, 2010; Järvenoja, Järvelä, & Malmberg, 2016). We also draw on our experience working with collaborative inquiries and computer-supported collaborative learning studies.

We start with discussing empirical findings on how inquiry-based learning environments challenge or support motivation. Then we turn to a conceptual discussion and review several relevant motivational constructs explaining motivation in learning contexts; we conclude by introducing motivation as a contextual, situated, and process-oriented construct. We continue discussing regulation of motivation and its role in overcoming socioemotional challenges in inquiry learning settings. Finally, we provide suggestions for designing and supporting motivation in inquiry learning and discuss future trends and developments.

What We Know about How Inquiry-Based Learning Environments Challenge or Support Student Motivation

Conditions and consequences of inquiry learning have been studied from various perspectives. Earlier studies showed positive but also some mixed results when studying the cognitive effects of inquiry-based learning approaches (De Simone, 2009; Derry, Hmelo-Silver, Nagarajan, Chernobilsky, & Beitzel, 2006; Gijbels, Dochy, Van den Bossche, & Segers, 2005; Kirschner, Sweller, & Clark, 2006). It is crucial to note that there are also variances in the quality of the learning processes among different students; some students have major difficulties in engaging in research-like inquiry working procedures, and their learning processes are more regressive than progressive (Krajcik et al., 1998). We claim that, like other learning approaches emphasizing learners' own agentic roles, advanced cognitive learning skills do not guarantee the adaptive and agentic learning process alone. Collaborative learning skills, motivation, and, particularly, regulation of motivation are crucial for the inquiry-based learning process to be successful. These are relatively demanding competences, and it has been suggested that they do not develop without specific engagement in educational practices that involve engagement in complex problem-solving and collaboration around messy problems (e.g., Barrie, 2012; Broussard, La Lopa, & Ross-Davies 2007).

Participation in inquiry strongly emphasizes *cognitive reconstructing* by changing the cognitive division of labor between teacher and student. When a student takes responsibility for higher cognitive activities, it enables him or her to go to a deeper level in the learning process. This shift from teacher-centeredness to student activity presupposes strong self-regulative efforts from students and, at the same time, offers more space for individual activities. This kind of meaningful and close relationship with learning tasks also may help students increase their interest and motivation (Järvelä & Renniger, 2014). However, the responsibility for setting up one's own learning goals and monitoring one's own learning activities can be quite demanding for some students, and, furthermore, collaborative interaction with other learners may be difficult to initiate (Rogat & Linnenbrink-Garcia, 2011). Motivational consequences of inquiry learning are therefore multifaceted, including factors that may increase motivation and engagement for learning but also factors potentially challenging motivation that can result in a decrease in commitment to inquiry and collaboration.

It is well established that there exist *motivational and socioemotional challenges* to effective group functioning during inquiry. In an ideal case, collaborative inquiry learning aims to bring a new culture of teaching and learning into the classroom, where students in groups engage in self-regulated learning activities supported by the teacher. Research shows that a process of collaborative inquiry is demanding in terms of social interaction and that groups often do not succeed (Kuhn, 2015). This is because effective and efficient collaboration entails much more than simply sharing ideas or working together. It involves building new knowledge together while adapting to different challenges with all of one's human mental capacities (Kirschner, Sweller, Kirschner, & Zambriano, 2018). It also involves showing tolerance, expressing and understanding different viewpoints, and coping with uncertainty (Muukkonen & Lakkala, 2009). Therefore, the core of collaborative inquiry involves a complex interaction of cognition, motivation, and emotions (Järvelä, Hadwin, Malmberg, & Miller, 2017). In addition, successful collaboration hinges on social, non-task-related affective interactions, such as feelings of group cohesiveness, team orientation, mutual trust, and sense of community (Fransen, Kirschner, & Erkens, 2011; Fransen, Weinberger, & Kirschner, 2013).

To promote these positive types of interactions, researchers have investigated a variety of instructional factors. One important factor appears to be the use of *complex and realistic tasks*. Muukkonen and Lakkala (2009) and Muukkonen, Lakkala, Kaistinen, and Nyman (2010) investigated the effects of this factor in a study of inquiry in a higher education context. A qualitative analysis of students' experiences examined how students cope with a knowledge-creation challenge based on developing a project for a customer (Muukkonen et al., 2010). Student teams were asked to create ideas and plans on future possibilities and challenges in digital services for a broadcasting company. The outcome of each team's work was a report and a presentation to the customer. Based on team interviews halfway through the course, the students described high interest but were confused with the open-ended assignment and expressed a heightened need for both a teacher-provided structure to inquiry and an awareness of ways to monitor and adjust inquiry efforts in the groups. At the end of the course, their self-reflections revealed a change to more positive appraisals of the assignment. It was evident from students' feedback that the authentic nature of the knowledge creation challenge as well as the presence of the customer in the process and their expectations for the outcomes provided a motivational driver to overcome the challenges in collaboration.

Muukkonen and colleagues (2010) suggested that as students tackled the challenge of knowledge creation, they engaged in two parallel processes—project work and inquiry—which might be best supported with different types of scaffolding. The first type is facilitating project work by pragmatic scaffolding and supporting the management of the practical and social aspects of collaboration—for instance, by providing timelines or templates for project management. The second type is facilitating the inquiry process by models and practices for epistemic advancement. This could be supported, for instance, by templates structuring the expected outcomes or questions helping to identify key concepts and their connections. Within the knowledge creation approach to learning, both of these processes are related to advancing *shared objects of inquiry* (Muukkonen & Lakkala, 2009). Shared objects of inquiry can be understood as both the general motivation (objective) for the inquiry (what are we aiming for?) and the more tangible outcomes (e.g., reports, presentations, plans, and designs) that are elaborated during the collaborative inquiry process (Paavola & Hakkarainen, 2005). *Open-endedness and the need to invest collective efforts* in the elaboration of shared goals and co-construction of tangible objects (e.g., presentation and design) have been emphasized as providing motivation for collaborative working (Damsa, 2014; Knorr-Cetina, 2001; Paavola & Hakkarainen, 2005). However, due to their collective construction, objects emerge that are only partially shared and sometimes fragmented (Damsa, 2014); this contributes to the experience of confusion and an accentuated need for negotiating the motivation and regulation of inquiry efforts. For instance, to alleviate confusion in open-ended processes, there is a need to engage the group in iterative negotiation of the goals of collaboration and the means of contributing to the development of the shared object (Muukkonen et al., 2010).

How successful groups deal with this and how less successful groups could be facilitated with timely prompts continue to be relevant research questions. From the pedagogical design point of view, providing a highly complex and realistic task needs to be adjusted every time to the knowledge and competence level of the participants while maintaining a projection that exceeds students' prior levels in order for learning and efforts in regulation of motivation to occur.

Motivation in Learning Contexts—Conceptual Discussion

Traditionally, in conceptual discussion, motivation is considered as a psychological phenomenon that is made up of individuals' former experiences and interests, beliefs, and appraisals of learning (success). This complex mental construction has an impact on individuals' ability and willingness to engage in learning activities. In consequence, motivation cannot be considered as a single variable affecting learning; it is a multifaceted phenomenon formed and maintained as a part of the learning process in interaction with a social context (Järvelä et al., 2010). For example, during a collaborative inquiry learning task, students' situational interest in the topic can emerge if collaboration with other group members is stimulating and captivating, which can boost self-efficacy through new discoveries gained in encouraging socioemotional interaction. This can result in increased motivation to commit to the group's joint goals and can gradually support students in developing greater personal interest in the topic as well as greater feelings of competence and deeper engagement in inquiry as such.

Several motivational constructs have been used when discussing motivation in learning in general. Motivation is a broad term that encompasses both engagement and interest, as well as other topics, such as perceptions or beliefs about achievement; capability and competence; and goals, values, and choice. These factors are influenced by a person's consideration of the possibility, utility, importance, and benefit of participating and belonging (Minnaert, Boekaerts, & de Brabander, 2007). Motivation also involves considering the choices people make without external influence and the conditions supporting the individual's experience of autonomy, competence, and relatedness (Ryan & Deci, 2000). We briefly overview several important constructs below.

Achievement goal theory provides a framework for understanding how students interpret and respond to various learning tasks and events. It posits two main explanations of students' achievement (Dweck & Leggett, 1988). These explanations are based on the way learners orient themselves toward learning, which are viewed as a strong indicator of engagement. Mastery goals refer to goals aimed at developing understanding, while performance goals reflect a focus on demonstrating one's ability or competence, often compared to others. These two primary goals have been further elaborated based on whether the student adopts an approach or avoidance focus (see Elliot, 1999). Achievement goals can explain and predict the students' behavior, affect, and strategic approaches (Linnenbrink-Garcia & Patall, 2016). Prior research generally suggests, for example, that mastery goals are beneficial for strategic regulation of learning and engagement, whereas performance goals, though useful in performance-oriented instructional settings, are considered as less adaptive in terms of adaptive learning processes and the use of regulation strategies (Payne, Youngcourt, & Beaubien, 2007; Volet, & Mansfield, 2006). Learning environments shape students' *goals*. Students' tendency to adopt mastery performance approaches can be both hindered or facilitated by the type of task, providing students' choices or reducing control, recognition, grouping, and evaluation (Maehr & Midgley, 1996). Although there is strong evidence of the influence of achievement goals on individual learning, not much is known about their influence on collaborative learning and inquiries. Mercier's (2017) study, however, showed that achievement goals influence interaction behaviors when students are engaged in collaborative activities. In her study, 45 pairs of students engaged in a building task. Groups with learning goals showed more knowledge convergence than groups with performance goals. They also engaged in qualitatively more advanced strategies, such as reflection and explaining.

Another, complementary, body of research has addressed *social goals*. Social and well-being goals expand achievement goal theory with a sociocognitive perspective that reflects the social dimension that is typically present in real-life learning situations (Patrick, Ryan, & Kaplan, 2007). There is substantial evidence that students' goals to engage in learning activities are not only directed at the task or their own performance but also reflect the social learning context.

Furthermore, real-life learning situations are not isolated from the surrounding world but can encompass multiple motivational goals, all related to academic achievement (Boekaerts, de Koning, & Vedder, 2006). This is highlighted in the range of social goals identified in the literature—for example, social approval goals, social responsibility goals, social interaction goals, social relationship goals, social status goals, contextual goals, or prosocial goals (Urdan & Maehr, 1995). In summary, inquiry learning contexts provide various ways to facilitate students' social goals and thus engagement in inquiries.

While achievement goal theory approaches motivation to learn from the desired and prioritized outcome and value perspective, *self-efficacy beliefs* are ability-related judgments that a person makes of his or her capabilities to learn and perform, develop skills, and master knowledge in relation to a certain learning task or domain. Self-efficacy is found to shape engagement and to affect how much effort a person is willing to invest in regulating his or her own learning and persistence in the face of difficulties (Schunk & DiBenedetto, 2009). Inquiry learning can offer opportunities for strengthening efficacy, as found by Jansen, Scherer, and Schroeders (2015) regarding perceived science self-efficacy.

Interest as a motivation concept describes meaningful participation with particular content: people's psychological state during engagement, as well as the likelihood that they will continue to reengage that content over time (Renninger & Hidi, 2016). Interest is a cognitive and affective motivational variable that develops through four phases, beginning with a triggering of interest that may or may not be sustained and extending through to a more well-developed individual interest. Interest as a concept has been useful to explain student motivation and engagement in science inquiries. This is mainly because inquiry learning supports learners' abilities to make connections to real disciplinary skills and content as well as to work with the language and tasks of the science content; inquiry learning thus develops learners' abilities to work through its challenges and thereby extend their current understandings (Renninger & Riley, 2015).

Motivation as a Contextual, Situated, and Process-Oriented Construct

The role of motivation in fostering learning and achievement has been widely acknowledged (Linnenbrink-Garcia & Pekrun, 2011). Motivation is not a static trait, however; instead, it develops in interaction with individual beliefs, contexts, learning situations, and social interactions. All of the motivational constructs presented above are involved in the ongoing, dynamic interplay between a person and the environment, as is emphasized in the sociocognitive theory of learning. In the next section, we will introduce *motivation as a contextual, situated*, and *process-oriented construct* (Järvelä et al., 2010; Järvenoja, Järvelä, & Malmberg, 2015). Our understanding of motivation is based on the assumption that, in a social learning context such as in collaborative inquiry, individual group members represent interdependent self-regulating agents who together constitute a social entity. The learners actively create affordances and constraints for motivation and engagement in the situation and during the activity. In the context of collaborative inquiries, participants bring along their motivational beliefs, tendencies, and goals, and these play a mediating role in their actual engagement in the group activity. As revealed in research on collaborative learning, each group generates its own social dynamics, and it is through members' interactions that engagement, as enacted motivation, is afforded or constrained (Järvenoja & Järvelä, 2009).

We also argue that, in collaborative inquiry, both social and individual processes of motivation occur concurrently and represent distinct systemic levels (Volet, Vauras, & Salonen, 2009). The social construction conceptualization of motivation provides a useful theoretical perspective to examine motivation as an enacted, dynamic, and social process (in inquiry learning). On an individual level, inquiry learning "motivates," "hooks," or "triggers" motivation or interest. On this level, motivation is a characteristic of individuals that is "*socially influenced*" by the context (e.g., situated interest in hands-on science inquiry activities). This level is the level that has been discussed as a main argument for designing motivating learning environments, but collaborative inquiry also provides students with socially constructed motivation (Nolen & Ward, 2008). On a social level, motivation is "*socially constructed*" in interactions between group members as they together engage in collaborative inquiry (e.g., through building up a joint engagement and goal commitment in disciplinary interactions). When considering motivation in collaborative inquiries, the social construction perspective to motivation is relevant, as it builds upon the idea that motivation emerges through interactions in social situations and that actual engagement represents enacted motivation (Järvelä & Järvenoja, 2009; Järvelä & Volet, 2004).

Regulation of Motivation and Emotions in Challenging and Open Learning Tasks

Grounding our analysis in a contextual and situated perspective on motivation, we review the role of motivation in a variety of learning environments. Many conventional studies on student motivation focus on students' perceptions but not on what they really do and how they act in the learning context to create, shape, maintain, or restore motivation (Järvelä et al., 2010; Järvenoja, Järvelä, &, Malmberg, 2016; Volet & Järvelä, 2001). A process-oriented perspective on studying motivation in social learning contexts instead investigates how motivation affects the groups' learning processes or inquiries in complex ways rather than just being a static motivational ground or condition for regulated learning. We discuss *regulation of motivation* as a part of the motivated and (self)-regulated learning process. This is particularly useful for inquiry learning settings that expect learners' interactions with a situated task and the associated social challenges.

Self-regulated learning theory explains the regulation processes in learning. Self-regulated learning refers to the process of an individual becoming a strategic learner by regulating his or her cognition, motivation, and behavior in order to optimize his or her learning (Schunk & Zimmerman, 1994). Motivation lies at the foundation of these regulatory processes and is critical to learning and achievement (Komarraju & Nadler, 2013). Research has defined different motivation and emotion regulation strategies that individuals use to purposefully influence their motivation (Gross & Thompson, 2007; Wolters, 2003). Motivation regulation strategies can, for example, aim to strengthen or redirect motivational goals through performance and mastery *self-talk* or make tasks more interesting through *interest enhancement strategies* (Wolters & Benzon, 2013). The studies on motivation and emotion regulation show that the regulation of motivation and emotions is composed of purposeful and appropriate activities through which individuals initiate, maintain, and supplement their willingness to complete a particular learning goal and overcome situations that challenge motivation and commitment. By engaging in regulation of motivation and emotions, not only individual learners but also groups can actively adjust their motivation and channel the emotional atmosphere within the group to overcome challenges (Boekaerts & Pekrun, 2015; Järvelä, Järvenoja, Malmberg, Isohätälä, & Sobocinski, 2016). Group members' personal experiences, group dynamics, and task characteristics can produce situated cognitive challenges (e.g., challenges in task understanding), motivational challenges (e.g., task commitment problems), and emotional challenges (e.g., dominating interaction). These challenges pose risks to motivated inquiry and joint engagement within collaborative groups. Through regulation of emotion and motivation, these conditions are actively shaped and adapted to create a ground for balanced collaboration and metacognitive processes, which is critical in inquiry learning success. For example, if a group gets stuck within an inquiry learning task and feel frustrated or willing to give up, group members can boost each other's efficacy by encouraging each other to invest more effort and emphasizing small success moments.

Overall, the ability to take an agentic role toward one's own motivation and to regulate feelings and engagement has been recognized as having a strong positive effect on students' development throughout their school years (Boekaerts, 2011; Zimmerman, 2011). When engaging in the regulation of emotions and motivation, the learner becomes aware of the motivation and emotions experienced and can strategically direct or control them to ensure engagement in learning (Boekaerts & Pekrun, 2015). Järvelä and her colleagues have been analyzing the socioemotional aspects of peer interaction and group learning and have illustrated how students' motivational accounts of their interactions reflect changes in engagement (Järvelä, Järvenoja, & Veermans, 2008; Järvelä, Veermans, & Leinonen, 2008). As an example, this was seen in students' goal-oriented discussions and thinking about various reasons for persisting in or completing a task in a situation where the students discussed which topic to choose for a task to create a poster, as in these examples: "Lets' take the topic 'metacognition'." That is also a good choice concerning the exam." Students' intrinsic motivation or situational interest were enhanced while completing the activity, as shown in statements such as: *"This is a brilliant idea!" "I can describe my example...."* Similarly, Vauras et al.'s (2009) micro-genetic analyses revealed how individuals' cognitive, affective, and motivational behaviors during real-time activities were related to change processes in their social relationship patterns. Together, these studies have shown that motivation is a critical component shaping the successful learning process.

Motivation Regulation in Collaborative Inquiry Learning

The actual process of collaborative inquiry involves opportunities for appraisals which may cause socioemotional challenges (e.g., situations presuming tolerance of ambiguity or differences in students' interest), which have a significant impact on motivation. When individuals' characteristics, goals, and situational demands clash and create conflicts, motivation and engagement are challenged, forcing individuals to exercise control over their emotions, their motivation, and sometimes their social environment. For example, in their case study Järvenoja and Järvelä (2013) describe a collaborative learning episode in which emotional balance within the case group falls apart as a result of group members' different opinions and their questioning of one member's personal experiences from childhood. The clash between the group members conflicts with their ability to continue joint learning. The case study illustrates that group members recognized the change in the atmosphere, which led them to exercise emotional regulation at a personal level, but also in coordination with each other to restore the secure and supportive emotional atmosphere. Given the challenging nature of most group activities, this type of regulation of both personal and joint motivation and emotions is needed for continued engagement and progress toward goal achievement (Järvenoja & Järvelä, 2005; Salonen, Vauras, & Efklides, 2005).

Process-oriented studies point out that such *motivational and socioemotional challenges* described in the above example act as triggers for motivation regulation and are typical in inquiry and collaborative learning tasks (Järvenoja et al., 2017; Näykki, Järvelä, Kirschner, & Järvenoja, 2014). These challenging situations are also triggers to activate motivation regulation. In the above example, the motivation to continue was endangered by the one group member who was heavily questioned by others. However, the challenging situation triggered the group's efforts to restore motivation and goal-oriented work. Students' interpretations of their interactions with peers have revealed, for example, how their goals are shaped through those interactions (Boekaerts & Minnaert, 2006) and how the actions of group members can have both positive and negative influences on individual motivation (Järvenoja & Järvelä, 2005; Volet & Mansfield, 2006). Similarly, self-efficacy beliefs can shape how people experience and the ways that an individual either on his or her own or in interaction with others is able to regulate these motivationally challenging situations. Again, going back to the previous example, without adaptive motivation and emotion regulation in the emotionally challenging situation, the questioned group member could have ended up giving up and questioning her self-efficacy. This could have further hampered the collaboration and motivation in the rest of the group. Motivation, however, is affected by the appraisals of the learning process and collaborative interactions in general.

To capture the social construction and enactment of motivation, researches must also consider the complementary cognitive angle, which explains the mediating role of individual member's metacognitive reflections and interpretations. For example, in a study by Järvenoja, Näykki, Törmänen, and Järvelä (2018), emerging challenges and related emotion regulation were studied as teacher education students worked collaboratively across six different mathematics tasks. The analysis revealed that, in collaborative learning situations, a wide range of micro-level challenges emerge, covering challenges with motivational and emotional issues, such as anxiety, annoyance or frustration, and a lack of self-efficacy or interest, as well as different cognitive and socially and contextually oriented challenges, such as difficulties in understanding the task or content and differences in working and communication styles (see also Järvenoja, Volet, & Järvelä, 2012). All of these challenging situations are possible triggers not only for decreasing motivation but also for regulation to emerge.

Recent research has shown that, when individuals work collaboratively, at least three types of regulated learning come into play for shaping motivation in the collaborative inquiry learning situation (Hadwin, Järvelä, & Miller, 2017). First, each group member takes responsibility for regulating his or her learning (self-regulated learning); second, each group member supports peers in regulating their learning (co-regulated learning); and third, the group comes together to collectively regulate learning processes in a synchronized manner (shared regulation of learning). Shared regulation refers to group members' deliberate and strategic adaptation during phases of collaborative planning, task enactment, and reflection. It involves multiple individual perspectives and fine-tuning of cognitive and motivational and emotional conditions as needed. For example, a study by Järvelä, Järvenoja, Malmberg, Isohätälä, and Sobocinski (2016) showed that motivation plays a role in successful collaborative inquiry. They studied how self- and shared regulation in computer-supported collaborative learning took place and whether they were useful for the learning outcomes. In their study, 44 teacher education students worked with open and challenging collaborative tasks, and temporal sequences of online chat discussions and log file traces were analyzed in online collaboration. The results showed that socially shared regulation of motivation is important in maintaining productive collaboration. When considering the contribution of socially shared regulation on collaborative learning outcomes, the correlation analyses showed that groups with higher learning outcomes tended to engage in socially shared planning and socially shared motivation, whereas the groups with low learning outcomes tended to engage more in self-regulated learning.

Designing and Supporting Motivation in Inquiry Learning: Principles, Tools, and Technologies

Even though there is an increasing interest in motivation in inquiry and collaborative learning groups, Belland, Kim, and Hannafin (2013) emphasized that, in the design of learning environments, in general, motivation has been ignored. Järvelä and Renniger (2014) claimed that the two main challenges to successful engagement in inquiry learning are as follows: (1) How do we enable those who are not yet engaged to develop their motivation for learning, and how can we help unmotivated learners become motivated to learn? and (2) How do we design in order to continue to support those who are already engaged so that they continue to deepen their interest and, as a result, their motivation to learn a particular disciplinary content? A third question could be added—how can a formal learning context create spaces to practice motivation regulation in action and generic or discipline-specific competences?

It is evident that students' motivation in various learning environments needs to be supported. We can classify motivation support into two levels: macro- and micro-levels of support for motivation. Macro-level support focuses on disciplinary practices, and micro-level support targets specific learning processes. We will describe both levels of motivation support as follows.

Macro-level support for students' interest, task engagement, and deepening of disciplinary work has been provided in many motivation intervention studies that provide principles for planning tasks and models for day's or week's working or principles applied in curriculum or study periods. For example, Renniger, Ren, and Kern (2018) have designed an intervention especially contributing to the development of science interest, in which they have implemented macro-level support through conducting out-of-school science workshops among middle-school-age students. The intervention was designed to support workshop participants' abilities to make connections to disciplinary skills and content workshops, consolidate their developing understanding and abilities to work with science skills and content, identify what they do and do not yet understand in science, and realize that they can do science in terms of skills and content knowledge. In practice, the intervention includes a brief writing assignment that is integrated into science activities. Overall, the study's findings showed that a motivation-based intervention was successful in supporting students' interest development and learning of disciplinary content.

Macro-level supports have also been investigated in higher education in a project designed to enhance competence and motivation through inquiries simulating knowledge work. Taking place in collaboration, knowledge work can be defined as co-developing knowledge objects (e.g., project plans, prototypes, articles) by a community's collective efforts and resources (Muukkonen et al., 2020). Studies on the development of knowledge work competence have examined the interplay of pedagogical design, assignment characteristics, engagement, and motivation as well as the learning of collaboration competence measured by the Collaborative Knowledge Practices (CKP) questionnaire (Muukkonen, Lakkala, Toom, & Ilomäki, 2017). When students in veterinary education had a peer-teaching activity included as an assignment in addition to collaboration during a dissection exercise task to learn the anatomical entities, they learned statistically significantly more about collaboration in order to advance a shared outcome and about the integration of individual and collective efforts (Laakkonen & Muukkonen, 2019). Preparation for a presentation of complex anatomy given to peers was experienced as promoting an increased need for socially shared planning, and it supported the motivation for in-depth inquiry to gain a full understanding of the complex subject. Another study using the CKP (Muukkonen et al., 2017) generated evidence on how the intensity of activities and the type of assignments affected the competence learning reported by students. Structured intense collaboration was related to higher ratings on learning about the iterative nature of development efforts and feedback practices. The courses had assignments that simulated multiple aspects of authentic professional tasks. Students related the authenticity to higher motivation to engage in the inquiry as a prolonged effort. These studies point out that the types of activities involved in inquiry learning courses correspond well with student self-assessment in learning the targeted collaboration competence, and these can be examined apart from the discipline-specific content.

Micro-level support is targeted toward groups' and group members' learning processes. When trying to understand social learning contexts, such as collaborative inquiry learning, educators must consider an extremely complex set of variables—cognitive, social, emotional, motivational, and contextual variables interacting with each other in a systemic and dynamic manner (Thompson & Fine, 1999); all of these contribute to students' motivational interpretations in a situation (Järvenoja et al., 2016). Based on our understanding of motivation as a social and situated phenomenon, we have targeted regulation of motivation as a way for micro-level support for motivation during collaborative inquiries (Järvenoja, Järvelä, & Malmberg, 2018). Regulating and controlling motivation, emotion, and task enactment during a learning process is the quintessential skill in collaborative inquiry because working together means co-constructing shared task representations, shared goals, and shared strategies (Järvelä & Hadwin, 2013). It also means regulating learning through shared metacognitive monitoring and control of motivation, cognition, and behavior (Hadwin et al., 2017).

In order to simplify design principles for motivational support in a complex intertwined process of cognition, motivation, and emotion in a learning process, we have used the concepts of *awareness*, *recognition*, and *regulation* as main principles in our tool development for supporting motivation. Awareness refers to student's meta-level acknowledgment that "something is wrong" and needs to be regulated (i.e., inquiry progress is endangered), recognition to an ability to accurately identify sources and reason for that (e.g., what causes a motivational problem), and regulation is to act, adapt, control behavior according to the recognized need (i.e., we need to adjust our joint goals as all group members are not committed to the current one). They are the main components of developing motivation in a learning task and continuing the motivated learning process during the challenging learning task progress. Next we introduce technological tools for supporting the individual and collaborative motivation implemented in our studies.

Individual-Level Motivational Support in Collaborative Inquiry Task

In a study by Järvenoja et al. (2018), we involved primary school students in a long-term inquiry learning project as a part of a biology curriculum during which they studied a science topic dealing with the vital conditions for life. The project included classroom lessons with the teacher, experimental field trips, collaborative group work, and individual work in the gStudy learning environment (Winne, Hadwin, Nesbit, Kumar, & Beaudoin, 2005). The study's pedagogical design emphasized both self-regulated learning and science inquiry skills; the students were encouraged to take responsibility for planning and directing their own learning, for example, by focusing their work according to their own interests and deciding how much time and effort they would invest in various subtopics of vital conditions for life—namely water, air, nutrition, heat, light, family, and human rights.

Because the science learning project inherently required high engagement and persistence from students as well as the ability to coordinate their learning, different types of motivation support were provided. At a *macro level*, the classroom teacher structured the work during the school day as well as within the lesson. That is, the teacher controlled the time both teachers and students spent with the project and with the different functions within the project, such as when there were teacher-led lessons, experimental field trips, or students individually working. The students themselves planned the flow of their independent working. The teacher provided hands-on support when it was requested, but the students were encouraged to perform independent inquiry and self-regulated learning. In addition to the teacher's support, *micro-level* support was also provided within the gStudy environment. The cognitive tools of the provided gStudy learning environment were complemented by the emotion awareness tool (EmAtool, Figure 9.1). The EmAtool (Järvenoja, Malmberg, Järvelä, Näykki, & Kontturi, 2018) was designed to support the students' motivation through increasing awareness of their situational motivation during inquiry learning. The students began every gStudy working session by spending a couple of minutes to evaluate their current emotional state and motivational goals for that particular inquiry learning session. This conscious consideration of these two components was supposed to increase students' awareness of their micro-level, situation-specific motivation so that the need for regulation could be recognized if the motivated learning was challenged, and further, the student could plan on how to proceed with motivated learning and activate accurate motivation regulation.

The EmAtool increases awareness of the user's current emotional state by asking the user to estimate the valence level (negative-positive) and then *recognize* the reason for this emotional state

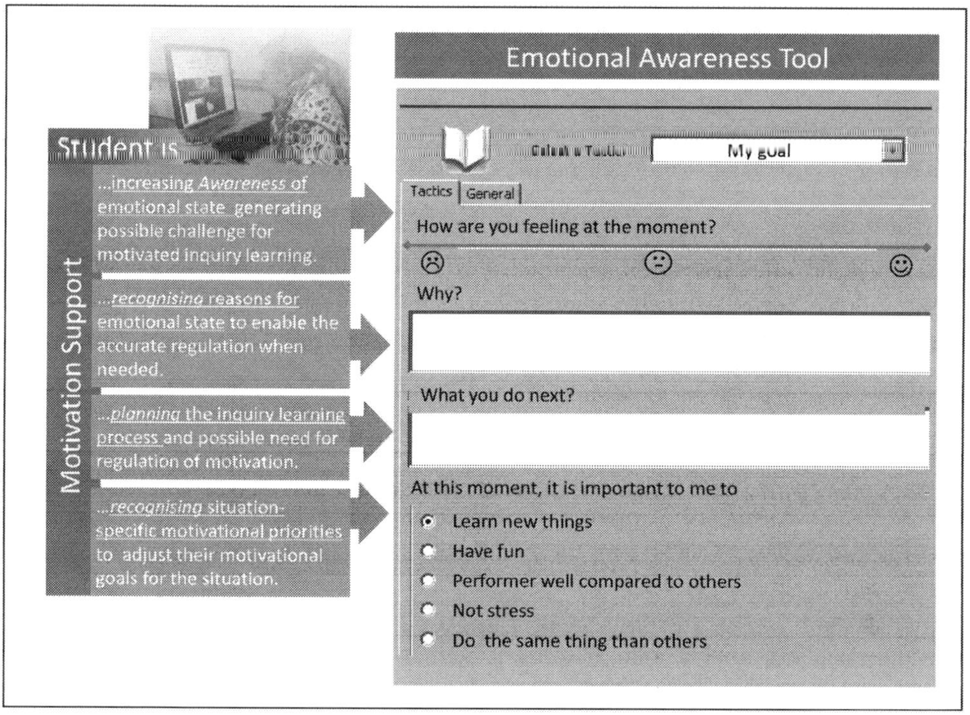

Figure 9.1 Emotion awareness tool

(i.e., what is the motivational, cognitive, and/or emotional source or reason for the current state). Then EmAtool prompts user to situate his or her current state with his or her motivational goals in that situation, which can help to adjust the goals and activate proper regulation strategies especially if the motivation is poor (Järvenoja et al., 2018).

Shared Motivation Support in Collaborative Group Task

Another tool that we developed—the socially shared regulated learning (S-REG) tool—extends our previous work on situated micro-level supports by providing targeted support for group work (for a review, see Järvelä et al., 2016; and for specific tool examples, see Järvenoja, Volet, & Järvelä, 2012; Järvenoja et al., 2018). Support is provided based on the challenges the groups have identified in their collaborative inquiry tasks. Similar to the EmAtool, S-REG elicits individual group member's awareness of motivational and emotional states but extends this to encompass group-level awareness and evaluations of the cognitive efficacy as well. After increasing the individual group member's awareness, the S-REG tool further prompts the groups to address the recognized challenges together. This change from individual- to group-level awareness, recognition, and, finally, regulation of the situation, takes place in a series of phases, as presented in Figure 9.2.

Figure 9.2 demonstrates how group members first evaluate their individual beliefs of efficacy related to their cognitive (*I know what I am supposed to do*), motivational (*I am willing to work*), and emotional (*I feel fine*) abilities (Figure 9.2, Phase 1). One group member can, for example, evaluate his or her cognitive starting point to be low ("I have no idea how to start"), but his or her motivation and emotions to be high ("I am committed and eager to start working"), while another group member may offer an opposite evaluation of his or her approach to working on that day.

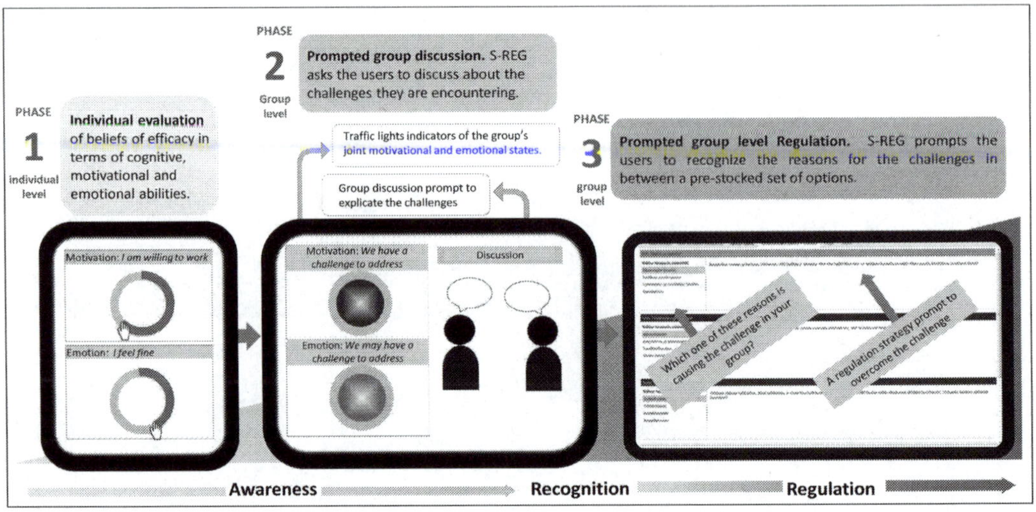

Figure 9.2 Socially shared regulated learning (S-REG) tool

In the next phases, S-REG indicates all the areas in which group members' evaluations clash or where they evaluate some challenges. The tool prompts the group members to recognize, through discussion, the "challenge areas" for the specific inquiry learning task and then consider how to regulate the situation to ensure the motivation for joint inquiry. The S-REG tool first initiates the discussion between the group members by providing a "traffic light" indicator to represent their joint motivational and emotional state (Figure 9.2, Phase 2). Next, the S-REG tool prompts the group members to discuss the traffic light. In this phase, group members can together recognize sources that can potentially create motivational challenges. For example, the group member doubting his or her ability to start working on a task has an opportunity to express this to other group members, or a group member having motivational problems can explain his or her standpoint. The discussion helps students become more aware and explicate the challenges the *group* encounters, and which may endanger the group members' joint motivation in order to continue the collaborative inquiry. After the discussion, the S-REG tool helps the group members recognize the reasons "behind" the challenges by providing a list of pre-stocked options from which to select (Figure 9.2, Phase 3). Finally, related to the groups' selected reason for a challenge in each of the three areas, the S-REG tool provides a regulation strategy that prompts the group to overcome their challenge (Figure 9.2, Phase 3). The use of the tool ends with a request to discuss the prompt or other alternatives to regulate the challenge in question. Empirical studies have shown that collaborating groups use the tool purposefully (e.g., Järvenoja, Järvelä, & Malmberg, 2017). In particular, the students became aware not only their own but the groups' emotional and motivational states by using S-REG tool. The results showed that when S-REG tool was implemented, the reported lower levels of group motivation and emotions were associated with the occurrence of co-regulation in the beginning of the learning sessions. The results of the study suggested that the S-REG tool balanced collaboration by prompting the groups to regulate emotions and motivation right in the beginning of the motivationally and emotionally challenging learning sessions.

To conclude, motivation in inquiry learning functions in several layers, which is important to acknowledge when designing and supporting motivated inquiry. While macro-level support provides means for addressing motivation and engagement, micro-level support targets the motivational challenges encountered in a situation during the process. In addition, motivation also functions on individual and social layers, particularly in collaborative inquiry. When support for motivation is designed, neither layer should not be neglected. Together, well-designed micro- and macro-level support implemented with technological tools will provide means to support students' ongoing motivation in inquiry learning, addressing the challenges deriving from overall unmotivation as well as more situated motivational challenges that endanger engaged learning and inquiry.

Future Trends and Developments

Motivation is a driving force for individual students and contributes to engagement among group members in collaborative inquiry. Motivation regulation keeps students on track while they are progressing in their inquiries, because motivation deals with processes involved in both initiating and sustaining behavior and engagement. As a construct, motivation is hard to operationalize in the practice of inquiry because its focus is on self-related beliefs that are cognitive, conscious, affective, and often under the control of the individual (Minnaert et al., 2007). More research is needed to understand how *inquiry learning challenges or supports student motivation to learn and especially what the settings, supports, and technologies are that make up the learning environment for motivating inquiries.* We suggest that theoretical approaches should extend well beyond the distinction between motivated and unmotivated and toward understanding motivation as a socially constructed and situated phenomena (Järvelä et al., 2010; Järvenoja et al., 2015), which can be supported by macro- and micro-level designs.

More research could focus on competence building in general and motivation support specifically with macro-level designs. Lakkala, Toom, Ilomäki, and Muukkonen's (2015) study examined how teachers redesigned their course according to pedagogical design principles supporting knowledge creation. They found that teachers took into account the benefit of the design principles as conceptual tools when redesigning their courses to integrate content learning with competence development objectives. Furthermore, teachers valued recommendations on how to model authentic professional practices in education and methods of scaffolding students' collaborative knowledge creation efforts, focusing on overcoming challenges to individual student's motivation and shared regulation of inquiry and motivation.

Integrating motivation scaffolds into technology in inquiry learning environments is promising (cf. Linn, McElhaney, Gerard, & Matuk, 2018). These scaffolds might include simple tools for prompting awareness of motivation in a collaborative inquiry situation, as we have introduced in this chapter (cf. Järvelä et al., 2014). Mobile tools implementing the experience sampling method can be used to trace fluctuations in motivation, challenge, and competence as well as emotions (e.g., Litmanen et al., 2012). In the future, through visualizations of ongoing activities, these may help regulate efforts or initiate interventions needed for achieving socially shared regulation of motivation in inquiry. Furthermore, situated self-reports could be implemented during the process of inquiry, and more adaptive support could be provided in online environments, such as through dashboards derived from machine learning and educational data mining (Dindar et al., 2018).

In the practical design of inquiry learning sessions, students should be engaged in reflecting on and talking about their motivation. This is especially a signal to teachers and teacher educators so that teachers and students learning to be teachers would themselves have an understanding of motivation as a phenomena and its driving force for successful inquiry. On the one hand, inquiry learning provides opportunities for individual and collective success for reinforcing motivation, and on the other hand, there are experiences of failures and learning challenges that provide opportunities for training motivation regulation. These situations are valuable for learners to become aware of their strengths and weaknesses in learning situations and "to investigate" their own learning.

References

Belland, B. R., Kim, C., & Hannafin, M. J. (2013). A framework for designing scaffolds that improve motivation and cognition. *Educational Psychologist*, *48*(4), 243–270. http://doi.org/10.1080/00461520.2013.838920

Blumenfeld, P. C., Soloway, E., Marx, R. W., Krajcik, J. S., Guzdial, M., & Palıncsar, A. (1991). Motivating project-based learning: Sustaining the doing, supporting the learning. *Educational Psychologist*, *26*(3–4), 369–398. https://doi.org/10.1080/00461520.1991.9653139

Boekaerts, M. (2011). Emotions, emotion regulation, and self-regulation of learning. In B. J. Zimmerman & D. H. Schunk (Eds.), *Handbook of self-regulation of learning and performance* (pp. 408–425). New York: Routledge.

Boekaerts, M., de Koning, E., & Vedder, P. (2006). Goal-directed behavior and contextual factors in the classroom: An innovative approach to the study of multiple goals. *Educational Psychologist*, *41*(1), 33–51. https://doi.org/10.1207/s15326985ep4101_5

Boekaerts, M., & Minnaert, A. E. M. G. (2006). Affective and motivational outcomes of working in collaborative groups. *Educational Psychology*, *26*(2), 187–208. https://doi.org/10.1080/01443410500344217

Boekaerts, M., & Pekrun, R. (2015). Emotions and emotion regulation in academic settings. In L. Corno & E. Anderman (Eds.), *Handbook of educational psychology* (3rd ed., pp. 76–90). New York: Routledge.

Broussard, S. R., La Lopa, J. M., & Ross-Davis, A. (2007). Synergistic knowledge development in interdisciplinary teams. *Journal of Natural Resources and Life Sciences Education*, *36*(1), 129–133. Retrieved from http://www.human-dimensions.org/images/JNRLSE_2007.pdf

Care, E., Griffin, P., & McGaw, B. (2012). *Assessment and teaching of 21st century skills*. Springer.

Damşa, C. I. (2014). The multi-layered nature of small-group learning: Productive interactions in object-oriented collaboration. *International Journal of Computer-Supported Collaborative Learning*, *9*(3), 247–281. https://doi.org/10.1007/s11412-014-9193-8

Derry, S. J., Hmelo-Silver, C. E., Nagarajan, A., Chernobilsky, E., & Beitzel, B. D. (2006). Cognitive transfer revisited: Can we exploit new media to solve old problems on a large scale? *Journal of Educational Computing Research*, *35*(2), 145–162. https://doi.org/10.2190/0576-R724-T149-5432

Desimone, L. M. (2009). Improving impact studies of teachers' professional development: Toward better conceptualizations and measures. *Educational Researcher*, *38*(3), 181–199. https://doi.org/10.3102/0013189X08331140

Dweck, C. S., & Leggett, E. L. (1988). A social-cognitive approach to motivation and personality. *Psychological Review*, *95*(2), 256–273. US: American Psychological Association. https://doi.org/10.1037/0033-295X.95.2.256

Elliot, A. J. (1999). Approach and avoidance motivation and achievement goals. *Educational Psychologist*, *34*(3), 169–189. https://doi.org/10.1207/s15326985ep3403_3

Fransen, J., Kirschner, P. A., & Erkens, G. (2011). Mediating team effectiveness in the context of collaborative learning: The importance of team and task awareness. *Computers in Human Behavior*, *27*(3), 1103–1113. https://doi.org/10.1016/j.chb.2010.05.017

Fransen, J., Weinberger, A., & Kirschner, P. (2013). Team effectiveness and team development in CSCL. *Educational Psychologist*, *48*(4), 9–24. https://doi.org/10.1080/00461520.2012.747947

Gijbels, D., Dochy, F., Van den Bossche, P., & Segers, M. (2005). Effects of problem-based learning: A meta-analysis from the angle of assessment. *Review of Educational Research*, *75*(1), 27–61. https://doi.org/10.3102/00346543075001027

Gross, J. J., & Thompson, R. A. (2007). Emotion regulation: Conceptual foundations. In J. J. Gross (Ed.), *Handbook of emotion regulation* (pp. 3–24). New York: Guilford Press.

Hadwin, A., Järvelä, S., & Miller, M. (2017). Self-regulation, co-regulation and shared regulation in collaborative learning environments. In D. Schunk & J. Greene (Eds.), *Handbook of self-regulation of learning and performance* (pp. 83–106). New York: Routledge.

Hadwin, A. F., Oshige, M., Gress, C., & Winne, P. (2010). Innovative ways for using gStudy to orchestrate and research social aspects of self-regulated learning. *Computers in Human Behavior*, *26*(5), 794–805. https://doi.org/10.1016/j.chb.2007.06.007

Jansen, M., Scherer, R., & Schroeders, U. (2015). Students' self-concept and self-efficacy in the sciences: Differential relations to antecedents and educational outcomes. *Contemporary Educational Psychology*, *41*, 13–24. https://doi.org/10.1016/j.cedpsych.2014.11.002

Järvelä, S., & Hadwin, A. (2013). New frontiers: Regulating learning in CSCL. *Educational Psychologist*, *48*(1), 25–39. https://doi.org/10.1080/00461520.2012.74800

Järvelä, S., Hadwin, A. F., Malmberg, J., & Miller, M. (2017). Contemporary perspectives of regulated learning in collaboration. In F. Fischer, C. E. Hmelo-Silver, P. Reimann, & S. R. Goldman (Eds.), *Handbook of the learning sciences* (pp. 127–136). New York: Taylor & Francis.

Järvelä, S., Järvenoja, H., Malmberg, J., Isohätälä, J., & Sobocinski, M. (2016). How do types of interaction and phases of self-regulated learning set a stage for collaborative engagement? *Learning and Instruction, 43*, 39–51. https://doi.org/10.1016/j.learninstruc.2016.01.005

Järvelä, S., Järvenoja, H., & Veermans, M. (2008). Understanding the dynamics of motivation in socially shared learning [Special issue]. *International Journal of Educational Research, 47*(2), 122–135. https://doi.org/10.1016/j.ijer.2007.11.012

Järvelä, S., Kirschner, P. A., Panadero, E., Malmberg, J., Phielix, C., Jaspers, J., … Järvenoja, H. (2014). Enhancing socially shared regulation in collaborative learning groups: Designing for CSCL regulation tools. *Educational Technology Research and Development, 63*(1), 125–142. https://doi.org/10.1007/s11423-014-9358-1

Järvelä, S., & Renninger, K. A. (2014). Designing for learning: Interest, motivation, and engagement. In D. Keith Sawyer (Ed.), *Cambridge handbook of the learning sciences* (2nd ed., pp. 668–685). New York: Cambridge University Press.

Järvelä, S., Veermans, M., & Leinonen, P. (2008). Investigating student engagement in computer-supported inquiry: A process-oriented analysis. *Social Psychology of Education, 11*(3), 299–322. https://doi.org/10.1007/s11218-007-9047-6

Järvelä, S., & Volet, S. (2004). Motivation in real-life, dynamic, and interactive learning environments: Stretching constructs and methodologies. *European Psychologist, 9*(4), 193–197. https://doi.org/10.1027/1016-9040.9.4.193

Järvelä, S., Volet, S., & Järvenoja, H. (2010). Research on motivation in collaborative learning: Moving beyond the cognitive-situative divide and combining individual and social processes. *Educational Psychologist, 45*(1), 15–27. https://doi.org/10.1080/00461520903433539

Järvenoja, H., & Järvelä, S. (2005). How students describe the sources of their emotional and motivational experiences during the learning process: A qualitative approach. *Learning and Instruction, 15*(5), 465–480. http://dx.doi.org/10.1016/j.learninstruc.2005.07.012

Järvenoja, H., Järvelä, S., & Malmberg, J. (2015). Understanding regulated learning in situative and contextual frameworks. *Educational Psychologist, 50*(3), 204–219. https://doi.org/10.1080/00461520.2015.1075400

Järvenoja, H., Järvelä, S., & Malmberg, J. (2017). Supporting groups' emotion and motivation regulation during collaborative learning. *Learning and Instruction*. Advance online publication. https://doi.org/10.1016/j.learninstruc.2017.11.004

Järvenoja, H., Malmberg, J., Järvelä, S., Näykki, P., & Kontturi, H. (2019). Investigating students' situation-specific emotional state and motivational goals during a learning project within one primary school classroom. *Learning: Research and Practice, 5*(1), 4–23. https://doi.org/10.1080/23735082.2018.1554821

Järvenoja, H., Volet, S., & Järvelä, S. (2012). Regulation of emotions in socially challenging learning situations: An instrument to measure the adaptive and social nature of the regulation process. *Educational Psychology, 33(1), 1–28*. https://doi.org/10.1080/01443410.2012.742334

Kirschner, P. A., Sweller, J., & Clark, R. E. (2006). Why minimal guidance during instruction does not work: An analysis of the failure of constructivist, discovery, problem-based, experiential, and inquiry-based teaching. *Educational Psychologist, 41*(2), 75–86. https://doi.org/10.1207/s15326985ep4102_1

Kirschner, P. A., Sweller, J., Kirschner, F., & Zambrano R., J. (2018). From cognitive load theory to collaborative cognitive load theory. *International Journal of Computer-Supported Collaborative Learning, 13*(2), 213–233. https://doi.org/10.1007/s11412-018-9277-y

Knorr-Cetina, K. (2001). Objectual practice. In T. R. Schatzki, K. Knorr-Cetina, & E. von Savigny (Eds.), *The practice turn in contemporary theory* (pp. 175–188). London: Routledge.

Komarraju, M., & Nadler, D. (2013). Self-efficacy and academic achievement: Why do implicit beliefs, goals, and effort regulation matter? *Learning and Individual Differences, 25*, 67–72. https://doi.org/10.1016/j.lindif.2013.01.005

Krajcik, J., Blumenfeld, P. C., Marx, R. W., Bass, K. M., Fredricks, J., & Soloway, E. (1998). Inquiry in project-based science classrooms: Initial attempts by middle school students. *Journal of the Learning Sciences*, 7(3–4), 313–350. https://doi.org/10.1080/10508406.1998.9672057

Kuhn, D. (2015). Thinking together and alone. *Educational Researcher, 44*(1), 46–53. http://doi.org/10.3102/0013189X15569530

Laakkonen, J., & Muukkonen, H. (2019). Fostering students' collaborative learning competencies and professional conduct in the context of two gross anatomy courses in veterinary medicine. Anatomical Sciences Education, 12(2), 154-163.

Lakkala, M., Toom, A., Ilomäki, L., & Muukkonen, H. (2015). Re-designing university courses to support collaborative knowledge creation practices. *Australasian Journal of Educational Technology, 31*(5), 521–536.

Linnenbrink-Garcia, L., & Pekrun, R. (2011). Students' emotions and academic engagement: Introduction to the special issue. *Contemporary Educational Psychology, 36*(1), 1–3. https://doi.org/10.1016/j.cedpsych.2010.11.004

Linnenbrink-Garcia, L., Patall, E. A. (2016). Motivation. In E. Anderman & L. Corno (Eds.), *Handbook of educational psychology* (3rd ed., pp. 91–103). New York: Taylor & Francis.

Litmanen, T., Lonka, K., Inkinen, M., Lipponen, L., & Hakkarainen, K. (2012). Capturing teacher students' emotional experiences in context: Does inquiry-based learning make a difference? *Instructional Science, 40*(6), 1083–1101. https://doi.org/10.1007/s11251-011-9203-4

Maehr, M. L., & Midgley, C. (1996). *Transforming school cultures*. Boulder, CO: Westview Press.

Mäkitalo-Siegl, K., & Fischer, F. (2013). Help seeking in computer-supported collaborative inquiry-learning environments. In S. A. Karabenick & M. Puustinen (Eds.), *Advances in help-seeking research and applications: The role of emerging technologies* (pp. 99–120). Charlotte, NC: IAP Information Age Publishing.

Mercier, E. M. (2017). The influence of achievement goals on collaborative interactions and knowledge convergence. *Learning and Instruction, 50*, 31–43. https://doi.org/10.1016/j.learninstruc.2016.11.006

Minnaert, A., Boekaerts, M., & de Brabander, C. (2007). Autonomy, competence, and social relatedness in task interest within project-based education. *Psychological Reports, 101*(2), 574–586. https://doi.org/10.2466/pr0.101.2.574–586

Muukkonen, H., & Lakkala, M. (2009). Exploring metaskills of knowledge-creating inquiry in higher education. *International Journal of Computer Supported Collaborative Learning, 4*(2), 187–211.

Muukkonen, H., Lakkala, M., Kaistinen, J., & Nyman, G. (2010). Knowledge creating inquiry in a distributed project management course. *Research and Practice in Technology-Enhanced Learning, 5*(2), 73–96. Retrieved from http://www.worldscinet.com/rptel/05/preserved-docs/0502/S1793206810000827.pdf

Muukkonen, H., Lakkala, M., Lahti-Nuuttila, P., Ilomäki, L., Karlgren, K., & Toom, A. (2020). Assessing the development of collaborative knowledge work competence: Scales for higher education course contexts. *Scandinavian Journal of Educational Research, 64*(7), 1071–1089. Retrieved from 10.1080/00313831.2019.1647284

Muukkonen, H., Lakkala, M., Toom, A., & Ilomäki, L. (2017). Assessment of competences in knowledge work and object-bound collaboration during higher education courses. In E. Kyndt, V. Donche, K. Trigwell, & S. Lindblom-Ylänne (Eds.), *Higher education transitions: Theory and research* (pp. 288–305). London: Routledge.

Näykki, P., Järvelä, S., Kirschner, P., & Järvenoja, H. (2014). Socio-emotional conflict in collaborative learning: A process-oriented case study in a higher education context. *International Journal of Educational Research, 68*, 1–14. https://doi.org/10.1016/j.ijer.2014.07.001

Nolen, S. B., & Ward, C. J. (2008). Sociocultural and situative approaches to studying motivation. In M. Maehr, S. Karabenick, & T. Urdan (Eds.), *Advances in motivation and achievement: Social psychological perspectives on motivation and achievement* (pp. 425–460). London: Emerald.

O'Donnell, A. M., & Hmelo-Silver, C. E. (2013). What is collaborative learning: An overview. In C. E. Hmelo-Silver, Chinn, C., Chan, C., & O'Donnell, A. M. (Eds.), *The international handbook of collaborative learning* (pp. 1–16). Abingdon: Routledge.

Paavola, S., & Hakkarainen, K. (2005). The knowledge creation metaphor – An emergent epistemological approach to learning. *Science & Education, 14*, 535–557. https://doi.org/10.1007/s11191-004-5157-0

Patrick, H., Ryan, A. M., & Kaplan, A. (2007). Early adolescents' perceptions of the classroom social environment, motivational beliefs, and engagement. *Journal of Educational Psychology, 99*(1), 83–98. https://doi.org/10.1037/0022–0663.99.1.83

Payne, S. C., Youngcourt, S. S., & Beaubien, J. M. (2007). A meta-analytic examination of the goal orientation nomological net. *Journal of Applied Psychology, 92*(1), 128–150. https://doi.org/10.1037/0021-9010.92.1.128

Renninger, K., & Hidi, S. (2016). *The power of interest for motivation and engagement*. New York: Routledge.

Renniger, K. A., Ren, Y., & Kern, H. M. (2018). Motivation, engagement, and interest. In F. Fischer, C. E. Hmelo-Silver, S. R. Goldman, & P. Reimann (Eds.), *International handbook of the learning sciences* (pp. 116–126). London: Routledge. https://doi.org/10.4324/9781315617572-12

Renninger, K. A., & Riley, R. R. (2015). The ICAN Intervention: Supporting learners to make connections to science content during science inquiry. *Science Scope, 29*(4), 49–53. https://doi.org/10.2505/4/ss15_039_04_49

Rogat, T. K., & Linnenbrink-Garcia, L. (2011). Socially shared regulation in collaborative groups: An analysis of the interplay between quality of social regulation and group processes. *Cognition and Instruction, 29*(4), 375–415. https://doi.org/10.1080/07370008.2011.607930

Rogat, T. K., Linnenbrink-García, L., & DiDonato, N. (2013). Motivation in collaborative groups. In C. E. Hmelo-Silver, C. A. Chinn, C. Chan, & A. M. O'Donnell (Eds.), *International handbook of collaborative learning* (pp. 250–267). London: Routledge.

Ryan, R., & Deci, E. (2000). Self-determination theory and the facilitation of intrinsic motivation, social development, and well-being. *The American Psychologist, 55*(1), 68–78. https://doi.org/10.1037/0003-066X.55.1.68

Salonen, P., Vauras, M., & Efklides, A. (2005). Social interaction: What can it tell us about metacognition and co-regulation in learning? *European Psychologist, 10*(3), 199–208. https://doi.org/10.1027/1016-9040.10.3.199

Schunk, D. H., & DiBenedetto, M. K. (2009). Self-efficacy theory in education. In K. R. Wentzel, & D. B. Miele (Eds.), *Handbook of motivation at school, 2* (pp. 34–54). New York: Routledge.

Schunk, D. H., & Zimmerman, B. J. (Eds.) (1994). *Self-regulation of learning and performance: Issues and educational applications.* Hillsdale, NJ: Lawrence Erlbaum.

Thompson, L., & Fine, G. A. (1999). Socially shared cognition, affect, and behavior: A review and integration. *Personality and Social Psychology Review, 3*(4), 278–302. https://doi.org/10.1207/s15327957pspr0304_1

Urdan, T. C., & Maehr, M. L. (1995). Beyond a two-goal theory of motivation and achievement: A case for social goals. *Review of Educational Research, 65*(3), 213–243. https://doi.org/10.3102/00346543065003213

Vauras, M., Salonen, P., Lehtinen, E., & Kinnunen, R. (2009). Motivation in school from contextual and longitudinal perspectives. In M. Wosnitza, S. A. Karabenick, A. Efklides, & P. Nenninger (Eds.), *Contemporary motivation research: From global to local perspectives* (pp. 1–23). Göttingen: Hogrefe.

Volet, S., & Järvelä, S. (Eds.). (2001). *Motivation in learning contexts: Theoretical advances and methodological implications.* London: Pergamon.

Volet, S., & Mansfield, C. (2006). Group work at university: Significance of personal goals in the regulation strategies of students with positive and negative appraisals. *Higher Education Research & Development, 25*(4), 341–356. https://doi.org/10.1080/07294360600947301

Volet, S., Vauras, M., & Salonen, P. (2009). Self- and social regulation in learning contexts: An integrative perspective. *Educational Psychologist, 44*(4), 215–226. https://doi.org/10.1080/00461520903213584

Winne, P. H., Hadwin, A. F., Nesbit, J. C., Kumar, V., & Beaudoin, L. (2005). gStudy: A toolkit for developing computer-supported tutorials and researching learning strategies and instruction (version 2.0) [computer program]. Simon Fraser University, Burnaby, BC.

Wolters, C. A. (2003). Understanding procrastination from a self-regulated learning perspective. *Journal of Educational Psychology, 95*(1), 179–187. https://doi.org/10.1037/0022-0663.95.1.179

Wolters, C. A., & Benzon, M. B. (2013). Assessing and predicting college students' use of strategies for the self-regulation of motivation. *The Journal of Experimental Education, 81*(2), 199–221, https://doi.org/10.1080/00220973.2012.699901

Zimmerman, B. J. (1989). A social cognitive view of self-regulated academic learning. *Journal of Educational Psychology, 81*(3), 329–339. https://doi.org/10.1037//0022–0663.81.3.329

Zimmerman, B. J. (2011). Motivational sources and outcomes of self-regulated learning and performance. In B. J. Zimmerman, & D. H. Schunk (Eds.), *Handbook of self-regulation of learning and performance* (pp. 49–64). New York: Routledge.

10

SCAFFOLDING INQUIRY

Reviewing and Expanding on the Function and Form of Scaffolding in Inquiry Learning

Chris Quintana

Introduction

As educational theory and practices continue to evolve, they inspire different learning and pedagogical approaches in different formal and out-of-class learning contexts. But across these learning contexts, one core idea remains constant: the need for more expert agents to support learners with their learning activity. This notion of *scaffolding* has been practiced and studied in many ways to better understand a variety of techniques for supporting learners over the challenges they encounter in their learning. While the contemporary idea of scaffolding emerged from studying the support provided to children during complex problem-solving activity (e.g., Wood, Bruner, & Ross, 1976), we continue to refine and expand the notion of scaffolding, especially with the evolving curricular activities and tools that learners have at their disposal. Recent efforts have helped develop more specific scaffolding descriptions and frameworks resulting in a corpus of structured scaffolding guidelines and principles that identify different conceptual approaches (or *scaffolding functions*) that support educational activity (e.g., Kali & Linn, 2007; Quintana et al., 2004). Other work, especially on scaffolded tools, provides examples of different *scaffolding forms*—the specific manner that scaffolding functions are implemented in a learning environment. Such work provides some foundations for discussing scaffolding, but new types of curricula, learning approaches, and tools open new scaffolding challenges and issues to explore in more detail.

One such learning approach is *inquiry learning*. Research on inquiry learning, an ongoing active and dynamic area of study, describes curricular and pedagogical approaches for inquiry as well as tools learners can use to engage in and learn inquiry. New inquiry standards and expectations—and the inquiry practices that can address these expectations—help expand the scaffolding functions needed to support learners with different inquiry practices. In addition, novel technologies and the blending of analog and digital tools that are being used within inquiry activity can also lead to new ideas about the specific implementations of scaffolding strategies in learning environments. Traditional discussions about scaffolding considered either face-to-face scaffolding that a teacher might use with a student, or technology-based scaffolding. But new technologies that are now being used in inquiry learning environments are leading to new research directions about different scaffolding forms and representational mechanisms that convey supportive information to learners.

Research on inquiry learning and scaffolding have been tightly connected for many years, and as the work on inquiry evolves, so too the work on how to potentially expand the notion of scaffolding. But before thinking about new directions for scaffolding inquiry, it is necessary to review the definitions and components of scaffolding, and to explicate how scaffolding is much more than simply support for learners in a particular learning environment.

Reviewing the Core Aspects of Scaffolding

The root description of scaffolding can be traced back to Wood, Bruner, and Ross (1976) in their influential paper on scaffolding and the role that tutoring plays in an instructional setting. That research explored situations where children were asked to build towers out of blocks, with the focus being on how an adult in the setting guided the children in this task. Within this context, Wood, Bruner, and Ross describe a "...kind of 'scaffolding' process that enables a child or novice to solve a problem, carry out a task or achieve a goal which would be beyond his unassisted efforts" (1976, p. 90). This definition, and the discussion that followed, set out many of the common features of scaffolding. One core feature is that a more expert agent can scaffold a learner through a difficult practice by "controlling" the aspects of a task that are too difficult for the learner, thus allowing the learner to focus on the aspects of the task that are within their range of competence. This mirrors Vygotsky's (1978) characterization of the "zone of proximal development (ZPD)," which represents the tasks that a learner can currently do *with assistance*. In this light, scaffolding is seen as that assistance in supporting a learner in their ZPD. Wood, Bruner, and Ross went on to describe six "scaffolding functions" that outline the manner in which an expert's activity can scaffold a novice through (1976):

- **Recruitment**: Setting the learner's interest and focus onto the important task at hand.
- **Reduction in degrees of freedom**: Simplifying the task in a productive manner to make a complex problem more doable by the learner (e.g., handling more complex parts of the task to allow the learner to engage in the aspects of the task they can currently handle themselves).
- **Direction maintenance**: Maintaining the learner's focus on the task and keeping them on the problem-solving track.
- **Marking critical features**: Accentuating or making explicit and relevant the critical and important aspects of the task (e.g., describing to the learner the difference between what the learner has produced and what the expert notes should be the correct production).
- **Frustration control**: Reducing the amount of frustration the novice learner may develop as they work on the task, though in ways that will reduce the learner's potential dependence on the tutor.
- **Demonstration**: Modeling or demonstrating a complex task to the learner.

Similar conceptual scaffolding ideas are also seen in Collins, Brown, and Newman's (1989) notion of *cognitive apprenticeship*—an apprenticeship model that can be used for learning cognitive skills. This model describes a mentor-apprenticeship relationship, and how reflection, monitoring, and self-correction through dialogue between the mentor and apprentice reflect many of the ideas about scaffolding, ZPD, and the expert-novice relationship. Note that the mentor-apprenticeship relationship may also include degrees of "expert-ness," especially when thinking about how more advanced learners may scaffold their peers, even as they are still learning themselves.

Taken together, these functions illustrate the fact that scaffolding should support a learner through the difficulties of a complex task, but in ways that still require the learner to expend cognitive effort on the tasks they are doing and learning. Reiser (2004) describes these conceptual issues in terms of the "structure" and "problematize" mechanisms of scaffolding. On the one hand, scaffolding should provide *structure* for learners to allow them to engage in a complex task by reducing the difficulty of the task. However, on the other hand, scaffolding should *problematize* the task for the learner, challenging the learner so that they expend the necessary effort in their engagement with the task. Consider an example of an inquiry project where students are working on selecting activities to add to their inquiry plan. Students with less experience in inquiry may not know what steps to take in order to drive their inquiry in a productive direction. For example, Symphony was a software environment that integrated a range of science inquiry tools behind an interface that scaffolded science inquiry processes (Quintana et al., 2004). The Symphony process map (Figure 10.1) scaffolds students by illustrating a set of possibilities for students to ponder and select. The process map provides structure by explicitly showing the inquiry possibilities that students may not be aware of. But it also problematizes the students' work by not explicitly showing the specific activity they should select for their plan—students still need to consider their options, discuss the possibilities, and select the next step for themselves. If the problematization vastly outweighs the structure (e.g., not using any sort of map to illustrate the possibilities), the task can remain too challenging and the learner may be unable to follow through with the task because of difficulty, loss of focus or interest, and so on. If the structure vastly outweighs the problematization (e.g., simply telling students what specific activity they should do next), the task may be made too easy, which can impede learning.

Another core aspect of scaffolding is that it should offer temporary support that ceases (or *fades*) when the learner is able to independently negotiate the task that was being supported by the scaffold. This is an important aspect of scaffolding that does not always receive the necessary depth of attention. Early scaffolding work pointed to the notion that the learner's need for scaffolding should be constantly gauged by the expert to determine whether it should be increased or reduced. For example, Wood and Middleton (1975) described observations of the mother-child instructional relationship and the mothers' use of two "rules" in a problem-solving context: If the child is doing well on the task, offer less help, but if the child is having problems with the task, offer more help. This connects to the notion of "contingent learning" (Wood & Wood, 1996, 1999) where the amount of instruction is contingent on the learner's performance on some learning activity. Here, a distinction is made between scaffolding, where additional instruction or support is added, and fading, where instruction or support is drawn back. The specific term "fading" was not necessarily mentioned in these discussions of contingent learning, but the concept of adding and removing scaffolding as needed through close monitoring of a learner's performance on a learning task is key. The term "fading" does arise in Collins, Brown, and Newman (1989) and their description of the scaffolding/fading process. There, the apprentice can observe the mentor

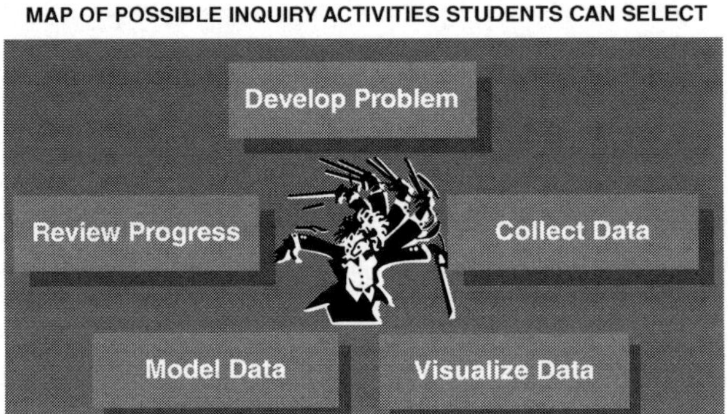

Figure 10.1 Symphony process map describes possible next steps (*structure*) without telling students what steps should be performed next, leaving that for students to determine (*problematize*)

as they *model* the target task. The apprentice can then attempt the task with *coaching* (i.e., scaffolding) from the mentor, and as the apprentice improves their performance of the task, the mentor can reduce (i.e., fade) the amount of scaffolding they are providing. Collins, Brown, and Newman (1989) summarize these concepts by describing scaffolding as "the supports the teacher provides to help the student carry out a task" (p. 482) and fading as the "gradual removal of supports until students are on their own" (p. 482).

Pea (2004) discussed the importance of the concept of fading when defining scaffolding, issuing a reminder that scaffolding discussions should not lose the idea of how (and whether) scaffolding fades. Pea (2004) describes fading as an "intrinsic component of the scaffolding framework" (p. 431), and if a given type of support does not or cannot fade, then it should not be qualified as a scaffold, but rather as a cognitive support that lies within a larger system of supports. This follows the idea of "distributed intelligence" (Pea, 1993), where a series of supports in a given context can be available to learners in the form of different supportive tools or interventions. Some supports may be intrinsic to a given task without which the task would not be possible (i.e., a cognitive support). Providing support alone does not make for a scaffold. Without fading, the supportive tool cannot exemplify the temporary nature of scaffolding described earlier and would then result in a situation where any supportive element is seen as scaffolding. As Stone (1998) describes in his review of the scaffolding metaphor that, in a learning situation, it is necessary that the guidance being provided to a learner should be temporary and dismantled as learners demonstrate their knowledge. A supportive tool that does not fade raises the question of whether the learner is actually learning anything or whether the tool has become a "crutch" that the learner cannot do without.

The idea of fading, along with other aspects of scaffolding defined earlier, helps move toward an integrative definition of scaffolding. For example, van de Pol, Volman, and Beishuizen (2010) provide a conceptual model of scaffolding (in teacher-student contexts) that illustrates the common aspects seen in several scaffolding characterizations:

- **Contingency**: This describes how teachers must use diagnostic strategies to determine the assistance the learner needs in the moment and then determine the scaffolding strategies that provide the requisite support.
- **Fading**: This describes how the teacher, in making these constant diagnoses, will begin to provide less support as the learner exhibits more expertise in their tasks.
- **Transfer of responsibility**: This is related to fading in that as the learner gains more expertise, they take more control of their learning (which can signal to the teacher that they can fade some scaffolding).

This model synthesizes many of the core ideas about scaffolding that help to conceptually clarify the concept for a general learning environment. These ideas began to expand as computers became used more frequently in education. For example, the idea of *software-realized scaffolding* was described by Guzdial (1994) in which he described three specific ways that software could scaffold learners: (1) by communicating processes to learners, (2) by providing hints and reminders to coach learners about their work, and (3) by encouraging reflection by eliciting articulation. These ideas were further expanded by Soloway, Guzdial, and Hay (1994) in their articulation of a *learner-centered design (LCD)* approach to software design. Work around software design at the time was focused on designing for software usability and supporting efficient activity. However, the concept of LCD was introduced to describe how, when designing software for learning contexts, designers also need to think about (1) the supportive needs learners faced in tackling complex, new tasks and material, and (2) the design of scaffolding features in software to provide that support by describing how software can change the nature of complex tasks to make them more accessible and can encourage and motivate learners as they are tackling complex activity.

These early ideas about scaffolding in technology reinforced and expanded many of the existing conceptual scaffolding descriptions, while also starting a discussion about what kinds of specific mechanisms could implement these scaffolding concepts. These ideas about scaffolding in software came at a pivotal point in which there was increasing interest in inquiry learning and the curricula and software tools that could support it. These discussions intersected with ideas about what it means to scaffold inquiry practices (i.e., scaffolding functions) and the specific techniques that realize these scaffolding approaches (i.e., scaffolding forms).

Scaffolding Function: What Kind of Scaffolding Is Needed in Complex Inquiry Practices?

Growing interest in inquiry learning, and how to support learners with such activity, increased awareness that it was becoming more important to systematically identify and organize different scaffolding approaches for inquiry. One research strand developed frameworks that organized and classified scaffolding features in ways that were not just useful from a scaffolding perspective but also for expanding descriptions of inquiry and inquiry practices themselves.

An example of research from this strand is the Scaffolding Design Framework (Quintana et al., 2004), which provides an organizational scheme to describe different scaffolding approaches for inquiry activity. The framework defined inquiry at a high level as "...the process of posing questions and investigating them with empirical data, either through direct manipulation of variables via experiments or by constructing comparisons using existing data sets" (Quintana et al., 2004, p. 341). Given this characterization of inquiry, three different "constituents of inquiry" organize the framework with a high-level view of inquiry to describe where learners need scaffolding as they iterate through different inquiry activities. These three components served as organizational categories to describe more focused scaffolding guidelines and strategies for inquiry:

- **Sensemaking**. This component includes the basic operations of testing hypotheses and interpreting data. The relevant scaffolding approaches include using representations and language that connect to and bridge a learner's understanding and allow learners to inspect data in different ways. Also, that tools and artifacts should be organized around the semantics of a discipline to help shape the learner's conception of inquiry activity.
- **Process management**. This component includes the strategic decisions made when planning and engaging in the inquiry process. These scaffolding approaches include providing structure and expert guidance for inquiry practices, tasks, and functionality, as well as having tools automatically handle routine tasks that may be less salient to the learner's inquiry activity so they focus on the more important aspects of their work.
- **Reflection and articulation**. This component includes the process of constructing, evaluating, and articulating different ideas during the inquiry process and what has been learned from it. These scaffolding approaches include facilitating ongoing support for reflection throughout the inquiry activity.

Another framework in this research tradition is the Design Principles Database framework (Kali & Linn, 2007), which had a stated goal of coalescing and synthesizing design knowledge about the use of technology for education. The framework organizes different supportive software features by using a set of "pragmatic principles," which themselves are organized into a set of higher-level "meta-principles." Taken together, these principles describe more conceptual scaffolding for learners during inquiry. The meta-principles and descriptions of some of the corresponding pragmatic principles in the database include:

- **Make science accessible**. This category includes features that connect learners to personally relevant examples and communicate the diversity of science inquiry to learners. The aim is to support students so that they can see how inquiry is done in real-world contexts and what kind of activity the inquiry process is composed of in a way that makes it seem less abstract or out of reach.
- **Make thinking visible**. This category includes features that help learners organize their thoughts and ideas through structured templates that provide learners with tools to represent their knowledge and ideas in different ways. These tools also enable learner view and manipulate data and other representations in different ways.
- **Help learners learn from each other**. This category includes features that encourage learners to learn from and work with others in the collaborative manner seen in inquiry activity, such as supporting learners to participate in online science discussions or collaboratively develop hypotheses during their classroom investigations.
- **Promote autonomous lifelong learning**. This category includes features that encourage learners to reflect on their work throughout their inquiry activity and to support learners with being able to explore data and phenomena by manipulating different factors and aspects of those models.

New Visions of Inquiry

These early frameworks were developed by examining scaffolded tools and curricula in a science context. But the way in which inquiry has been described over the years has evolved, and it is interesting to consider how these revised characterizations of inquiry now impact the scaffolding discussion. In previous characterizations, the term "inquiry" was seen in terms of an investigation to conduct and the different activities that are involved in that investigation. There were some overlaps in different descriptions of inquiry, but there was not necessarily a specific set of activities that were agreed upon as being "inquiry." Contemporary science standards like the Next Generation Science Standards (NGSS; National Research Council, 2013) largely replaced the notion of inquiry method or process with the idea of more specific science and engineering *practices*: asking questions and defining problems; developing and using models; planning and carrying out investigations; analyzing and interpreting data; using mathematics and computational thinking; constructing explanations and designing solutions; engaging in argument from evidence; and obtaining, evaluating, and communicating information. Many of these practices were described in previous characterizations of inquiry. However, in some respects, those descriptions of inquiry were also being developed ahead of or along with the different scaffolding frameworks that described ways of scaffolding inquiry. This meant that there were related, yet different, characterizations of inquiry and corresponding scaffolding ideas that made it challenging to compare or relate scaffolding ideas from different frameworks. For example, the Design Principles Database discusses ways of scaffolding collaboration or learning from others, while the Scaffolding Design Framework does not necessarily discuss the collaborative aspects of inquiry as a core aspect of inquiry that needs support. The NGSS practices are more comprehensive and specifically articulated to provide a more focused characterization of what needs to be scaffolded. This provides a more consistent platform with which to discuss scaffolding approaches for inquiry in science. The NGSS also describes how these practices support learning disciplinary core ideas (key disciplinary concepts), which adds another layer to consider whether scaffolding features need to be conceptualized around different disciplinary concepts. This conceptualization also leads to different possibilities to further expand the notion of scaffolding. One direction considers a differentiation between general approaches to scaffold disciplinary ideas and augmenting general scaffolding features with scaffolding "variants" that incorporate disciplinary knowledge. For example, given the NGSS description of modeling, we can focus on general scaffolding features to support the construction of models. But we can also consider how we might vary those scaffolding approaches to also include more nuanced disciplinary scaffolding, such as specific features to scaffold the development of a chemistry model versus features to scaffold an ecology model. Such work can contribute to thinking about how previous characterizations of and frameworks for scaffolding should evolve as the idea of "inquiry" evolves from the central (albeit, less clearly defined) concept being scaffolded to the NGSS distinction of a more defined "scientific practices."

Inquiry across Multiple Domains

While the notion of inquiry is evolving in science, there are also questions about inquiry in other domains to understand how inquiry is characterized in different fields. For example, Quintana, Zhang, and Krajcik (2005) put forth a more generalized and simplified view of inquiry in their Metacognitive Scaffolding Framework, which described scaffolding approaches for the metacognitive aspects of "online inquiry." Here, online inquiry could be seen as a more generalized view of inquiry where learners use web-based information to address questions they have posed in a variety of domains, not just science (Zhang & Quintana, 2011). Online inquiry is characterized by four high-level activities: asking questions, searching for online information, evaluating and reading that information, and synthesizing the information to answer the questions. These online inquiry activities are then crossed with three metacognitive challenges that learners face: task understanding and inquiry planning, monitoring and regulating an investigation, and reflection. For each online inquiry activity, there are scaffolding features identified to address each metacognitive challenge as it plays out in that activity. The Metacognitive Scaffolding Framework aimed to explicitly call out the need to scaffold metacognitive activity during inquiry, which is sometimes implied or less explicit in other scaffolding frameworks. For example, metacognitive scaffolding features could support learners with planning their inquiry activity or with monitoring their progress through their investigations and regulating their subsequent activity. This can lead to other avenues to explore in terms of scaffolding inquiry and considering scaffolding at these cognitive and metacognitive levels. The challenge involves developing scaffolding features to support metacognitive processes that can be difficult to express and gauge. Traditional metacognitive scaffolding features include textual prompts to support reflection or planning tools and grids that help learners develop an inquiry plan and track progress. But there is still room to consider different ways to articulate metacognitive process within inquiry and different features to scaffold those processes.

In history education, there are also efforts in incorporating inquiry practices in "historical inquiry" and illustrating what scaffolding looks like in for inquiry in this domain. For example, Li and Lim (2008) looked at the combination of online inquiry and historical inquiry where students use information gained from the internet to engage in their problem solving. They describe different references to historical inquiry to show how students should be able to create historical narratives and arguments using information in which they check the credibility of that information, validate and weigh evidence for claims being made, and search for causality as they make their arguments. Many of the conceptual scaffolding approaches in historical inquiry are similar to others mentioned earlier: use of prompts to support reflection and articulation, having teachers model the types of questioning activities that historians may use, and so on.

Similar work is seen in mathematics to explore inquiry practices in math education and the requisite scaffolding strategies. For example, Bakker, Smit, and Wegerif (2015) surveyed a range of scaffolding approaches in face-to-face mathematics education contexts to look at the intersection between the dialogic mathematics teaching and scaffolding concepts. They identify a range of scaffolding strategies in mathematics education, many of which are seen in science contexts (e.g., scaffolding approaches for progressing through tasks, analytic scaffolding for making sense of math concepts, placing math problems and concepts in language that makes more sense to learners, modeling math language and thinking). However, this review also identified other scaffolding approaches that support social and dialogic interactions, such as interactions to support math discourse during inquiry discussions, promoting argumentation in a collaborative fashion through peer and teacher discussion, and supporting mathematical conversation between students. While these examples (e.g., scaffolding discourse) are not necessarily exclusive to math, they can inform activities that exist but are not always spotlighted in science inquiry. Anghileri (2006) also outlines a three-level framework that describes teacher strategies for scaffolding learning in mathematics classrooms. These levels describe (1) scaffolding approaches that can come from the peers, experts, and artifacts in the classroom environment; (2) scaffolding approaches when explaining, reviewing, and restructuring math concepts for learners; and (3) scaffolding approaches to help learners develop conceptual thinking in math. Aside from these examples from non-technology contexts, other mathematics education work looked at scaffolding approaches when using technology. For example, Roschelle et al. (2010) describe a scaffolded handheld computer application that students use during mathematics inquiry. Multiple devices are integrated in a system that provides learning guidance as students work together on math problems to scaffold students by supporting repeated practice in different math activities, providing feedback, and supporting cooperative learning techniques.

The previous works serve as examples that have helped to consider the types of inquiry activity in multiple domains and to explore the manner in which these activities have been scaffolded. A productive line of future inquiry would be to compare conceptual scaffolding approaches in multiple domains in order to continue expanding the body of scaffolding approaches and frameworks and develop more ideas about the supportive functions that different scaffolding approaches can provide.

Scaffolding Forms: How Do Different Representations Inform Scaffolding Implementations?

Aside from work in articulating scaffolding function in different inquiry contexts, it is also important to explore the different *forms* that scaffolding can take. By looking at different scaffolding forms, we consider how we can implement different conceptual scaffolding approaches, which in turn can help us potentially consider different, or more nuanced, approaches to inquiry. Work on forms of scaffolding can leverage the different ways scaffolding is implemented, especially looking at scaffolding representations that arise from technology and media-rich tools. Initial characterizations of scaffolding included forms that were essentially limited to interpersonal communication as the expert interacted with the learner to provide different support via coaching, task demonstration, reminders, and so on. As computers began to be used for inquiry, different scaffolding approaches were developed that took advantage of the technology: task diagrams, reflection prompts, coaching from intelligent tutors, and so on. These forms helped to expand the discussion on scaffolding, which can be seen in different frameworks that incorporate a range of software-based scaffolding examples.

With the technology landscape continuing to evolve, new technologies are used to support inquiry in wider contexts, and these have the potential to continue expanding scaffolding ideas as we explore how these tools provide new forms that help us think about scaffolding in ways we might not have thought of previously. These developments can inform new forms of scaffolding and point toward new research directions: Do these technology contexts impact how we think about and enact scaffolding approaches for inquiry? Do these technologies inform ideas about new types of scaffolding we have not yet thought about? The next section poses some examples of how new technologies can be used to support inquiry and impact scaffolding research.

Example: Scaffolding Inquiry "in the Moment" through Mobile Technologies

One attractive aspect of inquiry has been to engage students in inquiry activities in different remote sites (e.g., doing inquiry about ecosystems by exploring and collecting data at a river, or gathering information for historical inquiry at a history museum). One question for doing such work is how to scaffold a number of students "in the moment" as they are working independently or in small teams at some field site. Mobile technologies show promise in supporting inquiry in these contexts. Such technologies began with "personal digital assistants" but now encompass tools such as smartphones and wearable devices. The emergence of mobile devices generated ideas about their use for learning (e.g., Roschelle & Pea, 2002), and with that came new work exploring how scaffolding features could be implemented on mobile devices. Initial work looked at how some scaffolding features available on computer-based inquiry tools could be designed on the smaller form factors of the mobile device (e.g., Luchini et al., 2002). But functionality of mobile technologies grew and began to be differentiated from that of more traditional desktop/laptop computers, which led to new ideas for scaffolding features. Examples include the use of mobile devices to support the collaborative activity that is part of inquiry (e.g., Roschelle et al., 2010), which connects to the "Help Learners Learn from Each Other" meta-principle in Kali and Linn (2007), or the use of mobile devices for information gathering—collecting different data and information in situ using data probes connected to the device or on-device cameras (e.g., Cahill et al., 2010). As mobile devices now transition to include wearable technologies, such as smartwatches, haptic technologies, location-sensing functionality, and different types of sensors, the questions continue to emerge regarding how to represent scaffolding information on such devices and what kind of inquiry activities are enabled with these devices in order to inform new scaffolding approaches. Some ideas include inquiry guidance and coaching while students are in their field investigation sites, for example, using the location-sensing capability of mobile devices to alert learners with different haptic or auditory modalities to aspects of the environment they are exploring that are relevant to their inquiry questions. Directions to explore include looking at how these devices can scaffold "in the moment" reflection on learner experiences in these environments and provide different modalities that learners can use to articulate information for their inquiry—using not just written text but also voice, photos, videos, and so on. Another option to be explored in this regard is how we can effectively demonstrate inquiry tasks (e.g., collecting information or identifying interesting phenomena) via video demonstrations or auditory guidance that students could view on a mobile device as they attempt to engage in those tasks in the field. These examples point us in different directions in exploring how mobile technologies can scaffold learners as they take their inquiry out of the classroom and into the field.

Example: Enacting Different Inquiry Contexts through Augmented and Virtual Reality

Another example is the growing interest in augmented and virtual reality tools and how they can be used to create more customized inquiry contexts to investigate different ideas and phenomena that would otherwise be difficult to explore. Many contemporary handheld devices now offer augmented reality (AR) functionality, where the device itself can act as a "lens" to view virtual content overlaid on a real-world item. Virtual reality (VR) is also becoming more commonplace as VR hardware is becoming increasingly mobile and wireless. These technologies have led to new discussions on how they might be used to enact and scaffold inquiry learning in a variety of situations. For example, Kyza and Georgiou (2019) describe an AR platform to support inquiry with information that can be overlaid over the actual physical content being studied. The platform can provide an overlay of location-based and other information that is aimed at supporting more reflection on the inquiry activity occurring at that location. This type of technology has also been used for historical inquiry during field trips where students can visit historical sites and see additional information about those sites using their AR devices (Efstathiou, Kyza, & Georgiou, 2018). Similarly, Chen and Tsai (2016) have looked at the use of AR to overlay geometric representations that students could manipulate in different ways as they are learning about particular geometry concepts. This use of AR can provide scaffolding in ways that would not be easy or possible in contexts where it would be difficult to convey the same information with a two-dimensional or textual description.

Virtual reality tools also hold promise for virtual environments where students can explore and engage in inquiry activities. These approaches can not only help students engage in more complex inquiry when going out to field sites is not possible, but the virtual environments can be structured in such a way as to embed a variety of scaffolds into them. For example, Dede et al. (2017) describe their EcoXPT virtual environment as one that "enables students to use the tools and the inquiry practices of ecosystem scientists" by embedding inquiry tools, data, and scaffolding for students. These types of environments allow exploration into different and more detailed scaffolds to help investigate a range of scaffolding forms that would be more complex to incorporate in a typical classroom inquiry setting. For example, EcoXPT uses a range of "Thinking Moves" that illustrate the questions scientists ask at key points in the environment as students explore an ecosystem. These reflective scaffolds can describe a range of questions to help students consider the history of the ecosystem, collect evidence, look for patterns in data, analyze causality, and construct explanations. While these conceptual scaffolding approaches are seen in the literature more abstractly, virtual environments like EcoXPT allow for more tailored and specific scaffolds that connect to the inquiry type (i.e., ecosystem inquiry) and use different forms (e.g., textual prompts overlaid on key aspects of the environment, and virtual characters providing the coaching and background information) that would be more complex to apply in other settings.

Example: Integrating Scaffolding within Physical Environments through Technology-Augmented Physical Spaces

The previous examples described individual technologies used for inquiry. But another possibility involves using different technologies in coordinated ways for inquiry activity in technology-augmented physical spaces that create a larger learning environment and include scaffolding in different forms. For example, Yoon et al. (2018) explored a museum setting that contained a range of features intended to scaffold students visiting the museum, especially during inquiry projects where they are working together to find and make sense of information about a historical question. These features scaffold sensemaking of historical information via AR-based scaffolding features at exhibits and text-based scaffolding features embedded in signage. Also, since students can work in groups on their inquiry, additional collaborative scaffolds are embedded in technology to support groups as they discuss and reach consensus about problems they are addressing at the exhibit. Such work helps uncover the scaffolding role that a technology or medium can play within the larger system of resources in the physical space. Similarly, another project, namely, the EvoRoom project (Lui et al., 2014), integrates two approaches for students to explore questions and engage in inquiry activity: (1) a physical space that includes multiple projection screens on which a virtual environment is projected for students to explore (e.g., creating a virtual rain forest that spans several chronological eras in a classroom), and (2) the Zydeco mobile device application that scaffolds students' data collection (e.g., taking photos in the virtual environment), data analysis (e.g., analyzing and describing the phenomenon they captured in the photo), and explanation construction (e.g., linking their data and reflections to start addressing their inquiry questions). The two are used in tandem as students use Zydeco to capture information from the virtual environmental simulation being projected in the physical space.

These studies not only illustrate the manner in which multiple resources can be combined to scaffold learners but also describe how to potentially integrate scaffolding features from different sources to provide a more comprehensive scaffolding approach. This fits with the idea of "synergistic scaffolding," an approach described by Tabak (2004) to show how individual scaffolding features can work together in a supportive manner, not in a distributed way where each feature independently scaffolds learners but where the scaffolding features can work together in a more integrated, holistic manner. Given the emergence of new technologies and the possibility that they each enable scaffolding forms in different ways for an array of inquiry activities, another research direction to consider is how this idea of synergistic scaffolding might be implemented in inquiry settings. This leads to many potential research directions about scaffolding inquiry. There is the challenge of fading: How do we think about a given scaffolding feature fading when it is integrated with other features—does the single feature fade, or does the larger cluster of scaffolding features with which the feature is integrated with also fade? There are also possibilities in terms of the specific type of scaffolding representations and forms to provide learners (e.g., Alavi & Dillenbourg, 2012): Can virtual characters act as expert agents to provide guidance and feedback to learners in different inquiry settings? How should we design more visual information that is intended to scaffold learners in these new AR/VR environments (e.g., how could we design a new generation of process maps using dynamic media?) that is more related to a given inquiry setting a student may be working in?

Articulating Scaffolding Descriptions: Integrating Scaffolding Form and Function

As more scaffolding features are developed, there is also an additional challenge for researchers and designers to articulate scaffolding information in ways that convey all the various components of the scaffolding, from the conceptual information about the scaffolding needs and goals, to the manner a conceptual scaffolding approach is implemented, to information about fading and the effectiveness of the scaffolding feature. Given the different elements of a scaffolding feature, more work is needed to think about standardizing ways of communicating scaffolding information so that these ideas can be tested, reused, and expanded for other contexts. This type of communication task is not new, especially in the design community, where there is often a goal of articulating design knowledge so others can use that information for their own designs. In the case of scaffolding, various aspects of the "form/function" dichotomy need to be described to fully understand the scaffolding feature—the function that a scaffold should provide to address that need, and the form of the scaffolding feature, the rationale for that feature, the implementation of that feature, and so on.

One approach to providing this type of multifaceted information is the *design pattern*, which was a concept first described by Christopher Alexander for architectural design (Alexander et al., 1977). Alexander identified the need for describing architectural features in ways that were informative but not prescriptive. Alexander wanted a descriptive representation that articulated the "how" and "why" of a given architectural feature, but in a way that would allow other architects to view a variety of design patterns and decide for themselves how they could use those features in their own work. Alexander proposed the design pattern as a representational mechanism with a set of dimensions for describing information about a given architectural feature that would encapsulate contextual information, design information, and design rationale for a given architectural feature. Specifically, a design pattern could include (Alexander et al., 1977):

- The name of the design pattern.
- The context in which the given architectural feature is being used.
- The problem or need that exists within the given context—why does the particular architectural feature need to be explored in that context?
- The conceptual solution that would address the identified problem.
- The physical implementation of that conceptual solution.

While the design pattern approach was developed for architecture, it inspired similar approaches in other domains, including software engineering and human-computer interaction to describe software and user-interface features (e.g., Gamma et al., 1994). Clancy and Linn (1999) also explored design patterns within computer science education—an approach that partially inspired the "design principles" used in the Design Principles Database project (Kali & Linn, 2007). Quintana, Krajcik, and Soloway (2003) expanded on the design pattern approach to explore how scaffolding features in software could be described using design patterns. The aim of the *scaffolding pattern* approach would be to encapsulate multiple scaffolding dimensions to illustrate the different aspects of scaffolding features. Quintana, Krajcik, and Soloway (2003) gave an example of a scaffolding pattern with similar dimensions to the Alexander patterns to name and describe the inquiry context and need for the scaffold in that context, the conceptual scaffolding strategy and physical implementation, plus:

- Information about how the scaffolding feature can fade and when it can fade.
- A discussion of how the software feature was used, its effectiveness, its tradeoffs, and so on.
- Potential connections to other scaffolding features (e.g., to describe possible synergistic scaffolding scenarios).

Other researchers have since looked at the idea of using design patterns to describe important aspects of approaches that support different learning tasks (e.g., Law et al., 2017). The utility of the pattern approach is to provide the community with a common representational form to describe different scaffolding features in a standardized way that integrates several pieces of information: information about conceptual scaffolding approaches that can connect to the literature (underlying theory for the scaffolding approach), examples describing different ways those conceptual approaches are implemented in software (descriptions of scaffolding forms), and the design rationale for different conceptual approaches and the way the scaffolding feature works within the given context (descriptions of the scaffolding function).

Concluding Remarks

Looking back at the work since Wood, Bruner, and Ross (2016) conceptualized scaffolding, the concept has inspired an active line of research that has seen the topic defined, debated, expanded, and implemented in a number of ways—in face-to-face instructional settings and in the development of different kinds of scaffolded tools. Specifically, there has been rich research in the area of inquiry learning, more so looking at inquiry from a science perspective, but with a growing amount of work looking at scaffolding inquiry in other fields.

Scaffolding research has seemingly come in waves. After initial characterizations of the term were followed by a multitude of examples of supportive interventions that were supposed to embody scaffolding, there were concerns that perhaps the term was becoming too generic, too all-encompassing, and losing some of its meaning and strength as a metaphor (e.g., Stone, 1998). In some respects, the discussions about the utility of the scaffolding concept led to projects, such as the various scaffolding frameworks described earlier, which aimed to organize the various scaffolding examples and provide frames and structures to more clearly define and explicate the scaffolding concept. These frameworks have helped to continue moving scaffolding research—alongside research on inquiry—in a productive direction. But we are now seemingly at a point with a changing landscape in terms of thinking about scaffolding and inquiry:

- The notion of inquiry is evolving and broadening over multiple domains. As we think about inquiry, how do we describe and generalize what inquiry is in order to articulate the necessary scaffolding to support the different aspects of inquiry?
- Powerful new technologies are now at our disposal, leading to new scaffolding possibilities for a larger number of contexts than ever before. How can we think about new ideas and new ways of scaffolding learners, especially now that we have the potential to create blended learning environments that incorporate technology and people together as potential sources of scaffolding?
- New pedagogical ideas are developing, leading to a continuing discussion about how we incorporate culture, diversity, learner development, multiple learner audiences, and new teaching strategies in learning environments. How do we incorporate these pedagogical ideas into the discussion about the dialogic and diagnostic aspects of scaffolding?

Perhaps we are now at another point in time where it is time to rethink and reorganize our ideas, strategies, and learning plans and methodologies, especially in inquiry-based learning, in the context of scaffolding. There are still many questions to address, some of which are brought on by these new possibilities for inquiry, scaffolding, and pedagogy. But we still also have the questions of the past to consider in terms of how contexts and activities can scaffold learners. It is important to continue addressing the questions about scaffolding inquiry, as this will continue to help think about learning at higher and broader levels, and the ways in which tools and people can continue to support learning via inquiry in a range of contexts and domains.

References

Alavi, H. S., & Dillenbourg, P. (2012). An ambient awareness tool for supporting supervised collaborative problem solving. *IEEE Transactions on Learning Technologies*, *5*(3), 264–274. https://doi.org/10.1109/tlt.2012.7

Alexander, C., Ishikawa, S., Silverstein, M., Jacobson, M., Fiksdahl-King, I., & Angel, S. (1977). *A pattern language: Towns, buildings, construction*. New York: Oxford University Press.

Anghileri, J. (2006). Scaffolding practices that enhance mathematics learning. *Journal of Mathematics Teacher Education*, *9*, 33–52. https://doi.org/10.1007/s10857-006-9005-9

Bakker, A., Smit, J., & Wegerif, R. (2015). Scaffolding and dialogic teaching in mathematics education: Introduction and review. *ZDM Mathematics Education*, *47*, 1047–1065. https://doi.org/10.1007/s11858-015-0738-8

Byrne, V., Kang, S., Norooz, L., Velez, R. A., Katzen, M., Addeh, A., … Clegg, T. L. (2018). Scaffolding authentic wearable-based scientific inquiry for early elementary learners. In *Proceedings of the Thirteenth International Conference for the Learning Sciences – ICLS 2018*. London.

Cahill, C., Kuhn, A., Schmoll, S., Pompe, A., & Quintana, C. (2010). Zydeco: Using mobile and web technologies to support seamless inquiry between museum and school contexts. *Proceedings of the 9th International Conference on Interaction Design and Children*, 174–177. Barcelona: ACM. https://doi.org/10.1145/1810543.1810564

Chen, M.-P., & Tsai, C.-C. (2016). Augmented-reality as a scaffolding tool for learning geometry. *Proceedings of EdMedia 2016—World Conference on Educational Media and Technology*, 1531–1535. Vancouver: Association for the Advancement of Computing in Education (AACE).

Clancy, M. J., & Linn, M. C. (1999). Patterns and pedagogy. *SIGCSE '99: The Proceedings of the Thirtieth SIGCSE Technical Symposium on Computer Science Education*. Presented at the SIGCSE '99, New Orleans. https://doi.org/10.1145/299649.299673

Collins, A., Brown, J. S., & Newman, S. E. (1989). Cognitive apprenticeship: Teaching the crafts of reading, writing, and mathematics. In L. B. Resnick (Ed.), *Knowing, learning, and instruction: Essays in honor of Robert Glaser*. Hillsdale, NJ: Lawrence Erlbaum Associates, Inc. https://doi.org/10.4324/9781315044408-14

Dede, C., Grotzer, T. A., Kamarainen, A., & Metcalf, S. (2017). EcoXPT: Designing for deeper learning through experimentation in an immersive virtual ecosystem. *Educational Technology & Society*, *20*(4), 166–178.

Efstathiou, I., Kyza, E., & Georgiou, Y. (2018). An inquiry-based augmented reality mobile learning approach to fostering primary school students' historical reasoning in non-formal settings. *Interactive Learning Environments*, *26*(1), 22–41. https://doi.org/10.1080/10494820.2016.1276076

Gamma, E., Helm, R., Johnson, R., & Vlissides, J. (1994). *Design patterns: Elements of reusable object-oriented software*. Boston, MA: Addison-Wesley.

Guzdial, M. (1994). Software-realized scaffolding to facilitate programming for science learning. *Interactive Learning Environments*, *4*, 1–44. https://doi.org/10.1080/1049482940040101

Kali, Y., & Linn, M. C. (2007). Technology-enhanced support strategies for inquiry learning. In J. M. Spector, M. D. Merrill, J. J. G. V. Merrienboer, & M. P. Driscoll (Eds.), *Handbook of Research on Educational Communications and Technology* (3rd ed., pp. 445–490). Mahwah, NJ: Lawrence Erlbaum Associates, Inc.

Kyza, E. A., & Georgiou, Y. (2019). Scaffolding augmented reality inquiry learning: The design and investigation of the TraceReaders location-based augmented reality platform. *Interactive Learning Environments*, *27*(2), 211–225. https://doi.org/10.1080/10494820.2018.1458039

Li, D. D., & Lim, C. P. (2008). Scaffolding online historical inquiry tasks: A case study of two secondary school classrooms. *Computers & Education*, *50*, 1394–1410. https://doi.org/10.1016/j.compedu.2006.12.013

Luchini, K., Quintana, C., Krajcik, J., Farah, C., Nandihalli, N., Reese, K., Wieczorek, A., & Soloway, E. (2002). Scaffolding in the small: Designing educational supports for concept mapping on handheld computers. *Extended Abstracts of the Conference on Human Factors in Computing Systems (CHI 2002)*, 792–793. Minneapolis, MN: ACM. https://doi.org/10.1145/506443.506600

Lui, M., Kuhn, A., Acosta, A., Quintana, C., & Slotta, J. D. (2014). Supporting learners in collecting and exploring data from immersive simulations in collective inquiry. *Human Factors in Computing Systems: CHI 2014 Conference Proceedings*, 2103–2112. https://doi.org/10.1145/2556288.2557162

National Research Council. (2013). *Next generation science standards: For states, by states*. Washington, DC: The National Academies Press.

Pea, R. D. (1993). Practices of distributed intelligence and designs for education. In G. Salomon (Ed.), *Distributed cognitions: Psychological and educational considerations*. New York: Cambridge University Press.

Pea, R. D. (2004). The social and technological dimensions of scaffolding and related theoretical concepts for learning, education, and human activity. *Journal of the Learning Sciences*, *13*(3), 423–451. https://doi.org/10.1207/s15327809jls1303_6

Quintana, C., Krajcik, J., & Soloway, E. (2003). Issues and approaches for developing learner-centered technology. In M. V. Zelkowitz (Ed.), *Advances in computing* (Vol. 57). Cambridge, MA: Academic Press. https://doi.org/10.1016/s0065-2458(03)57006-1

Quintana, C., Reiser, B. J., Davis, E. A., Krajcik, J., Fretz, E., Duncan, R. G., … Soloway, E. (2004). A scaffolding design framework for software to support science inquiry. *Journal of the Learning Sciences*, *13*(3), 337–386. https://doi.org/10.1207/s15327809jls1303_4

Quintana, C., Zhang, M., & Krajcik, J. (2005). A framework for supporting metacognitive aspects of online inquiry through software-based scaffolding. *Educational Psychologist*, *40*(4), 235–244. https://doi.org/10.1207/s15326985ep4004_5

Roschelle, J., & Pea, R. D. (2002). A walk on the WILD side: How wireless handhelds may change computer-supported collaborative learning. *International Journal of Cognition and Technology*, *1*(1), 145–168. https://doi.org/10.1075/ijct.1.1.09ros

Roschelle, J., Rafanan, K., Bhanot, R., Estrella, G., Penuel, B., Nussbaum, M., & Claro, S. (2010). Scaffolding group explanation and feedback with handheld technology: Impact on students' mathematics learning. *Educational Technology Research and Development*, *58*, 399–419. https://doi.org/10.1007/s11423-009-9142-9

Soloway, E., Guzdial, M., & Hay, K. E. (1994). Learner-centered design: The challenge for HCI in the 21st century. *Interactions*, *1*(2), 36–48. https://doi.org/10.1145/174809.174813

Stone, C. A. (1998). The metaphor of scaffolding: Its utility for the field of learning disabilities. *Journal of Learning Disabilities*, *31*(4), 344–364. https://doi.org/10.1177/002221949803100404

Tabak, I. (2004). Synergy: A complement to emerging patterns of distributed scaffolding. *Journal of the Learning Sciences*, *13*(3), 305–335. https://doi.org/10.1207/s15327809jls1303_3

van de Pol, J., Volman, M., & Beishuizen, J. (2010). Scaffolding in teacher–student interaction: A decade of research. *Educational Psychology Review*, *22*, 271–296. https://doi.org/10.1007/s10648-010-9127-6

Vygotsky, L. S. (1978). *Mind in society: The development of higher psychological processes*. Cambridge, MA: Harvard University Press.

Wood, D., Bruner, J. S., & Ross, G. (1976). The role of tutoring in problem solving. *Journal of Child Psychology and Psychiatry and Allied Disciplines*, *17*, 89–100. https://doi.org/10.1111/j.1469-7610.1976.tb00381.x

Wood, D., & Wood, H. (1996). Contingency in tutoring and learning. *Learning and Instruction*, *6*(4), 391–397. https://doi.org/10.1016/s0959-4752(96)00023-0

Wood, D. J., & Middleton, D. J. (1975). A study of assisted problem solving. *British Journal of Psychology*, *66*, 181–191. https://doi.org/10.1111/j.2044-8295.1975.tb01454.x

Wood, H., & Wood, D. (1999). Help seeking, learning, and contingent tutoring. *Computers & Education*, *33*, 153–169. https://doi.org/10.1016/s0360-1315(99)00030-5

Zhang, M., & Quintana, C. (2011). Scaffolding strategies for supporting middle school students' online inquiry processes. *Computers & Education*, *58*, 181–196. https://doi.org/10.1016/j.compedu.2011.07.016

11

INQUIRY-BASED PRACTICES

Opening Possibilities for (In)equitable Interactions in Classrooms

Dan Battey and Emily Wolf McMichael

Inquiry-based practices hold tremendous promise for transforming classrooms as students engage in challenging content and develop thinking practices that will allow them to learn science and mathematics in ways that go beyond rote learning. The impact of inquiry practices has been supported by research that shows student learning gains in science and mathematics (Laursen, Hassi, Kogan, & Weston, 2014; Rasmussen & Kwon, 2007; Rasmussen, Kwon, Allen, Marrongelle, & Burtch, 2006; Wilson, Taylor, Kowalski, & Carlson, 2010; Yager & Akcay, 2010). For example, Rasmussen and Kwon (2007) noted in their discussion of university-level student inquiry practices, "student inquiry serves ... to empower learners to see themselves as capable of reinventing mathematics and to see mathematics itself as a human activity" (p. 190). Similarly, in their discussion of the implementation of middle-school science inquiry instruction, Yager and Akcay (2010) described increases in student learning outcomes such as the "ability to apply concepts" and "creativity skills" (p. 11). Despite these overall positive effects, it is an open question whether inquiry is producing more equitable learning.

Research on the effectiveness of inquiry instruction that attends to equity often measures it in the classroom through quantitative student outcomes by comparing achievement or grades across student groups. Wilson, Taylor, Kowalski, and Carlson (2010) studied student outcomes to determine possible differences in student achievement following five lessons of inquiry-based instruction or "commonplace instruction" (p. 279). Overall, students in the inquiry-based condition performed better. Furthermore, the student outcomes demonstrated no difference in student post-test scores by gender or socioeconomic status for the inquiry-based classrooms. However, in the commonplace instruction classroom, "non-white" students scored significantly lower than white students on the written assessments for learning despite equal pre-test scores across groups. Although the authors found no significant difference in pre-test scores by student demographic variables in either classroom, they conclude that "inquiry-based instruction mitigated the expansion of existing gaps" (p. 291). While this research and other studies valuably take into account demographics when considering student outcomes (see Laursen, Hassi, Kogan, Hunter, & Weston, 2011; Laursen, Hassi, Kogan, & Weston, 2014), they also raise questions about the nature of inquiry at the classroom level that produces equitable or inequitable outcomes.

Differences in learning opportunities have been found between inquiry-based classrooms and traditional classrooms in undergraduate mathematics classrooms (Laursen, Hassi, Kogan, Hunter, & Weston, 2011; Laursen, Hassi, Kogan, & Weston, 2014). In a quasi-experimental study across four institutions and 100 introductory-level college mathematics classes, Laursen, Hassi, Kogan, and Weston (2014) note:

> On average, over 60% of IBL class time was spent doing and discussing mathematics through student-centered activities, including problem presentations, discussion, small group work, and computer work, while students in non-IBL courses spent 87% of class time listening to their instructors talk.
>
> *(p. 409)*

The authors discussed increases in learning opportunities and more positive affective variables for women in the inquiry-based classrooms compared with men in such settings. These studies showing positive instructional outcomes (or non-negative outcomes) in terms of student learning have been used to make the case that inquiry, by its nature, is equitable instruction.

Laursen and colleagues (2011, 2014) contribute valuable data regarding women's experiences in inquiry-based mathematics classrooms at the university level, but they did not examine the moment-by-moment production of learning opportunities for these women. For example, while students in these classrooms were practicing mathematical discussions or participating in small-group work, what was the nature of their interactions as well as their interactions with their teacher? For example, were women's contributions positioned as valuable in relation to their peers? Only knowing outcomes or differences in activities does not illustrate the ways in which the activities were used equitably to produce different outcomes. Research has echoed the effectiveness of inquiry-based mathematics learning, but more attention is needed to document the observable differences in learning opportunities engendered by these more student-centered contexts in order to consider classrooms equitable.

Inquiry practices certainly foster more engagement, higher-order thinking, and access to challenging content, but this simply produces an increase in the number of interactions in classrooms. However, nothing guarantees that the nature of those interactions is more equitable. For example, Battey and Neal (2018) illustrated how seven teachers, ranging from traditional to more inquiry-based mathematics practices, also differed in how they developed relationships with students in a predominantly Latinx and African American school. In particular, the study showed how inquiry-based classrooms increased the number of interactions between students and teachers, but that the increase in *quantity* of interactions did not parallel increases in the relational *quality* of interactions with students. Counter to what would be expected from the studies discussed previously, some of the teachers with the strongest inquiry practices were the most negative in relating to students around their mathematical contributions. For example, teachers positioned students' ideas shared through informal language as outside the discussion of mathematics. The lack of a correlation between inquiry practices and quality student-teacher relationships was affirmed in a study of teachers with mostly inquiry-based practices as well (Battey, Neal, Leyva, & Adams-Wiggins, 2016). While inquiry practices increase the number of interactions between students and teachers compared with traditional instruction, it cannot be assumed that the interactions are actually more equitable for historically marginalized students.

While we caution against the assumption that inquiry, on its own, will produce more equitable dynamics and outcomes, we do think inquiry, as an instructional approach, holds tremendous potential to address issues of equity. Inquiry opens space for students to take more ownership and authority through knowledge of content, allows for active participation, and makes students producers of knowledge rather than simply recipients of the knowledge others have produced. In this way, it holds promise, particularly for those who have often been excluded from knowledge production in science and mathematics, which thus perpetuates ideas that students of color and white women do not belong or are less able in these fields. Because student participation and authority over knowledge production are ways to increase equity in the inquiry context, some may wonder how to design or engineer inquiry instruction to ensure these take place for all students in their classrooms, regardless of their social identities. However, we will demonstrate how moment-to-moment teacher responsiveness to the social interactions of the inquiry classroom can foster or inhibit the creation of an equitable space where students' social identities are affirmed and they are learning substantive content. This may be less about "engineering" equity within inquiry classrooms and more about the way teachers use their knowledge of student academic and social dynamics to respond sensitively to the needs of their students as they navigate sharing their ideas in order to build solutions to the problems they have generated.

Some research has begun to examine inquiry classrooms for differences in the ways students equitably or inequitably experience daily inquiry learning and how these differences relate to social identities and power (Bell & Pape, 2012; Langer-Osuna, 2016; Tan & Barton, 2010). Specifically, some of this classroom-level research has examined the ways in which student identities shift from moment to moment as they are influenced by social interaction (Langer-Osuna, 2011; Wood, 2013). For example, Wood's (2013) work challenges the notion that contexts in which teaching and learning take place can be inherently equitable by examining the ways in which how students are positioned relate to their mathematical identities. In particular, Wood takes a perspective on identity to understand how it may shift from moment to moment in a classroom where complex instruction is utilized. In this sense, students can take on multiple identities in classrooms related to the type of content and the way the work is done, such as problem-solver, independent worker, or mathematical communicator. The classroom in the study was using complex instruction, which draws on sophisticated group-level work typical of inquiry-based classrooms (see Boaler & Staples, 2008). Wood argued that these moment-to-moment mathematical identities are intricately tied to opportunities for learning. Through her study of Jakeel, a Black fourth-grade boy, Wood demonstrated how two affirming mathematical identities that he took on as a result of interactions with his peers and teacher—mathematical explainer and capable mathematics student—led to significant mathematical learning as measured by shifts in his dialogue around mathematics. Contrastingly, for one disaffirming mathematical identity—menial worker—Jakeel's learning was not evidenced. In these moments, a fellow student told Jakeel what to do, including what to write, to cut out a shape, and even where to look. In these moments, which Jakeel resisted, he was seen as someone who needed to be directed, but his mathematical ideas were never sought out. Just as in any classroom, the instruction became a context in which issues of power and status influenced learning. Wood's findings on identity, status, and mathematical learning as influenced by social interaction and classroom context have been echoed in other research (Bell & Pape, 2012; Langer-Osuna, 2011, 2016).

Building on this work, other research has examined the ways in which societal-level narratives about race and/or gender influence students' positionality within classroom interactions and students' subsequent engagement in mathematical work (Battey, 2013; Hand, Penuel, & Gutiérrez, 2012; Mendick, 2005; Nasir, Snyder, Shah, & Ross, 2013). By positionality we mean that "students interactionally position themselves and one another with academic and social power that can affect collaborative mathematical work" (Langer Osuna, 2016, p. 108). This positioning occurs with respect to racial and gender identities in conjunction with student-student and teacher-student interactions that shape the context for student learning: "trajectories [of identity and engagement] develop in relation to both the classroom practices that serve to structure participation and the broader social worlds that at times support and other times conflict with classroom practices" (Langer-Osuna, 2011, p. 208). Langer-Osuna (2011) examined student positioning within a mathematics classroom designed to decrease inequities through Problem-Based Learning (PBL). PBL starts with an authentic open-ended problem that is designed to engage students in the range of knowledge and skills that are to be learned (Prince & Felder, 2007). While open inquiry has students determine a question, decide how to study the question, and conduct the investigation, PBL is more akin to guided inquiry where students are already given the question to begin with (Banchi & Bell, 2008). In studying the PBL mathematics class, Langer-Osuna found that students in the same cooperative group positioned each other's authority differently throughout the course of a school year. For example, Kofi, an African American[1] male student, was positioned as smart when he took on a leadership role within the group, while Brianna, an African American female student, was positioned as bossy during her experience as a leader. Langer-Osuna (2011) termed these as *positional identities* that are produced discursively through social interaction. These positional identities were formed, in part, based on narratives about race, gender, and leadership, and they influenced learning opportunities for both students in this case—that is, Brianna and Kofi. By the end of the year, Kofi expressed his interest in pursuing mathematics, whereas Brianna conveyed she didn't want to engage in mathematical work.

Aligned with this work, but focused on teacher-student interactions, a case study of an elementary mathematics teacher using inquiry-based practices showed that her ways of engaging with students aligned with deficit discourses, both for her Latinx and African American students (Battey, 2013). Deficit discourses entail both genetic and culturally based narratives that maintain the subordination of students of color (Solórzano & Yosso, 2001). Battey (2013) discussed an example of deficit discourses being applied during a discussion of why mathematics is important. A Black boy named David shared his experience of going to the store and being overcharged for an item. When he challenged the clerk about the charges, the clerk said it was due to tax. David noted that tax couldn't be $1 for a $2 item. David is sharing experiential knowledge using Black Vernacular English. However, instead of recognizing David's knowledge and perspective, the teacher devalued his contributions, positioned his informal knowledge as flawed, and critiqued his Black Vernacular English. While this research investigated just one classroom, its findings present a cautionary tale in assuming that inquiry practices necessitate equitable interactions.

The work examining the positioning of students with respect to each other and the teacher in inquiry-based instruction raises the need to consider the ways in which broader discourses around gender, race, and content still make their way into classrooms. Inquiry classrooms are just as susceptible to discourses about mathematics ability as being innate, and, if teachers are unwilling to value students' informal knowledge, students still may feel like their contributions and culture are not welcomed into the classroom. Along these lines, we adapt Hmelo-Silver, Duncan, and Chinn's perspective (2007) on inquiry:

> "Does it work?" is the wrong question. The more important questions to ask are under what circumstances do these guided inquiry approaches work, what are the kinds of outcomes for which they are effective, what kinds of valued practices do they promote, and what kinds of support and scaffolding are needed for different populations and learning goals.
>
> *(p. 105)*

We would reframe this to say "Is inquiry equitable?" is the wrong question. Instead, we should be asking under what circumstances are inquiry approaches in/equitable, for whom are they (not) working, and what kinds of scaffolding are needed to support historically marginalized students' learning.

Through this lens, we examine examples of inquiry classrooms that raise ways in which to explore how inquiry is implemented, and we do so with the aim of assisting teachers in working toward more equitable practices. First, we explore the power of uptaking student ideas by detailing one classroom case that denies a student voice to share his ideas and another that showcases a student's voice, even when his contribution could be seen as inaccurate. Following this juxtaposition and our discussion of the influence the uptake of student ideas may have on students' opportunities for learning, we move on to discuss additional examples of strong mathematics inquiry-based teaching and learning that provide equitable opportunities for student learning in various ways. We conclude with thoughts about further research on equity in inquiry-based instruction. We will focus on inquiry in mathematics given our expertise, but we believe much of what we uncover will likely generalize to science and potentially other domains.

Uptake of Student Contributions

As students and teachers take part in classroom communities that utilize inquiry-based learning strategies, interactions among students and between students and teachers become commonplace. While the members of these communities learn together through social interaction, their ideas relating to mathematical content are affirmed, denied, challenged, valued, ignored, and negotiated. This uptake of student contributions by teachers and other students in the classroom influences student positioning and intellectual authority, and, this, in turn, influences opportunities for student learning (Langer-Osuna, 2016; Wood, 2013). We argue that this common interactional practice in inquiry-based classrooms along with societal narratives about mathematical ability work in tandem to influence the availability of equitable learning experiences for students.

In the inquiry classroom, even though teachers may design engaging and collaborative group projects, student ideas can be ignored or repeatedly not taken up in favor of other students' ideas. This may be the case even when a student's ideas are mathematically accurate. Langer-Osuna (2016) described an elementary mathematics classroom where students worked collaboratively to solve open-ended problems. She focused on the activity of the teacher and one student group to demonstrate how a young African American boy, Jerome, was positioned without mathematical authority, which denied him, as well as his group, opportunities for learning. We draw on two excerpts from Langer-Osuna's work here to illustrate these interactions, which occurred in the context of inquiry-oriented practices. Specifically, Jerome's groupmate Ana, a Latina, was positioned with authority in the group when her contributions are received positively during the entire lesson, while Jerome's contributions were often received negatively or ignored. In this example, the students were working on the following problem:

> Avenue Crest Elementary is planning to design a fruit or vegetable garden. We have decided that it is best to divide our garden site into square sections that are one meter on each side. We will use four meters of rope to rope off the first section, and we'll only need 3 meters of rope for each additional section. How many meters of rope do we need if we plan on creating a garden with ten sections if the sections are in a single row?
>
> *(p. 111)*

As they worked, the teacher, Ms. Grand, circulated the room to scaffold their learning and provide real-time feedback. Jerome drew the garden on the group's poster paper following Ana's directive.

TEACHER: So, so if I asked you to draw a picture of this [points to word problem and reads], "We have decided that it is best to divide our garden site into square sections that are 1 meter on each side," What is a square section with one meter on each side look like? [Gaze shifts to Jerome.]

ANA: [simultaneously] A square.

JEROME: [simultaneously] [Quietly.] Like this. [Points to one square of the partitioned 2X5 drawing.]

ANA: [Draws a separate, individual square on the side of poster. Then draws tic marks on each side of square, as teacher watches.] One, one, one, one.

JEROME: [Keeps finger pointed on square of partitioned 2×5 drawing; shifts gaze to teacher.] Like a gate.
TEACHER: [To Jerome, pointing at Ana's drawing.] Does that look … does that look right? Is that a square with one meter on each side?
TEACHER: [Shifts gaze to Ana.]
ANA: Mm-Hmmm.
TEACHER: [simultaneously] Okay… okay.
ANA: [simultaneously] There's one on each side.
TEACHER: [simultaneously] So that…
JEROME: [simultaneously] [To himself.] In a single row.
TEACHER: That [pointing to Ana's drawing] looks good to me. (p. 116)

Here, Jerome's drawing of the garden (see Figure 11.1, two rows of five squares) was ignored by the teacher in favor of Ana's new drawing (upper right drawing with tick marks) as demonstrated by the teacher's shifts in gaze as well as the way the teacher directed Jerome's attention to Ana's drawing. When the teacher asked a direct question about visualizing a square section with one meter on each side, Jerome attempted to contribute multiple times by answering the teacher's question (pointing to one square of his own drawing), but his contributions were unacknowledged. During this exchange, Jerome also pointed out his group's mistake of drawing the garden sections in multiple rows, but was ignored by the teacher and his group mate.

Over 20 minutes later in the period, the teacher affirmed Ana's contribution about the single row even when she was having difficulty understanding the concept. Jerome's knowledge on this topic remained ignored while the teacher continued to engage with Ana:

TEACHER: And then what does this say down here? [Points to latter part of problem on poster.]
ANA: [Reads off the poster]: "How many meters of rope will you need if you plan on creating a garden with ten sections..." [Looks up to teacher.]
TEACHER: Keeping reading.
ANA: "…if the sections are in a single row?"
TEACHER: In a single row. So where's your single row? What does that mean? A single row?
ANA: [Puts hands up parallel to each other.] Like one … one row.

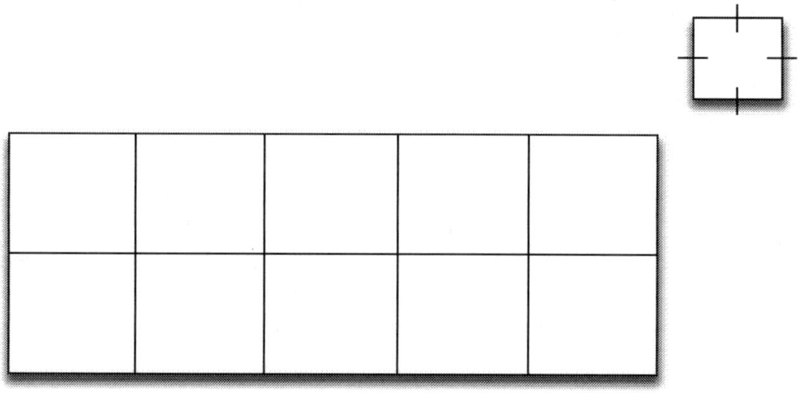

Figure 11.1 Depiction of Jerome's garden plot and Ana's tic-marked square. Reprinted from "The social construction of authority among peers and its implications for collaborative mathematics problem solving," by Jennifer M. Langer-Osuna, 2016, retrieved from *Mathematical Thinking and Learning*

TEACHER: One row. Okay. So where's that [in their drawing]?
ANA: [Swipes finger downward over first column of drawing. Looks back at teacher and smiles unsure.]
TEACHER: [Looks at Jerome.] All right, are you good? You think?
JEROME: Yeah. (p. 118)

In this example, Ana was struggling with understanding their representation needed to depict a single row (Figure 11.2). However, Ms. Grand did not clarify that Ana pointed to a column and attempted to share the mathematical authority with her. The students interpreted Ms. Grand's response as a positive evaluation of Ana's contribution. However, it was not the content of student answers that positioned students as competent or incompetent mathematically; rather, the teacher's positive engagement with Ana's contributions and lack of engagement with Jerome's ideas opened up learning opportunities for Ana, but silenced Jerome. While this can be seen as affirmative of Ana's mathematical identity, she was clearly confused, and the repercussions for Jerome are clear. In fact, she could have affirmed both students' ideas, but she never highlighted Jerome's thinking in the interactions throughout the entire lesson. Notice in the classroom excerpt the moments in which Jerome responded quietly or failed to challenge Ana's incorrect mathematical thinking even when he had knowledge to contribute. When the teacher missed opportunities for engaging Jerome in the work, she also stifled the group's ability to produce accurate work. Ana ultimately produced an incorrect diagram of the garden, and Jerome did not challenge her work. This sequence of interaction throughout the mathematics lesson spreads the idea that Jerome is mathematically incompetent repeatedly. This is particularly problematic for Jerome, an African American student, in conjunction with societal narratives about race and mathematical competence that frame African Americans as incapable of achievement in mathematics (Martin, 2009). These deficit narratives influence the daily action of the mathematics classroom by limiting access to math, devaluing mathematics contributions, and lowering cognitive demand.

While the case of Jerome and Ana demonstrates the possibility of inequitable learning experiences for students in mathematics classrooms that use inquiry practices, inquiry classrooms can also produce equitable learning opportunities for all students. One of the ways teachers can work toward equity is by deliberately taking up student ideas, which may be seen as difficult when incorrect answers or strategies are shared. Do teachers dismiss the ideas, correct the students, or find value in what was shared? To illustrate this, we draw on an example from Battey, Neal, Leyva, and Adams-Wiggins (2016), who studied Ms. Moore's class, an Asian American second-grade teacher using inquiry practices in a classroom that is made up of 75% Latinx and 25% Black students. In

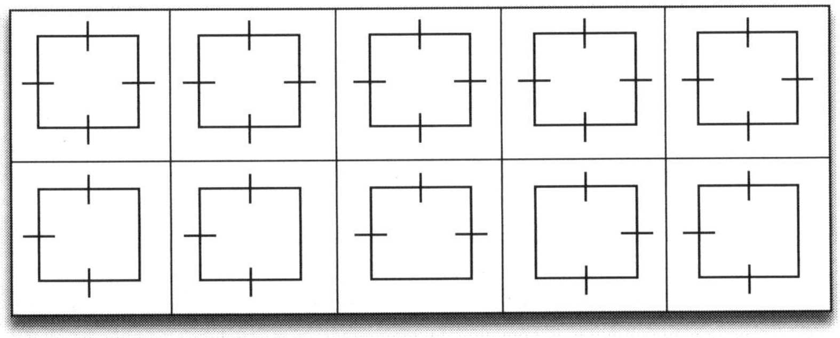

Figure 11.2 Depiction of the group's garden representation. Reprinted from "The social construction of authority among peers and its implications for collaborative mathematics problem solving," by Jennifer M. Langer-Osuna, 2016, retrieved from *Mathematical Thinking and Learning*

this classroom, Ms. Moore had students design problems so that she could pose them to the entire class to elicit their mathematical ideas. She intentionally chose student problems that could support building to some mathematical generalization. In the problem below, she was trying to get students to think about what happens when they see "x-x" (in this case 10-10) embedded on one side of an equation, while also challenging their ideas about the equal sign meaning "answer" or "operate" (Jacobs, Franke, Carpenter, Levi, & Battey, 2007). The following excerpt shows what occurred after one student, Jonathan, put 15 in the box rather than 5 in solving the problem 10 + 10 − 10 = 5 + □. As he shared his strategy, he clearly rewrote the problem as 10 + 10 + 10 − 10 = 5 + 15, adding an extra "+10." Ms. Moore supported Jonathan's mathematical competence around an incorrect answer. Italicized text in this and subsequent classroom episodes indicates vocal emphasis.

[Jonathan at the whiteboard presenting his solution of "15" for 10 + 10 − 10 = 5 + □]

STUDENTS [in unison]: I don't get it.

NIGEL: I don't get it. We gonna be on that problem for weeks! For months!

MS. MOORE: Hold on a second. Let's try and understand this, okay? Let's try to understand this.

STUDENT: We're going to be on that problem for months!

MS. MOORE: *We might be on this problem for weeks.* We might, and that's okay. Let's understand … let's understand the thinking. So, ten plus ten, and you added another ten [Jonathan incorrectly added another ten on the left side to get 30-10], so you had ten plus ten plus ten equals thirty. And then you minused ten and you got twenty. And then you took this side and five plus fifteen equals twenty. Ok, that makes sense.

NIGEL: I'll be dead by then, Ms. Moore. We're going to be on this problem for a month until we turn old. I'm taking my shoes off!

ALLISON: But it doesn't make fifteen or five.

MS. MOORE: *But that makes sense, what he did.* He added ten plus ten plus ten minus ten, that equals twenty.

Jonathan added an extra ten in his solution (10 + 10 + 10 − 10 = 5 + 15), and given that, he solved it correctly. Ms. Moore showed that the mathematics would be correct if the problem was written as Jonathan thought. In valuing his thinking, we argue that Ms. Moore also asserted Jonathan's mathematical competence, despite the incorrect answer to the problem originally posed. This is critical to value thinking broadly; otherwise, students can learn that mathematical thinking only matters when the answer is correct. Despite students saying they did not understand or that it was taking too long, she persevered in understanding Jonathan's mathematical thinking. To address these students in addition to highlighting Jonathan's thinking, Ms. Moore posed the problem Jonathan solved correctly to the entire class. Again, in both unpacking Jonathan's thinking and valuing the problem he solved, he is being positioned as competent within classroom discourse that could easily dismiss or devalue his thinking.

Across the two sets of examples in this section, we raise the possibilities that exist when instruction is based on inquiry-based practices. However, despite arguments from prior work that inquiry is in itself equitable, these examples show interactions in classrooms can go either way. In either of these examples, the opposite could have occurred. In the case with Jonathan, a teacher could have overlooked or dismissed his incorrect answer, attributing little to no value to it. And with Jerome, the teacher could have recognized and highlighted his thinking just as much as she did for Ana. The point is that inquiry-based practices open up more space for interaction, increasing their frequency and space for more student contributions. However, the degree to which those openings result in more equitable positioning is negotiable within each classroom.

Building Collective Competence

The uptake of individual students' ideas in inquiry-oriented classrooms is critical in terms of opening up or closing down equitable learning opportunities. In addition, teachers also negotiate whether and how students see themselves as competent within whole class discussions. During these classroom moments, teachers can be intentional about drawing on students' informal ideas, building on students' ideas, and crediting students for these ideas (Hand, 2012). This is especially critical when developing new concepts since students may not have the language proficiency to use formalized terms. While valuing informal language may seem obvious, teachers often view students' informal language as wrong, inaccurate, or not aligning with formal language in standards, even when the underlying mathematical ideas are valid.

Here we share an excerpt from Ms. Townsend's classroom. To provide context, Ms. Townsend is Black and 97% of her students are Black as well. The interaction we highlight here occurred in November while they were building a collective definition of a geometric net. In this interaction, students share informal language, but Ms. Townsend accepted it, combined it with contributions from other students, gave students credit for their ideas, and began to connect it with formal mathematics. In particular, Ms. Townsend used inquiry practices to engage in community knowledge building as a core practice.

MS. TOWNSEND: What's a net? If you know what a net is, let me get your hand. Who wanna help me out with a net? What a net? Net. Help me, what's a net? [points to Dante].

DANTE: It's a shape that's laid out.

MS. TOWNSEND: Ok, that's good. So you said a net is a shape that's laid out. Ok, Noah can you add to that?

NOAH: A thing that you can fold into a solid figure.

MS. TOWNSEND: Ok! So your net that's laid out [points to Dante] that you can fold into a solid figure [turns and points to Noah]. Before you can fold it into a solid figure, what do you have to do?

STUDENTS: [Students talking over each other]

MS. TOWNSEND: Ok, so let's, let's do it again. Dante said that a net was ... [pauses and points to Dante] Give it to me.

DANTE: A shape that's laid out.

MS. TOWNSEND: So a shape that's laid out, flat, on paper. What dimension is that?

STUDENTS: Two dimensions.

MS. TOWNSEND: And then Noah said when you fold it together, you get what, Noah?

NOAH: A solid figure.

MS. TOWNSEND: A solid figure. Which is what dimension?

SARAH: Three dimensional!

MS. TOWNSEND: [nods her head yes demonstratively] Three dimensional. There it is, that makes sense! So a net is a drawing that is laid out ... so that when you cut it out and fold it together, it gives you a solid figure that is three dimensional. You with me on that?

Ms. Townsend drew on students' ideas about what a net is. She accepted "A shape that's laid out" and the idea that it can be folded into a solid figure. In fact, she revoiced these ideas, named students in giving them credit for their thinking, and used the ideas to connect to where she wanted to go in comparing two-dimensional and three-dimensional figures. The above excerpt was intended to set up the idea of surface area. Ms. Townsend designed the discussion to draw out students' ideas of nets and two-dimensional figures to help them think about how to calculate the surface area of cylinders. In doing so, she showed students that they were drawing on ideas that they already know as they did something that they did not know yet. Again, we see this as building students' sense of competence in mathematics. What is unique in this case is that Ms. Townsend did this collectively, by giving students credit for their ideas and building their ideas off of one another. While she guided the discussion, it is clear that as they built toward surface area, students already had mathematical ideas to draw on. Again, this example shows multiple possibilities being raised by inquiry-based practices. A teacher could just as easily view the students' contributions as not entirely accurate or non-mathematical in nature. What we need to understand better as a field are the range of ways that teachers can build more equitable opportunities for students.

In a similar way, Ms. Carter drew on students' ideas to build a mathematical definition collectively. Ms. Carter is also Black, and her classroom is made up of 85% Black students. This was the first time that students had seen the word "collinear," and Ms. Carter accepted a broad range of answers to build from. Note the use of humor and the teacher's response to students' jokes.

MS. CARTER: Ok, we're going to do a little word study here and see if we can figure out what collinear means… Looking at this word, what is the mathematical, root word?
MONIQUE: Linear
MS. CARTER: Linear, very good [circles linear in collinear]. And we know when we see the word linear, what is that referring to?
MONIQUE: An equation.
MS. CARTER: It can be a linear equation. But linear means? What's the root word of linear?
DEVON & LAMAR: Ear! [multiple students smiling].
MS. CARTER: [Smiling] That's very funny.
DANIEL: Line.
MS. CARTER: *Line* [underlines line in linear]. So when we look at a linear equation, it's the equation of a…
DANIEL & MONIQUE: Line.

In the interaction above, Ms. Carter drew out students' prior knowledge of linear and line. She circled and underlined their ideas within collinear and focused their attention on the root words, showing them that they already knew a great deal about the word. Note the humor shared between the students and the teacher when the student said "ear" is the root word, as well. In some classrooms this would be grounds for reprimand or seen as a distraction. In this case it was normalized including the teacher smiling at the joke. This interaction continues but shifts to defining what "co" means in relationship to "linear."

MS. CARTER: Ok. So we see line. Who knows what the prefix co means [circles co in collinear]?
AALIYAH: Like you can say co-worker, co-council...
MS. CARTER: Coworker, co-council, they are//
AALIYAH: //Co-president, something like that. Don't it mean like second in line?
MS. CARTER: Well co-president, is one higher than the other?
AALIYAH: No.
MS. CARTER: Copresident, what do they do with the president position?
TAMIRA: They're doing it together.
MS. CARTER: They're doing it *together* [brings her hands together]. So co//
JUSTIN: //Oh, cooperate.
MS CARTER: Right *co—operate* [points to student]. Right, they're doing it together. You operate together. We come together, we cooperate with each other means we're doing it together. So as Tamira said and Justin brought out, the prefix co means together.

In this section, Ms. Carter drew on students' informal ideas of coworker, co-president, and cooperate to define "co." These are not mathematical in nature and could be dismissed in some contexts that focus only on formal terms. Note that as she begins to revoice Aaliyah's comment, she stops to discuss co-president. It is possible that Aaliyah could feel unacknowledged in this instance as her ideas are not credited later in the discussion. However, Ms. Carter does revoice and gives credit to Tamira and Justin for raising their point that "co" means together, building on their ideas. However, this example shows the constant interaction with students' ideas and the possibilities this raises for positioning students both as competent and incompetent within the same excerpt. In addition, this seems critical in building racially inclusive knowledge-building communities within inquiry classrooms.

Following this, Ms. Carter came back to a previous question that used the term "collinear." Here, she wanted them to connect their informal ideas back to the mathematics.

MS. CARTER: Now, look at the question. Are the points in question seven collinear? What do you think it might be asking you about the points that you used in the previous question?
JUSTIN: Are they all on the same line.
MS. CARTER: *Are they all on the same line.* That is *excellent.*

As Ms. Carter came back to the concept of "collinear," she related it to a problem they just worked on. Justin draws on their ideas of "co" and "line" to say they are "on the same line." Ms. Carter finishes with praise, but it is not empty praise as it builds on five different students' ideas, revoicing their thinking, and crediting them for their contributions. As with Ms. Townsend, Ms. Carter was also building a collective sense of competence in her classroom. Yet, even this is complicated by how Aaliyah could be positioned. While we did not note other instances of this in this lesson or the following lesson with Aaliyah, it raises the issue that students are being positioned constantly within inquiry-oriented classrooms.

Across both of these examples, teachers were doing more than recognizing individual student's competence. It should not be lost on the reader that both classrooms consisted predominantly of Black students. Therefore, framing the class as competent, noting multiple students' contributions, and relating these to substantive mathematics can mean something different in this context. Due to racialized discourses of a hierarchy of math ability (see Martin, 2009), Black students must deal with society, and sometimes schools and teachers as well, framing them as less able mathematically. What Ms. Carter and Ms. Townsend were doing was building a sense of collective competence, which could be a mechanism to challenge these deficit discourses. They did not let informal language, humor, or formal mathematics distract them in this. But for researchers, it is in looking at the micro-interactions of positioning that reveals the types of mechanisms in classrooms that result in more or less inequitable opportunities for learning for students.

Deficit Discourses and Positioning in Constructing Competence

While it is easy to see the work that Ms. Townsend and Ms. Carter were doing as routine, we should consider the stereotypes around mathematics ability that their students were navigating, as noted previously. As Martin (2009) noted, the deficit discourse of a racialized hierarchy of mathematics ability is prevalent in society and many students have teachers who share these views or are not consistently countering these views in society or in their classrooms. When inquiry practices open up the classroom space to discuss students' ideas, it raises the likelihood that racially marginalized students' ideas are going to be positioned as less competent. Instead of assuming that deficit discourses are not at play in researching classroom spaces, we should assume the opposite. Students are aware of stereotypes at early ages and are therefore looking for confirming and disconfirming evidence as to whether these stereotypes are real in their everyday lives.

This shift in approach means we should be documenting ways in which these discourses are affirmed, disconfirmed, or left implicit through social interaction in the classroom. When such discourses are left implicit in mathematics and science spaces, the default is that they are true, especially for young children trying to make sense of the world. Leaving children to make sense of entrenched stereotypes makes little sense, and yet that's generally what we do in K-12 education. This leaves inquiry classrooms complicit in perpetuating these stereotypes as much as traditional classroom environments.

In the excerpt from Langer-Osuna (2016), we see this play out for Jerome. The classroom interactions affirmed stereotypes for Jerome, an African American boy, but not for Ana, a Latina. However, we started by discussing Brianna from Langer-Osuna (2011), in which gender was used to position Brianna, an African American girl, as bossy. These examples show the ways in which students make sense of interactions and the ways in which classrooms can serve to perpetuate deficit discourses of students. As students' ideas are shared in inquiry-oriented classrooms, this raises numerous possibilities for the ways their ideas could be positioned in relation to other students. In addition, their ideas are constantly positioned with respect to broader racial and gender discourses. Furthermore, it is important that teachers are conscious that students are negotiating their identities with these discourses and that if their practices do not challenge these discourses, they are likely aligned with them.

This places work such as the studies by Wood and Langer-Osuna as central in documenting inquiry practices that support more equitable or inequitable participation. In particular, constructs such as positioning and positional identities hold potential for supporting researchers in documenting the dynamics at play in classrooms. It is through positioning that students' ideas play off one another, students see whose ideas are taken up for further discussion, and students construct who is and who is not competent. Therefore, documenting ways in which students position each other, but also how teachers position students, is critical in designing inquiry environments because these are the ways in which content domain competences are established.

Positioning with Respect to Subject, Peers, and Discourses

We want to return to the question we posed at the beginning of this chapter, which was adapted from Hmelo-Silver, Duncan, and Chinn's (2007) original question: Under what circumstances are inquiry approaches in/equitable, for whom are they (not) working, and what kinds of scaffolding are needed to support historically marginalized students' learning? For us, this requires attention to positioning of students. This means positioning students with respect to the subject, to each other, and to broader deficit discourses that may be at play. Therefore, we do not think this is simply an issue of "engineering" inquiry environments to be more equitable. It requires in-the-moment attention and consciousness on the part of the teacher for each of these forms of positioning in order to build students' competence in the field.

First, positioning with respect to the subject would consider how students are positioned with respect to mathematics (or other subjects, in other classes). Given the often-assumed formal nature of mathematics, equitable positioning with respect to the subject must take into consideration students' informal language and ideas. If the ways in which they present their ideas are not valued, this communicates that they are seen as less competent. Students can have insightful ideas that go overlooked or ignored due to informal expression. To be more equitable in terms of this positioning, it is imperative that teachers find ways to value their informal knowledge, build on it, and give them credit for their ideas. In addition, Ms. Moore even found ways to give credit to students' mathematical ideas when they provided incorrect answers by finding the correct mathematics that was shared. In the cases of Ms. Townsend and Ms. Carter, we see both teachers building collective competence, valuing informal language, and revoicing students' ideas in order to give them credit for those ideas. Therefore, while a principle of valuing students' ideas can be embedded in designing inquiry environments, the enactment of this needs to be done authentically in relation to the ideas students are generating, and therefore it can't be engineered ahead of time. However, positioning with respect to peers adds another layer of complexity to this.

Positioning students as competent with respect to one another is difficult. Positioning is always on the table as with Aaliyah in Ms. Carter's class when she shares the example of "co-president." We do not know how Aaliyah perceived this moment, but it's possible she saw this as the teacher positioning her as less competent. And, as in the example with Jerome and Ana, Ana was positioned as competent mathematically while Jerome was not. Much of this has to do with whose ideas are taken up, whose are not, and the ways in which students' ideas are taken up. Ms. Moore defends Jonathan in relation to his peers to position him as competent, even posing the problem he solved correctly to the entire class. Therefore, positioning is relational, both with the content and peers. And because of this, it requires consistently attending to relationships as they develop in classrooms.

Lastly, positioning is relational, as we mentioned previously, to broader societal discourses. While work has explored, through classroom discourse positioning of students with respect to each other and the content in a number of ways, documenting the extent to which these classroom moments perpetuate, or counter, existing deficit discourses is much less common. Ironically, in some ways this is easier to predict and therefore to engineer within inquiry environments. Given that deficit discourses around race, gender, and language play out in common ways in classrooms, we understand who among our students are often positioned as less competent or as not belonging in mathematics. Therefore, as educators, we can design opportunities for students to illustrate their competence and be intentional about highlighting students' ideas when their competence is made overt. However, in other ways this may be more difficult for educators to enact than the prior forms of equitable positioning. This takes an awareness and constant monitoring of the ways in which classroom moments might be interpreted in line with deficit discourses, intentional strategies to challenge these moments, and a deep understanding of the dynamics generated around issues of race, gender, and language. This takes a level of consciousness about equity that we struggle to develop in teachers, whether through preservice or in-service training. How does one engineer an equitable inquiry environment when the teacher does not know enough about how issues of equity play out in moment-to-moment interactions? We would suggest this can't be done.

We are not saying that teachers cannot learn to do this, but that sociopolitical consciousness, as Ladson-Billings (1995) terms it, is critical in addition to the inquiry design. This takes a concerted effort on the part of teachers to learn about race, racism, and the ways in which this impacts their behaviors and ideas. In addition, it requires learning about how societal and educational structures shape the classroom space for Black and Latinx students. And it takes putting these ideas into practice in building racially and culturally affirming relationships with students, parents, and the community. The practice of creating an equitable classroom community must happen in the moment-to-moment interactions in the classroom, consistently, and with careful consideration. Teachers may find this difficult given the many demands (e.g., classroom walkthroughs, scripted lessons, state testing, rigid lesson objectives) that already limit their ability to be responsive to their students. Still, we propose that the extent to which teachers create equitable learning conditions should be a tenet in what it means to be an effective teacher.

Conclusion

Given these issues, it is critical that researchers find ways to examine how inquiry-based practices are used to position students as both competent and incompetent, ways in which these align or challenge existing deficit discourses, and learn about classroom practices that disrupt these discourses. It is through classroom interactions that students develop their subject matter identities, make choices about pursuing content further or not, and learn about whether they feel they belong in the domain as racialized and gendered beings. As inquiry practices open up the classroom to increased interactions, we need to be able to support future and current teachers to draw on inquiry practices, in ways that do not reproduce racialized and gendered discourses so prevalent within mathematics and science classrooms. But we can only do this if we have a detailed enough understanding of how classroom practices reproduce and resist positioning within broader society.

Note

1 We use the race/ethnic term used within the original publication throughout.

References

Banchi, H., & Bell, R. (2008). The many levels of inquiry. *Science and Children, 46*(2), 26–29.

Battey, D. (2013). "Good" mathematics teaching for students of color and those in poverty: The importance of relational interactions in instruction. *Educational Studies in Mathematics, 82*(1), 125–144. https://doi.org/10.1007/s10649-012-9412-z

Battey, D., & Neal, R. A. (2018). Understanding the association between mathematics instruction and relational interactions in urban classrooms. *Mathematics Teacher Education and Development, 20*(1), 23–42. https://doi.org/10.1016/j.jmathb.2016.01.001

Battey, D., Neal, R., Leyva, L., & Adams-Wiggins, K. (2016). The interconnectedness of relational and content dimensions of quality instruction: Supportive teacher-student relationships in urban elementary mathematics classrooms. *Journal of Mathematical Behavior, 42*, 1–19. https://doi.org/10.1016/j.jmathb.2016.01.001

Bell, C. V., & Pape, S. J. (2012). Scaffolding students' opportunities to learn mathematics through social interactions. *Mathematics Education Research Journal, 24*(4), 423–445. https://doi.org/10.1007/s13394-012-0048-1

Boaler, J., & Staples, M. (2008). Creating mathematical futures through an equitable teaching approach: The case of Railside School. *Teachers College Record, 110*(3), 608–645.

Jacobs, V., Franke, M., Carpenter, T., Levi, L., & Battey, D. (2007). Professional development focused on children's algebraic reasoning in elementary school. *Journal for Research in Mathematics Education, 38*(3), 258–288.

Hand, V. (2012). Seeing culture and power in mathematical learning: Toward a model of equitable instruction. *Educational Studies in Mathematics, 80*(1–2), 233–247. https://doi.org/10.1007/s10649-012-9387-9

Hand, V., Penuel, W. R., & Gutiérrez, K. D. (2012). (Re) framing educational possibility: Attending to power and equity in shaping access to and within learning opportunities. *Human Development, 55*(5-6), 250–268. https://doi.org/10.1159/000345313

Hmelo-Silver, C. E., Duncan, R. G., & Chinn, C. A. (2007). Scaffolding and achievement in problem-based and inquiry learning: Scaffolding and achievement in problem-based and inquiry learning: A response to Kirschner, Sweller, and Clark. *Educational Psychologist, 42*(2), 99–107. https://doi.org/10.1080/00461520701263368

Ladson-Billings, G. (1995). Toward a theory of culturally relevant pedagogy. *American Educational Research Journal, 32*(3), 465–491. https://doi.org/10.3102/00028312032003465

Langer-Osuna, J. M. (2011). How Brianna became bossy and Kofi came out smart: Understanding the trajectories of identity and engagement for two group leaders in a project-based mathematics classroom. *Canadian Journal of Science, Mathematics and Technology Education, 11*(3), 207–225. https://doi.org/10.1080/14926156.2011.595881

Langer-Osuna, J. M. (2016). The social construction of authority among peers and its implications for collaborative mathematics problem solving. *Mathematical Thinking and Learning, 18*(2), 107–124. https://doi.org/10.1080/10986065.2016.1148529

Laursen, S., Hassi, M.-L., Kogan, M., Hunter, A.-B., & Weston, T. (2011). *Evaluation of the IBL mathematics project: Student and instructor outcomes of inquiry-based learning in college mathematics.* (Report to the Educational Advancement Foundation and the IBL Mathematics Centers) Boulder: University of Colorado, Ethnography & Evaluation Research. Retrieved from http://www.colorado.edu/eer/research/steminquiry.html.

Laursen, S. L., Hassi, M. L., Kogan, M., & Weston, T. J. (2014). Benefits for women and men of inquiry-based learning in college mathematics: A multi-institution study. *Journal for Research in Mathematics Education, 45*(4), 406–418. https://doi.org/10.5951/jresematheduc.45.4.0406

Martin, D. B. (2009). Researching race in mathematics education. *Teachers College Record, 111*(2), 295–338.

Mendick, H. (2005). Mathematical stories: Why do more boys than girls choose to study mathematics at AS-level in England? *British Journal of Sociology of Education, 26*(2), 235–251. https://doi.org/10.1080/0142569042000294192

Nasir, N. I. S., Snyder, C. R., Shah, N., & Ross, K. M. (2012). Racial storylines and implications for learning. *Human Development, 55*(5–6), 285–301. https://doi.org/10.1159/000345318

Prince, M., & Felder, R. (2007). The many faces of inductive teaching and learning. *Journal of College Science Teaching, 36*(5), 14.

Rasmussen, C., & Kwon, O. N. (2007). An inquiry-oriented approach to undergraduate mathematics. *The Journal of Mathematical Behavior, 26*(3), 189–194. https://doi.org/10.1016/j.jmathb.2007.10.001

Rasmussen, C., Kwon, O. N., Allen, K., Marrongelle, K., & Burtch, M. (2006). Capitalizing on advances in mathematics and K-12 mathematics education in undergraduate mathematics: An inquiry-oriented approach to differential equations. *Asia Pacific Education Review*, 7(1), 85–93. https://doi.org/10.1007/BF03036787

Solórzano, D. G., & Yosso, T. J. (2001). From racial stereotyping and deficit discourse toward a critical race theory in teacher education. *Multicultural Education, 9*(1), 2.

Tan, E., & Barton, A. C. (2010). Transforming science learning and student participation in sixth grade science: A case study of a low-income, urban, racial minority classroom. *Equity & Excellence in Education, 43*(1), 38–55. https://doi.org/10.1080/10665680903472367

Wilson, C. D., Taylor, J. A., Kowalski, S. M., & Carlson, J. (2010). The relative effects and equity of inquiry-based and commonplace science teaching on students' knowledge, reasoning, and argumentation. *Journal of Research in Science Teaching, 47*(3), 276–301. https://doi.org/10.1002/tea.20329

Wood, M. B. (2013). Mathematical micro-identities: Moment-to-moment positioning and learning in a fourth-grade classroom. *Journal for Research in Mathematics Education, 44*(5), 775–808. https://doi.org/10.5951/jresematheduc.44.5.0775

Yager, R. E., & Akcay, H. (2010). The advantages of an inquiry approach for science instruction in middle grades. *School Science and Mathematics, 110*(1), 5–12. https://doi.org/10.1111/j.1949-8594.2009.00002.x

12

HOW BEST TO ARGUE? EXAMINING THE ROLE OF TALK IN LEARNING FROM A SOCIOCULTURAL PERSPECTIVE

Alina Reznitskaya and Ian A. G. Wilkinson

Today researchers agree that the more ambitious goals of education, such as the development of reasoning and deep understanding, are better achieved by engaging students in dialogue, during which they participate in argumentation to articulate, explore, challenge, and justify their ideas (e.g., Asterhan & Schwarz, 2016; Kuhn, 1992; Mercer, Wegerif, & Dawes, 1999; Resnick, Asterhan, & Clarke, 2015). Theoretical justification for the use of dialogue in the classroom is often based on sociocultural perspectives, in which social interaction is viewed as the primary mechanism by which students advance their thinking (Vygotsky, 1968). Empirical support for this position comes from studies that examine the benefits of participating in argumentation through dialogue and document gains in students' reasoning, argumentative writing, inferential comprehension of text, and deep conceptual understanding of disciplinary concepts and principles (e.g., Gorard, Siddiqui, & See, 2015; Kuhn & Crowell, 2011; Mercer et al., 1999; Nussbaum & Sinatra, 2003; Osborne, 2010; Zhang et al., 2016).

Consider, for example, a study by Zhang et al. (2016), in which researchers evaluated the efficacy of different instructional approaches for supporting the development of sound decision making. Students in this study were assigned to three treatment conditions. In the first condition, students engaged in *Collaborative Reasoning* discussions of controversial issues, during which they participated in a "peer-led free-flowing discussion forum intended to encourage authentic argumentation" (p. 201). In the second condition, students received direct instruction in the form of "teacher-guided whole-class activities, whole-class question-and-answer sessions, and individual seat work" (p. 201). In the third condition, teachers continued to use their regular instructional methods, which—based on prior classroom studies (Alexander, 2018; Chen, Benus, & Hernandez, 2019; Howe & Abedin, 2013; Smith, Hardman, Wall, & Mroz, 2004)—were likely to be teacher-centered and to lack opportunities for open exchanges of ideas among students. Following the intervention, students in the *Collaborative Reasoning* group wrote essays that contained more varied reasons and more explicit explanations for why some reasons were better than others, compared to the other two conditions. However, their essays did not differ in terms of the number of arguments on either side of the issue.

The study by Zhang et al. (2016) is representative of a common type of research, including our own, in which dialogue-intensive interventions are contrasted with instructional environments that provide limited or no opportunities for students to engage in argumentation through dialogue (e.g., Dong, Anderson, Kim, & Li, 2008; Gorard et al., 2015; Mercer et al., 1999; Reznitskaya et al., 2009). Because the differences between dialogue—of any kind—and traditional teacher-centered approaches are so stark, it is common for researchers to find some benefits of dialogic engagement. Such studies help us understand the value of dialogue compared to traditional teaching and warrant its more prominent use in education. At the same time, by not taking into account specific characteristics related to the enactment of dialogue in a classroom, these studies provide little guidance as to how best to structure and support student participation in productive argumentation. Yet it is plausible that different realizations of dialogue can lead to unique affordances and limitations for argumentative discourse and have distinct implications for student learning (Asterhan & Schwarz, 2016).

In this chapter, we focus on two key aspects of dialogic engagement: dialogue type and degree of teacher support. We begin with a review of theoretical propositions frequently used by researchers of dialogue-intensive pedagogy to frame their studies, pointing out the need to further stipulate mechanisms responsible for different learning outcomes. Next, we closely examine the differences in implementation of dialogue by researchers who had similar educational aims and relied on similar theoretical justifications. We describe our use of inquiry dialogue in previous studies, and we compare it to another model, highlighting the differences in dialogue goals, practices, and levels of teacher involvement. This comparison is intended to illustrate important gaps in knowledge about the conditions that support student learning through social interaction. We then propose a way to refine sociocultural perspectives by integrating them with a recent framework developed by Asterhan and Schwarz (2016). Their framework identifies specific variables that shape the social context of argumentation and suggests related outcomes for student learning. We rely on this integrated model to develop new directions for studying the role of talk for learning and to address related methodological and practical implications.

Theoretical Framing of Dialogue and Argumentation

To explain the pedagogical potential of dialogue for individual learning and development of argumentation, researchers frequently rely on sociocultural theory (Asterhan & Schwarz, 2016; Webb, 2009; Wilkinson, Murphy, & Binici, 2015). They typically refer to some version of Vygotsky's (1978) general genetic law of cultural development and invoke the construct of *internalization*. According to this theory, thought is an interiorized external activity: "Every function in the child's cultural development appears twice: first, on the social level, and later, on the individual level; first, between people (interpsychological), and then inside the child (intrapsychological)" (Vygotsky, 1978, p. 57). Vygotsky was quite specific about the role of argumentation in the process of internalization, stating that "the higher functions of child thought first appear in the collective life of children in the form of argumentation and only then develop into reflection for the individual child" (Vygotsky, 1981, p. 157).

For Vygotsky, the external activity that is key to interiorized action is semiotically mediated social activity, and the primary semiotic tool is language. He regarded language as primary because it mediates both communication between people as well as thinking in the individual (Wells, 2007). Internalization is the process by which communicative exchanges between people are transformed into individual thought. From a sociocultural perspective, then, dialogue—whether with a more expert other (e.g., teacher) or with peers—enables students to construct new understandings and internalize new ways of thinking that foster the knowledge, skills, and dispositions which can be transferred to new tasks and contexts (Wells, 2007).

Language, of course, also provides participants with a means of thinking together. Dialogue in a discussion affords students the opportunity to combine their intellectual resources in order to collectively make sense of experiences and to solve problems. Mercer (1995) described this use of language as enabling a social mode of thinking or "interthinking." By using language to think together, students have the potential to co-construct knowledge and internalize ways of thinking that extend beyond the capabilities of the individual participants.

To illustrate, in a discussion focused on argumentation about a contestable issue, the process of internalization might proceed as follows. During the discussion, students take positions on an issue, support them with reasons and evidence, challenge other students' position or reasons, and respond to challenges from others. Over time, the skills and strategies of argumentation that are made visible in the group's discussion become part of an individual's thinking. For instance, a student who omits an important assumption during a discussion will, at first, only recognize the omission when someone else asks him or her for clarification. Eventually, the student might anticipate this reaction from his or her peers and self-edit his or her ideas before communicating them to the group. What began as interpersonal interaction in the group becomes an intrapersonal cognitive habit in the individual.

Moreover, because students in a discussion combine their intellectual resources—adding detail to given reasons, qualifying general statements, or finding flaws in each other's arguments—there is the opportunity for students to advance their thinking as a group. For example, a student from a refugee family might bring a unique personal experience to the discussion of immigration policies, thus enriching the collective understanding of his or her peers. The multiplicity of perspectives generated together enables students to test their ideas against those of others, providing a kind of self-correcting mechanism that helps to improve the overall quality of the group's argumentation (Kennedy, 2013; Splitter & Sharp, 1996). Splitter and Sharp (1996) explain how the group itself can act

> as a safeguard against sloppy thinking.... It is not that the group as a whole is incapable of making mistakes, nor that the majority opinion must rule, but that it is more likely that someone in the community will challenge what they deem to be unacceptable.
>
> *(p. 296)*

The group's capacity to self-correct depends on at least some of its members having the skills and knowledge to engage in productive argumentation during dialogue.

But, in the context of argumentative dialogue, what exactly is internalized? There are several schools of thought on this question. Some scholars suggest that the argumentative dialogue sensitizes students to different viewpoints and enables them to internalize a *perspective-taking process* (Ferretti & Fan, 2016; Ferretti & Graham, 2019). They point out that engagement in dialogue about contestable issues provides opportunities for students to understand the alternative perspectives on the issue and identify weaknesses in their own ideas. When students internalize this perspective-taking process, they can more adequately acknowledge the multiple viewpoints of others and strengthen the support they provide for their own position.

Other scholars posit a more structural and functional account of what happens when students engage in argumentation. They suggest that, through participation in dialogue, students internalize recurrent verbal patterns, or *argument stratagems* (Anderson et al., 2001). For example, students might refer to text to support their position, with a stratagem "In the story, it said [EVIDENCE]" (Anderson et al., 2001). With repeated exposure to various stratagems, learners abstract a more comprehensive generalized knowledge structure called an *argument schema* (Reznitskaya & Anderson, 2002). So, when students are prompted to provide reasons to support their positions or when they ask peers to justify their opinions, they make use of such argument stratagems, thus acquiring the knowledge, skill, and disposition to support and evaluate claims. In this way, the cognitive strategies of argumentation, such as generating and challenging other's reasons or questioning assumptions, serve as "psychological tools" (Vygotsky, 1981) that mediate the development of an individual argument schema.

Still other scholars take a more socially situated view of learning and suggest that, through argumentative dialogue, students "appropriate" ways of participating in the activity—the reasoning and rhetorical practices—and participate in these ways when they are engaged in subsequent related activities. In other words, through dialogue, students appropriate the semiotic tools and social practices of argumentation (Newell et al., 2011). Scholars from this school of thought often subscribe to Rogoff's (1990) notion that "learning is a process of changing participation in community activities" (p. 284). They tend to use the term "appropriation" rather than "internalization" to refer to the dynamic process by which individuals change in the ways they participate in activities. In preferring to use the term "appropriation," they seek to minimize the boundary between the social and the individual. For scholars who subscribe to this school of thought, the social and the individual are mutually constitutive, and it makes little sense to separate them—"participation is itself the process of appropriation" (Rogoff, 1995, p. 151).

Several studies conducted by Anderson and colleagues (Anderson et al., 2001; Dong et al., 2008; Kim, Anderson, Nguyen-Jahiel, & Archodidou, 2007; Lin et al., 2012; Lin, Anderson, et al., 2015) provide evidence that is consistent with these last two schools of thought. In detailed microgenetic analyses of students' participation in small-group *Collaborative Reasoning* discussions, Anderson and colleagues showed how students' use of various reasoning and rhetorical devices (argument stratagems, analogies) snowballed over time: Once a teacher or a student had successfully used a device in a discussion, other students used it with increasing frequency when engaged in the same activity. Presumably, students "appropriated" the social practices of argumentation for use in the same and subsequent discussions. Moreover, the argument stratagems made visible in the group later appeared in students' individual writing on a persuasive essay task, suggesting that students had "internalized" them.

We would like to see more studies that interrogate the mechanisms by which dialogue centered on argumentation helps students acquire new ways of speaking, acting, and thinking. Sociocultural theory yields promising insights into the process, but we lack a clear and nuanced understanding of what gets internalized or appropriated and under what circumstances. In fact, current theoretical accounts offer little guidance as to how to optimize the power of dialogue for teaching and learning argumentation. As a result, educators make different, and often opposing, assumptions about how best to structure and support dialogue in a classroom. We illustrate and discuss these assumptions next.

How Best to Argue?

To get a sense of existing variations in the enactment of dialogue aimed at supporting argumentation development, we compare discussion excerpts from two studies. The first excerpt comes from our own research and professional development project designed to help upper elementary school teachers conduct discussions around texts that engage students in argumentation (Reznitskaya & Wilkinson, 2017, 2019b; Wilkinson et al., 2017). During this project, we designed a professional development intervention, which we trialed and revised over three consecutive years.

Our project was motivated by the need for students to learn how to "think through complex problems in a deliberate, informed, and rational manner" (Reznitskaya & Wilkinson, 2015a, p. 279) and, as a result, develop a deeper understanding of the issues raised in the readings. As have many previous researchers of dialogue and argumentation (e.g., Billings & Fitzgerald, 2002; Lin et al., 2012; Wegerif, Mercer, & Dawes, 1999), we relied broadly on sociocultural theory to propose the mechanisms of learning through dialogue. That is, we posited that "during productive class discussions, students develop their cognitive capacities, as they internalize language practices from a social, external plane to an individual, internal plane (Vygotsky, 1978)" (Reznitskaya & Wilkinson, 2015b, p. 221).

Still, we believed it was important to further specify key features of interactions we wanted to promote in the classroom. To do so, we drew on a useful typology of dialogue types proposed by Walton (1998). According to Walton (1998), argumentation happens in different conversational contexts, or dialogue types, which have "distinctive goals and methods used by the participants to achieve these goals" (p. 3). Walton developed a taxonomy of six dialogue types—inquiry, persuasion, negotiation, information-seeking, deliberation, and quarrel—and described normative protocols for engagement within each type. For example, *inquiry dialogue* is defined as a collaborative process aimed at discovering the most reasonable answer to a controversial question. By contrast, *persuasion dialogue* is a competitive process aimed at defending chosen positions and undermining opponents' arguments. This difference in dialogue types is important because it determines argumentation practices and norms that are considered acceptable during a discussion.

In our project, we made a central assumption that *inquiry dialogue* was the normative model for engaging students in argumentation. Our choice was based on the work of a *Philosophy for Children* scholar, Maughn Gregory (2007), who applied Walton's work on dialogue types to education. Gregory (2007) explained that in inquiry dialogue participants are expected to not only defend their own positions and critically examine those of others (as in persuasion) but also to give up or qualify their viewpoints in the face of previously overlooked evidence or faulty reasoning (Gregory, 2007). As a result, inquiry dialogue should entail a systematic movement toward the truth, and it relies on epistemic commitments and evaluation standards that support such movement (Gardner, 2015; Gregory, 2007). Importantly, even though the truth remains an unreachable goal, it stands as a "regulative ideal" (Gardner, 2015) that serves "both to motivate the process [of inquiry] and regulate it" (Lipman, 1988, p. 148).

Gregory (2007) also suggested that during an actual classroom discussion, the discourse might shift from inquiry to other types of dialogue, depending on the stage of the discussion and the needs of the group. For example, students might ask an authoritative source, such as a teacher, about a specific fact as part of information-seeking dialogue, or engage in persuasion dialogue when they try to persuade someone of the merits of a particular position (Gregory, 2007). However, such "licit shifts" (Walton, 1998, p. 176) do not interfere with the overarching norms of inquiry dialogue, given that they are used in service of the larger goal of engaging in argumentation to collectively search for the most reasonable answer (Gregory, 2007).

Table 12.1 depicts an excerpt from our project that shows argumentation structured as inquiry dialogue. The excerpt comes from a discussion that took place in a fifth-grade language arts classroom. The teacher and his students were discussing a story *What Should Kelly Do?* (Weiner, 1980) about two children, Kelly and Evelyn, who are taking part in their school's art contest. In the story, Evelyn plans to submit a beautiful painting for the contest, but she becomes distracted and leaves it outside. As it starts to rain, Kelly notices Evelyn's painting and has to decide whether to alert Evelyn, probably losing her own chance of winning the contest. The question for discussion is: What should Kelly do?

The dialogue in Table 12.1 shows participants working together to formulate a well-justified conclusion. Note, for example, the frequent plural pronouns used by the teacher and his students to reflect the collaborative nature of engagement (e.g., "Are *we* then saying…?," "*We* are saying…" "What position are *we* connecting to?"). Note also that students both build on and challenge each other's ideas ("I agree with Daniel," "I'd like to disagree").

During our professional development work with teachers, we discussed these and other features of inquiry dialogue and contrasted them with other dialogue types, such as persuasion. Teachers were expected to develop and continually evaluate the "ground rules" for participating in inquiry dialogue with students. They also gave explicit discourse instructions to students prior to the discussion, explaining dialogue goals and expectations about participation. Below is an

Table 12.1 Example of argumentation structured as inquiry dialogue

Rosa:	I agree with Daniel and the reason is it does say in the story that Evelyn does not really care what she does. [Reading from the story] "She could turn out pictures that looked good enough to be on magazine covers, but she only painted when and what she wanted to." Which you could figure in two ways, but I am guessing it's the first way, which is a person who thinks they are so talented and they are amazing and they only paint when they want to! Because they are so good, so amazing that they deserve to do things whenever they want to. So, that's how I interpret it. ... And just to add on to Daniel ... Kelly wrapped hers in brown paper while Evelyn propped it against the wall of the school! Is that really respect for painting? That kind of hints to me that she does not really care about painting.
Teacher:	Evelyn?
Rosa:	Yeah. And she thinks she is so great she can just make another one just as amazing whenever she wants to and she does not have to follow the rules.
Teacher:	Can I just check on this? Cause. ... I am just trying to understand this, so you tell me if I got this right. Are we then saying if Evelyn doesn't have respect for her work, then her work should not be protected?
Colene:	We are saying, Evelyn does not protect her work, she does not care about it.
Teacher:	So, if Evelyn cares about it, then save it; if she does not care, then don't save it?
Daniel:	If Evelyn did care about it, she would not prop it against the school wall and go to play.
Teacher:	But I am wondering what position are we connecting to? ... Because we have evidence that Evelyn does not care, we should not save the painting? Is that what we are saying?
Rosa:	Partly, and the other part is if the person isn't going to follow the rules that they were specifically told to them, and they are just not going to bother, then what's the point of trying to help them? She propped the painting against the school wall! If Evelyn is going to treat it like it means nothing, I guess everyone else should too. Because that's how much it means to you!
Students:	[All at once] I disagree! I disagree! I disagree!
Chen:	I'd like to disagree. When she put the paining against the school wall, nobody could have known that it would rain. The weather reports could have said that it was sunny, or something. And I would also like to say that she has passion for painting. Like, the artist paints when she wants to...

example from our project, in which a teacher gave discourse instructions to students to explain their roles and responsibilities:

> When we do this kind of talk, it's important that we are not just sharing. So, our job is not just to get our ideas out so that everybody can hear them. It's actually to offer ideas up in the hopes that the group can determine what the most reasonable answer is, the best answer, the most thought through. So, our job is not just to share our answers, but also to consider other people's answers. And that means that we have to build on each other's ideas and make connections. So, the idea is to test, test each other's ideas. As a group, we should be able to think better than we can by ourselves. Does that make sense? All right.

Consistent with our assumptions about desirable features of dialogue, the teacher in the above excerpt placed emphasis on a collaborative versus competitive argumentation: "our job is..., " "we have to...," and "as a group, we should be able to think better than we can by ourselves." Also, he explained that the processes of argumentation should include both the co-construction of ideas (i.e., "we have to build on each other's ideas and make connections") and critical evaluation of each other's reasoning (i.e., "the idea is to test, test each other's ideas").

The excerpt in Table 12.1 reflects another important assumption we made in our work: that considerable teacher intervention is necessary to uphold the rigor of discussions. Teachers were expected to provide scaffolding through facilitation moves that were tailored to students' needs and gradually reduced over time (c.f. van de Pol, Volman, & Beishuizen, 2010). Because most students, especially those in primary grades, are not proficient in argumentation (Fischer et al., 2014; Means & Voss, 1996; Newell et al., 2011; Sadler, 2004), we assumed that the initial teacher involvement in discussions needed to be high: Teachers had to monitor the quality of students' arguments and intervene as necessary to model and promote the norms and criteria of argumentation that characterize inquiry dialogue.

The excerpt in Table 12.1 shows a rather prominent role on the part of the teacher during the discussion: He intervened, when needed, to enhance the quality of argumentation. Consider, for example, several facilitation moves used by the teacher to help students focus on the missing warrant in their arguments. In the discussion, Rosa took the position that Kelly should not alert Evelyn, thus possibly letting Evelyn's painting be ruined. Rosa, along with Colene and Daniel, supported this position with a reason that Evelyn did not care about her work. The teacher intervened multiple times to help students articulate the warrant that connects their reason with the taken position (e.g., "Are we then saying if Evelyn doesn't have respect for her work, then her work should not be protected?"). As a result of the teacher's probing, Rosa eventually voiced the key assumption in her argument: "If Evelyn is going to treat it like it means nothing, I guess everyone else should too." Once this previously unstated warrant was revealed and made available for public scrutiny, several students objected to it, and Chen offered an alternative perspective.

Such skillful scaffolding on the part of the teacher is likely to improve the quality of the group's argumentation. As students observe their teacher persistently probing for more explicit connections between positions and reasons, they are acculturated into a more rigorous approach to thinking through a complex issue together. As a result, students have the opportunity to internalize new "habits of mind," which might include specific reasoning skills that assist in uncovering unstated assumptions in the arguments of others, as well as an overarching epistemic commitment to truth-seeking (Gardner, 2015). Consistent with sociocultural perspectives (Vygotsky, 1981; Wells, 2007), the teacher acts as a more knowledgeable other, who models new dispositions and skills during a purposeful social activity, thus helping students acquire valuable cultural resources.

At the same time, providing high-quality scaffolding can impose heavy intellectual demands on the teacher. In the excerpt in Table 12.1, for example, the teacher had to track student arguments, analyze their structure and content, identify main weaknesses, and find ways to intervene to support his students, all during a real-time group discussion.

In our research and professional development program, we wanted teachers to develop advanced levels of expertise in facilitation and argumentation, so we provided lengthy and intensive professional development (Reznitskaya & Wilkinson, 2017, 2019a; Wilkinson et al., 2017). The program lasted from October through May and offered a total of 36 contact hours for teachers. During professional development, teachers participated in multiple workshops, study group meetings, and individual coaching sessions. Teachers learned about concepts and principles of dialogic teaching, inquiry dialogue, and argumentation. Much of the program focused on helping teachers acquire knowledge and skills on how to enhance the quality of argumentation through the use of strategically chosen facilitation moves, such as those used by the teacher in the excerpt in Table 12.1. Although teachers who took part in our program made considerable progress in acquiring new facilitation moves aimed at improving argumentation quality during discussions (Wilkinson et al., 2017), our analysis of their experiences also revealed that they found facilitation of argumentation quite challenging and struggled with implementing recommended practices (Reznitskaya & Wilkinson, 2019a).

Now we examine a discussion from another study, conducted in a sixth-grade classroom by MacArthur, Ferretti, and Okolo (2002). These researchers worked in a different disciplinary context—the discussion took place in a history classroom—but they had educational goals that were similar to those in our project: The study aimed to support the development of historical reasoning by having students "learn to make claims, support them with evidence, and warrant conclusions made." Engaging in historical reasoning was expected to help students acquire a deeper understanding of history.

MacArthur et al. (2002) used a general theoretical framing that was similar to that used in our project. They explained that their study was "based on sociocultural theory, which emphasizes the way learning is shaped by social context.... From this perspective, academic learning is a process of mastering the forms of discourse, that is, the ways of speaking and thinking, that are characteristic of particular disciplines" (p. 161).

An excerpt from the study of MacArthur et al. (2002) presented in their article is shown in Table 12.2. Prior to the discussion, students had read several sources about immigration to America in the early 20th century. They were assigned to represent opposing views of immigrants versus nativists and asked to debate each other.

As can be seen from Table 12.2, the similarity in goals and underlying theoretical assumptions between the two studies did not result in comparable instructional choices about how to implement dialogue in a classroom. In this excerpt, argumentation was structured as persuasion dialogue, a type of discourse aimed at winning over an opponent (Walton, 1998). Prior to the discussion, "the teacher gave clear procedures and expectations for the debate" (MacArthur et al., 2002, p. 163), but she did not participate in the discussion, except to keep time. In the excerpt, students showed high levels of participation, as well as readiness to represent views on immigration that may be different from their own. As noted by MacArthur et al. (2002), students used several sophisticated argument moves, including challenges (e.g., "How are we going to do that?") and rebuttals (e.g., "It's supposed to be free country"), even though these were not always clearly warranted. The authors concluded that the use of debates promoted student involvement in the discussion, improved students' knowledge about immigration, and encouraged perspective-taking. At the same time, they wondered whether "the competitive nature of the debates ... limited reasoned discussion" and whether "including a role for teacher mediation ... might lead to more productive discussions" (MacArthur et al., 2002, p. 171).

Table 12.2 Example of argumentation structured as persuasion dialogue

Arnie	Us nativists think you should go back to where you came from because you are going to take over the country.
Ariel	How are we going to do that?
Arnie	Because more and more immigrants are going to keep coming and then next thing you know there is going to be more immigrants than nativists.
Wendy	It's supposed to be free country.
Greg	I know, but some immigrants come to America and when voting time comes you all vote for what's best for you all, not what's best for the country.
Wendy	How can you say that when you don't know how we feel?
Arnie	Because you don't know anything about our country.
Greg	You just come to America and learning English and you might not know how the things are running and you are just picking names, and you vote for that person.
Wendy	But you don't own it. You don't own this country.
Arnie	Technically, we do, because we were born here.

The excerpts from two studies demonstrate some of the key differences in the actual implementation of dialogue in a classroom by educators and researchers. The observed variations in resulting argumentative discourse, despite the common educational goals and similar theoretical framing, are not necessarily all problematic: They reveal the creativity of individual scholars who designed instructional environments that generally reflect sociocultural perspectives. In fact, it is encouraging that today we have a number of well-established dialogue-intensive pedagogies focused on promoting argumentation, including *Philosophy for Children* (Lipman, 2003; Sharp, 1991), *Collaborative Reasoning* (Waggoner, Chinn, Yi, & Anderson, 1995), *Argue with Me* (Kuhn, Hemberger, & Khait, 2016), and *Thinking Together* (Dawes, Mercer, & Wegerif, 2004). Some of these approaches focus on inquiry (e.g., *Philosophy for Children*) and others on persuasion (e.g., *Argue with Me*). Moreover, some assume that a high level of teacher scaffolding is necessary until students acquire the necessary argumentation skills and thus require extensive and costly professional development for practitioners (e.g., *Philosophy for Children*). Others recommend minimal teacher scaffolding and provide limited professional development (e.g., *Argue with Me, Collaborative Reasoning*).

Although we appreciate the variation in instructional approaches, we also believe that the field is ready to develop a more precise and data-based understanding of specific ways in which argumentative discourse promotes student learning. We need to know whether participation in inquiry versus persuasion dialogue leads students to internalize different argumentation skills, epistemic commitments, content knowledge, and other competencies (cf. Asterhan et al., 2010; Felton, Garcia-Mila, & Gilabert, 2009). And we need to know how teachers can best support argumentation during the discussions and whether high investment in intensive professional development is well-justified (cf. Baker et al., 2017; Gardner, 2015).

Implications for Theory, Research, and Practice

When discussing future research on specific characteristics of argumentative discourse and related student learning, we do not mean to imply that researchers should simply contrast different established approaches, by, for example, comparing *Philosophy for Children* (Lipman, 2003; Sharp, 1991) with *Argue with Me* (Kuhn et al., 2016). This is because the numerous particularities of each approach would make results difficult to interpret. Rather, we argue for the need to conduct theoretically informed and systematic studies of the fundamental assumptions underlying these approaches. That is, in order to learn about the relative contributions of different ways of structuring and supporting argumentation, researchers need to focus on specific features of these learning environments. Fortunately, there is now relevant theory and emerging research to engage in this work.

For example, Asterhan and Schwarz (2016) presented a comprehensive *Argumentation for Learning Framework (AFL)* that classified the differences in how researchers have implemented and studied argumentation. The framework includes a number of variables grouped into the following three categories:

1 *Antecedents of argumentation* are variables that affect the characteristics of dialogic interaction: They act as enablers or inhibitors of the actual dialogue that takes place in a classroom. They include discourse instructions, ground rules, topics to be discussed, group composition, and so on.
2 *Dialogue characteristics* reflect the type of discourse resulting from different configurations of antecedents. Examples include inquiry versus persuasion dialogue.
3 *Learning outcomes* refer to the learning gains following the engagement in argumentation through dialogue, such as argumentation and social skills, content knowledge, epistemic cognition, and so on.

The *AFL* framework makes it clear that, because of the variation in the ways argumentative discourse has been enacted in previous studies, we know little about the relative value of particular conditions for promoting argumentation for learning. This is because variables listed in the *AFL* framework have been rarely isolated in research to examine their specific contributions to the development of particular skills, knowledge, or dispositions that students internalize from their engagement in dialogue with others. As succinctly put by the authors, "research in this field is abundant; however, causal evidence is not" (Asterhan & Schwarz, 2016, p. 165).

We see the *AFL* framework as a welcome elaboration of sociocultural theories. By enumerating evidence-based factors that can influence student experiences during dialogue, the framework provides a much-needed guidance for researchers who are interested in examining how and under what conditions dialogue supports learning. Using the *AFL* framework, researchers can manipulate some variables of interest, such as dialogue type and degree of teacher support, while controlling for other relevant factors, including topics to be discussed or group composition. Although such investigations are rare, in a few studies researchers have varied discourse instructions to examine their effects on students' argumentation and conceptual understanding (Asterhan et al., 2010; Felton et al., 2009). For example, Felton et al. (2009) found that students who were told to work collaboratively toward finding a solution were better at generating information for and against their own position on a posttest, compared to students who were instructed to persuade each other. On the other hand, Asterhan and Schwarz (2016) described their experimental study, in which the goal to persuade others resulted in more critical reasoning, compared with the goal to work toward better understanding. We need to learn more about how dialogue goals and instructions shape the social environment in a classroom and how this environment then affects the learning of individual students. For example, even if we assume that collaborative engagement in argumentation, such as inquiry dialogue, may be the normative model for reaching most reasonable conclusions (Gregory, 2007) and for promoting social values, such as respect for multiple viewpoints (Asterhan & Schwarz, 2016), it is entirely possible that the competitive, game-like nature of persuasion can activate unique psycho-educational mechanisms associated "with the efforts to triumph inherent in debate..." (Snow, 2017, p. ix). These mechanisms can, in turn, affect engagement and motivation of the students and impact their learning of certain argumentative competencies, such as finding flaws in the arguments of their opponents.

Following the *AFL* framework, future studies should also analyze the degree of teacher scaffolding needed to engage students in productive argumentation. Although researchers agree that simply putting students in groups is not sufficient and that teacher support should be contingent on student needs (Chiu, 2004; Littleton & Mercer, 2010; Webb, 2009), little is known about how the intensity of teacher scaffolding during discussion relates to the quality of group argumentation and subsequent individual performance. Some researchers suggest that teacher support during discussions should be minimal because constraining or routinizing interactions can disrupt student autonomy, impede authentic engagement, and otherwise turn a lively discussion into another tedious school task (e.g., Chiu, 2004; Lin, Jadallah, et al., 2015). In a study aptly titled "Less Is More: Teachers' Influence During Peer Collaboration," Lin et al. (2015) analyzed *Collaborative Reasoning* discussions and found that students were more likely to learn relational reasoning (i.e., how to relate two or more distinct concepts) from peers rather than from the teacher.

Other scholars maintain that, given well-documented problems with the quality of students' reasoning, teachers need to provide extensive scaffolding until students internalize the norms, criteria, and practices of rigorous argumentation (Gardner, 2015; Gregory, 2007). Susan Gardner, a co-director of the Vancouver Institute of *Philosophy for Children*, stressed the crucial role of teacher facilitation, suggesting that in its absence, discussions "can actually reinforce poor reasoning, since such reasoning will pass unnoticed and hence unchecked" (Gardner, 2015, p. 72).

Similarly, Splitter and Sharp (1996) suggested that "it is the teacher, who, at least in the first instance, must encourage students to talk and listen, who must weave into a coherent form their disparate thoughts and ideas, and who must exemplify modes of thoughtful and reasonable behaviour" (p. 285).

From a sociocultural perspective, it might be argued that considerable teacher involvement is necessary to initiate students into new ways of using language to enhance argumentation quality and provide them with necessary modeling and support. However, researchers need to learn more about how the intensity of teacher scaffolding during dialogue affects student engagement, motivation, learning, as well as the quality of argumentation. There may be a fundamental tension between the egalitarian nature of dialogue, in which "all participants' ideas, beliefs, and understandings ... are valued" (Billings & Fitzgerald, 2002) and the hierarchical, authoritative commitment to rigorous argumentation standards that are designed to eventually reveal that some ideas are better, more reasonable than others (c.f., Gardner, 2015).

Furthermore, although previous studies have examined the type (vs. the degree) of teacher intervention during dialogue (Billings & Fitzgerald, 2002; Nystrand, Wu, Gamoran, Zeiser, & Long, 2003; O'Connor, Michaels, & Chapin, 2015; Oyler, 2019; Reznitskaya et al., 2012), many important questions about the impact of teacher facilitation moves on student learning remain largely unanswered. This is because most prior research has focused on identifying teacher talk moves that characterize dialogic interactions or contrasting them with more traditional discourse patterns. For example, in our earlier study (Reznitskaya et al., 2012), we compared inquiry dialogues conducted by experienced facilitators trained in *Philosophy for Children* pedagogy to typical text-based discussions led by regular teachers in fifth-grade elementary school classrooms. Our analysis revealed several distinct discourse patterns frequently used by experienced facilitators to enhance the quality of discussions. For example, compared to regular teachers, *Philosophy for Children* facilitators asked about six times more Clarification Questions, during which they closely paraphrased a student's response and checked for accuracy in understanding (e.g., "So you're saying that a person cannot be intelligent unless they are educated?") (Reznitskaya et al., 2012). Such questions were intended not only to clarify students' ideas but also to draw the group's attention to potentially contentious statements so that they can be further discussed and challenged by the rest of the group.

Such studies are helpful for developing research-based understanding of effective facilitation, but they do not reveal how and under what conditions specific argumentative skills and dispositions are acquired by students as a result of particular talk moves used by the teacher. To be able to tease apart the affordances and limitations of different types and levels of teacher support, researchers need to rely on innovative multimethod approaches that allow for the detection and mapping of specific events, borrowed by students from a social activity and subsequently applied to new tasks performed independently (e.g., an argumentative essay). One example of such an approach comes from a recent study by VanDerHeide (2017), who used ethnographic methods, genre theory, and discourse analysis, to examine the content and processes of class discussion in relation to "writing moves" present in students' arguments. Similarly, in a study by Wagner, Ossa Parra, and Proctor (2017), the authors identified "tracers," or distinct ideas in the discussion transcripts, and then were able to link the content of dialogue to students' post-intervention writing performance.

Also, when investigating how different configurations of dialogue-based environments promote (or suppress) the internalization of new knowledge, skills, and dispositions, future studies will need to take into account that the actual argumentative discourse occurring in a classroom may differ from the discourse intended by researchers (Asterhan & Schwarz, 2016). That is, teachers and students may not follow given discourse instructions, norms, and practices for a variety of reasons, including lack of motivation and low competence in facilitation and argumentation.

This is why it is necessary for future studies to rely on psychometrically strong measures and data analytic procedures to assess the dialogue that actually takes place during the study.

In the past few decades, researchers have developed a variety of frameworks to analyze classroom interactions focused on argumentation, identifying important features of discourse productive for learning and suggesting new measurement strategies (Asterhan & Schwarz, 2009; Billings & Fitzgerald, 2002; Chinn & Anderson, 1998; Erduran, Simon, & Osborne, 2004; Felton, Crowell, Garcia-Mila, & Villarroel, 2019; Oyler, 2019). In such studies, researchers have systematically examined the distribution of functions of talk, the co-construction of student arguments, and teacher facilitation moves. In our own work, we recently designed and validated an observational rating scale that assesses the quality of teacher facilitation and student argumentation during inquiry dialogue in upper elementary classrooms (Reznitskaya & Wilkinson, 2017; Reznitskaya, Wilkinson, & Oyler, 2017).

At the same time, our measure, as well as most current analytic models used by researchers (for review, see Rapanta, Garcia-Mila, & Gilabert, 2013), was largely based on structural analysis of argumentation. That is, we identified and counted the presence of certain structural elements of the discourse (e.g., clarification questions from the teacher, consideration of alternative perspectives by the students), assuming that having more of these elements translated into better argumentation and more progress during the discussion. But it is possible that discussions with low-quality argumentation and little progress made by the students can have many of the desirable structural elements (Chinn, Duncan, Hung, & Rinehart, 2016). In a powerful example, Chinn et al. (2016) used an argument against vaccinations to demonstrate that seriously flawed reasoning can score high on several desirable discourse elements commonly assessed by researchers, such as elaborated reasoning, evidential support, and presentation and rebuttal of alternatives viewpoints. Future research should explore new approaches to measuring argumentation, including context-sensitive analyses that rely on argument reconstruction in order to get a more accurate assessment of quality and progress (e.g., Backman, Gardelli, Gardelli, & Persson, 2012; Björnsson, Kihlbom, & Ullholm, 2009; Chinn & Anderson, 1998).

Acquiring precise, evidence-based understanding of how to support student engagement in quality argumentation has direct implications for curriculum design and teacher professional development. On the one hand, studies show that learning how to scaffold student dialogue presents a serious challenge for teachers and appears to require extensive and sustained professional development (Gardner, 2015; Nguyen, Anderson, Waggoner, & Rowel, 2007; Reznitskaya & Wilkinson, 2019a). For example, to promote deep learning and long-term positive change, Weber and Gardner (2009) recommended a minimum of 5-course certification program to prepare skillful facilitators. In our own work, the professional development program lasted for an entire academic year and involved 36 contact hours with teacher participants, including resource-intensive individual coaching sessions, provided by project members with high levels of expertise in argumentation and facilitation.

On the other hand, there are educators who have achieved some success in engaging students in argumentation with comparatively little teacher professional development. For example, in the study of *Collaborative Reasoning*, Zhang et al. (2016) offered only a two-day workshop to teachers and were still able to demonstrate positive gains in student learning. If we are to confront the challenge of increasing the use of dialogue-intensive pedagogy in schools, then the benefits and costs of providing different amounts of support for teachers, and their students, need to be well understood. O'Connor and Snow (2018) expressed a related sentiment in their recent review of studies of classroom discourse:

> It may be that we are asking teachers to conduct discussions in formats that are more demanding than they need to be. Just as fitness programs lose many participants by featuring demanding routines that only those with the most leisure time (or other sources of support)

> can keep up with, it may be that we are asking teachers to do something that has so many dimensions of variation, so many degrees of freedom, so much to manage, that it is unlikely to go well in the majority of cases.
>
> *(p. 336)*

Indeed, are there some high-leverage practices that can be readily learned by teachers and yield substantial learning gains? What are those practices? More broadly, what do teachers absolutely need to know to become effective facilitators? Is it necessary, as some suggest (e.g., Bråten, Muis, & Reznitskaya, 2017), that teachers change their thinking about knowledge construction and justification, or epistemic cognition, in order to implement advocated discourse practices? In our professional development work, we had little research to draw on when we looked for answers to these important questions.

To conclude, in this chapter, we have argued for more research that addresses various assumptions underlying dialogue-based instruction to support the development of argumentation. We focused on two variables—how to structure the dialogue and how much teacher support to provide to students—because we believe that they capture major differences in how researchers have enacted argumentation in a classroom. Theoretically, we would like to see more studies that help demystify sociocultural perspectives by further specifying the mechanisms by which students internalize or appropriate new ways of speaking, acting, and thinking. Empirically, we need to learn more about the tradeoffs of persuasion versus inquiry dialogue for acquisition of argumentation skills and content knowledge and to gain insight into the role of teacher scaffolding in promoting or suppressing student engagement and learning. Methodologically, we need to find more creative approaches to study design, measurement, and data analysis in order to build a more accurate understanding of how and why dialogue works. Practically, we need to know whether there are considerable efficiencies in professional development, such as savings in duration and cost, which can be achieved without undermining the quality of instruction and student learning. Such efficiencies are important if we are serious about expanding the use of dialogue-intensive pedagogy to support the development of argumentation.

References

Alexander, R. J. (2018). Developing dialogic teaching: Genesis, process, trial. *Research Papers in Education*, 1–38. doi:10.1080/02671522.2018.1481140

Anderson, R. C., Nguyen-Jahiel, K., McNurlen, B., Archodidou, A., Kim, S., Reznitskaya, A., ... Gilbert, L. (2001). The snowball phenomenon: Spread of ways of talking and ways of thinking across groups of children. *Cognition and Instruction, 19*(1), 1–46. doi:10.1207/S1532690XCI1901_1

Asterhan, C. S. C., Butera, F., Nokes, T., Darnon, C., Schwarz, B. B., Butler, R., & Levin, J. (2010). Motivation and affect in peer argumentation and socio-cognitive conflict. In K. Gomez, L. Lyons, & J. Radinsky (Eds.), *Learning in the disciplines: Proceedings of the 9th international conference of the learning sciences* (pp. 211–218). Chicago, IL: International Society of the Learning Sciences.

Asterhan, C. S. C., & Schwarz, B. B. (2009). Argumentation and explanation in conceptual change: Indications from protocol analyses of peer-to-peer dialog. *Cognitive Science, 33*(3), 374–400. doi:10.1111/j.1551–6709.2009.01017.x

Asterhan, C. S. C., & Schwarz, B. B. (2016). Argumentation for learning: Well-trodden paths and unexplored territories. *Educational Psychologist, 51*(2), 164–187. doi:10.1080/00461520.2016.1155458

Backman, Y., Gardelli, T., Gardelli, V., & Persson, A. (2012). *Scientific thinking tools: A base for academic studies.* Lund: Studentlitteratur.

Baker, A. R., Lin, T.-J., Chen, J., Paul, N., Anderson, R. C., & Nguyen-Jahiel, K. (2017). Effects of teacher framing on student engagement during collaborative reasoning discussions. *Contemporary Educational Psychology, 51*(Supplement C), 253–266. doi:10.1016/j.cedpsych.2017.08.007

Billings, L., & Fitzgerald, J. (2002). Dialogic discussion and the Paideia seminar. *American Educational Research Journal, 39*(4), 907–941. doi:10.3102/00028312039004905

Björnsson, G., Kihlbom, U., & Ullholm, A. (2009). *Argumentation analysis: Skills for critical thinking*. Stockholm: Natur & kultur.

Bråten, I., Muis, K., & Reznitskaya, A. (2017). Teachers' epistemic cognition in the context of dialogic practice: A question of calibration? *Educational Psychologist, 52*(4), 253–269. doi:10.1080/00461520.2017.1341319

Chen, Y.-C., Benus, M. J., & Hernandez, J. (2019). Managing uncertainty in scientific argumentation. *Science Education, 0*(0). doi:10.1002/sce.21527

Chinn, C. A., & Anderson, R. C. (1998). The structure of discussions that promote reasoning. *Teachers College Record, 100*(2), 315–368.

Chinn, C. A., Duncan, R. G., Hung, L. C.-C., & Rinehart, R. W. (2016). *Epistemic criteria and reliable processes as indicators of argument quality in science students' argumentation*. Paper presented at the Annual Meeting of the American Educational Research Association, Washington, DC.

Chiu, M. M. (2004). Adapting teacher interventions to student needs during cooperative learning: How to improve student problem solving and time on-task. *American Educational Research Journal, 41*(2), 365–399. doi:10.3102/00028312041002365

Dawes, L., Mercer, N., & Wegerif, R. (2004). *Thinking together: A programme of activities for developing speaking, listening and thinking skills for children aged 8–11*. Birmingham: Imaginative Minds.

Dong, T., Anderson, R. C., Kim, I., & Li, Y. (2008). Collaborative reasoning in China and Korea. *Reading Research Quarterly, 43*(4), 400–424. doi:10.1598/RRQ.43.4.5

Erduran, S., Simon, S., & Osborne, J. (2004). TAPping into argumentation: Developments in the application of Toulmin's argument pattern for studying science discourse. *Science Education, 88*(6), 915–933. doi:10.1002/sce.20012

Felton, M., Crowell, A., Garcia-Mila, M., & Villarroel, C. (2019). Capturing deliberative argument: An analytic coding scheme for studying argumentative dialogue and its benefits for learning. *Learning, Culture and Social Interaction*, 100350. doi:10.1016/j.lcsi.2019.100350

Felton, M., Garcia-Mila, M., & Gilabert, S. (2009). Deliberation versus dispute: The impact of argumentative discourse goals on learning and reasoning in the science classroom. *Informal Logic, 29*, 417–446.

Ferretti, R. P., & Fan, Y. (2016). Argumentative Writing. In C. A. MacArthur, S. Graham, & J. Fitzgerald (Eds.), *Handbook of writing research* (2nd ed, pp. 301–315). New York: Guilford Press.

Ferretti, R. P., & Graham, S. (2019). Argumentative writing: Theory, assessment, and instruction. *Reading and Writing, 32*(6), 1345–1357. doi:10.1007/s11145-019-09950-x

Fischer, F., Kollar, I., Ufer, S., Sodian, B., Hussmann, H., Pekrun, R., … Eberle, J. (2014). Scientific reasoning and argumentation: Advancing an interdisciplinary research agenda in education. *Frontline Learning Research, 2*(3), 28–45.

Gardner, S. (2015). Commentary on 'Inquiry is no mere conversation'. *Journal of Philosophy in Schools, 2*(1), 71–91. doi:10.21913/JPS.v2i1.1105

Gorard, S., Siddiqui, N., & See, B. H. (2015). *Philosophy for children: Evaluation report and executive summary*. London: Education Endowment Foundation.

Gregory, M. (2007). Normative dialogue types in philosophy for children. *Gifted Education International, 22*, 160–171. doi:10.1177/026142940702200307

Howe, C., & Abedin, M. (2013). Classroom dialogue: A systematic review across four decades of research. *Cambridge Journal of Education, 43*(3), 325–356. doi:10.1080/0305764X.2013.786024

Kennedy, D. (2013). Developing philosophical facilitation: A toolbox of philosophical moves. In S. Goering, N. Shudak, & T. Wartenberg (Eds.), *Philosophy in schools: An introduction for philosophers and teachers* (pp. 110–118). New York: Routledge.

Kim, I., Anderson, R. C., Nguyen-Jahiel, K., & Archodidou, A. (2007). Discourse patterns during children's collaborative online discussions. *The Journal of the Learning Sciences, 16*(3), 333–370. 10.1080/10508400701413419

Kuhn, D. (1992). Thinking as argument. *Harvard Educational Review, 62*(2), 155–177.

Kuhn, D., & Crowell, A. (2011). Dialogic argumentation as a vehicle for developing young adolescents' thinking. *Psychological Science, 22*, 545–552. doi:10.1177/0956797611402512

Kuhn, D., Hemberger, L., & Khait, V. (2016). *Argue with Me: Argument as a path to developing students' thinking and writing*. New York: Routledge.

Lin, T.-J., Anderson, R. C., Jadallah, M., Kuo, L., Wu, X., Hummel, J. E., … Dong, T. (2012). Children's use of analogy during Collaborative Reasoning. *Child Development, 83*(4), 1429–1443. doi:10.1111/j.1467-8624.2012.01784.x

Lin, T.-J., Anderson, R. C., Jadallah, M., Nguyen-Jahiel, K., Kim, I., Kuo, L., … Li, Y. (2015). Social influences on children's development of relational thinking during small-group discussions. *Contemporary Educational Psychology, 41*, 83–97. doi:10.1016/j.cedpsych.2014.12.004

Lin, T.-J., Jadallah, M., Anderson, R. C., Baker, A. R., Nguyen-Jahiel, K., Kim, I.-H., … Wu, X. (2015). Less is more: Teachers' influence during peer collaboration. *Journal of Educational Psychology, 107*(2), 609–629. doi:10.1037/a0037758

Lipman, M. (1988). *Philosophy goes to school.* Philadelphia, PA: Temple University Press.

Lipman, M. (2003). *Thinking in education.* New York: Cambridge University Press.

Littleton, C., & Mercer, N. (2010). The significance of educational dialogue between primary school children. In C. Littleton & N. Mercer (Eds.), *Educational dialogues: Understanding and promoting productive interaction* (pp. 271–288). London: Routledge.

MacArthur, C. A., Ferretti, R. P., & Okolo, C. M. (2002). On defending controversial viewpoints: Debates of sixth graders about the desirability of early 20th-century american immigration. *Learning Disabilities Research & Practice (Wiley-Blackwell), 17*(3), 160–172. doi:10.1111/1540–5826.00042

Means, M. L., & Voss, J. F. (1996). Who reasons well? Two studies of informal reasoning among children of different grade, ability, and knowledge levels. *Cognition and Instruction, 14*(2), 139–178.

Mercer, N. (1995). *The guided construction of knowledge: Talk amongst teachers and learners.* Clevedon: Multilingual Matters Ltd.

Mercer, N., Wegerif, R., & Dawes, L. (1999). Children's talk and the development of reasoning in the classroom. *British Educational Research Journal, 25*(1), 95–111.

Newell, G. E., Beach, R., Smith, J., VanDerHeide, J., Kuhn, D., & Andriessen, J. (2011). Teaching and learning argumentative reading and writing: A review of research. *Reading Research Quarterly, 46*(3), 273–304. doi:10.1598/RRQ.46.3.4

Nguyen, K., Anderson, R. C., Waggoner, M., & Rowel, B. (2007). *Using literature discussions to reason through real life dilemmas: A journey taken by one teacher and her fourth-grade students.* In R. Horowitz (Ed.), *Talking texts: Knowing the world through the evolution of instructional discourse* (pp. 187–206). Erlbaum Associates.
Hillsdale, NJ: Erlbaum Associates.

Nussbaum, E. M., & Sinatra, G. M. (2003). Argument and conceptual engagement. *Contemporary Educational Psychology, 28*(3), 384–395. doi:http://dx.doi.org/10.1016/S0361-476X(02)00038-3

Nystrand, M., Wu, L., Gamoran, A., Zeiser, S., & Long, D. A. (2003). Questions in time: Investigating the structure and dynamics of unfolding classroom discourse. *Discourse Processes, 35*(2), 135–198. doi:10.1207/S15326950DP3502_3

O'Connor, C., Michaels, S., & Chapin, S. (2015). "Scaling down" to explore the role of talk in learning: From district intervention to controlled classroom study. In L. B. Resnick, C. Asterhan, & S. N. Clarke (Eds.), *Socializing intelligence through talk and dialogue* (pp. 111–126). Washington, DC: American Educational Research Association.

O'Connor, C., & Snow, C. E. (2018). Classroom discourse: What do we need to know for research and for practice? In M. Schober, A. Britt, & D. Rapp (Eds.), *The Routledge handbook of discourse processes* (2nd ed., pp. 315–342). New York: Routledge.

Osborne, J. (2010). Arguing to learn in science: The role of collaborative, critical discourse. *Science, 328*(5977), 463–466. doi:10.1126/science.1183944

Oyler, J. (2019). Exploring teacher contributions to student argumentation quality. *Studia Paedagogica, 24*(4), 173–198. doi:10.5817/SP2019-4-8

Rapanta, C., Garcia-Mila, M., & Gilabert, S. (2013). What is meant by argumentative competence? An integrative review of methods of analysis and assessment in education. *Review of Educational Research, 83*(4), 483–520. doi:10.3102/0034654313487606

Resnick, L. B., Asterhan, C. S. C., & Clarke, S. N. (2015). *Socializing intelligence through academic talk and dialogue.* Washington, DC: American Educational Research Association.

Reznitskaya, A., & Anderson, R. C. (2002). The argument schema and learning to reason. In C. C. Block & M. Pressley (Eds.), *Comprehension instruction: Research-based best practices* (pp. 319–334). New York: Guilford.

Reznitskaya, A., Glina, M., Carolan, B., Michaud, O., Rogers, J., & Sequeira, L. (2012). Examining transfer effects from dialogic discussions to new tasks and contexts. *Contemporary Educational Psychology, 37*, 288–306. doi:10.1016/j.cedpsych.2012.02.003

Reznitskaya, A., Kuo, L., Clark, A., Miller, B., Jadallah, M., Anderson, R. C., & Nguyen-Jahiel, K. (2009). Collaborative reasoning: A dialogic approach to group discussions. *Cambridge Journal of Education, 39*(1), 29–48. doi:10.1080/03057640802701952

Reznitskaya, A., & Wilkinson, I. A. G. (2015a). Positively transforming classroom practice through dialogic teaching. In S. Joseph (Ed.), *Positive psychology in practice* (2nd ed., pp. 375–399). Hoboken, NJ: John Wiley & Sons, Inc.

Reznitskaya, A., & Wilkinson, I. A. G. (2015b). Professional development in dialogic teaching: Helping teachers promote argument literacy in their classrooms. In D. Scott & E. Hargreaves (Eds.), *Sage handbook of learning* (pp. 219–232). London: Sage Publications.

Reznitskaya, A., & Wilkinson, I. A. G. (2017). *The most reasonable answer: Helping students build better arguments together.* Boston, MA: Harvard Education Press.

Reznitskaya, A., & Wilkinson, I. A. G. (2019a). Designing professional development to support teachers' facilitation of argumentation. In N. Mercer, R. Wegerif, & L. Major (Eds.), *The Routledge international handbook of research on dialogic education* (pp. 254–268). Abingdon: Routledge.

Reznitskaya, A., & Wilkinson, I. A. G. (2019b). Supporting teacher learning and use of inquiry dialogue with the argumentation rating tool. In R. Gillies (Ed.), *Promoting academic talk in schools* (pp. 128–143). Abingdon: Routledge.

Reznitskaya, A., Wilkinson, I. A. G., & Oyler, J. (2017). Supporting teacher spontaneous use of talk moves during inquiry dialogue. In E. Manalo, Y. Uesaka, & C. Chinn (Eds.), *Promoting spontaneous use of learning and reasoning strategies* (pp. 310–326). Singapore: Routledge.

Rogoff, B. (1990). *Apprenticeship in thinking: Cognitive development in social context.* New York: Oxford University Press.

Rogoff, B. (1995). Observing sociocultural activity on three planes: Participatory appropriation, guided participation, and apprenticeship. In J. V. Wertsch, D. Rio, & A. Alvarez (Eds.), *Socioculural studies of mind* (pp. 139–164). Cambridge: Cambridge University Press.

Sadler, T. D. (2004). Informal reasoning regarding socioscientific issues: A critical review of research. *Journal of Research in Science Teaching, 41*(5), 513–536. doi:10.1002/tea.20009

Sharp, A. M. (1991). The community of inquiry: Education for democracy. *Thinking: The Journal of Philosophy for Children, 9*(2), 31–37.

Smith, F., Hardman, F., Wall, K., & Mroz, M. (2004). Interactive whole class teaching in the national literacy and numeracy strategies. *British Educational Research Journal, 30*(3), 395–411. doi:10.1080/01411920410001689706

Snow, C. E. (2017). Foreword. In A. Reznitskaya & I. A. G. Wilkinson, *The most reasonable answer: Helping students build better arguments together* (pp. vii–x). Boston, MA: Harvard Education Press.

Splitter, L. J., & Sharp, A. M. (1996). The practice of philosophy in the classroom. In A. M. Sharp & R. F. Reed (Eds.), *Studies in philosophy for children: Pixie* (pp. 285–314). Madrid: Ediciones De La Torre.

van de Pol, J., Volman, M., & Beishuizen, J. (2010). Scaffolding in teacher–student interaction: A decade of research. *Educational Psychology Review, 22*(3), 271–296. doi:10.1007/s10648-010-9127-6

VanDerHeide, J. (2017). Classroom talk as writing instruction for learning to make writing moves in literary arguments. *Reading Research Quarterly, 53*(3), 323–344. doi:10.1002/rrq.196

Vygotsky, L. S. (1968). *Thought and language (newly revised, translated, and edited by Alex Kozulin).* Cambridge, MA: MIT Press.

Vygotsky, L. S. (1978). *Mind in society: The development of higher psychological processes.* Cambridge, MA: Harvard University Press.

Vygotsky, L. S. (1981). The genesis of higher-order mental functions. In J. V. Wertsch (Ed.), *The concept of activity in Soviet psychology* (pp. 144–188). Armonk, NY: Sharpe.

Waggoner, M., Chinn, C. A., Yi, H., & Anderson, R. C. (1995). Collaborative reasoning about stories. *Language Arts, 72*, 582–589.

Wagner, C. J., Ossa Parra, M., & Proctor, C. P. (2017). The interplay between student-led discussions and argumentative writing. *TESOL Quarterly, 51*(2), 438–449. doi:10.1002/tesq.340

Walton, D. (1998). *The new dialectic: Conversational contexts of argument.* Toronto, CA: Univeristy of Toronto Press.

Webb, N. (2009). The teacher's role in promoting collaborative dialogue in the classroom. *British Journal of Educational Psychology, 79*(1), 1–28. doi:10.1348/000709908X380772

Weber, B., & Gardner, S. (2009). "Back to the future" in philosophical dialogue: A plea for changing P4C teacher education. *Analytic Teaching and Philosophical Praxis, 29*(1), 25–30.

Wegerif, R., Mercer, N., & Dawes, L. (1999). From social interaction to individual reasoning: An empirical investigation of a possible sociocultural model of cognitive development. *Learning and Instruction, 9*(6), 493–516. doi:10.1016/S0959-4752(99)00013-4

Weiner, E. H. (1980). What should Kelly do? In E. H. Weiner (Ed.), *Unfinished stories: For facilitating decision making in the elementary classroom* (pp. 13–14). Washington, DC: National Education Association.

Wells, G. (2007). Semiotic mediation, dialogue and the construction of knowledge. *Human Development, 50*(5), 244–274. doi:10.1159/000106414

Wilkinson, I. A. G., Murphy, P. K., & Binici, S. (2015). Dialogue-intensive pedagogies for promoting reading comprehension: What we know, what we need to know. In L. B. Resnick, C. A. Asterhan, & S. N. Clarke (Eds.), *Socializing intelligence through academic talk and dialogue* (pp. 37–50). Washington, DC: American Educational Research Association.

Wilkinson, I. A. G., Reznitskaya, A., Bourdage, K., Oyler, J., Nelson, K., Glina, M., ... Kim, M.-Y. (2017). Toward a more dialogic pedagogy: Changing teachers' beliefs and practices through professional development in language arts classrooms. *Language & Education*, *31*(1), 65–82. doi:10.1080/09500782.2016.1230129

Zhang, X., Anderson, R. C., Morris, J., Miller, B., Nguyen-Jahiel, K. T., Lin, T.-J., ... Hsu, J. Y.-L. (2016). Improving children's competence as decision makers. *American Educational Research Journal*, *53*(1), 194–223. doi:10.3102/0002831215618663

13
ARGUMENTATION AND INQUIRY LEARNING

María Pilar Jiménez-Aleixandre and Pablo Brocos

This chapter explores interrelations among argumentation and inquiry, in particular features of inquiry learning environments (ILE) that promote argumentation, framing inquiry and argumentation as epistemic practices. Argumentation can be characterized as the evaluation of knowledge claims or competing models in the light of evidence and reasons, whereas inquiry may be defined as the endeavor of building knowledge through asking questions, generating and interpreting data, and drawing conclusions (Sandoval & Reiser, 2004). As such, they are intertwined, because evaluating knowledge generally entails the production of knowledge and vice versa. Thus, both inquiry and argumentation address epistemic goals about how knowledge claims are built, evaluated, and justified, seeking the development of epistemic cognition: the ability to construct, evaluate, and use knowledge. Inquiry and argumentation have been extensively developed and researched—particularly in science education—ascribing them a range of meanings, from being understood as specific practices to their characterization as overarching educational approaches aimed at promoting these practices. There is, however, consensus in considering that both are associated to innovative teaching and learning and should be integrated into education. Kuhn (2005) argues that inquiry and argumentation should be at the center of a *thinking curriculum*, oriented toward learners being able "to seek knowledge to solve problems and to achieve goals; to use reasoned argument to address issues and to make judgments" (p. 5), in a consideration of thinking as a social purposeful activity. From a sociocultural perspective, learning is situated in social practices (Kelly & Green, 2018), and there are reciprocal relationships between individual thinking and collective intellectual activities, of particular relevance for argumentation (Mercer, 2009).

Inquiry and argumentation share goals, and their classroom enactment have overlapping features, so it may be expected that their design principles have much in common. First, we discuss some theoretical approaches about inquiry and argumentation. Second, we examine critical components of ILE that foster argumentation, which is the main focus of the chapter. Third, the distinction between arguing to learn and learning to argue is briefly addressed.

Inquiry and Argumentation as Epistemic Practices: The Relevance of Goals

Inquiry has been conceptualized in a variety of ways, from Dewey in the 1930s to the National Research Council framework (NRC, 2012), a trajectory reviewed by Crawford (2014). There is consensus in emphasizing that inquiry involves two elements. First is the goal of equipping students to become independent learners, "to take charge of their own learning, choosing the questions they wish to investigate and seeking and finding answers to them" (Kuhn, 2005, p. 39). The second element is the engagement of students in processes of investigation rather than merely in instruction based on textbooks and lectures. Thus, for Kelly (2014), "Inquiry in science entails conducting an investigation into the natural or designed world, or even into the applications of scientific knowledge to societal issues" (p. 1364). Both aspects, for students to become active learners and to participate in investigations, are aligned with argumentation goals: pupils engage in argumentation rather than learning it secondhand, and participating in investigations creates opportunities for generating explanations to be evaluated and evidence to evaluate them. Thus, instructional environments deliberately designed to support authentic inquiry support students' engagement in argumentation practices (Rapanta & Felton, 2019).

Inquiry learning (IL) occurs in various educational domains, such as mathematics (Makar, Bakker, & Ben-Zvi, 2015), history (Monte-Sano, 2010; Monte-Sano & Budano, 2013), engineering (Kelly & Cunningham, 2019), or language arts (Kuhn, 2005; Reznitskaya & Gregory, 2013). Science may be the field in which inquiry has been more extensively researched and theoretically developed, and science education may have experienced a greater infusion of inquiry in curriculum standards and classrooms. However, this development has not resulted in a clear common understanding of what it means to teach science through inquiry (Osborne, 2014), which motivated the shift in the NRC (2012) from "inquiry" to "practices" as key to science learning. Beyond this lack of definition, Osborne (2014) argued that stepping away from inquiry as an overarching learning approach may be helpful to avoid the conflation between the goal of science, which is to develop new knowledge, and the goal of science education, which is "not to create new knowledge but rather to help students understand a body of existing, consensually agreed on and well-established old knowledge" (p. 580). The NRC framed the practices of scientists (and engineers) in three broad spheres of activity: investigation and empirical inquiry, construction of explanations using models, and evaluation of the fit of models and explanations to evidence. It needs to be noted that IL does not mean mere experimentation or "hands-on" activities but instead cognitive engagement in sense making and in developing evidence-based explanations (Hmelo-Silver, Duncan, & Chinn, 2007; Osborne, 2019). Science education approaches to inquiry highlight its connections to epistemic matters, and there is consensus in proposing that inquiry teaching should address epistemic goals with a focus on how we know what we know and why we believe what we do (Duschl & Grandy, 2008; Osborne, 2014).

Our analysis views inquiry and argumentation as ways of engaging in disciplinary knowledge construction, framing them in epistemic practices. Kelly and Licona (2018) defined epistemic practices as "the socially organized and interactionally accomplished ways that members of a group propose, communicate, evaluate, and legitimize knowledge claims" (p. 140). Epistemic practices afford a broader frame than previous characterizations of inquiry and argumentation as skills (e.g., Kuhn, 2005) or as genres of discourse (e.g., Clark & Sampson, 2007). Kelly and Licona considered that, in science education, inquiry can create opportunities for supporting epistemic goals defined as the "understanding of the reasons, evidentiary bases for conceptual knowledge and models" (p. 142). This characterization of epistemic goals and the proposal to achieve them through inquiry approaches can be extended and modulated for other disciplinary domains. Examples of epistemic learning goals that can be achieved through inquiry and argumentation may be evaluating causal explanations using epistemic criteria in science (Duschl, 2008) or using historical contextualization—empathy—in history (Huijgen, van de Grift, van Boxtel, & Holthuis, 2018).

Argumentation is thus an epistemic practice coherent with inquiry approaches. It corresponds to evaluating knowledge, one of the three broad scientific spheres in the NRC, alongside investigating and developing explanations. For Barzilai and Chinn (2018), arguments—like models or explanations—are *epistemic products* created, assessed, and communicated through *epistemic processes*. Jiménez-Aleixandre and Erduran (2008) considered two complementary processes intertwined in argumentation: evaluation of knowledge claims by coordinating them with available evidence and relevant theory, and persuasion of an audience. These processes draw respectively from Toulmin (1958), and Perelman and Olbrechts-Tyteca (1958). Rather than *persuasion*, the term *inquiry dialogue* has been proposed by Reznitskaya and Gregory (2013) for a communicative exchange whose main goal is "to collectively formulate reasonable judgments, adding to a group's existing body of knowledge and mutual understanding" (p. 115). This distinction is based on an analysis by Walton (1992), who claimed that these forms of dialogue have different goals. The goal of persuasion is to convince the other party, whereas the goal of inquiry dialogues is to *collectively* prove some proposition or to reach a conclusion. Collaboration is also emphasized in Kelly's (2008) characterization of inquiry as entailing a shift in the epistemic subject from the individual to the situated social group, where the shared norms for argumentation are agreed.

Aligning with the role of authentic issues of social relevance in inquiry approaches, the characterization of argumentation should be extended, beyond assessing explanations, to the evaluation of options or courses of action, relying on evidence, but also on values or ethical stances. For instance, socioscientific dilemmas as environmental management of foreign species (Evagorou, Jiménez-Aleixandre, & Osborne, 2012) or vegetarian diets (Jiménez-Aleixandre & Brocos, 2018); in history education evaluating the positions of actors in the Good Friday Agreement in Northern Ireland (López-Facal, Jiménez-Aleixandre, & Arcidiacono, 2015); or writing an essay about why did the United States drop an atomic bomb on Hiroshima (Monte-Sano, 2010).

In this chapter, we address learning environments from approaches, either called "inquiry" (in most domains) or "practices" (in science education, as in the NRC, 2012, framework). As Crawford (2014) argued, their central focus is the same "learner-constructed and -articulated science understandings based on logic and evidence as crucial components" (p. 537). Our interest is in the features of inquiry (or practices) environments promoting argumentation.

Critical Components of Inquiry Environments Promoting Argumentation

This section examines critical components of the design of inquiry environments that promote argumentation. ILE and argumentation environments share design principles (Jiménez-Aleixandre, 2008) and many features; in addition, their epistemic goals are normatively coincident to some extent. The characterization of components of ILE draws from Chinn, Duncan, and Rinehart's (2018) practical theory of epistemic design based on the AIR model of epistemic cognition. They analyze epistemic thinking in terms of three components: *epistemic aims or goals* (A), directed to the creation, evaluation, and critique of epistemic products, such as explanations or arguments; *epistemic ideals* (I), that is standards and criteria used to evaluate these products; and *reliable epistemic processes* (R) used to create and evaluate them. A fourth component, drawn from Berland and McNeill (2010), is *instructional context*, which creates adequate environments in order to support epistemic performances.

An argumentation task about diet choices designed in alignment with inquiry principles may illustrate the relationship between ILE and argumentation in regard to these components (Jiménez-Aleixandre & Brocos, 2018). Participants should develop *epistemic goals* in order to understand the issue at stake, for instance, the aim of finding out the nutritional value of certain foodstuff and its health implications, which involves the evaluation of evidence and arguments. This evaluation implies engagement in *epistemic processes*, such as selecting evidence—for instance, about the relationship between red meat intake and cardiovascular disease—and interpreting it. These processes are guided by *epistemic ideals*, such as epistemic criteria and disciplinary standards (e.g., evaluating whether the source of an information is reliable; that is, does it come from an experimental design or is it anecdotal evidence?). The *instructional context* determines key elements, such as the scaffolds to potentially promote participants' engagement in these epistemic performances. In real-life contexts, these four components are closely intertwined, although for analytical purposes we discuss them separately.

Most of the approaches informing our analysis correspond to engagement in inquiry projects over extended periods of time, such as Investigating and Questioning our World through Science and Technology (IQWST; Berland, 2011; Berland & Reiser, 2011); Promoting Reasoning and Conceptual Change in Science (PRACCIS; Chinn et al., 2018), framed using the AIR model; Biology Guided Inquiry Learning Environments (BGuILE; Sandoval & Reiser, 2004); Promoting historical contextualization (Huijgen et al., 2018); Engineering is Elementary (EiE; Kelly & Cunningham, 2019); and Reading Apprenticeship (Litman & Greenleaf, 2018). Others correspond to inquiry sequences for secondary school, such as production of historical narratives (Gómez-Carrasco & Miralles, 2016), or to inquiry laboratory activities aimed to scaffold students' engagement in argumentation, as in Argument-Driven Inquiry (ADI; Walker & Sampson, 2013). A fully comprehensive review of the literature on inquiry and argumentation is beyond the scope of this chapter. Rather, our purpose is to draw from studies in which several of the components are identified, to highlight the complementarities and synergies among them. Figure 13.1 summarizes our proposal about how these components of inquiry environments promote argumentation. However, for some of the components we have not identified clear evidence of the effect of inquiry on argumentation but rather synergies between both, as discussed for each case.

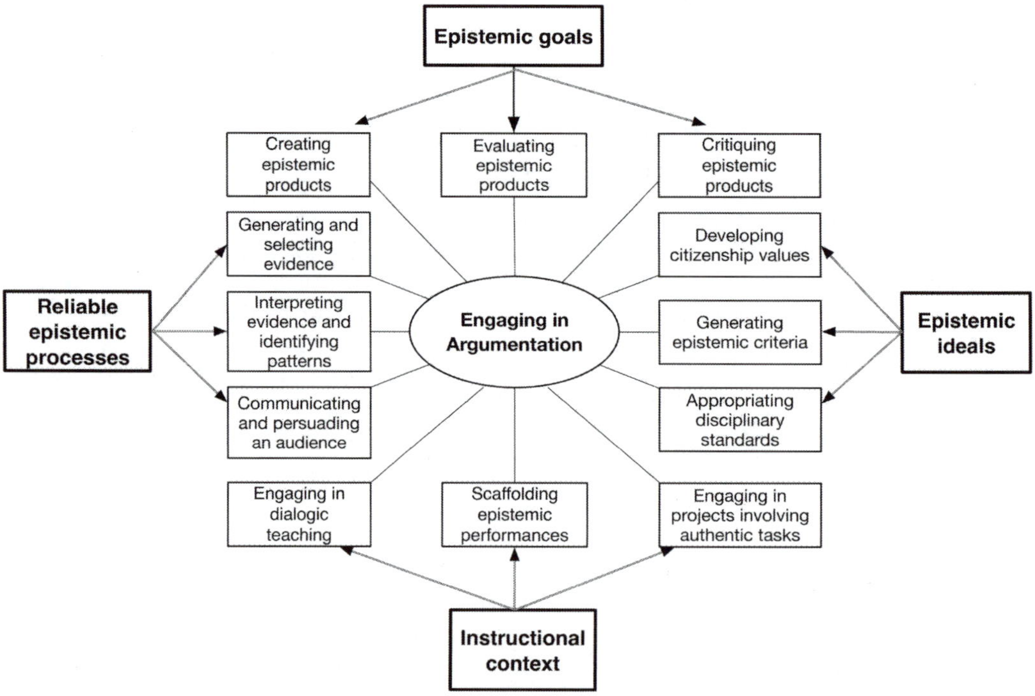

Figure 13.1 Critical components of inquiry learning environments promoting argumentation

Epistemic Goals

In ILE students set *epistemic goals*, such as constructing robust arguments or understanding the evidentiary bases for knowledge and models in science (Kelly & Licona, 2018) or for historical interpretations (VanSledright & Maggioni, 2016). Studies showing that epistemic goals influence reasoning and learning have focused on how individuals set and pursue epistemic goals, without connecting such personal knowledge construction to students' notions about the relevant community's goals (Sandoval, 2015). This suggests paying attention to both students' and disciplinary epistemic goals. The influence of different goal structures on students' performances has been explored by Berland (2011); the alignment of goals with existing practices in IQWST classrooms was carried over to students' argumentative interactions. Kim and Hannafin (2016) examined the effect of two types of goals embedded in an ILE task: Balanced reasoning (BR) goals asked students to support an informed decision while critically examining opposing arguments, whereas persuasion goals asked them to convince their peers. They found that BR goal instruction triggered high evaluation standards, an indicator of quality argumentation. The relationships between students' conceptions of inquiry and their epistemic beliefs have been examined by Getahun, Saroyan, and Aulls (2016), who found that more sophisticated epistemic beliefs corresponded to multidimensional conceptions of inquiry. VanSledright and Maggioni (2016) reviewed epistemic beliefs in connection to historical thinking, noting that some beliefs, as the idea that texts are authorless and therefore omniscient, may hamper the development of critical thinking. These results point to tight relationships among epistemic stances, argumentation, and learning.

We focus on three types of epistemic goals: creating, evaluating, and critiquing epistemic products. The first two goals draw from Barzilai and Chinn (2018), while critique has been emphasized by Ford (2015) and Osborne et al. (2016).

Creating Epistemic Products

Learning through inquiry involves creating epistemic products such as arguments (our focus in this chapter), explanations, models, and representations. In order to create a strong argument, students should embrace epistemic aims (Duncan & Chinn, 2018); in the context of PRACCIS model-based inquiry instruction, students constructed arguments comparing models. Duncan and Chinn proposed to evaluate the quality of arguments taking into account epistemic criteria. Brocos, Jiménez-Aleixandre, and Baker (under review) compared the construction of arguments driven by epistemic aims, such as supporting them in appropriate justification versus driven by pragmatic (non-epistemic) aims such as finishing the task quickly or preserving a positive self-image. The creation of arguments based in evidence has a range of meanings in different disciplines; for instance, in language arts data were drawn from journalistic or literary texts (Litman & Greenleaf, 2018). Constructing historical arguments is linked to a disciplinary way of thinking and working with evidence (Monte-Sano, 2010), including recognizing biases in sources or situating evidence in its context. The goal of historical interpretation is understanding the past, and the events cannot be replicated. Thus, historians do not look for generalizations. In Bravo-Torija and Jiménez-Aleixandre's (2018) study, the construction of arguments about marine resources management required the articulation of the use of evidence with the relevant ecological theory. Epistemic understanding of arguments thus involves a grasp of what counts as claims, evidence, and justification in a given disciplinary context.

Evaluating Epistemic Products

A relevant goal in ILE is evaluation of epistemic products. An evaluativist level of epistemic development is characterized by understanding that some knowledge claims or options may prove to be better, while a multiplist level involves considering all opinions as equally right. The influence of students' epistemic stances on the quality of their arguments and physics learning was explored by Nussbaum, Sinatra, and Poliquin (2008): The group that had previous information about the nature of arguments developed better ones, and evaluativists interacted more critically than multiplists. It needs to be noted that products are evaluated according to certain criteria, which will be examined in the next section.

Evaluation is central to the construction of arguments, as claims, models, or options do not exist in isolation but rather in competition with others (Osborne et al., 2016). Different discursive contexts pose different challenges to argumentation; we argue that when evaluating causal explanations, the focus of evaluation is on the trustworthiness of claims, whereas when choosing among options in socioscientific dilemmas the focus of evaluation may be on the potential of a given option (e.g., vegetarianism, renewable energy sources) to be carried out. There are also differences in the extent of individual versus social focus (Jiménez-Aleixandre & Brocos, 2018). Studies from Berland and McNeill (2010), Gotwals and Songer (2013), and Osborne et al. (2016) focused on learning progressions about argumentation. Gotwals and Songer identified reasoning—providing justifications for the relevant theory—as the most challenging aspect for sixth graders. Osborne et al. proposed levels of increasing complexity, according to the degree of coordination between claims and evidence and the competence to critique. Monteira and Jiménez-Aleixandre (2016) studied entry points for the use of evidence in early childhood, in the context of a five-month inquiry project about snails. The kindergartners were able to use evidence for evaluating alternative ideas, drawing patterns, or revising their initial ideas about snails' mouthparts, in order to account for particular marks (such as deep holes) in food and even for proposing a potential mechanism for its functioning. The authors proposed a rubric for examining children's use of evidence to evaluate claims at different epistemic levels, from closer to data to evaluative judgments. Current work on argumentation progressions has focused primarily on structural dimensions of arguments, and, in order to capture epistemic aspects, Duncan and Chinn (2018) proposed incorporating dimensions such as the fit with systematic evidence. In inquiry-oriented history education in high school, Monte-Sano (2010) identified trends about evidence's persuasiveness, sources, or contextualization. She highlighted the discipline-specific nature of data and warrants in students' arguments about the U.S. dropping the A-bomb. In contextualizing evidence, students' essays represented various levels of historical thinking: from demonstrating an understanding of causation, as what happened before and after the bombing of Hiroshima, to attempts to contextualize that resulted in distortion of the original meaning of the documents. To sum up, we may say that carrying out accurate judgments is a mark of progression in epistemic learning.

Critiquing Epistemic Products

There is an increasing consensus on the need for including critique in the epistemic goals set in ILE. A rigorous evaluation involves comparing alternative arguments, claims, or models, going beyond the articulation of support for one alternative and showing why others are flawed. Public expression of ideas is a feature of ILE and of argumentative interactions (Jiménez-Aleixandre & Erduran, 2008; Makar et al., 2015). Ford (2015) pointed out the centrality of evaluation and critique in scientific practices. Focusing on argumentation, Osborne et al. (2016) emphasized that it requires the ability to engage in both construction and critique, noting that critique is more demanding. A distinctive feature of inquiry-based argumentation, according to Rapanta and Felton (2019), is an emphasis on the analysis, critique, and interpretation of evidence. The object of critique may be varied, including texts in language arts (Litman & Greenleaf, 2018), which externalize intrapersonal literacy processes; historical sources subjected to critical examination in history education (Huijgen et al., 2018); or students' proposals for how to solve mathematical problems in mathematics (Makar et al., 2015).

As a summary of the relevance for argumentation of the epistemic goals of constructing, evaluating, and critiquing epistemic products, we may say that creating strong arguments requires the appropriation of the epistemic goals of knowledge-building. Productive engagement in the evaluation of alternative claims or options and in critique are related to an evaluativist level of epistemic development, which acknowledges that different people can hold different beliefs that have support, but that the support for some beliefs can be stronger than for others. At other levels, such as the multiplist, all claims are considered equally valid, making evaluation unnecessary. Constructing, evaluating, and critiquing arguments demand adaptation to disciplinary or discursive contexts. These goals promote the externalization of internal processes, as only claims that are publicly expressed may be subjected to evaluation and critique.

Epistemic Ideals

Epistemic ideals are defined by Chinn et al. (2018) as standards or criteria used to evaluate epistemic products. They used the terms *ideals* and *criteria* interchangeably, and we will employ *criteria*, which is more frequent in the literature. Inquiry-oriented pedagogies need to attend to the development of norms and practices that provide opportunities to learn through and about inquiry (Kelly, 2014). In a study focusing on norms of argumentation-based inquiry, Makar et al. (2015) defined norms as "classroom level cognitive and social structures operationalized through the collective expectations of the teacher and students about what count as appropriate activities and interactions" (p. 1108). They further proposed that in argumentation-based inquiry, normative practices would focus on shared goals of responding to the inquiry question, generating a justifiable solution, being explicit about the evidence and process, anticipating critique, and holding expectations to think mathematically. All of these, except the last one, apply to other disciplinary contexts.

We focus on three practices related to this component: generating epistemic criteria, appropriating disciplinary standards, and appropriating citizenship values.

Generating Epistemic Criteria

While engaged in ILE, students can generate epistemic criteria—rather than being provided with them—for the evaluation of epistemic products, such as models or arguments. Pluta, Chinn, and Duncan (2011) reported how seventh graders, after completing a series of model-evaluation tasks, elaborated criteria to evaluate scientific models, some of them epistemic, such as *good models fit all evidence* or *provide explanations of phenomena*. For the evaluation of the strength of evidence, Chinn et al. (2018) proposed criteria for strong evidence such as being diagnostic with respect to competing theories or models, or addressing core parts of the model. Ryu and Sandoval (2012) examined how a sustained focus on argumentation improved elementary children's epistemic criteria for scientific arguments: Children's arguments met evidentiary criteria, such as the articulation of causal claims and the explicit justification of claims with evidence. Improvement in the sophistication of sixth graders' criteria was also found by Lehrer and Schauble's (2012): They discussed the aesthetics of evidence and considered qualities of convincing evidence. Their initial criteria for good evidence emphasized direct experience; however, later in the year other criteria emerged tying evidence to data representations, culminating "in the statement that evidence deserves to be valued to the extent that it is germane to the research question being investigated" (p. 202), rather than simply whatever the investigator noticed. In our study regarding the use of evidence by kindergarteners (Monteira & Jiménez-Aleixandre, 2016), we found out that the teacher emphasis on the need for testing all claims contributed to create social norms that promoted children's engagement in argumentative discourse. Examples were that claims need to be supported by evidence and that experimentation is a valid procedure to generate data that might be used as evidence to confirm or disconfirm a claim. These kindergarteners applied the criteria rather than generating them. Walker and Sampson (2013) reported about the changes in students' criteria, such as what counts as quality evidence, to evaluate their own and others' arguments.

Appropriating Disciplinary Standards

A challenge for argumentation studies is the tension between domain-general and domain-specific dimensions or components. Although some argumentation skills have been viewed as being general, there is a growing consensus about the limitations, for instance, of domain-general epistemic criteria (Fischer et al., 2014), and the need for contemplating the interplay between domain-general and domain-specific elements. There are particular norms for knowledge construction within disciplines: Monte-Sano and Budano (2013) defined historical thinking as ways of thinking specific of the interpretive work of history, such as "recognizing multiple perspectives, situating events in historical context, analyzing the affordances and constraints of historical sources, constructing evidence-based arguments, or evaluating the merits of others' claims" (p. 181). Discussing norms in mathematical inquiry, Makar et al. (2015) suggested that learners embraced the complexity of the process of knowledge creation, managing doubt, ambiguity, anomalies, and contradictions as part of it. They emphasized the normative ways of reasoning with tools and representations, for instance including representations in explaining solutions. Becker et al. (2013) discussed *sociochemical* disciplinary norms shaping students' discourse, such as what can be accepted as a valid chemical representation. An example, recurrent in classroom discourse, was that particulate-level-based explanations about thermodynamics were valid justifications and could serve as a warrant. Particulate-level evidence was the most frequently used and accepted. In their study in engineering education, Kelly and Cunningham (2019) reported students' engagement in epistemic practices specific to engineering, such as making trade-offs between epistemic criteria and pragmatic constraints; typically engineering designs do not have unique solutions; they need to be optimized and tailored according to given constraints.

Developing Citizenship Values

Inquiry-based instruction is usually understood as having a focus on learning disciplinary content and practices. However, a central goal of school is the education of citizens who can participate in decisions (Schwarz, 2009). Therefore, to the criteria discussed above it will be necessary to add citizenship values, by which we understand to be ethical principles. For instance, in historical education the ethical dimension of knowledge should be taken into account; when learning about the Founding Fathers in the U.S. it is also necessary to consider the native people expelled from their traditional territories. For the purpose of educating citizens, there is consensus in assigning relevance to the development of critical thinking (CT). Jiménez-Aleixandre and Puig (2012) proposed a characterization of the components of CT, including: a) the use of epistemic criteria in evidence evaluation, b) the disposition to evaluate the reliability of sources, c) the capacity to develop independent opinions and to challenge socially established ideas, and d) the capacity to analyze and criticize discourses that justify inequalities. From these, the use of epistemic criteria and the evaluation of the reliability of the sources are relevant for a "post-truth" era, by which McIntyre (2018) means times in which actual facts are replaced by "alternative facts" and feelings are prioritized over evidence. The emergence of "post-truth" is drawing attention from educators; an example is the denial of human responsibility for climate change. The focus on understanding the nature of science is shifting from the acknowledgment of the tentativeness of scientific knowledge toward the relevance of epistemic education empowering students to face societal challenges. Reznitskaya and Wilkinson (2017) proposed argumentation through inquiry dialogue in order to support students in the appropriation of established methods to judge arguments. Chinn, Barzilai, and Duncan (2020) suggested the relevance of promoting apt epistemic performance to face post-truth reasoning problems. This could help to overcome difficulties such as lacking an understanding of the reliable processes that people can use to evaluate reports and of the need for a fit with evidence.

As a summary, we argue that epistemic criteria are a requisite for the evaluation processes central in argumentation. Given the importance of epistemic criteria for engaging in inquiry and argumentation, instruction should allow space for sharing them and making them explicit in the classroom. Research suggests that these efforts allow students to apply these criteria, improve them, or even elaborate their own criteria. In addition to domain-general criteria, there is a need for attending to specific disciplinary standards. The development of epistemic criteria is also relevant for fostering critical thinking and being able to assess the reliability of sources.

Reliable Epistemic Processes

In the AIR model, reliable epistemic processes (REPs) are defined as a variety of causal processes, such as perception, observation, or experimentation, used to generate knowledge (Duncan & Chinn, 2018). These processes are considered discipline-specific and social. Processes lie on a continuum from highly reliable, such as astronomical observation, to unreliable, such as astrology. Therefore, high-quality arguments should address an evaluation of the REP used. Rapanta and Felton (2019) pointed out: "Within an inquiry approach, the construction of arguments as both products (i.e. logical structures emerging in discourse) and processes (i.e. dialogical moves that promote argumentative reasoning) is an essential part of scientific discourse" (p. 290).

From a range of potential REPs in inquiry, we focus on three processes relevant for argumentation: generating and selecting data to become evidence, interpreting evidence in order to identify patterns and propose explanations, and communicating to and persuading an audience. The first two processes draw from Duschl's (2008) Evidence-Explanation (E-E) continuum; as he pointed out, each transition involves making epistemic judgments about "what counts" as data, evidence, or explanations. The third one draws from Kelly (2008) and Barzilai and Chinn (2018).

Generating and Selecting Evidence

Evidence is generated for answering questions; therefore, identifying valuable questions is essential. Students posing their own questions and designing investigations to answer them, rather than having them provided or designed by the teachers, are features of authentic inquiry (Chinn & Malhotra, 2002). In IQWST sixth-graders co-constructed questions recording them on a "Question board", which guided argumentation (Berland, 2011). In Lehrer and Schauble's (2012) inquiry project about change and variability in ecological systems, third-graders posed and revised questions that could be addressed by investigation, for instance: "I wonder if some bugs burrow in the mud to keep warm in winter?" Evidence was generated through experiments and through comparison, which is particularly relevant in biology studies. An inquiry project about snails (Monteira & Jiménez-Aleixandre, 2016) began with kindergarteners' list about "What do we want to know about snails?" Twenty questions were recorded in a display, and subsequently children engaged (with teacher scaffolding) in designing experiments and in *purposeful observation*, defined as prolonged, systematic observation used to test claims and answer questions related to processes. These investigations and observations generated evidence that the kindergarteners used to support their claims. In other inquiry projects, students have been provided with multiple pieces of evidence of different quality (Chinn et al., 2018), so they could learn to distinguish high-quality evidence from anecdotal evidence.

We distinguish *data* from *evidence*, characterizing *evidence* by its discursive role in knowledge evaluation. Koslowski et al. (2008) considered that information becomes evidence when an explanation can incorporate it into a causal framework. In the process of transforming data into evidence, external representations play an important role, in particular for young students. Discussing how children invented and used ways for measuring and representing nature, Lehrer and Schauble (2012) pointed out that inventing representations involves students in thinking about the functions and uses of inscriptions, and in understanding how inscribing involves reduction (selection) and amplification of data. Thus, in their study, a fifth-grader's drawing of an insect larva—previously identified as a "worm"—made visible the segments unnoticed by his classmates. This diagnostic feature allowed differentiation from worms, a step in answering the question about whether organisms living in compost were changing over time, and in building an argument. In an investigation of collaborative inquiry, Nichols, Gillies, and Hedberg (2016) compared sixth-year students' performances in Earth science as they used representations with a focus either on explanations or on argumentation. All improved in explaining and interpreting seismograms, but the argumentation group had the highest frequencies for knowledge construction discourse and for constructing representations. In these studies, it is not easy to disentangle features related to inquiry, modeling, and argumentation, and it seems that supporting students in the inquiry curriculum—as they engage in argumentation and in producing representations—creates synergies resulting in learning gains on several dimensions. In particular, the processes of data selection and the coordination of evidence with claims are relevant for the construction of arguments.

Interpreting Evidence and Identifying Patterns

Interpreting evidence to identify patterns is a second transformation involving epistemic judgments in the path from raw data to explanations (Duschl, 2008). It poses, however, some challenges for students. Researchers agree that data do not speak by themselves, but McNeill and Berland (2017) found that students see data as factual, rather than understanding evidence as constructed and needing to be interpreted. McNeill and Berland proposed a design heuristic in which information is transformable, so that students must manipulate it to find patterns and evaluate their fit to competing claims. To address challenges related to evidence-based practices, Duncan, Chinn, and Barzilai (2018) proposed a theoretical framework called *grasp of evidence*, with the purpose of facilitating more sophisticated ways of engaging with evidence. One of the five dimensions in their framework is evidence interpretation, and two REPs associated with it are evaluating model-evidence fit and developing arguments that systematically connect evidence to models in ways that meet ideals such as relevance or diagnosticity. They sought to promote a lay grasp of evidence, with the aim to help citizens learn to determine the credibility of scientific claims in everyday communication. It is challenging for students to recognize patterns in data and to explain these patterns by appealing to relevant theory (Bravo-Torija & Jiménez-Aleixandre, 2018). In EiE, Kelly and Cunningham (2019) studied elementary school children's ability to interpret data in tables of trial runs, finding that they could identify trends, for instance that parachutes with shorter suspension lines and bigger canopies had lower average drop speed.

Communicating and Persuading an Audience

Communicative processes, alongside creative and evaluative ones, are considered by Barzilai and Chinn (2018) to be part of apt epistemic performance. Although argumentation research has paid more attention to evaluation (drawing on Stephen Toulmin's influential work), persuasion was the focus of Chaïm Perelman's approach to argumentation. Perelman and Olbrechts-Tyteca (1958) characterized argumentation as the discursive techniques that promote adherences to proposed theses.

Persuasion is also emphasized as a goal of argument and as part of a process of social knowledge building by Osborne et al. (2016) and McNeill and Berland (2017). Kelly and Cunningham (2019) highlighted the relevance of knowledge communication in the EiE project: Students communicated through epistemic tools such as data tables, physical prototypes, graphs, and assessment rubrics specific to engineering. One example is writing a "persuasive letter to village elders" deploying an argument for the location of a bridge, weighing geotechnical criteria and cultural constraints.

As a summary, it may be said that students' engagement in argumentation is supported when a variety of REPs are incorporated into inquiry. Different ways of generating first-hand evidence—from designing experiments and prototypes to engaging in purposeful observation—contribute to students' understanding of the evidence-based nature of arguments. Data selection (either from first- or second-hand information) and transformation of data through representations play an important role. Interpreting evidence and identifying patterns require a problematization of engagement with evidence. Argumentation is a social process, hence the relevance of communication through the uses of verbal, written, and symbolic tools.

Instructional Context

An inquiry approach has consequences for how the curriculum and instructional tasks are designed, structured, and organized. IL environments are communities of practice, but teachers and students have different roles: Teachers steer the learning goals, model inquiry, and argumentation, and guide students' participation in the inquiry.

We focus on three features of instructional contexts: scaffolding epistemic performances, engagement in dialogic teaching, and engagement in projects involving authentic tasks. The first two features relate to the role of teachers, while the third one refers to curriculum design.

Scaffolding Epistemic Performances

Hmelo-Silver et al. (2007) discussed why IL should not be identified with unguided discovery, arguing that it is highly scaffolded, thereby reducing the cognitive load and providing learners with opportunities to engage in complex tasks that would otherwise be beyond their reach. Makar et al. (2015) reported a teacher's strategies in a fourth-grade mathematics classroom in order to successfully scaffold norms supporting argumentation-based inquiry. These included reminding students of norms such as justifying explanations. At the beginning of the year, the teacher made explicit whether the students were following the norms, then her scaffolding faded progressively. Eventually the students enacted the norms independently of her presence: They justified ideas to peers, built on the ideas of others, and challenged each other's ideas. This is evidence of how responsibility for creating and evaluating arguments was handed over to learners. Another example of effectively scaffolded argumentation is the Process-Oriented Guided Learning Inquiry (POGIL; Becker, Stanford, Towns, & Cole, 2015) in science. The teacher's strategies include questioning students, revoicing students' ideas, and especially supporting arguments connecting elements in the macro, sub-micro, and symbolic levels of representation. This is an example of the affordances of collaborative reasoning and of collaborative argumentation, which have proven effective in producing better learning outcomes (Chinn & Clark, 2013).

A scaffold designed to reduce cognitive load, the Model-Evidence Link (MEL) diagram, was generated and tested in PRACCIS (Chinn et al., 2018). It consists of a graphical representation and reasoning tool in which students use different kinds of arrows to denote relationships between multiple pieces of evidence and models, from "strongly supports" to "contradicts." MEL supports backing claims with evidence and more sophisticated understandings of how precisely evidence relates to claims. A successful attempt at developing software to promote students' argumentation in ILEs is

ExplanationConstructor (Sandoval & Reiser, 2004), a tool designed to support construction and evaluation of explanations attending to their epistemic features, specifically the articulation of coherent causal accounts and the fit of claims with data. Clark and Sampson (2007) reported the affordances of "personally-seeded discussions" in improving eighth-graders' arguments, compared to face-to-face discussions. This software demanded students to make sense of data they collected (e.g., drawing patterns). Students whose principles differ were connected, so that they had the chance to discuss the same data under different perspectives. Kelly and Cunningham (2019) also focused on epistemic tools, which they defined as physical, symbolic, or discursive artifacts that support knowledge building. They examined the use by elementary school pupils of epistemic tools specific to engineering design.

Engagement in Dialogic Teaching

A successful program focusing on promoting primary school children's use of language as a tool for reasoning, argumentation, and problem-solving is *Thinking Together*, implemented in the UK by Mercer and colleagues since the 1990s. Mercer (2009) pointed out that the success of the intervention required teachers to encourage *exploratory talk*, in which partners engage critically but constructively with each other's ideas. Children's performances showed significant changes after participating in the program, including becoming more effective at joint argumentation. Similarly, *dialogic teaching* (Alexander, 2008) is *supportive* of children's discourse; *reciprocal*—teacher and children share ideas; and *purposeful*—teachers steer classroom talk with specific goals in view. A form of dialogic teaching is *inquiry dialogue* (Reznitskaya & Gregory, 2013), which has been found to encourage students' metacognition, as well as epistemological understandings consistent with evaluativist epistemology, alongside argument skills and disciplinary knowledge. Reznitskaya and Wilkinson (2017) developed a professional development program for language arts teachers, with the objective of supporting them in fostering students' argumentation through inquiry dialogue. They developed the Argumentation Rating Tool (ART), to help students attend to four argumentation criteria: exploration of different perspectives, clarity in the structure of arguments, acceptability of evidence, and logical validity. ART proved useful in teachers' engagement in inquiry dialogue and in students' improved argumentation.

The PRACCIS project encourages a form of discourse that is a hybrid between the practical science content level and the meta-epistemic level, focused on ideals for good models, arguments, or evidence (Chinn et al., 2018). For instance, when students argue that their chloroplast model fits the evidence and explain why they think so, they are invoking the ideal of fit with evidence in their specific arguments about their model. PRACCIS design principles specify that students should be explicitly encouraged to reflect on what makes a model or argument a good one, and on what makes a process reliable or unreliable. Kim and Hannafin (2016) have argued that information evaluation is critical for successful inquiry and argumentation; they scaffold it through metacognitive tasks in order to help students monitor their knowledge sources, thus promoting engagement and transfer of metacognitive awareness.

Engagement in Projects Involving Authentic Tasks

Participation in practices involving argumentation requires extended engagement in meaningful inquiry; therefore, allowing sufficient time is key in designing ILEs (Chinn & Clark, 2013; Duschl & Grandy, 2008). Sustained participation allows opportunities to learn in depth (Fielding-Wells, 2016). Engagement in long-term projects has affordances, particularly in life sciences, as some processes can only be observed throughout an extended time span, such as the healing of a snail's broken shell or changes in organisms living in compost (Lehrer & Schauble, 2012). In a study by Monteira and Jiménez-Aleixandre (2016), kindergartners revisited a few topics over several sessions, revising and reconsidering previous observations and experiments, supported by the teacher. These recurring discussions allowed kindergartners to review their initial ideas under the light of new evidence, thus fostering their engagement in argumentation. Time and recurrence were linked in *purposeful observation*. Critical discussion, in which students think back on experiments and observations, has proven successful in promoting argumentation in eighth-graders engaged in open inquiry (Kim & Song, 2006). They were asked to produce an argumentative report about their experiments for peer review, followed by a critical discussion. Students supported their claims with evidence from the experiments and were able to refute and gave feedback to their peers. This feedback was used to think back about the experiments, leading to changes in the initial hypotheses, in the methods, and in data processing.

Inquiry curricula are organized around authentic tasks and problems that may have different, alternative solutions (Fielding-Wells, 2016). This design produces a diversity of outcomes—of epistemic products such as models or arguments (Chinn & Clark, 2013; Jiménez-Aleixandre, 2008) that may have different epistemic statuses for different participants. These statuses refer to the higher or lower plausibility or acceptability of these products to different students, and they may be modified during the process of inquiry (Jiménez-Aleixandre & Brocos, 2018). Duncan et al.'s (2018) design guidelines for developing a grasp of evidence emphasize diversity of evidence, for instance, including evidence that differs in quality and strength; they also recommend the development of shared epistemic criteria.

Contextualized tasks should be perceived as relevant to students' lives; as real-world problems, they are ill-structured, such as "what is the best route to school for the school bus?" (Makar et al., 2015); "Is climate change caused by human or by natural factors?" "Which fuel is best for the generation of electricity, natural gas or coal?" (Iordanou & Constantinou, 2015). Nichols et al. (2016) created a real-world context for their unit on natural disasters and geological events by including information on recent earthquakes; the students were asked to make sense of seismograms, drawing from plate tectonics, and to interpret different aspects of the relationships between representations, seismic waves, and ground shaking. The effect of task features on the quality of argumentation was explored by Kind et al. (2011), targeting issues in laboratory inquiry, such as treating data as unproblematic or lacking discussion about methods. Three types of tasks were compared: (a) collecting and making sense of complex data, about the influence of containers' surface color on the transportation of hot liquids; (b) collecting data to address conflicting hypotheses (predictions); and (c) discussing fictional data. The third task was more effective in generating more and better arguments; students' attention was focused on data and methods, and 50% of their time was used in hypothesizing or producing explanations. While the students actually performing the experiments took their own data as "correct," the students in the fictional data condition used methodological criteria to decide which experiment was best. This study points to the relevance of critical discussion in overcoming problems of laboratory inquiry, such as seeing data gathering as the main focus and neglecting other dimensions of inquiry like evidence evaluation.

These features of ILE, then, support students' engagement in argumentation: first, scaffolding complex performances, such as justification or backing claims with evidence, through teachers' strategies or epistemic tools; second, inquiry dialogue with extensive sharing of ideas encouraging participation in the discourses of science; and third, projects involving authentic tasks that support a diversity of potential outcomes, or produce a diversity of students viewpoints or positions, which is a requisite for argumentation.

Arguing to Learn and Learning to Argue

In the context of inquiry, researchers have distinguished between arguing to learn and learning to argue. *Arguing to learn* (AL) involves engaging in argumentation in order to develop disciplinary knowledge, while *learning to argue* (LA) means learning the components of argumentation and how to engage in its practice (Chinn & Clark, 2013). Schwarz (2009) reviewed research about both aspects, suggesting that in AL argumentation may be considered as a tool to achieve goals such as content learning, whereas in LA argumentation is the object of the learning. We agree with Schwarz in seeing learning to argue and arguing to learn as intertwined in classroom discourse, rather than as independent, although in research they are frequently addressed separately. In their study of 40 teachers of language, history, and science, Litman and Greenleaf (2018) found that 58% of argumentation tasks had an AL focus, whereas only 17% had an LA focus and 25% had a dual one.

The impact of argumentation on learning content has been explored in several studies. von Aufschnaiter, Erduran, Osborne, and Simon (2008) showed that engagement in argumentation enabled high school students to elaborate their science understandings at relatively high levels of abstraction. They also found out that students could only engage in argumentation when they understood both the content of the task and the level of abstraction with which it was presented. The main predictor of high-quality arguments was students' familiarity and understanding of the task content. Sampson and Clark (2009) examined the differences between individual and collaborative argumentation conditions. The students in the collaborative condition demonstrate superior mastery and transfer performances about heat and temperature than those who wrote individual arguments. They also produced significantly better arguments. In a study about the effect of a ten-week Argument-Driven Inquiry instruction with chemistry undergraduates, Walker and Sampson (2013) found that it had a positive impact on the quality of written and oral arguments and on the development of content knowledge. These studies point to the positive effects of argumentation on learning, although when comparing explanation and argumentation conditions Nichols et al. (2016) found that the explanation group had higher scores in conceptual understanding. Chinn and Clark (2013) suggested three processes that may explain why argumentation may promote content learning: explicit elaborative processing, such as articulating their explanations, or modification of ideas; learning from others, in particular their peers; and stronger reasons to believe in the claims that they are building, developed in the process of providing evidence for claims.

Learning to argue has been discussed in the central section of this chapter. As Chinn (2006) pointed out, it can involve either formal preparation of a "case" for individual or collective claims and conclusions, or the discursive process of working out the best model based on evidence and relevant theory. There are a variety of approaches to interpret what are better arguments and how to evaluate the development of argumentation. Chinn (2006) suggested that the improvement in the ability to argue can be explained in terms of students developing better argument schemas, i.e. mental representations of the conditions for good arguments, such as sample size in a given piece of evidence. The need of domain-specific knowledge for the construction of quality arguments has been examined in a number of studies. Some instances can be knowledge of: evidence typical of a domain, relevant theories, or specific criteria for evaluating evidence (Chinn & Clark, 2013). Without it, as Monte-Sano's (2010) study showed, students may exhibit features of argumentation while revealing fundamental flaws in historical thinking. Historical arguments involve conceptual understanding and procedural knowledge of historical analysis; this would make possible to construct plausible arguments, select relevant evidence, and explain its significance. An integrated approach is also suggested by Walker and Sampson (2013): Laboratory instruction involving argumentation and disciplinary engagement, such as ADI, can foster both the development of argumentation and of content knowledge.

Concluding Thoughts

This review about the relationships between inquiry learning and argumentation suggests two main implications: First, there are interactions and synergies between IL and argumentation, rather than clear-cut effects of one on the other. This is coherent with their shared epistemic goals and with the fact that "educators who have sought to promote inquiry in classrooms have often sought to build argumentation into their inquiry-based classroom interventions" (Chinn & Clark 2013, p. 327). Second, the review points toward a constellation of components of inquiry learning environments that promote argumentation in combination, rather than to the effect of isolated factors. Classrooms are complex systems where many factors interact, including explicit shared goals, students in charge of their own learning, strategies used by teachers to scaffold epistemic performances, curricula oriented to the creation of epistemic products and to engaging students in inquiry for extended periods of time, and the development of epistemic criteria, which are relevant for the evaluation processes making part of argumentation. Even when several or most of these components are incorporated into ILEs, productive argumentation does not always occur, as it is challenging for students. Nevertheless, the studies reviewed here show potential for improving our efforts toward integrating argumentation in teaching and learning.

Acknowledgments

Work supported by the Spanish Ministry of Science, Education and Universities, partly funded by the European Regional Development Fund (ERDF). Contract grant PGC2018-096581-B-C22. Thanks to Sabela F. Monteira for her support with the literature review and the first draft of the chapter.

References

Alexander, R. J. (2008). *Towards dialogic teaching. Rethinking classroom talk* (4th ed.). York: Dialogos.

Barzilai, S., & Chinn, C. (2018). On the goals of epistemic education: Promoting apt epistemic performance. *The Journal of the Learning Sciences*, *27*(3), 353–389. https://doi.org/10.1080/10508406.2017.1392968

Becker, N., Rasmussen, C., Sweeney, G., Wawro, M., Towns, M., & Cole, R. (2013). Reasoning using particulate nature of matter: An example of a sociochemical norm in a university-level physical chemistry class. *Chemistry Education Research and Practice*, *14*(1), 81–94. https://doi.org/10.1039/c2rp20085f

Becker, N., Stanford, C., Towns, M., & Cole, R. (2015). Translating across macroscopic, submicroscopic and symbolic levels: The role of instructor facilitation in an inquiry-oriented physical chemistry class. *Chemistry Education Research and Practice*, *16*, 769–785. https://doi.org/10.1039/c5rp00064e

Berland, L. K. (2011). Explaining variation in how classroom communities adapt the practice of scientific argumentation. *Journal of the Learning Sciences*, *20*(4), 625–664. https://doi.org/10.1080/10508406.2011.591718

Berland, L. K., & McNeill, K. L. (2010). A learning progression for scientific argumentation: Understanding student work and designing supportive instructional contexts. *Science Education*, *94*(5), 765–793. https://doi.org/10.1002/sce.20402.

Berland, L. K., & Reiser, B. (2011). Classroom communities' adaptation of the practice of scientific argumentation. *Science Education*, *95*(2), 191–216. https://doi.org/10.1002/sce.20420.

Bravo-Torija, B., & Jiménez-Aleixandre, M. P. (2018). Developing an initial learning progression for the use of evidence in decision-making contexts. *International Journal of Science and Mathematics Education*, *16*(4), 619–638. https://doi.org/10.1007/s10763-017-9803-9.

Chinn, C. A. (2006). Learning to argue. In A. M. O'Donnell, C. E. Hmelo-Silver, & G. Erkens (Eds.), *Collaborative learning, reasoning and technology* (pp. 355–383). Mahwah, NJ: Erlbaum.

Chinn, C. A., & Barzilai, S., & Duncan, R. G. (2020). Education for a "post-truth" world: New directions for research and practice. *Educational Researcher.* https://doi.org/10.3102/0013189X20940683.

Chinn, C. A., & Clark, D. B. (2013). Learning through collaborative argumentation. In C. E. Hmelo-Silver, C. A. Chinn, C.K. Chan, & A. M. O'Donnell (Eds.), *The international handbook of collaborative learning* (pp. 314–332). New York: Routledge. https://doi.org/10.4324/9780203837290.ch18.

Chinn, C. A., Duncan, R. G., & Rinehart, R. (2018). Epistemic design: Design to promote transferable epistemic growth in the PRACCIS project. In E. Manalo, Y. Uesaka, & C. A. Chinn (Eds.), *Promoting spontaneous use of learning and reasoning strategies. Theory, research and practice for effective transfer* (pp. 243–259). New York: Routledge. https://doi.org/10.4324/9781315564029-16.

Chinn, C. A., & Malhotra B. A. (2002). Epistemologically authentic inquiry in schools: A theoretical framework for evaluating inquiry tasks. *Science Education*, *86*(2), 175–218. https://doi.org/10.1002/sce.10001

Clark, D. B., & Sampson, V. D. (2007). Personally-seeded discussions to scaffold online argumentation. *International Journal of Science Education, 29*(3), 253–277. https://doi.org/10.1080/09500690600560944
Crawford, B. A. (2014). From inquiry to scientific practices in the science classroom. In N. G. Lederman & S. K. Abell (Eds.), *Handbook of research on science education* (Vol. II, pp. 515–541). New York: Routledge. https://doi.org/10.4324/9780203097267.ch26
Duncan, R. G., & Chinn, C. A. (2018, October). Evaluating the quality of argumentation: Going beyond structure to incorporate epistemic practices. Paper presented at the meeting of the Argumentation SIG, European Association for Research on Learning and Instruction (EARLI).
Duncan, R. G., Chinn, C. A., & Barzilai, S. (2018). Grasp of evidence: Problematizing and expanding the next generation science standards' conceptualization of evidence. *Journal of Research in Science Teaching, 55*, 907–937. https://doi.org/10.1002/tea.21468.
Duschl, R. (2008). Science education in three-part harmony: Balancing conceptual, epistemic and social learning goals. *Review of Research in Education, 32*, 268–291. https://doi.org/10.3102/0091732X07309371.
Duschl, R. A., & Grandy, R. E. (2008). Reconsidering the character and role of inquiry in school science: Framing the debates. In R. A. Duschl & R. E. Grandy (Eds.), *Teaching scientific inquiry: Recommendations for research and implementation* (pp. 1–37). Rotterdam: Sense. https://doi.org/10.1163/9789460911453_002.
Evagorou, M., Jiménez-Aleixandre, M. P., & Osborne, J. (2012). "Should we kill the grey squirrels?" A study exploring students' justifications and decision-making. *International Journal of Science Education, 34*(3), 401–428. https://doi.org/10.1080/09500693.2011.619211.
Fielding-Wells, J. (2016). "Mathematics is just 1+1=2, what is there to argue about"? Developing a framework for argument-based mathematical inquiry. In B. White, M. Chinnappan, & S. Trenholm (Eds.), *Opening up mathematics education research* (Proceedings of the 39th annual conference of the Mathematics Education Research Group of Australasia), pp. 214–221. Adelaide: MERGA.
Fischer, F., Kollar, I., Ufer, S., Sodian, B., Hussmann, H., Pekrun, R., … Eberle, J. (2014). Scientific reasoning and argumentation: Advancing an interdisciplinary research agenda in education. *Frontline Learning Research, 5*, 28–45. https://doi.org/10.14786/flr.v2i2.96.
Ford, M. (2015). Educational implications of choosing "practice" to describe science in the Next Generation Science Standards. *Science Education, 99*(6), 1041–1048. https://doi.org/10.1002/sce.21188.
Getahun, D. A., Saroyan, A., & Aulls, M. W. (2016). Examining undergraduate students' conceptions of inquiry in terms of epistemic belief differences. *Canadian Journal of Higher Education, 46*(2), 181–205.
Gómez-Carrasco, C., & Miralles, P. (2016). Historical skills in compulsory education: Assessment, inquiry based strategies and students' argumentation. *New Approaches in Educational Research, 5*(2), 130–136. https://doi.org/10.7821/naer.2016.7.172.
Gotwals, A. W., & Songer, N. B. (2013). Validity evidence for learning progression-based assessment items that fuse core disciplinary ideas and science practices. *Journal of Research in Science Teaching, 50*(5), 597–626. https://doi.org/10.1002/tea.21083.
Hmelo-Silver, C. E., Duncan, R. G., & Chinn, C. A. (2007). Scaffolding and achievement in problem-based and inquiry learning: A response to Kirschner, Sweller, and Clark (2006). *Educational Psychologist, 42*(2), 99–107. https://doi.org/10.1080/00461520701263368.
Huijgen, T., van de Grift, W., van Boxtel, C., & Holthuis, P. (2018). Promoting historical contextualization: The development and testing of a pedagogy. *Journal of Curriculum Studies, 50*(3), 410–434. https://doi.org/10.1080/00220272.2018.1435724.
Iordanou, K., & Constantinou, C. P. (2015). Supporting use of evidence in argumentation through practice in argumentation and reflection in the context of SOCRATES learning environment. *Science Education, 99*(2), 282–311. https://doi.org/10.1002/sce.21152.
Jiménez-Aleixandre, M. P. (2008). Designing argumentation learning environments. In S. Erduran & M. P. Jiménez-Aleixandre (Eds.), *Argumentation in science education: Perspectives from classroom-based research* (pp. 91–115). Dordrecht: Springer. https://doi.org/10.1007/978-1-4020-6670-2_5.
Jiménez Aleixandre, M. P., & Brocos, P. (2018). Shifts in epistemic statuses in argumentation and in conceptual change. In T. Amin & O. Levrini (Eds.), *Converging perspectives on conceptual change: Mapping an emerging paradigm in the learning sciences* (pp. 171–179). Oxford: Routledge.
Jiménez-Aleixandre, M. P., & Erduran, S. (2008). Argumentation in science education: An overview. In S. Erduran & M. P. Jiménez-Aleixandre (Eds.), *Argumentation in science education: Perspectives from classroom-based research* (pp. 3–27). Dordrecht: Springer. https://doi.org/10.1007/978-1-4020-6670-2_1.
Jiménez-Aleixandre, M. P., & Puig, B. (2012). Argumentation, evidence evaluation and critical thinking. In B. Fraser, K. Tobin, & C. McRobbie (Eds.), *Second international handbook for science education* (Vol. 2, pp. 1001–1017). Dordrecht: Springer. https://doi.org/10.1007/978-1-4020-9041-7_66.

Kelly, G. J. (2008). Inquiry, activity and epistemic practice. In R. A. Duschl, & R. E. Grandy (Eds.), *Teaching scientific inquiry: Recommendations for research and implementation* (pp. 99–117). Rotterdam: Sense Publishers. https://doi.org/10.1163/9789460911453_009.

Kelly, G. J. (2014). Inquiry teaching and learning: Philosophical considerations. In M. R. Matthews (Ed.), *International handbook of research in history, philosophy and science teaching* (pp. 1363–1380). Dordrecht: Springer. https://doi.org/10.1007/978-94-007-7654-8_42.

Kelly, G. J., & Cunningham, C. (2019). Epistemic tools in engineering design for K–12 education. *Science Education, 103*(4), 1080–1111. https://doi.org/10.1002/sce.21513.

Kelly, G. J., & Green, J. (2018). Framing issues of theory and methods for the study of science and engineering education. In G. J. Kelly & J. Green (Eds.), *Theory and methods for sociocultural research in science and engineering education* (pp. 1–28). London: Routledge. https://doi.org/10.4324/9781351139922-1.

Kelly, G. J., & Licona, P. (2018). Epistemic practices and science education. In M. R. Matthews (Ed.), *History, philosophy and science teaching* (pp. 139–165). Dordrecht: Springer. https://doi.org/10.1007/978-3-319-62616-1_5.

Kim, H., & Song, J. (2006). The features of peer argumentation in middle school students' scientific inquiry. *Research in Science Education, 36*, 211–233. https://doi.org/10.1007/s11165-005-9005-2.

Kim, S. M., & Hannafin, M. J. (2016). Synergies: Effects of source representation and goal instructions on evidence quality, reasoning, and conceptual integration during argumentation-driven inquiry. *Instructional Science, 44*(5), 441–476. https://doi.org/10.1007/s11251-016-9381-1.

Kind, P. M., Kind, V., Hofstein, A., & Wilson, J. (2011). Peer argumentation in the school science laboratory—Exploring effects of task features. *International Journal of Science Education, 33*(18), 2527–2558. https://doi.org/10.1080/09500693.2010.550952.

Koslowski, B., Marasia, J., Chelenza, M., & Dublin, R. (2008). Information becomes evidence when an explanation can incorporate it into a causal framework. *Cognitive Development, 23*(4), 472–487. https://doi.org/10.1016/j.cogdev.2008.09.007.

Kuhn, D. (2005). *Education for thinking*. Cambridge, MA: Harvard University Press.

Lehrer, R., & Schauble, L. (2012). Supporting inquiry about the foundations of evolutionary thinking in the elementary grades. In S. M. Carver & J. Shrager (Eds.), *The journey from child to scientist* (pp. 171–205). Washington, DC: American Psychological Association. https://doi.org/10.1037/13617-009.

Levstik, L., & Barton, K. (2015). *Doing history. Investigating with children in elementary and middle school*. New York: Routledge.

Litman, C., & Greenleaf, C. (2018). Argumentation tasks in secondary English language arts, history, and science: Variations in instructional focus and inquiry space. *Reading Research Quarterly, 53*(1), 107–126. https://doi.org/10.1002/rrq.187.

López-Facal, R., Jiménez-Aleixandre, M. P., & Arcidiacono, F. (2015). Le territoire comme composante de l'identification nationale dans l'argumentation des élèves du secondaire. In N. Muller Mirza & C. Buty (Eds.), *L'argumentation dans les contextes de l'éducation* (pp. 323–354). Bern: Peter Lang.

Makar, K., Bakker, A., & Ben-Zvi, D. (2015). Scaffolding norms of argumentation-based inquiry in a primary mathematics classroom. *ZDM Mathematics Education, 47*, 1107–1120. https://doi.org/10.1007/s11858-015-0732-1.

McIntyre, L. C. (2018). *Post-truth*. Cambridge, MA: MIT Press. https://doi.org/10.7551/mitpress/11483.001.0001.

McNeill, K. L., & Berland, L. (2017). What is (or should be) scientific evidence use in K-12 classrooms? *Journal of Research in Science Teaching, 54*(5), 672–689. https://doi.org/10.1002/tea.21381.

Mercer, N. (2009). Developing argumentation: Lessons learned in the primary school. In N. Muller-Mirza & A.-N. Perret-Clermont (Eds.), *Argumentation and education: Theoretical foundations and practices* (pp. 177–194). Dordrecht: Springer. https://doi.org/10.1007/978-0-387-98125-3_7.

Monteira, S. F., & Jiménez-Aleixandre, M. P. (2016). The practice of using evidence in kindergarten: the role of purposeful observation. *Journal of Research in Science Teaching, 53*(8), 1232–1258. https://doi.org/10.1002/tea.21259.

Monte-Sano, C. (2010). Disciplinary literacy in history: An exploration of the historical nature of adolescents' writing. *Journal of the Learning Sciences, 19*(4), 539–568. https://doi.org/10.1080/10508406.2010.481014.

Monte-Sano, C., & Budano, C. (2013). Developing and enacting pedagogical content-knowledge for teaching history: An exploration of two novice teachers' growth over three years. *Journal of the Learning Sciences, 22*(2), 171–211. https://doi.org/10.1080/10508406.2012.742016.

National Research Council. (2012). *A Framework for K–12 science education: Practices, crosscutting concepts, and core ideas*. Washington, DC: The National Academies Press. https://doi.org/10.17226/13165.

Nichols, K., Gillies, R., & Hedberg, J. (2016). Argumentation-based collaborative inquiry in science through representational work: Impact on primary students' representational fluency. *Research in Science Education, 46*, 343–364. https://doi.org/10.1007/s11165-014-9456-4.

Nussbaum, E. M., Sinatra, G., & Poliquin, A. (2008). Role of epistemic beliefs and scientific argumentation in science learning. *International Journal of Science Education, 30*(15), 1977–1999. https://doi.org/10.1080/09500690701545919

Osborne, J. (2014). Scientific practices and inquiry in the science classroom. In N. G. Lederman, & S. K. Abell (Eds.). *Handbook of research on science education* (Vol. II, pp. 579–599). New York: Routledge. https://doi.org/10.4324/9780203097267.CH29.

Osborne, J. (2019). Not "hands on" but "minds on": A response to Furtak and Penuel. *Science Education, 103*, 1280–1283. https://doi.org/10.1002/sce.21543.

Osborne, J., Henderson, J. B., MacPherson, A., Szu, E., Wild, A., & Yao, S-Y. (2016). The development and validation of a learning progression for argumentation in science. *Journal of Research in Science Teaching, 53*(6), 821–846. https://doi.org/10.1002/tea.21316.

Perelman, C., & Olbrechts-Tyteca, L. (1958). *Traité de l'argumentation. La nouvelle rhétorique*. Bruxelles: Éditions de l'Université de Bruxelles. (*The new rhetoric: A treatise on argumentation*. Notre Dame: University of Notre Dame Press, 1969).

Pluta, W. J., Chinn, C. A., & Duncan, R. G. (2011). Learners' epistemic criteria for good scientific models. *Journal of Research in Science Teaching, 48*, 486–511. https://doi.org/10.1002/tea.20415.

Rapanta, C., & Felton, M. (2019). Mixed methods research in inquiry-based instruction: an integrative review. *International Journal of Research & Method in Education, 42*(3), 288–304. https://doi.org/10.1080/1743727X.2019.1598356.

Reznitskaya, A., & Gregory, M. (2013). Student thought and classroom language: Examining the mechanisms of change in dialogic teaching. *Educational Psychologist, 48*(2), 114–133. https://doi.org/10.1080/00461520.2013.775898.

Reznitskaya, A., & Wilkinson, I. A. G. (2017). Truth matters: Teaching young students to search for the most reasonable answer. *Phi Delta Kappan, 99*(4), 33–38. https://doi.org/10.1177/0031721717745550.

Ryu, S., & Sandoval, W. A. (2012). Improvements to elementary children's epistemic understanding from sustained argumentation. *Science Education, 96*, 488–526. https://doi.org/10.1002/sce.21006.

Sampson, V., & Clark, D. (2009). The impact of collaboration on the outcomes of argumentation. *Science Education, 93*(3), 448–484. https://doi.org/10.1002/sce.20306.

Sandoval, W. A. (2015). Epistemic goals. In R. Gunstone (Ed.), *Encyclopedia of science education* (pp. 393–398). Dordrecht: Springer. https://doi.org/10.1007/978-94-007-2150-0_245.

Sandoval, W. A., & Reiser, B. J. (2004). Explanation-driven inquiry: Integrating conceptual and epistemic scaffolds for scientific inquiry. *Science Education, 88*, 345–372. https://doi.org/10.1002/sce.10130.

Schwarz, B. B. (2009). Argumentation and learning. In N. Muller Mirza & A.-N. Perret-Clermont (Eds.), *Argumentation and education* (pp. 91–126). Dordrecht: Springer.

Toulmin, S. (1958). *The uses of argument*. Cambridge: Cambridge University Press. https://doi.org/10.1007/978-0-387-98125-3_4.

VanSledright, B. & Maggioni, L. (2016). Epistemic cognition in history. In J. A. Greene, W. A. Sandoval, and I. Bråten (Eds.) *Handbook of epistemic cognition* (pp. 128–146). New York: Routledge.

von Aufschnaiter, C., Erduran, S., Osborne, J., & Simon, S. (2008). Arguing to learn and learning to argue: Case studies of how students' argumentation relates to their scientific knowledge. *Journal of Research in Science Teaching, 45*(1), 101–131. https://doi.org/10.1002/tea.20213.

Walker, J. P., & Sampson, V. (2013). Learning to argue and arguing to learn in science: Argument-Driven Inquiry as a way to help undergraduate chemistry students learn how to construct arguments and engage in argumentation during a laboratory course. *Journal of Research in Science Teaching, 50*(5), 561–596. https://doi.org/10.1002/tea.21082.

Walton, D. N. (1992). Types of dialogue, dialectical shifts and fallacies. In F. H. van Eemeren, R. Grootendorst, J. A. Blair & C. A. Willard (Eds.), *Argumentation illuminated* (pp. 133–147). Amsterdam: SicSat.

14

COLLABORATIVE INTERACTIONS IN INQUIRY LEARNING

Asmalina Saleh, Cindy E. Hmelo-Silver, and Krista D. Glazewski

In this chapter, we discuss the value of collaborative interactions in inquiry learning, or collaborative inquiry. Inquiry is an instructional method where students engage in the design and conduct of scientific research (National Research Council, 2000). Grounding students' experiences in the process of doing research has proven beneficial in supporting individual learning gains (Furtak et al., 2012; Minner et al., 2010). In addition, research has also demonstrated that engagement in inquiry learning can promote outcomes such as knowledge production, inquiry skills, and practices that benefit both the individual and the community. Rather than assuming that these outcomes are related only to the individual engagement in inquiry practices, we draw on the assumption that the processes of knowledge production are social in nature (Grandy & Duschl, 2008). Collaborative inquiry thus can be defined as the social process of knowledge generation, which is distributed and mediated across multiple participants and tools, while solving a problem or addressing a driving question (Chernobilsky et al., 2004). Based on our definition, there are several elements of collaborative inquiry that need to be unpacked: (1) the problem or goal of inquiry, (2) the social processes and interactions in meaning-making, and (3) the cultural and material elements that shape and scaffold these processes.

Goals of Collaborative Inquiry

Traditionally, inquiry learning aims to support students' construction of knowledge and engagement in practices by following inquiry cycles that mirror the practices of professional scientists (Pedaste et al., 2015). Collaborative inquiry learning has the similar pedagogical goal of helping students develop group inquiry skills and generate collective knowledge. The challenge in supporting collaborative inquiry is supporting the shift from the perspective of students as individual learners to the view of learning as collective advancement of knowledge in a classroom community (Slotta et al., 2018). As part of this collaborative knowledge construction, individuals share and build on ideas to advance individual and collective learning (Kimmerle et al., 2010; Scardamalia & Bereiter, 2014). In short, collaborative inquiry learning focuses on a collective goal, which in turn mediates learning activities (Jeong & Hmelo-Silver, 2016).

Social Interactions and Processes in Meaning-Making

From a sociocultural perspective on learning, inquiry means engaging in practices related to cultural traditions of disciplines ranging from the sciences to the humanities. Learning originates from an inter-psychological plane (i.e., social interactions) and then shifts to an individual plane (Vygotsky, 1978). Thus, participating in inquiry with others helps students understand how to use specific kinds of processes. These processes include engaging in various discourses, practices, and representations that are critical to each community. From a disciplinary standpoint, there have been several ways of collaborative meaning construction, ranging across argumentation (Chin & Osborne, 2010; Schwarz et al., 2003), collaborative representations (Suthers & Hundhausen, 2003), collective epistemology (Slotta & Najafi, 2013), explanation-driven inquiry (Sandoval & Reiser, 2004), and theory-building (Scardamalia & Bereiter, 2014). The nature of these scientific enterprises is inherently social in that it involves the creation of shared meaning.

Material and Cultural Foundations of Collaborative Inquiry

The material and cultural base of collaborative inquiry refer to material products that are informed by culture or our way of life (Faulkner et al., 2006). The material foundation of collaborative inquiry involves the use of conceptual tools and physical resources, ranging from technological tools such as computers to curricular materials such as textbooks. These materials are utilized as individuals engage in collaborative inquiry and are inherently *cultural products*. This is because physical and conceptual tools are influenced by culture. Understanding cultural products therefore include understanding norms, or expectations about practices that are not always visible. These norms may include disciplinary norms and classroom expectations (e.g., how to invite diverse perspectives). More generally, disciplinary norms include norms that are focused on the process of generating knowledge (e.g., how to generate data collaboratively) and epistemic norms that center on what counts as a good inquiry product (e.g., standards for a good explanation). On the other hand, everyday assumptions about classroom expectations (e.g., being respectful, managing collaborative timelines, deadlines) are just as critical in supporting collaborative inquiry. Clarifying norms is important, given that there might be a mismatch between students' everyday practices and the classroom's inquiry practices and expectations (Nasir et al., 2005). Moreover, these norms are often invisible, making it critical to surface them so that students can be successful in engaging in collaborative inquiry.

For students to engage in successful knowledge generation or the creation of products, they must be able to recognize that there are different disciplinary norms and practices associated with each disciplinary framework. As guiding structures, disciplinary frameworks such as argumentation, problem-based learning (PBL), and accountable talk shape the social processes of inquiry (Hmelo-Silver, 2004; Michaels et al., 2010; Osborne, 2010). Because of the similar assumptions underpinning these disciplinary frameworks, these guiding principles can often be integrated to support collaborative inquiry learning. For example, Saleh et al. (2019) highlighted how a PBL inquiry process and framework for argumentation was integrated into the design of a game-based learning environment. Students engaged in the process of investigating and collecting information about why the fish in a hatchery were sick. As students engage in the PBL inquiry process, they learn to be accountable to their peers, by building on their peers' ideas and collaboratively deciding which explanations were more viable given the available data. As students generate explanations collectively, they draw on epistemic norms, utilize various cultural products such as a collaborative whiteboard or concepts, and are held accountable to classroom and social expectations. These explanations must then be defended and critiqued within the community of inquirers.

Because collaborative inquiry is often an ill-defined phenomenon, scaffolds are critical to the inquiry process. These scaffolds or instructional supports have the aim of helping students in tasks that they would not otherwise accomplish on their own (Wood et al., 1976). To support collaborative inquiry, scaffolds are often embedded in artifacts and curricular materials and must support content learning and social interactions. It is therefore critical to be aware of the desired disciplinary practices, associated inquiry cycles, norms, tools, and the nature of the problem to be solved so that we can support collaborative inquiry effectively.

Challenges for Teachers and Learners

Given the complexity of inquiry processes, we outline three challenges that teachers and learners face as they engage in collaborative inquiry: (1) operationalizing collaborative inquiry in practice, (2) determining the processes of interest, and (3) designing scaffolds to support collaborative inquiry.

Operationalizing Collaborative Inquiry in Practice

Although we have sought to define collaborative inquiry, in practice, there are multiple frameworks that one can utilize. Examples include knowledge building, knowledge community and inquiry, inquiry learning, project-based learning (PjBL), PBL, and group investigation. The multiple frameworks also mean that there are different ways to approach learning and teaching, making it challenging to know where to start. Nonetheless, these frameworks share similar fundamental assumptions about the social nature of learning and highlight several core practices associated with the collaborative inquiry process: collaborative knowledge (co-)construction and engaging in the social practice of regulating learning processes (Järvelä & Hadwin, 2013; Pedaste et al., 2015; Quintana et al., 2004). We distinguish regulation processes such as task management from the co-construction of knowledge because these two processes require different sets of practices (Järvelä & Hadwin, 2013). Collaborative knowledge construction includes sharing, negotiating, and integrating multiple perspectives through discussion. Regulatory processes refer to how the group sets goals, plans, and enacts strategies to execute these goals and address challenges that arise in their implementation efforts (Quintana et al., 2004). This involves the coordination of the materials, people, and learning activities in the inquiry process.

Determining Which Processes to Target for Support

As noted earlier, because of the multiple frameworks associated with collaborative inquiry, deciding which processes to support can also be challenging. Once these processes are determined, it is necessary to know how to instruct and assess learners as they engage in collaborative inquiry. Disciplinary practices can provide guidance on key competencies to support. In K-12 education, standards such as the Next Generation Science Standards (NGSS); College, Career, and Civic Life (C3) Framework for Social Studies State Standards; National Council of Teachers of Mathematics (NCTM); and Standards for the Assessment of Reading and Writing highlight practices that align with specific disciplines (IRA/NCTE Joint Task Force, 2010; NCSS, 2013; NCTM, 2000; NGSS Lead States, 2013). These standards focus on practices such as problem-solving processes that support the development of scientific understanding, English literacy, and civics education. Once the processes of interest are defined, the challenges for students must be clarified. First, learners may not know all the steps in the inquiry process, lack strategic knowledge to select the appropriate analysis, or how to separate observations from inferences (Quintana et al., 2004). The challenges of managing the inquiry process increase when students must work with one another, especially if students prefer working alone (e.g., the lone wolf) or do not know what it means to collaborate effectively. Ultimately, the biggest challenge of attempting to support collaborative inquiry is that it is inherently a time-consuming process. This is in part because of the commitment to the advancement of social knowledge, rather than individual cognition alone (Slotta et al., 2018). Thus, teachers must be share similar epistemological commitments to support students in achieving this goal.

Scaffolding Targeted Processes

Identifying the framework and the associated targeted processes are initial steps that must be taken to understand how to support collaborative inquiry. Once these processes are identified, the challenge now becomes how to understand the forms and functions of scaffolds or instructional supports that can be designed to support collaborative inquiry (Saye & Brush, 2007). The function, or what the scaffold aims to support, must be clearly specified. However, the challenge is often to unpack whether there needs to be a one-to-one mapping between scaffolds, or if one scaffold can support multiple processes (Martin et al., 2019; Reiser & Tabak, 2014; Saleh et al., 2020). Similarly, the form in which the scaffolds are delivered must be considered. For instance, the scaffold can take the form of preplanned instructional materials, a hard scaffold, or a just-in-time scaffold such as prompts, and questions provided by teachers (Saye & Brush, 2017). As we have noted earlier, collaborative inquiry includes the co-construction of knowledge, which is distinct from process management. Although these processes often intersect, it is helpful to separate them because task-related aspects of inquiry might be easily automated by tools and technology, whereas meaning-making requires students to attend to complex social interactions involving knowledge building. In the following section we expand on how to support collaborative inquiry.

Scaffolding Collaborative Inquiry

Given the body of work that has shaped our understanding of how to support collaborative inquiry, we will broadly highlight how to support regulatory processes and co-construction of knowledge as it relates to the different phases of inquiry. Figure 14.1 highlights a general model for collaborative inquiry, and we situate where in this inquiry cycle these scaffolds might be useful.

Notably, these examples are meant to present the reader with an initial idea of some of the work in the field of the learning sciences and are neither a comprehensive nor exhaustive review of the

Figure 14.1 Scaffolds for *regulatory processes (asterisks) and **co-construction of knowledge (double asterisks) in the general inquiry model

literature. Given that the inquiry process is complex, the various phases of inquiry are meant to guide students and build awareness of critical different features of scientific thinking. We will articulate how coordinating collaborative inquiry requires attending to (1) regulative process, or the coordination of learning materials and social interactions, and (2) co-construction of knowledge that is supported by discursive interactions. We will highlight how both regulation processes and co-construction are critical to the phases of inquiry, regardless of the inquiry framework that one uses (Bybee, 2006; National Research Council, 2000; Pedaste et al., 2015; White & Frederiksen, 2000).

Supporting Regulation Processes

Often, the inability to manage the process of inquiry has direct consequences in collaborative inquiry. For example, students spend less time on problem-solving or the inquiry process and report frustrations with group work. Below, we provide four strategies to manage the process of collaborative inquiry: (1) communicating process as they relate to phases of collaborative inquiry, including goal setting, knowledge management, and automating or fading prompts as needed (Hmelo-Silver, 2006), (2) providing procedural roles, (3) designing the social configuration of inquiry, and (4) setting norms and expectations related to what it means to engage in collaborative inquiry.

Communicating the Collaborative Inquiry Processes

To support how students might organize the materials they use and plan their inquiry, it is important to encourage students to share how they might regulate group processes and outcomes. To make this more salient to students, providing representations of group processes and task progression is recommended. Such tools should be embedded with representations that support joint attention of (1) shared goals and plans, (2) task knowledge, (3) the team's strengths and weaknesses, (4) strategy knowledge and use, and (5) the team's engagement and emotional processes (Järvelä et al., 2015). Externalizing these learning processes help students share ideas, promote interactions, and prompt regulatory processes where appropriate. For the purposes of collaborative inquiry, representations that help students manage group awareness should include several elements of the inquiry process. Teachers can provide students with checklists that provide an overview of the areas of inquiry that students need to attend to and provide reflection time for students to evaluate their group processes. These checklists can be crucial for collaborative inquiry, in that they hold the group accountable for the management of group processes. Students can also be encouraged to understand peer activities to better develop a sense of their individual work. This can include attending to how others contribute to group work in terms of work products or discussions, their responsiveness, and quality of contributions that peers in the group provide. However, participation should not be conflated with the quality of learning, and other indicators such as quality of explanations and cognitive strategies should be considered.

Providing Procedural Roles to Support Inquiry

Due to the complexity of the inquiry process, it is important to specify roles that help students manage different aspects of the problem. The decomposition of tasks or problems can be undertaken at the group level by assigning roles. It should be noted that roles can support both regulatory processes and knowledge building. For example, in scientific communities, students learn about three strategic steps in science, predicting and theorizing, summarizing results, and, finally, relating these two steps (Herrenkohl, 2006). As they engage in these steps, groups of students adopt procedural, communicative, and intellectual roles. Procedural roles allow students to share tasks among group members with the aim of efficiently completing investigations by engaging all members. Communicative roles allow students to work in small groups, where students must work together to prepare reports that are delivered to the classroom. Intellectual roles, on the other hand, help students generate questions and provide feedback on their peer's reasoning.

In this section, we focus on procedural roles to illustrate how these roles can support socially shared regulation of learning. In her work in elementary science classrooms, Herrenkohl (2006) distributed procedural roles among groups of four students as they engage in the science investigation phase (i.e., someone in charge of materials, facilitator, clean-up manager, and recorder). Although these roles were distinct, students had to coordinate with one another to make sure that all members were aware of each other's tasks. This communication promoted group awareness and was critical for students to ensure they were discharging their responsibilities for the benefit of the group. As students finalized their scientific investigations, a next set of roles, communicative roles, was then used to help students report their findings to their classroom. To support reporting of information and because reporting is a difficult task, this role was also distributed among students. Thus, in a group of four students, roles included two scribes and two reporters. Students were required to work collaboratively with the reporters to structure their report and decide what information to provide to their audience. This included discussing their ideas and making sure that the group is meeting the required goals. After generating their reports, the communicators share their findings with their classmates. Although adopting these roles was challenging for students, over 78% of fifth-grade students participated in classroom conversations ($N = 24$). This was particularly compelling because 18 out of the 24 students who participated in the study were from underserved populations. Because of the support that students received, they could contribute to classroom conversations and collaborate with their peers. When students are aware of their roles, they are more likely to work efficiently and be more aware of group interactions and collaboration.

Social Configuration of Collaborative Inquiry

Another way that teachers can support collaborative inquiry is to vary the social configurations of group work. Zhang et al. (2009) report on a three-year design experiment wherein three social configurations of collaborative inquiry were used; fixed, interacting, and opportunistic collaboration. In fixed groups, students work in their small groups with no changes in members, whereas in interacting groups, students engage with other groups to share ideas. In opportunistic collaboration, groups are formed and re-formed with newer members. In these configurations, all groups were aware of inquiry goals and worked together to achieve them. The researchers found that students working in interacting groups performed better in measured outcomes than those in fixed groups, whereas students working in opportunistic groups outperformed students in both fixed and interacting groups. Students in the opportunistic model had the freedom to group and regroup based on emergent goals. Because of this flexibility, students were in frequent contact with diverse ideas and perspectives. Students were then more aware of the gaps in knowledge for the *community*, not just within their groups, providing an impetus for further whole-classroom knowledge construction. However, the fixed or interacting groups were still beneficial for students. Thus, depending on the teacher's aims and the needs of the students, different social configurations can support collaborative sense-making in various ways. Ultimately, a combination of visual representations, group norms, prompts, and social configuration need to be balanced to support collaborative inquiry.

Externalizing Expectations and Setting Norms

Teachers can support regulatory processes by attending to norms or externalizing expectations about how to manage the group and the inquiry by generating, engaging, and maintaining classroom norms. Creating a knowledge-building community requires commitment to several principles such as authentic problems, diversity of ideas, and community knowledge (Scardamalia & Bereiter, 2014). Because the aim of the knowledge-building community is to support theory-building, it is critical to highlight these norms. To ensure that students can engage in collaborative inquiry productively, teachers must approach inquiry as a set of practices. This perspective means that students are expected to take on the role of epistemic agents or agents who shape the practices of a community (Stroupe, 2014). We highlight three norms that must be externalized for successful collaborative inquiry: (1) epistemic norms that focus on what counts as good collaborative inquiry products and processes, (2) norms of social interaction, and (3) norms of valuing students' own everyday knowledge and practices.

First, clarifying epistemic norms is critical to support students' evidentiary practices (Duncan et al., 2018). As epistemic agents, the community of learners should have shared goals of inquiry or epistemic aims. The community should use criteria to evaluate whether the community aims have been achieved and acknowledge the diverse ways that knowledge construction can occur (Barzilai & Chinn, 2018). Second, norms of social interactions, especially in the context of a learning community, involve responding to peer work and practices salient to the community. In fact, responsiveness to ideas is an important characteristic of successful groups (Barron, 2003). Students must be aware of each other's ideas and proposals and respond to these proposals by questioning, agreeing, echoing ideas, or extending them. Finally, a key factor in supporting successful collaborative inquiry is to leverage students' funds of identity. The funds of identity approach builds on prior work in funds of knowledge (González et al., 2005) and can be defined as "historically accumulated, culturally developed, and socially distributed resources" that are exercised in their everyday practice (Esteban-Guitart & Moll, 2014, p. 31). Often, there is a disconnect between students' interests and the teachers' role in ensuring that learning has happened. Detecting students' funds of identity can highlight the connections between multiple individuals in the community. Civil (2007) noted that teachers can ask students to represent what is important to them and share it with the community. In this way, students realize that there are commonalities in their expertise and interests, which encourages them to rely on their peers more and to collectively pursue group objectives align with inquiry practices.

Supporting Collaborative Knowledge Construction

Although we have characterized generating and maintaining norms of collaborative inquiry as related to regulatory processes, the reality is that the process of managing inquiry and generating collective knowledge are tightly coupled. For instance, the norm of accountability highlights how the advancement of knowledge is a communal effort and related to scientific inquiry and argumentation. Supporting group sense-making practices also requires structuring prompts and representing key processes. However, a key difference is that these prompts and processes target knowledge building and not regulating group tasks and goals. In this section, we highlight how to support knowledge construction, by attending to (1) questioning strategies, (2) problematizing gaps in student understanding, (3) cognitive role specialization, (4) using representations to externalize knowledge, and (5) varying social configurations for group formation. Notably, these suggestions are broad and can be applicable in targeting general sense-making inquiry practices such as hypothesis testing and data interpretation, as well as supporting specific collaborative disciplinary practices such as argumentation (Chin & Osborne, 2010), and shared representations (Suthers & Hundhausen, 2003).

Questioning Strategies

To support collaborative sense-making practices, teachers and facilitators can pose different types of questions to the group, such as short, long, or meta-category questions that support student sense-making (Hmelo-Silver & Barrows, 2008). Short-answer questions such as simple yes/no responses or forced-choice scenarios can help ground students' understanding of the fact whereas long-answer questions are focused on elaborating understanding, inferencing, and reasoning that lead to knowledge building (Chin & Brown, 2002). On the other hand, meta-category questions support task-related understanding related to group dynamics and monitoring group progress. van Zee et al. (2001) suggest using "reflective toss" which would build on the groups' ideas and toss them back to the learners for further reflection and explanation and deepening their collaborative inquiry. One example illustrated in *Wise Practice Video Database* (Callahan, 2016) depicted a case of collaborative historical inquiry that struggled to construct an argument about bias from a primary source newspaper article during study of the US Civil Rights Movement in the 1950s and 1960s. As the group struggled to make determinations about bias, the teacher engaged with one student in particular, modeling and supporting the ability to make inferences and reason about the issues through questioning techniques that ranged from factual ("*Who is the author? Where was it written?*") to inferential ("*What was their point of view?*") to reflective ("*Do they show you one side and then show you the other and then let you make the decision, or do they just show you one side and try to get you to lean that way, perhaps?*"). Throughout the exchange, the student moved from a high degree of uncertainty at the beginning ("*I don't see how*") to one of certainty about her explanation following guidance from the teacher ("*I mean, I see what he's talking about.... He might be writing it—He might be writing it to show that whites should stick to their side and not associate....*"). This example illustrates how moves between levels of questions can result in deeper student reasoning and stronger explanations, especially if the teacher encourages different students to build on ideas. In addition, this level of questioning can support group inquiry by asking how ideas are different or if the group members agree with each other as well bringing other students into the conversation through questions (Hmelo-Silver & Barrows, 2008).

These examples illustrate how facilitators can scaffold collaborative inquiry through questioning strategies. To ensure effective collaborative inquiry, it is necessary to scaffold students to use these questioning strategies. This is because student-generated questions that target knowledge building often generate productive discussions in collaborative learning. This suggests that there must be a shift from teacher questioning to student-generated questions (Chin & Brown, 2002). Chin and Osborne (2010) further recommended that teachers provide support by making sure that students write down their questions and present them to their group. Often, students ask factual questions, which results in less productive discussions. By writing their questions, students can begin to engage with their peers and deepen their discussions. Similarly, conceptual resources such as evidence statements or sentence starters can be integrated into curricular materials to help students share their ideas with the group and to ask for feedback these ideas.

The success of group sense-making depends on both holding students accountable to the claims that they make (i.e., norm setting) and for the teacher to ask students to explain their thinking rather than to simply restate or summarize their findings (Webb, 2009). Deciding when to intervene in group sense-making however can be challenging. Teachers can listen to group discussions and then prompt students to explain as needed. This is especially important because different group dynamics might mean more adversarial style of discussion, but this does not mean that these discussions are not productive even if they appear problematic on the surface (Nussbaum, 2002). A key aspect of teacher facilitation, however, is the fading of scaffolds. Rather than providing instructional support to students during the entire inquiry process, it is important for students to appropriate practices such as questioning, hypothesis generation, and argumentation. Ultimately, scaffolds should be removed, and students will be able to engage in their own inquiry investigation with minimal support.

Problematizing Gaps in Student Understanding

An ill-defined or complex problem is particularly useful for supporting collaborative inquiry. Such complex problems may be too complicated for individual investigation, thus requiring sharing of knowledge and negotiation of ideas between members (Cohen, 1994). A good problem also allows group members and teachers to share and evaluate different ideas and provide feedback on these perspectives (Hmelo-Silver, 2004). Sharing and evaluating ideas means that students can publicly present their arguments, representations, or models so that others may build on these ideas (Berland & Reiser, 2009). To scaffold collaborative knowledge building, teachers can problematize gaps in students' collective understanding (i.e., established as "learning issues" in PBL) related to the problem by supplying contradictory examples or data and deliberately assigning students with contrasting views of the problem.

By challenging the group's assumptions and viewpoints about the problem, students can then work toward integrating these different perspectives and work toward knowledge generation. The aim of problematizing learning issues is to help students notice gaps in their understandings and encourage students to seek novel solutions to solve complex issues (Reiser, 2004). This can include asking students to propose specific solutions to a problem or inquiry question. Subsequently, both students and teachers can point out possible discrepancies in these solutions or approaches (Wood et al., 1976). The teacher's role is to provide guidance as needed and offer insights and evaluations of the different perspectives and approaches that students may adopt. Teachers can also encourage different group members to provide alternative perspectives or reflect on their proposals. One way to support the generation of alternative views is through accountable talk, a form of structured discussion that holds students accountable to the learning community and processes of knowledge and reasoning (Michaels et al., 2010). In accountable talk, all students are valued contributors and must (1) listen to ideas, (2) build on the ideas of others, and (3) ask questions to clarify or expand ideas. Encouraging students to listen and build on their peers' ideas promotes the diversity of ideas. At the same time, the group can also examine possible gaps in their thinking and address these gaps. Collaborative inquiry requires that groups achieve consensus on the issues that they are examining (Barron, 2003). Given that argumentation and reflection are critical elements of collaborative inquiry, problematizing learning issues can be useful in the conceptualization, investigation, and reporting phases of inquiry. As students engage in these phases, teachers can request students to articulate their ideas and justify the decisions that they make. In addressing the group this way, the teacher can support joint attention to the problem and ask the group to devote resources to resolve these discrepancies (Reiser, 2004).

Assigning Intellectual Roles to Support Collaborative Sense-making

If procedural roles can be helpful in ensuring that all students remain engaged, intellectual roles have the function of supporting sense-making in groups. In problem-solving groups, taking on unique roles allows students to attend to different aspects of inquiry and ensure that students are dependent on each other instead of simply doing parallel work. For instance, students can take on roles such as the group leader or tutoring positions (Belland et al., 2009). Leadership roles are made possible when other tasks are distributed (i.e., procedural roles). For example, some students can unpack what is needed to engage in the tasks and others can execute or perform tasks such as searching for information to share with the team. Thus, students can gain more leadership skills as they become more familiar in their roles. In collaborative inquiry, groups may function well when leaders emerge among the students in the group (Gressick & Derry, 2010; Hmelo-Silver et al., 2007; Sun et al., 2017).

Intellectual roles moreover have the function of providing students with the necessary information about how to engage in a task. In the communities of inquiry approach, for example, students use intellectual roles to engage in collaborative sense-making (Herrenkohl et al., 1999). Intellectual roles align with the inquiry process, in that students in these roles are tasked to engage in predicting and theorizing, summarizing results, and relating evidence to predictions and theories. In their work with third-, fourth- and fifth-grade students, Herrenkohl et al. (1999) noted that students were able to engage in productive explanations when supported by intellectual tools and two roles: the intellectual and audience roles. The teacher and students co-construct the definitions of these roles by identifying the criteria for which the community must be held accountable. For instance, in the intellectual role, students must generate claims and support those claims with evidence. These criteria are publicly visible in the classroom to remind students of these roles. Another key element in supporting collaborative inquiry is the audience role. As audience members, students can evaluate other groups' reports as their peers share their findings and provide evidentiary support to the presenting groups in their argumentation. In Herrenkohl et al.'s (2009) work, the audience role supported the collaborative inquiry process by encouraging students to hold each other accountable for the practices that they must engage in. This is important because both the construction and the critique of claims are critical aspects of inquiry (Ford, 2008). As part of this process, students engage in collective meaning-making (i.e., construction of claims) and challenge (i.e., critique) each other as they attempt to address their research questions.

Representing and Externalizing Knowledge

Just as it was as important to externalize the regulatory processes related to inquiry, it is also critical to externalize sense-making prompts and conceptual resources so that students are better aware of the group's sense-making processes, especially while generating theories about a problem (Scardamalia & Bereiter, 2014). Hmelo-Silver and Barrows (2008) for example showed the ways that a structured PBL whiteboard and a prompt to "create a drawing" provided a focus for supporting group collaboration and negotiation of shared understanding. More recently, participatory simulations that leverage the use of the body and externalized representations have demonstrated how students can use these resources to engage in collaborative inquiry. Danish et al. (2020), for instance, highlighted how groups of first and second graders collaboratively learned about states of matter by role-playing as particles in a computer simulation. When each student moved their body in the classroom, their individual movements were projected on a screen. Students must then coordinate with their peers to discuss how to make states of matter by engaging in multiple cycles of inquiry. The use of students' movements as a resource for public negotiation, visual representations in the computer simulation, and the sense-making prompts provided to students helped students orient, conceptualize the problem, and support collaborative meaning-making (Fiore et al., 2018).

Technology and Resources That Support Collaborative Inquiry

Recently, Jeong and Hmelo-Silver (2016) have suggested a framework that outlines the affordances needed for computer-supported collaborative learning. This framework highlights how collaborative inquiry can be supported by two broad categories: (1) attending to the context of collaborative inquiry and (2) knowledge construction processes. In prior sections, we have discussed how to support the process of knowledge construction. In this section, we will focus on the contexts of collaborative inquiry. Creating meaningful contexts for the support of collaborative inquiry includes providing groups with (1) a joint task, (2) communication tools and shared resources, and (3) opportunities to create a community.

Meaningful Joint Tasks in Collaborative Inquiry Learning Environments

To make collaborative inquiry meaningful, it is critical to design joint tasks or tasks that foster interdependence among collaborators. As noted earlier, a complex inquiry problem often means that multiple individuals must work together to solve it. Recent developments in technology have allowed learners to leverage their bodies for learning. For example, Danish et al. (2020) highlight how joint tasks meant that students must work together to successfully achieve targeted states of matter or collect nectar for the hive by using their bodies. Similarly, inquiry-based environments such as the Web-based Inquiry Science Environment (WISE) provided supports for joint tasks by integrating peer learning into the curricular units (Linn et al., 2003). Joint tasks included encouraging students to generate group norms and criteria that support knowledge construction, as well as having pairs of students work together to solve problems. To support the coordination of these joint tasks, WISE has several features such as the inquiry map, show and tell, and debates with explicit scaffolds that ask students to respond to each other's ideas. Central to these features is the ability to make students' thinking visible to others by inviting learners to gather and explain their findings and, in turn, invite peers to respond. By sharing and discussing ideas, students work interdependently and have access to multiple perspectives about the problem.

Multiuser games have also been successful in providing immersive experiences that support collaborative inquiry play (Saleh et al., 2019). The collaborative inquiry play framework integrated a PBL approach with Vygotsky's (1978) conceptualization of play in the design of a game-based learning environment called CRYSTAL ISLAND: ECOJOURNEYS.[1] In the game-based learning environment, students have the joint task of solving an aquatic problem. Groups of students engage in multiple phases of inquiry and collaborate using a whiteboard, a virtual collaborative space that helps manage, externalize group processes, and support knowledge co-construction (Hmelo-Silver & Eberbach, 2012). Each student explored a different path in the story and must share their unique observations with their peers. The success with problem-solving therefore was contingent on student working collaboratively by sharing, drawing on each other's observations, and negotiating explanations to the problem. Studies with middle-school students suggested that students built on each other's ideas and had significant gains in ecosystems learning (Mott et al., 2019). One particularly salient design feature that fostered collaborative inquiry play was the intentional integration between the joint tasks that centered on a robust inquiry question that required interdependency among students in a fun, immersive environment. Technology-supported environments therefore highlight how joint tasks can be designed to support collaborative inquiry. The examples above range from more technologically involved platforms such as motion-tracking software to more ubiquitous platforms such as online portals and games. Although not all these tools can be easily imported into the classroom, findings from these learning environments are still broadly relevant.

Communication Tools and Shared Resources

Participants in collaborative inquiry have resources that they need to share with their collaborators. Technological tools can support sharing resources directly as well as providing communication spaces for knowledge co-construction. If learners meet in person, communication spaces may not be necessary; however, to the extent that discussions and negotiations are recorded in some way (e.g., through online discussions), there is an enduring record of the process that supports reflection on the collaborative inquiry process. When collaborative inquiry is distributed, this is even more necessary. Teams can use tools such text-editing software, threaded discussion tools, web conferencing, and other technologies to foster communication. These services are made possible by different communication spaces such as discussion forums and wiki. Wikis are an example of how knowledge can be jointly constructed using Web 2.0 tools. Learning management systems (LMS) also provide teachers with a suite of integrated tools that they can use to support collaborative inquiry, such as wiki, chat, discussion boards, videos, and other multimedia resources. The benefits of LMS is the ease of providing access to all students, and its adaptability to teachers. At the same time, teachers and students might require support to use these systems effectively in their classrooms.

Opportunities to Create Communities

The affordances of tools that support communication and sharing resources also mean that these tools can support and sustain collaborative learning communities. For instance, Wikis such as Wikipedia allow community members to write, edit, and sustain the written artifacts. On the other hand, there are video-based teaching channels that foster discussions among teachers about how to support meaningful learning experiences for their students. In a traditional classroom, the creation of a classroom community can be facilitated by regular group norming discussions and expectations about how to engage in a community. A key element of these communities is whether the community is working together toward a shared goal. From a learning perspective, it is important for members of these collaborative learning communities to work together and create a shared understanding about ideas that are of interest to the community. Authority moreover is distributed among members, and no single person is the source of the knowledge. Examples of this include knowledge communities that aim to create a community where students and teachers generate collective learning goals and engage in the process of meeting these goals by negotiating and building on ideas presented by members in the community (Slotta et al., 2018).

Examples of Collaborative Inquiry

Given the importance of collaborative inquiry skills in the 21st century, it is beneficial to support both content and process outcomes. Here, we highlight several models of collaborative inquiry that have been implemented in various educational contexts, from K-12, college to computer-supported collaborative learning (CSCL) environments. For the purposes of this chapter, we will describe three models of collaborative inquiry: (1) group investigation, (2) problem-based learning and project-based science, and (3) knowledge building and community of inquiry. We provide examples from research that highlight how the different models can be implemented with and without technology. In each of the examples, we first define the features of each model and elaborate aspects of each model according to our definition of collaborative inquiry: (1) the nature of social interactions, (2) the problem or goals of the activity, and (3) conceptual, physical, and/or cultural tools.

Group Investigation

Group investigation is a form of cooperative learning, in which students form small interest groups to pursue topics of interest (Sharan et al., 2013). Group investigations invite students to engage as a community of inquiry and are focused on four principles: investigation, interaction, interpretation, and intrinsic motivation. These principles are instantiated in the six stages of group investigation in which students (1) are introduced to a multifaceted problem that allows the classroom to generate questions; (2) sign up to explore questions of interest, form groups of three to five, create a group action plan, and pose additional questions (i.e., interaction); (3) investigate questions; (4) plan their classroom presentations; (5) present their projects; and (6) evaluate peers' projects. In terms of materials, students typically use a collection of resources that include newspaper clippings, videos, and books.

To understand the impact of the group investigation method, Tan, Sharan, and Lee (2007) conducted a comparison study in which students were assigned to either a traditional whole-class lecture method ($n = 103$) or the group investigation method ($n = 138$). Results indicated that students in both conditions learned the targeted geography content, which meant that students using the group investigation method did learn as well as their peers. This is critical given that cognitive learning outcomes can be difficult to achieve when using an inquiry learning approach. Moreover, students using the group investigation method noted that they had better social relationships with their peers. Another critical takeaway was that high-achieving students were better able to gauge their successes with problem-solving without teacher feedback, whereas lower-achieving students needed external support from the teachers. This may suggest high-achieving and low-achieving students would benefit from different types of scaffolds (i.e., metacognitive vs. cognitive). Another key implication was that the implementation of group investigation should be supported by both classroom and school norms regarding how students engage academically. This is especially critical when students and teachers are used to specific methods of instruction, which suggests that attending to cultural norms of investigations has to be of primary importance to ensure that these practices endure beyond that of a research implementation.

Problem-Based Learning (PBL) and Project-Based Learning (PjBL)

As a student-centered approach, PBL aims to promote collaborative inquiry learning by engaging students in ill-defined problems. In problem-solving groups, taking on unique roles allow students to attend to different aspects of inquiry and ensure that students are dependent on each other instead of simply doing parallel work. Collaborative work is supported by scaffolds, which can be provided by facilitators, multimedia resources, and the use of a PBL whiteboard (Hmelo-Silver & Eberbach, 2012). Similarly, PjBL shares similar constructivist assumptions about the nature of student learning and engages students with a driving question. Students' inquiry is authentic, collaborative, and supported by learning technologies. The process places critical emphasis on group-created products or artifacts. In their work with project-based science, Krajcik et al. (2007) pointed out that supporting seventh-grade science explanations about chemistry should be supported by careful articulation of curricular standards by determining which elements of scientific concepts and practices may be problematic for students. By unpacking inquiry practices in a systematic manner, students who engaged in their curricular unit had significant gain scores in their pre- and post-tests. Another key takeaway from this work was the importance of acknowledging inquiry practices as indicators of learning, in addition to content learning. This suggests that collaborative inquiry practices as measures of student competence can be included as a learning goal.

Both PBL and PjBL can be applied in other disciplines such as English as a second language, engineering, history, and social studies. In problem-based historical inquiry for instance, groups of students used an open learning environment that had over a thousand multimedia artifacts related to the Civil Rights Movement (Saye & Brush, 2007). In their analysis of a nine-year research program involving this learning environment, Saye and Brush (2007) showed that students remained engaged in the tasks, developed empathy for historical individuals (i.e., perspective recognition), and adopted more complex epistemological assumptions about knowledge and history. However, students' ability to reason critically and construct knowledge were mixed. Without just-in-time adaptive scaffolding, students were less likely to learn about the desired content. Thus, for successful problem-based historical inquiry, groups of students must be supported by preplanned scaffolds, a targeted problem space, and jigsaw strategies, as well as adaptive scaffolds like questioning and prompting.

Knowledge Building, Knowledge Community, and Inquiry

The knowledge building and knowledge community inquiry models draw on a social constructivist framework but leverage digital scaffolds on a higher scale compared to models used in PBL and project-based science (Slotta et al., 2018). At the core of both approaches is the focus on advancing communal knowledge by building a knowledge base. Students must engage in knowledge-building discourse and be committed to improving ideas. Students' collaborative inquiry learning moreover is supported by scaffolds that aim to support the generation of student explanations. In both instances, members in the community engage in the production of designs and theories. The community defines and shapes the inquiry question to be resolved. In the knowledge-building framework, there are 12 principles that shape how technology can translate these principles, by providing indicators of progress and to reduce barriers to implementation (Zhang et al., 2011). These tools include collaborative workspaces, analytic tools that support individual and group progress, a note-creating system that is integrated with analytic tools and scaffolds, and a communal database.

Concluding Thoughts

Collaborative inquiry learning, broadly defined, is characterized by social processes and interaction that are problem-driven in nature and scaffolded by cultural and material resources. Student group processes include orienting to the problem, conceptualizing the issues, investigating, and documenting observations, constructing explanations, and refining their ideas. Challenges include identifying both what processes we should support and how to support those processes. As such, we have summarized recommendations for regulating group processes and co-construction of knowledge, which are crucial for a range of inquiry settings. In presenting examples from a range of disciplines, we demonstrate the importance of recognizing that disciplinary norms for problem-solving need to be considered. Ultimately, we argue that collaborative inquiry skills are essential for both learning and engagement.

Note

1 https://projects.intellimedia.ncsu.edu/ecojourneys/

References

Barron, B. (2003). When smart groups fail. *Journal of the Learning Sciences*, *12*(3), 307–359. https://doi.org/10.1207/S15327809JLS1203_1

Barzilai, S., & Chinn, C. A. (2018). On the goals of epistemic education: Promoting apt epistemic performance. *Journal of the Learning Sciences*, *27*(3), 353–389. https://doi.org/10.1080/10508406.2017.1392968

Belland, B. R., Glazewski, K. D., & Ertmer, P. A. (2009). Inclusion and problem-based learning: Roles of students in a mixed-ability group. *RMLE online*, *32*(9), 1–19. https://doi.org/10.1080/19404476.2009.11462062

Berland, L. K., & Reiser, B. J. (2009). Making sense of argumentation and explanation. *Science Education*, *93*(1), 26–55.

Bybee, R. W. (2006). Scientific inquiry and science teaching. In L. B. Flick & N. G. Lederman, (Eds.), *Scientific inquiry and nature of science* (Science & Tehcnology Library, vol. 25, pp. 1–14). Springer. https://doi.org/10.1007/978-1-4020-5814-1_1

Chernobilsky, E., DaCosta, M. C., & Hmelo-Silver, C. E. (2004). Learning to talk the educational psychology talk through a problem-based course. *Instructional Science*, *32*, 319–356. https://doi.org/10.1023/B:TRUC.0000026552.14289.2c

Chin, C., & Brown, D. E. (2002). Student-generated questions: A meaningful aspect of learning in science. *International Journal of Science Education*, *24*(5), 521–549. https://doi.org/10.1080/09500690110095249

Chin, C., & Osborne, J. (2010). Students' questions and discursive interaction: Their impact on argumentation during collaborative group discussions in science. *Journal of Research in Science Teaching, 47*(7), 883–908. https://doi.org/10.1002/tea.20385

Civil, M. (2007). Building on community knowledge: An avenue to equity in mathematics education. In N. S. Nasir & P. Cobb (Eds.), *Improving access to mathematics: Diversity and equity in the classroom* (pp. 105–117). New York: Teachers College Press.

Cohen, E. G. (1994). Restructuring the classroom: Conditions for productive small groups. *Review of Educational Research, 64*(1), 1–35. https://doi.org/10.3102/00346543064001001

Danish, J. A., Enyedy, N., Saleh, A., & Humburg, M. (2020). Learning in embodied activity framework: A sociocultural framework for embodied cognition. *International Journal of Computer-Supported Collaborative Learning, 15*(1), 49–87. https://doi.org/10.1007/s11412-020-09317-3

Danish, J. A., Enyedy, N., Saleh, A., Lee, C., & Andrade, A. (2015). Science through technology enhanced play: Designing to support reflection through play and embodiment. In O. Lindwall, P. Häkkinen, T. Koschman, P. Tchounikine, & S. Ludvigsen (Eds.), *Exploring the material conditions of learning: The computer supported collaborative learning (CSCL) conference* (Vol. 1). International Society of the Learning Sciences. https://doi.org/10.22318/cscl2015.313

Duncan, R. G., Chinn, C. A., & Barzilai, S. (2018). Grasp of evidence: Problematizing and expanding the next generation science standards' conceptualization of evidence. *Journal of Research in Science Teaching, 55*(7), 907–937. https://doi.org/10.1002/tea.21468

Esteban-Guitart, M., & Moll, L. C. (2014). Funds of identity: A new concept based on the funds of knowledge approach. *Culture & Psychology, 20*(1), 31–48. https://doi.org/10.1177/1354067X13515934

Faulkner, S. L., Baldwin, J. R., Lindsley, S. L., & Hecht, M. L. (2006). Layers of meaning: An analysis of definitions of culture. In J. R. Baldwin, S. F. Faulkner, M. L. Hecht, & S. L. Lindsley (Eds.), *Redefining culture* (pp. 51–76). New York: Routledge. https://doi.org/10.4324/9781410617002

Fiore, S. M., Graesser, A., & Greiff, S. (2018). Collaborative problem-solving education for the twenty-first-century workforce. *Nature Human Behaviour, 2*(6), 367. https://doi.org/10.1038/s41562-018-0363-y

Ford, M. (2008). "Grasp of practice" as a reasoning resource for inquiry and nature of science understanding. *Science & Education, 17*(2–3), 147–177. https://doi.org/10.1007/s11191-006-9045-7

Furtak, E. M., Seidel, T., Iverson, H., & Briggs, D. C. (2012). Experimental and quasi-experimental studies of inquiry-based science teaching: A meta-analysis. *Review of Educational Research, 82*(3), 300–329. https://doi.org/10.3102/0034654312457206

Grandy, R., & Duschl, R. (2008). Consensus: Expanding the scientific method and school science. In *Teaching scientific inquiry*. Leiden: Brill | Sense. https://doi.org/10.1163/9789460911453_022Gonzalez, N., Moll, L. C., Tenery, M. F., Rivera, A., Rendon, P., Gonzales, R., & Amanti, C. (1995). Funds of knowledge for teaching in Latino households. *Urban Education, 29*(4), 443–470. https://doi.org/10.1177/0042085995029004005

Gressick, J., & Derry, S. J. (2010). Distributed leadership in online groups. *International Journal of Computer-Supported Collaborative Learning, 5*(2), 211–236. https://doi.org/10.1007/s11412-010-9086-4

Herrenkohl, L. R. (2006). Intellectual role taking: Supporting discussion in heterogeneous elementary science classes. *Theory into Practice, 45*(1), 47–54. https://doi.org/10.1207/s15430421tip4501_7

Herrenkohl, L. R., Palincsar, A. S., DeWater, L. S., & Kawasaki, K. (1999). Developing scientific communities in classrooms: A sociocognitive approach. *Journal of the Learning Sciences, 8*(3–4), 451–493. https://doi.org/10.1080/10508406.1999.9672076

Hmelo-Silver, C. E. (2004). Problem-based learning: What and how do students learn? *Educational Psychology Review, 16*(3), 235–266. https://doi.org/10.1023/B:EDPR.0000034022.16470.f3

Hmelo-Silver, C. E. (2006). Design principles for scaffolding technology-based inquiry. In A. M. O'Donnell, C. E. Hmelo-Silver, & G. Erkens (Eds.), *Collaborative learning, reasoning, and technology* (pp. 147–170). New York: Routledge. https://doi.org/10.4324/9780203826843

Hmelo-Silver, C. E., & Barrows, H. S. (2008). Facilitating collaborative knowledge building. *Cognition and Instruction, 26*(1), 48–94. https://doi.org/10.1080/07370000701798495

Hmelo-Silver, C. E., & Eberbach, C. (2012). Learning theories and problem-based learning. In S. Bridges, C. McGrath, & T. Whitehill (Eds.), *Problem-based learning in clinical education. Innovation and change in professional education* (vol. 8). Dordrecht: Springer. https://doi.org/10.1007/978-94-007-2515-7_1

Hmelo-Silver, C. E., Katic, E., Nagarajan, A., & Chernobilsky, E. (2007). Soft leaders, hard artifacts, and the groups we rarely see: Using video to understand peer learning processes. In R. Goldman, R. Pea, B. Barron, & S. J. Derry (Eds.), *Video research in the learning sciences.* (pp. 255–270). New York: Routledge. https://doi.org/10.4324/9780203877258

IRA/NCTE Joint Task Force on Assessment, International Reading Association, & National Council of Teachers of English. (2010). *Standards for the assessment of reading and writing*. Newark, DE: International Reading Association.

Järvelä, S., & Hadwin, A. F. (2013). New frontiers: Regulating learning in CSCL. *Educational Psychologist*, *48*(1), 25–39. https://doi.org/10.1080/00461520.2012.748006

Järvelä, S., Kirschner, P. A., Panadero, E., Malmberg, J., Phielix, C., Jaspers, J., Koivuniemi, M., & Järvenoja, H. (2015). Enhancing socially shared regulation in collaborative learning groups: designing for CSCL regulation tools. *Educational Technology Research and Development*, *63*(1), 125–142. https://doi.org/10.1007/s11423-014-9358-1

Jeong, H., & Hmelo-Silver, C. E. (2016). Seven affordances of computer-supported collaborative learning: How to support collaborative learning? How can technologies help? *Educational Psychologist*, *51*(2), 247–265. https://doi.org/10.1080/00461520.2016.1158654

Kimmerle, J., Cress, U., & Held, C. (2010). The interplay between individual and collective knowledge: technologies for organisational learning and knowledge building. *Knowledge Management Research & Practice*, *8*(1), 33–44. https://doi.org/10.1057/kmrp.2009.36

Krajcik, J., McNeill, K. L., & Reiser, B. J. (2007). Learning-goals-driven design model: Developing curriculum materials that align with national standards and incorporate project-based pedagogy. *Science Education*, *92*(1), 1–32. https://doi.org/10.1002/sce.20240

Linn, M. C., Clark, D., & Slotta, J. D. (2003). WISE design for knowledge integration. *Science Education*, *87*(4), 517–538. https://doi.org/10.1002/sce.10086

Martin, N. D., Dornfeld Tissenbaum, C., Gnesdilow, D., & Puntambekar, S. (2019). Fading distributed scaffolds: The importance of complementarity between teacher and material scaffolds. *Instructional Science*, *47*(1), 69–98. https://doi.org/10.1007/s11251-018-9474-0

Michaels, S., O'Connor, M. C., Hall, M. W., & Resnick, L. B. (2010). *Accountable talk sourcebook: For classroom conversation that works*. Pittsburgh, PA: University of Pittsburgh Institute for Learning. Retrieved from https://ifl.pitt.edu/how-we-work/sourcebook.cshtml

Minner, D. D., Levy, A. J., & Century, J. (2010). Inquiry-based science instruction—what is it and does it matter? Results from a research synthesis years 1984 to 2002. *Journal of Research in Science Teaching*, *47*, 474–496. https://doi.org/10.1002/tea.20347

Mott, B. W., Taylor, R. G., Lee, S. Y., Rowe, J. P., Saleh, A., Glazewski, K. D., Hmelo-Silver, C. E., & Lester, J. C. (2019). Designing and developing interactive narratives for collaborative problem-based learning. In R. E. Cardona-Rivera, A. Sullivan, & R. M. Young (Eds.), *Interactive storytelling: 12th international conference on interactive digital storytelling, ICIDS 2019* (pp. 19–22). Little Cottonwood Canyon, UT: Springer Cham.

Nasir, N., Rosebery, A., Warren, B., & Lee, C. (2005). Learning as a cultural process: Achieving equity through diversity. In R. K. Sawyer (Ed.), *The Cambridge handbook of the learning sciences* (Cambridge Handbooks in Psychology, pp. 489–504). Cambridge: Cambridge University Press. doi:10.1017/CBO9780511816833.030

National Council for the Social Studies (NCSS). (2013). *The college, career, and civic life (C3) framework for social studies state standards: Guidance for enhancing the Rigor of K-12 civics, economics, geography, and history*. Silver Spring, MD. Retrieved from www.socialstudies.org/C3.

National Council for Teachers of Mathematics. (2000). *Principles and standards for school mathematics*. Reston, VA.

National Research Council. 2000. *How people learn: Brain, mind, experience, and school: Expanded Edition*. Washington, DC: The National Academies Press. https://doi.org/10.17226/9853.

NGSS Lead States. 2013. *Next generation science standards: For states, by states*. Washington, DC: The National Academies Press.

Nussbaum, E. M. (2002). How introverts versus extroverts approach small-group argumentative discussions. *The Elementary School Journal*, *102*(3), 183–197. https://doi.org/10.1086/499699

Osborne, J. (2010). Arguing to learn in science: The role of collaborative, critical discourse. *Science*, *328*(5977), 463–466. https://doi.org/10.1126/science.1183944

Pedaste, M., Mäeots, M., Siiman, L. A., De Jong, T., Van Riesen, S. A., Kamp, E. T., Manoli, C. C., Zacharia, Z. C., & Tsourlidaki, E. (2015). Phases of inquiry-based learning: Definitions and the inquiry cycle. *Educational Research Review*, *14*, 47–61. https://doi.org/10.1016/j.edurev.2015.02.003

Quintana, C., Reiser, B. J., Davis, E. A., Krajcik, J., Fretz, E., Duncan, R. G., Kyza, E., Edelson, D., & Soloway, E. (2004). A scaffolding design framework for software to support science inquiry. *Journal of the Learning Sciences*, *13*(3), 337–386. https://doi.org/10.1207/s15327809jls1303_4

Reiser, B., & Tabak, I. (2014). Scaffolding. In R. K. Sawyer (Ed.), *The Cambridge handbook of the learning sciences* (Cambridge Handbooks in Psychology, pp. 44–62). Cambridge: Cambridge University Press. https://doi.org/10.1017/CBO9780511816833.030

Saleh, A., Hmelo-Silver, C. E., Glazewski, K. D., Mott, B., Chen, Y., Rowe, J. P., & Lester, J. C. (2019). Collaborative inquiry play: A design case to frame integration of collaborative problem solving with story-centric games. *Information and Learning Sciences, 120*(9/10), 547–566. https://doi.org/10.1108/ILS-03-2019-0024

Saleh, A., Yuxin, C., Hmelo-Silver, C. E., Glazewski, K. D., Mott, B. W., & Lester, J. C. (2020). Coordinating scaffolds for collaborative inquiry in a game-based learning environment. *Journal of Research in Science Teaching,* (57), 1490-1518. https://doi.org/10.1002/tea.21656

Sandoval, W. A., & Reiser, B. J. (2004). Explanation-driven inquiry: Integrating conceptual and epistemic scaffolds for scientific inquiry. *Science Education, 88*(3), 345–372. https://doi.org/10.1002/sce.10130

Saye, J. W., & Brush, T. (2007). Using technology-enhanced learning environments to support problem-based historical inquiry in secondary school classrooms. *Theory & Research in Social Education, 35*(2), 196–230. https://doi.org/10.1080/00933104.2007.10473333

Scardamalia, M., & Bereiter, C. (2014). Knowledge building and knowledge creation. In R. K. Sawyer (Ed.), *The Cambridge handbook of the learning sciences* (Cambridge Handbooks in Psychology, pp. 397–417). Cambridge: Cambridge University Press. https://doi.org/10.1017/CBO9781139519526.025

Schwarz, B. B., Neuman, Y., Gil, J., & Ilya, M. (2003). Construction of collective and individual knowledge in argumentative activity. *The Journal of the Learning Sciences, 12*(2), 219–256. https://doi.org/10.1207/S15327809JLS1202_3

Sharan, S., Sharan, Y., & Tan, I. G.-C. (2013). The group investigation approach to cooperative learning. In C. E. Hmelo-Silver, C. A. Chinn, C. K. K. Chan, & A. M. O'Donnell (Eds.), *The international handbook of collaborative learning* (pp. 351–369). Accessed January 1, 2020, Routledge Handbooks Online.

Slotta, J. D., & Najafi, H. (2013). Supporting collaborative knowledge construction with Web 2.0 technologies. In C. Mouza & N. Lavigne (Eds.), *Emerging technologies for the classroom. Explorations in the learning sciences* (pp. 93–112). New York: Springer. https://doi.org/10.1007/978-1-4614-4696-5_7

Slotta, J. D., Quintana, R. M., & Moher, T. (2018). Collective inquiry in communities of learners. In F. Fischer, C. E. Hmelo-Silver, S. R. Goldman, & P. Reimann (Eds.), *International handbook of the learning sciences* (pp. 308–317) Abingdon: Routledge. https://doi.org/10.4324/9781315617572-30

Stroupe, D. (2014). Examining classroom science practice communities: How teachers and students negotiate epistemic agency and learn science-as-practice. *Science Education, 98*(3), 487–516. https://doi.org/10.1002/sce.21112

Sun, J., Anderson, R. C., Perry, M., & Lin, T.-J. (2017). Emergent leadership in children's cooperative problem solving groups. *Cognition and Instruction, 35*(3), 212–235. https://doi.org/10.1080/07370008.2017.1313615

Suthers, D. D., & Hundhausen, C. D. (2003). An experimental study of the effects of representational guidance on collaborative learning processes. *The Journal of the Learning Sciences, 12*(2), 183–218. https://doi.org/10.1207/S15327809JLS1202_2

Tan, I. G. C., Sharan, S., & Lee, C. K. E. (2007). Group investigation effects on achievement, motivation, and perceptions of students in Singapore. *The Journal of Educational Research, 100*(3), 142-154. https://doi.org/10.3200/JOER.100.3.142-154

van Zee, E. H., Iwasyk, M., Kurose, A., Simpson, D., & Wild, J. (2001). Student and teacher questioning during conversations about science. *Journal of Research in Science Teaching, 38*(2), 159–190. https://doi.org/10.1002/1098-2736(200102)38:2<159::Aid-tea1002>3.0.Co;2-j

Vygotsky, L. S. (1978). *Mind in society: The development of higher psychological processes.* England: Harvard University Press. https://doi.org/10.2307/j.ctvjf9vz4

Webb, N. M. (2009). The teacher's role in promoting collaborative dialogue in the classroom. *British Journal of Educational Psychology, 79*(1), 1–28. https://doi.org/10.1348/000709908X380772

White, B. Y., & Frederiksen, J. R. (2000). Technological tools and instructional approaches for making scientific inquiry accessible to all. In M. Jacobson (Ed.), *Innovations in science and mathematics education: Advanced designs for technologies of learning* (pp. 321–359). New York: Routledge. https://doi.org/10.4324/9781410602671

Wood, D., Bruner, J. S., & Ross, G. (1976). The role of tutoring in problem solving. *Journal of Child Psychology and Psychiatry, 17*(2), 89–100. https://doi.org/10.1111/j.1469-7610.1976.tb00381.x

Zhang, J., Hong, H.-Y., Scardamalia, M., Teo, C. L., & Morley, E. A. (2011). Sustaining knowledge building as a principle-based innovation at an elementary school. *The Journal of the Learning Sciences, 20*(2), 262–307. https://doi.org/10.1080/10508406.2011.528317

Zhang, J., Scardamalia, M., Reeve, R., & Messina, R. (2009). Designs for collective cognitive responsibility in knowledge-building communities. *Journal of the Learning Sciences, 18*(1), 7–44. https://doi.org/10.1080/10508400802581676

15

COMMUNITY-LEVEL DESIGN CONSIDERATIONS IN CREATING COMMUNITIES OF INQUIRY

Katerine Bielaczyc

A major emphasis in contemporary inquiry models is on creating learning contexts that mirror disciplinary cultures (e.g., Edelson & Reiser, 2006; Gresalfi & Cobb, 2006; Herrenkohl, Palincsar, DeWater, & Kawasaki, 1999; Hogan & Corey, 2001). Socializing students into ways of talking, thinking, and acting as a community of inquiry provides a means for developing a deeper understanding of the nature of knowledge creation through disciplinary norms and practices.

Knowledge creation is a collective endeavor, extending beyond individual inquiry. As Ford (2010) points out, "individuals do not construct scientific knowledge, communities do" (p. 269). Thus, in order to fully understand how to cultivate community-based models in classrooms, it is critical to look beyond engaging students in inquiry at the *individual level* (e.g., positioning a student as a biologist or an historian) to also consider educational implications at the *community level* (e.g., students participating in collective practices and social interactions across a community of biologists or historians). The "community level" is not seen as simply the summation of individual activity; instead, it centers on the joint enterprise engaged in by participants. The units of interest concern the shared identity, joint activity and collective norms, and collaborative achievements of participants functioning as a whole.

Because traditional schooling has long emphasized individual knowledge and performance, understanding and creating supports at the community level may be unfamiliar. In order to guide teachers and designers interested in cultivating classrooms based on community-based models of inquiry, this chapter highlights four key design considerations focused specifically at the community level:

- Cultivating a social identity of a collective enterprise
- Attending to communal knowledge spaces
- Framing social interactions using multiplayer epistemic games
- Supporting metalevel reflections on the community inquiry

In brief, *cultivating a social identity of a collective enterprise* refers to socializing students into seeing themselves and each other as engaged in a joint undertaking of the inquiry. The aim is to develop a shared understanding of "who we are," "what we do," and "what we know." *Attending to communal knowledge spaces* concerns creating public spaces where the processes and products of the community's inquiry are made visible and available for interaction among participants. The idea is to develop explicitly recognized places to conduct "our work" and keep track of "where we are" in the inquiry. *Framing social interactions using multiplayer epistemic games* is viewed as a means of scaffolding interactions among members of the community. The multiplayer game structures are intended to clarify and guide the various ways that students can work together to advance their collective inquiry. *Supporting metalevel reflections on the community inquiry* relates to engaging participants in constructing understandings of the ways in which the community is engaged in inquiry. The aim is to cultivate practices that permit analysis of the work of the collective, such as stepping back and assessing the community's progress, developing a sense of productive or nonproductive ways of working together, or creating representations of the collective processes. Although each design element is discussed separately, they tend to be interdependent and mutually supportive in communities of inquiry.

Within this chapter, I will frame and discuss these four design issues in general terms applicable across a variety of types of community-based models of inquiry. In addition, I will also provide direct examples drawn from research in classrooms enacting the Knowledge Building Communities (KBC) model (Chan & van Aalst, 2018; Scardamalia, 2002; Scardamalia & Bereiter, 2006). The KBC model was created by Marlene Scardamalia, Carl Bereiter, and their colleagues in the 1990s and has developed as one of the "longest running design experiments in education" (Bereiter, 2005/2006, p. 18). This research is rich with examplars, because working together as a community engaged in collective knowledge building is central to the KBC model. The research associated with this model also has a wide international footprint including classroom and school implementations on several continents.[1]

Cultivating a Social Identity of a Collective Enterprise

Students' *social identity* refers to how they view themselves as learners and how they perceive the role that other students in the class (and others in their social network) play with regard to their own learning (Bielaczyc, 2006, 2013). In a community of inquiry, students are meant to see each other as co-investigative resources, where the diverse knowledge and skills among the community members can be brought together to advance the collective understanding of various problems under investigation. It is important to develop a shared understanding of "who we are," "what we do," and "what we know." However, as pointed out by Grossman and her colleagues, a sense of working together as a community is not brought into being simply by "linguistic fiat" (Grossman, Wineburg, & Woolworth, 2001, p. 943). Even in classrooms where extended inquiry and collaborative activities are common, there is a tendency to focus on investigations local to the individual or collaborative group, rather than working as a classroom collective functioning similar to a disciplinary community. Thus, it is critical to consider how to cultivate a social identity of working together on a joint enterprise among students.

Cultivating social identities consistent with a community of inquirers involves supporting students in developing individual skills or areas of expertise of value to the community, setting communal norms, and engaging in shared practices and interactions. By working toward common goals and developing a collective awareness of the expertise available among the members of the community, a sense of "who we are" can be fostered. Over time, as community members contribute to each other's investigations and help advance the collective knowledge, the students are meant to develop a sense of what their community is able to accomplish as a whole.

In working toward cultivating the social identity of a collective enterprise, it may be helpful for teachers and designers to attend to issues such as positioning participants as members of a community (who we are), establishing community practices and norms (what we do), and recognizing collective achievements (what we know and what we can accomplish). The two examples below are intended to deepen the understanding of these issues and the means for creating relevant supports.

Example of Cultivating a Social Identity of a Collective Engaged in Science Inquiry

This example is from *Ideas First*, a design research project involving Primary 3 and 4[2] classrooms in Singapore (Bielaczyc & Ow, 2014). The aim was to cultivate science classrooms as knowledge-building communities as cohorts moved across two school years. The emphasis here is on the use of visual images and artifacts as a means of cultivating a social identity of a collective enterprise.

The first day of Primary 3 Science class opens with discussing "How do Scientists make sense of the world?" The discussion highlights the underpinnings of Ideas First, such as working as a science community to understand questions that we have about the world and how, like scientists, we keep working to improve our ideas and explanations. These early discussions about the parallels between the classroom community of inquiry and the science community are supported by the *We Work as a Science Community* handout. One side of the handout has photographs of students from their own school carrying out investigations along with the quote "I am doing my part in a community that is making progress on important problems."[3] The intention is to signal students' social identity within knowledge-building classrooms: *We can work together on problems and carry out investigations in many different ways.* The flipside of the handout presents parallels between the students' work and how scientists "make sense of the world" (Figure 15.1). This handout is used as a constant referent throughout the year to name and help support the development of community norms and practices (e.g., "when we are working on a problem, we share our ideas," "we support

IDEAS FIRST

How do Scientists make sense of the world?

In Ideas First we learn how to make sense of our world in the same way that scientists do:

- **We work as a Science Community.**
  - We work together to share our ideas with each other.
  - The community can only move ahead, if we help all of the members of our community to move ahead.
- **We work to answer questions that we have about the world**
  - When we are working on a problem, we share our ideas (*My Idea is...*)
  - We support our ideas with evidence (*My evidence is..*)
  - We explain why our ideas answer our questions (*Why? Because..*)
  - We ask questions (*INTU...* (INTU = I need to understand))
  - We know that we can find out information by taking to others, doing research in the library or on the Internet (*Plan...*)
  - We bring in information from different sources (*New information...*)
  - We work to improve our ideas and explanations (*A better idea is...*)
- **We understand that scientists keep working to better understand the world. We keep working to improve our ideas and explanations.**

Figure 15.1 "We Work as a Science Community" handout (one side of two-sided handout)

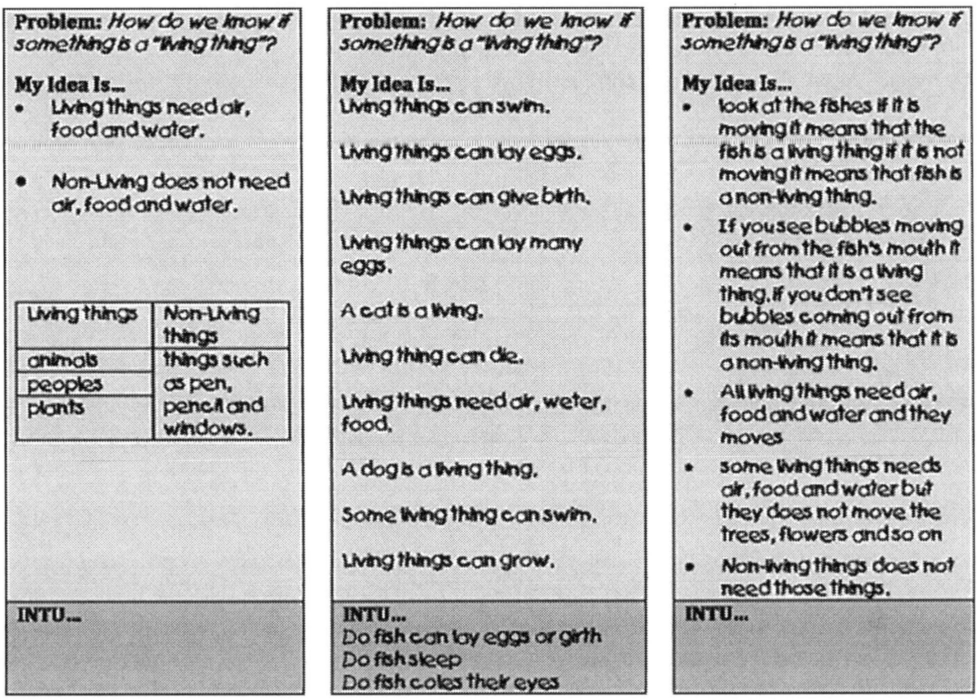

Figure 15.2 *My Idea is...* cards from three different students in one of the Primary 3 classes

our ideas with evidence"). These initial discussions, visual images of students, and articulation of parallels between the work of the classroom community and science community provide first steps in positioning participants as members of a community (who we are) and establishing community practices and norms (what we do).

In another early Primary 3 Science class, students begin working together on a joint inquiry problem—*How do we know if something is a "living thing"?* Another set of artifacts, Think Cards, are used to support the collective inquiry. Prior to doing any formal research, students are encouraged to generate ideas and explanations using the *My Idea Is...* Think Card as a support. Figure 15.2 shows the responses of three different students. These *My Idea is...* Think Cards are then shared publicly (via the visualizer or whiteboard for the whole class, or in small-group discussions), making visible the diversity of ideas available as community resources. The aim is to signal that what begins as "My Idea is..." becomes "Our Ideas are...." This collection of ideas is also used to highlight how much knowledge is available when we work together and how, even prior to carrying out the inquiry, students bring many powerful perspectives to the community. Sharing the collective knowledge available across the *My Idea is...* Think Cards provides foundational steps toward recognizing collective achievements (what we know and what we can accomplish).

Example of Cultivating a Social Identity of a Collective Engaged in Historical Inquiry

The second example comes from a five-week summer research seminar focused on cultivating a community of "critical researchers" among high schoolers developed as part of UCLA's IDEA Institute (Rogers, Morrell, & Enyedy, 2007). The aim was to create a youth-led public history project examining racial segregation and struggles for educational justice across Los Angeles (LA).

The emphasis here is on how interactions with persons outside of the research seminar contributed to fostering a social identity of a collective enterprise.

Over the course of the seminar, the youth interacted with various members of the LA community. On the first day, they met with five UCLA undergraduates who had similarly participated in the summer seminar when they were high school students. The undergraduates shared their own experiences, discussing how participating in the research enterprise "offers young people a meaningful social role that can affect their daily lives" (p. 3). The alumni messaged that the youth are joining an enterprise with a history, as part of an even larger group of participants than their present cohort.

In carrying out their research, the youth collected data at an LA historical archive. Not only did the archives director treat "the students as she would any 'sanctioned' researchers who visited the archive" (p.11), she also asked if the research groups would contribute their video-based oral histories of community members to the archive. Students also carried out interviews in which they documented the perspectives of various LA citizens. Taking on different roles as they engaged with various people had an impact on the youth:

> While in the field, students took on multiple roles with implications for their development as researchers and activists. For instance, when approaching well-known activists and respected community members, the students took on the formal roles of oral historians. They became young scholars armed with notebooks and cameras to record for posterity these seemingly forgotten stories of educational activism amid changing schools and changing communities ... they gained confidence in their research capabilities when others treated them with respect. Nothing we might have fabricated in the formal seminar space could match the reaction to the students by other members of their own communities. As a consequence, the students took themselves and their work very seriously. ...The MV clearly saw these students as legitimate researchers and, even more, as the guardians of their community's historical narrative, with the ability to carry their stories to places the MV were unlikely to travel.
>
> *(Rogers, et al., 2007, pp. 10–11)*

In the final stages of their work, the research groups gave formal presentations on their work in the university's faculty center. After the presentations, a group of invited panelists "responded as they would at a professional research conference. Students answered questions about their methods and findings and pointed to future directions in historical and social science research" (p. 12).

During the course of the seminar, the students were positioned to interact with others as authentic researchers doing work of real importance (who we are). They engaged in research processes that were recognized as legitimate (what we do), and the products of their inquiry were treated authentically—subject to critique as if they were "at a professional research conference" and qualified to be archived along with other oral histories of community members (what we know and what we can accomplish). In this way, the students came to see that their research identities and their work were validated and valued by members of the LA community, impacting their sense of social identity.

Attending to Communal Knowledge Spaces

Communal knowledge spaces play a critical role in supporting the work of communities of inquiry. Historical analyses of knowledge-creating communities in industry (e.g., Krugman, 1991), organizations (e.g., Brown & Duguid, 2000), and science (e.g., Sagan, 1980), all point to the free exchange of ideas in spaces accessible to all members of the community as a key element of knowledge advancement (Bielaczyc & Collins, 2006). Similarly, in student inquiry communities it is important to attend to public knowledge spaces (e.g., whiteboards, online forums) where the processes and products of the community's inquiry can be made visible and available for further work by participants. Such communal knowledge spaces provide explicitly recognized places to conduct "our work" and keep track of "where we are" in the joint inquiry.

In theorizing about the role of communal knowledge spaces in communities of inquiry, my colleagues and I (Bielaczyc, Paik, & Ow, 2012) highlighted four ways that such spaces support the collective enterprise:

1 *Validating multiple perspectives in a shared problem space*
When a community pools together their work on a problem via a communal space, diverse perspectives can be brought together. Multiple perspectives can foster creativity in a number of ways, including providing a variety of solution paths, a richness to draw from in better understanding the problem itself, a set of ingredients for inventing new methods for knowledge work, and opportunities to surface new insights or problems from conflicting viewpoints.

2 *Objectifiying concepts as shared artifacts to be worked with*
Representing and reifying concepts in the communal space permit the creation of public *conceptual artifacts* (Bereiter, 2002). Conceptual artifacts serve as objects of inquiry that community participants can tinker with, critique, combine with other knowledge objects, and improve upon. New conceptual artifacts can also be constructed from existing artifacts, providing a way to enrich and advance the knowledge available to the community.

3 *Capturing traces of the community's knowledge work*
Community members work with the conceptual artifacts in the communal space in a variety of ways. When operations on conceptual artifacts and other processes involved in the community's knowledge work are captured in the space, then traces of the knowledge work themselves become available for reflection and advancement.

4 *Representing "what the community knows"*
The community knowledge space is where the community shares its ideas and work in a common and public arena. The contents of the space can thus be seen as a representation of "what we know."

By supporting diverse perspectives and continual improvement, a community knowledge space communicates to participants that knowledge is dynamic—something that members can continually contribute to and advance through multiple means. Capturing traces of various aspects of the inquiry provides a means for gaining insight into and reflecting upon the enterprise of knowledge creation. Treating the ideas of all members as valued efforts toward the joint inquiry, sharing and reflecting on knowledge as objects, and considering "what we collectively know," all signal a different type of epistemology than that found in traditional classrooms. Such spaces may also contribute to cultivating a social identity of a collective enterprise (the design element discussed in the previous section).

There are three primary types of spaces that teachers and designers may attend to in creating communal knowledge spaces: (a) talk-based spaces, (b) physical spaces, and (c) online spaces. Each is discussed in turn below.

Talk-Based Communal Knowledge Spaces

One way that inquiry communities share and construct collective knowledge is through public talk. The inquiry-based research literature provides numerous examples of participant structures that have been used in order to support the exchange of knowledge among community members. For example, the *jigsaw method* (Aronson, 1978) has been used to create an interlocking structure of social interactions, where members of a small-group configuration also have roles that are common across the small groups (e.g., Brown & Campione, 1994; Engle & Conant, 2002). Over the course of the inquiry, participants meet in both their small groups and their role groups, thus providing a means for knowledge to move throughout the community, promoting "knowledge diffusion" (Barab, Hay, Barnett, & Keating, 2000).

Whole-class discussion is perhaps the most common way to create a talk-based space that permits "pulling together what we know" as a community of inquiry. Whole-class discussions provide a means for collectively working with and advancing knowledge, such as when community members engage in argumentation, debates, and the co-construction of new ideas. For example, "science circle" is a public talk space created by a teacher in order to support students' strengths in argumentation and storytelling:

> Science circle was a time to hear students' questions, for students to read aloud from their journals, to share observations, to try out theories, argue claims, and the like. The focus was on the student to elaborate or clarify what he or she meant. The teachers talked relatively little. When they did, they asked genuine questions. Science circle became a place where students talked to students, challenged each other, asked each other to clarify, even joked and told stories.
>
> *(Warren, Ballenger, Ognowski, Rosebery, & Hudicourt-Barnes, 2001, p. 535)*

Typically, members of inquiry communities work individually or in small groups with interspersed opportunities for collective public talk via whole-class discussion (e.g., Herrenkohl & Mertl, 2010; Kapur & Bielaczyc, 2012). Several researchers have documented how knowledge is constructed in moving across such local and public spaces in inquiry-based classrooms (Barab et al., 2000; Enyedy, 2003; Hall & Rubin, 1998).

Talk-based communal spaces provide opportunities for inquiry communities to exchange ideas and engage in high-bandwidth interactions (including gestures and body movements, puzzled looks, etc.) to co-construct meanings and advancements in knowledge. However, some of the challenges raised by talk-based spaces include the need for co-location of participants and for synchronous in-the-moment participation. Furthermore, public talk "produces no *permanent* record, so there is nothing to *reproduce, distribute, modify, navigate, or survey*.... This means that if something is forgotten, it cannot be recovered. If a good idea is produced, it cannot easily be distributed or studied" (Collins, Neville, & Bielaczyc, 2000, p. 148). Sometimes writing spaces are used to document elements of whole-class discussions, thus augmenting the oral exchange with a written record. It is also possible to record and transcribe public talk. For example, Hennessey (2003) described how her students used videorecordings of inquiry group discussions in order to compare earlier and later discussions for idea improvement.

Physical Communal Knowledge Spaces

Physical objects such as whiteboards, chart paper, and walls can be used as public spaces in support of collective knowledge work. For example, Wells (2000) describes a middle-school community of inquiry that created a "knowledge wall" on one wall of their classroom for posting and manipulating questions, ideas, and other knowledge objects. The conceptual artifacts that are collected in the public space can include not only language but also visuals and other products of inquiry that are collected together in order to make visible "what we know." For instance, Harvard's Project Zero has created a variety of "thinking routines" to make visible participants' conceptions (Ritchhart, Church, & Morrison, 2011). These involve the creation of charts, maps, and visuals that can then be posted in a public space for examination and further work by the inquiry

Figure 15.3 Gund Hall in the Harvard Graduate School of Design

community. Externalization into a shared visual form can surface gaps in understanding or areas in need of further investigation (e.g., Hmelo-Silver & Barrows, 2008).

Sometimes the 3D physical workspace of an inquiry community can be set up in ways that processes and products remain visible as members carry out their work, in addition to being purposely examined by the collective at given points throughout the inquiry process. This can often be seen in arts- and design-based inquiry communities. For example, the architecture of Gund Hall at the Harvard Design School (Figure 15.3) has an open and step-like structure permitting continuous visibility of students' design projects and encouraging discussions across peripheral workspaces. An example from a classroom-based science inquiry community comes from a study by Lehrer, Schauble, and Lucas (2008) in which students developed models of pond ecologies within one-gallon jars: "just looking around the classroom at the collection of jars provided opportunities to learn about the dilemmas posed by other jars, as well as the potential answers that they may afford" (p. 526).

Physical communal knowledge spaces allow an inquiry community to capture more lasting records of communal knowledge work. Physical spaces can also afford asynchronous engagement in communal knowledge work. They often permit community members to both view and manipulate a range of types of knowledge objects (e.g., language-based, drawings, data graphics). Such manipulation can include pulling together objects into categories, drawing connections, and elaborating or annotating the content of various knowledge objects—operations that help organize and advance the communal knowledge. One challenge in a physical space is that once the knowledge objects are manipulated to create a representation of the communal knowledge, that representation must often be deconstructed in order to create other representations. For example, if one group of students organize the artifacts on a "knowledge wall" to show a particular representation of the community's knowledge, then the artifacts need to be rearranged if another group wants to show a different representation. Similarly, it is difficult to afford a means for each member of the community to work in parallel with the knowledge objects to manipulate and create their own representations.

Online Communal Knowledge Spaces

Digital media offer opportunities for sharing and working with communal knowledge in a variety of ways, particularly shared knowledge bases. Examples of shared, multimedia knowledge bases specifically designed to support community-based inquiry include *Knowledge Forum* (Scardamalia, 2004; Scardamalia & Bereiter, 2006) and *Scratch* (Resnick et al., 2009; Roque, Rusk, & Resnick, 2016). Such environments provide public online spaces that collect together "our work" and where inquiry processes and products are made available for further work by community participants. In interviews with students working in Knowledge Forum databases, they described how the public nature of the database led to an awareness of how others contributed to the collective inquiry and a feeling for how "we as a class" are building knowledge over time (Bielaczyc, 2018). In gaining a communal sense of their work, students spoke of becoming motivated to read the database more widely and co-construct knowledge with others.

Online communal knowledge spaces have many of the same affordances of physical communal knowledge spaces, such as the creation of lasting records of community work and permitting asynchronous interaction. In addition, online communal knowledge spaces tend to afford much wider access, greater manipulation capabilities, and more varied forms of visualization than do physical spaces. For example, in regard to wider access, community members need not be co-located and can access online spaces in an anytime-anywhere manner. Furthermore, these online spaces may be extended, "via the Internet, to the worldwide community of knowledge workers. Thus work between individuals and the community—work of benefit personally and collectively—is easily extensible to work between one community and multiple communities beyond the classroom" (Zhang, Scardamalia, Lamon, Messina, & Reeve, 2007, p. 120).

Online communal spaces also tend to be searchable. Digital objects within communal spaces can often be tagged with metadata, permitting a variety of forms of indexing and display. Some digital objects also afford reworking or "remixing," where the original object is able to keep its form intact, while participants in the community are able to extend or make alterations that transform the original. For example, members of the Scratch community author and share programmable objects in a communal space, permitting others to learn by "going beneath the hood" to investigate the code of each other's projects and to draw from, remix, and extend each other's work (Roque et al., 2016).

Framing Interactions Using Multiplayer Epistemic Games

One way that the inquiry practices of disciplinary communities can be conceptualized is playing the "epistemic games" of those communities (Collins & Ferguson, 1993; Perkins, 1997). Like most games, epistemic games consist of forms that provide a structure along with rules, strategies, and different moves that guide play. What makes these games "epistemic" is that they are directed toward building knowledge and understanding (Perkins, 1997). The construct of epistemic games can be used to make visible the forms, goals, and rules of the work involved in disciplinary inquiry practices to be explicitly discussed. In working to cultivate communities of inquiry in classrooms, epistemic games can serve as a means of scaffolding students in disciplinary practices. For instance, many of the inquiry models used in K-12 education support students in approaching their investigations based on some sort of "research cycle." These cycles can be viewed as an epistemic form that guides the inquiry.

Much of the research concerned with epistemic game play has focused on guiding the actions of individual participants as they engage in inquiry (e.g., Collins & Ferguson, 1993; Sandoval, Bell, Coleman, Enyedy, & Suthers, 2000). More recent research by my colleagues and I have extended the construct of epistemic games to "multi-player epistemic games" in order to guide teachers and students engaged in community-based models of inquiry (Bielaczyc & Kapur, 2010; Bielaczyc & Ow, 2014). It is this construct of multiplayer epistemic games that teachers and designers may find useful as a community-level support. Multiplayer epistemic game play is intended to mirror the *distributed* efforts within disciplinary inquiry communities that result in the collective construction of knowledge. In multiplayer epistemic games, the moves can be distributed across multiple players—where individuals (or small groups) make contributions, others act upon such contributions (improve upon, synthesize, argue against, etc.), and knowledge is created and refuted through the collective workings of the whole.

Example of the Multiplayer "Progressive-Improvement Game"

As an example, I again draw from Ideas First, a project enacting the KBC model in primary school classrooms in Singapore (Bielaczyc & Ow, 2014). As part of this design research, the central work of the classroom community was characterized as the "Progressive Improvement Game" (Figure 15.4). In the Progressive-Improvement Game, players work on a common problem (*Our Problem*) by proposing *Initial Theories*. They may also generate *Questions* that identify areas in need of further investigation in order to refine their initial ideas. The players then work to gather further information through *Investigative Work* and/or the *Exchange of Ideas*. This, in turn, leads to theory refinement and further questions to pursue (*Improved Theories and Questions*). To encourage consideration of how various aspects of an investigation fit together, it is also important to engage in periodic *Pull-Together*'s. The epistemic form in Figure 15.4 was intended to make visible the practice of continual idea improvement and provide a shared reference for scaffolding the community's inquiry.

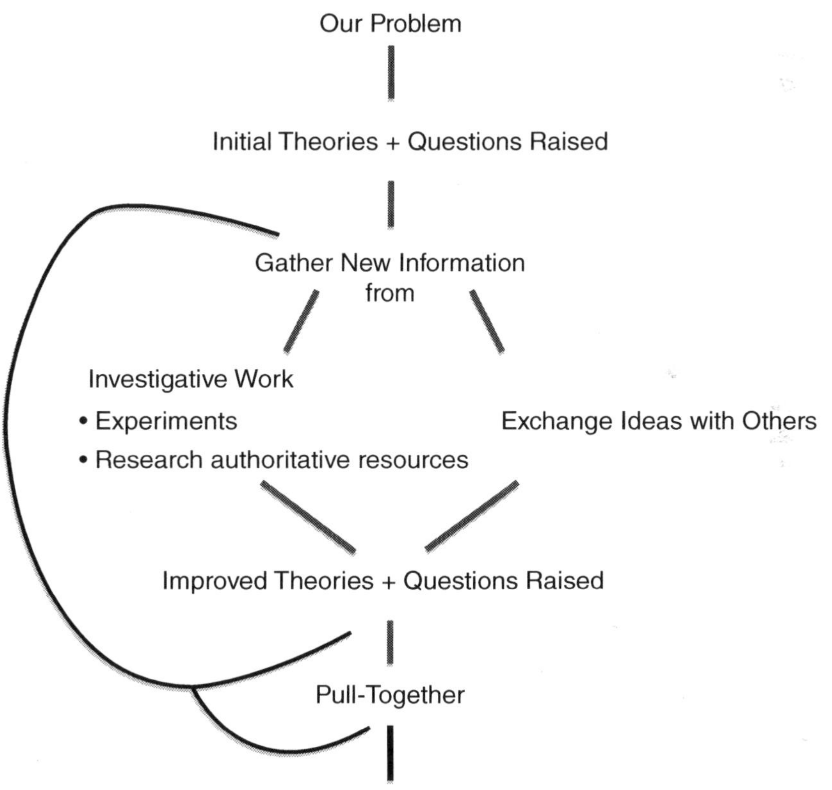

Figure 15.4 The basic moves of the progressive improvement game

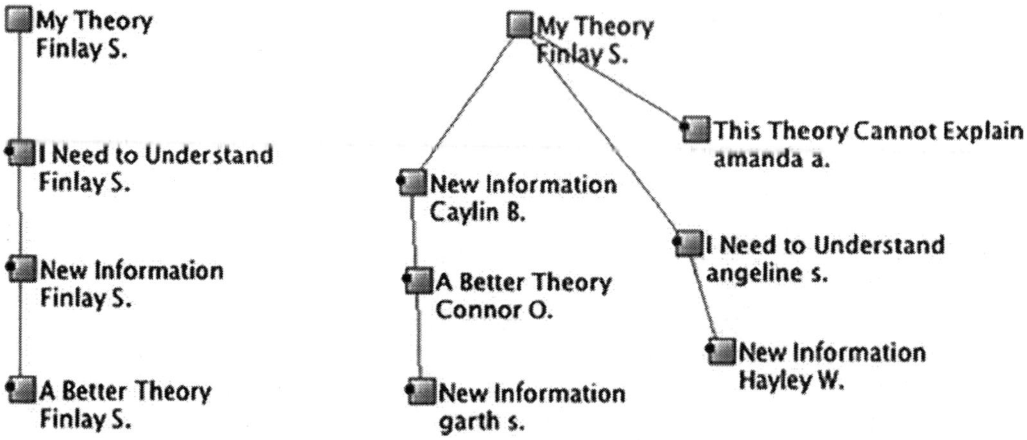

Figure 15.5 Single-player knowledge moves (left) compared to distributed, multiplayer knowledge moves (right)

The students played the Progressive-Improvement Game in the online communal space of Knowledge Forum. The Knowledge Forum View was positioned as the "game board" where game pieces in the form of Notes and Build-On's were used to make knowledge-building moves—actions that players take in order to advance knowledge given a particular board configuration. Figure 15.5 (left) shows a single student (Finlay) making a sequence of knowledge-building moves across Notes (*My Theory, I Need to Understand, New Information*, and a *Better Theory*). "Multiplayer" idea improvement is achieved by actions distributed across students building upon each other's moves (Figure 15.5, right). One student may propose an initial idea related to the community's inquiry, a different student may independently carry out investigative work related to this idea, and yet a different student may contribute an insight that comes from synthesizing the investigative work with the contributions made by others.

As noted in the previous section, communal knowledge spaces make it possible to capture the community's knowledge work. Because the Notes and their configurations on the Knowledge Forum View provide concrete, point-at-able visualizations of the multiplayer epistemic game play, they can visually aid metadiscourse concerning "strategic knowledge-building moves" (the importance of metadiscourse is discussed below in the section on metalevel reflections). In one study, the online configurations were used by students and teachers to talk about how to work as a collective toward progressively improving the knowledge within a given problem space. Over time, the teachers and students discussed and documented a repertoire of strategic and non-strategic knowledge-building moves. Across the two years, students were found to improve in their ability to generate strategic knowledge-building moves: from 183 students (66%) in year 1 to 247 students (94%) in year 2 (Bielaczyc & Ow, 2014).

Example of the Multiplayer "Scientific Presentation Game"

Although their work does not specifically term what students are doing as a "multi-player epistemic game," another example can be drawn from the work of Herrenkohl and her colleagues (Herrenkohl & Guerra, 1998; Herrenkohl & Mertl, 2010). Students in the fourth-grade science community involved in this research can be seen as positioned as players of a "Scientific Presentation Game."

This research investigated means of supporting students in becoming members of a community of inquiry that paralleled a community of scientists. The students engaged together in a variety of balance and building investigations, working in small groups interspersed with public presentations of their work. One particular focus was on helping students to develop theoretically based arguments concerning their investigations. Students' explanation construction was supported by introducing three "focal practices of thinking like a scientist" (Herrenkohl & Mertl, 2010, p. 32): (1) predicting and theorizing, (2) summarizing results, and (3) relating predictions and theories to results. Based on these focal practices, students played particular intellectual roles during the public presentation of the small group work: *reporter and scribe roles* to report the group work, and *audience roles* to critique and help co-construct improved arguments with the reporters. Each group had two reporters and two scribes who worked together with the three focal practices in order to structure their report. Certain students in the audience were assigned the intellectual role of supporting improvements in the group's predictions and theorizing (first focal practice); other audience members were assigned roles relating to the second focal practice and third focal practice, respectively. According to Herrenkohl and Mertl (2010):

> These roles structured discussion of important epistemological ideas for young science learners. Students needed support to understand what kinds of thinking practices were important to privilege in science (Cobb & Yackel, 1996). These roles gave specific guidance to students who began to learn techniques for how to have discussions about their small-group investigations.
>
> *(p. 34)*

During each public presentation, a "scientific presentation game" could be seen to ensue, with the thinking-like-a-scientist focal practices providing guidance for the moves of the "players." As reporters shared their work, various audience members made moves relating to improving predictions or theories, ways of summarizing results, and relating the outcomes of the groupwork to the group's theoretical positions. This multiplayer epistemic game play provided a supportive structure for students to publicly enact focal practices, receive responses to their moves, and co-construct improved arguments, thus coming to a better understanding of how these focal practices work together as part of a process contributing toward the progressive improvement of theoretically based arguments.

Supporting Metalevel Reflections on the Community Inquiry

Supporting metalevel reflections on the community inquiry relates to engaging participants in constructing understandings of the ways in which the community is engaged in inquiry. In some ways, it serves as a communal-level parallel to individual metacognition, where an individual makes his or her own thoughts the objects of self-reflection (Brown, 1987). Community participants make the work of the collective the object of communal reflection. Through analysis of the community's inquiry processes and products, such metalevel reflection is intended to deepen understanding of the community's ways of working. This might include stepping back and assessing the collective's progress, developing a sense of productive or nonproductive ways of working together, or determining which areas of the inquiry are in need of further investigation.

Working together to construct metalevel understandings of the community inquiry can occur in many ways. Sometimes community members engage in verbal "de-briefing sessions" in order to share their impressions of how the inquiry is proceeding and to discuss and work through challenges with content, processes, or even each other. Community members may create a visual representation of the communal inquiry, using it as a means to express and capture key elements of the work in a visible form that can support further dialogue among participants. For example, students in one of my team learning courses created a 3D physical representation involving a base with a central post rising upward marked with a timeline, along with pipe cleaners, labels, and cards containing brief personal and collaborative narratives. The students represented their communal interactions and knowledge work over a nine-week period—with pipe cleaners in upward and outward movements to express their ever-expanding knowledge, with key points and "a-ha moments" marked along the way, and intertwining and varying pipe cleaners of different colors indicating emerging and interweaving areas of inquiry, including threads of investigation that "went no-where" yet spawned important insights. Although the representation may not be fully communicative to outside observers, the participants spoke of how constructing the representation together facilitated their own understanding of their knowledge advancements, inquiry processes, and social interactions.

When lasting records of the work of the community are available in either physical or online communal spaces, this can support more detailed analysis of the collective inquiry. Participants are able to engage in "metadiscourse," that is, discourse on the knowledge objects, processes, and unfolding progress of the communal discourse. Furthermore, it may be possible to physically or digitally capture the metadiscourse itself and add it to the communal space, thereby constructing metalayers annotating the community's work. Lee, Chan, and van Aalst (2006) provide an example of this from a knowledge-building classroom where students examined the types of collective knowledge advances occurring in their Knowledge Forum database, which they documented in Portfolio Notes added to the database.

A related area of research concerns "reflective structuration," the reflective process where community members co-develop shared inquiry structures in order to support and guide their ongoing knowledge work (Tao & Zhang, 2018; Zhang, et al., 2018). These collective inquiry structures "serve as a social mediating mechanism to help channel students' ongoing participation, action, and collaboration" (Zhang, et al., 2018, p. 396). Studies by Tao and Zhang and their colleagues (e.g., Tao & Zhang, 2018; Tao, Zhang, & Gao, 2017) have documented a variety of inquiry structures co-constructed by students and teachers in knowledge-building classrooms, including the use of tree charts to highlight areas of investigation, concept maps to show relationship among knowledge objects and chart the progress of inquiry, and research cycles to serve as a guide to collective work. As the community's inquiry progresses over time, students often re-visit and re-work their collective inquiry structures in order to update them based on the current state of the communal work.

In contexts where communal inquiry involves digital media, several developers have created tools that automate the analysis and visualization of the community's work. Such automated analysis and visualization tools provide representations of the collective processes and products that can then be used to support metalevel reflections by community members. For example, several tools exist to provide group-level visualizations of knowledge building in Knowledge Forum databases, including the *Analytic Toolkit* (Burtis, 1998), which provides analyses such as the frequency of use for specific knowledge-building objects, and *KBDeX* (Matsuzawa, Oshima, Oshima, Niihara, & Sakai, 2011; Oshima, Oshima, & Matsuzawa, 2012), which supports social network analyses. Another example comes from work in the area of generative designs (Davis, 2009; Stroup, Ares, & Hurford, 2007). Generative designs collect up each individual participant's work on a shared problem from their personal handheld device and projects the work of the entire class onto a physical communal display space at the front of the classroom. Davis and her colleagues (Davis & Brady, 2010; Davis & Effendi, 2010a, 2010b) created a portfolio of metalevel visualization tools that made visible different features of the participants' contributions as a means of supporting metalevel reflections on the work of the collective.

Example of Using Visualization Tools to Support Metalevel Reflections

I draw from research on KBC classrooms in order to provide a more detailed illustration of the use of visualization tools to support metadiscourse. The research of Resendes and her colleagues

(Resendes, 2014; Resendes, Scardamalia, Bereiter, Chen, & Halewood, 2015) highlights that it is possible for even young learners to engage in metalevel reflections on their community inquiry.

One study examined how automated collective-level feedback tools were used in second-grade classrooms in order to support metadiscourse on their ongoing inquiry in Knowledge Forum (Resendes et al., 2015). Two types of visualization tools captured the database work, a *Word Clouds* tool highlighted the use of new domain vocabulary, and an *Epistemic Discourse Moves* tool produced bar graphs of the frequency of use of various scaffolds in Knowledge Forum. For instance, Figure 15.6 shows how the Words Cloud tool was used to create a set of comparative word clouds: a cloud of word frequencies in the student database ("Our Words"), a cloud of authoritative source material on the same topic ("Expert Words"), and a cloud based on their intersection ("Shared Words"). As the collective inquiry progressed over time, the tool captured relevant changes in the database, producing "a variety of results to fuel knowledge-building metadiscourse" (p. 314).

These visualizations enabled new types of metalevel conversations about the collective inquiry. According to one of the teachers involved in the work:

> Typically … KB talks focus on developing and discussing theories, posing questions, and bringing new information to the group. The talk around the graphs and the word clouds added a new focus: that of helping children be aware of the quantity and type of notes they wrote in the view. Through discussions of this sort, children saw how those notes often affected the direction of their learning.
>
> *(Resendes, et al., 2015, p. 316)*

Figure 15.6 Comparative word clouds (from Resendes et al., 2015, p. 315)

The study examined whether the formative feedback provided by the visualizations supported students in carrying out metadiscourse supporting productive knowledge building, such as evaluating their work in Knowledge Forum, along with strategizing and setting new directions for their inquiry. According to the researchers, "our findings support a qualified 'yes'" (p. 329). Their qualification was due to what they observed as a dependency on the teacher because of the active role that the teacher needed to take in facilitating the student conversations. However, with the support of the tools and their teachers, the second graders engaged in metalevel reflections on their community inquiry. Furthermore, in comparison with a control group, analyses of the work carried out by students in Knowledge Forum subsequent to engaging in such metadiscourse showed advances in the "scientificness" and complexity of their knowledge-building discourse, increased use of domain vocabulary and epistemic discourse moves, and more connected and coherent communication networking.

Example of Using Tools for Assessing Interactions to Support Metalevel Reflections

The second example highlights the use of computer-based tools to scaffold groups in monitoring and regulating their collaborative interactions toward improving their collaborative knowledge-building discourse. The work of Borge and her colleagues (Borge, Ong, & Rosé, 2018; Borge & Shimoda, 2019) centers on helping learners to cultivate *socio-metacognitive expertise*, metacognitive regulation where participants work to improve their collective processes.

In the CREATE system, learners engage in joint sense-making discussions in an online text-based environment. Afterwards, the system supports learners in examining and assessing their archived discussions, including scaffolding learners in assessing collective contributions and identifying "the gap between existing and desired collaborative processes with concrete research-based reflective assessments that provide a model of desired activity" (p. 73). The key "micro-patterns" used to guide the assessments include *verbal equity, joint idea building, exploring alternative perspectives*, and *proposing high-quality claims*. Learners use rubrics associated with these micro-patterns to assess their team's communication patterns and engage in reflective discussions to plan improvements for their next cycle of collaborative interactions and assessments.

The CREATE system was used to investigate two- to three-person groups engaged in sense-making around course readings in a university-level online course on information sciences and technology. The quality of collaborative communication patterns was found to significantly improve across five sessions over ten weeks: "in Session 5, students discuss ideas in more depth and display longer, more diverse, and more cohesive communication acts" (p. 88). Participants used the rubric and analysis supports provided in CREATE to treat their collaborative interactions as objects of individual and collaborative reflection, discussing strengths and weaknesses in their online discussions and improving their interaction strategies over time.

Conclusion

This chapter highlights four central community-level design considerations of use to teachers and designers in creating communities of inquiry: (1) cultivating a social identity of a collective enterprise, (2) attending to communal knowledge spaces, (3) framing social interactions using multiplayer epistemic games, and (4) supporting metalevel reflections on the community inquiry. Although presented in a linear fashion, in practice these elements tend to be interdependent and mutually supportive.

The chapter is premised on the idea that teachers and designers may need such support because of traditional schooling's emphasis on individual knowledge and performance. Schooling's focus on the individual also points to a need to attend to students' comfort in shifting to a community of inquiry approach. A shift to working together with one's peers, sharing ideas and artifacts of inquiry in a public manner, and reflecting on "our collective inquiry" may be challenging to students who have been socialized into traditional forms of schooling. For example, Lampert and her colleagues (Lampert, Rittenhouse, & Crumbaugh, 1996) describe how creating a mathematics learning community in a fifth-grade classroom led to student discomfort in engaging in mathematical argumentation with community members. Several students described their difficulties with the shift, with one student saying:

> it can get sort of embarrassing at times, because like everybody else, like you say something and everybody will raise their hand and want to say something different or they all disagree with you. And it makes you sort of feel like you want to crawl into a hole and die.
>
> *(p. 742)*

Similar worries concerning the public visibility of one's work have been raised by students in knowledge-building classrooms (Bielaczyc, 2013, 2018). Researchers have explored strategies for supporting students in making such transitions, such as forms of anonymity in publicly shared work (Davis, 2005, 2007), teacher guidance and modeling (Herrenkohl & Mertl, 2011), and implementation paths that provide phased approaches to transitioning into collective inquiry work (Bielaczyc, 2013; Bielaczyc & Ow, 2014). Given how students have been socialized into "right answer approaches" and a focus on individual work, such transition challenges are understandable, and not insurmountable, but do require attention and care.

A related area concerns attending to the linguistic and cultural strengths of individual students within the collective. It is important that a collective approach not lead to the exclusion of individual participants or mask the individual strengths that each student brings to the inquiry. As noted by Warren and Rosebery (2011):

> diverse points of view, histories, meanings, and sense-making practices come into contact in real time as students and teachers navigate academic subject matter, and likewise understanding that this navigation inevitably takes place at powered boundaries of culture, race, class, and language.... These boundaries are powered because they are governed by "the settled expectations of Whites" (Harris, 1993/1995, p. 1731) regarding what counts as knowing and who counts as knowledgeable (Martin, 2009). Through these expectations, certain meanings and certain practices—certain ways of knowing, seeing, speaking, writing, acting, valuing—are privileged over others, in society as in school.
>
> *(p. 99)*

Diversity should be a strength of communities of inquiry, but because certain views and normative approaches are privileged, it is critical to attend to means for navigating interculturality (Bang, Warren, Rosebery, & Medin, 2012; Warren & Rosebery, 2011). Teachers and students need to become familiar with, deeply understand, and value the sense-making resources that learners from ethnically, culturally, and linguistically diverse backgrounds contribute to the work of the collective. Recognition, understanding, and valuing of diverse sense-making resources among classroom members may increase validation and, in turn, participation across "powered boundaries of culture, race, class, and language" and lead to powerful co-constructed meanings and practices.

Notes

1 Please refer to ikit.org.
2 Equivalent to Grades 3 and 4 in U.S. classrooms.
3 Quote adapted from Bereiter (2002).

References

Aronson, E. (1978). *The jigsaw classroom*. Beverly Hills, CA: Sage.

Bang, M., Warren, B., Rosebery, A. S., & Medin, D. (2012). De-settling expectations in science education. *Human Development*, *55*(5), 243–358. https://doi.org/10.1159/000345322

Barab, S. A., Hay, K. E., Barnett, M., & Keating, T. (2000). Virtual solar system project: Building understanding through model building. *Journal of Research in Science Teaching*, *37*(7), 719–756. https://doi.org/10.1002/1098-2736(200009)37:7<719::AID-TEA6>3.0.CO;2-V

Bereiter, C. (2005/2006). Design research: The way forward. *Education Canada*, *46*(1), 16–19.

Bielaczyc, K. (2006). Designing social infrastructure: Critical issues in creating learning environments with technology. *Journal of the Learning Sciences*, *15*(3), 301–329. https://doi.org/10.1207/s15327809jls1503_1

Bielaczyc, K. (2013). Informing design research: Learning from teachers' designs of social infrastructure. *Journal of the Learning Sciences*, *22*(2), 258–311. https://doi.org/10.1080/10508406.2012.691925

Bielaczyc, K. (2018). Learning from the knowledge builders: Students making sense of the change to a classroom knowledge building community. Paper presented at *Knowledge Building Summer Institute*, University of Toronto, Canada.

Bielaczyc, K., & Kapur, M. (2010). Playing epistemic games in science and mathematics classrooms. *Journal of Educational Technology*, *50*(5), 19–25

Bielaczyc, K., & Ow, J. (2014). Multi-player epistemic games: Guiding the enactment of classroom knowledge building communities. *Journal of Computer-Supported Collaborative Learning*, *9*(1), 33–62. https://doi.org/10.1007/s11412-013-9186-z

Bielaczyc, K., Paik, S., & Ow, J. (2012). Investigating teacher change in creating classroom knowledge building communities. Poster presented at *International Conference of the Learning Sciences*, Sydney, Australia.

Borge, M., Ong, Y. S., & Rosé, C. P. (2018). Learning to monitor and regulate collective thinking processes. *Journal of Computer-Supported Collaborative Learning*, *13*(1), 61–92. https://doi.org/10.1007/s11412-018-9270-5

Borge, M., & Shimoda, T. (2019). Designing a computer-supported-collective regulation system: A theoretically informed approach. *Technology, Instruction, Cognition, & Learning*, *11*(2), 193–217.

Brown, A. (1987). Metacognition, executive control, self-regulation, and other more mysterious mechanisms. In F. E. Weinert & R. H. Kluwe (Eds.), *Metacognition, motivation, and understanding* (pp. 65–116). Hillsdale, NJ: Lawrence Erlbaum.

Brown, A. L., & Campione, J. C. (1994). Guided discovery in a community of learners. In K. McGilley (Ed.), *Classroom lessons: Integrating cognitive theory and classroom practice* (pp. 229–270). Cambridge, MA: MIT Press/Bradford Books.

Brown, J. S., & Duguid, P. (2000). *The social life of information*. Cambridge, MA: Harvard Business School Press.

Burtis, J. (1998). Analytic toolkit for knowledge forum. Toronto: The Ontario Institute for Studies in Education, University of Toronto.

Chan, C. K. K., & van Aalst, J. (2018). Knowledge building: Theory, design, and analysis. In F. Fischer, C. E. Hmelo-Silver, S. R. Goldman, & P. Reimann (Eds.), *International handbook of the learning sciences* (pp. 295–307). New York: Routledge. https://doi.org/10.4324/9781315617572-29

Collins, A., & Ferguson, W. (1993). Epistemic forms and epistemic games: Structures and strategies for guiding inquiry. *Educational Psychologist*, *28*(1), 25–42. https://doi.org/10.1207/s15326985ep2801_3

Collins, A., Neville, P., & Bielaczyc, K. (2000). The role of different media in designing learning environments. *International Journal of Artificial Intelligence in Education*, *11*, 144–162.

Davis, S. M. (2005). What's in a name? Students' use of anonymity within next-generation classroom networks. Doctoral dissertation, University of Texas at Austin.

Davis, S. M. (2007). Impact of anonymity of input in next-generation classroom networks. In C. A. Chinn, G. Erkens, & S. Puntambekar (Eds.), *Proceedings of the 7th International Computer Supported Collaborative Learning (CSCL) 2007*, Part 1 (pp. 162–164). NJ. https://doi.org/10.3115/1599600.1599631

Davis, S. M. (2009). Generative activities: Making sense of 1098 functions. In R. Lesh, P. L. Galbraith, C. R. Haines, & A. Hurford (Eds.), *Modeling students' mathematical modeling competencies ICTMA 13* (pp. 189–200). New York: Springer. https://doi.org/10.1007/978-1-4419-0561-1_16

Davis, S. M., & Brady, C. (2010). *GenSing visualizer.* Singapore: Learning Sciences Lab, National Institute Education.
Davis, S. M., & Effendi, D. (2010a). *GenSing spiral viewer.* Singapore: Learning Sciences Lab, National Institute Education.
Davis, S. M., & Effendi, D. (2010b). *GenSing wave visualizer.* Singapore: Learning Sciences Lab, National Institute Education.
Edelson, D. C., & Reiser, B. J. (2006). Making authentic practices accessible to learners: Design challenges and strategies. In R. K. Sawyer (Ed.), *The Cambridge handbook of the learning sciences* (pp. 335–354). New York: Cambridge University Press. https://doi.org/10.1017/CBO9780511816833.021
Engle, R. A., & Conant, F. R. (2002). Guiding principles for fostering productive disciplinary engagement: Explaining an emergent argument in a community of learners classroom. *Cognition and Instruction, 20*(4), 399–483. https://doi.org/10.1207/S1532690XCI2004_1
Enyedy, N. (2003). Designing for the intersection of culture and cognition: How different forms of talk, distributed across different social configurations, interact to shape conceptual and community development in a computer-mediated mathematics classroom. *Journal of the Learning Sciences, 12*(3), 361–407. https://doi.org/10.1207/S15327809JLS1203_2
Ford, M. J. (2010). Critique in academic disciplines and active learning of academic content. *Cambridge Journal of Education, 40*(3), 265–280. https://doi.org/10.1080/0305764X.2010.502885
Gresalfi, M., & Cobb, P. (2006). Cultivating students' discipline-specific dispositions as a critical goal for pedagogy and equity. *Pedagogies, 1,* 49–58. https://doi.org/10.1207/s15544818ped0101_8
Grossman, P., Wineburg, S., & Woolworth, S. (2001). Toward a theory of teacher community. *The Teachers College Record, 103,* 942–1012. https://doi.org/10.1111/0161-4681.00140
Hall, R., & Rubin, A. (1998). There's five little notches in here: Dilemmas in teaching and learning the conventional structure of rate. In J. Greeno & S. Goldman (Eds.), *Thinking practices in mathematics and science learning* (pp. 189–235). Mahwah, NJ: Lawrence Erlbaum.
Hennessey, G. (2003). Metacognitive aspects of students' reflective discourse: Implications for intentional conceptual change teaching and learning. In G. M. Sinatra & P. R. Pintrich (Eds.), *Intentional conceptual change* (pp. 103–132). Mahwah, NJ: Lawrence Erlbaum.
Herrenkohl, L. R., & Guerra, M. R. (1998). Participant structures, scientific discourse, and student engagement in fourth grade. *Cognition and Instruction, 16*(4), 433–475. https://doi.org/10.1207/s1532690xci1604_3
Herrenkohl, L. R., & Mertl, V. (2010). *How students come to be, know, and do: A case for a broad view of learning.* New York: Cambridge University Press. https://doi.org/10.1017/CBO9780511777608
Herrenkohl, L. R., Palincsar, A. S., DeWater, L. S., & Kawasaki, K. (1999). Developing scientific communities in classrooms: A sociocognitive approach. *Journal of the Learning Sciences, 8*(3), 451–493. https://doi.org/10.1207/s15327809jls0803&4_4
Hmelo-Silver, C. E., & Barrows, H. S. (2008). Facilitating collaborative knowledge building. *Cognition and Instruction, 26,* 48–94. https://doi.org/10.1080/07370000701798495
Hogan, K., & Corey, C. (2001). Viewing classrooms as cultural contexts for fostering scientific literacy. *Anthropology & Education Quarterly, 32*(2), 214–243. https://doi.org/10.1525/aeq.2001.32.2.214
Kapur, M., & Bielaczyc, K. (2012). Designing for productive failure. *Journal of the Learning Sciences, 21*(1), 45–83. https://doi.org/10.1080/10508406.2011.591717
Krugman, P. (1991). *Geography and trade.* Cambridge, MA: MIT Press.
Lampert, M., Rittenhouse, P., & Crumbaugh, C. (1996). Agreeing to disagree: Developing sociable mathematical discourse. In D. Olson & N. Torrance (Eds.), *Handbook of education and human development* (pp. 731–764). Oxford: Blackwell's Press.
Lee, E. Y. C., Chan, C. K. K., & van Aalst, J. (2006). Students assessing their own collaborative knowledge building. *International Journal of Computer-Supported Collaborative Learning, 1*(1), 57–87. https://doi.org/10.1007/s11412-006-6844-4
Lehrer, R., Schauble, L., & Lucas, D. (2008). Supporting development of the epistemology of inquiry. *Cognitive Development, 23*(4), 512–529. https://doi.org/10.1016/j.cogdev.2008.09.001
Matsuzawa, Y., Oshima, J., Oshima, R., Niihara, Y., & Sakai, S. (2011). KBDeX: A platform for exploring discourse in collaborative learning. *Procedia-Social and Behavioral Sciences, 26,* 198–207. https://doi.org/10.1016/j.sbspro.2011.10.576
Oshima, J., Oshima, R., & Matsuzawa, Y. (2012). Knowledge building discourse explorer: A social network analysis application for knowledge building discourse. *Educational Technology Research & Development, 60,* 903–921. https://doi.org/10.1007/s11423-012-9265-2
Perkins, D. (1997) Epistemic games. *International Journal of Educational Research, 27*(1), 49–61. https://doi.org/10.1016/S0883-0355(97)88443-1

Resendes, M. (2014). Enhancing knowledge building discourse in early primary education: Effects of formative feedback. Doctoral dissertation, University of Toronto.

Resendes, M., Scardamalia, M., Bereiter, C., Chen, B., & Halewood, C. (2015). Group-level formative feedback and metadiscourse. *International Journal of Computer-Supported Collaborative Learning, 10*(3), 309–336. https://doi.org/10.1007/s11412-015-9219-x

Resnick, M., Maloney, J., Monroy-Hernández, A., Rusk, N., Eastmond, E., Brennan, K., Millner, A., Rosenbaum, E., Silver, J., Silverman, B., & Kafai, Y. (2009). Scratch: Programming for all. *Communications of the ACM, 52*(11), 60–67. https://doi.org/10.1145/1592761.1592779

Roque, R, Rusk, N., & Resnick, M. (2016). Supporting diverse and creative collaboration in the Scratch online community. In U. Cress, H. Jeong, & J. Moskaliuk (Eds.), *Mass collaboration and education* (pp. 241–256). Switzerland: Springer International. https://doi.org/10.1007/978-3-319-13536-6_12

Ritchhart, R., Church, M., & Morrison, K. (2011). *Making thinking visible: How to promote engagement, understanding, and independence for all learners.* San Francisco, CA: Jossey-Bass.

Rogers, J., Morrell, E., & Enyedy, N. (2007). Studying the struggle: Contexts for learning and identity development for urban youth. *American Behavioral Scientist, 51*(3), 419–443. https://doi.org/10.1177/0002764207306069

Sagan, C. (1980). *Cosmos.* New York: Ballantine.

Sandoval, W. A., Bell, P., Coleman, E., Enyedy, N., & Suthers, D. (2000, April). Designing knowledge representations for learning epistemic practices of science. Paper presented at the *Annual Conference of the American Educational Research Association*, New Orleans, US.

Scardamalia, M. (2002). Collective cognitive responsibility for the advancement of knowledge. In B. Smith (Ed.), *Liberal education in the knowledge society* (pp. 67–98). Chicago, IL: Open Court.

Scardamalia, M. (2004). CSILE/Knowledge Forum®. In A. Kovalchick and K. Dawson (Eds.)
Education and technology: An encyclopedia (pp. 183–192). Santa Barbara: ABC-CLIO.

Scardamalia, M., & Bereiter, C. (2006). Knowledge building: Theory, pedagogy and technology. In R. K. Sawyer (Ed.), *Cambridge handbook of the learning sciences* (pp. 97–115). Cambridge: Cambridge University Press. https://doi.org/10.1017/CBO9780511816833.008

Stroup, W. M., Ares, N. M., & Hurford, A. C. (2005). A dialectic analysis of generativity: Issues of network supported design in mathematics and science. *Mathematical Thinking and Learning,* 7(3), 181–206. https://doi.org/10.1207/s15327833mtl0703_1

Tao, D., & Zhang, J. (2018). Forming shared inquiry structures to support knowledge building in a Grade 5 community. *Instructional Science, 46*(4), 563–592.

Tao, D., Zhang, J., & Gao, D. (2017). Reflective structuration of knowledge building practices in Grade 5 science: A two-year design-based research. In B. K. Smith, M. Borge, E. Mercier, & K. Y. Lim (Eds.), *Making a difference: Prioritizing equity and access in CSCL, 12th international conference on computer supported collaborative learning (CSCL) 2017* (Vol. 2). Philadelphia, PA.

Warren, B., Ballenger, C., Ogonowski, M., Rosebery, A. S., &Hudicourt-Barnes, J. (2001). Re-thinking diversity in learning science: The logic of everyday sense-making. *Journal of Research on Science Teaching, 38*(5), 529–552. https://doi.org/10.1002/tea.1017

Warren, B., & Rosebery, A. (2011). Navigating interculturality: African American male students and the science classroom. *Journal of African American Males in Education, 2*(1), 98–115.

Wells, G. (2000). Dialogic inquiry in education. In C. Lee & P. Smagorinsky (Eds.), *Vygotskian perspectives on literacy research* (pp. 51–84). Cambridge, MA: Cambridge University Press.

Zhang, J., Scardamalia, M., Lamon, M., Messina, R., & Reeve, R. (2007). Socio-cognitive dynamics of knowledge building in the work of nine- and ten-year-olds. *Educational Technology Research and Development (ETR&D), 55*(2), 117–145. https://doi.org/10.1007/s11423-006-9019-0

Zhang, J., Tao, D., Chen, M-H., Sun, Y., Judson, D., & Naqvi, S. (2018). Co-organizing the collective journey of inquiry with Idea Thread Mapper. *Journal of the Learning Sciences, 27*(3), 390–430. https://doi.org/10.1080/10508406.2018.1444992

SECTION 3

Inquiry and Learning across Disciplines and Contexts

16
INQUIRY AND LEARNING IN LITERATURE

Carol D. Lee

Reading comprehension is particularly challenging because it entails a form of ill-structured problem solving (Simon, 1977; Hatano & Inagaki, 1986). This is because the demands of comprehension will differ substantively by the nature of the text, the goals, motivations and resources the learner brings, the nature of the task to be addressed through reading, and the resources available in the contexts in which the reading occurs (Goldman & Lee, 2014; Valencia et al., 2014). Standards and pedagogical strategies for reading comprehension highlight generic reasoning processes (e.g., asking questions, making predictions, making connections). However, this multidimensional system coordinating text, reader, task, and context means that it is challenging, especially for novice readers, to determine which such generic processes should be invoked and when. The demands of texts also differ by genre (e.g., informational versus narrative), but equally important within these broad genre categories differ substantively within disciplines (e.g., reading in history, in science, in mathematics, and in literary studies) (Goldman et al., 2016). This chapter focuses explicitly on the demands of comprehending and interpreting literature and the role of inquiry in such learning. The problem space of necessity includes the resources readers bring, the demands of literary texts including generative tasks, and the features of robust learning environments that facilitate learning and the disposition to engage in such problem solving. I define inquiry as pedagogical practices that support learners over time in designing and carrying out investigations of ill-structured problems with decreasing direct supports from teachers.

Literary Reasoning

Literature examines the dilemmas of being human (Van Peer, 1991; Lee, 2011). Archetypal themes include human dilemmas that persist across time and space (Hogan 1997) (good versus evil, coming of age, courageous action) and prototypical kinds of people (the mythic hero, the tragic hero, the trickster) with whom we interact and observe. The targets of interrogating literary texts are not about pre-determined right or wrong answers. Ideally, we examine literature to extrapolate lessons about the self and the human condition, interrogate the structural and rhetorical choices authors make and how such choices convey meaning, to make connections across texts (literary and non-literary) and to position texts within particular literary, historical, ideological, and philosophical systems (Hillocks, 2016; Rabinowitz, 1987). In literary inquiry, the claims made are likely to fall into one or more of these comprehension targets and the criteria for what constitutes warrantable evidence are wide ranging. Warrants to support evidence for claims may come from the reader's personal experiences or belief systems, may be informed by particular literary traditions, or by shared norms by a particular community of readers. Claims that readers make are substantiated by the nature of evidence and warrants on which they draw. Traditions of literary criticism warrant the salience of particular kinds of evidence. For example, New Criticism privileges the text, while other traditions privilege orientations that the reader brings either as an individual (reader response) or the reader as a member of a particular community (Black Aesthetic, Marxist, Feminist). Literary reasoning privileges such diversity in modes of reasoning and targets of human meaning-making across time and space. This has implications for how we conceptualize trajectories of learning across K-12 education. Implications include, among others: How do we take into account the developmental niche of students in terms of readiness to wrestle with human conundrums? How do we decide on the range of national traditions from which to draw literary texts for the curriculum? When do we introduce the range of traditions of literary criticism? We can identify categories of requisite prior knowledge that serve as generative resources for interpreting literary works: narrative text structures, figuration, and social and ethical knowledge.

Regardless of the targets for comprehension, attention to text structure is important. In the reading comprehension literature, the ability to detect text structure serves as a resource for the reader to make predictions about the logical relations among propositions in a text. With informational texts, complexities of text structure include whether there is a single text structure or multiple text structures (cause-effect, problem-solution, sequence, etc.) and whether the indicators of text structure are explicit (e.g., use of words like because, if-then, next) or implied. Even though this conception of text structure is generic, it applies to texts in history, science, and mathematics, for example. Text structure in literature, however, is different. We can think of text structures in literature as more akin to the idea of genres. Literary genres include romance, tragedy, the Western, fables, magical realism, among others. There is common-sense evidence of the predictive power of these literary genres. For example, if a movie is advertised with symbolic images of a Western, we go to the theater with expectations about the kinds of people we will meet and the kinds of challenges that will unfold. In addition to recognizing the indicators of literary genres, knowledge of prototypical character types is equally generative (mythic hero, tragic hero, trickster).

Such genres are presented in prose, poetry, or plays. But there are common practices that support meaning-making with poems (e.g., the function of the final couplet in sonnets) and plays (use of soliloquy, etc.). While literature anthologies in middle and high school, especially in freshman-level classes, highlight what are purported distinctions between novels, short stories, plays, and poetry, these distinctions are not actually powerful levers for meaning-making for novice readers.

A second category of requisite knowledge is about how readers conceptualize themes. Themes may be local to the text as well as broader extrapolations to the world outside the text. Readers explicitly and implicitly activate criteria for what constitutes evidence of a particular theme (criteria for distinguishing good versus evil, for what constitutes good parenting). Such criteria derive from experience in the world, from prior reading history, from the social networks in which reading unfolds (which can be formal classrooms as well as communities of readers, such as the community of readers of *Harry Potter* novels or book clubs).

A third category of requisite knowledge involves techniques that writers create to invite the reader into the world of the text and to focus the reader's attention. Many of these techniques are inherited across literary and national traditions. These include structural forms like inverted chronologies, shifts in point of view, use of metaphor, symbolism, and irony. Others are uniquely created by particular writers, often inspiring new writing traditions (e.g., free verse). The most complex exemplars of literary reasoning invite an epistemological orientation that privileges complexity, multiple points of view, personal relevance, multiple readings, and attention to structure and language.

Resources of the Reader

As noted, current research in reading comprehension conceptualizes the problem space as including the reader, text, task, and context. Reading comprehension works as a form of ill-structured problem solving where the solution pathways are not straightforward and simply pre determined. With this framing, we need to conceptualize the resources that readers bring to wrestling with literary texts. For the purposes of this chapter we consider students in grades 6–12 because there are developmental considerations around the kinds of texts that younger children typically read and the psychosocial resources they are more likely to bring. While the kinds of texts and tasks become increasingly more complex across the grades, the curriculum in grades 6–12 unfolds more closely connected. There are certainly texts that middle-school students typically are asked to read that they may meet again in high school (e.g., *To Kill a Mockingbird*) (Wolf, 1995).

Resources readers bring are multidimensional and come both from individual attributes and experiences and from resources and repertoires from social networks in which the reader is routinely engaged. Repertoires include the stock of routine practices, epistemic dispositions, and ways of using language that people develop as a consequence of their participation in routine cultural practices. As we engage new experiences in the world, we typically recruit from such repertoires we have developed over time as resources for tackling new problems. Individual attributes include knowledge with regard to literary text structures, linguistic repertoires particularly with regard to figuration (Lee, 1995a, 1995b), dispositions around uncertainty and probabilistic reasoning (Chinn et al., 2011), and knowledge about the social world embodied in texts (Hynds, 1989). What we might think of as community resources include shared practices and beliefs around narrative (Bruner, 1990), where narrative texts include music lyrics, visual texts such as movies, oral storytelling genres, and around language use (e.g., attention to figuration, to story structure). For example, Heath (1983) documented differences in how a southern white working-class community and southern African American community valued and socialized how children were encouraged to tell stories. Figuration, rhetorical creativity, and issues of point of view were valued in the African American community, whereas literal narratives were valued in the white working-class community.

In addition to text and linguistic knowledge, readers bring both phenomenological and epistemological orientations that are relevant to dispositions that may be taken up in acts of reading. In terms of phenomenological orientations, the readers' perceptions of themselves in terms of efficacy (the ability to carry out the task), relevance (does the work entailed in interrogating the literary text fulfill some ego-focused goals?), the task (is the goal to get a grade or to interrogate one's self?), and the setting (is it safe to expose one's frailties and uncertainties?), all matter (Maslow, 1954; Dweck, 1999; Spencer, 2006). In terms of epistemological orientations, does the reader value both content and structure, multiple possible explanations of phenomenon encountered during reading, imagining entering the subjunctive fictional world of the literary text (Hart, 2001; Galda & Liang, 2003; Chinn et al., 2011)? These resources that readers bring to instructional settings matter and need to be considered in the design of instruction in ways that invite and support inquiry. However, these reader resources are typically not highlighted in commercial literature curriculum and literature anthologies used in grades 6–12 (Applebee et al., 2000). Equally important, they are not easily subject to measurement in schools, although I will illustrate a longitudinal study in which these factors were measured and taken up in the design of instruction.

There is no question that generic reading skills are an important part of the resources that readers bring (Snow et al., 1998). However, the most common ways in which such skills are considered in instruction are not as simply predictive as often assumed. First, the most competent reader in terms of generic skills (e.g., decoding, vocabulary, syntactic) can meet a text he or she doesn't understand, even with effort. For example, most people wrestle with technical legal and medical documents or texts in disciplines to which they bring little relevant prior knowledge. The Educational Testing Service (Shore et al., 2017), for example, has designed a reading test which includes measures of prior knowledge and its correlates to comprehension of related texts. With literature, in particular, there are texts that are relatively simple in terms of standard reading-level measures but entail complex problems of figuration, thematic abstractions, and character development such that generic reading skills alone do not predict their complexity (Lee & Goldman, 2015). For example, Alice Walker's story "The Flowers" is 561 words with a Flesch-Kincaid reading level of 5.5 (using the old Lexile grade levels, but with new Common Core would be considered appropriate for 3rd graders). However, the patterns of parallelism, disjunctures, and allusions are quite complex. On the other hand, a novel like Steinbeck's *The Grapes of Wrath* has a lexile level of 680 (roughly sixth grade using old Lexile levels and roughly 3rd grade with new Common Core transformations). One can imagine students with reading scores at or above grade level still wrestling with the problems of the novel, while others who read just below the fifth-grade level whose families are migrant workers may well bring prior knowledge that makes the themes of the text more accessible than their counterparts with somewhat higher reading-level scores but whose life experiences are far afield from the themes of the text. The point here is that the resources the reader brings are complex and multidimensional and in the end not deterministic. The pedagogical question is how those who design instruction (commercial curriculum designers, teachers, school communities) conceptualize the demands of literary reading, at what particular point in the life course of students instruction takes place (Eccles et al., 1993; Damon & Lerner, 2008), and the relevant resources that students as readers bring to the work.

Pedagogical Implications for Inquiry-Focused Instruction with Literature

I should begin by defining what I mean by inquiry instruction. This handbook focuses on inquiry that supports learning content as well as inquiry that socializes epistemological dispositions with regard to complex reasoning. The literature on epistemology is mixed with regard to the question of whether an epistemological disposition valuing complexity transfers across contexts and tasks (Hofer, 2000). For example, even if I have a general disposition to value complexity, this does not mean I can address a complex problem about economic investments. It may be that even though I generally value complexity, I do not wish to invest time and effort into thinking systematically about this problem. In addition, the epistemological demands of reasoning within disciplines differ substantively (Goldman et al., 2016; Lee et al., 2016). For example, the disposition to value examining multiple primary-source documents to interrogate a historical phenomenon is not a requisite for examining literature. At one level one may think of content learning with regard to literature as coming to know the plot, perhaps historical background information around the author or the writing, and production of the text (e.g., understanding *The Scarlet Letter* in its historical context of 17th-century Salem). There is no question that a good deal of instruction in grades 6–12 focuses on such goals. It is also possible that students can be engaged in inquiry-related practices (e.g., annotations, using graphic organizers, collaborative discussions) aimed at such content-focused goals (Greenleaf et al., 2007). However, the focus of this chapter is on inquiry-based tasks that support wrestling with relationships between content and structure, with constructing arguments in which claims are supported with evidence from the text content, but equally importantly, with warrants and backings rooted in disciplinary claims (often rooted in an array of traditions of literary criticism) about implications of structure and language (Toulmin et al., 1984; Scholes, 1985; Lee, 2011; Hillocks, 2016). I will illustrate such complex inquiry with an example from work conducted in the Cultural Modeling Project (Lee, 2016):

> In two versions of this unit—one 8th grade and one 12th grade—students were supported in interrogating the short story "Damballah" by John Edgar Wideman. It is a complex story about a character named Orion during the African Holocaust of Enslavement who

> symbolically resists the de-humanization of slavery and in so doing provides an example for a boy on the plantation. Students were supported in investigating the following: the significance of the title, of the main character's name and names, of the differentiated narrative points of view in the text, of the symbolism of characters and actions in the story, and potential symbolic import of Orion as a messianic figure. With the supports outlined below of robust learning environments, qualitative analyses of classroom discourse and pre-post assessments of these comprehension targets, students showed evidence of learning.

This kind of reasoning distinguishes novice from expert readers of literature where expert readers are not simply professional critics but people who read widely and deeply (Zeitz, 1994; Peskin, 1998). In fact, this attention to relations of content, structure, and language is also taken up in other expert-like communities around non-text-based narratives, such as communities of those who listen widely to hip hop music or aficionados of film noir.

Robust learning environments are designed to address the following (Nasir et al., 2006; Lee, 2017b):

- Position the learner as competent
- Anticipate sources of vulnerability
- Examine and scaffold resources the learner brings
- Make public the social good and utility
- Make problem solving explicit and public
- Provide supports as learners are engaged in complex problem solving
- Provide expansive opportunities
- Remain adaptive and dynamic

To design for such goals requires deep knowledge of the cognitive, social, and emotional demands of complex learning in ways that are specific to disciplines. I will seek to illustrate these demands with respect to inquiry engaging literary texts.

Knowledge Required to Design Robust Learning Environments for Inquiry in Literary Reasoning

That new learning builds on prior knowledge is well established in cognitive psychology (Anderson & Pearson, 1988; McNamara & Kintsch, 1996; Bransford et al., 1999). A central question around new learning involves understanding relationships between existing schemas and the targets of new learning. Research on conceptual change has shown that if tensions and contradictions between existing schema and new targets of learning are not addressed in how people learn, the contradictory concepts can be maintained in long-term memory (diSessa & Sherin, 1998). For example, a study of college engineering students documented how despite learning in physics classes about multiple forces acting on falling objects, these students continued to hold on to the belief that gravity was the only force acting on falling objects (diSessa, 1982). diSessa argues that growth in conceptual knowledge involves expanding one's understandings of relationships among factors embedded in the target concept and understanding relationships among relevant concepts. For example, understanding relationships between structural and rhetorical choices made by authors as windows into particular literary constructs reflects relational conceptual knowledge. For example, in the short story "Damballah" recognizing that titles are important alone is not sufficient, but knowing that associations one might make with a title (both inside the text and outside) may be a segue into a symbolic meaning reflects relational conceptual knowledge. It's not just pieces of knowledge, but how they fit together that is most generative.

One particular affordance for literary reasoning is that it embodies reasoning endemic to the human species: narrative. Literature is a specialized form of narrative. We know from our evolutionary history that humans are pre-disposed to produce narratives as a way of making sense of experience in the world (Mandler, 1987; Bruner, 1990; Sugiyama, 2001). Over cultural-historical time, humans have come to produce narratives in an array of embodiments (e.g., oral storytelling, written texts from both non-alphabetic graphic representations to how we think of written texts today, in visual forms like visual arts as well as film). Across embodiments, narratives entail agents with internal states and goals that drive actions in which they engage and actions that bear some chronological and logical set of relations and often some thematic abstraction or takeaway around the significance of the story (Trabasso et al., 1983; Trabasso & Sperry, 1985). Research shows that even very young children have an intuitive sense of narrative or what is called story grammar (Applebee, 1978). The diversity of narrative genres, goals for their use, and the ways in which the young and old are socialized to engage in the narrative sense-making of their communities and social networks are vast. And the social processes through which narrative traditions change and evolve are also complex, informative, and interesting (Champion et al., 1995; Heath, 2001).

I raise this framing as a universal but diverse human practice for several reasons. It certainly suggests that understanding the narrative sense-making practices and traditions in which students as novice readers engage outside of formal schooling is a useful resource to examine when conceptualizing robust pedagogical practices of inquiry to support literary reasoning. However, how both common sense and scientific knowledge are taken up in the public arena and by extension taken up in public institutions, such as public schooling, is influenced by societal ideological beliefs. In the U.S. and much of the Western world, there is a historical metanarrative about human hierarchies where people of color and people from lower economic statuses are viewed as having fewer intellective resources (Gould, 1981). Such deficit belief systems around literacy instruction in schools have demonized the language practices of those who are seen as the other. Historically in the U.S. these have included speakers of African American English and speakers whose first language is other than English (Farr, 1991; Wolfram et al., 1999; Lee, 2005a). There is a long and arduous history around deficit attributions to African American English as inhibiting students' abilities to learn to read and write and efforts to see a major goal of education to get rid of non-English-speaking students' first language (Ball & Farr, 2003; Gándara et al., 2004; August & Shanahan, 2006). During the late 1960s and 1970s, literacy researchers developed what were called dialect readers for speakers of African American English amid arguments that AAE dialect interfered with children learning to decode and what came to be called Direct Instruction developed with a heavy focus on decoding at the expense of comprehension instruction, a practice that continues today in many early reading programs aimed at African American and children of the poor (Bereiter & Engelmann, 1966). The idea of dialect interference was debunked (Piestrup, 1973; Rickford & Rickford, 1995). With regard to students whose first language is other than English, studies have gone on to document the ways that linguistic repertoires in the first language actually facilitate reasoning and reading in the second language (Langer et al., 1990; Jimenez et al., 1995; Carlson & Meltzoff, 2008). This of course is connected to many factors, including whether the child learned to read in the first language and linguistic relations between the two languages. I raise these issues because they remain a major influence on how educators and literacy researchers are able to conceptualize what intellective resources particular groups of students bring and what to make of such resources as supports for inquiry in literary reasoning.

Because literary texts share many features in common with other narrative genres (e.g., music lyrics, narrative films, visual art that tells a story, everyday storytelling traditions), it is not uncommon that students from across diverse communities bring concepts around story structures (Gee, 1989), around language figuration (Smitherman, 1977), around ways of enticing the listener/reader into a subjunctive world (Heath, 1983), as well as epistemological resources around valuing figuration, valuing visualization, manipulating structure, and perceiving telling stories as a way to self-reflect and connect with others (Lee, 2005). These are all forms of knowledge and dispositions that are essential to the enterprise of literary reasoning (Lee, 2011; Goldman et al., 2016).

Another set of factors influencing how prior knowledge is entailed in reading comprehension is the phenomenon of relations between top-down and bottom-up processes. Kintsch (1998) and others have shown how reading comprehension is an outgrowth of dynamic relations between the two processes (Anderson, 2004). Bottom-up processes entail the reader extrapolating directly from the text base while top-down processes entail the reader bringing prior knowledge from outside the text to bear. While these interactive meaning-making processes are embodied in reading any text, the particulars of how they play out will differ substantively by distinct disciplinary traditions around language use, text structure, and concepts routinely drawn upon. I will illustrate these distinctions in a literary text.

The text below is from the second paragraph of the opening of John Edgar Wideman's short story "Damballah."

> He watched the clear water race and ripple and pucker. Where the sun cut through the pine trees and slanted into the water he could see the bottom, see black stones, speckled stones, shining stones whose light came from within. Above a stump at the far edge of the river, clouds of insects hovered. The water was darker there, slower, appeared to stand in deep pools where tangles of root, bush and weed hung over the bank. Orion thought of the eldest priest chalking a design on the floor of the sacred *obi*. Drawing the watery door no living hands could push open, the crossroads where the spirits passed between worlds. His skin was becoming like that in-between place the priest scratched in the dust.

A literary reading will entail bottom-up processes of understanding what is literally in the text and will focus primarily on deriving the content of the text (who are the characters, what do they do). Top-down processes involve the reader bringing knowledge not directly stated in the text, the interpretation of which requires both prior knowledge of that to which the language is referring, but equally importantly, to the potential significance of the language, akin to what Rabinowitz (1987) calls "rules of notice" (what features of language and structure draw our attention) and "rules of signification" (on what reasoning we draw to impute significance or meaning to that which draws our attention). In Table 16.1 below, I illustrate what we would attend to from bottom-up processes and what we might as literary readers attend to from top-down processes.

People engage in similar processes in making sense of everyday texts, "reading" advertisements, music lyrics, movies, and cartoons. In such everyday texts, people draw on intuitive understandings where a literal interpretation is not sufficient. For example, people typically understand the satire of cartoons and the symbolism of images in film, beyond their attention to simply what happened. However, these intuitive understandings are typically not recruited in the teaching of literary reasoning. Ironically, the commercial interests that produce such everyday texts (advertisements we see on tv, songs that make millions of dollars, commercially popular movies) bet on the fact that a general audience is likely able to interpret such tropes. At the same time, there are certainly everyday texts for which some people do not have the requisite knowledge to interpret. One can think of older people listening to rap as one possible example—like me.

The question then is how to make everyday narrative sense-making repertoires public and an object of interrogation in instruction in ways that invite inquiry—inquiry here defined as individual and collective actions (in this case by students and teachers) to examine phenomenon in ways that enable extrapolations of patterns that inform conceptual understanding. In the two earlier examples of interrogating "Damballah," inquiry is focused on students understanding patterns they notice as instances of broader concepts, like symbolism, like archetypal messiah characters. Conceptual understanding is here defined as understanding processes of reasoning to solve problems

Table 16.1 Bottom-up and top-down processes in literary reasoning: "Damballah"

Bottom-up	*Top-down*
There is a man in a river looking at stones at the bottom, tangled roots. He is thinking about a priest.	Orion is a celestial constellation named after the Greek mythic hero/hunter whom Zeus placed as a star in the constellation. Obi originates among the Yoruba of West Africa and represents an orisha or sacred spirit, embodied by the kola nut in West Africa and the coconut in extensions of Yoruba in the African diaspora through religions such as Santeria. The kola nut or coconut as a representation of the Orisha is used to see into the future. This involves a process of actively making real-world associations with salient details of the text, to be used as an evolving database from which the reader can impute symbolic significance to the rich description of the action of bathing in the river.
Content focus	Interpretive focus
Plot—what is happening	What do the tensions (watery door no living hands could push open) and unusual patterns (his skin was becoming like that in-between place the priest scratched in the dust) suggest? What patterns do I see (eldest priest, Obi, root/bush/weed, and the watery door no living hands could push open)? Why is the character named Orion? Posing these particular questions reflects an inquiry process of seeking to attribute a specific category of literary significance (e.g., construct) to details noted by their salience/rules of notice (repeated, unusual, in tension).

that do not simply involve following procedures but also include weighing competing evidence and articulating warrants and backing to support claims. Everyday narrative sense-making repertoires are not always understood in explicit and publicly articulated ways. They are often intuitive, but such intuitive understandings do not mean people cannot engage meaningfully in the practice. At the same time, the more explicit the user's understanding becomes, the greater the likelihood he or she can creatively build on and extend the practice in new ways. This expansion of existing knowledge often entails a restructuring of schemas and connects back to diSessa's (diSessa & Sherin, 1998) argument about conceptual change involving expanding one's understandings of relationships of factors within concepts and relationships across relevant concepts.

Returning to the propositions about what makes learning environments robust, I now turn to several illustrations of pedagogical programs that enable these features by scaffolding students' everyday narrative repertoires (knowledge, linguistic, epistemological, and phenomenological) to support conceptual change in interrogating literary texts. These features include positioning the learner as competent, anticipating sources of vulnerability, making tasks relevant, supporting processes of learning in situ, and recruiting diverse repertoires of knowledge and dispositions that learners bring.

Cultural Modeling

Cultural Modeling (Lee, 1995a, 1995b, 1997, 2007) is an instructional framework to scaffold everyday narrative repertoires to support literary reasoning. Most work has been with middle- and high-school African American students who are speakers of African American English Vernacular. The components of the framework include the following:

- Identifying what are called cultural data sets—everyday narrative texts in which the interpretive problems embodied are similar to those in literary texts targeted in instruction

- Designing and coordinating metacognitive instructional conversations in which students work individually and in groups to identify salient features of the everyday texts that contribute to their understanding of the text
- Creating case studies or gateway activities (Smagorinsky et al., 1987) built on the work of Hillocks (1971, 2007, 2011) where students examine contrastive cases in order to extrapolate criteria on which to make judgments about themes and/or character types
- Extrapolating from the metacognitive instructional conversations and the contrastive case studies heuristics or what Rabinowitz (1987) calls "Rules of Notice" to guide what features of the literary texts draw their attention
- Using heuristic organizers derived from such conversations to guide problem solving while reading
- Addressing what Hillocks (Hillocks & Ludlow, 1984) calls author generalization and structural generalization questions by weighing evidence students have generated from their heuristic organizers in order to construct oral and written formal arguments that include claims, evidence, backing, and warrants.

Units of instruction focus on a generative set of questions that include interrogating a theme (such as coming of age) or character type (e.g., the trickster) along with an interpretive problem (e.g., symbolism, irony, satire, unreliable narration). These instructional targets are considered generative because they are foundational to literary reasoning and relevant regardless of the national tradition (e.g., American Literature, British Literature, African Literature), are taken up regardless of the literary critical theory upon which the reader may draw, and are relevant across genres. To the extent then that students across the grade 6–12 span repeatedly have opportunities to engage inquiry focused on themes, character types, and interpretive problems, they can over time develop conceptually rich dispositions toward literature as a meaningful resource across the lifespan. Themes and character types are selected that offer students opportunities to wrestle with conundrums in their own lives, in the lives of their families, social peer networks, and broader communities, rather than arbitrary choices on which to focus based on curricular content arbitrarily passed on in school curricula.

The selection of texts requires a careful analysis of the complexity demands that include but go beyond readability levels. This includes understanding the ways that structure and language are organized by the author in ways that focus or at least attract attention to details that not only move the plot forward but also help us understand the characters, but often in ways that are not explicit but must be inferred. In order to select cultural data sets drawn from the everyday practices of students, the curriculum designer or teacher must first construct a detailed documentation of the demands of text complexity.

Cultural data sets may include rap songs, tv commercials, clips from films or short films, covers from CDs, works of art—any representation that embodies an interpretive move (e.g., symbolism, irony, satire, unreliable narration) which the teacher/curriculum designer can expect students will already recognize. Metacognitive instructional conversations are student driven but guided by the teacher to identify what are the features of these everyday texts that draw the students' attention and what students think such features convey. These conversations inevitably invite contestations that provoke students into articulating warrants and backings for their claims (e.g., why anybody should believe their evidence makes the case). Students create external representations of their arguments that are available publicly to the class. This issue of creating external representations is an important pedagogical move to support inquiry for several reasons. In disciplines such as mathematics and science, students routinely create external representations of internal meaning-making processes that embody shared disciplinary artifacts that convey processes of reasoning (Schoenfeld, 1987). Outside of written essays, there is not a widely implemented set of practices around creating external representations of internal meaning-making processes in the teaching of literary reasoning in K-12 settings. It is precisely the creation of these external representations that invite inquiry driven by contestations over ideas.

These external representations are then linked to what are called heuristic organizers. They differ from the ways that routine graphic organizers are used in reading instruction in that such graphic organizers routinely ask students for an outcome of comprehension. Heuristic organizers in Cultural Modeling guide students through a process of reasoning. The guidance in these organizers are extrapolations of syntheses of work in literary criticism and literary theorizing that interestingly map on to what students typically already do with everyday narrative texts that involve these same interpretive problems (Lee, 2011). These heuristic organizers also serve as external representations of students' reasoning processes that are now public to the student, to other students, and to the teacher. We have found these external representations as an essential component to support inquiry. Because the problems with which students are wrestling are complex problems for which there are not simple right or wrong answers, it can take time for both students (individually and in groups) and teachers to process the arguments being laid out. When such arguments are only articulated in discussion, they are ephemeral. And it is important to note that the bones of these arguments, embodied in the heuristic organizers, are created while students are reading and not simply after they have finished reading. They are constructed individually but interrogated collectively in small and whole groups and are subject to revision based on feedback loops, loops that demand students are able to support their claims with evidence, backing, and warrants. Figure 16.1 provides an example of a heuristic organizer for symbolism. The headings guide students into the questions they should ask themselves. Their answers will provide both evidence and backing for their claims. Before students use this heuristic organizer, they would have been using another organizer that captures what Rabinowitz (1988) calls rules of notice (e.g., moves that writers use to gain the reader's attention).

Because students will ultimately engage in argumentation around their interpretations of the literary texts, Cultural Modeling draws on research on argumentation from Toulmin and colleagues (Toulmin et al., 1984) and Hillocks (1995, 2011). Toulmin defines arguments as entailing claims, evidence, backing, and warrants. Backing and warrants provide the reasons why someone should believe the evidence. Backing and warrants—in literature—can be both personal and disciplinary. Students may make claims that the flowers in Alice Walker's short story "The Flowers" are symbolic and not simply literal by invoking warrants about their personal associations with flowers as well as disciplinary norms about repetition and parallelism as evidence of a significance beyond

Heuristic Organizer for Symbolism

What I think is symbolic: Image, event, character, action, object, name, places	**What the text says (p. #)**	**Associations I can make with the image, event, character, action, object, name, or place**	**What do the words in the text and the associations I make lead me to think about what the symbol means?**

Figure 16.1 Heuristic organizer for symbolism

the literal. In making arguments around themes and character types, the framework draws on pedagogical strategies developed by Hillocks and colleagues that support students in developing criteria (shared or contested) about how you recognize the embodiment of a theme or character type. For example, Hillocks (2011) has designed contrastive case studies to interrogate criteria for what constitutes courageous action. In one of these, there is a fire in a building on the block. In one case, an ordinary citizen—Joe Blow—goes into the burning house to save someone inside. In the second case, a fireman goes into to save those trapped inside the burning house. Both cases are clearly courageous, but they entail different kinds of courageous action where the contrastive criterion is whether you are trained to carry out the act. These student-developed criteria (shared or contested) are then drawn upon as students interrogate themes and character types within and across texts in the literature unit. These activities (scaffolding through cultural data sets and contrastive cases, engaging in metacognitive instructional conversations, developing and using heuristic organizers) prepare students to wrestle with what Hillocks (Hillocks & Ludlow, 1984) calls author generalizations (e.g., what the reader thinks the text says about the world beyond the text) and structural generalizations (e.g., how does the author's use of language and structure work to convey meaning?) as arguments supported by evidence, backing, and warrants.

I offer Cultural Modeling as an extended example of inquiry-based instruction focused on generative and complex literary reasoning that scaffolds everyday narrative repertoires of students, particularly students from minoritized communities.

Many of the foundational propositions undergirding Cultural Modeling were influenced by my training with Dr. George Hillocks. Hillocks distinguished between declarative knowledge (e.g., knowing that) and procedural knowledge (e.g., knowing how). He explored the pedagogical implications of this distinction particularly in the field of written composition but also in his conception of what he called gateway activities used to establish criteria for making judgments. I have incorporated the use of gateway activities but have also expanded this distinction in what I call heuristic organizers, as illustrated in heuristics for detecting symbolism and satire and drawing on similar heuristics developed by Michael Smith for irony and unreliable narration. Several other of Hillocks' former students have built pedagogical models for heuristics to guide students' literary reasoning (Smith, 1989, 1991a, 1991b; Levine & Horton, 2013).

Smith conducted several studies engaging students in inquiry around detecting irony and use of unreliable narrators. These heuristics were built on the work of Wayne Booth (1983). Understanding how literary forms are often represented in everyday narrative genres, Smith used cartoons as illustrations that students examine to extrapolate how they know there is an unreliable narrator. Smith (1991b) found positive transfer of this skill set to a close transfer test. In a similar vein, Levine and Horton (2013) developed heuristics for detecting internal states of character and thematic extrapolations by focusing students' attention to the emotional valence in literary texts. This includes the ways that authors draw the reader's attention by crafting emotionally dense descriptions and actions. Emotions serve a catalytic role in human sense-making, allowing us to distinguish what is unsafe and what is rewarding (Clore & Ortony, 2000; Dai & Sternberg, 2004). Our repertoires for examining emotional valence are central to human functioning and therefore serve as a generative resource. Through several studies, Levine tested this model in middle- and high-school classrooms, with positive transfer to close transfer tasks.

Literary Reasoning as Identity Wrestling

As discussed, a particular strength of literature is its invitation to wrestle with the conundrums of the human experience. Literature that lasts across time, often interrogating what are called archetypal themes, does so precisely because they are works that wrestle with persistent human challenges. How do we understand Raskolnikov in *Crime and Punishment* or Cholly, the father who rapes his daughter in *The Bluest Eye*, or how humans survived holocausts in Toni Morrison's *Beloved* or Anne Frank's *Diary*? It is most unfortunate that these conundrums persist, but great writers, I argue, are like mystics who somehow have the gift of second sight. In the evolution of Cultural Modeling, we have begun to focus conceptually and methodologically more on how supporting students to develop a sense of efficacy in this complex reasoning and a sense of relevance for their lives can be designed for and documented. Such complex reasoning entails the conceptual and epistemological demands of literary reasoning (Lee, 2017a) I have described as well as phenomenological reasoning entailing conceptions of the self along multiple dimensions (personal, racial/ethnic, gender, class; senses of self-efficacy and coping) (Spencer, 2006).

In a recent longitudinal study funded by the Institute of Education Sciences in Project READi (https://www.projectreadi.org), carried out in an urban charter school serving a predominantly low-income African American population, the design intently focused on identity wrestling (Lee, 2016). Wrestling with conceptions of the self is a life-long task, but one especially salient at particular points of life course transition, such as adolescence. For youth placed at risk due to societal structures and stereotypes, identity wrestling, particularly during adolescence, is complex as it involves both the normative tasks of adolescent development and the additional stressors arising from racism and poverty, for example. We sought in this project to support African American adolescents' sense of self-efficacy and positive racial identity through learning to engage in inquiry practices that support literary reasoning, based on the Cultural Modeling Framework. The study included pre-post measures of students' perceptions of instruction, their epistemological orientations toward reading literature, their racial identity, their coping strategies as these correlated with grades and tests of literary reasoning in a close-transfer task designed by the project and far transfer to standardized measures of reading comprehension (Lee, 2016; Lee, Mandara, & Buell, 2016). Overall, we found positive correlations between these identity measures, perceptions of instruction, epistemological orientations, and the reading and, specifically, literary reasoning outcome measure (an assessment of students' abilities to analyze a literary text that embodied the same problems as the unit of instruction but which they had not read in class). One limitation is there is no comparison group, but it is the first study to document the facilitation of identity development specifically through literature instruction that includes empirically established measures of identity, particularly racial identity, epistemology, and coping.

Other Exemplars of Scaffolding Repertoires of Practice Developed out of People's Participation in Routine Cultural Practices

A growing body of research expands the concept of culturally relevant instruction, much situated in literacy research and inquiry. These include what is called culturally humanizing pedagogy (Paris, 2012; Paris & Winn, 2013; Paris & Alim, 2014) and social design experiments (Gutiérrez, 2016; Gutiérrez & Jurow, 2016). Culturally humanizing pedagogy expands our understanding of cultural repertoires to include the understanding that youth participate in multiple communities of practice. Some are inherited across family, ethnicity, and nation. Others are specific to particular moments in cultural historical time, such as current youth culture that is both shared and diverse in this era, expanding in many ways across the globe. For example, Alim et al. (2008) and Alim (2009) have documented hip hop communities in Shanghai and rural China as well as among the Afrikaners in South Africa, all engaging in the creation of narratives as hip hop lyrics and social practices associated with producing, listening to, and sharing the music.

Scaffolding everyday repertoires is one model of inquiry practices. Drawing on everyday repertoires is a powerful model of inquiry as it empowers students to draw on what is often complex tacit knowledge as a resource for meaning-making. While tacit knowledge from observations in the world have been documented in domains of physics and mathematics (Mintzes, 1984; Dunbar et al., 2007), I have argued for exemplars of such knowledge as people engage with narrative genres in the everyday world. Another generative exemplar of inquiry practices in literary reasoning and other domains is the role of creating external representations of internal processes. In mathematics, for example, algorithms and data displays illustrate such external representations. In the teaching of literary reasoning and literacy broadly speaking, three forms of external representations have been documented. These include discussion, writing, and the production of art.

Discussion, Writing, Performance, and Art as External Representations

The power of dialogic discussion has been widely documented to support student learning (Nystrand, 1997; Cazden, 2000; Michaels et al., 2002; Applebee et al., 2003). It is a widely advocated practice in the teaching of literature but still remains a challenge to design and carry out. Among its challenges are how to engage a majority of participants, how students can learn to build off of one another's ideas, and how teachers can understand ideas that emerge in the moment in order to build upon. There are also issues of what language repertoires and norms for interaction will be privileged in classroom discussions and what is opened up and closed off by these considerations. In Cultural Modeling studies, in working with speakers of African American English, we have found that inviting AAE interactional styles draws more students to engage and allows for more diverse ideas to emerge (Lee, 2001, 2006). Similar results have been found with regard to inviting multiple national language and varieties as medium for discussion (Jimenez et al., 1995; Ball & Farr, 2003; Orellana et al., 2003; Valdes et al., 2005; August & Shanahan, 2006). I want to highlight several programs of research that illustrate culturally responsive designs for discussion.

Gutierrez (Gutierrez et al., 1999; Gutiérrez, 2008) offers the construct of the third space, defined as forms of interaction and content focus that emerge when teachers are open to what may appear in the beginning as dissident positions and interests of students, creating a hybrid space that brings the teacher's goals and the students' goals in dialogue. She also includes examples of the third space discussion that brings contested worldviews in dialogue. Discussion as contested territory is not typically the goal of discussion in classrooms, including literature classes, where there is often the goal of leading students toward a preconceived assumption of "the right answer" to questions that the teacher has posed. This is reflected in the well-documented pattern of discussion called IRE where the teacher initiates the questions, students respond, and the teacher then evaluates (Mehan, 1979). The kinds of discussion that Gutierrez documents in the third space are often heavily driven by students who themselves are not seeking to reach consensus. Such dialogue in literature classrooms is particularly impactful and actually most reflective of the broad norms of the discipline because of the very nature of literary texts and tasks. Even studies of expert readers of literature as assumed by the academy (critics, literature professors, etc.) do not agree on the interpretations of texts. In fact, the whole field of literary theorizing and criticism is built on the premise and value of contested readings.

Winn (2010a, 2010b, 2013) has carried out longitudinal ethnographies of youth from minoritized communities living in poverty, and in particular her work with incarcerated girls, in programs designed to support literacy development in tandem with identity wrestling around self-efficacy in light of their circumstances. The students examine texts with themes of resilience, share their own stories of struggle, and create their own written stories. She calls the discussions Restorative Justice Circles and has studied them in incarcerated spaces as well as schools. In a similar vein, San Pedro (Grande et al., 2015), Kinloch (2010), Cammarota and Fine (2010), Morrell (2002), Orellana (2009), and D'Andrade and Morrell (2005) have carried out similar studies of dialogic discussions in the vein of what Gutierrez calls the third space in classrooms and informal spaces, inviting everyday language repertoires and interactional styles as a medium of communication, examining texts—both canonical across national and ethnic traditions and texts from youth's everyday experiences—that summon critical interrogations of the historical and contemporary positioning of power of these youth and their communities. Dialogic discussion where students are empowered contributors, toward goals jointly articulated by students and teachers and in some cases by community members, is foundational to these case illustrations. This family of research programs shares a common set of design principles. They integrate attention to the development of technical skills of comprehension with identity wrestling and social justice action. They consciously expand the range of texts to be interrogated beyond the typical Eurocentric canon promoted by schools in the U.S. to include not only what we might think of as multicultural literary texts but, equally importantly, as texts of political and cultural critical theorizing. Attention to such texts of critical theorizing is an important component of the range of texts that support literary reasoning. Understanding the contexts of a work's production, the historical, cultural, political contexts of the subjunctive world captured by the literary text, and the responses and critiques of others are a common part of the literature curriculum, particularly in high school, but doing so with social justice goals in mind and in ways that interrogate dominant ideologies and power relations is unusual in public schooling.

Writing is well documented as a meaning-making mediational tool to support text comprehension (Applebee, 1984; Tierney et al., 1989). In particular, the construction of arguments—often initially explored through discussion—is a tool of inquiry as it requires the writer to figure out how to gather evidence to support claims and ideally to figure out how to convince others that one's evidence should be believed through the invocation of backing and warrants (Hillocks, 2011). Unless the teacher provides the student with an actual outline of what claims to make and what evidence to present, the act of constructing an argument, especially in written form, positions the writer as an active agent in an inquiry process. In all the programs I have described, students produce written artifacts as external representations of their understandings of texts (typically essays). But they also often ask students to create other imaginative written genres that are an outgrowth of their explorations of identity-related themes embodied in texts they have read and discussions they have had. These genres include students writing original stories, poems, and plays, sometimes individually and sometimes collaboratively. It is common in these programs for student writing to be made public and often performed. With the social justice focus of these programs, student writing as public and performative is intended not simply to motivate students, but equally importantly, to stimulate community building and interrogation of historical and local political and economic power wrestling. I argue that literature plays a foundational role in this body of work because literature most essentially entails interrogations of the conundrums of the human experience through narrative, with narrative sense-making serving as an evolutionary disposition of our species.

Finally, Smagorinsky and colleagues (Smagorinsky et al., 2012; Smagorinsky & O'Donnell, 1998; Smagorinsky, Cameron, & O'Donnell, 2007) have explored artistic production—including multimedia—as a tool to focus students' attention in examining literary works. Students create what they call a body biography, a life-size production that they fill with images that represent their understanding of characters in a literary work. They argue that these body biographies represent external representations of students' thinking, often created through social interactions with one another, and in so doing open up opportunities through inquiry to interrogate one another's thinking. In other studies, they have examined how the act of creating a work of art in the process of interpreting a literary work has facilitated attention and engagement. This body of work conceptualizes the production of art as multimodal artifacts that recruit a broader range of sense-making resources than what are typically recruited by having students' representations of their literary reasoning solely through oral and written language. Much of this work has also been shaped by the proposition that literary reasoning can serve as a medium for identity wrestling, and the production of artistic artifacts beyond the traditional essay opens up new opportunities for how students can engage in inquiry.

Conclusion

I have tried to capture the multidimensional nature of literary reasoning, the complexity of the problem space, and implications for the design of learning environments—in and out of formal schooling—that engage students in complex and thoughtful reasoning about literary texts. The possibilities of such inquiry to engage youth in wrestling with the challenges of identity development, particularly during the critical transition period of adolescence, make this work especially compelling.

References

Alim, H. S. (2009). "Hip hop nation language." In A. Duranti (Ed.), *Linguistic anthropology: A reader* (pp. 272–289). Malden, MA: Blackwell Publishing.

Alim, H. S., et al. (2008). *Global linguistic flows: Hip hop cultures, youth identities, and the politics of language.* London: Routledge.

Anderson, R. (2004). Role of the reader's schema in comprehension, learning, and memory. In R. B. Ruddell and N. J. Unrau (Eds.), *Theoretical models and processes of reading* (pp. 469–482). Newark, DE: International Reading Association.

Anderson, R. C., & Pearson, P. D. (1988). A schema-theoretic view of basic processes in reading comprehension. In P. L. Carrell, J. Devine, & D. E. Eskey (Eds.), *Interactive approaches to second language reading* (pp. 37–55). Cambridge, UK: Cambridge University Press.

Applebee, A., et al. (2000). Creating continuity and coherence in high school literature curricula. *Research in the Teaching of English, 34*(3), 396–429.

Applebee, A. N. (1978). *The child's concept of story: Ages two to seventeen.* Chicago, IL: University of Chicago Press.

Applebee, A. N. (1984). Writing and reasoning. *Review of Educational Research, 54*(4), 577–596.

Applebee, A. N., et al. (2003). Discussion-based approaches to developing understanding: Classroom instruction and student performance in middle and high school English. *American Educational Research Journal, 40*(3), 685–730.

August, D., & Shanahan, T. (2006). *Developing literacy in second-language learners: Report of the National Literacy Panel on language-minority children and youth.* Mahwah, NJ: Lawrence Erlbaum.

Ball, A., & Farr, M. (2003). Language varieties, culture and teaching the English Language Arts. In J. Flood, D. Lapp, J. Squire and J. Jensen (Eds.), *Handbook of research on teaching the English Language Arts* (pp. 435–445). Mahwah, NJ: Lawrence Erlbaum.

Bereiter, C., & Engelmann, S. (1966). *Teaching disadvantaged children in pre-school.* Englewood Cliffs, NJ: Prentice Hall.

Booth, W. (1983). *A rhetoric of fiction.* Chicago, IL: University of Chicago Press.

Bransford, J., et al. (1999). *How people learn: Brain, mind, experience and school.* Washington, DC: National Academy Press.

Bruner, J. (1990). *Acts of meaning.* Cambride, MA: Harvard University Press.

Cammarota, J., & Fine, M. (2010). *Revolutionizing education: Youth participatory action research in motion.* London: Routledge.

Carlson, S. M., & Meltzoff, A. N. (2008). Bilingual experience and executive functioning in young children. *Developmental Science, 11*(2), 282–298.

Cazden, C. (2000). *Classroom discourse: The language of teaching and learning.* Portsmouth, NH: Heinemann.

Champion, T., et al. (1995). Narrative discourse among African American children. *Journal of Narrative and Life History, 5*(4), 333–352.

Chinn, C. A., et al. (2011). Expanding the dimensions of epistemic cognition: Arguments from philosophy and psychology. *Educational Psychologist, 46*(3), 141–167.

Clore, G. L., & Ortony, A. (2000). Cognition in emotion: Always, sometimes, or never? In L. Nadel, R. Lane, & G. L. Ahern (Eds.), *The cognitive neuroscience of emotion* (pp.24–61). New York: Oxford University Press.

Dai, D. Y., & Sternberg, R. (2004). *Motivation, emotion, and cognition: Integrative perspectives on intellectual functioning and development.* Mahwah, NJ: Lawrence Erlbaum.

Damon, W., & Lerner, R. M. (2008). The scientific study of child and adolescent development: Important issues in the field today. In W. Damon & R. M. Lerner (Eds.), *Child and adolescent development an advanced course.* Hoboken, NJ: Wiley and Sons.

diSessa, A. (1982). Unlearning Aristotelian physics: A study of knowledge-base learning. *Cognitive Science, 6*, 37–75.

disessa, A. A., & Sherin, B. L. (1998). What changes in conceptual change? *International Journal of Science Education, 20*(10), 1155–1191.

Dunbar, K., Fugelsang, J., & Stein C. (2007). Do naïve theories ever go away? Using brain and behavior to understand changes in concepts. In M.C. Lovett & P. Shah (Eds.) *Thinking with data* (pp. 193–206). Mahwah, NJ: Lawrence Erlbaum Associates.

Duncan-Andrade, J. M., & Morrell, E. (2005). Turn up that radio, teacher: Popular cultural pedagogy in new century urban schools. *Journal of School Leadership, 15*(3), 284.

Dweck, C. S. (1999). *Self-theories: Their role in motivation, personality and development.* Philadelphia, PA: The Psychology Press.

Eccles, J., et al. (1993). Deveopment during adolescence: The impact of stage-environment fit on young adolescents' experiences in schools and families. *American Psychologist, 48*(2), 90–101.

Farr, M. (1991). Dialects, culture and teaching the English language arts. In J. Flood, J. Jenson, D. Lapp, & J. Squire (Eds.), *Handbook of research on teaching the English Language Arts* (pp. 365–371). New York: Macmillan.

Galda, L., & Liang, L. A. (2003). Literature as experience or looking for facts: Stance in the classroom. *Reading Research Quarterly, 38*(2), 268–275.

Gándara, P., et al. (2004). Chapter 2: Legacy of brown: Lau and language policy in the United States. *Review of Research in Education, 28*(1), 27–46.

Gee, J. P. (1989). The narrativization of experience in the oral style. *Journal of Education, 171*(1), 75–96.

Goldman, S. R., et al. (2016). Disciplinary literacies and learning to read for understanding: A conceptual framework for disciplinary literacy. *Educational Psychologist, 51*(2), 219–246.

Goldman, S. R., & Lee, C. D. (2014). Text complexity: State of the art and the conundrums it raises. *Elementary School Journal, 115*(2), 290–300.

Gould, S. J. (1981). *The mismeasure of man.* New York: Norton.

Grande, S., et al. (2015). Indigenous peoples and identity in the 21st century: Remembering, reclaiming, and regenerating. In D. Koslow & L. Salett (Eds), *Multicultural perspectives on race, ethnicity, and identity* (pp.105–122). Washington, DC: NASW Press.

Greenleaf, C., et al. (2007). *Reading apprenticeship academic literacy course.* San Francisco, CA: West Ed.

Gutiérrez, K. (2008). Developing a sociocritical literacy in the third space. *Reading Research Quarterly, 43*(2), 148–164.

Gutierrez, K., et al. (1999). Rethinking diversity: Hybridity and hybrid language practices in the Third Space. *Mind, Culture, and Activity, 6*(4), 286–303.

Gutiérrez, K. D. (2016). "2011 AERA presidential address: Designing resilient ecologies social design experiments and a new social imagination. *Educational Researcher, 45*(3), 187–196.

Gutiérrez, K. D., & Jurow, A. S. (2016). Social design experiments: Toward equity by design. *Journal of the Learning Sciences, 25*(4), 565–598.

Hart, F. E. (2001). The epistemology of cognitive literary studies. *Philosophy and Literature, 25*(2), 314–334.

Hatano, G., & Inagaki, K. (1986). Two courses of expertise. In H. W. Stevenson, H. Azuma, & K. Hakuta (Eds.), *Child development and education in Japan* (pp. 262–272). New York: Freeman.

Heath, S. B. (1983). *Ways with words: Language, life and work in communities and classrooms.* New York: Cambridge University Press.

Heath, S. B. (2001). What no bedtime story means: Narrative skills at home and school. In A. Duranti (Ed.), *Linguistic anthropology* (pp. 318–342). Malden, MA: Blackwell.

Hillocks, G. (1971). *Observing and writing.* Urbana, IL: National Council of Teachers of English.

Hillocks, G. (1995). *Teaching writing as reflective practice.* New York: Teachers College Press.

Hillocks, G. (2007). *Narrative writing: Learning a new model for teaching.* Portsmouth, NH: Heinemann.

Hillocks, G. (2011). *Teaching argument writing, grades 6–12.* Portsmouth, NH: Heinemann.

Hillocks, G. (2016). The territory of literature. *English Education, 48*(22), 109–126.

Hillocks, G., & Ludlow, L. (1984). A taxonomy of skills in reading and interpreting fiction. *American Educational Research Journal, 21*, 7–24.

Hofer, B. (2000). Dimensionality and disciplinary differences in personal epistemology. *Contemporary Educational Psychology, 25*(4), 378–405.

Hogan, P. C. (1997). Literary universals. *Poetics Today, 18*(2), 223–249.

Hynds, S. (1989). Bringing life to literature and literature to life: Social constructs and contexts of four adolescent readers. *Research in the teaching of english*, 23(1), 30–61.

Jimenez, R., et al. (1995). Three children, two languages, and strategic reading: Case studies in bilingual/monolingual reading. *American Educational Research Journal, 32*, 31–61.

Kinloch, V. (2010). *Harlem on our minds: Place, race, and the literacies of urban youth*. New York: Teachers College Press

Kintsch, W. (1998). *Comprehension: A paradigm for cognition*. New York: Cambridge University Press.

Langer, J., et al. (1990). Meaning construction in school literacy tasks: A study of bilingual students. *American Educational Research Journal, 27*(3), 427–471.

Lee, C. D. (1995a). A culturally based cognitive apprenticeship: Teaching African American high school students' skills in literary interpretation. *Reading Research Quarterly, 30*(4), 608–631.

Lee, C. D. (1995b). Signifying as a scaffold for literary interpretation. *Journal of Black Psychology, 21*(4), 357–381.

Lee, C. D. (1997). Bridging home and school literacies: A model of culturally responsive teaching. In J. Flood, S. B. Heath & D. Lapp (Eds.), *A handbook for literacy educators: Research on teaching the communicative and visual arts* (pp. 330–341). New York, Macmillan Publishing Company.

Lee, C. D. (2001). Is October Brown Chinese: A cultural modeling activity system for underachieving students. *American Educational Research Journal, 38*(1), 97–142.

Lee, C. D. (2005a). Culture and Language: Bi-dialectical Issues in Literacy. In J. Flood & P. L. Anders (Eds.), *The Literacy Development of Students in Urban Schools* (pp. 241–274) .

Newark, DE: International Reading Association.

Lee, C. D. (2005b). Double voiced discourse: African American vernacular english as resource in cultural modeling classrooms. In A. F. Ball & S. W. Freedman (Eds.), *New literacies for new times: Bakhtinian perspectives on language, literacy, and learning for the 21st century* (pp. 129–147). New York: Cambridge University Press.

Lee, C. D. (2006). Every good-bye ain't gone: Analyzing the cultural underpinnings of classroom talk. *Qualitative Studies in Education, 19*(3), 305–327.

Lee, C. D. (2007). *Culture, literacy and learning: Taking bloom in the midst of the whirlwind*. New York: Teachers College Press.

Lee, C. D. (2011). Education and the study of literature. *Scientific Study of Literature, 1*(1), 49–58.

Lee, C. D. (2016). A longitudinal study of disciplinary literacy development in literature and history as a resource for identity development and psycho-social well being. Project READI Technical Report #11.

Lee, C. D. (2017a). Eco-cultural modeling framework: Designing literacy as resource for imagining future selves and possibilities. Paper presented at the Annual Meeting of the American Educational Research Association: San Antonio, TX.

Lee, C. D. (2017b). Integrating research on how people learn and learning across settings as a window of opportunity to address inequality in educational processes and outcomes. *Review of Research in Education, 41*(1), 88–111.

Lee, C. D., et al. (2016). Epistemic cognition in literary reasoning. In J. Green, W. Sandoval, & I. Bråten (Eds.), *Handbook of epistemic cognition* (pp. 163–183). New York: Taylor & Francis.

Lee, C. D., & Goldman, S. R. (2015). Assessing literary reasoning: Text and task complexities. *Theory into Practice, 54*(3), 213–227.

Lee, C. D., Mandara, J., & Buell, J. (2016). Slipping into the breaks and looking around: Exploring the roles of racial identity and psycho-social development on academic outcomes through literature. Paper presented at the Annual Meeting of the American Educational Research Association: Washington, DC.

Levine, S., & Horton, W. S. (2013). Using affective appraisal to help readers construct literary interpretations. *Scientific Study of Literature, 3*(1), 105–136.

Mandler, J. (1987). On the psychological reality of story structure. *Discoure Processes, 10*, 1–29.

Maslow, A. H. (1954). *Motivation and personality*. New York: Harper.

McNamara, D. S., & Kintsch, W. (1996). Learning from text: Effects of prior knowledge and text coherence. *Discourse Processes, 22*, 247–287.

Mehan, H. (1979). *Learning lessons*. Cambridge, MA: Harvard University Press.

Michaels, S., et al. (2002). *Accountable talk: Classroom conversation that works (3 CD-ROM set)*. Pittsburgh, PA: University of Pittsburgh.

Mintzes, J. J. (1984). Naive theories in biology: Children's concepts of the human body. *School Science and Mathematics, 84*(7), 548–555.

Morrell, E. (2002). Toward a critical pedagogy of popular culture: Literacy development among urban youth. *Journal of Adolescent & Adult Literacy, 46*(1), 72–78.

Nasir, N., et al. (2006). Learning as a cultural process: Achieving equity through diversity. In K. Sawyer (Ed.), *Handbook of the learning sciences*, (pp. 686–706). New York: Cambridge University Press.

Nystrand, M. (1997). *Opening dialogue: Understanding the dynamics of language and learning in the English classroom*. New York: Teachers College Press.

Orellana, M. (2009). *Translating immigrant childhoods: Children's work as culture and language brokers*. New Brunswick, NJ: Rutgers University Press.

Orellana, M., et al. (2003). In other words: Translating or "para-phrasing" as a family literacy practice in immigrant households. *Reading Research Quarterly*, *38*(1), 12–34.

Paris, D. (2012). Culturally sustaining pedagogy: A needed change in stance, terminology, and practice. *Educational Researcher*, (41), 3.

Paris, D., & Alim, H. S. (2014). What are we seeking to sustain through culturally sustaining pedagogy? A loving critique forward. *Harvard Educational Review*, *84*(1), 85–100.

Paris, D., & Winn, M. T. (2013). *Humanizing research: Decolonizing qualitative inquiry with youth and communities*. Thousand Oaks, CA: Sage.

Peskin, J. (1998). Constructing meaning when reading poetry: An expert-novice study. *Cognition and Instruction*, *16*(3), 235–263.

Piestrup, A. M. (1973). Black dialect interference and accomodation of reading instruction in first grade. *Monographs of the Language-Behavior Research Laboratory*, (p. 4) Berkeley, CA: University of California, Language-Behavior Research Laboratory.

Rabinowitz, P. (1987). *Before reading: Narrative conventions and the politics of interpretation*. Ithaca, NY: Cornell University Press.

Rickford, J., & Rickford, A. (1995). Dialect readers revisited. *Linguistics and Education*, *7*, 107–128.

Schoenfeld, A. H. (1987). *Cognitive science and mathematics education*. Hillsdale, NJ: Lawrence Erlbaum Associates.

Scholes, R. (1985). *Textual power, literary theory and the teaching of English*. New Haven, CT: Yale University Press.

Shore, J. R., Wolf, M. K., O'Reilly, T., & Sabatini, J. P. (2017). Measuring 21st-century reading comprehension through scenario-based assessments. In M.K. Wolf & Y.G. Butler (Eds.) *English language proficiency assessments for young learners*, (pp. 234–252). NY: Routledge.

Simon, H. A. (1977). The structure of ill-structured problems. In *Models of discovery* (pp. 304–325). Dordrecht, Netherlands: Springer.

Smagorinsky, P., Cameron, T., & O'Donnell-Allen, C. (2007). Achtung maybe: A case study of the role of personal connection and art in the literary engagement of students with attentional difficulties. *Reading & Writing Quarterly*, *23*(4), 333–358.

Smagorinsky, P., et al. (1987). *Explorations: Introductory activities for literature and composition* (pp. 7–12). Urbana, IL: National Council of Teachers of English.

Smagorinsky, P., et al. (2012). Identity, meaning, and engagement with school: A Native American student's composition of a life map in a senior English class. *Journal of American Indian Education*, *51*(2), 22–44.

Smagorinsky, P., & O'Donnell-Allen, C. (1998). The depth and dynamics of context: Tracing the sources and channels of engagement and disengagement in students' response to literature. *Journal of Literacy Research*, *30*(4), 515–559.

Smith, M. (1989). Teaching the interpretation of irony in poetry. *Research in the Teaching of English*, *23*, 254–272.

Smith, M. (1991a). Constructing meaning from text: An analysis of ninth-grade reader responses. *Journal of Educational Research*, *84*(5), 263–271.

Smith, M. (1991b). *Understanding unreliable narrators: Reading between the lines in the literature classroom*. Urbana, IL: National Council of Teachers of English.

Smitherman, G. (1977). *Talkin and testifyin: The language of Black America*. Boston, MA: Houghton Mifflin.

Snow, C., et al. (1998). *Preventing reading difficulties in young children*. Washington, DC: National Academy Press.

Spencer, M. B. (2006). Phenomenology and ecological systems theory: Development of diverse groups. In W. Damon & R. M. Lerner (Eds.), *Handbook of child psychology* (vol. 1, pp. 829–893). New York: Wiley.

Sugiyama, M. S. (2001). Narrative theory and function: Why evolution matters. *Philosophy and Literature*, *25*(2), 233–250.

Tierney, R. J., et al. (1989). The effects of reading and writing upon thinking critically. *Reading Research Quarterly*, *24*, 134–173.

Toulmin, S., et al. (1984). *An introduction to reasoning*. New York: Macmillan Publishing Company.

Trabasso, T., et al. (1983). Causal cohesion and story coherence. In H. Mandl, N. L. Stein & T. Trabasso (Eds.), *Learning and comprehension of text* (pp. 83–111). Hillsdale, NJ: Lawrence Erlbaum.

Trabasso, T., & Sperry, L. L. (1985). Causal relatedness and importance of story events. *Journal of Memory and Language*, *24*, 595–611.

Valdes, G., et al. (2005). Enhancing the development of students' language(s). In L. Darliing-Hammond & J. Bransford (Eds.), *Preparing teachers for a changing world: What teachers should learn and be able to do* (pp. 126–168). San Francisco, CA: Jossey-Bass.

Valencia, S. W., et al. (2014). Putting text complexity in context: Refocusing on comprehension of complex text. *Elementary School Journal,* 115(2), 270–289.

Van Peer, W. (1991). But what is literature? Toward a descriptive definition of literature. In R.D. Sell, (Ed.), *Literary pragmatics* (pp. 127–141). NY: Routledge

Winn, M. T. (2010a). "Betwixt and between": Literacy, liminality, and the celling of Black girls. *Race Ethnicity and Education, 13*(4), 425–447.

Winn, M. T. (2010b). 'Our side of the story': moving incarcerated youth voices from margins to center. *Race Ethnicity and Education, 13*(3), 313–325.

Winn, M. T. (2013). Toward a restorative English education. *Research in the Teaching of English, 48*(1), 126.

Wolf, D. P. (1995). *Reading reconsidered: Literature and literacy in high school.* New York: College Entrance Examination Board.

Wolfram, W., et al. (1999). *Dialects in schools and communities.* Mahwah, NJ: Lawrence Erlbaum.

Zeitz, C. M. (1994). Expert-novice differences in memory, abstraction, and reasoning in the domain of literature. *Cognition and Instruction, 12*(4), 277–312.

17

INQUIRY LEARNING IN HISTORY

Carla van Boxtel, Michiel Voet, and Gerhard Stoel

Introduction

Inquiry learning in history education is typically about students developing or evaluating interpretations of the past. Students are expected to do so through inquiry tasks that usually center on investigations of authentic historical questions, and on the reading, analysis, and synthesis of multiple sources, which can include historical documents, artifacts, and accounts created by historians. These inquiry tasks focus on distinct issues in history, such as exploring causes and consequences of the French Revolution, evaluating different interpretations of the collapse of the Soviet Union, or comparing how people in the past and in the present times have dealt, and are dealing, with immigration challenges and issues. In this chapter, we use the term *inquiry learning* but would like to point out that the history education literature, in addition to using "inquiry learning" (e.g., Goldman et al., 2016; Seixas, 1993), also uses other, interchangeable terms like "inquiry-based learning" (e.g., Pellegrino & Kilday, 2013; Voet & De Wever, 2017), "(problem-based) historical inquiry" (Brush & Saye, 2014), "document-based lessons" (e.g., Reisman, 2012), or "doing history" (e.g., Barton & Levstik, 2004; Levstik & Barton, 2015). So far, the main focus of research on this pedagogical approach has been to uncover the disciplinary reasoning and knowledge that underlie successful inquiry learning, students' ability and difficulties when engaging in such disciplinary reasoning, and ways in which inquiry learning in history can be facilitated.

In this chapter, we first discuss how inquiry learning has been conceptualized by history education researchers and how students engage in historical inquiry. We then examine instructional strategies that are advocated and found to be effective for engaging students in historical inquiry and developing historical inquiry competences. In addition, we address the role of teachers as the orchestrators of inquiry learning in history. Finally, we will formulate challenges for future research and implications for educational practice. We will argue that successful implementation of inquiry learning in the history classroom requires a clear view of the learning goals that are aimed at and the processes that students should engage in.

Conceptualizations of Inquiry Learning in History

In order to understand inquiry learning in history, we first look at the connection with the academic discipline. What is characteristic of historical inquiry practices? Then we look at conceptualizations in which inquiry learning is presented as a learner-centered approach, during which students engage in domain-specific reasoning and construct their own account of the past or evaluate a given account.

Historical Inquiry as a Specific Form of Academic Inquiry

History education researchers refer to historical inquiry as a specific form of academic inquiry and have argued that, if students are to understand historical inquiry and use disciplinary strategies, they should first of all become familiar with the nature and construction of historical knowledge (Maggioni, VanSledright, & Alexander, 2009; Stoel, Logtenberg, Wansink, Huijgen, Van Boxtel, & Van Drie, 2017). This claim is based on observations that, while historical inquiry shares some common attributes of inquiry with other disciplines, there are also important differences (Levy, Thomas, Drago, & Rex, 2013). For instance, historical inquiry resembles research in other disciplines in that it typically starts with a question or a tentative thesis. Unlike researchers in many disciplines, however, historians cannot directly observe or reenact the subject of investigation. As such, their task consists in creating, through inquiry of primary and secondary sources, the subject that they work on (Maza, 2017).

However, the variety in historical inquiry practices that exist within the discipline is often not discussed in history education research. Experts in the philosophy of history, who discuss how historians conduct research and compose historical narratives, point out that historical inquiry is not a singular scientific practice (Paul, 2015; Tosh, 2015). There are many sub-disciplines and methods of historical inquiry. There are, for example, different ideas about how to explain historical events. Retz (2016) argued that the intentionalist philosophy of history has had a profound influence on the work of history education researchers. Influential scholars, such as Wineburg and Seixas, clearly align themselves with this view that reconstructing and contextualizing the intentions of human agents is key to the process of historical inquiry. The focus is on the specific situation and human agency rather than on any overarching universal laws or categories. Chapman (2017), however, mentions not only the intentions of historical actors and the context for their actions as important aspects of causal explanation but also the unintended consequences of intentional action and the impact of factors of change that lack intention and belief, such as states of affairs, nonhuman "agents," and structures.

Another specific characteristic of historical inquiry is the idea that the narratives by historians do not present the past as it was but, instead, offer representations of what the past can be expected to have been like. This view is rooted in common agreement that historical inquiry centers on a specific form of theory-evidence coordination: Because historical claims cannot be empirically tested, they need to be argued for and supported by evidence from historical sources (Kuhn, Weinstock, & Flaton, 1994). As a consequence, historians may arrive at different accounts of the past as they ask different questions, use different sources, or draw on different interpretative frameworks (e.g., focusing on either the political or the social dimension, or using a different periodization). Recently, this view has become even more prevalent due to increasing attention for research on collective memory and sensitive history. The work in these interdisciplinary fields clearly shows how sociocultural contexts also affect the construction of historical narratives.

Historical Inquiry as a Pedagogic Approach

When we look at historical inquiry as a pedagogic approach, inquiry learning is often regarded as the opposite of more explanatory approaches, during which a readymade historical narrative is presented to students. Inquiry learning does, however, not mean that students need to discover all of history by themselves, but rather that they form their own conclusions about particular historical phenomena, under the expert guidance of the teacher. Most researchers emphasize the application of disciplinary methods of collecting data and drawing conclusions, but others have also emphasized the importance of dialogue in inquiry (Barton & Levstik, 2004; Van Boxtel & Van Drie, 2017; Dobber & Van Oers, 2015). More specifically, Dobber and Van Oers (2015) stated that inquiry learning implies learning to talk, think, and work as researchers within a community of inquiry and therefore considered interactions within the classroom and with others from outside of the classroom as central aspects of inquiry.

Historical Inquiry Processes

Several researchers have tried to unravel historical inquiry in terms of its components and underlying knowledge, skills, and attitudes. Perhaps the most influential definition of historical inquiry processes has been provided by Wineburg (1991). Wineburg and history education researchers who have built upon his work focus on the strategies that are characteristic of the analysis of historical information sources, such as contextualization, sourcing, evaluating reliability, corroboration, and close reading (Breakstone, Smith, & Wineburg, 2013; Nokes, 2017; Nokes, Dole, & Hacker, 2007; Reisman, 2012; Wineburg, 1991). The act of contextualizing (i.e., considering how a historical context may have shaped actions or interpretations) in particular has been considered as a strategy that sets historical inquiry apart from that in other disciplines. Historians aim to reconstruct the larger processes, atmosphere, and mentality of the context and try "to understand each age in its own terms, to take on its own values and priorities, instead of imposing ours" (Tosh, 2015, p. 6).

Other scholars have pointed out that an analysis of historical sources is only a part of historical inquiry and that historical inquiry neither starts nor ends with it (Nokes, 2017; Van Boxtel & Van Drie, 2018; Voet & De Wever, 2016). These scholars emphasize that other processes also play a key role in historical inquiry. For example, historical inquiry typically starts with a historical question or problem (Logtenberg, Van Boxtel, & Van Hout-Wolters, 2011), focusing on themes such as change and continuity, causes and consequences, ways in which the past has been or is represented, or ethical judgment. Given the centrality of these questions to historical inquiry, the act of problem-finding, forming historical questions, and formulating hypotheses can be regarded as another key activity of historical inquiry (e.g., Van Drie & Van Boxtel, 2008; Logtenberg et al., 2011; Schreiber et al., 2006; Voet, 2017).

Another contribution to the identification of reasoning processes involved in historical inquiry comes from scholars who focus more on the synthesis of information from multiple sources and the construction of evidence-based written arguments (e.g., Monte-Sano, De La Paz, & Felton, 2014; Nokes, 2017). After all information has been analyzed, one needs to weigh different interpretations to formulate a claim about the past. This claim then needs to be substantiated with arguments based on relevant evidence, examples, details, footnotes, and quotations. In addition, the argumentation must address historical evidence that goes against the claim (Chapman, 2017). Research on the written and oral language forms that are used to construct historical arguments further points out that historical arguments may take on different structures. To be more specific, Goldman et al. (2016) made a distinction between descriptive, explanatory, and narrative structures. Later, Chapman (2017) added an evaluative structure as another form of historical writing.

Several scholars brought several inquiry activities together in a definition or integrative framework. Levstik and Barton (2015), for example, conceptualized "doing history" as the asking of questions, gathering data from primary and secondary sources, organizing and interpreting data, and sharing the results with particular audiences. Recently, Voet (2017) discussed different conceptualizations of inquiry learning in history education and stated that these conceptualizations revolve around working with an open-ended historical question, which drives the investigation, using multiple information sources representing different perspectives on a topic in order to construct an argumentative account. Van Boxtel and Van Drie (2018), and Van Drie and Van Boxtel (2008) developed a framework of historical reasoning, including inquiry activities. They defined historical reasoning as an activity in which a student attempts to reach justifiable conclusions about processes of continuity and change, causes and consequences, and/or differences and similarities between historical phenomena or periods. Historical reasoning is constructed through asking historical questions, constructing temporal and causal relationships and historical contextualization, and supporting assertions with arguments based on critical analysis and evaluation of available historical interpretations and primary sources. Based on the model of expertise development of Alexander (2003), Van Boxtel and Van Drie (2018) pointed out that students' historical reasoning in the context of historical inquiry is dependent on historical interest, substantive historical knowledge (historical facts, concepts, and chronology), understanding of metahistorical concepts (e.g., causation in history, change, historical significance), and epistemological beliefs. When a student does not consider a historical question or topic relevant, it is not likely that he or she will make much effort to critically examine historical sources and come to an elaborate historical argument. In addition, students need knowledge of historical events, developments, and chronology to contextualize, explain, or compare historical phenomena. Furthermore, students' questions and argumentation are shaped by their understanding of what historical change or causation can entail and their understanding of the nature of historical knowledge. Maggioni et al. (2009) showed that students often consider historical claims as either correct or wrong or as a matter of opinion, whereas historians understand the constructed nature of history and use scientific criteria for evaluating the quality of interpretations.

Potential Benefits of Inquiry Learning in History

Above we discussed the processes involved in historical inquiry and the role of available mental resources. But what do scholars consider potential benefits of inquiry learning in history? Why do history education researchers emphasize engagement in historical inquiry, rather than having students learn about the outcomes of historical inquiries by reading a textbook or listening to their teachers? Over the years, researchers have mentioned different reasons for doing so.

First, they emphasized that historical inquiry allows students to develop a deeper understanding of how historical accounts are created and historical thinking and reasoning skills (e.g., Levstik & Barton, 2015; Stoel, Van Drie, & Van Boxtel, 2017). Nuanced beliefs about the nature and construction of historical knowledge and historical reasoning skills are important for the critical examination of historical representations in the media, films, museums, and other settings (Trautwein et al., 2017; Van Boxtel & Van Drie, 2018). When students engage in the analysis of multiple sources and historical argumentation, they are likely to discover that there is typically more than one plausible answer and that the validity of their claims therefore rests on their arguments and use of evidence. Some researchers have found positive effects of inquiry learning on historical thinking and reasoning skills, for example, sourcing and close reading skills (Britt & Aglinskas, 2002; Nokes, Dole, & Hacker, 2007; Paxton, 2002; Reisman, 2012; Rouet, Britt, Mason, & Perfetti, 1996; Wiley & Voss, 1999).

Second, it has been argued that inquiry learning helps students to reach a deeper historical understanding of how people lived in the past. The investigation of primary sources, such as historical images or diaries that provide concrete details, can help students imagine how life in the past was different (Lévesque, 2008). Through historical investigation, students can construct a vivid image of how things looked like, how people lived, and the ideas and emotions they had (De Leur, Van Boxtel, & Wilschut, 2017). Inquiry learning enhances deep elaboration of the learning content.

A third expected benefit of inquiry learning in history is the assumed contribution to *generic* literacy skills, which includes reading comprehension, critical analysis of sources, and construction of arguments (e.g., Reisman, 2012; De La Paz & Felton, 2010; Wineburg & McGrew, 2018). Skills related to the evaluation of historical sources, for example, partly overlap with media literacy skills. To illustrate this, the educational materials that have been developed for the critical analysis of primary historical sources are currently expanded to help students to spot fake information online (the project MediaWise, co-developed with the Stanford History Education Group of Sam Wineburg).

Finally, some scholars state that inquiry learning can increase motivation and student engagement. Working with historical sources, such as objects or a photograph, can stimulate curiosity, particularly when they puzzle students (Barton, 2005). As such, Stoel, Van Drie, & Van Boxtel (2017) found a significant increase in students' interest when strategy instruction was embedded in a historical inquiry task. It has, however, also been argued that large amounts of source work can be quite boring for students. Counsell (1998) even used the phrase "death by sources." Several researchers have therefore emphasized the importance of inquiry questions that students consider meaningful or that originate in students' own curiosity and interest (Logtenberg, 2012; Saye & Brush, 2002).

Instructional Strategies and Approaches

History educators usually conceptualize inquiry learning as guided or scaffolded discovery learning. This approach is in line with more general research showing that inquiry is most effective when students are guided by an expert (Hmelo-Silver, Duncan, & Chinn, 2007). This guidance is provided by designing instruction, activities, materials, and feedback in such a way that they foster concrete aspects of historical thinking and reasoning. In this paragraph, we discuss several approaches that research on history education has shown to be effective.

Historical questions are important starting points for historical inquiry. Historical questions can be taken from the discipline of history, or from the daily life, or interests of students. Van Drie, Van Boxtel, and Van der Linden (2006) showed that an evaluative historical question ("to what extent were changes in the 1960s revolutionary or not?") was more effective in stimulating historical reasoning than a descriptive historical question ("what has changed in the 1960s?"). Similarly, Monte-Sano and De La Paz (2012) found that analytical questions (i.e., asking to consider various causes, compare multiple sources, or explore bias in sources) elicited more awareness of differing perspectives in historical sources than a question in which students had to imagine themselves as an historical agent.

Considering the effects of historical questions from a more affective point of view, Barton and Levstik (2004) argued that questions from academic history are not necessarily meaningful for students. Instead, questions related to students' own reality or interests may be more able to generate an interest in historical inquiry. Along these lines, Brush and Saye (2008) focused on persistent societal problems in a historical context to promote student engagement. In their study, students took the roles of consultants to Civil Rights leaders in 1968 to discuss the strategies that should be pursued in the struggle for a more equal society. Interview and classroom observation data showed that students were highly engaged. Likewise, Van Straaten, Wilschut, and Oostdam (2018) suggested that inquiries into enduring human issues and historical analogies can stimulate interest in history, due to the connections among past, present, and future. Finally, Logtenberg (2012) went a step further by suggesting that students should be given the opportunity to formulate their own questions. From his point of view, the process of formulating personal historical questions does not only make the inquiry more relevant but may also serve as an engine that triggers other historical reasoning processes

In addition to working with authentic and meaningful questions, researchers have also reported that explicit attention to reasoning strategies can be effective (Stoel, Van Drie, & Van Boxtel, 2015). Most empirical studies to date have focused on the strategies related to the analysis of multiple sources (Nokes et al., 2007; Reisman, 2012; Rouet et al., 1996; Wiley & Voss, 1999). For instance, Nokes et al. (2007) showed how explicit strategy instruction on sourcing, contextualizing, and corroborating embedded in inquiry tasks effectively fostered students' ability to reason with multiple historical sources. In recent years, the focus of researchers has broadened from strategies used to critically analyze and compare historical sources to include the additional strategies and concepts needed to synthesize historical information and construct an historical account. This holds especially true for the construction of causal explanations. For instance, a study by Stoel, Van Drie, & Van Boxtel (2017) showed that students' ability to use causal reasoning strategies and the language needed to express causation in a nuanced manner increased after a lesson unit that combined historical inquiry with explicit instruction about how to categorize causes and practice in using the vocabulary related to causal relationships.

An important characteristic of explicit strategy instruction is that not only the thinking of the teacher becomes explicit through instruction and modeling but also that the reasoning of the students becomes explicated and visualized through scaffolded inquiry activities. This can be achieved by using graphical organizers, e.g., card sorting, matrices, and (causal) concept maps (Chapman, 2003; Stoel et al., 2015; Van Drie, Van Boxtel, Jaspers, & Kanselaar, 2005). During group work these graphical representations function as concrete "objects" that structure the discussion and elicit historical reasoning. Teachers can see what students are thinking, ask questions, and provide feedback. This "just-in-time" teacher feedback is an important aspect of a learning environment that fosters historical reasoning. For instance, Saye and Brush (2002) investigated the extent to which expert guidance embedded in a multimedia learning environment (i.e., a storyboard that guided students through the process of constructing an historical argument) supported students' critical reasoning about ill-structured problems. They found that this scaffolding provided limited support in the process of historical inquiry and suggested that complex inquiry tasks also require spontaneous support that can only be provided by a teacher.

A growing body of work emphasizes the need also to pay explicit attention to the demands of historical literacy and the role of language. Historians use everyday language, but often do so in domain-specific and nuanced ways (e.g., they use concepts like *reliable, representative, short-term, process*, and *precondition*). Furthermore, they use specific genres or text structures that allow them to express their analysis (Coffin, 2006; Goldman et al., 2016; Monte-Sano, 2010; Schleppegrell, Greer, & Taylor, 2008). Finally, historians write accounts in which the author is clearly present; they argue for a certain perspective, discuss the evidence for their claim, and reference the sources they use. In contrast, students often write rather linear and factual recounts and tend to use sources only as carriers of information (McCarthy Young & Leinhardt, 1998; Stoel, 2017; Wineburg, 1991). Several recent studies have shown that an explicit (discipline-based) writing instruction positively affects the ability of students to articulate historical reasoning in their writing (De La Paz & Felton, 2010; De La Paz & Wissinger, 2015; Van Drie, Braaksma, & Van Boxtel, 2015). Other research showed positive effects of instruction on referencing sources and integrating source information in a written essay (Britt & Aglinskas, 2002; De La Paz, 2005). It is important to acknowledge and carefully scaffold the linguistic demands that historical inquiry tasks place on students—especially if students have to generate a written answer. Otherwise, the result might not represent a student's actual ability to reason historically (Reisman, 2012).

In the finishing phases of historical inquiry, whole-class discussion is advocated as an effective way to foster historical thinking and literacy (Reisman et al., 2018; Van Boxtel & Van Drie, 2017; Dobber & Van Oers, 2015). Through whole-class discussion students can compare findings, while teachers can provide feedback, ask (epistemological) questions, and reflect with the students on learning outcomes (Stoel et al., 2015; Van Drie & Van Boxtel, 2011). In a recent study, Van Drie and Van de Ven (2018) found that students who participated in whole-class discussion included and transformed ideas from this discussion in subsequent writing. Furthermore, they found that discussion contributed to students' ability to use abstract historical concepts in their writing.

The Implementation of Inquiry Learning by Teachers

Despite the potential of inquiry learning to support history learning, and despite examples of effective instructional approaches, studies have shown that it is still far from common practice in most history classrooms (see e.g. Cuban, 2016; VanSledright, 2011). A relatively large body of research on history education has therefore focused on the question as to why teachers' adoption of inquiry learning remains rather low and how the implementation of inquiry learning can be enhanced and supported.

Why Are Many History Teachers Reluctant to Use Inquiry Learning?

Studies on the adoption of inquiry learning reveal the existence of several barriers to inquiry learning, spread out across the macro-, meso-, and micro-level of history teachers' working context. One of the main problems at macro-level is that current history textbooks and teaching materials typically offer little support for the organization of inquiry learning. Instead, their contents are often dominated by a desire to provide students with an outline of national or world history (Loewen, 2018). Most history textbooks also tend to reduce history to a fixed narrative, rather than presenting it as the result of disciplinary inquiry (Paxton, 1999). This suggests to teachers that history teaching mainly revolves around covering a vast narrative and that stories and lectures are effective ways to teach history (VanSledright & Limón, 2006). Although some scholars have taken it upon themselves to create more inquiry-oriented curriculum materials (e.g., Reisman, 2012), educational publishers have yet to follow suit. Another macro-level barrier consists of restrictions imposed on teachers by limited time and demands related to high-stakes testing (Haydn, 2011). Such restrictions force teachers to make choices about what to teach, and when they do so, they tend to drop the most time-consuming activities, such as inquiry learning (Van Hover & Yeager, 2003). Moving on to the meso-level, teachers also have to take into account the views of their colleagues. In some cases, these colleagues may act as mentors that support inquiry learning (Achinstein & Fogo, 2015). More often than not, however, it appears that teachers' options to organize inquiries are instead constrained by their colleagues' expectations to cover particular content (Fehn & Koeppen, 1998). At the micro-level, the presence of low-ability students, who sometimes lack even basic reading skills, may further dissuade teachers from organizing classroom inquiries (Van Hover & Yeager, 2003), despite research suggesting that such students may also benefit from historical inquiry activities (e.g., De La Paz & Wissinger, 2017).

The barriers associated with history teachers' working context make it clear that implementing inquiry learning in history classrooms is no simple matter. Even so, it also appears that teachers cope differently with these constraints (Voet & De Wever, 2017). Some studies suggest that this is largely due to differences in teachers' subject matter knowledge and, in particular, their understanding of the nature of history (Bouhon, 2009; McCrum, 2013). According to these studies, teachers with a sound understanding of history's interpretative nature are more inclined to organize historical inquiries, in order to convey this understanding to their students. Other studies have cast doubt on this proposition, however, by demonstrating that even teachers with a very nuanced understanding of history may still choose to teach through traditional, expository approaches (Hartzler-Miller, 2001; VanSledright, 1996). A study by McDiarmid (1994) even showed that, after student teachers had been taught through an inquiry-based curriculum, lectures and stories kept on dominating their thinking about instruction. In summary, it is clear that history teachers' classroom instruction does not necessarily reflect their own subject matter knowledge (Williamson McDiarmid, 1994). That teachers' subject matter knowledge appears to have little effect on the decision to implement historical inquiry does not mean that this kind of knowledge is irrelevant, however. After all, teachers cannot properly introduce students to historical inquiry if they are not familiar with it themselves (Martin & Monte-Sano, 2008; Fehn & Koeppen, 1998) or if they are unable to transform content into inquiry activities that allow students to further develop their understanding of history (Monte-Sano & Budano, 2013).

As researchers failed to find strong influences of subject matter knowledge on history teachers' adoption of inquiry learning, they turned instead to teachers' beliefs about education. These beliefs are a set of ideas that teachers hold about different aspects of their work, such as the purpose of education, their own teaching abilities, and the school environment (Pajares, 1992). They differ from knowledge in that they are not so much a consensus about reality but rather a personal view that others do not necessarily have to agree with (Rokeach, 1968). Another important aspect of beliefs is that they generally carry a strong affective and evaluative component (Nespor, 1987). What this means, in essence, is that teachers can be expected to attach different values to various aspects of their work and to judge instructional situations differently. Beliefs thus function as a kind of lens through which teachers interpret and organize their work.

Teachers' beliefs are largely developed through experience, which includes a large number of observations during teachers' own careers as students (Lortie, 1975). As a consequence, studies have found history teachers are generally inclined to recreate for others the kind of instruction that worked well for them (Hicks, 2005). In particular, Virta (2002) discovered that novice history teachers generally accepted, or even praised, the lecture-based approaches through which charismatic teachers had been able to capture their interest. Similarly, McDiarmid (1994) noted how she was struck by the extent to which novice history teachers were prisoners of their own experiences as students, when she found that they generally equated history teaching with telling about events in the past and explaining why these had happened.

This led Barton and Levstik (2003) to conclude that the main reason history teachers are reluctant to adopt inquiry learning is that doing so conflicts with what they believe to be two of their primary tasks: controlling students' behavior and covering content. This claim is supported by several studies, such as by Hicks (2005) and Van Hover and Yeager (2003), who found that novice history teachers' work is often driven by concerns about behavior management and a desire to pass down historical narratives. More recent work by Voet and De Wever (2019) starts from a different, but complimentary, point of view and argues that adoption of inquiry learning remains limited due to negative perceptions of its expected value. This expected value is the function of the extent to which history teachers value the outcomes of inquiry learning and the extent to which they then feel capable to realize these outcomes (Pollock, 2006). Empirical data show that this framework is able to explain about 38% of the variance in history teachers' adoption of inquiry learning (Voet & De Wever, 2019). To sum up, there is thus ample evidence that teachers' adoption of inquiry learning depends in significant part on their beliefs.

How Can History Teachers Be Stimulated to Adopt Inquiry Learning?

Initiatives to facilitate history teachers' adoption of inquiry learning generally take the form of teacher training (e.g., Levy et al., 2013; Martin & Monte-Sano, 2008; Voet & De Wever, 2017), as it has been firmly established that this approach is effective in altering teachers' practice (Brouwer & Korthagen, 2005). Some have proposed other approaches, such as the use of educative curriculum materials, which not only provide an outline of instructional activities but also try to address teachers' subject matter and pedagogical knowledge (Davis & Krajcik, 2005). Even so, others have noted that differences in the impact of such materials can often be traced back to teachers' training (Reisman & Fogo, 2016).

There exists quite a large body of research on what makes teacher training effective, with some studies providing a number of criteria for the design of training programs (e.g., Desimone, 2009). Recent work, however, has rightly argued that the design of effective training programs starts with being familiar with teachers' decision-making and the particular problems that they face (Kennedy, 2016). Bearing in mind the research on history teachers' adoption of inquiry learning, this means that initiatives to facilitate high-quality inquiry learning in history classrooms should primarily address teachers' history subject matter and pedagogical knowledge and their beliefs.

Although there are only a few studies that have looked into the matter of preparing history teachers for inquiry learning, their findings are fairly consistent. These studies first of all point toward the benefits of an inquiry-based teacher training curriculum, which engages trainees in inquiries and provides models of inquiry lessons. More specifically, engagement in historical inquiry has been found to improve teachers' understanding of history (Williamson McDiarmid, 1994) and positively affect their beliefs regarding inquiry learning's expected value (Voet & De Wever, 2018). Furthermore, teachers' observations of inquiry learning show them how they can structure similar activities in their own classroom (Levy et al., 2013). Second, the available research stresses the importance of providing teachers with concrete information about how inquiry learning can benefit history learning and how it can then be organized in classrooms. In a recent study, Voet and De Wever (2017) were able to positively affect teachers' attitudes toward inquiry learning, by discussing its relative benefits, compared to more expository teaching approaches, and by addressing various popular misconceptions about historical inquiry. Examples of such misconceptions include beliefs that secondary-school students lack the intellectual maturity to carry out historical inquiries (Booth, 1994) or that inquiry learning tends to focus on skills while neglecting content (Martin & Monte-Sano, 2008). When it comes to giving practical information on how to organize inquiry learning, Levy et al. (2013) noted that it is important to ensure that teachers are able to locate resources that can assist them in preparing inquiry activities, such as online repositories for source materials or lesson plans. In addition, teacher trainers should also make sure that their trainees are able to develop appropriate scaffolds for inquiry activities. Such scaffolds may vary from simple adjustments that make source materials more accessible, to more elaborate support for students' reasoning during the inquiry (see e.g. De La Paz & Felton, 2010).

Although research has shown that training that follows these directions may have a positive effect on teachers' knowledge and beliefs in general, it appears that such training also has its limitations. In particular, it has been found that the impact of training on teachers' beliefs tends to die out as they reenter the classroom (Fehn & Koeppen, 1998; Voet & De Wever, 2017). It thus seems that when history teachers are confronted with the various barriers to inquiry learning that exist within their work environment, they tend to fall back on their old beliefs (Kagan, 1992). It is therefore particularly important for training to provide teachers with extended support after the training has ended. One of the most common approaches is to give teachers the opportunity to continue exchanging ideas with teacher trainers and their colleagues after training has ended (Levy et al., 2013). Other promising approaches include the use of professional learning communities and lesson study protocols (e.g., Callahan, 2018; Saye, Kohlmeier, Brush, Mitchell, & Farmer, 2009), where teachers work together to design, implement, evaluate, and revise lessons. So far, however, research has not investigated how such extended support after training might affect history teachers' use of inquiry learning in the long term.

Conclusions

This chapter has focused on specifics of inquiry learning in history education. Our discussion started with conceptualizations of this approach in history education research. These conceptualizations range from a focus on the analysis of historical sources or historical argumentation to more integrative approaches that allow us to gain deeper understanding of the interrelatedness of the processes and resources that are central to inquiry learning and might contribute to a more common language to talk about historical inquiry processes. In recent decades, more researchers have emphasized the social nature of historical inquiry practices. This approach raises new questions for the design and implementation of inquiry learning in history, for example, about the potential of dialogic teaching approaches, collaborative learning, and professional learning communities. More research is needed to investigate the potential of such approaches.

We showed that the literature mentions a variety of reasons to implement inquiry learning in history education. These entail that inquiry learning contributes to more nuanced epistemological ideas, historical and more generic thinking and reasoning skills, historical understanding, historical interest and motivation. To substantiate these claims, more research is needed. Given the limited availability of valid and reliable instruments to measure learning outcomes in history, this is a challenge.

In the available studies, students are supported in a variety of ways, for example, by explicit instruction about how to corroborate between sources or to construct a historical explanation or by scaffolds that support the writing of a historical argument. We know little about how students' proficiency in historical inquiry develops in primary and secondary education with effective support. At present, there is also little research on how to adjust inquiry learning to the needs of students, for example, high-ability students or students with low language proficiency. In addition, more research is needed on the potential of inquiry tasks that more explicitly connect past, present, and future. The historical questions that students investigate do not always seem meaningful from a student perspective.

It is widely acknowledged that the adoption of inquiry learning is still limited. Researchers have emphasized the importance of information about how inquiry learning can benefit history learning, because teachers often have negative perceptions of its expected outcomes. Furthermore, teachers can be supported by practical information on how to organize inquiry lessons and collaboration in professional learning communities. There is a need for more longitudinal designs that allow to map the effect of extended support on history teachers' work after training has ended.

The research that we discussed in this chapter can inform teachers who want to implement inquiry learning in the classroom about the processes that students need to engage in and about effective instructional strategies. Precisely because teachers may not have a clear view of potential benefits of inquiry learning, and because different goals are possible and inquiry learning can be filled in different ways, it seems important that teachers implement inquiry learning with a clear view on what their goals exactly are. Goals give direction to the reading, thinking, reasoning, argumentation, and writing processes that students should engage in during an inquiry task and, subsequently, to the kind of tasks, instruction, and scaffolds that can provoke and support these processes. For example, when teachers aim at the development of nuanced views on the interpretative nature of history, they should engage students in the critical examination of multiple (partly conflicting) sources, the development of claims and arguments, and enhance dialogue in which different answers are compared and students reflect on epistemic questions. When development of historical thinking and reasoning skills is aimed at enhancing students' understanding of present issues and reflection on future possibilities, teachers need to engage students in authentic inquiry questions, such as questions asked by the students themselves or enduring issues in society, and support particular thinking and reasoning processes (e.g., evaluating reliability of sources or causal reasoning) by providing explicit instruction or scaffolds. If teachers want to adopt inquiry learning to help students form a concrete picture of a complex historical development or phenomenon, they can select sources that shed light on concrete aspects of daily life and ideas of people in the past and support students in processes of identifying aspects of change and continuity and historical contextualization. We propose that researchers should also be clear about the learning processes and outcomes that are central to their studies. Just as historical inquiry is not a single academic practice, inquiry learning in the classroom is not one single practice but needs to take different forms according to the goals that are central and the level and experience of the students.

References

Achinstein, B., & Fogo, B. (2015). Mentoring novices' teaching of historical reasoning: Opportunities for pedagogical content knowledge development through mentor-facilitated practice. *Teaching and Teacher Education, 45*(1), 45–58. https://doi.org/10.1016/j.tate.2014.09.002

Alexander, P. A. (2003). The development of expertise: The journey from acclimation to proficiency. *Educational Researcher, 32*(8), 10–14. https://doi.org/10.3102/0013189X032008010

Barton, K. C. (2005). Primary sources in history: Breaking through the myths. *Phi Delta Kappan, 86*(10), 745–753. https://doi.org/10.1177/003172170508601006

Barton, K. C., & Levstik, L. S. (2003). Why don't more history teachers engage students in interpretation? *Social Education, 67*(6), 358–361.

Barton, K. C., & Levstik, L. S. (2004). *Teaching history for the common good.* Mahwah, NJ: Erlbaum.

Booth, M. (1994). Cognition in history: A British perspective. *Educational Psychologist, 29*(2), 61–69. https://doi.org/10.1207/s15326985ep2902_1

Bouhon, M. (2009). *Les représentations sociales des enseignants d'histoire relatives à leur discipline et à son enseignement.* Université Catholique de Louvain. Retrieved from http://hdl.handle.net/2078.1/30401

Breakstone, J., Smith, M., & Wineburg, S. (2013). Beyond the bubble in history/social studies assessments. *The Phi Delta Kappan, 94*(5), 53–57. https://doi.org/10.1177/003172171309400512

Britt, M. A., & Aglinskas, C. (2002). Improving students' ability to identify and use source information. *Cognition and Instruction, 20*(4), 485–522. https://doi.org/10.1207/S1532690XCI2004_2

Brouwer, N., & Korthagen, F. (2005). Can teacher education make a difference? *American Educational Research Journal, 42*(1), 153–224. https://doi.org/10.3102/00028312042001153

Brush, T., & Saye, J. (2008). The effects of multimedia-supported problem-based inquiry on student engagement, empathy, and assumptions about History. *Interdisciplinary Journal of Problem-Based Learning, 2*(1), 21–56. https://doi.org/10.7771/1541-5015.1052

Brush, T., & Saye, J. (2014). An instructional model to support problem-based historical inquiry: The persistent issues in history network. *Interdisciplinary Journal of Problem-Based Learning, 8*(1), 39–50. https://doi.org/10.7771/1541-5015.1409

Callahan, C. (2018). Promoting second-order historical domain knowledge through recursive and collaborative professional development. *The Journal of Social Studies Research, 42*(3), 287–297. https://doi.org/10.1016/j.jssr.2017.06.001

Chapman, A. (2003). Camels, diamonds and counterfactuals: A model for teaching causal reasoning. *Teaching History, 112*, 46–53.

Chapman, A. (2017). Causal explanation. In I. Davis (Ed.), *Debates in history teaching* (2nd ed., pp. 1–22). London: Routledge.

Coffin, C. (2006). Learning the language of school history: The role of linguistics in mapping the writing demands of the secondary school curriculum. *Journal of Curriculum Studies, 38*(4), 413–429. https://doi.org/10.1080/00220270500508810

Counsell, C. (1998). Editorial. *Teaching History, 91*, 2–3.

Cuban, L. (2016). *Teaching history then and now: A story of stability and change in schools.* Cambridge, MA: Harvard Education Press.

Davis, E. A., & Krajcik, J. S. (2005). Designing educative curriculum materials to promote teacher learning. *Educational Researcher, 34*(3), 3–14. https://doi.org/10.3102/0013189X034003003

De La Paz, S. (2005). Effects of historical reasoning instruction and writing strategy mastery in culturally and academically diverse middle school classrooms. *Journal of Educational Psychology, 97*(2), 139–156. https://doi.org/10.1037/0022-0663.97.2.139

De La Paz, S., & Felton, M. K. (2010). Reading and writing from multiple source documents in history: Effects of strategy instruction with low to average high school writers. *Contemporary Educational Psychology, 35*(3), 174–192. https://doi.org/10.1016/j.cedpsych.2010.03.001

De La Paz, S., & Wissinger, D. R. (2015). Effects of genre and content knowledge on historical thinking with academically diverse high school students. *Journal of Experimental Education, 83*(1), 110–129. https://doi.org/10.1080/00220973.2013.876228

De Leur, T., Van Boxtel, C., & Wilschut, A. (2017). 'I saw angry people and broken statue': historical empathy in secondary history education. *British Journal of Educational Studies, 65*(3), 331–352. https://doi.org/10.1080/00071005.2017.1291902

Desimone, M. (2009). Improving impact studies of teachers' professional development: Toward better conceptualizations and measures. *Educational Researcher, 38*(3), 181–199. https://doi.org/10.3102/0034654315626800

Dobber, M., & Van Oers, B. (2015). The role of the teacher in promoting dialogue and polylogue during inquiry activities in primary education. *Mind, Culture, and Activity, 22*(4), 326–341. https://doi.org/10.1080/10749039.2014.992545

Fehn, B., & Koeppen, K. E. (1998). Intensive document-based instruction in a social studies methods course and student teachers' attitudes and practice in subsequent field experiences. *Theory and Research in Social Education, 26*(4), 461–484. https://doi.org/10.1080/00933104.1998.10505861

Goldman, S. R., Britt, M. A., Brown, W., Cribb, G., George, M., Greenleaf, C., ... Project READI. (2016). Disciplinary literacies and learning to read for understanding: A conceptual framework for disciplinary literacy. *Educational Psychologist, 51*(2), 219–246. https://doi.org/10.1080/00461520.2016.1168741

Hartzler-Miller, C. (2001). Making sense of "best practice" in teaching history. *Theory & Research in Social Education, 29*(4), 672–695. https://doi.org/10.1080/00933104.2001.10505961

Haydn, T. (2011). Secondary history: Current themes. In I. Davies (Ed.), *Debates in history teaching* (pp. 30–45). Oxon: Routledge.

Hicks, D. (2005). Continuity and constraint: Case studies of becoming a teacher of history in England and the United States. *International Journal of Social Education, 20*(1), 18–40.

Hmelo-Silver, C., Duncan, R., & Chinn, C. (2007). Scaffolding and achievement in problem-based and inquiry learning: A Response to Kirschner, Sweller, and Clark. *Educational Psychologist, 42*(2), 99–107. https://doi.org/10.1080/00461520701263368

Kagan, D. M. (1992). Implications of research on teacher belief. *Educational Psychologist, 27*(1), 65–90. https://doi.org/10.1207/s15326985ep2701_6

Kennedy, M. M. (2016). How does professional development improve teaching? *Review of Educational Research, 86*(4), 945–980. https://doi.org/10.3102/0034654315626800

Kuhn, D., Weinstock, M., & Flaton, R. (1994). Historical reasoning as theory-evidence coordination. In M. Carretero & J. F. Voss (Eds.), *Cognitive and instructional processes in history and the social sciences* (pp. 377–401). Hillsdale, NJ: Erlbaum.

Lévesque, S. (2008). *Thinking historically: Educating students for the twenty-first century.* Canada: University of Toronto Press.

Levstik, L., & Barton, K. C. (2015). *Doing history. Investigating with children in elementary and middle schools.* New York and London: Routledge.

Levy, B. L. M., Thomas, E. E., Drago, K., & Rex, L. A. (2013). Examining studies of inquiry-based learning in three fields of education: Sparking generative conversation. *Journal of Teacher Education, 64*(5), 387–408. https://doi.org/10.1177/0022487113496430

Loewen, J.W. (2018). *Lies my teacher told me: everything your American history textbooks got wrong.* New York, London: The New Press.

Lortie, D. (1975). *Schoolteacher: A sociological Study.* Chicago, IL: University of Chicago Press.

Logtenberg, A. (2012). *Questioning the past. Student questioning and historical reasoning.* University of Amsterdam: Dissertation. https://doi.org/11245/1.374232

Logtenberg, A., van Boxtel, C., & van Hout-Wolters, B. (2011). Stimulating situational interest and student questioning through three types of historical introductory texts. *European Journal of Psychology of Education, 26*(2), 179–198. https://doi.org/10.1007/s10212-010-0041-6

Maggioni, L., VanSledright, B., & Alexander, P. A. (2009). Walking on the borders: A measure of epistemic cognition in history. *The Journal of Experimental Education*, 77(3), 187–214. https://doi.org/10.3200/JEXE.77.3.187–214

Martin, D., & Monte-Sano, C. (2008). Inquiry, controversy, and ambiguous texts: Learning to teach for historical thinking. In W. J. Warren & A. D. Cantu (Eds.), *History education 101: The past, present, and future of teacher preparation* (pp. 167–186). Charlotte, NC: Information Age.

Maza, S. (2017). *Thinking about history.* Chicago, IL: The University of Chicago Press.

McCarthy Young, K. M., & Leinhardt, G. (1998). Writing from primary documents. A way of knowing in History. *Written Communication, 15*(1), 25–68. https://doi.org/10.1177/0741088398015001002

McCrum, E. (2013). History teachers' thinking about the nature of their subject. *Teaching and Teacher Education, 35*(1), 73–80. https://doi.org/10.1016/j.tate.2013.05.004

McDiarmid, G. W. (1994). Understanding history for teaching: A study of the historical understanding of prospective teachers. In M. Carretero & J. F. Voss (Eds.), *Cognitive and instructional processes in history and the social sciences* (pp. 159–185). Hillsdale, NJ: Lawrence Erlbaum.

Monte-Sano, C. (2010). Disciplinary literacy in history: An exploration of the historical nature of adolescents' writing. *Journal of the Learning Sciences, 19*(4), 539–568. https://doi.org/10.1080/10508406.2010.481014

Monte-Sano, C., & Budano, C. (2013). Developing and enacting pedagogical content knowledge for teaching history: An exploration of two novice teachers' growth over three years. *Journal of the Learning Sciences, 22*(2), 171–211. https://doi.org/10.1080/10508406.2012.742016

Monte-Sano, C., & De La Paz, S. (2012). Using writing tasks to elicit adolescents' historical reasoning. *Journal of Literacy Research*. https://doi.org/10.1177/1086296X12450445

Monte-Sano, C., De La Paz, S., & Felton, M. (2014). Implementing a disciplinary-literacy curriculum for US history: learning from expert middle school teachers in diverse classrooms, *Journal of Curriculum Studies, 46*(4), 540–575. https://doi.org/10.1080/00220272.2014.904444

Nespor, J. (1987). The role of beliefs in the practice of teaching. *Journal of Curriculum Studies, 19*(4), 317–328. https://doi.org/10.1080/0022027870190403

Nokes, J. D. (2017). Exploring patterns of historical thinking through eighth-grade students' argumentative writing. *Journal of Writing Research, 8*(3), 437–467. https://doi.org/10.17239/jowr-2017.08.03.02

Nokes, J. D., Dole, J. A., & Hacker, D. J. (2007). Teaching high school students to use heuristics while reading historical texts. *Journal of Educational Psychology, 99*, 492–504. https://doi.org/10.1037/0022-0663.99.3.492

Pajares, M. F. (1992). Teachers' beliefs and educational research: Cleaning up a messy construct. *Review of Educational Research, 62*(3), 307–332. https://doi.org/10.3102/00346543062003307

Paul, H. (2015). *Key issues in historical theory*. London and New York: Routledge.

Paxton, R. J. (2002). The influence of author visibility on high school students solving a historical problem. *Cognition and Instruction, 20*(2), 197–248. https://doi.org/10.1207/S1532690XCI2002_3

Paxton, R. J. (1999). A deafening silence: History textbooks and the students who read them. *Review of Educational Research, 69*(3), 315–339. https://doi.org/10.3102/00346543069003315

Pellegrino, A. M., & Kilday, J. (2013). Hidden in plain sight: Preservice teachers' orientations toward inquiry-based learning in history. *Journal of Social Studies Education Research, 4*(2), 1–26.

Pollock, J. L. (2006). *Thinking about acting. Logical foundations for rational decision making*. Oxford: Oxford University Press.

Reisman, A. (2012). Reading like a historian: A document-based history curriculum intervention in urban high schools. *Cognition and Instruction, 30*(1), 86–112. https://doi.org/10.1080/07370008.2011.634081

Reisman, A., & Fogo, B. (2016). Contributions of educative document-based curricular materials to quality of historical instruction. *Teaching and Teacher Education, 59*, 191–202. https://doi.org/10.1016/j.tate.2016.05.018

Reisman, A., Kavanagh, S. S., Monte-Sano, C., Fogo, B., McGrew, S. C., Cipparone, P., & Simmons, E. (2018). Facilitating whole-class discussions in history: A framework for preparing teacher candidates. *Journal of Teacher Education, 69*(3), 278–293. https://doi.org/10.1177/0022487117707463

Retz, T. (2016). At the interface: Academic history, school history and the philosophy of history, *Journal of Curriculum Studies, 48*(4), 503–517. https://doi.org/10.1080/00220272.2015.1114151

Rokeach, M. (1968). *Beliefs, attitudes and values: A theory of organization and change*. San Francisco, CA: Jossey-Bass.

Rouet, J.-F., Britt, M. A., Mason, R. A., & Perfetti, C. A. (1996). Using multiple sources of evidence to reason about history. *Journal of Educational Psychology, 88*, 478–493. https://doi.org/10.1037/0022-0663.88.3.478

Saye, J. W., & Brush, T. (2002). Scaffolding critical reasoning about history and social issues in multimedia-supported learning environments. *Educational Technology Research & Development, 50*(3), 77–96. https://doi.org/10.1007/BF02505026

Saye, J. W., Kohlmeier, J., Brush, T., Mitchell, L., & Farmer, C. (2009) Using mentoring to develop professional teaching knowledge for problem-based historical inquiry. *Theory & Research in Social Education, 37*(1), 6–41. https://doi.org/10.1080/00933104.2009.10473386

Schleppegrell, M. J., Greer, S., & Taylor, S. (2008). Literacy in history: Language and meaning. *Australian Journal of Language and Literacy, 31*(2), 174–188.

Schreiber, W., Körber, A., von Borries, B., Krammer, R., Leutner-Ramme, S., Mebus, S., … Ziegler, B. (2006). *Historisches Denken. Ein Kompetenz-Strukturmodell* [Historical thinking. A competence structure model], 2. Auflage, Neuried, Germany: Ars Una.

Seixas, P. (1993). Historical understanding among adolescents in a multicultural setting. *Curriculum Inquiry, 23*(3), 301–327. https://doi.org/10.1080/03626784.1993.11076127

Stoel, G., Logtenberg, A., Wansink, B., Huijgen, T., van Boxtel, C., & van Drie, J. (2017). Measuring epistemological beliefs in history education: An exploration of naïve and nuanced beliefs. *International Journal of Educational Research, 83*, 120–134. https://doi.org/10.1016/j.ijer.2017.03.003

Stoel, G. L. (2017). *Teaching towards historical expertise: Developing students' ability to reason causally in history*. University of Amsterdam: Dissertation. Retrieved from http://hdl.handle.net/11245.1/1cfaaed8-9929-462e-b2e0-ad1945f1f034

Stoel, G. L., van Drie, J. P., & van Boxtel, C. A. M. (2015). Teaching towards historical expertise. Developing a pedagogy for fostering causal reasoning in history. *Journal of Curriculum Studies, 47*(1), 49–76. https://doi.org/10.1080/00220272.2014.968212

Stoel, G. L., van Drie, J. P., & van Boxtel, C. A. M. (2017). The effects of explicit teaching of strategies, second-order concepts, and epistemological underpinnings on students' ability to reason causally in history. *Journal of Educational Psychology, 109*(3), 321–337. https://doi.org/10.1037/edu0000143

Tosh, J. (2015). *The pursuit of history. Aims, methods and new directions in the study of history.* London: Routledge.

Trautwein, U., Bertram, C., von Borries, B., Brauch, N., Hirsch, M., Klausmeier, K., ... & Neureiter, H. (2017). *Kompetenzen historischen Denkens erfassen. Konzeption, Operationalisierung und Befunde des Projekts «Historical Thinking-Competencies in History» (HiTCH).* Münster, New York: Waxmann.

Van Boxtel, C., & Van Drie, J. (2017). Engaging students in historical reasoning: The need for dialogic history education. In M. Carretero, S. Berger, & M. Grever (Eds.), *Palgrave handbook of research in historical culture and education. Hybrid ways of learning history* (pp. 573–589). London: Palgrave Macmillan.

van Boxtel, C. A. M., & Van Drie, J. P. (2018). Historical reasoning: conceptualizations and educational applications. In S. A. Metzger & L. McArthur Harris (Eds.), *The Wiley international handbook of history teaching and learning* (pp. 149–176). Hoboken, New Jersey: Wiley-Blackwell.

Van Drie, J., Braaksma, M., & van Boxtel, C. (2015). Writing in history: Effects of writing instruction on historical reasoning and text quality. *Journal of Writing Research*, 7(1), 123–156. https://doi.org/10.17239/jowr-2015.07.01.06

Van Drie, J., & van Boxtel, C. (2011). In essence I'm only reflecting: teaching strategies for fostering historical reasoning through whole-class discussion. *International Journal of Historical Learning, Teaching and Research, 10*(1), 55–66. https://doi.org/10.18546/HERJ.10.1.05

Van Drie, J., & van Boxtel, C. (2008). Historical reasoning: Towards a framework for analyzing students' reasoning about the past. *Educational Psychology Review, 20*(2), 87–110. https://doi.org/10.1007/s10648-007-9056-1

Van Drie, J., van Boxtel, C., Jaspers, J., & Kanselaar, G. (2005). Effects of representational guidance on domain specific reasoning in CSCL. *Computers in Human Behavior, 21*(4), 575–602. https://doi.org/10.1016/j.chb.2004.10.024

Van Drie, J., van Boxtel, C., & van der Linden, J. L. (2006). Historical reasoning in a computer-supported collaborative learning environment. In A. M. O'Donnell, C. E. Hmelo, & G. Erkens (Eds.), *Collaborative learning, reasoning, and technology* (pp. 265–296). Mahwah NJ: Lawrence Erlbaum Associates.

Van Drie, J., & van de Ven, P-H. (2017). Moving ideas: An exploration of students' use of dialogue for writing in history. *Language and Education, 31*(6), 526–542. https://doi.org/10.1080/09500782.2017.1326504

Van Hover, S. D., & Yeager, E. A. (2003). Challenges facing beginning history teachers: An exploratory study. *International Journal of Social Education, 19*(1), 8–21.

VanSledright, B. (1996). Closing the gap between school and disciplinary history? Historian as high school teacher. In J. Brophy (Ed.), *Advances in research in teaching*, 6, *Teaching and learning history* (pp. 257–289). Greenwich, CT: JAI Press.

VanSledright, B., & Limón, M. (2006). Learning and teaching social studies: a review of cognitive research in history and geography. In P. A. Alexander & P. H. Winne (Eds.), *The handbook of educational psychology* (2nd ed., pp. 545–570). Mahwah, NJ: Lawrence Erlbaum.

VanSledright, B. A. (2011). *The challenge of rethinking history education.* New York: Routledge.

Van Straaten, D., Wilschut, A., & Oostdam, R. (2018). Exploring pedagogical approaches for connecting the past, the present and the future in history teaching. *Historical Encounters, 5*(1), 46–67.

Virta, A. (2002). Becoming a history teacher: Observations on the beliefs and growth of student teachers. *Teaching and Teacher Education, 18*(6), 687–698. https://doi.org/10.1016/S0742–051X(02)00028-8

Voet, M. (2017). *Inquiry-based learning in history education: Exploring teachers' beliefs, knowledge and use of technology, and preparing future teachers for implementation in class.* Ghent University: dissertation. Retrieved from http://hdl.handle.net/1854/LU-8521306

Voet, M., & De Wever, B. (2016). History teachers' conceptions of inquiry-based learning, beliefs about the nature of history, and their relation to the classroom context. *Teaching and Teacher Education, 55*, 57–67. https://doi.org/10.1016/j.tate.2015.12.008

Voet, M., & De Wever, B. (2017). Preparing pre-service history teachers for organizing inquiry-based learning: The effects of an introductory training program. *Teaching and Teacher Education, 63*, 206–217. https://doi.org/10.1016/j.tate.2016.12.019

Voet, M., & De Wever, B. (2018). Effects of immersion in inquiry-based learning on student teachers' educational beliefs. *Instructional Science, 46*(3), 383–403. https://doi.org/10.1007/s11251-017-9439-8

Voet, M., & De Wever, B. (2019). Teachers' adoption of inquiry-based learning activities: The importance of beliefs about education, the self, and the context. *Journal of Teacher Education, 70*(5), 423–440. https://doi.org/10.1177/0022487117751399

Wiley, J., & Voss, J. F. (1999). Constructing arguments from multiple sources: Tasks that promote understanding and not just memory for text. *Journal of Educational Psychology, 91*(2), 301–311. https://doi.org/10.1037/0022-0663.91.2.301

Wineburg, S. (1991). Historical problem solving: A study of the cognitive processes used in the evaluation of documentary and pictorial evidence. *Journal of Educational Psychology, 83*(1), 73–87. https://doi.org/10.1037/0022-0663.83.1.73

Wineburg, S., & McGrew, S. (2018). Lateral reading and the nature of expertise: Reading less and learning more when evaluating digital information. *Teachers College Record, 121*(11), 1–40. https://doi.org/10.2139/SSRN.3048994

18

BROADENING PARTICIPATION IN MATHEMATICAL INQUIRY

A Problem of Instructional Design

Ilana Seidel Horn and Melissa Gresalfi

Introduction

Mathematics instruction, with its long history of rote memorization, often stands out in the school curriculum for its perceived irrelevance to everyday life. Indeed, hating mathematics has become cliché in popular culture, usually conveyed through images of blathering teachers subjecting bored, passive children to mind-numbingly dull content (TV Tropes, n.d.). Such widespread images stand in stark contrast to the engaged and active learning that inquiry-oriented mathematics instruction strives toward. In fact, eliciting and supporting children's mathematical thinking through active sense-making is a primary goal of inquiry, which, as the trope suggests, goes against the grain of cultural expectations for math class. Our first claim, then, is that inquiry-oriented instruction challenges many common assumptions about mathematics teaching and learning.

Broadly, by *inquiry-oriented instruction*, we refer to a range of teaching approaches that share the goal of eliciting and building on children's ideas in disciplinarily authentic ways to develop deep and robust mathematical understandings. These approaches often center rich mathematical tasks (Stein, Remillard, & Smith, 2007), emphasize classroom dialogue that supports exploration (Sfard, 2001; Staples, 2007; Yackel & Cobb, 1996), and position teachers as facilitators of mathematical sense-making rather than purveyors of information (Humphreys & Boaler, 2005; Stein, Engle, Smith, & Hughes, 2008).

Why press toward forms of math instruction that challenge people's expectations? Inquiry-oriented mathematics instruction is rooted in several empirical findings about children's learning. First, children learn better when they make sense of mathematical ideas. Memorization may "work" as a learning strategy for simple mathematical procedures, but it soon dissembles when the content becomes more complex (OECD, 2016a). Second, inquiry-oriented mathematics more authentically reflects the practices of mathematicians (Lehrer & Schauble, 2004; Schoenfeld & Hermann, 1982; Sinclair, 2006), with its emphasis on persuasion, insight, and enjoyment. Finally, because inquiry-oriented instruction focuses on children's sense-making, it fosters autonomy and agency in ways that support the development of positive mathematical dispositions (Boaler & Greeno, 2000; Gresalfi, 2007; Horn, 2008).

In addition, inquiry mathematics is seen as a means to rectify inequalities in schools. Because mathematics serves as a gatekeeping course, students' educational outcomes are highly dependent on achievement in that domain. Scholars who study equity in mathematics education often take *critical approaches* in their research, analyzing how power operates in schooling and increases the likelihood of reproducing unequal educational outcomes based on race, socioeconomic status, and gender. Their work frequently reminds us that inclusive mathematics classrooms play an important role in redressing longstanding educational inequalities by emphasizing diverse approaches to thinking and valuing student voice, helping a wider range of students meaningfully engage with the content (Cabana, Shreve, Woodbury, & Louie, 2014; Gutiérrez, 2008; Martin, Gholson, & Leonard, 2010; Nasir & Shah, 2011). Looking at consensus documents about mathematics teaching (e.g., NCTM, 2000; OECD, 2016b), we find that inquiry-oriented mathematics instruction is widely viewed as a central strategy for broadening participation in mathematics in particular and STEM disciplines in general. Success in mathematics classes supports students' STEM advancement, so by broadening participation in mathematics, educators can offer more people access to advanced STEM learning. Thus, our second claim is that inquiry-oriented mathematics instruction matters for redressing educational inequalities.

However, although educators have been pressing for a shift toward inquiry-oriented mathematics instruction for decades (NRC, 1989, 2001; NCTM, 1989; Van den Heuvel-Panhuizen, 2003), such approaches remain relatively rare in most classrooms around the globe, with inquiry methods less likely to be used in the least-resourced classrooms (OECD, 2016b). In other words, the instructional approach most likely to broaden participation is, paradoxically, seldom used in classrooms where there is great need to deeply engage in mathematical ideas to remedy inequity. This situation comes from numerous interrelated root causes, including traditions of schooling that focus on students' compliance over learning (Erickson et al., 2007), institutional structures that press teachers toward traditional instruction (Gutiérrez, 2016), standardized assessment practices that require all students to cover the same content at the same time (Shepard, 2010), the maldistribution of well-prepared teachers (OECD, 2005), insufficient and inadequately effective professional development (Garet, Porter, Desimone, Birman, & Yoon, 2001; Hill, 2007), widespread beliefs that only "capable" students can learn through inquiry (Jackson, Gibbons, & Sharpe, 2017; Zohar & Dori, 2003), and teachers' own histories and knowledge as mathematics learners (Lortie, 1975; Heaton, 1992). Our third claim, then, is that the project of normalizing inquiry-oriented mathematics instruction in schools is a project of cultural change.

Given the potential for inquiry-oriented instruction to broaden participation in mathematics, along with its concomitant challenges, how should educators approach this task? We offer a classroom ecology perspective (Doyle, 1988; Janssen, Westbroek, & Doyle, 2015), described in the next section, to address this question.

The Ecology of Mathematics Classrooms

As stated, myriad forces work against the widespread actualization of inquiry-oriented mathematics instruction, and these forces are often mutually reinforcing—such as when the use of high-stakes standardized assessments creates a rationale to press teachers towards traditional instruction. Any model of change must account for these interrelations. To this end, we view mathematics classrooms as places with their own cultures—they have norms, values, and practices that are reenacted with both similarity and variation across the globe. To take on the cultural change project of normalizing inquiry-oriented mathematics instruction, we require a lens for seeing the potential leverage points for this work.

To identify these leverage points, we examine mathematics classrooms as complex systems. Indeed, decades of research on mathematics classrooms demonstrates the utility of conceptualizing them as *interactive systems* whose elements impact and influence one another in both predictable and unforeseen ways. As Walter Doyle's (1983, 1988) foundational research showed, classrooms, as complex systems, shape the tasks teachers require students to work on. Not only do the details of tasks matter, but, in addition, their history and place within any classroom setting shape what, how—and, crucially, whether—students learn. One finding in this research is that novel tasks are less likely to succeed than routine tasks, as they heighten uncertainty (Cohen, 2011; Doyle, 1988). This poses a problem for inquiry-oriented instruction, since novel tasks often provoke the questions and curiosity that support inquiry. Academic tasks are a critical part of the classroom ecology, shaping and being shaped by students, teachers, and other institutional conditions.

To extend this perspective on classroom ecologies, we turn to systems theory, a field that has emerged from mathematics and the sciences (Abraham & Shaw, 1992). Specifically, systems theory explores and describes connections between elements of a system to understand changes in the system's behavior resulting from these connections (Vallacher, Read, & Nowak, 2002). As one of many examples, consider the development of a secondary forest: the process of succession, wherein new plants replace existing ones (such as the transition from grassland to forest). This process is predictable and appears to be almost determined. At the same time, scientists recognize that there is no "blueprint" for this change; instead, it comes about through interactions among elements in the system (such as changes in the soil, climate, and animals). Thus, the process of succession cannot be understood through the isolation of individual elements: examining the emergence of one tree species does not explain how grassland changed into a secondary forest. Rather, multiple components of the system interact and have to be analyzed together to gain insight into how succession works in nature.

Building on Doyle and others, we make a similar argument about classrooms. Spending time in schools, we encounter some behaviors that are so typical that they could easily be mistakenly taken as predetermined: Students get wild on the last day of school before a vacation, a substitute teacher struggles to persuade children to cooperate, a new textbook slows a class's progress through the curriculum. Although they may be familiar to many, these examples are not predetermined outcomes. Instead, microanalyses of participation—interactionist methods we use to understand classroom systems (Jordan & Henderson, 1995)—show that stabilities can be seen as emerging across *elements* in a *system*. In other words, students' actions are shaped by the stated expectations of the teacher, utterances of other students, the structure of the task, and their own knowledge, histories, expectations, social locations, and so on. As just two brief examples of such distal interactions in classroom ecologies that researchers have identified, there is a connection between teachers' knowledge of and beliefs about mathematics teaching and their ability to maintain the richness of mathematical tasks (Wilhelm, 2014). In another analysis, investigators found that teachers' approaches to setting up mathematical tasks were predictive of students' subsequent opportunities to learn in concluding discussions of the same lessons (Jackson, Garrison, Wilson, Gibbons, & Shahan, 2013).

This view of the classroom as a system grounds our understanding of what it means to successfully conduct inquiry-oriented mathematics lessons. Importantly, we see the issue as going beyond *implementation*—a word that too often sounds like turning on an appliance, something that works basically the same way irrespective of context, thus reducing the complexity of the change. Rather, we see conducting inquiry-oriented mathematics lessons as a problem of *design*. For that reason, we read the literature with attention to key elements that could operate as leverage points for educators aiming toward inquiry-oriented mathematics instruction. We conceptualize these leverage points as important components of the system that help us understand both successes and failures of inquiry-oriented instruction. Using this systems lens, we consider not only how something worked but also how its success might influence the behavior of other key elements. That is, we do not simply track one species of tree; we see how its proliferation shifts the broader landscape of the secondary forest.

In what follows, we share our reading of the literature on inquiry-oriented mathematics instruction with attention to three leverage points that have been the focus of significant research. These leverage points are: (1) teachers' knowledge about inquiry mathematics, (2) curricular connections to other contexts, and (3) classroom norms and practices. For each of these leverage points, we describe their role in inquiry-oriented mathematics instruction, as well as some key research on the promises and challenges they pose for such modes of teaching.

Leverage Point 1: Teachers' Knowledge for Inquiry Mathematics

To successfully implement inquiry lessons, teachers need opportunities to reconceptualize *what it means to do math* and *how students learn math.* This reconceptualization points to two important novel forms of teacher knowledge to support inquiry instruction—one that centers on content and one that centers on students.

Mathematically, inquiry instruction shifts lesson goals from *answer-getting* to *problem-solving* (Lampert, 1990). Teachers' ability to support children's problem-solving requires them to listen to emerging ideas, pose useful questions, and offer strategic hints—all of which demand that they know more than how to do a task themselves. Although many details of what that knowledge consists of, how to develop it, and the ways it plays out in teaching are still under investigation (Rowland & Ruthven, 2011), researchers generally agree that, to support inquiry, teachers require mathematical knowledge that goes beyond personal understandings and extends to ways of representing ideas, how to best explore them, and how they develop in children (Ball & Bass, 2000; Goulding, Rowland, & Barber, 2002).

One line of research that seeks to specify teacher knowledge in support of student sense-making looks at *mathematical knowledge for teaching* (MKT; Hill, Rowan, & Ball, 2005; Hill, 2010) as a key resource for successful inquiry-oriented math instruction. While there may only be one correct answer to 372 divided by 9 in the base 10 number system, there are many ways to visualize, approach, and resolve that problem. Developing different strategies, explaining how and why they work, and how they might be related get to the heart of the disciplinary thinking that inquiry-oriented instruction aims to develop, and MKT seeks to identify and trace the influence of some aspects of teachers' knowledge for inquiry mathematics on their subsequent instruction. For instance, Hill and colleagues (2008) found that MKT was strongly associated with the quality of their mathematical instruction, including responsiveness to students' mathematical thinking.

What teachers know about mathematics—and about teaching mathematics—therefore has multiple points of connection with other elements of the classroom system that impact whether mathematical inquiry actually occurs. If teachers haven't had an opportunity to consider the wealth of approaches students might take to solving a problem, they might not recognize the logic or meaning of student thinking as they first work on a novel task. In "helping" such a student, teachers might shift the direction of their thinking, thereby narrowing the scope of the problem. In this vein, Wilhelm's (2014) research found that teachers' MKT and their conceptions of teaching strongly correlated with their ability to maintain the cognitive demand of rich tasks. Maintaining the cognitive demand has an impact on students' learning, since it keeps students in the realm of problem-solving instead of answer-getting. This, in turn, influences student learning. In a small-scale comparative analysis, Kazemi and Stipek (2009) found teachers' use of mathematical disciplinary practices of *making mathematical arguments*, *connecting problem-solving approaches*, and *argumentation* during classroom were associated with a measurable increase of children's conceptual understanding.

With regards to student learning, teachers' understandings of students-as-learners shape their capacity to support for inquiry mathematics. These include their *visions of students' mathematical capabilities* (Jackson et al., 2017) and notions about which students can do challenging mathematics. In their study, Jackson and colleagues found that most mathematics teachers viewed students as having limited capacity for learning mathematics, making inquiry instruction difficult to get off the ground. Indeed, this is a part of a larger picture: A large-scale study in the U.S. documented teachers' persistent bias against female, Black, and Latinx students in mathematics (Copur-Gencturk, Cimpain, Lubienski, & Thacker, 2020), making explicit anti-bias work a crucial part of teacher development for productive inquiry instruction. Other scholars point to the importance of taking *asset-based* stances on students as sense-makers—working from students' strengths as a starting point rather than focusing on their deficits—to support inquiry learning (Cohen & Lotan, 2014; Horn, 2012). Together, these studies show how strong content knowledge, mathematical knowledge for teaching, and robust asset-oriented conceptions of student learning that includes specific attention to bias are essential to teachers' capacity to support inquiry instruction.

When teachers successfully reconceptualize mathematics and student learning in ways that support inquiry instruction, powerful teaching results. Perhaps the best-documented instance of this can be seen in one of the most well-known professional development efforts in mathematics education—Cognitively Guided Instruction (CGI; Carpenter & Franke, 2004). CGI aims to support teachers to develop an understanding of how students' ideas develop and progress in different mathematical domains. The CGI team anchored their work in the ways students intuitively thought about particular kinds of problems and how their thinking was related to instructional tasks. CGI professional development helped teachers see these strategies as reasonable, coherent, and, importantly, part of an emergent trajectory of student learning. This helped teachers to develop instructional strategies that allowed them to both understand and build on student thinking. Notably, in a longitudinal study of teacher engagement with CGI, researchers found a relationship between teachers' level of inquiry practice and their beliefs about mathematics teaching (Fennema et al., 1996). As in other studies of inquiry teaching, teachers' conceptions about their work matter as much as their detailed knowledge of research-based interventions.

Reconceptualizing mathematics, teaching, and student learning is nontrivial, and we suspect that overlooking the leverage point of teachers' knowledge in shifting to inquiry instruction may explain some cases where the shift is not successful. The research literature is rife with examples of teachers believing that they are using inquiry-oriented math instruction, with that view often disputed by educational researchers. In one such study, Spillane and Zeuli (1999) looked at 25 teachers who believed that their instruction had shifted and found that only 4 teachers had really achieved a shift in ways that reflected consensus documents on mathematics teaching. They explain this disparity in terms of teachers' giving greater attention to *behavioral changes* in the classroom over *epistemological ones*. That is, the materials (e.g., inquiry-oriented curriculum) and social organization (e.g., groupwork) of the classroom may have changed, but the types of interactions (e.g., answer-getting) did not, leading to the interpretive conflict between the teachers and researchers. On a more fine-grained level, teachers' inattention to the ways their classrooms are embedded in broader systems, such as racism, xenophobia, and sexism, can reproduce stereotypical achievement patterns, even when they are making efforts to broaden participation (Hand, 2010).

A primary challenge is illuminated by these findings: What do we do when teachers' mathematical knowledge for teaching and conceptions of students' capabilities hinder their attempts at inquiry instruction? This question connects to multiple potential leverage points in the system. For example, although we know that Mathematical Knowledge for Teaching matters for student achievement (Hill et al., 2005), we also know that taking more mathematics content courses does not necessarily lead to more productive ways of thinking about mathematics teaching (Ma, 2010). Likewise, although inquiry-oriented instruction requires that teachers follow students' understanding as they design and pace curriculum and activities, teachers are almost always asked to follow pacing guides as a part of the standardization movement in mathematics education (OECD, 2016b). As a result, teachers are faced with a persistent dilemma: Do we follow the children or the curriculum?

As these examples make clear, focusing on teacher and student knowledge is just one part of the complex system of classrooms. Even in cases when teachers know and understand the power of student inquiry and are able to anticipate their students' thinking, content issues extend beyond teachers' knowledge into the broader organization of school and community (Herbel-Eisenmann, Lubienski, & Id-Deen, 2006). In one classroom the first author recently visited, a highly accomplished geometry teacher concluded that having students explore the reasons behind triangle properties was not a worthwhile use of time, because it got her "too far behind" her pacing guide. Although the exploration helped students understand why the triangle properties worked as they did, she thought it would be more efficient to simply tell them and have them memorize the facts to get through the lesson more quickly. The constraints of the system in which she worked, seen here in the use of a common accountability tool, inhibited her from making decisions that would have centered student learning and understanding.

Leverage Point 2: Curriculum with Connections

Returning to the cultural impediments to inquiry mathematics, we point back to the frequency with which mathematics is described as *abstract, meaningless*, or *irrelevant*. This cultural belief plays out in typical answer-seeking instruction, where students are commonly asked to acquire a set of facts and procedures, which they seldom connect to each other or to contexts of use. Reflecting this lack of connection, a student said in an interview with the second author, "We learn to do it one way on one [textbook] page. And then you turn the page and you learn to do it a different way. I have no idea why." Inquiry-oriented teachers engage students by using tasks and activities that support meaningful connections to other mathematical methods, ideas, or real-world contexts. As with all learning, connecting new understandings to familiar ones supports students' retention of information, interest, and motivation.

For this reason, inquiry-oriented mathematics instruction emphasizes connections, whether these are to prior mathematical learning or to the real world. In this way, inquiry instruction not only offers a context of use that helps students see the relevance of mathematics in their lives (Gutstein, 2003) but also offers new information that can serve to push back on and refine student understanding. The emphasis on connections supports students' deep mathematical engagement, because considering the usefulness, impact, or significance of particular tools on outcomes shapes understandings of how and why they work (Cobb, McClain, & Gravemeijer, 2003). Of course, contexts do not have to be "stories" like word problems. Legitimate disciplinary dilemmas—such as considering whether parallel lines truly never meet on Euclidean versus spherical planes—can push back significantly on students' thinking, even though the "push back" remains situated in the world of mathematics (Ball, 1993; Greeno, 1991).

When it comes to building math content from real-world contexts, topics such as number, shape, data, and measurement are easy to connect. For that reason, such topics have been the primary focus of project-based learning seeking to connect mathematics with contexts of use. These studies suggest that opportunities to consider math as it influences and connects to various situations supports both rich conceptual understanding of mathematics (CTGV, 1997; Hall & Rubin, 1998; Lehrer & Schauble, 2002) and the development of productive relationships to the discipline of mathematics (Boaler, 2002; Gresalfi, 2015; Jurow, 2005).

Mathematics has social power, and that too can be used in inquiry instruction to promote students' sense-making. A prominent example of this approach is *Teaching Mathematics for Social Justice* (TMSJ), which involves empowering students to identify dilemmas and problems in their lives and then use mathematics to understand and change the world around them (Bartell, 2013; Gutstein, 2003, 2006; Frankenstein, 1990; Leonard, Brooks, Barnes-Johnson, & Berry, 2010). In this approach, mathematics as a discipline is no longer viewed as a neutral and abstract subject, but rather as a tool for making sense and making change in ways that are consequential.

Returning to our systems perspective, it is imperative to consider the ways that tasks interact with other elements of the classroom. Connecting the symbol system of mathematics to other contexts does not happen without trouble. Often, real-world examples provide their own fictions, creating cognitive dissonance for children (Wisittanawat & Gresalfi, 2020). For example, Walkerdine (1988) found that working-class children may have the psychological experience of "splitting" when the disjuncture between the fictive quantities of school mathematics collides with the well-known (to them) material realities. She illustrates this through working-class 7-year-old girls playing a shopping game where all the items, large and small, cost less than ten pence. The ludicrousness of this situation is not lost on them, and Walkerdine argues that such nonsensical abstraction of quantity—a common ploy in school mathematics—is class-based luxury.

Finally, many studies of project-based instruction and TMSJ caution about the dilemmas of balancing classroom conversations about mathematical content and exploration of problem contexts. To get the sense-making dividends, students need opportunities to think about the contexts, yet, without careful facilitation, those same contexts can sometimes overtake mathematical thinking and learning. This dilemma again highlights the interconnectedness of the classroom system. Transforming tasks to connect with and across contexts requires teachers to think carefully about the mathematics in those tasks and, in turn, requires them to develop ways of anticipating the diverse ways students might reason about them (Jackson et al., 2013). As Cohen and Ball (1990) wrote decades ago, changing the text (or textbook) changes nothing if the norms, practices, and values of teachers are unchanged.

Leverage Point 3: Classroom Norms and Practices

When we think of classrooms as interactive systems, we cannot overlook the dense social relationships that exist. The mandate in inquiry-oriented mathematics instruction to follow students' thinking seems obvious at first blush. However, with only a little more consideration, the complexity of this mandate quickly becomes evident. Namely, teachers do not typically teach *individual* children whose thinking could guide their work. Rather, they teach *groups* of children whose ideas and learning needs may diverge widely from one another. What is more, the classroom is a densely social space, which means it invites many of the complexities of any social milieu. In addition, they are evaluative spaces, marked by the surveillance of teachers and peers and the related judgments about competence in both academic and social tasks (Erickson, Bagrodia, Cook-Sather, Espinoza, Jurow, Schultz, & Spencer, 2007).

Of the three leverage points we highlight, classroom norms and practices are perhaps most critical to efforts to broaden participation in mathematical learning. For these reasons, accounts of successful inquiry-oriented mathematics instruction often address the need for teachers to build classroom communities (Goos, 2004; Hufferd-Ackles, Fuson, & Sherin, 2004; Sherin, 2002). When norms of interaction normalize mistakes (Horn, 2012), value multiple forms of mathematical competence (Gresalfi, Martin, Hand, & Greeno, 2009), emphasize mutual respect (Boaler & Staples, 2008), and are marked by supportive relationships with teachers (Battey, Neal, Leyva, & Adams-Wiggins, 2014), students are more willing to take risks and share their fledgling thinking.

One well-studied and critical facet of mathematics classrooms' social relations involves issues of academic and social *status*—perceptions of students' academic ability and social desirability (Cohen & Lotan, 2014; Langer-Osuna, 2011). When teachers attend to and interrupt these perceptions, which are often based on stereotypes rooted in race and gender (Leyva, 2017; Joseph, Hailu, & Matthews, 2019; McGee & Martin, 2011), students' mathematical engagement and understanding can improve (Boaler & Staples, 2008; Horn, 2008). If students' ideas are genuinely invited, they experience a sense of belonging that can ease the vulnerability of sharing ideas and support deeper engagement (Horn, 2017).

Classrooms are spaces where students learn not only about disciplines but also about themselves. Classroom norms inform students about what "knowing" math looks like and what counts as evidence of understanding. These same norms also serve as resources for students to learn about themselves in relation to those categories. Mathematics education research has been prolific in documenting the wide range of norms that can organize classrooms. The norms of inquiry classrooms often emphasize collaboration and communication, for example, through inviting partial answers and offering different approaches to solving problems. Research shows that classroom norms shaping what counts as competent mathematical behavior have significant implications for the kinds of relationships students are likely to develop to school mathematics (Boaler & Greeno, 2000; Boaler & Staples, 2008; Cobb, Gresalfi, & Hodge, 2009).

As an example, Sengupta-Irving and Enyedy (2015) contrasted two different statistics units, taught by the same teacher to two different seventh-grade classes, which intentionally contrasted Open versus Guided styles of inquiry. Although there were overlapping norms since both classes were taught by the same teacher, the authors also documented the different expectations that developed in the two classes. In the Open class, students were asked to articulate problems, invent strategies, and explore different solutions, while students in the Guided class were given the problems and, through structured inquiry, were scaffolded to see to a variety of possible solutions. These different practices led to very different interactions among the students and, in turn, different kinds of mathematical conversations. For example, students in the Open class independently generated new mathematical ideas in their discussions (coded as "strategy talk"), while students in the Guided class only did so in response to their teacher's opening. This resulted in very different amounts of *new mathematical talk*—only 3% of coded utterances in the Guided classroom, but 59% of coded utterances in the Open classroom. In addition, there was a different distribution of *personal authority*, with students in the Open class seeing new mathematical ideas as central to their problem-solving endeavor. For example, students in the Open classroom held peers accountable both to each other and to disciplinary norms, as seen in the content of their questions to one another. While students in the Guided classroom tended to ask each other questions about completing the procedures of the task (in the vein of answer-getting), students in the Open class tended to ask questions that focused on the data they were analyzing (in the vein of problem-solving; 16% of questions were coded as focusing on data for the Guided class, and 44% were focused on data for the Open class). Although both classes showed the same learning gains about statistics, students developed very different attitudes toward what they were doing, with those in the Open class being significantly more positive about mathematics than those in the Guided class.

Transforming classroom norms can be a significant challenge, because norms are subtle and often invisible, particularly to those who, like teachers, have power. Changing norms to emphasize the importance of making mistakes, for instance, cannot be accomplished simply by telling students that "making mistakes is okay." This message can be undermined by other common practices, such as only asking students to explain their thinking ("How did you get that answer?") if they have made a mistake. Students pick up what is truly valued—*the teacher only asks me to explain my thinking when I am wrong*—even when these expectations remain tacit (Schoenfeld, 1988). Transforming classroom norms thus involves reconceptualizing both mathematics and student learning. Norms that emphasize explanation, exploration, and collaboration also inherently push toward slower-paced instruction, which might conflict with institutional pressures to "cover" content.

Design Thinking as a Framework for Supporting Mathematical Inquiry

We have argued here that inquiry-oriented mathematics instruction is a cultural change project, one that is urgent for redressing educational inequality. As we have shown, every leverage point plays off of other elements in the classroom system. For that reason, interventions focusing on a single element—teacher knowledge, curriculum, *or* classroom norms—are likely to fall short. With so many forces working against the widespread adoption of inquiry-oriented mathematics instruction, how are educators, persuaded by the research and committed to inquiry-oriented mathematics instruction, to proceed?

We propose that they focus on implementation processes that take a *design-thinking* approach (Razzouk & Shute, 2012). Design thinking involves both analytic and creative engagement where teachers experiment, prototype, gather feedback, and redesign their inquiry teaching practices. In contrast to methods-focused approaches to teaching (Bartolomé, 1994), design thinking presumes that any pre-established routine for inquiry instruction will need to go through ongoing cycles of revision in response to feedback.

Conceptualizing inquiry-oriented instruction as an act of design thinking highlights that changing instruction is not an all-or-nothing affair—changing routines, introducing new practices, attending to classroom norms and practices, and even changing curricula, all have far-reaching consequences—consequences that influence one another. Indeed, as our systems perspective suggests, focusing on one leverage point influences others in ways that might not have been anticipated. Thus, rather than asking teachers to change their practice whole-cloth, we propose that teachers think about exploring how different leverage points of inquiry-oriented teaching influence their overall classroom settings.

The design-thinking sequence of experimenting, prototyping, gathering feedback, and redesign resembles the work in Realistic Mathematics Education (RME) of using iterative cycles of *preliminary instructional design*, *teaching experiments*, and *retrospective analyses* in support of the development of inquiry-oriented math instruction (Gravemeijer, 2004). Researchers in RME have used all three leverage points to support inquiry. For leverage point 1, teachers' knowledge, researchers have provided teachers' specific trajectories of students' thinking about mathematical content to support inquiry teaching (Clements & Sarama, 2004; Confrey, Malone, & Corely, 2014; Van den Heuvel-Panhuizen, 2003). For example, when asked to solve the problem 9 + 5, experienced inquiry teachers know that students often begin to reason by using a strategy called *direct modeling*, where they lay out 9 objects, then 5 objects, and count for the total. This can move through *partial modeling*—starting with 9 and using 5 fingers to *count on* to 14—before students begin to naturally use *benchmark facts* (e.g., 9 + 5 = 10 + 4, which can be easily calculated). Understanding this development can help teachers resist simply teaching students a strategy that involves "making tens." This popular strategy is useful and builds naturally on a base-10 system, but introducing it before students have had a chance to represent these quantities in ways that make sense to them can render such strategies as yet another meaningless approach. Although research-based learning trajectories vary in specificity, they tend to focus on elementary mathematics topics, making more advanced topics important sites for systematic investigation.

For leverage point 2, curriculum with connections, RME relies on *didactic phenomenological analysis* (Freudenthal, 1986). Using this design principle, mathematical concepts are analyzed from an instructional perspective. Instead of looking for material that illustrates a concept, phenomenological analysis beckons educators to look for phenomena that might invite learners to develop the concept. For example, to motivate the need for a coordinate system, teachers might ask students to describe the location of points scattered on a coordinate plane to a classmate. The difficulty of the task becomes quickly apparent, and the usefulness of ordered pairs a relief to all (Meyer, 2014), supporting an understanding of how coordinate systems (whether Cartesian or polar) locate points in space.

Finally, RME addresses leverage point 3, classroom norms and practices, by inviting educators to attend to sociomathematical norms in the classroom (Yackel & Cobb, 1996). Sociomathematical norms are agreed-upon ways of talking about consensus and arguments in mathematics classrooms. In inquiry-oriented classrooms, educators strive to have norms that make disagreements, mistakes, and challenges socially viable in the classroom. In addition, RME focuses on norms and practices through a design principle to imagine potentially productive discourse topics for the activity (Stephan, Bowers, Cobb, & Gravemeijer, 2003). For instance, in the Cartesian coordinate system example, teachers could anticipate students' emergent strategies for locating the points. They could listen for and elicit the variety of strategies students use, with particular attention to ones that focus on horizontal and vertical locations.

RME illustrates a deeply comprehensive approach to addressing classroom norms and practices. We note, however, that some of the research on inquiry-oriented mathematics instruction does not explicitly address key issues affecting students—namely, the status issues and stereotype threats—that other research has found to be so consequential for children's engagement and participation.

Discussion

Inquiry mathematics teaching approaches elicit and build on children's ideas in disciplinarily authentic ways. They have long been pursued to deepen students' understanding of and broaden participation in school mathematics. While educational research has identified the possibilities for inquiry-oriented mathematics instruction, it also highlights numerous challenges. In this chapter, we have summarized the nature of these possibilities and challenges to invite a shift in how we think about teachers' development of these practices and their uptake in classrooms. As we mentioned earlier, instead of viewing this as a challenge of implementation, we propose that inquiry-oriented instruction is better engaged as a problem of cultural change that demands design thinking around key leverage points in the classroom system—namely, teachers' knowledge, curriculum with connections, and classroom norms and practices. Researchers can support these designs through documentation of and strategies for addressing these leverage points.

In particular, we propose that researchers interested in supporting inquiry-oriented instruction pursue work that addresses the following questions:

- What kinds of knowledge, beliefs, and practices do mathematics teachers need to productively support inquiry-oriented instruction? How do we support mathematics teachers' development toward these?
- What kinds of contexts and situations can deepen students' mathematical thinking without distracting them or simply offering entertainment that obscures the underlying mathematics and its meanings?
- What kinds of strategies are useful for ensuring that classroom interactions support the development of productive mathematical identities for all students, especially as students are encouraged to display their mathematical thinking and uncertainty?
- What facets of classroom ecologies are vital to supporting inquiry-oriented mathematics instruction? How do we help teachers to reflect on their work toward inquiry-oriented instruction in ways that productively reflect on their classroom ecologies?
- Since much of the research on inquiry-oriented mathematics instruction focuses on elementary grades, what additional knowledge do we need to promote this form of instruction for older students? What are the unique challenges and affordances of those settings, and how does prior research apply?
- What changes would we need to see in broader systems of schooling—pacing guides, accountability schemes, and so on—to reduce teachers' dilemmas about inquiry-oriented instruction?

Progress on these and related questions could contribute to our knowledge base for supporting widespread implementation of inquiry-oriented mathematics instruction and, in turn, broaden participation in mathematics learning.

References

Ball, D. L. (1993). With an eye on the mathematical horizon: Dilemmas of teaching elementary school mathematics. *The Elementary School Journal, 93*(4), 373–397. https://doi.org/10.1086/461730.

Ball, D. L., & Bass, H. (2000). Interweaving content and pedagogy in teaching and learning to teach: Knowing and using mathematics. In J. Boaler (Ed.), *Multiple perspectives on the teaching and learning of mathematics* (pp. 83–104).Westport, CT: Ablex Publishing.

Bartell, T. G. (2013). Learning to teach mathematics for social justice: Negotiating social justice and mathematical goals. *Journal for Research in Mathematics Education, 44*(1), 129–163. https://doi.org/10.5951/jresematheduc.44.1.0129.

Bartolomé, L. (1994). Beyond the methods fetish: Toward a humanizing pedagogy. *Harvard Educational Review, 64*(2), 173–195. https://doi.org/10.17763/haer.64.2.58q5m5744t325730.

Battey, D., Neal, R. A., Leyva, L., & Adams-Wiggins, K. (2016). The interconnectedness of relational and content dimensions of quality instruction: Supportive teacher–student relationships in urban elementary mathematics classrooms. *The Journal of Mathematical Behavior, 42*, 1–19. https://doi.org/10.1016/j.jmathb.2016.01.001.

Boaler, J. (2002). *Experiencing school mathematics: Traditional and reform approaches to teaching and their impact on student learning.* London: Routledge. https://doi.org/10.4324/9781410606365.

Boaler, J., & Greeno, J. G. (2000). Identity, agency, and knowing in mathematics worlds. In J. Boaler (Ed.), *Multiple perspectives on mathematics teaching and learning* (pp. 171–200). Westport, CT: Ablex Publishing.

Boaler, J., & Staples, M. (2008). Creating mathematical futures through an equitable teaching approach: The case of Railside School. *Teachers College Record, 110*(3), 608–645.

Cabana, C., Shreve, B., Woodbury, E., & Louie, N. (2014). *Mathematics for equity: A framework for successful practice.* New York: Teachers College Press.

Clements, D. H., & Sarama, J. (2004). Learning trajectories in mathematics education. *Mathematical Thinking and Learning, 6*(2), 81–89. https://doi.org/10.1207/s15327833mtl0602_1.

Carpenter, T. P., & Franke, M. L. (2004). Cognitively guided instruction: Challenging the core of educational practice. In T.K. Glennan, S.J. Bodilly, J.R. Galegher, and K.A. Kerr (Eds.), *Expanding the reach of education reforms: Perspectives from leaders in the scale-up of educational interventions*, 41-80. Santa Monica, CA: RAND Education.

Cobb, P., Gresalfi, M., & Hodge, L. L. (2009). An interpretive scheme for analyzing the identities that students develop in mathematics classrooms. *Journal for Research in Mathematics Education, 40(1)*, 40–68.

Cobb, P., McClain, K., & Gravemeijer, K. (2003). Learning about statistical covariation. *Cognition and Instruction, 21*(1), 1–78. https://doi.org/10.1207/S1532690XCI2101_1.

Cohen, D. K. (2011). *Teaching and Its Predicaments.* Cambridge, MA: Harvard University Press. https://doi.org/10.4159/harvard.9780674062788

Cohen, D. K., & Ball, D. L. (1990). Relations between policy and practice: A commentary. *Educational Evaluation and Policy Analysis, 12*(3), 331–338. https://doi.org/10.3102/01623737012003331.

Cohen, E. G., & Lotan, R. A. (2014). *Designing groupwork: Strategies for the heterogeneous classroom* (3rd ed.). New York: Teachers College Press.

Confrey, J., Maloney, A. P., & Corley, A. K. (2014). Learning trajectories: A framework for connecting standards with curriculum. *ZDM, 46*(5), 719–733. https://doi.org/10.1007/s11858-014-0598-7.

Copur-Gencturk, Y., Cimpian, J. R., Lubienski, S. T., & Thacker, I. (2020). Teachers' bias against the mathematical ability of female, black, and Hispanic students. *Educational Researcher, 49*(1), 30–43. https://doi.org/10.3102/0013189X19890577

Doyle, W. (1983). Academic work. *Review of Educational Research, 53*(2), 159–199. https://doi.org/10.3102/00346543053002159.

Doyle, W. (1988). Work in mathematics classes: The context of students' thinking during instruction. *Educational Psychologist, 23*(2), 167–180. https://doi.org/10.1207/s15326985ep2302_6.

Erickson, F., Bagrodia, R, Cook-Sather, A., Espinoza, M. L., Jurow, A. S., Shultz, J. J., & Spencer, J. (2007). Students' experience of school curriculum: The everyday circumstances of granting and withholding assent to learn. In F. M. Connelly (Ed.) *The Sage handbook of curriculum and instruction* (pp. 198–218). Thousand Oaks, CA: Sage Publications. https://doi.org/10.4135/9781412976572.n10.

Fennema, E., Carpenter, T. P., Franke, M. L., Levi, L., Jacobs, V. R., & Empson, S. B. (1996). A longitudinal study of learning to use children's thinking in mathematics instruction. *Journal for Research in Mathematics Education*, 403–434. https://doi.org/10.2307/749875.

Frankenstein, M. (1990). Incorporating race, gender, and class issues into a critical mathematics literacy curriculum. *The Journal of Negro Education, 59*(3), 336–347. https://doi.org/10.2307/2295568.

Freudenthal, H. (1986). *Didactical phenomenology of mathematical structures* (Vol. 1). Springer Science & Business Media.

Garet, M. S., Porter, A. C., Desimone, L., Birman, B. F., & Yoon, K. S. (2001). What makes professional development effective? Results from a national sample of teachers. *American Educational Research Journal, 38*(4), 915–945. https://doi.org/10.3102/00028312038004915.

Goos, M. (2004). Learning mathematics in a classroom community of inquiry. *Journal for Research in Mathematics Education, 35*(4), 258–291. https://doi.org/10.2307/30034810.

Goulding, M., Rowland, T., & Barber, P. (2002). Does it matter? Primary teacher trainees' subject knowledge in mathematics. *British Educational Research Journal, 28*(5), 689–704. https://doi.org/10.1080/0141192022000015543a.

Gravemeijer, K. (2004). Local instruction theories as means of support for teachers in reform mathematics education. *Mathematical Thinking and Learning, 6*(2), 105–128. https://doi.org/10.1207/s15327833mtl0602_3.

Greeno, J. G. (1991). Number sense as situated knowing in a conceptual domain. *Journal for Research in Mathematics Education, 22*(3), 170–218. https://doi.org/10.2307/749074.

Gresalfi, M., Martin, T., Hand, V., & Greeno, J. (2009). Constructing competence: An analysis of student participation in the activity systems of mathematics classrooms. *Educational Studies in Mathematics, 70*(1), 49–70. https://doi.org/10.1007/s10649-008-9141-5

Gresalfi, M. S. (2009). Taking up opportunities to learn: Constructing dispositions in mathematics classrooms. *The Journal of the Learning Sciences, 18*(3), 327–369. https://doi.org/10.1080/10508400903013470.

Gutiérrez, R. (2008). A "gap gazing" fetish in mathematics education? Problematizing research on the achievement gap. *Journal for Research in Mathematics Education, 39*, 357–364.

Gutiérrez, R. (2016). Strategies for creative insubordination in mathematics teaching. *Special Issue Mathematics Education: Through the Lens of Social Justice,* 7(1) 52-62.

Gutstein, E. (2003). Teaching and learning mathematics for social justice in an urban, Latino school. *Journal for Research in Mathematics Education, 34*(1), 37–73. https://doi.org/10.2307/30034699.

Gutstein, E. (2006). *Reading and writing the world with mathematics: Toward a pedagogy for social justice*. New York: Taylor & Francis.

Hall, R., & Rubin, A. (2013). There's five little notches in here: Dilemmas in teaching and learning the conventional structure of rate. In J. Greeno & S. Goldman (Eds.) *Thinking Practices in Mathematics and Science Learning* (pp. 199–246). London: Routledge.

Hand, V. M. (2010). The co-construction of opposition in a low-track mathematics classroom. *American Educational Research Journal, 47*(1), 97–132. https://doi.org/10.3102/0002831209344216.

Heaton, R. M. (1992). Who is minding the mathematics content? A case study of a fifth-grade teacher. *The Elementary School Journal, 93*(2), 153–162. https://doi.org/10.1086/461719.

Herbel-Eisenmann, B. A., Lubienski, S. T., & Id-Deen, L. (2006). Reconsidering the study of mathematics instructional practices: The importance of curricular context in understanding local and global teacher change. *Journal of Mathematics Teacher Education, 9*(4), 313–345. https://doi.org/10.1007/s10857-006-9012-x.

Hill, H. C. (2007). Learning in the teaching workforce. *The Future of Children, 17*(1), 111–127. https://doi.org/10.1353/foc.2007.0004.

Hill, H. C. (2010). The nature and predictors of elementary teachers' mathematical knowledge for teaching. *Journal for Research in Mathematics Education, 41*(5), 513–545.

Hill, H. C., Blunk, M. L., Charalambous, C. Y., Lewis, J. M., Phelps, G. C., Sleep, L., & Ball, D. L. (2008). Mathematical knowledge for teaching and the mathematical quality of instruction: An exploratory study. *Cognition and Instruction, 26*(4), 430–511, https://doi.org/10.1080/07370000802177235.

Hill, H. C., Rowan, B., & Ball, D. L. (2005). Effects of teachers' mathematical knowledge for teaching on student achievement. *American Educational Research Journal, 42*(2), 371–406. https://doi.org/10.3102/00028312042002371.

Horn, I. S. (2008). Turnaround students in high school mathematics: Constructing identities of competence through mathematical worlds. *Mathematical Thinking and Learning, 10*(3), 201–239. https://doi.org/10.1080/10986060802216177.

Horn, I. S. (2012). *Strength in numbers: Collaborative learning in secondary mathematics*. Reston, VA: National Council of Teachers of Mathematics.

Horn, I.S. (2017). *Motivated: Designing Math Classrooms Where Students Want to Join In*. Portsmouth, NH: Heinemann.

Hufferd-Ackles, K., Fuson, K. C., & Sherin, M. G. (2004). Describing levels and components of a math-talk learning community. *Journal for Research in Mathematics Education, 35*(2), 81–116. https://doi.org/10.2307/30034933.

Humphreys, C., & Boaler, J. (2005). *Connecting mathematical ideas: Middle school video cases to support teaching and learning*. Portsmouth, NH: Heinemann.

Jackson, K., Garrison, A., Wilson, J., Gibbons, L., & Shahan, E. (2013). Exploring relationships between setting up complex tasks and opportunities to learn in concluding whole-class discussions in middle-grades mathematics instruction. *Journal for Research in Mathematics Education, 44*(4), 646–682. https://doi.org/10.5951/jresematheduc.44.4.0646.

Jackson, K., Gibbons, L., & Sharpe, C. J. (2017). Teachers' views of students' mathematical capabilities: Challenges and possibilities for ambitious reform. *Teachers College Record, 119*(7), 7.

Janssen, F., Westbroek, H., & Doyle, W. (2015). Practicality studies: How to move from what works in principle to what works in practice. *The Journal of the Learning Sciences, 24*(1), 176–186. https://doi.org/10.1080/10508406.2014.954751.

Jordan, B., & Henderson, A. (1995). Interaction analysis: Foundations and practice. *The Journal of the Learning Sciences, 4*(1), 39–103. https://doi.org/10.1207/s15327809jls0401_2.

Joseph, N. M., Hailu, M. F., & Matthews, J. S. (2019). Normalizing Black girls' humanity in mathematics classrooms. *Harvard Educational Review, 41*(1), 203–227. https://doi.org/10.17763/1943-5045-89.1.132.

Jurow, A. S. (2005). Shifting engagements in figured worlds: Middle school mathematics students' participation in an architectural design project. *The Journal of the Learning Sciences, 14*(1), 35–67. https://doi.org/10.1207/s15327809jls1401_3.

Kazemi, E., & Stipek, D. (2009). Promoting conceptual thinking in four upper-elementary mathematics classrooms. *Journal of Education, 189*(1–2), 123–137. https://doi.org/10.1177/0022057409189001-209.

Lampert, M. (1990). When the problem is not the question and the solution is not the answer: Mathematical knowing and teaching. *American Educational Research Journal, 27*(1), 29-63.

Langer-Osuna, J. M. (2011). How Brianna became bossy and Kofi came out smart: Understanding the trajectories of identity and engagement for two group leaders in a project-based mathematics classroom. *Canadian Journal of Science, Mathematics and Technology Education, 11*(3), 207–225. https://doi.org/10.1080/14926156.2011.595881.

Lehrer, R., & Schauble, L. (Eds) (2002). *Investigating Real Data in the Classroom: Expanding Children's Understanding of Math and Science.* Williston, VT: Teachers College Press

Lehrer, R., & Schauble, L. (2004). Modeling natural variation through distribution. *American Educational Research Journal, 41*(3), 635–679. https://doi.org/10.3102/00028312041003635.

Leonard, J., Brooks, W., Barnes-Johnson, J., & Berry III, R. Q. (2010). The nuances and complexities of teaching mathematics for cultural relevance and social justice. *Journal of Teacher Education, 61*(3), 261-270.

Leyva, L. A. (2017). Unpacking the male superiority myth and masculinization of mathematics at the intersections: A review of research on gender in mathematics education. *Journal for Research in Mathematics Education, 48*(4), 397–433. https://doi.org/10.5951/jresematheduc.48.4.0397.

Lortie, D. C. (1975). *Schoolteacher: A sociological study.* Chicago, IL: University of Chicago Press.

Ma, L. (2010). *Knowing and teaching elementary mathematics: Teachers' understanding of fundamental mathematics in China and the United States.* London: Routledge. https://doi.org/10.4324/9780203856345.

Martin, D. B., Gholson, M. L., & Leonard, J. (2010). Mathematics as gatekeeper: Power and privilege in the production of knowledge. *Journal of Urban Mathematics Education, 3*(2), 12–24.

McGee, E. O., & Martin, D. B. (2011). "You would not believe what I have to go through to prove my intellectual value!" Stereotype management among academically successful Black mathematics and engineering students. *American Educational Research Journal, 48*(6), 1347–1389. https://doi.org/10.3102/0002831211423972.

Meyer, D. (2014, February 12). Pick a point. Retrieved January 22, 2019 from http://blog.mrmeyer.com/2014/pick-a-point/

Nasir, N. I. S., & Shah, N. (2011). On defense: African American males making sense of racialized narratives in mathematics education. *Journal of African American Males in Education, 2*(1), 24–45.

National Council of Teachers of Mathematics (Ed.). (2000). *Principles and standards for school mathematics* (Vol. 1). Reston, VA: National Council of Teachers of Mathematics.

National Council of Teachers of Mathematics. Commission on Standards for School Mathematics. (1989). *Curriculum and evaluation standards for school mathematics.* Reston, VA: National Council of Teachers of Mathematics.

National Research Council. (1989). *Everybody counts: A report to the nation on the future of mathematics education.* Washington, DC: National Academies Press.

National Research Council. (2001). *Adding it up: Helping children learn mathematics.* Washington, DC: National Academies Press.

OECD. (2005). *Teachers matter: Attracting, developing and retaining effective teachers.* Paris: Organization for Economic Co-operation and Development Publishing.

OECD. (2016a). Is memorisation a good strategy for learning mathematics?, *PISA in Focus*, No. 61, OECD Publishing, Paris, https://doi.org/10.1787/5jm29kw38mlq-en.

OECD. (2016b), *Equations and inequalities: Making mathematics accessible to all*, PISA, OECD Publishing, Paris, http://dx.doi.org/10.1787/9789264258495-en

Razzouk, R., & Shute, V. (2012). What is design thinking and why is it important? *Review of Educational Research*, *82*(3), 330–348. https://doi.org/10.3102/0034654312457429.

Rowland, T., & Ruthven, K. (2011). *Mathematical knowledge in teaching*. Dordrecht: Springer. https://doi.org/10.1007/978-90-481-9766-8

Schoenfeld, A. H. (1988). When good teaching leads to bad results: The disasters of 'well-taught' mathematics courses. *Educational Psychologist*, *23*(2), 145–166. https://doi.org/10.1207/s15326985ep2302_5.

Schoenfeld, A. H., & Herrmann, D. J. (1982). Problem perception and knowledge structure in expert and novice mathematical problem solvers. *Journal of Experimental Psychology: Learning, Memory, and Cognition*, *8*(5), 484. https://doi.org/10.1037/0278-7393.8.5.484.

Sengupta-Irving, T., & Enyedy, N. (2015). Why engaging in mathematical practices may explain stronger outcomes in affect and engagement: Comparing student-driven with highly guided inquiry. *The Journal of the Learning Sciences*, *24*(4), 550–592. https://doi.org/10.1080/10508406.2014.928214.

Sfard, A. (2001). There is more to discourse than meets the ears: Looking at thinking as communicating to learn more about mathematical learning. *Educational Studies in Mathematics*, *46*(1–3), 13–57. https://doi.org/10.1023/A:1014097416157.

Shepard, L. (2010). What the marketplace has brought us: Item-by-Item teaching with little instructional insight. *Peabody Journal of Education*, *85*(2), 246–257. https://doi.org/10.1080/01619561003708445.

Sherin, M. G. (2002). A balancing act: Developing a discourse community in a mathematics classroom. *Journal of Mathematics Teacher Education*, *5*(3), 205–233. https://doi.org/10.1023/A:1020134209073.

Sinclair, N. (2006). The aesthetic sensibilities of mathematicians. In *Mathematics and the Aesthetic* (pp. 87–104). New York: Springer. https://doi.org/10.1007/978-0-387-38145-9_5.

Spillane, J., & Zeuli, J. (1999). Reform and teaching: Exploring patterns of practice in the context of national and state mathematics reforms. *Educational Evaluation and Policy Analysis*, *21*(1), 1–27. https://doi.org/10.3102/01623737021001001.

Staples, M. (2007). Supporting whole-class collaborative inquiry in a secondary mathematics classroom. *Cognition and Instruction*, *25*(2–3), 161–217. https://doi.org/10.1080/07370000701301125.

Stein, M. K., Engle, R. A., Smith, M. S., & Hughes, E. K. (2008). Orchestrating productive mathematical discussions: Five practices for helping teachers move beyond show and tell. *Mathematical thinking and learning*, *10*(4), 313-340.

Stein, M. K., Remillard, J., & Smith, M. S. (2007). How curriculum influences student learning. In F. K. Lester (Ed.), *Second handbook of research on mathematics teaching and learning* (Vol. 1, issue 1, pp. 319–370). Charlotte, NC: Information Age Publishing.

Stein, M. K., & Smith, M. (2011). *5 practices for orchestrating productive mathematics discussions*. Reston, VA: National Council of Teachers of Mathematics.

Stephan, M., Bowers, J., Cobb, P., & Gravemeijer, K. P. (Eds.) (2003). Supporting students' development of measuring conceptions: Analyzing students' learning in social context. *Journal for Research in Mathematics Education Monograph, 12*.

TV Tropes. (n.d.) Everybody hates mathematics. Retrieved from https://tvtropes.org/pmwiki/pmwiki.php/Main/EverybodyHatesMathematics. January 8, 2019.

Vallacher, R. R., Read, S. J., & Nowak, A. (2002). The dynamical perspective in personality and social psychology. *Personality and Social Psychology Review*, *6*(4), 264-273.

Van den Heuvel-Panhuizen, M. (2003). The didactical use of models in realistic mathematics education: An example from a longitudinal trajectory on percentage. *Educational Studies in Mathematics*, *54*(1), 9–35. https://doi.org/10.1023/B:EDUC.0000005212.03219.dc.

Walkerdine, V. (1988). *The mastery of reason: Cognitive development and the production of rationality*. Milton Park, UK: Taylor & Frances/Routledge.

Wilhelm, A. G. (2014). Mathematics teachers' enactment of cognitively demanding tasks: Investigating links to teachers' knowledge and conceptions. *Journal for Research in Mathematics Education*, *45*(5), 636–674. https://doi.org/10.5951/jresematheduc.45.5.0636.

Wisittanawat, F., & Gresalfi, M. S. (2020). The "tricky business" of genre blending: Tensions between frames of video game play and school mathematics. *The Journal of the Learning Sciences*. https://doi.org/10.1080/10508406.2020.1817747

Yackel, E., & Cobb, P. (1996). Sociomathematical norms, argumentation, and autonomy in mathematics. *Journal for Research in Mathematics Education*, *27*(4), 458–477. https://doi.org/10.2307/749877.

Zohar, A., & Dori, Y. J. (2003). Higher order thinking skills and low-achieving students: Are they mutually exclusive? *The Journal of the Learning Sciences*, *12*(2), 145–181. https://doi.org/10.1207/S15327809JLS1202_1.

19

INQUIRY AND LEARNING IN SCIENCE

Ravit Golan Duncan, Na'ama Y. Av-Shalom, and Clark A. Chinn

Recent educational reforms internationally have placed inquiry at the center of science education (e.g., Ministry of Education, 2012; National Research Council, 2012; Province of British Columbia, 2020). Although inquiry in science education is often not explicitly defined, it typically involves students working with evidence to construct and/or critique scientific explanations or models (cf. Ford, 2008). Moreover, students need a significant degree of epistemic agency—the autonomy to make sense of evidence themselves, to reach their own conclusions, and typically to engage in a social community with classmates, sharing and arguing over different explanations of evidence (Damşa et al., 2010; Miller et al., 2018; Stroupe, 2014). Researchers and practitioners alike regard inquiry learning as conferring a variety of benefits to science students. In this chapter, we discuss these benefits of inquiry learning and how they can be supported by innovative and effective inquiry learning environments in science education.

One impetus for the move toward inquiry in science education was the recognition that science education has, since its inception, focused teaching on the "final form" content of science—the theories, laws, and explanations that have already been well established (Duschl & Grandy, 2008; Duschl & Tahrisylaj, this volume). In contrast, curricula have until recently focused much less on science as a process—how scientists developed this final form knowledge. When scientific processes were introduced in classrooms, they were typically oversimplified (Chinn & Malhotra, 2002). For instance, students were taught to conduct simple observations of what they saw without mobilizing these observations in tandem with other evidence to support models or explanations. Or they were shown how to control variables on highly constrained tasks with just a few variables—tasks very different from the complexity of real science. These oversimplified forms of inquiry not only fail to give students a grasp of how scientific inquiry occurs; they may also actually mislead students into thinking that science is much simpler and more straightforward than it really is (Chinn & Malhotra, 2002). The movement toward scientific inquiry in science education has accordingly sought to enable students to gain a better grasp of the real practices of scientific inquiry.

But what is the value of gaining a grasp of the practices of inquiry? One potential benefit is that because students find inquiry to be more interesting than traditional forms of science instruction, inquiry learning may spur more students to consider careers in science, including students in groups that are underrepresented in science (NRC, 2011). This addresses one important goal of science education: developing pathways to science careers. Equally, if not more, important are the potential benefits for laypeople who do not plan to become scientists. Laypeople often need to make medical and health decisions such as whether to undergo a treatment, vaccinate their children, eat food that might have been exposed to certain pesticides, or whether to stay at home or wear a mask to avoid COVID-19. People also need to vote about scientific issues, such as whether oil pipelines should be built or whether genetically modified food should be labeled. They also need to decide whether to believe (and share) what they hear on the news, read on the Internet, or discuss with others. In order to do that, lay individuals need to be able to identify relevant expertise, level of consensus, and other considerations necessary to ascertain the credibility of a claim (Chinn et al., 2020a; Duncan et al., 2018; Feinstein et al., 2013), and they need to be able to do this across issues, new and old, that they encounter. They also need to be able to understand how to evaluate rejections of science—from unfounded claims that the earth is flat to assertions that vaccinations are harmful and that humans are not causing climate change. Yet, at the same time, it is important to learn to evaluate legitimate critiques of science, such as the sexism in medical research that often treats findings with men as applicable equally to women (Criado-Perez, 2019).

In this chapter, we focus particularly on inquiry learning in science classes geared toward preparing students to interact productively with science as lay citizens. The goal is to promote what Feinstein (2011) has called *competent outsiders*—adults who are able to use scientific information to solve problems individually and in groups, but without an expectation that they approach the expertise of scientists. These competencies are not easy to develop, and it is unclear that schools are developing them well or at all (Feinstein, 2011; Grandy & Duschl, 2007; McNeill & Berland, 2017). As we will discuss, inquiry learning can bridge this learning gap and support the development of individuals who can productively engage with science to attain both personal and civic aims.

Scientific Inquiry

We begin by first positioning scientific inquiry learning in the broader context of scientific inquiry. These changes in views of what scientific inquiry entails inform views of what science students need to know about scientific inquiry. Over the last 80 to 90 years, views of scientific inquiry have broadly shifted (Grandy & Duschl, 2007; NRC, 2007) from an emphasis on science as verified through observation, to an emphasis on theory change in science, and lastly to emphasizing the social context of scientific knowledge building:

- *Science as verified through observations.* In the late 19th and early 20th centuries, science was becoming valued as an observation-driven process (including experimentation) in which all scientific knowledge was verified through being grounded, ultimately, in observations (Grandy & Duschl, 2007; NRC, 2007; Oreskes, 2019). Views tended to be domain-general: One could identify an "effective method of inquiry into any subject-matter" (Dewey, 1910, p. 124). Associated with these views were simplified representations of scientific inquiry, such as the five-step "scientific method" (Rudolph, 2005, 2019), that are still prevalent today, as seen in many textbooks and posters on classroom walls.
- *Science as theory change.* In the second half of the 20th century several seminal works emerged conceptualizing science as a process of fundamental theory change in which scientists abandon one configuration of theories and methods in favor of another (e.g., T. Kuhn, 1962). At certain points, such as when anomalies accumulate that an established theory cannot explain, the field can undergo a major shift, with that theory being replaced in part or in totality. Previous scientific "knowledge" may now be reconceived in new ways according to the new theory (T. Kuhn, 1962). For example, when scientists understood that diseases were caused by microscopic organisms and not miasma (a kind of pollution of the air with a bad smell), this new theory changed not only future research and knowledge but also how all of the prior knowledge about diseases was (re)interpreted. Furthermore, in this conceptualization science is a joint endeavor of communities of scientists who collectively arrive at

a consensus about scientific theories, rather than individual scientists carrying out logical, justificatory methods (Grandy & Duschl, 2007).

- *Science as social.* Building on the idea of the scientific community, a new conceptualization emerged from anthropological and psychological research that emphasized the social nature of science (Brown et al., 1989, Longino, 1990; Nersessian, 2005). Scholars have recognized science as being a more complex and dialogic process. Not only do scientists often disagree about the meaning or relevance of data, but a diversity of interpretations within the scientific community is now seen as a positive and necessary aspect of scientific practice (Brickhouse, 2008; Longino, 1990; Oreskes, 2019; Solomon, 2008). In this conceptualization of science, researchers are understood to be acting within wider social structures which shape their processes of knowledge generation, as well as their motives, values, resources, and other aspects (Duschl, 2008; Erduran & Dagher, 2014). These are dynamic structures and can be within and beyond the domain of science, including other researchers, funding bodies, the public, and others. Communities of researchers and others engage in argumentation and other forms of dialogue about different ideas; these processes not only develop conceptual understanding but also refine and adapt the broader inquiry practices and underlying epistemologies (Duschl & Grandy, 2011; Erduran & Dagher, 2014). The objectivity of scientific knowledge arises not from the reasoning of individual scientists but from community processes of social critique and the willingness to take these critiques seriously (Longino, 2002; Oreskes, 2019). Furthermore, there is great variation in the practices (including the methodologies) of different areas of science, so that there is no single overarching method of science (Galison & Stump, 1996).

One other important contemporary trend in studies of science is relevant to inquiry learning in science. Specifically, the processes of knowledge construction by scientists are now widely understood as situated in model building (Duschl & Grandy, 2008; Giere, 1988; Nersessian, 2005; Windschitl et al., 2008). There are a variety of perspectives about the nature of models, but generally they are considered to be reasoning aids, helping to represent theoretical structures or systems (Windschitl et al., 2008). Models are not evaluated as "true" or "false"; rather, they are evaluated for how closely they resemble the world in desired respects. Newtonian physics is false in the light of relativity, but it provides models that resemble the world sufficiently well to send spacecraft to the moon. Models are developed through dialogue, disagreement, and other social knowledge-building practices, and support the disciplinary activities of a scientific community (Lehrer & Schauble, 2003; Windschitl et al., 2008).

The recent vision of science as a social practice of model building provides a much more complex picture of science than a view of science as a straightforward application of a scientific method. Science educators conceptualize scientific inquiry as a continuing, dialogic process of developing and refining scientific models and engaging in argumentation, which is situated within, and responsive to, wider social structures (Duschl, 2008; Erduran & Dagher, 2014; Grandy & Duschl, 2007; NRC, 2007). Science is not a straightforward method for attaining truth but rather a community practice that engages in a social struggle to achieve consensual knowledge (Duschl, 2020). Real inquiry is a "mangle of practice" in which there is constant interplay between different kinds of epistemic products and the many rich processes used to generate them (Pickering, 1995). Current work to promote inquiry learning in science education has increasingly adopted this more complex portrait of scientific inquiry.

Inquiry Learning to Develop Competent Outsiders

To develop a lay population able to productively engage with science, it is important to move away from canonical approaches to science education, which focus heavily on preparing students for science careers through the accumulation of scientific facts or concepts (Feinstein et al., 2013). Rather, as noted earlier, we need to move toward the goal of developing "competent outsiders" (Feinstein, 2011), people who are able to aptly engage with scientific issues in their personal lives as active, scientifically literate citizens, regardless of whether or not they go on to pursue a science career.

One assumption behind inquiry learning in science is that engaging students in the practice of science will enable them to understand the practices of science and perhaps to evaluate scientific evidence on important public issues themselves (American Association for the Advancement of Science [AAAS], 1990). But more recent approaches have questioned this assumption. Laypeople are limited in their ability to reason with scientific evidence because each discipline has a variety of highly specialized methods, protocols, and bodies of knowledge (Duncan et al., 2018). Thus, another important aspect of scientific knowledge that students need to develop is understanding how laypeople can aptly engage with science and when they might need to (Duncan et al., 2018; Feinstein et al., 2013). For example, this involves developing sophisticated reasoning skills, understanding when and how to trust experts or reports of evidence, and learning how to use these to make choices in daily lives. Engaging with inquiry in science will help students grapple with these issues as they discover the bounds of their knowledge and develop strategies to continue in their inquiry processes (Bromme & Goldman, 2014; Duncan et al., 2018).

This *scientific literacy perspective* requires situating science inquiry much more in the context of the practical problems that are faced by laypeople (Feinstein & Waddington, 2020). This requires different competencies from the skills of a scientist (Keren, 2018). For example, if a student sees an article on the Internet about a new vaccination that might be helpful (or harmful) to her, it is first important that she be able to identify that this is an area that she can address using science. Then, she needs to be able to assess the article: Is the author trustworthy? Does the venue use reliable practices of vetting information before publishing or posting it? Do the claims align with established scientific claims? Is compelling evidence presented? Has the information been cherry-picked? Do scientists have consensus on this issue? Have disinformation techniques been used, such as creating a false level of uncertainty, or using financially tainted experts? Laypeople need to be able to answer questions like these, and they are not expected to engage in original science themselves to answer questions or to have the technical competence to engage with evidence in the same way that scientists do (Duncan et al., 2018). Science inquiry instruction should be oriented toward helping students use science to solve real-world problems faced by individuals and citizens in their capacity as laypeople.

New Perspectives on Inquiry Learning in Science

In the prior section, we provided an image of science as a knowledge-building endeavor generating scientific models and explanations that are evidence-based. The development of these epistemic products involves dialogic processes carried out in the social contexts of the scientific community (Latour, 1999). We have also emphasized that learning to use science as competent outsiders is not the same thing as learning to be a scientist, so inquiry learning must take this into account.

What are the implications of this view of science on what students and teachers should be doing in the science classroom? We can think about these implications through the lens of the AIR model of epistemic thinking, which identifies three components of epistemic thinking: *A*ims, *I*deals, and *R*eliable processes (elaborated on below; Chinn et al., 2014). This model can be operationalized in the context of science inquiry to derive three key implications.

First, this view implies that we need to engage students with the *epistemic aims* of both science and lay application of science. Students should be figuring out key science ideas through investigation with the central *aim* of developing new models that explain natural phenomena (Berland et al., 2016; Osborne, 2014), and they should use scientific ideas and evidence to solve practical problems (Duncan et al., 2018). Second, toward this aim students should be engaged in using a wide array of *reliable epistemic processes* to generate the knowledge. This can include scientific inquiry processes such as careful observation, experimentation, development of explanatory models, co-constructing ideas with fellow students through argumentation and other forms of discourse, and more. It can also include processes that are reliable for competent outsiders such as determining who the most reliable experts are, finding out whether experts are in consensus, and adapting knowledge to local, particular circumstances. Third, the work of building knowledge about phenomena should be done in the context of a community with *shared epistemic ideals* (criteria) about (a) what count as appropriate aims, i.e., which questions should be taken up and investigated by the class; (b) what count as reliable processes for generating knowledge, e.g., what are the standards for determining whether observations are valid or for determining whether experts have established a stable consensus; and (c) what count as good epistemic products, e.g., what count as good models and good arguments.

In the next section, we will focus on model-based inquiry (MBI), a promising approach for engaging students in scientific inquiry in accordance with the implications outlined above. Our aim is to illustrate, through exemplar MBI environments, how this approach engages students in the epistemic aims, ideals, and reliable processes through typical tasks, talk, and teaching strategies.

Model-Based Inquiry Learning

As we have discussed, much scientific inquiry involves building explanations and models of the world around us (Giere et al., 2006; Nersessian, 2002). Such models can take a variety of forms, including equations, taxonomies, computational models, causal models, and system models. Most models make explicit ideas about underlying mechanisms—how entities and interactions at lower scalar levels bring about phenomena observed at higher scalar levels (Krist et al., 2018). Model-based inquiry learning environments take as their epistemic aim the construction, critique, and revision of (predominantly) mechanistic models based on evidence. In contrast to their use in current classrooms as teaching tools to show concepts, models in MBI environments are seen as tools-to-think-with that can be used to explain, to predict, and to raise new questions for further investigation and modeling (Gilbert, 2004; Windschitl et al., 2008).

Different learning environments foreground and background different aspects of modeling practices, affording different kinds of discussions about the epistemic aims, ideals, and reliable processes of inquiry. Our first exemplar is the research of Lehrer and Schauble (2003, 2004) with its focus on data modeling. They engage students with questions about how one can extract useful information regarding a phenomenon and represent this information in ways that make patterns of interest salient. Students participate in extensive experimentation with and discussions about what to measure, how to measure it, and how to represent the data. Through these activities, students develop an understanding that any set of measures and any choice of its representation can show certain qualities of the data (and certain phenomena) while hiding others. These tasks and conversations emphasize that science involves transforming the phenomena through experimental designs and tools that make it accessible for investigation, which Lehrer and Schauble term as *arranging the conditions for seeing* (Lehrer & Schauble, 2010). Arranging the conditions for seeing entails reasoning about reliable processes of transforming phenomena; for example, what should we measure in order to determine variation in the growth of plants? Students could suggest multiple variables in this situation—plant height, width, number of leaves, or canopy volume. Moreover, students could suggest multiple ways of measuring each variable, with some methods being more accurate and reliable than others (measuring height with string, and not a ruler, may be more accurate when plant stalks are bendy rather than straight). Deciding which variables to measure and how to go about measuring them involves considerable uncertainty (Manz, 2015; Manz & Renga, 2017) and inventiveness.

This exemplar highlights the importance of providing students with opportunities to engage with the messiness of arranging the conditions for seeing and the reliability of the processes used to see patterns of interest. Allowing students to identify the variables to measure, invent ways to measure them, and tackle issues of how to best represent the data in ways that help with the "seeing" (data modeling) is critically important in inquiry learning (Ford, 2005). The implication here is that rather than teaching students about methods (e.g., that they need to control variables), we need to engage them in activities and discussions that will help them understand the epistemic purpose of using particular methods and research designs (Berland et al., 2016; Ford, 2008) and the conditions under which these are reliable (Duncan et al., 2018). Research has shown that when students *do* understand the purpose of specific methods, such as controlling variables, they are more likely to use these in novel contexts (Ford, 2008).

Our next exemplar, the IQWST middle-school curriculum, emphasizes the iterative development of class models that represent the consensus of the learning community's current state of understanding of the phenomenon under investigation (Krajcik et al., 2008; Schwartz et al., 2008). IQWST units are grounded in natural phenomena and progress through the investigation of driving questions (e.g., how can I smell things from a distance? Why do organisms look the way they do?). As students explore these questions, they develop progressively more sophisticated and comprehensive models of the natural phenomenon at hand. The models are based on evidence that the students collect through designed experiments and observations or receive as representations of data collected by others (e.g., data from studies conducted by scientists). Using these models, students engage in the writing of scientific explanations that include a claim, supporting evidence, and reasoning that justifies the connection of the evidence to the claim (McNeill & Krajcik, 2008).

IQWST units are grounded in phenomena that are likely to be meaningful and interesting to the students and are built around storylines that chart out a path through iterative cycles of questioning and investigations such that prior activities set up new questions for investigation that are explored in the next "chapter" of the storyline. As the storyline unfolds, students progressively build more nuanced understandings through these cycles of questioning and investigation. Students work as a learning community to construct knowledge that is meaningful and valued by their own community and is legitimate from the perspective of the scientific community (Berland et al., 2016). That is, students decide what questions they wish to address (their aims), how they are going to address them using scientific practices that they see as useful in their situation (the reliable processes), and what will count as an appropriate explanation that is based on evidence that the community finds compelling (ideals for explanations). The strong emphasis of IQWST units on student ownership over the goals, process, and norms of knowledge construction is intended to engender meaningful engagement with epistemic considerations of scientific inquiry.

This exemplar highlights the importance of engaging students in doing science, rather than doing the lesson (Jiménez-Aleixandre et al., 2000), in ways that afford them with meaningful opportunities to pursue scientifically legitimate epistemic goals of answering questions, amassing relevant evidence, and constructing knowledge. Rather than carrying out inquiry activities in a rote or perfunctory manner, students in epistemically authentic inquiry environments such as IQWST and others (Calabrese-Barton & Tan, 2010; Passmore, Gouvea, & Giere, 2014) engage with epistemic considerations about the nature of the desired knowledge product, its generality (how it relates to other explanations and phenomena), the justifications of the desired knowledge (e.g., strength of evidentiary support), and the intended audience of the products generated (Berland et al., 2016). When students have a purpose for their inquiry, they are able to leverage personal and cultural knowledge and resources to generate legitimate scientific knowledge and present it in ways that resonate with their home cultures and communities (Calabrese Barton & Tan, 2010). The implication here is that inquiry-based learning environments need to engage students with these epistemic considerations (epistemic ideals) and the epistemic goals (or aims) of knowledge construction in ways that students will see as worthy and meaningful while maintaining fidelity to the epistemic aims and practices of science.

The third and final exemplar draws on our own work with the Promoting Reasoning and Conceptual Change in Science (PRACCIS) project in middle-school classrooms (Chinn et al., 2018; Rinehart et al., 2016). PRACCIS units are also anchored in a phenomenon and engage students with the construction, evaluation, and revision of models based on a set of multiple pieces of evidence that vary in strength and quality. In these units, students consistently consider two or more competing models, either those that they constructed or those that were provided to them, and evaluate these against the set of evidence. Based on their evaluation of the models, students typically write a scientific argument to support the model they think is best.

A key feature of PRACCIS is an explicit focus on epistemic criteria for judging epistemic products and processes. In the course of an activity involving scaffolded comparisons of models of varying forms and quality, students develop a class list of criteria (ideals) for good models. Such lists include criteria that underscore the communicative aspects of models—secondary epistemic criteria, such as *has labels*, *is organized*, and *is easy to understand*—as well as primary epistemic criteria that underscore the accuracy of the model, such as *is supported by evidence*, *does not have evidence that contradicts it*, and *is accurate* (Pluta et al., 2011). Criteria lists are taken up as shared norms that are used by students when generating and critiquing models. As the community's understandings of the modeling practice evolves, the list is periodically revised to reflect the change in shared ideals. Class discussions about these epistemic ideals focus on both the application of ideals and the justifications for their worthiness (e.g., a model supported by multiple studies is better than a model supported by only one study because replication of results provides stronger support). In addition to developing and using criteria about model quality, PRACCIS also supports students in developing standards for what counts as good evidence. Toward this end, a key feature of PRACCIS is providing students with evidence that varies in form and quality. Given that a substantial portion of the evidence that individuals (students and adults) encounter in the public realm is of low quality, engaging students with poor-quality evidence is important if we want them to be savvy evaluators of evidence in the real world (Duncan et al., 2018). Evaluating evidence quality is part of the epistemic messiness that should be part and parcel of doing science inquiry in the classroom.

This exemplar highlights the importance of epistemic criteria and their justifications. If the aim of inquiry in science and in the science classroom is to construct knowledge, then there need to be some standards by which to judge these knowledge products and the processes used to generate them. These standards need to be meaningful to the community and taken as shared ideals toward which the community and its knowledge products strive. The implication here is that inquiry-based learning environments need to afford opportunities for students to develop and be held accountable to epistemic ideals about what count as good models, good evidence, good explanations, and good arguments. Moreover, these ideals should be driven by a genuine valuing of shared standards. Thus, the learning community should be vested in these ideals because it can justify their utility in helping to generate better knowledge products. As the community's understanding of inquiry practices evolves so should the community's shared ideals.

The three exemplars of innovative science inquiry learning environments illustrate thick authenticity (Shaffer & Resnick, 1999), in which students' goals are both meaningful to them and reflect the aims of the discipline. In such environments, students engage with the epistemic messiness of science inquiry through activities that make salient (a) that model and theory construction are the core epistemic aims of science inquiry and involve a great deal of inventiveness and justification to generate valued epistemic products; (b) that nature needs to be transformed through (reliable) processes in order to allow us to see and interpret patterns of interest; and (c) that the products and processes of inquiry are evaluated based on agreed shared communal criteria that allow us to judge whether the products achieve the epistemic aims set by the community. Discourse plays a key role in engendering the saliency of these core epistemic considerations of inquiry; in model-based inquiry, the pervasive form of discourse is argumentation, and we discuss the importance and crucial role of argumentation in talk and writing in meaningful epistemic engagement with inquiry.

Features of Effective Inquiry Learning

What kinds of instruction can promote students' appropriation of productive aims, ideals, and reliable processes? Features of effective instruction that can be incorporated into inquiry learning environments include the following:

- *Engagement in inquiry.* Although there are approaches to learning that stress direct instruction with practice, the evidence is strong that learning to engage in inquiry requires instruction that actually engages students in inquiry as a means of instruction (Chinn et al., 2013; Furtak et al., 2012; Hmelo-Silver et al., 2007; Minner et al., 2010). This is not to exclude a role for interleaving occasional episodes of direct instruction with inquiry (e.g., introducing students explicitly to the Claim-Evidence-Reasoning components of a good argument as a tool that students can then use while engaging in inquiry to construct models that best fit the evidence). But learning to engage in inquiry requires experience in negotiating the complex interactions of successful inquiry. Each of the projects described above engages students in rich inquiry environments.
- *Scaffolds of epistemic practices.* Engaging students in inquiry, however, without supports is ineffective. Each of the three exemplar projects we discussed provides scaffolds to students that help make epistemic practices more visible to them. For example, IQWST uses a "CER" scaffold to encourage students to construct more complete arguments in terms of *C*laims, *E*vidence, and *R*easoning connecting claims and evidence (McNeill et al., 2006; McNeill & Krajcik, 2012). IQWST has also used technology tools to help students understand the critical components of explanations (Sandoval & Millwood, 2005). PRACCIS has used diagrams that systematically organize students' analyses of all the evidence with respect to each model. Such scaffolds are critical to fostering successful learning through inquiry (Hmelo-Silver et al., 2007). This approach to supporting learning can be viewed as guided inquiry or guided discovery, where some help is provided to facilitate discovery while still allowing students to make the discoveries themselves; guided discovery has been found to be more effective than direct explanation or pure discovery (Hmelo-Silver et al., 2007; Mayer, 2004). Quintana (this volume) discusses effective scaffolds for inquiry in more detail.
- *Epistemic agency.* All of the programs described above afford students with extensive epistemic agency to make up their own minds about which models to create or choose, how to evaluate and interpret evidence, and so on. Effective inquiry environments seek multiple ways of providing such autonomy (Miller et al., 2018; Stroupe, 2014), not only in constructing and evaluating models but even in developing the very aims to be pursued, the ideals or norms to be used in the community (e.g., community-developed ideals in PRACCIS), and the reliable processes to be used (e.g., the social negotiation of processes of observations in Lehrer and Schauble's data modeling).
- *Metacognitive understanding and regulation.* The programs described above all encourage students to reflect on their practices, thereby developing a metacognitive understanding of relevant aims, ideals, and processes. Metacognitive understanding of the aims, ideals, and

processes of epistemic thinking is an important goal of education (Barzilai & Chinn, 2018). Such metacognitive understanding supports better reasoning (for discussions of evidence for this, see Barzilai & Chinn, 2018; Chinn et al., 2020b). Promoting metacognitive understanding involves discourse that describes appropriate aims, ideals, and processes (e.g., stating that *fit with evidence* is an ideal for models) and discourse that evaluates and justifies aims, ideals, and processes (e.g., using empirical evidence on the placebo effect to justify that blind observation is a reliable research process) (Chinn et al., 2020b). Among our three exemplars, PRACCIS places a strong emphasis on metacognitive understanding, as students reflect on ideals of good models and processes of producing good evidence. IQWST also promotes such understanding through its emphasis on promoting students' understanding of the structure of arguments.

- *Fostering social communities of inquiry.* Most effective inquiry learning environments also place a strong emphasis on developing community norms that support inquiry. In terms of the AIR model, we can view these efforts as promoting shared commitments to seeking epistemic aims such as explanations of phenomena (Sandoval & Millwood, 2005), epistemic ideals such as fit with evidence and clarity of communication (Pluta et al., 2011; Ryu & Sandoval, 2012), and reliable processes such as seeking out and weighing multiple alternative theories (Chinn et al., 2018). PRACCIS achieves these goals through having students develop shared, public class lists of relevant ideals and processes. Teachers can promote shared commitments by pressing students to give relevant justifications, such as supporting a norm of demanding that models fit the evidence by pressing students to justify their ideas using evidence; these norms can spread thereby throughout a classroom (e.g., Hennessey, 2003; Ryu & Sandoval, 2012). Moreover, these shared epistemic criteria and norms are likely to change over time within the community as students learn more about different types of processes and what makes them reliable (or not), as they learn more about convincing ways to argue using evidence, and as they learn more about what kinds of knowledge are more valuable to them.

Internalist versus Contextual Approaches to Inquiry Learning in Science

The three examples we have discussed to this point can all be characterized as *internalist* approaches to science education (Feinstein & Waddington, 2020). The term *internalist* refers to the focus of the curricula on engaging students as if they were "inside" science—as if they were young scientists working in the manner of scientists. Feinstein and Waddington (2020) argued that, while effective internalist approaches to science education are needed, there is also a need for *contextual* approaches that engage students with science not as if they were scientists building models but as citizens using science in non-science settings. An overemphasis on "internalist" approach to scientific inquiry will fall short of enabling students to engage with science as competent outsiders. Feinstein and Waddington (2020) further argue that contextual approaches have been much less emphasized in science education.

With some science topics, students could pursue contextual approaches to inquiry. Instead of being placed in the role of scientists gathering and reviewing evidence, they could work as citizens, searching for information to inform local actions, but focused heavily on evaluating source credibility, trying to ascertain whether expertise exists and on which issues, and so on. These engage students in evaluating both expert testimony and scientific evidence as they take the role of laypersons (Duncan et al., 2018).

Another approach could involve students in metacognitive reflection on the implications of what they have learned about science through internalist inquiry. For example, effective internalist inquiry might engage students in realistic processes of seeing how scientists use social critique to improve ideas over time, that scientists work out better methods over time through such critiques, that scientific claims are tentative, and so on. These understandings could help students appreciate why ideas with a broad scientific consensus are credible, giving them deeper reasons to trust science than just treating science as an authority (Chinn & Duncan, 2018). It could also help them grasp why corporate-funded science sometimes falls short (e.g., ideas may not be subject to full scrutiny because many ideas are viewed as proprietary). It could help them understand why one would expect the science of COVID-19 to change rapidly over even short periods of time. Thus, effective internalist inquiry could be coupled with lessons and units that enable students to apply their growing understanding of scientific practices to lay reasoning about science.

Instruction can also engage students directly in the practices of outsiders dealing with science. One form that instruction can take is engaging students in *socioscientific* problems in which they use the scientific knowledge they are developing to solve practical problems. Recent work has emphasized the value of engaging students in *consequential* problems that matter to them (Birmingham et al., 2017; Tan et al., 2019). These may be problems that are place-based—that is, current problems in students' own communities. Students may also be involved in choosing these problems themselves. Educators may involve students in using science to address problems of social justice in their communities (Tan et al., 2019). Consequential problems hold great promise for enhancing students' engagement, motivation, and learning.

To learn how to deal with science in real contexts, problems should be authentic as well as consequential. *Authentic* learning environments capture as much of the messiness of real world thinking as possible (Chinn et al., 2020a). For example, they expose students to bad evidence as well as good evidence, to a variety of conflicts as is found in the real world and problems that tempt the use of motivated forms of reasoning as well as emotional commitments that may conflict with evidence. Chinn et al. (2020a) argued that such environments in schools are needed to prepare students to reason on such problems in the real world.

Benefits of Engaging Students in Inquiry

There are many benefits to engaging students in inquiry learning in science; in this section, we discuss three of them. When designed appropriately, inquiry learning leads to (1) *increased motivation,* (2) *deeper content learning,* and (3) *improved reasoning.*

Increased Motivation

Inquiry learning in science increases students' motivation. Recent perspectives consider motivation to be "in the interaction between individual and subject matter" (D. Kuhn, 2007, p. 109). One way to do this is to help students identify the areas in which science is relevant to their lives and to the areas that they care about (Feinstein, 2011). Inquiry learning environments in science afford students opportunities to engage in scientific communities and guide investigations themselves through the questions and methods that they choose to pursue. Having a meaningful problem to pursue and more ownership over the process and products can increase student motivation. For example, Lynch et al. (2005) found that a high-quality inquiry-based science curriculum increased students' motivation and engagement when compared with students using other kinds of curricula. Students especially improved in orienting toward mastery goals, which suggests that students became more focused on developing their own understanding and skills. Other research on inquiry-based curricula has also shown student gains in motivation (e.g., Engle & Conant, 2002), including among students who started with lower motivation and who struggled with low feelings of self-efficacy (Mistler-Jackson & Songer, 1999). These studies show that active participation in inquiry learning environments can encourage students to take ownership of their own learning, develop their interest, self-efficacy, and other aspects of motivation.

Supports Content Learning

Alongside the increased emphasis on science practices, recent reforms continue to emphasize learning content as an important goal (Hmelo-Silver et al., 2007), and improving best practices for content teaching continues to be particularly important. Inquiry learning has been shown to be a very effective tool for improving content learning in science. Several meta-analyses of research on inquiry learning environments found that a majority of studies on inquiry instruction show positive effects across science domains on student content learning (Furtak et al., 2007), such as on learning concepts, facts, and principles, and on retention (Minner et al., 2010). Inquiry tasks, such as working with evidence and models, can also help students attend to relevant information and areas that need explanation (Chinn et al., 2013). In addition, several studies suggest that inquiry learning can have differential effects particularly benefitting the lowest-performing students (Geier et al., 2008; Lynch et al., 2005) and historically underserved students (Geier et al., 2008), thereby helping to close achievement gaps.

Inquiry learning environments can take on a variety of forms (Furtak et al., 2012) that can be challenging for students, requiring a high cognitive load and more time (Chinn et al., 2013; Kirschner et al., 2006). However, learning science through inquiry enhances inquiry skills useful for daily life, motivation to engage with science and science learning, and content understanding. Effective learning environments function as knowledge-building communities (e.g., Engle & Conant, 2002), and the resulting knowledge is both deeper and more robust (see Stroupe, 2017). Through engaging in inquiry learning environments, students can come to understand scientific practices and the nature of science.

Supports Growth in Reasoning

A main focus of inquiry learning in science is to improve students' competence in reasoning—that is, their competence in the aims, ideals, and processes used to engage in productive reasoning. Environments that engage students in inquiry environments are effective in promoting students' competence in reasoning, including argumentation and use of evidence (Chinn & Clark, 2013; Chinn et al., 2013; Ryu & Sandoval, 2012). Abrami et al. (2008) found that learning environments that placed students in authentic situations (such as problem-solving) promoted greater development of critical thinking skills. As we have noted earlier, these positive results are contingent on developing learning environments with supportive features including scaffolding, epistemic agency, metacognitive support, and fostering social communities engaged in inquiry.

Inquiry learning environments can also promote movement toward becoming more competent outsiders. As we noted earlier, there is a need for much more research on how to promote competent outsiders. However, two lines of research provide support for the claim that inquiry-based learning can support development of at least some facets of the reasoning needed by competent outsiders. Research on the use of socioscientific issues in inquiry learning has shown that appropriately designed learning environments support growth in reasoning skills needed to address such real-world problems (Zeidler et al., 2019). The second line of research comes from studies of students' use of multiple, conflicting documents to reach conclusions about complex problems. These studies show that, with appropriate scaffolding and guidance, students gain skill in reasoning with information from multiple documents, including deeper consideration of source quality and perspective, as well as better integration of information (e.g., Barzilai & Ka'adan,

2017; Barzilai et al., 2020). Effective support includes engaging students in reflection on source evaluation (e.g., what are the characteristics of good sources), in considering multiple perspectives found across documents, and in carefully analyzing how different sources and ideas are related (e.g., Barzilai et al., 2018; Barzilai et al, 2020; Wiley et al., 2009).

Challenges in the Learning and Teaching of Model-Based Inquiry

Engaging in MBI is not trivial for students or teachers. In this section, we discuss some of these challenges. We then provide a brief overview of how instruction can be informed by a learning progression for modeling practice as a way to address some of these challenges.

Disciplinary Literacy

The first challenge we discuss is one broadly associated with inquiry and that is not specific to model-based inquiry—the challenge of disciplinary-specific forms of literacy. Scientific inquiry involves sophisticated literacy skills such as the ability to make sense of scientific data representations, terminology, and the norms of scientific writing (Lemke, 1990; Moje, 2008; Shanahan & Shanahan, 2008). While these disciplinary-specific ways of reading, writing, and talking are central to the scientific knowledge-building endeavor, they are rarely the focus of instruction (Goldman et al., 2016). For example, students' struggles in constructing evidence-based models and explanations (Berland & Reiser, 2009; McNeill & Krajcik, 2012) are partly due to difficulties with the science concepts and with understanding disciplinary norms of what counts as an acceptable written or oral explanation in science (Moje, 2008). Science instruction should also include efforts to make the norms of reading, writing, and talking in the discipline explicit to students and to engage them in discussing why these norms exist (Goldman et al., 2016).

Understanding Models as Abstractions

The benefits of models are not immediately obvious to students; they do not readily understand why it is helpful to abstractly represent a phenomenon or a variable when one can simply go and observe it (Lehrer & Schauble, 2010). This perspective reflects the early trends in scientific reports that were predominantly narrative accounts of phenomena that others could also go and observe (Bazerman, 1988). This initial perspective of "seeing is believing" shifted in science as reports began to include more details about the conditions for seeing and ultimately provided representations of phenomena that omit many features while making salient only the theoretically relevant ones. Students' initial models tend to preserve much of the original phenomena, for example, students may add fingers to a model of a joint (elbow) even when figures are immaterial to the mechanism of joint movement (Penner et al., 1997), or students may prefer to use string to represent the length of plant roots because it looks more like roots (Lehrer & Schauble, 2010).

Increasing the Repertoire of Representational Forms

To young students the inclusion of more features of the phenomenon in the representation makes it seem more realistic and believable. This is not necessarily a problem; however, too many unnecessary details can occlude important aspects of the phenomenon and interfere with productive sense-making. Thus, a key challenge in supporting modeling with younger students is helping them enlarge and evolve their repertoire of representational forms such that they come to see the advantages of representations that omit irrelevant features and emphasize important ones. Developmentally, the earlier (more detailed) representations still serve to anchor the representation as a reference, and subsequent representations maintain coherence with earlier ones while moving away from the details of the phenomenon toward illuminating essential patterns and mechanisms (Lehrer & Schauble, 2010).

Purpose and Use of Models

An additional challenge is students' perceptions of the purpose and use of models. There is extensive research documenting changes to students' perceptions of the purpose of models and what can be done with them. Initially students do not really see a role for models in inquiry; rather, science is construed as an effort to identify and quantify relationships between variables. This relation-based view of science (Driver et al., 1996) is commensurable with the traditional instructional focus on the scientific method and controlling variables (Windschitl et al., 2008). In a relation-based view of science, models do not play a role in knowledge building but are viewed as replicas of the phenomenon (e.g., model of the cell or DNA) that are created by experts in order to show the phenomenon (e.g., see organelles in the cell). Students do not see much of a role for themselves in creating models; rather, they view their role as consuming knowledge that can be gleaned by viewing the models of experts (Harrison & Treagust, 2000).

As students engage more deeply with inquiry, they develop a somewhat more sophisticated view in which models are seen as representations of phenomena that are abstractions that show relationships between components and processes of the phenomenon. Students may recognize that models have explanatory power, but still see their main purpose as mostly communicative. While students may view models as ideas one can test, such tests serve to validate the models but not to refute or revise them; models are seen as correct depictions because they were created (and can only be created) by experts. Therefore, models are not seen as contestable or amenable to revision in light of evidence.

A more sophisticated and expert-like view of models and modeling comes about as students begin to see the role of models as part of knowledge building. This model-based reasoning affords seeing models as tools to think with and as having working value in generating ideas (Driver et al., 1996). Students with a model-based reasoning perspective see themselves as capable of generating and testing models; such engagement is no longer considered as the purview of only experts. Students also understand that different individuals can create different models, that none of these models are objectively correct, and that all models need to be evaluated against data and revised accordingly.

Developmental Considerations: A Progression for Models and Modeling

There have been research efforts to more fully characterize the continuum of students' developing understandings of scientific modeling in order to inform instructional efforts of engaging students in this core practice (Schwarz et al., 2009). Schwarz et al. (2009) organized their progression around two commitments. Modeling entails (a) integrating meta-knowledge about models with elements of the practice, and (b) integrating the sense-making and communicative goals of modeling. Meta-modeling knowledge has long been recognized as important for developing a model-based reasoning perspective of inquiry and involves understanding why models are used in science, how they are used, and what are their strengths and limitations (Schwarz & White, 2005). Meta-modeling knowledge mutually supports and is deepened by engagement with elements of the modeling practice: creating, using, evaluating, and revising models. The integration of meta-modeling knowledge and elements of modeling is in service of two core goals of modeling—using models as thinking tools to make sense of and explain phenomena, and using models to communicate these explanations and ideas to others.

The learning progression proposed by Schwarz et al. (2009) therefore describes growth in sophistication along two integrated dimensions (constructs): *understanding models as generative tools for predicting and explaining*, and *understanding models as changeable entities*. Each of these constructs includes multiple levels that describe more sophisticated ways of reasoning. For example, there are four levels in the second construct (models as changeable entities) that describe a shift from viewing models as unchanging even in light of new information (level 1), to changing models based on information from authority (e.g., teacher or textbook) rather than based on fit with evidence (level 2), to changing models in light of evidence in order to generate a more accurate model (level 3), and finally to considering changes to models in ways that enhance their explanatory power and fit with evidence and that may involve combining ideas from different models (level 4).

Using examples from late elementary and middle school, Schwarz et al. (2009) illustrated student reasoning along these levels and showed that core aspects of the modeling practice elements are within reach of elementary and middle-school students. Furthermore, they showed that students were able to develop some understandings about this practice (meta-modeling knowledge). However, relatively few students showed reasoning at the highest level of the progressions. This is in part because of the conflicting expectations and norms of the traditional ways of teaching science and the model-based science approach. For example, the common perception of science as a fixed body of facts to be learned (Duschl, 2008; Duschl & Duncan, 2009) is at odds with a view of science as an effort to build knowledge that is contestable. Both how science is currently learned and how the discipline is perceived present obstacles to engendering model-based reasoning. In addition, the kinds of everyday experiences that students may draw on to make sense of modeling do not really provide much traction for grounding meta-modeling knowledge such as what is the benefit of modeling, why are explanatory scope and parsimony important criteria for evaluating models, and so on. Traditional science instruction and everyday experience do not create a need-to-know for these aspects of modeling practice (Edelson, 2001; Lehrer & Schauble, 2006). As we have noted before, key to engendering model-based inquiry is designing thickly authentic learning environments that generate a genuine need for epistemic engagement with scientific inquiry practices.

Conclusions

Inquiry learning has been a focus of science education reforms since the late 1950s. It has taken on different forms, with an early focus on science skills (e.g., varying-one-thing-at-a-time), to a focus on "the" scientific method, and, most recently, a focus on scientific practices for knowledge building. These shifts came as science education researchers, educators, and policymakers realized that the typical instruction of the time was insufficient to foster deep and meaningful engagement with science, especially in terms of engendering an understanding of the epistemic commitments and aims of science inquiry. Understanding these commitments is important for both advanced STEM courses and for laypeople's engagement with science on a personal and civic level.

The shift to using scientific practices and language, and the exhortation that students should be learning core ideas in science through engagement in these scientific practices, reflects the idea that science knowledge is built in the context of a scientific community with shared norms and standards for its processes and products. The focus in the US and elsewhere on modeling and argumentation as core practices of inquiry (Hazelkorn et al., 2015; NRC, 2012) emphasizes that a fundamental epistemic game in science is one of making and critiquing claims (Collins & Ferguson, 1993; Ford, 2008), which often come in the form of models.

However, shifting the classroom toward a learning community in which evidence is used to create and critique models through argumentation is not trivial. Over the past three decades, there has been extensive research devoted to designing and studying learning environments that can support meaningful inquiry. There are several important insights and implications from this body of work that we have discussed in this chapter, which we briefly summarize here. First, the epistemic aim of science is knowledge building, and this should be reflected in the activities and discourse in the classroom: Students should be engaged in the development, evaluation, and revision of explanatory models. Second, the process of building and critiquing models is inherently epistemically messy, and students need to experience and tackle this messiness rather than avoid it. Epistemically friendly environments neither prepare students for advanced studies in science nor civic (or personal) engagement with science (Duncan et al., 2018; Goldberg, 2013). Figuring out how to make a phenomenon accessible to study, what to measure and how to measure it, and how to deal with the uncertainly involved is a core part of actually doing science (Lehrer & Schauble, 2010; Manz, 2015). Third, the messiness and uncertainty do not mean that "anything goes" and that any evidence or model is as good as any other. Scientists employ multiple criteria for determining the adequacy, trustworthiness, and utility of epistemic products and processes (Barzilai & Chinn, 2018; Chinn et al., 2014; Duncan et al., 2018). Students can also develop their own criteria for judging epistemic products that their learning community creates or evaluates (Pluta et al., 2011). Fourth and last, learning communities and the students that make them up need to find the engagement with inquiry practices meaningful, and they need to understand, at a meta-level, why they are doing what they are doing (Berland et al., 2016). It is not enough that the teacher and the designers of the environment know why certain activities and talk are important; students must feel a need to know themselves (Edelson, 2001).

Moving forward, given the challenges involved, further research and expansion of professional development opportunities for educators will be necessary to support wider-scale implementation of inquiry learning environments. However, we can build on these insights to support educators in using inquiry-based methods and support students as they become scientifically literate citizens.

References

Abrami, P. C., Bernard, R. M., Borokhovski, E., Wade, A., Surkes, M. A., Tamim, R., & Zhang, D. (2008). Instructional interventions affecting critical thinking skills and dispositions: A stage 1 meta-analysis. *Review of Educational Research, 78*(4), 1102–1134. https://doi.org/10.3102%2F0034654308326084

American Association for the Advancement of Science. (1990). *Science for all Americans*. New York: Oxford University Press.

Barzilai, S., & Chinn, C. A. (2018). On the goals of epistemic education: Promoting apt epistemic performance. *Journal of the Learning Sciences, 27*(3), 353–389. https://doi.org/10.1080/10508406.2017.1392968

Barzilai, S., & Ka'adan, I. (2017). Learning to integrate divergent information sources: The interplay of epistemic cognition and epistemic metacognition. *Metacognition and Learning, 12*(2), 193–232. https://doi.org/10.1007/s11409-016-9165-7

Barzilai, S., Mor-Hagani, S., Zohar, A. R., Shlomi-Elooz, T., & Ben-Yishai, R. (2020). Making sources visible: Promoting multiple document literacy with digital epistemic scaffolds. *Computers & Education, 157*. doi:10.1016/j.compedu.2020.103980

Barzilai, S., Zohar, A. R., & Mor-Hagani, S. (2018). Promoting integration of multiple texts: A review of instructional approaches and practices. *Educational Psychology Review, 30*(3), 973–999. https://doi.org/10.1007/s10648-018-9436-8

Bazerman, C. (1988). *Shaping written knowledge: The genre and activity of the experimental article in science* (Vol. 356). Madison: University of Wisconsin Press.

Berland, L. K., & Reiser, B. J. (2009). Making sense of argumentation and explanation. *Science Education, 93*(1), 26–55. https://doi.org/10.1002/sce.20286

Berland, L. K., Schwarz, C. V., Krist, C., Kenyon, L., Lo, A. S., & Reiser, B. J. (2016). Epistemologies in practice: Making scientific practices meaningful for students. *Journal of Research in Science Teaching, 53*(7), 1082–1112. https://doi.org/10.1002/tea.21257

Birmingham, D., Calabrese Barton, A., McDaniel, A., Jones, J., Turner, C., & Rogers, A. (2017). "But the science we do here matters": Youth-authored cases of consequential learning. *Science Education, 101*(5), 818–844. https://doi.org/10.1002/sce.21293

Brickhouse, N. (2008). What is inquiry? To whom should it be authentic? In R. A. Duschl & R. E. Grandy (Eds.), *Teaching scientific inquiry* (pp. 284–287). Rotterdam: Sense Publishers. https://doi.org/10.1163/9789460911453_021

Bromme, R., & Goldman, S. R. (2014). The public's bounded understanding of science. *Educational Psychologist, 49*(2), 59–69. https://doi.org/10.1080/00461520.2014.921572

Brown, J. S., Collins, A., & Duguid, P. (1989). Situated cognition and the culture of learning. *Educational Researcher, 18*(1), 32–42. https://doi.org/10.3102/0013189X018001032

Calabrese Barton, A., & Tan, E. (2010). We be burnin'! Agency, identity, and science learning. *Journal of the Learning Sciences, 19*(2), 187–229. https://doi.org/10.1080/10508400903530044

Chi, M. T. H. (1992). Conceptual change within and across ontological categories: Examples from learning and discovery in science. In R. Giere (Ed.), *Cognitive models of science: Minnesota studies in the philosophy of science* (pp. 129–186). Minneapolis: University of Minnesota Press. https://doi.org/10.5749/j.ctttsr75.9

Chinn, C. A., Barzilai, S., & Duncan, R. G. (2020a). Education for a "Post-Truth" world: New directions for research and practice. *Educational Researcher.* https://doi.org/10.3102/0013189X20940683

Chinn, C. A., Barzilai, S., & Duncan, R. G. (2020b). Disagreeing about how to know: The instructional value of explorations into knowing. *Educational Psychologist, 55*(3), 167–180. https://doi.org/10.1080/00461520.2020.1786387

Chinn, C. A. & Clark, D. B. (2013). Learning through collaborative argumentation. In C. E. Hmelo-Silver, C. A. Chinn, C. Chan, & A. M. O'Donnell (Eds.), *The international handbook of collaborative learning* (pp. 314–332). London: Routledge. https://doi.org/10.4324/9780203837290-27

Chinn, C. A., & Duncan, R. G. (2018). What is the value of general knowledge of scientific reasoning? In *Scientific reasoning and argumentation: The roles of domain-specific and domain-general knowledge* (pp. 77–101). Taylor and Francis. https://doi.org/10.4324/9780203731826

Chinn, C. A., Duncan, R. G., Dianovsky, M., & Rinehart, R. (2013). Promoting conceptual change through inquiry. In S. Vosniadou (Ed.), *International handbook of research on conceptual change* (2nd ed., pp. 539–559). New York: Routledge. https://doi.org/10.4324/9780203154472

Chinn, C. A., Duncan, R. G., & Rinehart, R. W. (2018). Epistemic design: Design to promote transferable epistemic growth in the PRACCIS project. In E. Manalo, Y. Uesaka, & C. A. Chinn (Eds.), *Promoting spontaneous use of learning and reasoning strategies: Theory, research, and practice for effective transfer.* New York: Routledge. https://doi.org/10.4324/9781315564029-16

Chinn, C. A., & Malhotra, B. A. (2002). Epistemologically authentic inquiry in schools: A theoretical framework for evaluating inquiry tasks. *Science Education, 86*(2), 175–218. https://doi.org/10.1002/sce.10001

Chinn, C. A., Rinehart, R. W., & Buckland, L. A. (2014). Epistemic cognition and evaluating information: Applying the AIR model of epistemic cognition. In D. Rapp and J. Braasch (Eds.), *Processing inaccurate information: Theoretical and applied perspectives from cognitive science and the educational sciences* (pp. 425–453). Cambridge, MA: MIT Press. https://doi.org/10.7551/mitpress/9737.001.0001

Collins, A., & Ferguson, W. (1993). Epistemic forms and epistemic games: Structures and strategies to guide inquiry. *Educational Psychologist, 28*, 25–42. https://doi.org/10.1207/s15326985ep2801_3

Criado-Perez, C. (2019). *Invisible women: Data bias in a world designed for men.* New York: Abrams Press.

Damşa, C. I., Kirschner, P. A., Andriessen, J. E., Erkens, G., & Sins, P. H. (2010). Shared epistemic agency: An empirical study of an emergent construct. *The Journal of the Learning Sciences, 19*(2), 143–186. https://doi.org/10.1080/10508401003708381

Dewey, J. (1910). Science as subject-matter and as method. *Science, 31*(787), 121–127.

Driver, R., Leach, J., Millar, R., & Scott, P. (1996). *Young people's images of science.* Buckingham: Open University Press.

Duncan, R. G., Chinn, C. A., & Barzilai, S. (2018). Grasp of evidence: Problematizing and expanding the next generation science standards' conceptualization of evidence. *Journal of Research in Science Teaching, 55*(7), 907–937. https://doi.org/10.1002/tea.21468

Duschl, R. A. (2008). Science education in three-part harmony: Balancing conceptual, epistemic and social learning goals. *Review of Research in Education, 32*, 268–291. https://doi.org/10.3102/0091732X0730937

Duschl, R. A. (2020). Practical reasoning and decision making in science: *Struggles for truth, Educational Psychologist, 55*(3), 187–192. https://doi.org/10.1080/00461520.2020.1784735

Duschl, R. A., & Duncan, R. G. (2009). Beyond the fringe: Building and evaluating scientific knowledge systems. In S. Tobias, S., and T. M. Duffy (Eds.), *Constructivist Instruction: Success or Failure?* (pp. 311–332). London: Taylor & Francis. https://doi.org/10.4324/9780203878842

Duschl, R. A., & Grandy, R. E. (2008). Reconsidering the character and role of inquiry in school science: Framing the debates. In R. A. Duschl & R. E. Grandy (Eds.), *Teaching scientific inquiry* (pp. 1–37). Rotterdam: Sense Publishers. https://doi.org/10.1163/9789460911453_002

Duschl, R. A., & Grandy, R. E. (2011). Demarcation in science education: Toward an enhanced view of scientific method. In R. S. Taylor & M. Ferrari (Eds.), *Epistemology and science education: Understanding the evolution vs. intelligent design controversy* (pp. 3–19). London: Routledge. https://doi.org/10.4324/9780203839638

Duschl, R. A., & Tahirsylaj, A. (this volume). Evolving conceptions of educational research and inquiry. In R. G. Duncan & C. A. Chinn (Eds.), International Handbook of Inquiry and Learning. New York; Routledge.

Edelson, D. C. (2001). Learning-for-use: A framework for integrating content and process learning in the design of inquiry activities. *Journal of Research in Science Teaching, 38*(3), 355–385. https://doi.org/10.1002/1098-2736(200103)38:3%3C355::AID-TEA1010%3E3.0.CO;2-M

Engle, R. A., & Conant, F. R. (2002). Guiding principles for fostering productive disciplinary engagement: Explaining an emergent argument in a community of learners classroom. *Cognition and Instruction, 20*(4), 399–483. https://doi.org/10.1207/S1532690XCI2004_1

Erduran, S., & Dagher, Z. R. (2014). *Reconceptualizing the nature of science for science education* (Vol. 43). Dordrecht: Springer. https://doi.org/10.1007/978-94-017-9057-4

Feinstein, N. (2011). Salvaging science literacy. *Science Education, 95*(1), 168–185. https://doi.org/10.1002/sce.20414

Feinstein, N. W., Allen, S., & Jenkins, E. (2013). Outside the pipeline: Reimagining science education for nonscientists. *Science, 340*(6130), 314–317. https://doi.org/10.1126/science.1230855

Feinstein, N. W., & Waddington, D. I. (2020). Individual truth judgments or purposeful, collective sensemaking? Rethinking science education's response to the post-truth era. *Educational Psychologist, 55*(3), 155–166. https://doi.org/10.1080/00461520.2020.1780130

Ford, M. J. (2005). The game, the pieces, and the players: Generative resources from alternative instructional portrayal of experimentation. *The Journal of The Learning Sciences, 14*(4), 449–487. https://doi.org/10.1207/s15327809jls1404_1

Ford, M. J. (2008). "Grasp of practice" as a reasoning resource for inquiry and nature of science understanding. *Science & Education, 17*, 147–177. https://doi.org/10.1007/s11191-006-9045-7

Furtak, E. M., Seidel, T., Iverson, H., & Briggs, D. C. (2012). Experimental and quasi-experimental studies of inquiry-based science teaching: A meta-analysis. *Review of Educational Research, 82*(3), 300–329. https://doi.org/10.3102/0034654312457206

Galison, P. L., & Stump, D. J. (1996). *The disunity of science: Boundaries, contexts, and power.* Stanford, CA: Stanford University Press.

Giere, R., Bickle, J., & Maudlin, R. (2006). *Understanding scientific reasoning* (5 ed.). Belmont: Thomson/Wadsworth Publishing.

Geier, R., Blumenfeld, P. C., Marx, R. W., Krajcik, J. S., Fishman, B., Soloway, E., & Clay-Chambers, J. (2008). Standardized test outcomes for students engaged in inquiry-based science curricula in the context of urban reform. *Journal of Research in Science Teaching, 45*(8), 922–939. https://doi.org/10.1002/tea.20248

Giere, R. N. (1988). *Explaining science: A cognitive approach.* Chicago, IL: University of Chicago Press.

Gilbert, J. K. (2004). Models and modelling: Routes to more authentic science education. *International Journal of Science and Mathematics Education, 2*(2), 115–130. https://doi.org/10.1007/s10763-004-3186-4

Goldberg, S. (2013). Epistemic dependence in testimonial belief, in the classroom and beyond. *Journal of Philosophy of Education, 47*(2), 168–186. https://doi.org/10.1111/1467-9752.12019

Goldman, S. R., Britt, M. A., Brown, W., Cribb, G., George, M., Greenleaf, C., Lee, C. D., Shanahan, C., & Project READI. (2016). Disciplinary literacies and learning to read for understanding: A conceptual framework for disciplinary literacy. *Educational Psychologist*, https://doi.org/10.1080/00461520.2016.1168741

Grandy, R., & Duschl, R. A. (2007). Reconsidering the character and role of inquiry in school science: Analysis of a conference. *Science & Education, 16*(2), 141–166. https://doi.org/10.1007/s11191-005-2865-z

Harrison, A. G., & Treagust, D. F. (2000). A typology of school science models. *International Journal of Science Education, 22*(9), 1011–1026. https://doi.org/10.1080/095006900416884

Hazelkorn, E., Ryan, C., Beernaert, Y., Constantinou, C. P., Deca, L., Grangeat, M., Karikorpi, M., Lazoudis, A., Casulleras, R. P., Welzel, M., Europäische Kommission, & Europäische Kommission (Eds.). (2015). *Science education for responsible citizenship: Report to the European Commission of the Expert Group on Science Education.* Publications Office of the European Union. https://doi.org/10.2777/12626

Hennessey, M. G. (2003). Metacognitive aspects of students' reflective discourse: Implications for intentional conceptual change teaching and learning. In G. M. Sinatra & P. R. Pintrich (Eds.), *Intentional conceptual change* (pp. 105–134). Mahwah NJ: Erlbaum.

Hmelo-Silver, C. E., Duncan, R. G., & Chinn, C. A. (2007). Scaffolding and achievement in problem-based and inquiry learning: a response to Kirschner, Sweller, and Clark (2006). *Educational Psychologist, 42*(2), 99–107. https://doi.org/10.1080/00461520701263368

Jiménez-Aleixandre, M. P., Rodríguez, A. B., & Duschl, R. A. (2000). "Doing the lesson" or "doing science": Argument in high school genetics. *Science Education*, *84*(3), 757–792. https://doi.org/10.1002/1098-237X(200011)84:6%3C757::AID-SCE5%3E3.0.CO;2-F

Keren, A. (2018). The public understanding of what? Laypersons' epistemic needs, the division of cognitive labor, and the demarcation of science. *Philosophy of Science*, *85*(5), 781–792. https://doi.org/10.1086/699690

Kirschner, P. A., Sweller, J., & Clark, R. E. (2006). Why minimal guidance during instruction does not work: An analysis of the failure of constructivist, discovery, problem-based, experiential, and inquiry-based teaching. *Educational Psychologist*, *41*(2), 75–86. https://doi.org/10.1207/s15326985ep4102_1

Krajcik, J. S., McNeill, K. L., & Reiser, B. (2008). Learning-goals-driven design model: Developing curriculum materials that align with national standards and incorporate project-based pedagogy. *Science Education*, *92*(1), 1–32. https://doi.org/10.1002/sce.20240

Krist, C., Schwarz, C. V., & Reiser, B. J. (2018). Identifying essential epistemic heuristics for guiding mechanistic reasoning in science learning. *Journal of the Learning Sciences*, *28*(2), 160–205. https://doi.org/10.1080/10508406.2018.1510404

Kuhn, D. (2007). Is direct instruction an answer to the right question? *Educational Psychologist*, *42*(2), 109–113. https://doi.org/10.1080/00461520701263376

Kuhn, T. S. (1962). *The structure of scientific revolutions*. Chicago, IL: University of Chicago Press.

Latour, B. (1999). *Pandora's hope: Essays on the reality of science studies*. Cambridge, MA: Harvard university Press.

Lehrer, R., & Schauble, L. (2003). Origins and evolution of model-based reasoning in mathematics and science. In R. Lesh & H. M. Doerr (Eds.), *Models and modeling in mathematics teaching, learning, and problem solving* (pp. 59–70). Mahwah, NJ: Erlbaum. https://doi.org/10.4324/9781410607713

Lehrer, R., & Schauble, L. (2004). Modeling natural variation through distribution. *American Educational Research Journal*, *41*(3), 635–679. https://doi.org/10.3102/00028312041003635

Lehrer, R., & Schauble, L. (2006). Scientific thinking and science literacy: Supporting development in learning in contexts. In W. Damon, R. M. Lerner, K. A. Renninger, & I. E. Sigel (Eds.), *Handbook of child psychology* (6th ed., Vol. 4). Hoboken, NJ: John Wiley and Sons.

Lehrer, R., & Schauble, L. (2010). What kind of explanation is a model? In M. K. Stein (Ed.), *Instructional explanations in the disciplines* (pp. 9–22). New York: Springer. https://doi.org/10.1007/978-1-4419-0594-9_2

Lemke, J. L. (1990). *Talking science: Language, learning, and values*. Norwood, NJ: Ablex.

Longino, H. E. (1990). *Science as social knowledge: Values and objectivity in scientific inquiry*. Princeton, NJ: Princeton University Press. https://doi.org/10.2307/j.ctvx5wbfz

Longino, H. E. (2002). *The fate of knowledge*. Princeton, NJ: Princeton University Press.

Lynch, S., Kuipers, J., Pyke, C., & Szesze, M. (2005). Examining the effects of a highly rated science curriculum unit on diverse students: Results from a planning grant. *Journal of Research in Science Teaching*, *42*(8), 912–946. https://doi.org/10.1002/tea.20080

Manz, E. (2015). Resistance and the development of scientific practice: Designing the mangle into science instruction. *Cognition and Instruction*, *33*(2), 89–124. https://doi.org/10.1080/07370008.2014.1000490

Manz, E., & Renga, I. P. (2017). Understanding how teachers guide evidence construction conversations. *Science Education*, *101*(4), 584–615. https://doi.org/10.1002/sce.21282

Mayer, R. E. (2004). Should there be a three-strikes rule against pure discovery learning? The case for guided methods of instruction. *The American Psychologist*, *59*(1), 14–19. https://doi.org/10.1037/0003-066X.59.1.14

McNeill, K. L., & Berland, L. (2017). What is (or should be) scientific evidence use in k-12 classrooms? What is (or should be) scientific evidence use. *Journal of Research in Science Teaching*, *54*(5), 672–689. https://doi.org/10.1002/tea.21381

McNeill, K. L., & Krajcik, J. (2008). Inquiry and scientific explanations: Helping students use evidence and reasoning. In J. Luft, Bell, R. L., & Gess-Newsome, J. (Eds.), *Science as inquiry in the secondary setting*, (pp. 121–134). Arlington, VA: NSTA Press.

McNeill, K. L., & Krajcik, J. S. (2012). *Supporting grade 5-8 students in constructing explanations in science: The claim, evidence, and reasoning framework for talk and writing*. Boston, MA: Pearson.

McNeill, K. L., Lizotte, D. J., Krajcik, J., & Marx, R. W. (2006). Supporting students' construction of scientific explanations by fading scaffolds in instructional materials. *The Journal of the Learning Sciences*, *15*(2), 153–191. https://doi.org/10.1207/s15327809jls1502_1

Miller, E., Manz, E., Russ, R., Stroupe, D., & Berland, L. (2018). Addressing the epistemic elephant in the room: Epistemic agency and the next generation science standards. *Journal of Research in Science Teaching*, *55*(7), 1053–1075. https://doi.org/10.1002/tea.21459

Ministry of Education. (2012). *Science syllabus: lower secondary—express course/normal (academic) course*. Singapore: Curriculum Planning & Development Division, Ministry of Education.

Minner, D. D., Levy, A. J., & Century, J. (2010). Inquiry-based science instruction—what is it and does it matter? Results from a research synthesis years 1984 to 2002. *Journal of Research in Science Teaching, 47*(4), 474–496. https://doi.org/10.1002/tea.20347

Mistler-Jackson, M., & Butler Songer, N. (2000). Student motivation and internet technology: Are students empowered to learn science? *Journal of Research in Science Teaching: The Official Journal of the National Association for Research in Science Teaching, 37*(5), 459–479. https://doi.org/10.1002/(SICI)1098-2736(200005)37:5%3C459::AID-TEA5%3E3.0.CO;2-C

Moje, E. B. (2008). Foregrounding the disciplines in secondary literacy teaching and learning: A call for change. *Journal of Adolescent & Adult Literacy, 52*, 96–107. https://doi.org/10.1598/JAAL.52.2.1

National Research Council. (2007). *Taking science to school: Learning and teaching science in grades K-8*. Washington, DC: The National Academies Press. https://doi.org/10.17226/11625

National Research Council. (2011). *Successful K-12 STEM education: Identifying effective approaches in science, technology, engineering, and mathematics*. Committee on Highly Successful Science Programs for K-12 Science Education, Board on Science Education and Board on Testing and Assessment, Division of Behavioral and Social Sciences Education. Washington, DC: The National Academies Press. https://doi.org/10.17226/13158

National Research Council. (2012). *A framework for K-12 science education: Practices, crosscutting concepts, and core ideas*. Washington, DC: The National Academies Press. https://doi.org/10.17226/13165

Nersessian, N. (2002). The cognitive basis of model-based reasoning in science. In P. Carruthers, S. Stich, & M. Siegal (Eds.), *The cognitive basis of science* (pp. 133–153). Cambridge: Cambridge University Press. https://doi.org/10.1017/CBO9780511613517.008

Nersessian, N. J. (2005). Interpreting scientific and engineering practices: Integrating the cognitive, social, and cultural dimensions. In M. Gorman, R. Tweney, D. Gooding, & A. Kincannon (Eds.), *Scientific and technological thinking* (pp. 17–56). Mahwah, NJ: Lawrence Erlbaum Associates. https://doi.org/10.4324/9781410611314

Oreskes, N. (2019). *Why trust science?* Princeton, NJ: Princeton University Press.

Osborne, J. (2014). Teaching scientific practices: Meeting the challenge of change. *Journal of Science Teacher Education, 25*(2), 177–196. https://doi.org/10.1007/s10972-014-9384-1

Passmore, C. M., Gouvea, J. S., & Giere, R. (2014). Models in science and in learning science: Focusing scientific practice on sense-making. In M. R. Matthews (Ed.), *International handbook of research in history, philosophy and science teaching* (pp. 1171–1202). Netherlands: Springer. https://doi.org/10.1007/978-94-007-7654-8_36

Penner, D., Giles, N., Lehrer, R., & Schauble, L. (1997). Building functional models: Designing an elbow. *Journal of Research in Science Teaching, 34*(2), 125–143. https://doi.org/10.1002/(SICI)1098-2736(199702)34:2%3C125::AID-TEA3%3E3.0.CO;2-V

Pickering, A. (1995). *The mangle of practice: Time, agency, and science*. Chicago, IL: University of Chicago Press.

Pluta, W. J., Chinn, C. A., & Duncan, R. G. (2011). Learners' epistemic criteria for good scientific models. *Journal of Research in Science Teaching, 48*(5), 486–511. https://doi.org/10.1002/tea.20415

Province of British Columbia. (2020). Science. BC's New Curriculum. https://curriculum.gov.bc.ca/curriculum/science/core/introduction

Quintana, C. (this volume). Scaffolding inquiry: Reviewing and expanding on the function and form of scaffolding in inquiry learning.

Rinehart, R., Duncan, R., Chinn, C., Atkins, T., & DiBenedetti, J. (2016). Critical design decisions for successful model-based inquiry in science classrooms. *International Journal of Designs for Learning, 7*(2). https://doi.org/10.14434/ijdl.v7i2.20137

Rudolph, J. (2005). Epistemology for the masses: The origins of "The Scientific Method" in American schools. *History of Education Quarterly, 45*(3), 341–376. https://doi.org/10.1111/j.1748-5959.2005.tb00039.x

Rudolph, J. (2019). *How we teach science: What's changed, and why it matters*. Cambridge, MA: Harvard University Press.

Ryu, S., & Sandoval, W. A. (2012). Improvements to elementary children's epistemic understanding from sustained argumentation. *Science Education, 96*(3), 488–526. https://doi.org/10.1002/sce.21006

Sandoval, W. A., & Millwood, K. A. (2005). The quality of students' use of evidence in written scientific explanations. *Cognition and Instruction, 23*(1), 23–55. https://doi.org/10.1207/s1532690xci2301_2

Schwarz, C. V., Reiser, B. J., Davis, E. A., Kenyon, L., Achér, A., Fortus, D., ... & Krajcik, J. (2009). Developing a learning progression for scientific modeling: Making scientific modeling accessible and meaningful for learners. *Journal of Research in Science Teaching: The Official Journal of the National Association for Research in Science Teaching, 46*(6), 632–654. https://doi.org/10.1002/tea.20311

Schwarz, C. V., & White, B. Y. (2005). Metamodeling knowledge: Developing students' understanding of scientific modeling. *Cognition and Instruction*, *23*(2), 165–205. https://doi.org/10.1207/s1532690xci2302_1

Shaffer, D. W., & Resnick, M. (1999). "Thick" authenticity: New media and authentic learning. *Journal of Interactive Learning Research*, *10*(2), 195–216.

Shanahan, T., & Shanahan, C. (2008). Teaching disciplinary literacy to adolescents: Rethinking content-area literacy. *Harvard Educational Review*, *78*(1), 40–59. https://doi.org/10.17763/haer.78.1.v62444321p602101

Shwartz, Y., Weizman, A., Fortus, D., Krajcik, J. S., & Reiser, B. (2008). The IQWST experience: Using coherence as a design principle for a middle school science curriculum. *The Elementary School Journal*, *109*(2), 199–219. doi.org/10.1086/590526

Solomon, M. (2008). Social epistemology of science. In R. A. Duschl & R. E. Grandy (Eds.), *Teaching scientific inquiry* (pp. 86–94). Rotterdam: Sense Publishers. https://doi.org /10.1163/9789460911453_007

Stroupe, D. (2014). Examining classroom science practice communities: How teachers and students negotiate epistemic agency and learn science-as-practice. *Science Education*, *98*(3), 487–516. https://doi.org/10.1002/sce.21112

Stroupe, D. (2017). Conclusion: Themes across chapters and lingering questions. In D. Stroupe (Ed.). *Reframing science teaching and learning* (pp. 165–170). New York: Routledge. https://doi.org/10.4324/9781315639031-11

Tan, E., Calabrese Barton, A., & Benavides, A. (2019). Engineering for sustainable communities: Epistemic tools in support of equitable and consequential middle school engineering. *Science Education*, *103*(4), 1011–1046. https://doi.org/10.1002/sce.21515

Windschitl, M., Thompson, J., & Braaten, M. (2008). Beyond the scientific method: Model based inquiry as a new paradigm of preference for school science investigations. *Science Education*, *92*(5), 941–967. https://doi.org/10.1002/sce.20259

Zeidler, D. L., Herman, B. C., & Sadler, T. D. (2019). New directions in socioscientific issues research. *Disciplinary and Interdisciplinary Science Education Research*, *1*(1), 1–9. https://doi.org/10.1186/s43031-019-0008-7

20
INQUIRY AND LEARNING IN ENGINEERING

Anette Kolmos, Pia Bøgelund, and Jette Egelund Holgaard

Introduction

In engineering education, the main pedagogical change in recent years has been the introduction of problem-based and project-organized learning (PBL) (Capraro & Slough, 2013; Han, Capraro, & Capraro, 2015; Kolmos & de Graaff, 2014). In science education, one of the main pedagogical changes has been inquiry-based learning (IBL) (Kearney, 2011; Rocard et al., 2007). PBL and IBL involve different ways of organizing the learning process: PBL reflects professional practice, whereas IBL is mainly a reflection of scientific practice, and the two learning approaches thus have different starting points. IBL is more often initiated by an urge to understand a phenomenon, whereas PBL and project-organized learning are more often triggered by a complex and real-life problem. However, at the same time, these learning approaches share an active, collaborative, and experience-based learning philosophy, and, in practice, a mixture of different learning approaches typically exists.

In this chapter, we will start by introducing the engineering domain, as this forms the basis for understanding why and how the concept of inquiry differs in an engineering context compared to a science context. We then turn to the implications for pedagogical approaches and outline two responses to the call for specified models for engineering education, i.e., PBL and design-based learning (DBL), and highlight their differences from IBL. DBL is introduced as a complementary approach to PBL in engineering education due to its specific focus on technological innovation processes. DBL reflects professional practice, in the same way as PBL, but is centered around industrial design practices. Having accounted for the contextual and philosophical roots of the two pedagogical approaches in this way, we then set out to show how the three learning approaches of PBL, IBL, and DBL are merged in a specific learning context at Aalborg University (AAU). Ultimately, the aim of the chapter is to illustrate inquiry and learning in an engineering context.

Understanding Engineering

Engineering is closely related to science, as engineers apply scientific theories aimed at understanding "what is" in order to create and appropriate future technology to diverse societies. From a narrow perspective, engineering could be confused with applied science, as scientific knowledge is applied to solve practical problems by means of technology. However, in a broader understanding, the emphasis on distributed and contextual creation and appropriation processes makes engineering a much wider discipline than applied science (Jamison, Kolmos, & Holgaard, 2014), just as the use of technology within science does not reduce science to applied engineering. This contextual understanding of engineering underlines the interplay between science, technology, and society.

From the point of view of the educational system, engineering has been integrated into existing STEM subjects in many countries, although some have established it as a separate subject in primary school, such as Sweden and Finland (De Vries, Gumaelius, & Skogh, 2016). In the US, engineering is integrated into the existing STEM subjects regulated at the national and state levels, and, thus, the integration has been diverse. In the school system, the concept of engineering has therefore also become quite diverse, which also is to be found in professional life as many engineers have different understandings of the role of engineering and the epistemology of engineering practices.

A narrow understanding of engineering is found in studies on the perceptions of school-going children. In one US study, elementary school students' conceptions of engineering and technology were analyzed. At this level, perceptions of what engineers do are still very much connected to technologies such as repairing cars, installing wiring, constructing buildings, and setting up factories (Cunningham, Lachapelle, & Lindgren-Streicher, 2005). These results are echoed in other studies from the US, in which students have been shown to see engineers as male persons fixing, building, or using machines (Capobianco, Diefes-Dux, Mena, & Weller, 2011). In such studies, there is no understanding of engineering as a working process that includes teamwork and design processes or that engineering involves humanistic elements. Here, engineering becomes a matter of a man-machine interaction.

Studies present engineering in a more process-oriented way. One US study has revealed that engineering is described in the form of standards integrated into existing STEM subjects, where the most frequently used concepts are design, technology, use, process, and problem (Carr, Bennett, & Strobel, 2012). The study concluded that there is a surprising overlap in the understanding of an engineering process including the identification of a problem, the design of solutions, and the evaluation of the impact and effectiveness of these applied solutions. Along these lines, Dym et al. have presented the following definition: "Engineering design is a systematic, intelligent process in which designers generate, evaluate, and specify concepts for devices, systems, or processes whose form and function achieve clients' objectives or users' needs while satisfying a specified set of constraints" (Dym, Agogino, Eris, Frey, & Leifer, 2005, p. 104). Engineering thus becomes a matter of creating and appropriating technology to meet human needs.

Furthermore, aspects of engineering as a distributed and collaborative process are emphasized. Several qualitatively oriented studies of engineering practice have reached the conclusion that the abilities to communicate and to collaborate are important skills for engineers (Henriksen, 2013; Trevelyan, 2007, 2010). In a study of six companies of different sizes, the clear conclusion was drawn that across the different engineering branches and organizational cultures, engineers saw their work as consisting of problem-solving, either in teams or through more informal collaboration (Anderson, Courter, McGlamery, Nathans-Kelly, & Nicometo, 2010).

With this additional focus on collaboration and distribution, engineering can be seen as a distributed process of creating and appropriating technology to meet human needs. This approach can be identified in the learning outcomes presented by the American Accreditation Board for Engineering (ABET) in 2014, which emphasize the abilities to design a system, to function as part of a multidisciplinary team, and to identify, formulate, and solve engineering problems through effective communication and social professional responsibility (ABET, 2014).

Finally, some studies have highlighted the contextual nature of engineering (see, for example, Jamison et. al., 2014). This focus on contextual learning in engineering represents a view of this field that sees engineers as broadly educated citizens who are aware of the environment and other contextual issues. This is clearly emphasized in the 2017 revision of the suggested learning outcomes from ABET, which stress the "ability to design a system, component, or process to meet desired needs within realistic constraints such as economic, environmental, social, political, ethical, health and safety, manufacturability, and sustainability" (ABET, 2017, p. 4).

Hence, the concept of engineering is expanded. In short, we can define engineering as a distributed process of creating sustainable technology that is appropriate to human needs and diverse societal contexts. Thus, the abovementioned "man-machine" understanding of engineering represented in school children's approaches to engineering varies significantly from the understanding of engineering presented in ABET 2017, which will frame many future engineering programs. This does not mean, however, that the understanding of engineering as a concept is unified or that there is a stable or closed discourse; on the contrary, the interpretation of this concept can differ widely depending on the specific aspect of society in question.

IBL, PBL, and DBL—Different Perspectives, Merged Practices

In the previous section, we have outlined the engineering domain and characterized engineering as a distributed process of creating sustainable technology that is appropriate to human needs and diverse societal contexts. This perspective is common for professional engineering in the work place and the challenge now is to align this perspective with the views found in the educational system. Recent research on engineering education strongly indicates that active learning methodologies such as group-based project work can contribute to bridging the gap between engineering education and engineering work and are a motivation for learning (Kolmos & Bylov, 2016; Prince, 2004).

Over the past two decades, there has been a tremendous change in engineering education to more active learning methodologies, both at course level and at a more systemic level (Graham, 2018; Kolmos & de Graaff, 2014; Prince, 2004; Prince & Felder, 2006). Many international societies such as the Conceive-Design-Implement-Operate (CDIO) society, the Project Approaches in Engineering Education (PAEE) society, and the International Research Symposium on PBL (IRSPBL) society (Crawley, Malmqvist, Östlund, Brodeur, & Edström, 2014; Edström & Kolmos, 2012; De Campos, Dirani, & Manrique, 2012) reflect this direction. These active learning methodologies are characterized by the approach that disciplines can be learned with a contextual purpose, and they involve problem identification, relation to creative practice, and highly collaborative processes. IBL, PBL, and DBL are examples of such specific active learning-based models, and in this section, we will relate them to the engineering domain and discuss in more detail how these approaches can supplement each other.

IBL in an Engineering Context

Examples of IBL in relation to higher education in engineering and science are mainly related to science domains such as chemistry (Madhuri, Kantamreddi, & Prakash Goteti, 2012) and nanotechnology (Cheng, Yang, Chang, & Kuo, 2015) and are often related to experimental design. IBL has been used directly and explicitly as the conceptual framework for transforming engineering education on only very few occasions; one example is the exclusive use of IBL in an introductory course on Civil and Environmental Engineering at the University of South Carolina, Columbia (Friedman et al., 2010).

However, indirectly through reference to active learning framed by other educational approaches such as PBL, DBL, and CDIO, notions of inquiry as introduced by Dewey (1938) have become more prominent. Bruce Alberts, previously the president (1993–2005) of the National

Academy of Sciences, Washington DC, has characterized inquiry as partly a state of mind that involves inquisitiveness, for example, being curious and asking "how" and "why" questions (NRC, 2000). In this broad sense of IBL as presented by Bruce Alberts, there is no doubt that the principles of IBL have a place in engineering education. However, since IBL has historically been related more closely to science education than to engineering education, the starting point and perspective of inquiry differs due to the different epistemological conditions for learning in science and engineering.

In 2012, the National Research Council (NRC), USA, published a report on future science education for grades K-12 (National Research Council, 2012). As part of this work, analyses were carried out to identify various practices within engineering and science in order to identify different epistemological roots. One finding of this report was that there are considerable differences in the initiating processes of science and engineering; for science, it is stated that "science begins with a question about a phenomenon, such as 'Why is the sky blue?' or 'What causes cancer?'" and seeks to develop theories that can provide exemplary answers to such questions? For engineering, it is argued that "Engineering begins with a problem, need, or desire that suggests an engineering problem that needs to be solved." This study supports the argument that IBL is more closely linked to science (staring from an inquiry), whereas engineering has been more closely linked to PBL (starting from a problem).

Nevertheless, engineering students also find themselves in situations in which they have to ask more fundamental questions in order to understand a phenomenon. For example, if engineering students want to design an edutainment app for pupils to learn maths, they have to ask themselves "What is learning?" in order to understand the core purpose of the design.

PBL in an Engineering Context

While IBL has been more strongly conceptualized within science education, PBL has been more widely adopted in engineering education to capture the constructivist turn of the educational discourse. The philosophical aim of IBL is to raise questions, and the specific outcomes are targeted toward a conceptual understanding of science principles (Unver & Arabacıoğlu, 2014). The aim of PBL is more pragmatic or holistic in nature; it focuses on what the problem calls for. The philosophical aim of PBL can be characterized as problem identification and problem-solving, and the learning outcomes are directed toward problem-solving skills (Unver & Arabacıoğlu, 2014).

Following Kolmos (2003), a PBL environment refers to a comprehensive learning environment at the curriculum level that combines specific cognitive, collaborative, and content-related strategies to address authentic problems. Cognitively, the learning is problem- and project-based and situated in a specific domain combined with real-life problems. Collaboratively, the learning takes place in participant-directed teams, while from a content perspective, the learning is interdisciplinary and exemplary and emphasizes theory as well as practice, including research methodologies. This aims to model real-world situations, to guide learners to develop interdisciplinary deep content learning within an exemplary discipline area and to foster problem-solving and collaborative skills. PBL has been shown to be effective to increase motivation for learning, reinforce competence development, and decrease drop-out rates (Dochy, Segers, Van den Bossche, & Gijbels, 2003; Strobel & van Barneveld, 2009).

A specific example of this could be a group of engineering students who are looking at the problem of atomic waste in a sustainable development context, with the aim of defining and scrutinizing different technological strategies for storing waste products in an environmentally safe way in order to identify and create the best storage solution from technological, environmental, and economic perspectives.

DBL in an Engineering Context

In engineering education, a problem-solving approach typically implies the design of new artifacts, processes, or services. Savin-Baden (2014) outlines a specific constellation of PBL for DBL and mentions that "in this constellation the activities and problem scenarios most commonly focused on are the creation of an article or product, the development of a representation of the artifact within the guidelines of the particular discipline, and a focus on the function of the particular production or artifact" (Savin-Baden, 2014, p. 206). As such, DBL relates to problems, where a new design of a tangible product is the answer, and thereby design thinking as well as design methodology somehow predetermine the structure of the DBL process.

Hence, as an independent approach, DBL has adopted specific aspects from PBL (Gómez Puente, van Eijck, & Jochems, 2011). Like PBL, DBL has also been linked directly to IBL and has been defined as "an educational approach method grounded in the processes of inquiry and reasoning towards generating innovative artefacts, systems and solutions" (Gómez Puente, Van Eijck, & Jochems, 2013). In a study exploring the effects of DBL at Eindhoven University of technology, Puente et. al (2014) concluded that DBL makes students take a broad approach in exploring problems and searching for design alternatives as a result of open-ended, authentic, and hands-on activities within DBL.

DBL has also been characterized as part of the discourse about inquiry, as it "requires students to utilize and therefore demonstrate, their declarative (knowing that), procedural (knowing how), schematic (knowing why) and strategic (knowing when and where) cognitive abilities" (Wells, 2016a, p. 6). This discourse clearly involves inquisitiveness by stressing the type of questions that need to be asked to appropriate the design process to the situation at hand. A specific example of DBL in an engineering context could be a group of engineering students looking at the development of a particular mobile phone antenna, for which the user needs and design criteria have been obtained from collaboration with a mobile company.

IBL, PBL, and DBL in Engineering

In Table 20.1, we have highlighted the core differences between IBL, PBL, and DBL based on the above discussion. In practice, the design of learning processes for engineering is much more complex, and although one learning approach may be declared a framework for educational practice, the others will typically present themselves due to the existence of common philosophical ground. As an example, we will of course find students in IBL working on real-life problems, such as students in industrial design who grapple with more fundamental "why" questions. In other words, although the different frameworks each have a different emphasis, they mutually inform each other. As an example, an engineering student working on a design problem in a PBL environment will most likely be heavily influenced by a DBL approach, but the PBL approach will re-enforce the incentive to move beyond user needs and picture the design in a broader societal context.

In the following, we describe an institutional case example of inquiry and learning in engineering in which PBL is the fundamental educational approach, but at the same time the PBL model clearly integrates IBL and DBL perspectives.

Table 20.1 Differences in emphasis between IBL, PBL, and DBL conceptualizations

	IBL	*PBL*	*DBL*
Reflection of	Scientific practice	Professional practice	Industrial design
Initiated by	Why and what questions	Real-life problems	Ideas/user needs
Aims to	(Re)construct knowledge	Impact (sub)societies	Design tangible products

IBL in a PBL context—the Aalborg Model

Problem- and project-based learning combines design and inquiry in a learning process in which student teams identify problems, methodologies, and possible solutions to these problems (Kolmos & Graaff, 2014). This type of collaborative knowledge construction corresponds to the core of engineering as a distributed process of creating sustainable technology that is appropriate for human needs and diverse societal contexts.

In Table 20.2 below, we compare approaches to engineering and science identified by the NRC (2012) to the phases of an engineering and science project in a PBL environment (Algreen-Ussing & Fruensgaard, 1990). Although these eight practices supplied by the NRC are not intended as phases, and are primarily defined with a starting point based in scientific rather than in engineering thinking, a comparison indicates a more comprehensive learning process, as it is important to be able to master all phases of a project, no matter whether it is a research project or an innovation process.

From the above comparison, we can see that there seems to be considerable overlap. Typically, the problem analysis in PBL (point 2) will include the main aspects of points 1–4 in the overview from the NRC (asking questions, using models, carrying out investigations, and analyzing and interpreting data). Likewise, the problem-solving process in PBL will typically include the use of mathematical and computational thinking (point 1), a design (point 2), and argumentation and evidence for findings (point 3). Furthermore, both perspectives include an evaluation of the findings.

There are, however, differences between the two perspectives shown in Table 20.2. First, the project phases defined by Algreen-Ussing and Fruensgaard (1990) have a more explicit focus on what has been called *problem design*, including identification, analysis, and formulation (see the examples in Section "Inquiry in Relation to the Design of a Problem and a Solution"). Problem analysis is very important in both engineering and science, but the difference is that the product

Table 20.2 Approaches to engineering and science identified by the NRC (2012) compared to the phases of an engineering and science project in a PBL environment (Algreen-Ussing & Fruensgaard, 1990)

	National Research Council (2012)	*Project phases (Algreen Ussing & Fruensgaard, 1990)*
Problem analysis	1 Asking questions (for science) and defining problems (for engineering) 2 Developing and using models 3 Planning and carrying out investigations 4 Analyzing and interpreting data	1 Initiating problem (the trigger for the problem—what starts it out) 2 Problem analysis (analysis of the problem)—for whom, what, and why) 3 Literature review 4 Definition and formulation of problem (specification requirement)
Problem-solving	1 Using mathematics and computational thinking 2 Constructing explanations (for science) and designing solutions (for engineering) 3 Engaging in argument based on evidence 4 Obtaining, evaluating, and communicating information	4 Problem-solving methodologies (overview of possible solutions and assessment of impact) 5 Demarcation (argumentation for the choice of solution) 6 Specification of requirements 7 Solving the problem (carry out a first prototype: construction/design and further analysis) 8 Implementation (prototype and sometimes real systems) 9 Evaluation and reflection (impact, effect, and efficiency of solution)

of the engineering process needs to fit into a system and/or address the needs of customers or the population as a whole (Holgaard, Guerra, Kolmos, & Petersen, 2017). Problem analyses therefore involve a combined study of the context, human beings, the system, scientific knowledge, and the expected impact. Second, the phases outlined by Algreen-Ussing and Fruensgaard (1990) relate to the *design of solutions* (see the examples in Section "Inquiry in Relation to the Design of a Problem and a Solution"), typically through prototyping, implementing, and evaluating products (including technological services). Third, Algreen-Ussing and Fruensgaard (1990) see the project as a way of organizing the design and solving the problem, and hence *project management* is also stressed as being an important part of engineering (see the examples in Section "Inquiry in Process Management").

In the following, we will use our experiences with the Aalborg University PBL model to stress the ways in which IBL and DBL are integrated into this problem- and project-organized approach to engineering education. The purpose is to show how the different approaches can be combined—not to imply that this is the best way or to argue for one particular approach. First, we emphasize the inquiry processes with regard to the design of the problem and the solutions, which concerns what students work on during the project. In the second part, we emphasize the inquiry process in terms of project management, which from a metalearning perspective relates to how students work.

Inquiry in Relation to the Design of a Problem and a Solution

Problem design in PBL can be summarized as the identification, analysis, and formulation of a problem (Holgaard, Guerra, Kolmos, & Petersen, 2017). DBL approaches have also stressed the problem identification phase, which involves specifying the need and defining and formulating the problem, and is initiated by the teacher asking more open questions in relation to a theme (Wells, 2016b). DBL mirrors the design process, which in essence is concerned with formulating a plan representing an artifact that, once it is made, will fulfil certain needs (de Vries, 2006). In the same way as PBL environments, DBL situations are realistic learning situations that are designed to encourage students to apply real-life and domain knowledge and skills when doing project-like work (de Vries, 2006).

At AAU, IBL adds to the understanding of the problem design process in PBL by highlighting the need to reach a deeper understanding of a given phenomenon in the problem space. Through a comparison of IBL with PBL, Unver and Arabacıoğlu (2014) distinquished differences in the learner's role. In IBL, this role is described as interpreting, explaining, hypothesizing, designing, and directing the learner's own tasks and sharing the answers with authority, whereas in PBL, this role is described as determining whether a problem exists; creating an exact statement of the problem; identifying information, data, and learning goals; and creating a work plan (Unver & Arabacıoğlu, 2014). In the Aalborg PBL model, engineering students also interpret, explain, and hypothesize about different phenomena in different ways depending on the kind of problems that

Table 20.3 Different types of problems in the technological innovation process

	Technology specified	*Technology unspecified*
Problem specified	Redesign to meet user requirements	Design to meet user requirements
Problem unspecified	Top-down problem analysis Human-technology interaction in CONTEXT	Bottom-up problem analysis User needs in CONTEXT

they choose to study, as they are trained to work with different types of problems at different stages in the technological innovation process (see Table 20.3).

If both the problem and the technology are specified, students have more time to work with the redesign of a particular product, and learn to work creatively, although within a rather narrow set of boundaries. In these types of projects, students have the opportunity to carry out testing in more depth and have time to experience the continuous phases of prototyping. One example could be students who work to redesign an app that can help people to handle food waste in accordance with a particular waste-handling system. Typical questions of inquiry are: Why do the users experience problems with the product? What kinds of functionalities would fit with the new user requirements? How can such a solution be designed in alignment with the other functionalities of the product? How can this new function be implemented for testing at the beginning of the prototyping process? How should such a test be carried out? Although students apply inquiry in this process, uncertainties—which call for a more fundamental understanding of the phenomena emphasized in IBL—are limited.

If the problem is specified but the technology is unspecified, students have a list of user requirements and aim to develop technological solutions that meet these requirements. In this type of project, the intended learning objectives are oriented toward design capabilities, and the students go into more depth with the design methodology. In the example above, students know that they are working to help households handle their waste, but they need to move into the design funnel at an early stage, meaning that their learning is more design-based. Typical questions of inquiry are: How can user requirements be translated into success criteria for the product? How can we manage the creative process of divergent thinking to find new inventions for this problem? How can we explore these emergent ideas via interaction with the users? Which solution should be implemented and why? How can we prototype this solution for testing as early as possible to reach inputs and move further in the iterative design process? The more fundamental understanding of phenomena that is emphasized in IBL is mostly related to natural science, e.g., in this case, an understanding of the nature of the bacterium "Ideonella sakaiensis," which is capable of breaking down and consuming certain forms of plastic.

If the problem is unspecified and the technology is specified, we have what is popularly known as a solution in search of a problem. This calls for what has been characterized as a top-down problem analysis (Holgaard et al., 2017). In this type of problem, the focus is on human-technology interactions and divergence of use. Let us imagine that a new scanning device can identify the type of plastic contained in a product. This could be used to create a more advanced waste-handling system, in which users are assisted in sorting different types of plastics, instead of putting all plastic products into the same bin, but it could also be used to help parents buy toys for their children or to help allergic people get safe products. The problems that could be addressed with a particular technology are many, but the actual design of the product will be highly dependent on the chosen problem and target group. Typical questions for inquiry are: What functionalities can be delivered by this technology? What is the state of the art in relation to similar types of technologies? Where and when have these similar technologies been put into use? What use patterns are related to the use of this technology? Where can we find similar use patterns? What problems are these use patterns addressing? The more fundamental understanding of phenomena emphasized in IBL is mostly related to the social sciences and humanities, e.g., understanding the types of (social) psychology, human behavior, or actor networks that could hinder or promote the technology.

If both the problem and the technology are unspecified, students have the maximum possible degrees of freedom to choose, although this is delimited by their domain knowledge and experience. From a curriculum development perspective, this type of project is typically arranged to allow students to gain competence in problem design, as the content of the learning cannot be specified in advance in the curriculum. The project starts with students searching for a problem, and when they find a potential problem that would be of interest in both their own learning and that of others, they make this problem the focus of a bottom-up problem analysis. This group may involve media technology students moving around the city center in search of a problem, one of whom notices that in a certain area there is much more garbage outside than inside the dustbin. Maybe that could be something to work with—the students go home and start their problem analysis. Typical questions are: What is the problem? Who considers this to be a problem? Why is it a problem? Who benefits from the problem (if anyone)? In which situations does the problem arise? What has been done previously to address this problem? Why has this not worked? Who has an interest in solving this problem? In these kinds of projects, the emphasis will be on problem analysis. Students typically find this very challenging, and to scaffold the learning process, attempts are made in most cases to delimit both the problem and the solution space. One way of achieving this is to set a theme for the semester; for example, sustainable lifestyles can initiate attention being paid to waste. This was in fact the case in the previous example mentioned, where students started to explore how people handled their waste in the city. They ended up with a low-fi model of an intelligent waste bin that would, among other functionalities, inform people if they had missed when they attempted to throw litter into the bin. Although they did not move far in terms of prototyping, they learned how to explore new problems and market potential. This combination of unspecified problems and technologies means that students can be challenged to understand a phenomenon in relation to natural science, social science, humanities, or whatever the problem calls for. In this specific case, for example, the students had to investigate the phenomenon of cognitive dissonance to understand why people did not throw their garbage into the bin in contrast to their values and beliefs that this was the right thing to do.

Inquiry in Process Management

The processes of inquiry go beyond what is needed to design a problem or a product, since in PBL, inquiry also has a metalearning perspective, meaning that students seek inquiry in relation to the learning process itself. In the following, we elaborate on this and give some specific examples of how to scaffold the inquiry process in the first year of study for all engineering students at AAU in terms of process competences related to collaboration, learning, and project management.

Process management (PM) competences are understood to form a comprehensive approach that includes the ability to lead a project process, manage time and other resources, guide group collaboration and communication, and be self-directed in terms of personal and cognitive development. At AAU, all engineers are taught these competences during the entire education as each semester entails a specific PBL project. In the first year of study, when the students are doing semester-long projects, they have a specific course and a specific task that is designed to facilitate the inquiry process of PM and also to support them in self-directed teamwork and reflection on their own learning. The course consists of a mixture of short introductory theory sessions and longer sessions of group work, in which different exercises and other activities are undertaken to facilitate cognitive understanding and bodily awareness of different PM dimensions. Supervisors (academic staff) provide feedback on the way students solve the group work exercises and, in some instances, give feedback on written material. Table 20.4 shows an overview of the tools employed as part of the course.

Some of these tools are intended to provide students with a mental map that will help them reflect on their own position; these include team profiles, motivational types, conflict style tests, and learning styles. They raise questions such as: who am I/who are we, and how can I/we best deal with these issues? How shall I/we plan the use of time, participate in group work, find the motivation to work, deal with conflicts, and learn new material?

Table 20.4 Overview of some tools that can facilitate reflection in both course and process analysis tasks

	Course activity tools to spur reflection on PM	*Process analysis tools to spur reflection on PM*
Learning to lead a project process and manage resources	Templates for chairing a meeting Time management tools (e.g., Gantt charts) How to delegate work Team profiles and roles	Collect data during the project process Discuss with other groups and own team mates Write a reflective text about project leadership and resource management on the basis of the Kolb circle: experience, reflection, generalization, and future actions (Kolb, 1984)
Learning to collaborate and communicate externally and internally	Group collaboration agreements Communicative diagrams and active listening exercises Conflict-style tests and feedback modes Peer-learning activities and co-writing templates	Collect data during project process Discuss with other groups and own team mates Write a reflective text on team competences on the basis of the Kolb circle (Kolb, 1984)
Individual, self-directed learning and PBL	Apply learning styles Create personal learning objectives Motivation	Collect data during project process Discuss with other groups and own teammates Write a reflective text on learning on the basis of the Kolb circle (Kolb, 1984)

Other kinds of tools provide the group members with "best practice" approaches: templates for chairing a meeting, peer learning activities, and Gantt charts, to mention just a few. They point in the direction of how to deal efficiently with project management issues and require some kind of trial-and-error process to be carried out. Yet other types of tools require students to pay attention to bodily experiences, such as active listening exercises, communicative diagrams, and feedback modes. In this case, the inquiry process is again not only related to knowing "how" to apply the tools; it is also a process through which students question their personal actions and team behavior and seek inquiry to explain—e.g., a lack of resilience or motivation, or the social interaction experienced.

The inquiry process inherent in these last two kinds of tools links directly to the specific task that all groups must carry out as part of the PBL project in the first year of their study—the process analysis. At the end of the project, after the group has handed in the main report, group members join their peers to discuss the process of carrying out the PBL project. Finally, based on these discussions and reflections within the group, group members write a report on the main aspects of working in a problem-based and project-organized way. In this sense, the inquiry process that takes place as the students work out their process analysis is a metalearning process asking questions in relation to the Kolb circle (Kolb, 1984): what happened? What does that mean? How does this relate to others' experiences? What conclusions can we draw? And how can we use this knowledge in the future? In this way, the approach used in IBL—interpreting, explaining, hypothesizing, designing, directing, or interpreting tasks—is an integrated part of PBL, even from a metalearning perspective.

Final Remarks

In this chapter, we have shown that IBL is embedded within the problem design process, and in particular in identifying, analyzing, and formulating the problem, where the last of these includes questions for further inquiry. Likewise, IBL is embedded within the product design process, where both PBL and DBL come into play and become interlinked with IBL. But there are important differences in the focus on product development, and especially the process of creation and designing can be a key factor in increasing motivation for all STEM subjects. We have also stressed that within PBL, IBL has metalearning and collaborative aspects, which are highly implicit in the way engineering has been characterized. Inquiry is not only related to the design of a problem or a product but is also related to understanding both individual and social learning processes and aligning the process management accordingly.

As a reference for our discussion of pedagogical frameworks for engineering, we have specifically focused on problem- and project-based learning (PBL), DBL, and IBL. These three pedagogical frameworks are all built on a constructivist learning philosophy and serve as umbrella frameworks for different and overlapping educational models. However, we would argue that these three approaches reflect different practices, have different starting points, and differ in their primary scope.

In a problem-based and project-organized approach, students are faced with uncertainties that require them to search for a deeper understanding of the phenomena involved in problem design, product design, and their own collaborative learning and project management experiences. In this way, IBL adds an important dimension to engineering education.

Based on the reflections provided in this chapter, we would argue for a more explicit focus on the different types of inquiry that relate to different engineering practices. We emphasize that the diversity and the suitability of the questions that students need to ask themselves in order to become engineers and to master engineering must be considered in the design of the curriculum. A more casual approach to inquiry carries a risk of reductionism, in the sense that engineering is reduced to a reactive mode of implementing what others ask for. Much more is required of the engineer of the future.

References

ABET. (2014). Criteria for accrediting engineering programs. Retrieved from http://abet.org/eac-current-criteria/

ABET. (2017). *Criteria for accrediting engineering programs*. Baltimore, MD: ABET.

Algreen-Ussing, H., & Fruensgaard, N. O. (1990). *Metode i projektarbejde*. Aalborg: Aalborg University Press.

Anderson, K. J. B., Courter, S. S., McGlamery, T., Nathans-Kelly, T. M., & Nicometo, C. G. (2010). Understanding engineering work and identity: A cross-case analysis of engineers within six firms. *Engineering Studies*, *2*(3), 153–174. https://doi.org/10.1080/19378629.2010.519772

Capobianco, B. M., Diefes-Dux, H. A., Mena, I., & Weller, J. (2011). What is an engineer? Implications of elementary school student conceptions for engineering education. *Journal of Engineering Education*, *100*(2), 304–328. https://doi.org/10.1002/j.2168-9830.2011.tb00015.x

Capraro, R. M., & Slough, S. W. (2013). Why PBL? Why STEM? Why now? An introduction to STEM project-based learning. In *STEM Project-Based Learning* (pp. 1–5). Springer. https://doi.org/10.1007/978-94-6209-143-6_1

Carr, R. L., Bennett, L. D., & Strobel, J. (2012). Engineering in the K-12 STEM Standards of the 50 US States: An analysis of presence and extent. *Journal of Engineering Education*, *101*(3), 539–564. https://doi.org/10.1002/j.2168-9830.2012.tb00061.x

Cheng, P-H., Yang, Y-T. C., Chang, S-H. G., & Kuo, F-R. R. (2015). 5E mobile inquiry learning approach for enhancing learning motivation and scientific inquiry ability of university students. *IEEE Transactions on Education*, *59*(2), 1–7. https://doi.org/10.1109/TE.2015.2467352.

Crawley, E. F., Malmqvist, J., Östlund, S., Brodeur, D. R., & Edström, K. (2014). The CDIO approach. In *Rethinking Engineering Education* (pp. 11–45). Springer. https://doi.org/10.1007/978-3-319-05561-9_2

Cunningham, C. M., Lachapelle, C., & Lindgren-Streicher, A. (2005). *Assessing elementary school students' conceptions of engineering and technology*. Portland, OR: American Society of Engineering Education.

de Campos, L. C., Dirani, E. A. T., & Manrique, A. L. (2012). *Project approaches to learning in engineering education: The practice of teamwork*. Springer Science & Business Media. https://doi.org/10.1007/978-94-6091-958-9

de Vries, M. J., Gumaelius, L., & Skogh, I.-B. (2016). Pre-university engineering education. In *Pre-university Engineering Education* (pp. 1–12). Springer. https://doi.org/10.1007/978-94-6300-621-7_1

de Vries, E. (2006). Students' construction of external representations in design-based learning situations. *Learning and Instruction, 16*(3), 213–27. doi:10.1016/j.learninstruc.2006.03.006

Dewey, J. (1938). *Logic – the theory of inquiry.* New York: Henry Holt and Company

Dochy, F., Segers, M., Van den Bossche, P., & Gijbels, D. (2003). Effects of problem based learning: A meta-analysis. *Learning and Instruction, 13*(5), 533–568. https://doi.org/10.1016/S0959-4752(02)00025-7

Dym, C. L., Agogino, A. M., Eris, O., Frey, D. D., & Leifer, L. J. (2005). Engineering design thinking, teaching, and learning. *Journal of Engineering Education, 94*(1), 103–120. https://doi.org/10.1002/j.2168-9830.2005.tb00832.x

Edström, K., & Kolmos, A. (2012). Comparing two approaches for engineering education development. *Proceedings of the 8th International CDIO Conference.* http://cdio2012.com/.

Friedman, D. B., Crews, T. B., Caicedo, J. M., Besley, J. C., Weinberg, J., & Freeman, M. L. 2010. An exploration into inquiry-based learning by a multidisciplinary group of higher education faculty. *Higher Education, 59*, 765–83. doi:10.1007/s10734-009-9279-9

Gómez Puente, S. M., Van Eijck, M., & Jochems, W. 2011. Towards characterising design-based learning in engineering education: A review of the literature. *European Journal of Engineering Education, 36*(2), 137–149. doi:10.1080/03043797.2011.565116

Gomez Puente, S. M., van Eijck, M. W., & Jochems, W. (2014). Exploring the effects of design-based learning characteristics on teachers and students. *International Journal of Engineering Education*, 30(4), 916–928.

Gómez Puente, S. M., Van Eijck, M., & Jochems, W. (2013). A sampled literature review of design-based learning approaches: A search for key characteristics. *International Journal of Technology and Design Education, 23*(3), 717–732. https://doi.org/10.1007/s10798-012-9212-x

Graham, R. (2018). *The global state of the art in engineering education.* Retrieved from United States of America: neet.mit.edu

Han, S., Capraro, R., & Capraro, M. M. (2015). How science, technology, engineering, and mathematics (STEM) project-based learning (PBL) affects high, middle, and low achievers differently: The impact of student factors on achievement. *International Journal of Science and Mathematics Education, 13*(5), 1089–1113. https://doi.org/10.1007/s10763-014-9526-0

Henriksen, L. B. (2013). The engineering project as story and narrative. In *Enterprise Resource Planning: Concepts, Methodologies, Tools, and Applications* (pp. 854–865). IGI Global. https://doi.org/10.4018/978-1-4666-4153-2.ch050

Holgaard, J. E., Guerra, A., Kolmos, A., & Petersen, L. S. (2017). Getting a hold on the problem in a problem-based learning environment. *International Journal of Engineering Education, 33*(3), 1070–1085.

Jamison, A., Kolmos, A., & Holgaard, J. E. (2014). Hybrid learning: An integrative approach to engineering education. *Journal of Engineering Education, 103*(2), 253–273. https://doi.org/10.1002/jee.20041

Kearney, C. (2011). Efforts to increase students' interest in pursuing science, technology, engineering and mathematics studies and careers. *National measures taken by, 21.*

Kolb, D. (1984). *Experiential learning: Experience as the source of learning and development.* Upper Saddle River, NJ: Prentice Hall P T R.

Kolmos, A. (2003). Characteristics of problem-based learning. *International Journal of Mechanical Engineering Education, 19*(5), 657–662.

Kolmos, A., & Bylov, S. M. (2016). Ingeniørstuderendes Forventning Og Parathed Til Det Kommende Arbejdsliv: Arbejdsrapport No. 1. UNESCO.

Kolmos, A., & Graaff, E. (2014). Problem-based and project-based learning in engineering education. In B. M. Olds & A. Johri (Eds.), *Cambridge handbook of engineering education research* (pp. 141–161). Cambridge: Cambridge University Press. https://doi.org/10.1017/CBO9781139013451.012

Madhuri, G. V., Kantamreddi, V. S. S. N., & Prakash Goteti, L. N. S. (2012). Promoting higher order thinking skills using inquiry-based learning. *European Journal of Engineering Education, 37*(2), 117–123. doi:10.1080/03043797.2012.661701

National Research Council (NRC). (2000). *Inquiry and the national science education standards. A guide for teaching and learning.* Washington, DC: National Academies Press. https://doi.org/10.17226/9596

National Research Council (NRC). (2012). *A framework for K-12 science education: Practices, crosscutting concepts, and core ideas.* Washington, DC: National Academies Press.

Prince, M. (2004). Does active learning work? A review of the research. *Journal of Engineering Education, 93*(3), 223–231. doi:10.1002/j.2168-9830.2004.tb00809.x

Prince, M. J., & Felder, R. M. (2006). Inductive teaching and learning methods: Definitions, comparisons, and research bases. *Journal of Engineering Education, 95*(2), 123. https://doi.org/10.1002/j.2168-9830.2006.tb00884.x

Rocard, M., Csermely, P., Jorde, D., Lenzen, D., Walberg-Henriksson, H., & Hemmo, V. (2007). *Science Education NOW: A renewed pedagogy for the future of Europe*. Brussels: European Commission. Luettu: http://ec. europa. eu/research/science-society/document_library/pdf_06/report-rocard-onscience-education_en. pdf (21.10. 2016).

Savin-Baden, M. (2014). Using problem-based learning: New constellations for the 21st century. *Journal on Excellence in College Teaching, 25*, 197–219.

Strobel, J., & van Barneveld, A. (2009). When is PBL more effective? A meta-synthesis of meta-analyses comparing PBL to conventional classrooms. *Interdisciplinary Journal of Problem-based Learning, 3*(1), 4.

Trevelyan, J. (2007). Technical coordination in engineering practice. *Journal of Engineering Education, 96*(3), 191–204. https://doi.org/10.7771/1541-5015.1046

Trevelyan, J. (2010). Reconstructing engineering from practice. *Engineering Studies, 2*(3), 175–195. https://doi.org/10.1080/19378629.2010.520135

Unver, A. O., & Arabacıoğlu, S. (2014). A comparison of inquiry-based learning (IBL), problem-based learning (PBL) and project-based learning (PJBL) in science education. *Academia Journal of Educational Research, 2*(7), 120–128.

Wells, J. G. (2016a). Efficacy of the technological engineering design approach: Imposed cognitive demands within design-based biotechnology instruction. *Journal of Technology Education, 27*(1), 4–20. doi:10.21061/jte.v27i2.a.1

Wells, J. G. (2016b). I-STEM Ed Exemplar: Implementation of the PIRPOSAL Model. *Technology and Engineering Teacher, 76*(2), 16–23. http://proxy.library.vcu.edu/login?url=http://search.proquest.com/docview/1871579422?accountid=14780%5Cnhttp://vcu-alma-primo.hosted.exlibrisgroup.com/openurl/VCU/vcu_services_page?url_ver=Z39.88-2004&rft_val_fmt=info:ofi/fmt:kev:mtx:journal&genre=article.

21

INQUIRY AND LEARNING IN INFORMAL SETTINGS

Jennifer D. Adams and Susan McCullough

Inquiry and Learning in Informal Settings

In this chapter, we describe inquiry and learning in informal settings. In the first section, we will provide an overview of informal learning. In the United States, the National Science Foundation has dedicated a lot of resources to studying informal science learning. Because of this, much of the definitions around informal learning environments, and correspondingly informal science learning, emerge from this literature. In arts education, the emphasis has been on building visual literacy, which has evolved to embed elements of learner-centered meaning-making during interactions with objects of art. In this chapter, we will first discuss the contexts of informal learning followed by an overview of inquiry as a pedagogical approach. We then discuss informal science learning and how inquiry is used both as a pedagogical approach and a way to engage learners in the practices of scientific knowledge production. As informal learning institutions often provide teacher education and professional development, we will also describe how inquiry is used to support teacher learning in arts and science informal contexts and how this is a way of creating a continuum between formal and informal learning and between the classroom and informal learning contexts. We will conclude with a discussion of the challenges to and structures that support learning in informal settings.

The Contexts of Informal Learning

The authors of this chapter are co-researchers in a collaborative project to learn about teacher identity in relation to teacher learning in informal science contexts. One of the teachers in our collaborative research described herself as "teaching on a continuum" between formal and informal learning. She had teacher learning experiences in collaboration with a natural history museum and incorporated some of the practices she learned in her classroom. For her, informal science learning was a low-stakes way to get her students engaged in inquiry in the classroom. She viewed informal science learning as collaborative and hands-on versus the "chalk and talk" and standardized testing-focus of formal learning. Hofstein and Rosenfield (1996) noted the difficulty in defining informal science learning, noting, "informal learning experiences can occur in formal learning environments as well as informal learning environments" (p. 90). They advocate for integrating informal learning experiences in the school curriculum to foster equity in science learning. This is because informal learning is associated with learner-centered and self-directed approaches and allows learners to leverage their own existing funds of knowledge and experiences while engaging with new information. In the United States, the term "informal" has largely described most learning experiences that happen outside of the classroom regardless of who determines the objectives and approach and often in contrast or opposition to formal learning that is classroom/school based and structured by curricula, assessments, and standards.

Inquiry in informal settings. When one talks about inquiry in informal environments, it brings to mind many images but most probably centers on notions of observing, asking questions, and conducting some kind of investigation. In educational contexts, this notion is augmented with particular teaching and learning goals in mind, whether it is about the skills associated with inquiry or learning about the phenomena being investigated. It is important to distinguish between inquiry as a pedagogical approach and inquiry as a scientific practice (Gyllenpalm & Wickman, 2011). In education settings, this is critical because inquiry could be used as an approach to learn more about something, or it could be taught as an essential part of the skills and process of doing science. We are starting from the definition of inquiry as a process of searching for information that begins with engaging learners' interests and curiosities. This means: looking—centering observations of a work of art, artifact, or the natural world; asking—generating questions based on observations; discovering—using questions to engage in a deeper investigation of the object, artifact, or the natural world; and connecting—making meaning from the observations and investigations through connecting and comparing findings, reflecting on new understandings, and applying and extending new understandings to other contexts.

During the past two decades, researchers in informal science learning have done much to theorize learning in out-of-school settings. A considerable amount of this theorizing is grounded in a constructivist view of learning and attends to the notion that learners are bringing experiences and perspectives into a setting that influences the learning that happens. Museums and other similar sites of learning have been germane to building theory in this area because these are spaces that afford self-guided, learner-choice experiences. For example, in 2000, John Falk and Lynn Dierking introduced the Contextual Model of Learning to describe the learning that occurs in informal settings. It posits that three overlapping contexts—the personal, the sociocultural, and the physical—interact and influence learning and meaning-making across a lifespan. The personal refers to what a learner brings to a learning situation—their experiences, beliefs, identities, interests, and motivations. The sociocultural recognizes that learning happens both individually and in groups and is inextricably bound to social, historical, cultural, and political contexts. Knowledge and meaning-making is a shared process and occurs in interactions between people and places. The physical context describes the materiality of learning—that it occurs in the interaction with objects and the real world (Falk & Dierking, 2004). Because informal learning environments are artifact-driven and self-guided, learning programs within these spaces are often designed with a notion of inquiry in mind.

Interestingly, it has been noted that only 13% of our lifelong learning actually happens in formal schooling (NRC, 2009). While this number is specific to science learning, we imagine that it could extend to the arts. Mocker and Spear (1982) describe informal learning as one of the three modes of lifelong learning and define these modes in terms of learner control, formal learning, informal learning, and nonformal learning. Formal learning—the learner decides neither the approach nor learning objectives; this largely describes K-12 learning, university degree programs, and professional certification. Informal learning—the objectives are predetermined; however, the learner's approach is self-directed; this would describe most visitor experiences in informal institutions. Nonformal learning—the learner determines both the learning objectives and approach; this describes everyday learning that largely happens through everyday conversations and activities and is often closely related to learners' cultures and communities (Eshach, 2007). There are elements of formal, informal, and nonformal in all learning contexts (Colley, Hodkinson, & Malcolm, 2002); therefore, when attempting to make the distinction it is important to understand the aspects and interrelationships of the learning approaches as situated in the contexts in which they occur.

Literature on informal learning has focused on both engaging the learner and understanding how learning occurs in diverse informal settings ranging from museums to family settings. In the United States, much of the early literature around informal learning was based on studies of museum interactions. In 2002, Scott G. Paris published the volume, *Perspectives on Object-Centered Learning in Museums*, which was amongst the first collaborative efforts to theorize museum and or object-based learning. This book aimed to generate an "object-based epistemology that stands in contrast to the traditional methods of learning through text and discourse" (p. xvi). Overall, the chapters in the book emphasized the importance of dialogues in learning with objects, including the dialogues that people have with each other and in relation to objects of science, history, and art in museums. This coupled with the nature of learning in museums—freedom to explore, intellectual safety, and personal choice—affords naturalistic inquiry that emerges from people's innate curiosities about familiar and unfamiliar objects.

Presently, informal learning research has moved beyond the halls of museums and science centers and extended into parks, zoos, botanical gardens, place-based contexts, citizen science, and even in people's homes and communities. Learning in these contexts privileges open-ended approaches that stem from learners' lived experiences with the subject or phenomena. This learning is often framed using inquiry questions that prompt learners to reflect on what they already know and pose questions about what they would like to learn. For example, the information display in front of a giant erratic in the Okotoks, Alberta, Canada poses the question, "how did it get here?" This would probably be the first question one would ask upon seeing a giant boulder in the prairies with no other similar rocks nearby. This question accesses a learners' curiosity and allows them to engage with deeper questions about geological processes (i.e., the relationship between the erratic and glaciers and the Canadian Rocky Mountains, on view in the distance) behind the composition of the rocks and, because Indigenous connections to the landscape are important to the local culture, the significance of this feature to the local Blackfoot Indigenous people. These kinds of questions form the foundation for self-guided or educator-facilitated inquiry in ways that allow learners to explore their own questions and curiosities at their own pace.

Inquiry as Pedagogy

As a pedagogical approach, inquiry-based learning is learner-centric and designed to inspire curiosity and motivation to delve deeper into the objects or phenomena under investigation. More importantly, inquiry-based learning affords learners a sense of agency in allowing them to guide much or all of their learning process. Inquiry allows learners to generate their own questions and chart their own paths to understanding. Doris Ash and Gordon Wells (2006) describes inquiry as:

> learners build[ing] on their existing understandings and make sense of the world through material and symbolic actions and interactions. By engaging with materials, ideas, and utterances, learners are active agents, constructing knowledge rather than passively receiving it.
>
> *(p. 36)*

This is a constructivist stance on inquiry that emphasizes inquiry as leveraging learners' prior experiences. Due to the emphasis on investigations, inquiry, as a learning strategy, has gained much traction in relation to science teaching and learning. For example, Pedaste et al. (2015) describe inquiry-based instruction as "an educational strategy in which students follow methods and practices similar to those of professional scientists in order to construct knowledge" (p. 48). If applied uncritically, this notion of inquiry follows the "scientific method" in that it asks learners to construct hypotheses, design an experiment, and draw conclusions based on observations. In these instances, inquiry is structured as a direct path or a one-way approach of problem-solving. Interestingly, even in the practice of scientific research, the notion of a single universal scientific method is obsolete. However, a pedagogy of inquiry that centers learners' perspective and curiosities values multiple entry points and paths to gathering information and problem-solving about an object or phenomena at hand. Thus, it makes perfect sense that a pedagogy of inquiry aligns with informal education as it allows for learners to make meanings through their interactions with the artifacts, objects, and phenomena.

Describing Inquiry in Informal Science

Because the nature and definitions of inquiry are often associated with science, much of the articulations around inquiry have been described in relation to science teaching and learning settings. The *Learning Science in Informal Environments* (NRC, 2009) report outlines six strands that describe the goals and practices of science learning with inquiry woven throughout; however, inquiry is embedded in some strands more than others.

For example, Strand 3, "Engaging in Scientific Reasoning," describes inquiry as one of the skills of science: "the outcomes of this strand include scientific inquiry skills, such as asking questions, exploring, experimenting, applying ideas, predicting, drawing conclusions from evidence, reasoning, and articulating one's thinking in conversation with others" (p. 66). Similarly, for Strand 4,

> Direct experience with the process of knowledge construction through the types of inquiry-based activities characteristic of informal environments can serve as an important departure for ... recognizing that people are involved in the interpretive aspects of evaluating theories, evidence, and the relationship between the two; that scientific knowledge is uncertain and changeable; and that a diversity of strategies and methods are employed in scientific research.
>
> *(p. 67)*

Both of these descriptions highlight that inquiry is not only central to scientific practice but also a way to engaging learners in the scientific enterprise of knowledge production in informal learning environments.

Inquiry in informal settings can range from entirely open-ended to a more structured process. Open-ended inquiry is good for exploring or immersion into a topic and/or for assessing people's prior experiences with phenomena. Open-ended inquiry is also a way to engage learners in a creative approach to inquiry-based learning through an ideation process. This would begin with divergent thinking that allows learners to generate as many ideas and questions as possible about their observations and then choose the most salient questions and ideas (as a form of convergent thinking). From there they could embark on a more structured inquiry that aims at gathering more information to address questions or confirm (or debunk) ideas or even designing something that solves a problem in relation to their inquiries.

The Resiliency Schools Consortium was a NOAA-funded project in which students in an afterschool setting learned about climate resiliency, assessed the climate vulnerabilities of their school building and community, and then designed approaches to mitigate these vulnerabilities. In order to do this, students first used NOAA's online tools to learn climate-related science and completed an experiential assessment of their school building, which included examining infrastructure that would be vulnerable to floods, heat, and other extreme weather events. Based on their assessments, they first brainstormed different mitigation strategies and then decided on the most salient ideas to move forward. The second year of the project entailed them implementing their ideas with some funding from the project and other sources. While this open-ended approach to inquiry centers agency on the learner, the facilitator has to be comfortable with having less control of the outcomes and with the diversity of questions, observations, and ideas that emerge.

On the other hand, guided inquiry is particularly useful for informal learning in partnerships with schools and teachers where there are curricular goals as well as the desire to take advantage of informal approaches to learning. Structured or "guided inquiry" is described as "purposeful informal experiences tied to the curriculum can help students develop an understanding of the enterprise of science as a whole—the wondering, investigating, questioning, data collecting, and analyzing" (Miele & Adams, 2016, p.52), all while giving students choice in how they pursue their inquiry. In keeping with the dialogic nature of inquiry, Miele and Adams (2016) suggest incorporating "accountable talk" to allow students to defend and justify their observations and claims. In using accountable talk during an inquiry exercise, a facilitator poses questions, such as "Can you tell me more about...?" or "What is your evidence for...?" and/or prompts, "I agree with ... because...," in order to foster learning discussions. Regardless of how the inquiry is structured, it is important to allow learners some element of choice and to engage in dialogues in order to deepen and expand the learning opportunities.

Another project, this time in the United Kingdom, views inquiry in both formal and informal learning contexts as a way to get youth interested in science. Anastopoulou et al. (2012) advocated for a Personal Inquiry Learning approach that extends science learning beyond the classroom, emphasizing that learning science by inquiry allows students to learn to think like scientists, do authentic science, and engage in scientific discourse. "By carrying out authentic scientific investigations students can also come to understand the natural world as an arena of investigations, where they have agency in deciding what, where and how to study," in addition to learning the process of scientific knowledge production through experimental design, data collection and making choices about data, and "take part in discussion about scientific phenomena that affect, for instance, their health and environment" (Anastopoulou et al., 2012, p. 252). This is all the more important in both the increasing mistrust and politicization of science and global scope of socio-scientific issues as well as issues that are central to a learner's lived experiences, like environment and health.

Inquiry and Science Teacher Learning in Informal Settings

The examples above bring to the surface the overlap between inquiry in informal learning and inquiry in school settings. As teachers are largely responsible for designing learning in school settings, understanding how science teachers define, understand, and enact informal science learning is helpful in thinking about teacher learning and professional development. In our collaborative project, we interviewed 20 teachers who participated in informal science professional learning—this included either credit-bearing courses and/or extended professional development in partnership with an informal science institution—about their teaching enactments. We designed the interviews to be dialogic (Knight & Saunders, 1999) so that they would elicit a dialogue between the interviewer (all of whom had experiences as classroom teachers) and teachers around teaching practices. One of the questions specifically asked was, "how do you define informal science education?" We used key-words-in-context (KWIC) to analyze the culture and implications of the words used (Leech & Onwuegbuzie, 2008). This enabled us to learn how teachers used the words "informal" or "informal science," and the words and phrases that were associated with those words.

Our findings resonated with other researchers (Sevdalis & Skoumios, 2014) who found that media and other resources brought into the classroom were often associated with informal learning;

however, the association with place commonly remained—taking students outside of the classroom for learning experiences. Therefore, it was no surprise that teachers associated the term *informal science education* with field trips. They mentioned their experiences of working and collaborating with students in specific places they visited and programs that they participated. However, teachers also described characteristics of informal versus formal learning in a strict dichotomy; for example, they used words like "rigid" and "structured" in describing formal learning and words like "flexible" and "dynamic" in describing informal learning. They also viewed informal science as being more "authentic" and having more relevance to students' lives. There was also a notion of unexpectedness and not being able to control the outcome. For these teachers, the pedagogy of informal science learning was associated with authentic science learning (where students were collecting real data or engaged in field-based activities) and open-ended inquiry. With this in mind, teacher learning could be structured to allow teachers to shift perceptions of authentic and inquiry-based science learning. Activities that model scientific inquiry for the classroom could allow teachers to view formal and informal learning as a continuum of practices with different approaches having a particular purpose for engaging learners in scientific endeavor.

Informal science teacher learning contributes to developing a teaching philosophy that centers inquiry. Skayia, Avraamidou, and Evagorou (2019) studied a cohort of teachers enrolled in a teacher preparation program in Southern Europe. They all took a course which included three specially designed activities that took place in informal science settings: (a) working with a scientist, (b) carrying out a field study, and (c) participating in a science festival. They visited the scientists' labs to become familiar with the physical setting of a laboratory and the tools that scientists use in their investigations. The field study entailed teachers shadowing an educator in an environmental center and assisting with the facilitation of studies about the flora and fauna of the city and local parks with elementary students. For the third activity, they prepared and demonstrated science activities to young visitors at a science festival. Once in the classroom, Skayia et al. (2019) learned through interviews, classroom observations, and examination of classroom artifacts that the participants emphasized experiential and inquiry-based approaches in their classroom that included taking students out into the schoolyard to do investigations and using questions to guide students' curiosity and learning. In articulating their personal philosophies, they emphasized inquiry-based learning and,

> Interestingly, the participants also highlighted the importance of utilizing out-of-school settings and adopting informal science approaches to science teaching and learning for the purpose of making strong connections between school science and students' everyday lives, making science fun, motivating, and engaging students in the activities.
>
> *(pp. 81–82)*

This and the preceding example demonstrate how informal science contexts and learning experiences are valuable in allowing teachers to experience inquiry first-hand in ways that they could transfer into the classroom. Inquiry-based teacher education is salient in promoting student-centered learning and expanding opportunities for meaningful and personally relevant science learning.

Describing Inquiry in Art Museum Education

The forerunner of art museum education in the United States as we currently know it emerged in the 1960s when paid educators led visitors in groups through the galleries, sharing art historical information with them (Hein, 2013; Mayer, 2005; Rice & Yenawine, 2002). Deepening the concept of visitor participation, educators in the 1970s art museum espoused the goal of "visual literacy" (Fischer & Levinson, 2010; Mayer, 2005). Patterson Williams, a Master Teacher at the Denver Art Museum, describes the goal of visual literacy in this way: "we wanted people to practice looking at art, responding to it, and get good at those visual skills" (Fischer & Levinson, 2010, p. 322). Mayer describes the importance of this shift: "art museum educators moved the center of the educational endeavor from works of art to visitors, rewriting their beliefs and practices of teaching in the art museum" (2005, p. 357). Suddenly, visitors were no longer passive recipients of knowledge, and they began to add their own voices to the interpretations offered by experts in art history. Visitors were encouraged to share their ideas in group tours and even question art historical interpretations offered by curators. They were even invited to share their own experiences and understanding of the historical contexts around the works of art they saw at the museum. Making meaning about an art object came from the discussions or exchange of information, interpretation, experience, and social contexts among visitors. As such, museum education began to chip away at the conventional hierarchies of knowledge within the museum institution. What the visitor of any age brought to a discussion of an image was just as important as art historical information provided by curators in these conversations facilitated by museum educators.

Until the mid-1980s, as we know from Eisner and Dobbs' seminal report *The Uncertain Profession* published in 1986, most museum educators had been trained in art history and art historical knowledge that guided the "tours" they gave to museum visitors of all ages and experience levels (Mayer, 2005). But in the mid-1980s progressive museum educators began to question this strategy and considered how inquiry-based teaching, a pedagogical approach that is learner-centered and allows the learner to guide the process of making meaning about the art object while drawing on prior knowledge and experiences, might play a role in gallery teaching. This shift to inquiry produced a continuum of strategies ranging from what might be called "pure" inquiry—meaning-making about an art object drawn only from the learners' ideas and observations—to guided inquiry as a process that integrates a facilitated learner exploration and relevant information about the art object. In both cases, asking a series of open-ended questions was the method of inquiry. Philip Yenawine, designer of a pervasive inquiry strategy used in many art museums known as the Visual Thinking Strategy (VTS), describes his "conversion" or shift to inquiry-based teaching:

> There was a time when I thought my responsibility as a museum educator was to carefully consider the art on view ... and decide what key elements needed to be made clear for visitors to be able to "enter" the work. I now think it more appropriate to reverse the equation. Now I often seek to grasp what people already know that I can help them use to begin to decode unfamiliar work.
>
> *(Rice & Yenawine 2002, p. 291)*

Yenawine's strategy was considered controversial by some, as one of its primary tenets was that no information at all need be shared with the viewer. Another key component to inquiry-based teaching in art museums is the facilitation of dialogue used to make meaning as a group. In their study of young children in museums in New Zealand, Clarkin-Phillips, et al. (2018) remind us that "through listening and accepting the ideas of the group, the museum educators assisted students to hear different perspectives and build meaning from multiple voices highlighting the role of dialogue" (p. 35).

Danielle Rice writes that when she started out in museum education she believed that "the role of the museum educator was to deconstruct the museum, to give people a sense that art was part of a social and political context and that museums participated in this contextualization as well" (Rice & Yenawine, 2002, p. 291). This of course cannot be accomplished by sharing art historical information alone; rather, it relies on a process of inquiry. Art historical information can provide facts about when, where, and how the object was made. Alongside this information, institutions often provide a singular interpretation of the object that emphasizes the institution's perspective. However, in order to understand the social and political context in which an object was created, as well as engage with questions about historical and contemporary meanings of the object, viewers must engage in creating their own interpretation drawn from their own examinations of the work. This includes processing the given information and connecting it to their own prior knowledge and experiences. This goal continues to be critical to progressive museum educators. As Nina Simon and others note, "Another important goal of museum education is to interrupt the established authority of the art museum. Museum education increasingly prioritizes the task of empowering visitors to create meaning for and amongst themselves" (McCullough, Dewhurst, & Du, 2018, p. 33). Another reason to use inquiry to engage students is that by asking them to share their ideas they are being invited to participate in the meaning-making process.

The inquiry strategies described above serve to help the learner look inward toward objects within a museum's collection as well as to investigate the nature of the art museum as an institution. This is still best accomplished in a group discussion facilitated by a museum educator, though some museums do attempt to engage the general visitor with didactic panels offering questions to ponder about the objects or by sharing contextual or historical information the visitor might relate to. It is possible to construct interpretive labels "in an accessible and straightforward way, resembling conversations" in a sense mimicking the inquiry process that might happen in a group discussion (Dovydaitytė, 2018, p. 276). Much like the guided inquiry in informal science described earlier in this chapter, guided inquiry in the art museum begins by asking students to create a narrative about an art object. They are then required to provide visual evidence for their ideas based on what they see in the art object. Providing this evidence allows students to hone their observation skills, draw on prior knowledge of art, and integrate their own experiences into the conversation. For example, a student looking at Starry Night by Vincent Van Gogh may share that we are looking at a windy night scene of a small town with a church. When asked how can they tell all this by looking, the student can provide evidence such as the presence of stars to indicate nighttime, the strong lines painted by the artist communicating wind, and their own experience of having seen a steeple on a church before in their own neighborhood. However, these strategies can also be used to look outward from the museum as well. Many museums incorporate inquiry strategies in their programs for school groups, teens, and families both in the galleries and the art studio. These practices guide participants to explore, research, and create art about issues of interest to them (Dewhurst, 2010).

Connecting Collections through Inquiry

The Museum of Modern Art (MoMA) has a long history of using inquiry in its gallery practice. The Visual Thinking Curriculum was first developed there by Philip Yenawine and the staff of the MoMA Education Department in the late 1980s. In 2004 in her role as Director of School and Family programs at the Museum of Modern Art (MoMA), Susan McCullough (second author) joined the teacher programs staff from the Metropolitan Museum of Art, The Solomon R. Guggenheim Museum, and the Whitney Museum of American Art in a collaborative week-long summer institute for teachers. The institute was called Connecting Collections and featured a day at each museum. Although our initial idea was to demonstrate how each museum engages school audiences differently, our colleagues found that we shared more commonalities in gallery pedagogy than differences. As such, the structure of the institute came to focus on the elements of that pedagogy including inquiry-based teaching, object selection, and sequencing of gallery activities.

This common inquiry-based strategy used across all four institutions consisted of three questions in reference to an artwork: What's going on here? What do you see that makes you say that? And what more can you find? In its earliest form, the strategy called for the museum educator to offer no information about the artwork, including the title, and share no personal or institutional opinions. However, at MoMA, it was more pedagogically effective for teachers to have some art and historical information. In addition, it was useful to structure the inquiry around a compelling and visually evident theme. These thematic, inquiry-based discussions are led by experienced museum educators and include a careful selection and sequencing of objects and writing questions that will serve to deepen the inquiry.

During Connecting Collections and other professional development and preservice teacher education sessions facilitated for teachers, it became clear that question development is a surprisingly difficult component of the inquiry strategy. Hence, we developed a facilitated experiential approach for generating and honing guided-inquiry questions. This process is first modeled for teachers, followed by a reflection on and dissection of the process.

Facilitated Experiential Inquiry with Art

We begin by introducing the theme and asking participants what they know about that theme (for a discussion about the relative merits of using a thematic approach see Hubard, 2014). For example, if the theme we are exploring is power, participants would be asked to share the forms of power they are familiar with. Once notions of power have been explored, including a variety of definitions of power, a consideration on who has power, and how an artist might represent power, we move from a discussion of the theme to a discussion of the artwork. This is followed by the sharing of an image of the artwork with participants and asking them to take a minute to look and then posing the question, "what is going on here?" As participants offer ideas and begin to construct narratives about the work, they are asked to provide visual evidence for their ideas with the prompt, "what do you see that makes you say that?" The role of facilitator of this inquiry-based process also involves the facilitator making connections between ideas that are offered, asking participants to explain why they agree or disagree with an idea that has been shared and making sure that all aspects of both the theme—referring back to the initial conversation about the theme—and the artwork have been explored. This is augmented by asking additional open-ended questions and sharing background information about the artwork when it seems relevant to the conversation and useful to the meaning-making process.

At this point, teachers are asked to reflect on the conversation by asking participants to dissect what happened as a part of the inquiry around the artwork—what was the role of the facilitator? What was their role as the audience? What is always interesting about this part of the process is participants will often misremember questions that were asked even if they were short and simple. For example, while the first question is always "what is going on here?" participants will often recall, "What do you see here?" However, this leads to a fruitful conversation about the critical differences between these two questions. If participants were asked about what do they *see* one could expect to hear a laundry list of objects, colors, or materials present in the artwork, information that often fails to generate an interesting or productive conversation. However, when asked, "what is *going on*?," participants immediately began to construct a narrative, giving visual evidence for their ideas that can be debated and/or built upon by other participants. Likewise, they will sometimes remember the posed questions as yes/no questions, for example, "is this an image of power?" as opposed to "in what ways is power represented here?" This also leads to a generative discussion about how convergent questions do not lend themselves as productively to inquiry as divergent questions. In these instances, reflections on the types of questions posed allowed the teachers to understand the importance of structuring inquiry questions in ways that generate deeper discussions and meaning-making around the art being viewed.

The participants are then invited to choose an artwork and develop some questions that will help to guide students through an inquiry-based discussion. Participants are often challenged by this task, though it looked easy when done by an experienced museum educator. They struggle to create questions that are divergent, don't rely on prior art historical knowledge, aren't leading or opinion based, and do not ask students to guess at an answer (e.g., why did the artist use this material?) instead of using the visual evidence in front of them. Participants also learn the importance of sequencing to build meaning. The way questions are sequenced at an individual artwork, asking students to start with description and move to interpretation, is an important component in the meaning-making process and in their ability to think critically about the artwork they are discussing. Likewise, the choice of artworks, and the order in which they are viewed and discussed with students, contribute to this process. Oftentimes art museum educators will begin a gallery lesson with narrative, representational images, and then move to more complex and abstract images as the lesson goes on. Participants learn through this process that they could assess the success of an inquiry if, by the final work of art, they have to ask few questions or none at all because students have become familiar with the inquiry process. Students know that they are building on the meaning-making done at previous artworks to add to their understanding of the artwork as well as the theme that has been consistent throughout the gallery lesson.

The inquiry-based pedagogy that is shared by many art museum educator colleagues is focused on a process that, as a field, we often struggle to name. The elements in an inquiry-based process centering on an artwork are: describe, interpret, share relevant information, make multiple meanings, debate multiple meanings, and respond creatively to the artwork and the ideas that have been generated in discussing it. These are not necessarily steps to be taken in a linear fashion; rather, these are components that weave throughout the inquiry process. It is also critical to remember that once the inquiry process has been introduced to participants the inquiry is not bound to the artworks in a museum but can be extended to the institutions of museums themselves and beyond. After students learn that their opinions and ideas about artworks are valuable to the meaning-making process, they feel free to ask other questions such as "what makes this art?" and "why is this object on view?" or "why is one object displayed more prominently than another?" Art museum educators are able to push students to consider the role of the museum in society with critical questions such as "which objects should be collected?" "What is considered valuable and why?" "Where and how are objects displayed?" At many encyclopedic museums, for example, art from non-Western continents and indigenous cultures are on view on the first floor, while traditional Western painting and sculpture is displayed on upper-level floors. This allows us to question the hierarchy of art and consider which artists are present and celebrated in art museums? Who is missing? And, importantly, who decides? These questions can lead to examinations of the role of museums in codifying certain artists and art historical knowledge and the role of donors and philanthropists in the decision-making process for exhibiting art.

Challenges to Inquiry in Informal Learning

While inquiry is a common pedagogical approach in science and art education, there are challenges to enacting inquiry in informal settings. For one, although inquiry-based approaches emphasize learner agency in observing and questioning, effective inquiry benefits from assessing learners' prior knowledge and scaffolding questions and exploration prompts in ways that allow them to build on that knowledge. In many informal contexts, learners are only there for a limited time, often for one-off visits, so there may not be sufficient time to assess knowledge and scaffold and extend learning. To overcome this challenge, questions or prompts in supporting exhibit texts that encourage learners to observe and exchange information with other learners in their group would help to stimulate potentially generative conversations. For example, labeling in a zoo may prompt learners to look for particular primate behaviors and have them discuss how this is similar and different from human behavior. A gallery guide in an art museum may have visitors discover a common theme among works of art and encourage them to engage with questions about the ways that the art connects to their personal history and/or everyday life. In these instances, the questions are often broad and open-ended but help to ignite the learners' curiosity that might have brought them to the exhibit or learning context in the first place.

Another challenge of inquiry in informal settings is being comfortable with the diversity of perspectives and understandings that learners bring with them to the learning context. In other words, being comfortable with the unexpected. In informal settings, audiences are diverse in age, education level, race and cultural backgrounds, political viewpoints, and so on, and these positions contribute to the possible messiness that comes with inquiry: unexpected questions, dialogues, and engagements may emerge. If a facilitator is present, they would have to manage their own expectations and biases that may emerge as well as learn to be comfortable with not knowing the answers or outcome. This includes being able to let go of "canonical" or given knowledge about particular artifacts, even in scientific settings, and listening to the different viewpoints that emerge as it could be an opportunity to learn a new angle or stance toward the topic at hand. Another important aspect is being able to leverage this difference toward a greater collective meaning-making and understandings of artifacts and issues.

Structures That Support Inquiry in Informal Learning

Central to inquiry in informal learning environments is questioning and predicting: "questioning is widely regarded by educators as one of, if not the, central inquiry behaviors that support learning in informal environments" (NRC, 2009, pp. 144–145). Questions structure the learning dialogues that happen in relation to the objects or phenomena under investigation. In a study of floor facilitator identity and practice in a science center, Jennifer D. Adams (first author) and collaborator Preeti Gupta learned that central to visitor interactions was "asking questions, eliciting thoughts and inviting them to physically interact with the exhibit" (Adams & Gupta, 2013, p. 99), all of which are done through guiding questions. Similarly, when preservice science teachers completed a practicum as floor facilitators in a science center, they shifted from more activity-based approaches (such as doing demonstrations and describing an exhibit) to more inquiry-based approaches: "I am helping kids understand exhibits by letting them perform the activities instead of me showing it to them" (Gupta & Adams, 2010). In both of these studies, the questions structured the inquiries, and knowing how to formulate and pose questions were important in assessing one's skills as a floor facilitator.

In both informal science and art contexts, the sequencing of questions is critical to planning an inquiry-based learning cycle. The questions should be structured so that they (a) encourage careful looking and observing, (b) engage learners in dialogues between the objects/art/display/phenomena and between each other, (c) encourage learners to build on ideas that emerge from the dialogues, and (d) prompt learners to make connections and extensions that relate their inquiries to other things in the learning context and in their lived experiences. These kinds of questions are not meant to be linear in approach but rather represent the different kinds of questions that could be used to access different ways of looking and learning in informal places and spaces.

Questions are one element that supports authentic inquiry in informal environments. In extending inquiry to creative engagement, it is also important to design learning environments that allow inquiry to emerge and grow. This includes embedding collaboration, fostering a sense of distributed expertise (no one person is the expert; all contribute equally but differently), and allowing learners to play with ideas, objects—putting different elements together to create new knowledge, new artifacts, and new connections.

Conclusions

Inquiry-based learning is primarily used in art museums to develop visual literacy. Research in art museum education has demonstrated that an inquiry-based approach to looking at art can also develop critical thinking skills in students (Kisida, Bowen, & Green, 2016). When the gallery conversation extends beyond objects and images to include social issues related to museums and their collections, students have the opportunity to connect their ideas and knowledge to an investigation of the role of cultural institutions to explore issues of social justice and equity. Inquiry-based learning in informal science setting allows learners to engage with scientific objects and phenomena in personally meaningful ways. It is both a pedagogical approach and central to the process of scientific discovery. Inquiry also allows learners to consider the ways that science impacts their daily lives and well-being. However, both the challenge and the value of inquiry-based learning in an informal setting is that the conversation can go in unexpected ways. While it is sometimes difficult to codify these "teachable moments," the range of learning opportunities in informal environments should be researched further so this resource can be used more fully. For example, we could study the kinds of questions and prompts, both in art and science, that support productive conversation. We could also examine the role that digital technologies that are increasingly present in informal settings, play in supporting inquiry. Moving forward, it will be increasingly important for researchers to consider the sociocultural aspects of inquiry; what are the different ways that questions could be asked and what is considered scientific evidence or artistic interpretation. This will allow us to move beyond hegemonic notions of what is considered science and art toward a more holistic understanding of our humanity and world.

Acknowledgments

The Resiliency Schools Consortium project is supported by the National Oceanic and Atmospheric Administration (U.S.) ref: NA16SEC0080004; the ILETES project is supported by the National Science Foundation (U.S.) ref: NSF. 1844256.

References

Adams, J., & Gupta, P. (2013). "I learn more here than I do in school. Honestly, I wouldn't lie about that": Creating a space for agency and identity around science. *International Journal of Critical Pedagogy, 4*(2), 87–104.

Anastopoulou, S., Sharples, M., Ainsworth, S., Crook, C., O'Malley C., & Wright, M. (2012). Creating personal meaning through technology-supported science inquiry learning across formal and informal settings. *International Journal of Science Education, 34*(2), 251–273. https://doi.org/10.1080/09500693.2011.569958

Ash, D., & Wells, G. (2006). Dialogic inquiry in classroom and museum: Actions, tools, and talk. *Counterpoints, 249*, 35–54.

Clarkin-Phillips, J., Carr, M., Thomas, R., Tinning, A., & Waitai, M. (2018). Fostering the artistic and imaginative capacities of young children: Case study report from a visit to a museum. *International Journal of Early Childhood, 50*(1), 33–46. https://doi.org/10.1007/s13158-018-0211-2.

Colley, H., Hodkinson, P., & Malcolm, J. (2002). Non-formal learning: Mapping the conceptual terrain, a consultation report. Other. Leeds: University of Leeds.

Dewhurst, M. (2010). An inevitable question: Exploring the defining features of social justice art education. *Art Education, 63*(5), 6–13. https://doi.org/10.1080/00043125.2010.11519082.

Dovydaitytė, L. (2018). The problem of public participation in art museums. *Kunstiteaduslikke Uurimusi, 27*(1–3), 265–280.

Eshach, H. (2007). Bridging in-school and out-of-school learning: Formal, non-formal, and informal education. *Journal of Science Education and Technology, 16*(2), 171–190. https://doi.org/10.1007/s10956-006-9027-1

Falk, J. H., & Dierking, L. D. (2004). The contextual model of learning. In G. Anderson (Ed.), *Reinventing the museum: Historical and contemporary perspectives on the paradigm shift* (pp. 139–142). Walnut Creek: AltaMira Press.

Fischer, D. & Levinson, L. (2010). Redefining successful interpretation in art museums. *Curator: The Museum Journal, 53*(3), 299–323. https://doi.org/10.1111/j.2151-6952.2010.00031.x

Gupta, P., & Adams, J. (2010). Museum University partnerships for pre service education. In B. Fraser, K. Tobin, & C. McRobbie (Eds.), *Second international handbook of science education*. Amsterdam, NL: Kluwer Academic Publishers.

Gyllenpalm, J., & Wickman, P. O. (2011). "Experiments" and the inquiry emphasis conflation in science teacher education. *Science Education, 95*(5), 908–926. https://doi.org/10.1002/sce.20446

Hein, G. E. (2013). Progressive museum education: Examples from the 1960s. *International Journal of Progressive Education, 9*(2), 61–76.

Hofstein, A., & Rosenfeld, S. (1996). Bridging the gap between formal and informal science learning. *Studies in Science Education, 28*(1), 87–112. https://doi.org/10.1080/03057269608560085

Hubard, O. (2014). Concepts as context: Thematic museum education and its influence on meaning making. *The International Journal of Art and Design Education, 33*(1), 103–115. https://doi.org/10.1111/j.1476-8070.2014.12001.x.

Kisida, B., Bowen, D., & Green, J. P. (2016). Measuring critical thinking: Results from an art museum field trip experiment. *Journal of Research on Educational Effectiveness, 9*(1), 171–187. https://doi.org/10.1080/19345747.2015.1086915.

Knight, P., & Saunders, M. (1999) Understanding teachers' professional cultures through interview: A constructivist approach. *Evaluation & Research in Education, 13*(3), 144–156. https://doi.org/10.1080/09500799908666954

Leech, N. L., & Onwuegbuzie, A. J. (2008). Qualitative data analysis: A compendium of techniques and a framework for selection for school psychology research and beyond. *School Psychology Quarterly, 23*(4), 587. https://doi.org/10.1037/1045-3830.23.4.587

Mayer, M. (2005). A postmodern puzzle: Rewriting the place of the visitor in art museum education. *Studies in Art Education, 46*(4), 356–368. https://doi.org/10.1080/00393541.2005.11651796.

McCullough, S., Du, J., & Dewhurst, M. (2018). Engaging audiences, building community, challenging power: Museum education and public art. In C. K. Knight and H. Senie (Eds.), *Museums and Public Art?* (pp. 28–40). Newcastle: Cambridge Scholars Publishing.

Miele, E. A., & Adams, J. D. (2016). Guided-choice learning in out-of-school environments. *Science Scope, 39*(6), 52.

Mocker, D. W., & Spear, G. E. (1982). Lifelong learning: Formal, nonformal, informal, and self-directed. Information Series No. 241. http://hdl.voced.edu.au/10707/116040

National Research Council. (2009). *Learning science in informal environments: People, places and pursuits*. Washington, DC: The National Academies Press. https://doi.org/10.17226/12190.

Paris, S. G. (2002). *Perspectives on object-centered learning in museums*. London: Routledge.

Pedaste, M., Mäeots, M., Siiman, L. A., De Jong, T., Van Riesen, S. A., Kamp, E. T., ... & Tsourlidaki, E. (2015). Phases of inquiry-based learning: Definitions and the inquiry cycle. *Educational Research Review, 14*, 47–61. https://doi.org/10.1016/j.edurev.2015.02.003

Rice, D., & Yenawine. P. (2002) A conversation on object-centered learning in art museums. *Curator: The Museum Journal, 45*(4), 289–301. https://doi.org/10.1111/j.2151-6952.2002.tb00066.x.

Sevdalis, C., & Skoumios, M. (2014). Non-formal and informal science learning: Teachers' conceptions. *International Journal of Science in Society, 5*(4), 13–25. https://doi.org/10.18848/1836-6236/CGP/v05i04/59287

Skayia, A., Avraamidou, L., & Evagorou, M. (2019). How preservice elementary teachers develop their personal philosophies about science teaching: The role of informal science approaches. *Journal of Research in Science, Mathematics and Technology Education, 2*(2), 72–83. https://doi.org/10.31756/jrsmte.222

INDEX

Note: **Bold** page numbers refer to tables and *italic* page numbers refer to figures.

Made in the USA
Las Vegas, NV
29 October 2024

17af4448-76b3-4533-8e75-e9582296b5b4R01